FOREST TREES
OF THE PACIFIC SLOPE

George B. Sudworth at his desk in the Bureau of Forestry, shortly before his death. *Courtesy of the U.S. Forest Service.*

FOREST TREES
OF THE PACIFIC SLOPE

by

GEORGE B. SUDWORTH

With a New Foreword by

WOODBRIDGE METCALF
Extension Forester, Emeritus
University of California, Berkeley

and

A New Table of Changes in Nomenclature by

E. S. HARRAR
Dean of the School of Forestry
Duke University

DOVER PUBLICATIONS, INC.

NEW YORK

Published in Canada by General Publishing Company, Ltd., 30 Lesmill Road, Don Mills, Toronto, Ontario.
Published in the United Kingdom by Constable and Company, Ltd., 10 Orange Street, London WC 2.

This Dover edition, first published in 1967, is an unabridged republication of the work originally published by the Forest Service of the U. S. Department of Agriculture in 1908. It contains a new Foreword by Woodbridge Metcalf and a new Table of Changes in Nomenclature by E. S. Harrar.

Standard Book Number: 486-21752-3

Library of Congress Catalog Card Number: 65-27018

Manufactured in the United States of America
Dover Publications, Inc.
180 Varick Street
New York, N.Y. 10014

FOREWORD TO THE DOVER EDITION

Since this manual first appeared in 1908 as a publication of the United States Forest Service, it has been studied by thousands of students of forestry and botany throughout the United States and has been a standard piece of equipment for every field forester and in every forest office throughout the Pacific Coast country from Alaska to the Mexican border. For some years now it has been out of print, and this new edition will be welcomed by many who have had to do without it as a field companion, and have only been able to consult library copies.

George B. Sudworth was born at Kingston, Wisconsin in 1864 and received his early education in the public schools of Kalamazoo, Michigan, the Kalamazoo Baptist College and the University of Michigan, from which he graduated with a Bachelor of Arts degree in 1885. In 1886 he joined the old Bureau of Forestry, serving as botanist on valuation surveys throughout the Great Lakes region. He was appointed dendrologist in 1895 and became chief of that department in 1904. Throughout these years he was occupied in extensive field studies of trees in various forest regions and compiled the *Check List of Forest Trees of the United States* in 1898. This he revised a short time before his death in 1927. It continued to be a standard reference on name and range of trees of the United States until it was again revised by Elbert Little, Jr. in 1953 and issued by the United States Forest Service as the *Check List of Native and Naturalized Trees of the United States* (Agricultural Handbook No. 41).

The author was thoroughly convinced of the value of accurate and "full-sized" illustrations as aids in identification (see page 11) and the excellent line drawings by C. L. Taylor, A. E. Hoyle, N. Brenizer and others contribute greatly to the value of the publication. Sudworth knew trees from thousands of miles of field travel at a time when much of the western country could be reached only by pack train or on foot, and his field notebooks are fascinating records of these expeditions (1899-1904). The detailed notes on range and occurrence of each species were compiled from these records and supplemented by the observations of other scientists, such as Dr. C. Hart Merriam, who made available extensive notes on tree distribution in California.

Sudworth appreciated the difficulties faced by those who want to perfect their knowledge of trees. He points out, on page 10, that the

George B. Sudworth and assistant on mules in Hassic Meadow, Middle Tule, Sequoia National Forest. *Courtesy of the U.S. Forest Service.*

student "will be able to settle doubtful points only by much careful field study and the observation of all that can be found distinctive in trees. In order to know even a few trees well, a multitude of details must be learned and remembered, especially if the species are closely related. Much of the dendrologist's knowledge of trees is gained through long study by a partly unconscious absorption of small, indescribable, but really appreciable details. To meet as many as possible of these difficulties, common and striking differences in the leaf and fruit forms of a number of trees have been specially pointed out in illustrations or descriptions." These words are as true today as when they were written nearly sixty years ago, and the modern reader should give careful attention to the other points which Sudworth emphasizes in his introduction.

Sudworth's skill in forest description is well illustrated in this excerpt from his Field Notebook No. 4, of October, 1901, on the Middle Fork of the Kaweah River in Tulare County, California:

This is a large and important watershed. Its headwaters comprise, beginning on the east, Deer Creek, Cliff Creek, the Main Channel, Boulder Creek, and Alta Creek. The divide at the head of this system is high and rugged (reference to photos). Tharp's Mountain (Tharp's Peak) forms an immense high barrier on the N., 11,200 ft. in elevation. From Timber Gap trending northward and westward, this divide is a broken succession of peaks and sharp ridges composed of bare granite rock; this continues to the head of Marble Fork of the Kaweah and Mt. Silliman forming a continuous divide between the headwaters of Kings River and the above-mentioned Kaweah watersheds. From 500 to 600 ft. of this divide is bare of tree growth. Patches of Foxtail Pine form timberline at 10,500 ft. extending down about 500 ft. This is succeeded by a pure growth of California Red Fir with 5-10% of Silver Pine on the Ridges.

This belt descends to about 8,000 ft. where it is mingled with White Fir and Jeffrey Pine extending down to 7500 ft. Here the California Red Fir disappears and Sugar Pine and Bull (Ponderosa) Pine with White Fir form a heavy commercial forest down to 5,000 ft.; when the White Fir disappears and the forest is composed of mainly Bull Pine and Incense Cedar with occasional Sugar Pine.

A fringe of Lodgepole Pine prevails about Alta Meadow and at the head of marshy little meadows at all tributaries at the same level. California Red Fir is more or less closely mingled with this pine on the upper side.

Bigtrees (Sequoia) at Redwood Meadow (notes of 1900) cover about 50 acres and comprise two separate groves. A small grove of 80-100 trees (largest 17-18 ft. diameter) are located at head of a small tributary of Cliff Creek, and is separated from the main grove at Redwood Meadow by a ridge. One mile N. of Redwood Meadow near top of ridge from which the trail descends into the first creek east of Main Channel of Middle Kaweah the stands are Bigtree. No other trees of the kind in the vicinity. Note also that scattering Bigtrees extend S. from Redwood Meadow grove down the slope

View of Mineral King Sawtooth Peak (Miners' Peak) at headwaters of Eastfork Kaweah River, shows portion of this head valley to N.E. of Farewell Gap. *Juniperus occidentalis* on right in thin stand. (15112)

among Sugar Pines for about ½ to ¼ mile, extending limits of the grove over 50-60 acres more than originally (1900) determined.

The lower (to 1 mile up from the channels) slopes of the Middle Kaweah tributaries bear but little pine at their junction. Kellogg Oak of brushy size with Manzanita brush and Ceanothus form the principal cover. The timbered slopes are covered with loose boulders, exposed small areas of granite rock and rich loam soil.

The heaviest body of commercial timber in this basin is situated from a point 3-4 miles N.W. of Redwood Meadow to Timber Gap and southward along the north-west slope of Middle Kaweah—This body of timber continues eastward over the divide into East Kaweah Basin over both slopes and above and below the region of Atwood's Mill (extent defined by notes and views of 1900).

Toward the junction of the Middle and Marble forks of Kaweah River the brush area immediately above the channels increases to 1-1½ miles on either side. (A sample ¼ acre at 8800 ft. on the W. slope of Mt. Silliman shows 27 California Red Fir 16″ to 54″ diameter, Av. ht. 128 ft., 4 Western White Pine 20-25″ diam. by 90 ft., and 11 Lodgepole Pine 16″-45″ diam. by 85 ft. average height.)

On his trips of exploration, Sudworth took hundreds of photographs which are carefully described in his field notebooks. Some of these photographs and thirteen of the notebooks are at the University of California, Berkeley, in the Forestry Library, where they are available for study. Three pictures of the Kaweah River country are reproduced herein with Sudworth's captions. A fourth photograph describes the largest of the Sequoias.

In 1904 Sudworth visited the Inverness Peninsula and then made a trip from King City to the summit of the Santa Lucia Mountains through some of the steepest and brushiest country in the south coast ranges of California. In this record he notes:

The slopes of the main Santa Lucia range (on the E. side) carry a chaparral largely of *Quercus dumosa* (2 to 10 ft. high), a shrubby Tanbark Oak, *Quercus chrysolepis, Arbutus menziesii,* a low form of *Adenostema* and of *Arctostaphylos glauca.* From the head of San Miguel Canyon westward the slopes carry *Pinus ponderosa, P. coulteri, P. lambertiana,* and *P. attenuata* extends throughout the eastern and western slopes.

The rarest tree of the canyons near the Santa Lucia Range divide on either side is *Abies venusta* (now *bracteata*)—Santa Lucia Fir. Some 75 to 80 trees stand in San Miguel Canyon, extending from near the head of the canyon downstream for ½ mile. Five or six trees were also seen in a deep gulch one mile N.E. of San Miguel Canyon.

External form of *Abies venusta* and Other Characteristics: The trees of San Miguel Canyon are uniformly broadly conical for ⅔ of their height; the upper ⅓ of the crown then contracts sharply in a narrow, sharply pointed spire—very similar to the sharp-pointed "leader" of *Abies lasiocarpa.* It is

General Sherman Bigtree in N.W. corner of Giant Forest; 80 ft. 6 inches in circumference, 285 ft. high. (15061)

Old and young Sequoias in side gulch of East Tule River; medium-sized trees with abundant reproduction 2 to 30 ft. high in washed bottom of the gulch. (25993)

Bigtrees scarred by fires, Redwood Meadow; part of a group of 13 on one quarter acre. (15096)

unique in this character among all other associated species. Its branches are given off in regular whorls (5 to 6 in each) and stand out horizontally. A distinctive feature are long, pendant lateral branchlets of the main branches— often 2½ to 4 ft. long.

The buds of this tree are likewise very distinctive—large, slender, sharp-pointed, bright russet-brown. The bark of young trees (2 to 8 inches in diam.) is a dull ashy grey and smooth; while that of larger trees is shallowly furrowed; the bark being exceedingly hard; interiorly (when cut into) the bark is a bright red-purple. Branches (extend) quite to the ground. These trees grow only in the bottom of the canyon from 10 to 50 ft. above the dark, rocky stream-bed, in a rich, moist soil. The trees in Big Creek Canyon are said to extend from the stream far up the rocky, dry sides of the canyon.

This description of one of the least known of American trees is typical of the notes made by Sudworth on the characteristics and distribution of various tree species as he saw them in the field; and often there are comments on timber growth and quality with counts of sample quarter acres of typical stands.

Forest fires, logging operations and the march of civilization have changed the appearance of much of the western mountain country since the turn of the century when Sudworth described it, but the same species of trees are there as young stands and the early records are becoming increasingly valuable for historical reference.

Research during the past fifty years has resulted in a number of changes in both the scientific and common names of trees. These changes are listed in the table by Professor E. S. Harrar (see page 411), and the reader will find them also in the above-mentioned *Check List*.

The reader should realize that this volume deals only with *native* trees of the country which drains into the Pacific Ocean. Thus, for identification of the many ornamental trees which have been brought from around the world and planted throughout this region, he must consult other books.

WOODBRIDGE METCALF

Berkeley, California
September, 1966

OTHER UNITED STATES FOREST SERVICE TREE BULLETINS
BY GEORGE B. SUDWORTH

Pine Trees of the Rocky Mountain Region
Spruce and Balsam Fir Trees of the Rocky Mountain Region
Cypress and Juniper Trees of the Rocky Mountain Region
Miscellaneous Conifers of the Rocky Mountain Region

FOREST TREES
OF THE PACIFIC SLOPE

CONTENTS.

3

4   CONTENTS.

8   CONTENTS.

INTRODUCTION.

This volume is the first of four which are to deal with all the native forest trees of North America north of the Mexican boundary. It contains an account of the tree species known to inhabit the Pacific region, 150 in all. Part II will be devoted to the Rocky Mountain trees, Part III to the trees of the southern States, and Part IV to the trees of the northern States.

The region covered by Part I includes Alaska, British Columbia, Washington, Oregon, and California (see maps, frontispiece). Many trees described occur wholly within this region, but none are represented throughout it. A few are found on its southern border and range into Mexico, while three or four trees stretch from within the Pacific region to the Atlantic.

DEFINITION OF A TREE.

The definition of a tree followed by the author includes woody plants having one well-defined stem and a more or less definitely formed crown (but not excluding unbranched cactuses, yuccas, and palms), and attaining somewhere in their natural or planted range a height of at least 8 feet and a diameter of not less than 2 inches. It has been difficult to apply this definition in all cases, for there is no sharp line between some shrub-like trees and some tree-like shrubs. However, though wholly arbitrary, it has been serviceable. A considerable number of species included are, over much of their range, little more than chaparral shrubs, becoming tree-like only in exceptionally favorable places. Recent discoveries in this region have made it necessary to class as trees several species previously regarded as shrubs. Some species are shrubs within this territory, but are trees outside of it. There still remain for further careful consideration several species of Arctostaphylos, Ceanothus, and Styrax, which may prove to be trees.

DESCRIPTIONS AND ILLUSTRATIONS OF SPECIES.

Since this work was prepared solely for the layman, the use of technical terms has been avoided. In describing species the writer has endeavored to define essential and simple characters in plain

9

terms. It is believed that the chief distinguishing characters of trees may be readily observed by laymen if clearly pointed out in ordinary language. The color of wood given refers to heartwood; sapwood is described only when it is materially different from the usual whitish color of such wood.

The illustrations are relied upon chiefly to define the important distinctive characters. Additional characters, difficult or impossible to show in drawings, such as the roughness, very minute hairiness, etc., of foliage or other parts, are briefly described. No attempt has been made to translate exactly the technical terms used by botanists to describe, for example, the different types of hair, wool, and other appendages which often mark the leaves and twigs of trees. Little attention has been given to defining or illustrating such transient characters as flowers and young or immature foliage. Mature foliage, fruits, bark, form of trunk and crown, and some other features, always present, or at least persisting longer than the flowers, are those most readily observed, and for this reason have been singled out and emphasized. Some trees are very easily identified by the special shape of their leaves, the color and character of their bark, or the form of their crown, whereas the recognition of others requires all available evidence. It must be borne in mind also that some trees, especially conifers, have very dissimilar leaves, buds, and bark on different parts of the crown and trunk.

A long experience has taught the author that it is difficult for lay students of trees to appreciate the variation in shape and size possible in the leaves and fruits, and in the bark characters of a single species. It is hard for them to understand that such minor differences in the size and form of leaves and fruits as may characterize different individuals of the same species are really within the limits of one recognized species. They look for absolute uniformity in the characters of species presented in different individuals, when it really is not to be found. The student will, therefore, often find it exceedingly difficult to identify some forms of a species. Representative leaves, fruits, and other characters have been illustrated and described according to the best judgment of the author, who has tried to give the best of the knowledge he applies in making an identification. The student may find tree forms slightly or considerably different in details from those illustrated and described here, and will be in doubt. He will be able to settle doubtful points only by much careful field study and the observation of all that can be found distinctive in trees. In order to know even a few trees well, a multitude of details must be learned and remembered, especially if the species are closely related. Much of the dendrologist's knowledge of trees is gained through long study by a partly unconscious absorption of small, indescribable, but really appreciable, details.

To meet as many as possible of these difficulties, common and striking differences in the leaf and fruit forms of a number of trees have been specially pointed out in illustrations or descriptions.

VALUE OF FULL-SIZED ILLUSTRATIONS.

Nearly all figures show leaves, etc., of natural size. In the writer's experience, nothing is more helpful, particularly to untrained students, than illustrations practically the exact size of specimens they will find in the field. In reduced illustrations of the leaves, fruits, and seeds of some trees distinctive characters are lost, so that even specialists find them useless. Reduced figures are used only when the natural sizes of the object are too large for the pages of this book. It is believed, however, that in these cases distinctive characters have not been lost.

OMISSION OF ARTIFICIAL KEYS FOR IDENTIFICATION.

Keys leading up to the identification of families, genera, and species are omitted, chiefly to prevent further delay in publication. They appear to be little used, if at all, by lay students, who prefer to identify trees by elimination, i. e., by comparing the specimen with the illustrations until a " picture " is found that " fits." This method is wholly unscientific, but is nevertheless the one which busy, untrained lovers of trees are most likely to follow.

TECHNICAL NAMES OF TREES.

The technical nomenclature does not correspond wholly with that of any one author. Tree names adopted here are based upon the generally accepted law of priority, which demands that the earliest tenable name be retained. The period in which this law is here held to be operative is from 1753, when the general application of binominal names of plants began. This is in accordance with the usage of most dendrologists.

Many changes of technical names have been necessary since the publication of the author's " Nomenclature of North American Trees " and " Check List of the Forest Trees of the United States," upon which the nomenclature is based. It is regrettable, but inevitable, that authors should differ in judgment regarding the retention of certain tree names, even if they do accept as a working principle priority of publication for every name used. The intricacies of nomenclatural law are too great to be discussed here, but for the sake of illustrating one of the many points of disagreement among dendrologists, the two names *Sequoia wellingtonia* and *Sequoia washingtoniana,* now retained for the bigtree of the California Sierras, are cited.   Each name is held by its advocates to be correctly founded. In this case the difference of opinion does not involve priority, but the question of whether or not the earliest name (*S. washingtoniana*) was properly established by publication.   The author of *Taxodium washingtonianum*, on which *Sequoia washingtoniana* is based, described it in untechnical language in a San Francisco newspaper, and not, as his opponents maintain he should have done, in technical terms and in a recognized plant journal.   The point, in the case of publication in a newspaper, that the announcement of a new species is not made to technical readers but to the general public does not, in the writer's judgment, affect the principle of publicity.   In deciding questions of this kind the writer has felt that if a tree has been named and definitely enough described or figured in public print to enable a reader to recognize the tree designated, the author's name of the tree is justly entitled to recognition, whether or not the description was technical or was printed in some appropriate journal of standing. This opinion does not, of course, question the entire propriety and desirability of describing new species in technical language and announcing them either in botanical journals or at least in those devoted to biological subjects.

COMMON NAMES OF TREES.

The selection of common names given here is based upon the widest usage over most of the trees' ranges.   The ideal common name is one exclusively used for a tree throughout its range.   Such names are rare, but every effort should nevertheless be made to establish them.   The stability of scientific names (which are never knowingly duplicated), though yet imperfect, is what gives them their chief advantage over common names.

Unfortunately common names of trees are not always appropriate or well chosen.   They do not, as they should, refer to some striking characteristic of the tree or of its habitat.   Inappropriate names, however, when once established, can not well be discarded, since usage, as in language, is really a law, and since if not duplicated for other trees they may serve as well as more appropriate ones the practical purpose of names—convenient handles.   The deliberate and senseless application of the same name to two or more species is, however, something to be avoided and discouraged.   It is both unnecessary and perplexing to have several very different pines called " white pine."   Still more pernicious is the deliberate use of the same name for two or more trees belonging to entirely distinct genera; for example, " larch " applied to fir or balsam (a species of Abies), " pine " applied to spruce (a species of Picea) is inexcusable and misleading. This misuse of names is most to be deplored when it is intended, as it has been in some cases, to overcome prejudices against a certain timber and, in effect, to deceive consumers. In this way " white pine," a wood of good reputation, is used for a wood of less excellent quality derived from pines in Arizona, although true timber white pine does not grow there; so also " satin walnut," an invented name, has been commonly used for plain sweet or red gum. Many other examples might be cited.

The locally accepted names of a few trees have been replaced or modified, for the purpose of avoiding duplication. Thus " red cedar " of the northwest (*Thuja plicata*) is made into " western red cedar " in order to avoid confliction with the eastern red cedar (*Juniperus virginiana*), which became well known long before the western tree was discovered. Another suggestion made in cases where it seemed proper is that of perpetuating the use of such patronymic common names as Engelmann spruce (*Picea engelmanni*), Brewer oak (*Quercus breweri*), etc., particularly for trees which have received no common distinctive names because they are still little known. It is exceedingly helpful to use such names for trees which do not readily suggest good common names. *Salix nuttallii* is a good example. Lay observers would see in this tree just a " variety of willow," and " Nuttall willow " is a convenient common name. Often the use of such names will emphasize what the original describer of the tree sought to perpetuate by naming it in honor of some worthy or distinguished person.

SIZES OF TREES.

For the most part, the heights and diameters given for trees are intended to be those ordinarily found. Extreme sizes, when given, are purposely guarded by some modifying statement, to show that they are exceptional. Lumber operations are rapidly changing the forests of nearly every region. The largest trees of certain species once common are now rare or even wanting.

There appears to be a popular tendency to overestimate and to overstate the size of trees, particularly of large trees. The California Sierra bigtree (*Sequoia washingtoniana*) is often spoken of as being 400 or more feet high and 30 or more feet in diameter. According to the writer's experience it would be extremely difficult to find one of these trees now standing which is over 300 feet high or over 27 feet in diameter. Most of the large ones are under 275 feet in height and under 18 feet in diameter (6 feet above the swelled bases).

RANGE OF TREES.

In giving the range of trees, departure has been made from the usual practice of describing only the general region of occurrence.

This is briefly recorded for the benefit of those who desire just this information.   But for the benefit of very many more it has seemed proper to include also a brief detailed description of the local range, vertical and horizontal, by States, Territory, and other geographical subdivisions in the region occupied by the species or subspecies.   The fullest information possible has been given for commercial trees.

A very much more definite knowledge is greatly and generally needed of the local distribution of our trees.   Extreme extensions or outlying stations for each tree require to be recorded.   No observers have done more along this line than authors of State and county floras, by whom actual limits of range have been carefully worked out for the trees and other plants of their special localities.   There are too few of these painstaking workers, and their work can not be too highly praised.   The writer wishes to emphasize the fact also that the numerous unpublished silvical, National Forest boundary, and other field reports by members of the Forest Service, as well as special field reports by members of the U. S. Geological Survey and the Biological Survey, have proved rich sources of new information on the local and general range of Pacific trees.   Through these sources the distribution of some trees has been extended hundreds of miles beyond previously recorded limits.   Finally, it is hoped that by giving, in detail, what is now known the many observers and lovers of trees who are scattered throughout this region will be stimulated to make further contributions.   Much is yet to be learned of where the trees of this region grow.

OCCURRENCE OF TREES.

Closely connected with a study of the areal and altitudinal range of trees is the equally important determination of where, in their respective ranges, this or that species lives—by necessity or by virtue of special fitness.   Like animals, trees have what may be termed a more or less definite habitat, defined by such physical conditions as soil, moisture, topography, and, to a greater or less extent, temperature.   The likes and dislikes, as it were, of one species are, of course, shared by a number of others, so that several species may have their habitat in wet, in moist, or in dry situations; while different individuals of the same species may accommodate themselves to all of these situations.

It would lead too far, for present purposes, to discuss, even briefly, the factors upon which the adaptation of trees to environment appear to depend.   The effects of mutual likes and dislikes upon species are to be seen in the occurrence of certain trees in pure stands only and the occurrence of others with different kinds of trees or with different species of the same kind.

The occurrence of trees is also influenced by their tolerance—that is, their ability to exist, for a part or the whole of their lives, in dense shade or their requirement of various degrees of shade or of full light. To what extent, however, tolerance—inherent or acquired—may be accounted for by the amount of soil moisture a given species requires can not be stated now. Finally, the characteristic habits and methods of reproduction, by seed or by sprouts, most important factors in the life history of a tree, have much to do with the occurrence of a species.

It may be said here, in passing, that dendrology, the botany of trees, properly includes a study of the distinguishing characteristics of tree species for the purpose of identification and, naturally, of the affinities which determine their classification into orders and other natural groups. The characteristics of a tree include the definition of both external and internal form characters—the morphology of its trunk, root, branches, twigs, buds, leaves, flowers, fruit, seed—as well as of the anatomical structure of the tissues, including characteristic secretions—gums, resins, etc.—of which these parts are composed. A study of the physiological processes which characterize the life of the tree organism are a part, too, of dendrology. It deals also with the natural range—horizontal and vertical and its peculiar climatic conditions, as well as with the habitat or occurrence—including the character of site and soil the tree chooses either in pure or mixed growths. What the forester has long called silvics, a study of the habits and life history of trees in the forest, therefore falls naturally under dendrology. Silvics, as the basis for all practical silvicultural operations, deals with the factors which influence the life and growth of trees in their natural or adopted habitat. In recent years the new science of ecology, a study of plant associations, has included, in so far as the life habits of trees are concerned, a part of dendrology as one of its natural subdivisions. It appears logical, however, to consider dendrology as still including the study of tree associations. This leaves forest ecology in its proper place as a department of general ecology, and at the same time preserves the identity of an essential part of dendrology, a distinct division of general botany. However this may be, the serious student of tree life—dendrology— can make no mistake in taking the broadest view of the field and in striving to familiarize himself with all that pertains to trees, from a study of their distinguishing characteristics to their modes of life and associations.

ACKNOWLEDGMENTS.

Grateful acknowledgment is here made to Dr. C. Hart Merriam, who placed at the writer's disposal transcripts of his voluminous notes on the distribution and occurrence of California trees. The unpublished data thus made available is the result of over twenty years of field observations made while studying life zones and during thousands of miles of travel, on foot and on horseback, especially in unfrequented and little-known sections of the State.   Doctor Merriam's rare and accurate knowledge of Pacific trees renders the information contributed exceptionally valuable.

Special acknowledgment is due the American Museum of Natural History, New York, for diameter measurements and corresponding age determinations, taken from the Jesup Collection of North American woods, through the cordial cooperation of the director, Dr. H. C. Bumpus. With these determinations, together with similar ones obtained through personal field studies and from unpublished records of the Forest Service, the author has been able to present statements of the ages attained by practically all of the Pacific trees.

It is difficult to abandon wholly the terse and exact language of technical science and to convey in ordinary terms an accurate impression of a tree's distinguishing characteristics. The writer has endeavored to make this work simple and at the same time thoroughly accurate. If it proves helpful at all in acquainting the uninitiated with the characters and habits of Pacific trees, he will be greatly encouraged in the preparation of the other regional floras designed to follow this part.

GEORGE B. SUDWORTH.

PLATE I.

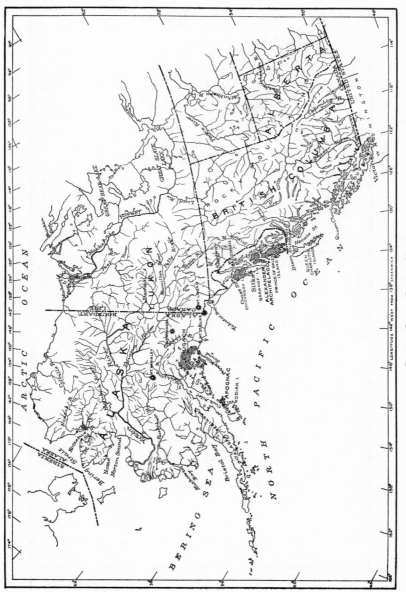

PACIFIC COAST REGION NORTH.

PLATE II.

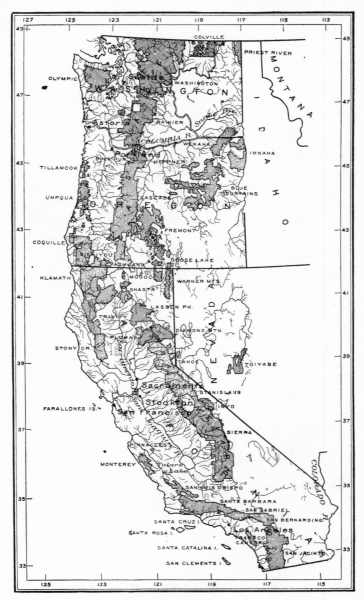

PACIFIC COAST REGION SOUTH.

GYMNOSPERMÆ.

The Gymnosperms are technically distinguished from other seed-bearing trees by having their ovules borne naked or without the usual covering provided in other trees. They have resinous wood formed in concentric rings, which are laid on each year, one outside of the preceding one, and just beneath the bark. As with other classes of our trees which grow in this manner, the age can be accurately told by counting the rings shown on a cross-section of the stem at the ground just above where the root is given off. Some of these trees bear male and female flowers separately on different branches of the same tree, and some bear male flowers on one tree and female flowers on a different tree. The male flowers produce pollen (resembling yellowish powder) in large quantities and the wind conveys it to the female or fruit ("seed") bearing flowers for the purpose of fertilization. It is light and easily blown by wind for 50 or more yards. According to the character of their fruits, Gymnosperms are divided into two families, Coniferæ (cone-bearers), and Taxaceæ (yew-like).

Family CONIFERÆ.

This family includes the pines (*Pinus*), spruces (*Picea*), larches or true tamaracks (*Larix*), hemlocks (*Tsuga*), false or bastard hemlocks (*Pseudotsuga*), firs or "balsam trees" (*Abies*), "bald" cypress (*Taxodium*), arborvitæs or "cedars" (*Thuja*), true cypresses (*Cupressus* and *Chamæcyparis*), redwood and bigtree (*Sequoia*), and junipers or "cedars" (*Juniperus*). In all but the last group these trees bear a fruit which is a distinctly woody cone, with from two to several naked seeds under each of its overlapping or otherwise closed scales. The junipers produce a berry-like fruit, which, though not woody, is, however, morphologically a cone. The seeds of most conifers have a thin wing which helps them greatly to be scattered by the wind far from the parent tree, and so provides for their reproduction over a wide area. The seeds of some conifers have no wing, or merely a rudimentary one. The berry-like fruits of the junipers are largely dependent for their distribution upon birds which eat them and upon flood waters which distribute them. The hard seed loses only its pulpy coating by being eaten. The leaves of conifers are small and scale-like, or long and needle-like. In all but the bald cypresses (*Taxodium*) and larches (*Larix*), the leaves remain on the trees for several years, which has given them the names of "evergreens." The seed leaves (cotyledons) number from 2 to about 18.

PINUS. PINES.

The pines are all evergreen trees. Their branches are more or less thickly clothed with clusters of needle-like leaves in bundles of two, three, four, or five. One species has solitary leaves. New leaves are formed each year on the young twigs which lengthen the previous year's growth. The leaves produced in a season may remain on the tree from two to six or eight years. They die and

19

fall when a set of new leaves is being formed at the ends of the branches. The fruits of pines are woody, scaly cones, matured in from two to three years. The cones of some pines remain on the trees only a few weeks after ripening, while those of others persist for many years, or even are so firmly attached as to be entirely enveloped by the annual diameter growth of the tree. At maturity most pine cones open under the heat of the sun and liberate their seeds; a few pines, however, rarely open their cones except under the heat of a forest fire. This fact explains how certain pines often reproduce themselves after the original forest has been killed by fire, since not all of the cones are burned enough to destroy their seeds, and the seeds are scattered after the fire. The flowers of the pines are of two sexes, male and female, borne usually on different branches of the same tree. Male flowers, which produce pollen, are short, oval, and bud-like, or long cylindrical bodies, clustered at the ends of mature leafy branches. They are bright red, yellow, or orange. The female flowers, which produce cones and seed, are small, greenish, scaly, cone-like bodies, produced singly or in pairs or groups near the ends of young growing shoots of the spring. After fertilization of the two ovules (under each scale) these flowers develop into small cones during the first season, as a rule completing their growth and maturing their seeds at the end of the second summer. Ripe cones vary from an inch in length and three-fourths inch in diameter, to 2 feet in length and 6 or 8 inches in diameter. The seed of most pines bears a thin papery wing at one end. In a few species, however, the seed has only the rudiment of a wing, which remains attached to the cone scale when the seed is shed. The piñon or "nut" pines bear wingless seeds. Pine seeds vary from one-half the size of a kernel of wheat to nearly the size of a small hazel nut. Seeds of the "nut" pines are gathered by western Indians for food. The needle-like foliage of pines varies from an inch to 14 or 15 inches in length. Seed-leaves (cotyledons) of pines are needle-shaped and from 3 to 15 in number. Succeeding these, pine seedlings produce temporary or primary leaves, which are single; but later, commonly at the beginning of the second year, they begin to bear their leaves in clusters. Leaves are borne in clusters during the remainder of the tree's life.

The pines are among our most important commercial trees. Because they have straight, unbranched, cylindrical trunks, they furnish large amounts of excellent saw timber, without waste. Pine timber is widely used for all construction purposes on account of its straight grain, strength, and other qualities.

The naval stores used in the United States, as well as the large quantities exported to other countries, are derived by distillation from the crude resin of the more resinous-wooded pines. Recently the wood of stumps and old logs is being distilled for turpentine. Some 70 species of pines are known in the world. Thirty-four pines inhabit the United States, 17 of which occur in the Pacific region.

Pines are of ancient origin, some of them having existed in the Cretaceous and Miocene periods in North America and Europe.

WHITE PINES.

Western White Pine; Silver Pine.

Pinus monticola Dougl.

DISTINGUISHING CHARACTERISTICS.

This species is more commonly called "white pine" where it is cut for lumber. The name western white pine is proposed for this tree in order to distinguish it from the eastern white pine (*Pinus strobus*).

In dense forests, in which its most characteristic form is found, this pine has a tall, slender shaft, with a peculiarly short-branched, narrow, symmetrical crown; the branches are usually slender and drooping and in early life extend over one-half or two-thirds the length of the trunk. Its height ranges from 90 to 100 feet, and its diameter from $2\frac{1}{2}$ to $3\frac{1}{2}$, or, exceptionally, 4 feet. In open forests, where the conditions are less favorable to its better development, it is a short-bodied tree, 50 or 60 feet in height, with one or several very long, stout, horizontal branches extending from 10 to 15 feet or more beyond the other slender branches. This striking character distinguishes the tree as far as it can be seen. The bark of trees a foot or more in diameter is distinctly broken into peculiar small, square blocks. No other tree associated with it has this bark character. Bark of mature trees is rarely over $1\frac{1}{4}$ inches thick. In dense stands the color of the bark is grayish-purple, while in open, wind-swept stands it is a distinct cinnamon color. The action of wind constantly tears off thin outer scales of bark and exposes the red-brown interior. Young trees have thin, smooth, bright gray bark, as do also the branches and upper stems of old trees. The foliage of this pine is bluish-green, with a whitish tinge. The leaves are from 2 to about 4 inches long, borne 5 in a bundle (fig. 1). The cones are matured at the end of the second summer, usually by the first of September. They shed their seed soon afterward and fall from the trees within a few months. The cones (fig. 2) vary in length from about 6 to 10 inches— occasionally slightly longer or shorter. In unweathered mature cones the tips of the scales are red-brown or yellow-brown, the inner portion of the scales being a deep red. The seeds (fig. 2, *a*) are reddish brown, with small blackish spots. Seed leaves, 6 to 8 or 9.

Wood, very light and soft; heartwood, pale brown, of high commercial value.

LONGEVITY.—A long-lived tree, attaining an age of from 200 to 500 years.

RANGE.

Middle and upper slopes of northwestern mountains from west side of Continental Divide in northern Montana and southern British Columbia to Washington, Oregon, and California.

BRITISH COLUMBIA.—Lateral valleys east of Columbia-Kootenai Valley, northward to Donald, on Gold and Selkirk ranges (in region of heavy rainfall), northward to Great Shuswap and Adams lakes; also on central ranges, in southwest to Coast Range, there extending 51 miles up Homathco River to 2,235 feet elevation. On interior mountains of Vancouver Island and southwest coast, but not yet found on Queen Charlotte Islands.

WASHINGTON.—Mountains of Northeast, Blue Mountains, and westward to Cascade and Coast ranges, at elevations from 300 up to 6,000 feet. In northern Cascades, from near sea level on Puget Sound up to about 3,000 feet; farther south on west side, at from 2,000 to 6,000 feet, and on the east side, at from 1,150 to 4,700 feet; eastward 5 miles above Lake Chelan, and in Okanogan County to mountains west of Okanogan River (T. 36 N., R. 24 E.). Farther south, noted up to 6,000 feet, Tolt, Snoqualmie, Cedar, Green, White, Yakima, Wenache, and Entiat river basins. In Olympics, from near sea level up to 1,800 feet.

OREGON.—On both sides of Cascades and on coast ranges, at from 3,000 to 6,000 feet in north and 5,000 to 7,500 feet in south, extending eastward to Blue and Warner mountains. On north side Mount Hood from 20 miles south of Hood River on the Columbia at 2,000 to 4,300 feet; on south side from Camas Prairie to Government Camp. Cascade National Forest (North) at 1,500 to 6,100 feet, throughout west slope north of McKenzie River, on east slope south of Mount Hood in White River Basin, and at headwaters of Warm Springs River and Beaver Creek. Eastward in Deschutes River Valley east of Cascades to upper Paulina Creek Canyon. Cascade National Forest (South) only on main divide southward (to T. 39, S., R. 5 E.), on west side at 5,000 to 7,500 feet, and not over 14 miles west of summit, except upper South Umpqua River Basin and on Siskiyous between Siskiyou and Sterling peaks. Frequent on east side of Cascades, but confined to declivities at 5,500 to 6,000 feet. Noted on Mount Mazama (Crater Lake) from 5,000 to above

6,000 feet. Also in coast ranges on Iron Mountain and Rusty Butte. Noted in Upper Klamath River basin on Gearhart Mountains, head of Sprague River. Farther east, in Goose Lake National Forest, noted on Cottonwood Creek, head of Deep Creek, and in north Warner Mountains (east of Goose Lake), at 7,500 to 8,500 feet.

CALIFORNIA.—Northern cross ranges and southward in Sierras. On Siskiyous at 6,000 to 7,000 feet elevation, summit of Glass Mountain (border Siskiyou and Modoc counties) ; on Mount Shasta at 6,000 to 7,200 feet ; south of Brewer Creek up to 7,200 feet, near

FIG. 1.—*Pinus monticola.*

Inconstance Creek, in Mud Creek Canyon, near top of Red Cone (east of Wagon Camp). Lassen Peak at 6,000 to 7,000 feet ; down to 5,500 feet on south side, and on north side at upper Hat Creek ; east Trinity Mountains on Canyon Creek at 4,500 feet to outlet of Twin Lakes (5,500 feet). Reported on high summits of Trinity and Klamath National Forests. In northern Sierras, generally at 6,000 to 7,500 feet, but at 8,400 feet on Pyramid Creek. Region of Donner Lake (Nevada and Placer counties), westward to Cisco and eastward to near Truckee ; also east side of Sierras facing Reno, Nevada.

FIG. 2.—*Pinus monticola: a,* seed.

Noted in mountains about Lake Tahoe, Glen Alpine Canyon, Grass Lake, from summit on west side Sierras at 7,500 feet to Echo at 5,500 feet. *Alpine County:* Silver Creek Canyon above 7,500 feet; on and near summit of Mokelumne Pass, at 8,800 feet, and divide between Mokelumne and Pacific valleys at 7,900 feet. *Tuolumne County:* West to just east of Eureka Valley and eastward nearly to Sonora Pass, at 9,000 feet; on White Mountain, Mount Conness, ridge between Dingley and Delaney creeks at 9,000 to 9,500 feet; north side Lambert Dome, Tuolumne River Canyon, Middle Fork Tuolumne westward nearly to White Wolf, between Tuolumne Meadows and Lake Tenaya, about Cathedral Lakes and southward. *Mariposa County:* Near Sunrise Ridge at 9,300 feet, and into Little Yosemite at 6,000 feet; ridge west of Lake Tenaya and westward to beyond White Wolf, from Porcupine Flat southward to 7,800 feet. *Mono County:* Bloody Canyon (east side Mono Pass), at about 9,300 feet. In southern Sierras, at 8,000 to 10,000 feet, while on divide between Middle and South forks of Kings River, and on divide between East and Middle forks of Kaweah River, it goes to 11,000 feet elevation; upper Kings River Canyon above Junction Meadow and below Vidette Meadow; Giant Forest and from Clover Creek Divide to Rowell Meadow; Alta Peak (between Marble and East Forks Kaweah River); south side North Fork of Kaweah; on Mount Silliman, at 8,900 to 10,200 feet, and above Mineral King, at 9,600 to 10,400 feet. On west slopes of Sierras, extends southward to head of Soda Creek (branch Little Kern River, in T. 19 S., R. 32 W.), and on divide between Kern River and its south fork, to a point about opposite lower end of Monache Valley (T. 19 to 21 S., R. 34 E., lat. 36° 10'). On east side of Sierras it extends from Truckee to head of Cottonwood Creek. In south, reported on Mount Wilson in San Gabriel Range, on San Bernardino Mountains, at 10,000 feet, at Round Valley in San Jacinto Mountains at 8,900 to 9,500 feet, and on Tahquitz Peak at 8,600 feet.

The detailed range of this pine in Idaho and Montana will be dealt with in a subsequent publication.

OCCURRENCE.

Not confined to any definite type of locality. At north, most abundant and largest in moist valleys, growing also in dry, exposed subalpine regions. Adapted to variety of soils. Best growth occurs in deep, porous soils. Most common in poor, sandy situations.

Greatest development in northern Idaho, on gentle north slopes and flats. Less frequent west of Continental Divide in Montana and of Cascades in Oregon. In northern California, on north slopes, and on south and west slopes in protected coves, broad valleys, and mountain benches; in southern California rather abundant on high, west slope of Sierras. Occurs commonly as scattered trees or small groups with other species; very rarely in pure stands and only on exposed high slopes. In Cascades and Sierras occasionally forming 50 to 70 per cent of stand on small areas, but throughout its range not exceeding 3 or 4 per cent. In Washington associated with western hemlock, amabilis fir, lowland fir, and Douglas fir; in Oregon, with Douglas fir, lowland fir, and amabilis fir; in California, with Douglas fir, lodgepole pine, red fir, and Shasta fir.

CLIMATIC CONDITIONS.—Throughout its range the approximate seasonal temperature varies between —26° F. and 98° F. Mean annual rainfall in north, from 15 inches in parts of Montana and Idaho to about 60 inches near Puget Sound; in California, probably between 20 and 30 inches. Humidity is great in western Washington, where over two-thirds of the days are cloudy or foggy, while it is smaller in east and south, where one-half of the days are overcast. Snow falls throughout its range, less near sea than in northern Rocky and California mountains, where it reaches a depth of several feet.

TOLERANCE.—Endures shade for a relatively long period in youth, later requiring an abundance of light for its development. It prunes well. Does not recover well after suppression during pole stage.

REPRODUCTION.—Reproduces itself only sparingly and at irregular intervals of about two years. Not a prolific seeder; bears seed only when of considerable age (40 to 60 years). Seed germinates poorly on heavy humus, unless the humus is moist during most of growing season; best on exposed moist mineral soil.

Sugar Pine.

Pinus lambertiana Dougl.

DISTINGUISHING CHARACTERISTICS.

The largest and most magnificent of Pacific white pines, if not of all the timber pines of the region, the western yellow pine being its only rival. Its massive trunk attains a height of from 160 to 180 feet, with a diameter of from 4 to 7 feet. Somewhat taller and larger trees are occasionally found. The trunk of mature trees is very straight, and tapers but little until the few large, very long, horizontal limbs of its wide, flat crown are reached. These huge branches stand out so prominently at right angles from the upper trunk as to distinguish it from associated pines. Its long, cylindrical cones, suspended from the tips of the branches, also serve to distinguish the tree at a long distance. Trees from pole size to a foot in diameter bear distinct whorls of branches at long intervals down to the ground. Later in life the lower whorls are shaded out and two or more of the upper limbs develop enormously in the full light. This usually takes place as the tree attains its main height growth. Old bark

FIG. 3.—*Pinus lambertiana.*

is deeply furrowed longitudinally, the ridges being broken into long, irregular plates. It is from $1\frac{1}{2}$ to $2\frac{1}{2}$ inches or more in thickness and grayish brown in color. In exposed situations the force of high winds tears off the weathered flakes of bark, leaving the exposed surface a deep red-brown color. The smooth, thin bark of the young trunks and branches of old trees is a dull, dark gray. The foliage is a deep blue-green, with a whitish tinge. The leaves (fig. 3), in bundles of 5, are from $2\frac{3}{4}$ to about 4 inches long. Those of each year's growth persist two or three years. The cones (fig. 4), which are unique among

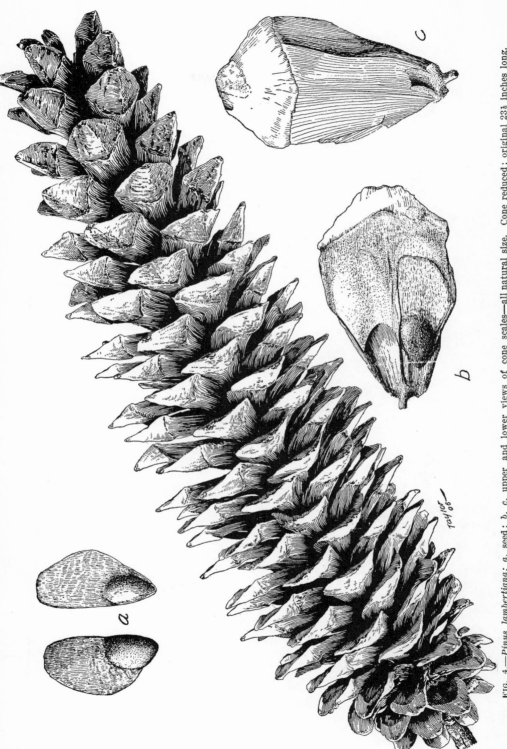

FIG. 4.—*Pinus lambertiana*: *a*, seed; *b*, *c*, upper and lower views of cone scales—all natural size. Cone reduced; original 23½ inches long.

all our pines in their huge size and form, are from 12 to 16 inches long and from $2\frac{1}{2}$ to $3\frac{1}{2}$ inches in diameter; occasionally, 18 to 23 inches in length. The tips of the scales are shiny and pale reddish brown, the inner part of the scale being a deep purple brown. Cones ripen during August of the second year and shed their seeds by October. Cones seldom fall until the third spring or summer, and sometimes they remain on the trees until the autumn of that year, The seeds (fig. 4, *a*) are smooth, and vary from a dark chocolate to a blackish brown. Seed leaves, 12 to 15. The wood is light and soft, but somewhat less so than that of the western white pine; heartwood, pale reddish-brown; of great commercial value.

LONGEVITY.—A very long-lived tree, reaching an age of from 300 to 500, and, in occasional instances, nearly 600 years.

RANGE.

Mountains from North Fork of Santiam River, Oregon, southward in Coast and Cascades ranges, Sierras, and southern California cross ranges, to Mount San Pedro Martir, Lower California.

OREGON.—Mainly on west side of Cascades and northward to within a few miles northwest of Mount Jefferson; on Siskiyous and mountains of Klamath Basin and eastward to Goose Lake, generally at 2,000 feet to 3,000 feet elevation, but near coast down to 1,000 feet, while on east side of Cascades it goes to 5,000 feet. In northern Cascade National Forest, only on North Fork of Santiam River, at 1,700 to 3,700 feet elevation, from Chimney Peak to Humbug Creek Basin (T. 9 S., R. 6 E., lat. 44° 47′, long. 122° 4′), the northern limit. South of this it occurs on headwaters of Willamette River (T. 22 S., R. 1 and 3 E., T. 23 S., R. 2 to 4 E., T. 24 S., R. 3 to 4 E.), south of Fish Lake on main divide (T. 27 S., R. 6½ E.); in Rogue River Valley; on Rogue-Umpqua river divide (T. 30 S., R. 1 to 5 E., T. 31 S., R. 1 to 6), and more abundantly southward on Cascades to Siskiyous. Crosses Cascades south of Fish Lake and occurs on headwaters of Deschutes River between Sink Creeks, Walker Range, and Pengra, also on south and east basal slopes of Mount Mazama. Extends along east slopes at elevations of 4,500 to 6,500 feet to beyond the Klamath Marshes and Klamath Gap. Extends southeastward between these marshes and upper Klamath Lake, while farther east, in Yamsay Range, it occurs on Fuego Mountain, in Black Hills, and eastward to Klamath-Deschutes divide, where it ranges from head of Deschutes River to Gearhart Mountains and Drew Valley, west of Goose Lake. Ashland National Forest, up to about 5,400 feet. A few trees at about 1,700 feet in southern coast ranges of Curry County (S. 2, T. 38 S., R. 14 W., and S. 35, T. 37 S., R. 14 W.), about 5 miles from coast.

CALIFORNIA.—In Siskiyous and southward over northern California abundant save on higher peaks and in Shasta Valley, at elevations of 3,000 to 6,000 feet throughout western two-thirds of State. Extends eastward to Mount Shasta and summits in Shasta National Forest north of Shasta, but unknown on Modoc and Warner mountains in northeastern California. Noted in Siskiyou County eastward to near Beswick (on Klamath River, just south of Oregon line); also on Shovel Creek Ridge (near Klamath Falls), Little Shasta Valley, and on Goosenest Mountain. Western limit, same as that of yellow pine, follows inland margin of fog belt 20 to 30 miles from coast. Klamath National Forest, at 3,000 to 5,000 feet elevation; reported also to extend nearly to sea-level on flats of Smith River (Del Norte County); western limits in Siskiyou County at least to west slope of Marble Mountain Divide and (west of it) Russian Creek basin; northward on Salmon River to junction with Klamath River, and to 5,500 feet on Salmon Summit (on west) and basin betwen Salmon Summit and Trinity Summit. Humboldt County; sparingly on west slope of Trinity Mountain, between about 3,700 and 5,000 feet; about 2½ miles from Hoopa Valley at 1,600 feet, and a little farther west common at 1,800 to 2,100 feet; here up north side of Supply Canyon to 2,600 feet (westmost limit). Mount Shasta National Forest, at from 3,000 to 6,000 feet, sometimes up to 6,500 and down to 2,000 feet, and extending southward in Sacramento Canyon to the "Loop," while on Mount Shasta it occurs only from a point 4½ miles southeast of Edgewood, on northwest side, around west and south sides to Ash Creek, reaching about 6,000 feet, but on south slopes going to 7,500 feet. Farther south in Shasta County, east limits are Soldier Mountain (1 mile northwest of Dana), ridge east of Fall River Valley (Shasta-Lassen county boundary); noted westward to point 3 miles east of Montgomery, and on McCloud River south to Baird. In Trinity National Forest it goes eastward to Lewiston on west border of Sacramento Valley; Coast Range at 2,300 to 4,150 feet and southward to Bully Choop and Yola Buli ranges and westward to upper Mad River; on north slopes and flats, generally at 3,000 to 6,000 feet, but on South Fork Mountain it grows at 5,000 feet elevation, on South Fork of Trinity River at 3,500 to 5,000 feet, on Hay Fork Mountain and Bear Wallow Creek at 5,500 feet, and in Rattlesnake Basin at 3,900 feet. In Stony Creek National Forest, north of Clear Lake, on slopes of north and south ranges between 2,000 and 5,000 feet; especially abundant on Pine and Sanhedrin Mountains, and headwaters of the South Fork of Eel River. On Mayacamas mountains, extending to Bartlett Mountain (northeast of Clear Lake), here on south side above 3,000 feet, and on west side above 3,800 feet—and to Glenbrook and Cobb Mountain, in Lake County; southward, it goes to Sutro Ranch, near Oakhill Mountain; also on north and northeast slopes of Mount St. Helena, and on south side above Tollhouse and eastward, also at intervals down ridge southeast of mountain (south limit in northern coast ranges). Once found on Pope and Howell mountains; also reported from many points in Mendocino County and from Galloway and Austin creeks, in Sonoma County. Not detected in mountains about San Francisco Bay, but is found in westmost coast range at Palo Alto. In Santa Lucia Mountains, south of Monterey Bay, grows on north slopes of Santa Lucia and Cone Peaks in San Antonio and Arroyo Seco river basins at 4,000 to 5,900 feet. In northern Sierras, mainly on west slopes, at 3,500 to 6,500 feet elevation, occasionally extending down to 2,000 feet and up to 7,500 feet. *Tehama County:* Westward on Sierras to near Lyonsville and 10 miles east of Payne. *Lassen County:* northwest corner from point 5 miles west of Bieber westward; not east of Big Valley; in southern part of county, eastward to Susanville; general in Lassen Peak, Plumas, and Diamond Mountain National forests; in Plumas Forest two belts occur east and west of divide, mainly at 3,000 to 5,500 feet elevation, but some trees at 7,500 feet. Westward in Butte County to Magalia, North Fork Feather River, and to point about 4 miles north of Bidwell Bar (1,300 feet). *Yuba County:* To North Fork Yuba River and Oregon Hills. Eastward in Plumas County to Mount Dyer, Greenville, Quincy, and ridge west of Sierra Valley. *Sierra County:* East slope of mountains west of Sierra Valley, reaching 6,000 feet on west side of Yuba Pass. *Nevada County:* To country north of Lake Tahoe. In Tahoe National Forest, eastern limits are main Sierra divide, except that it extends to east slopes of Sierras at head of North Fork of American River, and near shores of Lake Tahoe (at 6,250 feet elevation); thence descending Truckee River Canyon into Nevada to a point opposite Reno, where it is scattered above 6,000 feet. Westward in Placer County to Colfax (2,500 feet), Applegate, and 5 miles east of Forest Hill; westward in Eldorado County to Placerville, Pleasant Valley, 6 miles east of Nashville (at about 2,000 feet), and eastward on west slopes of Sierras to about 5,500 feet (Echo and elsewhere). Occurs generally in Stanislaus National Forest, but not throughout yellow pine belt, at 3,000 to 5,000 feet, and sometimes at 2,000 feet and 7,000 feet. *Amador County:* Westward to Oleta and Pinegrove, and eastward on west slope Sierras to Volcano. *Calaveras County:* Westward to point (1,500 feet) 6 miles east of San Andreas, and 4 miles east of Murphys; eastward to West Point, Railroad Flat, Big Trees, and 10 miles west of Bloods at 6,600 feet. *Tuolumne County:* Westward to Soulsbyville and Bigoak Flat; eastward (at about 6,200 feet) to between Cold Spring and Eureka Valley, at Aspen Meadows (6,200 feet), North Crane Creek (about 6,000 feet). *Mariposa County:* Westward to Ball Creek (east Coulterville), points (3,000 feet) 4 miles east of Mariposa, and 3 miles east of Wassama. Extends eastward to Yosemite Valley, occurring here as follows: Little Yosemite and eastward at 6,800 to 7,000 feet, and Sunrise Ridge at 7,600 feet; Yosemite Falls trail (near top of fall) at about 7,000 feet, and Indian Canyon Basin; south of Yosemite from head of Nevada Fall (6,000 feet) to Glacier Point (7,300 feet), and southwestward to Yosemite, Wawona road (at Chinquapin); Sentinel Dome at about 7,500 to 7,700 feet, or more. In southern Sierras it grows at elevations between 5,500 and 9,000 feet, or occasionally down to 4,500 feet. *Fresno County:* Eastward to Bubbs Creek (tributary of Kings River); Summit Meadow at 8,000 feet. *Tulare County:* In Sequoia National Park and adjacent parts of Kaweah watersheds; in Buck Canyon, near Bear Paw Meadow, and between Cliff, Canyon, and Deer creeks (tributaries of Middle Fork Kaweah); Kern River Canyon (near Kern Lakes); part of Tule River Indian Reservation (South Fork of Tule River) and eastward on Sierras. Occurs on Greenhorn and Piute ranges at 6,000 to 7,000 feet, Mount Breckenridge, on other mountains south of South Fork of Kern River, and on Tehachapi Mountains, where, as in Tejon Canyon, it grows at 6,000 to 7,500 feet. Quite general in southern California mountains at from about 5,000 to over 8,500 feet. In Santa Barbara National Forest, at 5,000 to 7,500 feet and sometimes up to 8,800 feet, on San Rafael to San Emigdio Mountains, Mount Pinos, and other mountains in basins of Piru-Sespe and Santa Maria rivers. In Sierra Madre Mountains, it grows between 5,500 and 8,500 feet at Strands, near Pasadena, on Waterman Mountain, Mount Gleason, Strawberry Peak, Mount Wilson, Pine Flats, Mount Islip, Prairie Forks, and on Mount San Antonio; on San Bernardino Mountains between 4,500 to 8,000 feet, and occasionally from 4,000 to 10,500 feet, but mainly on top of range from T. 2 N, R. 5, W, eastward to Bear Lake. In timbered portions of San Jacinto Mountains, generally at elevations of 5,800 to 9,000 feet, sometimes descending to 5,000 and ascending to 9,800 feet; common on westside trail at 6,000 feet, and also on southwest side of Tahquitz-Strawberry Divide. In Cuyamaca Mountains, at from 5,500 feet, on east side Cuyamaca Peak, to 6,500 feet on summit.

LOWER CALIFORNIA.—Frequent in forests of San Pedro Martir Plateau at elevations from 8,000 to 10,000 feet.

OCCURRENCE.

Chiefly on north slopes and benches and in ravines and canyons; occasionally on low mountain summits; found also on south and west slopes at higher altitudes. Grows on variety of soils from glacial drift and volcanic ash to deep, loose sands and clays; fresh, rich, well-drained, sandy loam or gravelly soils are most characteristic.

Never in pure stands. At lower elevations, mainly with western yellow pine, incense cedar, Kellogg oak, and, in northern California, also with Douglas fir; occasionally with tanbark oak. At high elevations yellow pine and incense cedar decrease, and white fir, and occasionally red fir, together with the big tree, become chief associates, especially on east and north slopes.

CLIMATIC CONDITIONS.—Atmospheric moisture is essential; hence it prefers cool, moist sites on north and east slopes and in heads of gulches and canyons. Doubtless on account of this requirement its altitudinal range of 1,000 to 3,000 feet at the north increases, going southward, roughly at the rate of about 500 feet to every 200 miles, until, at its southern limit, 9,000 feet is reached.

TOLERANCE.—In early youth requires partial shade, especially on dry, south slopes; when older it becomes very intolerant, even more intolerant than western yellow pine.

REPRODUCTION.—Not a regular or prolific seeder. A little seed is produced locally each year, but good crops occur locally at intervals of about from four to six years; regularity in seed years doubtful. Trees below 20 inches in diameter seldom bear seed to any extent. Ordinarily trees shed seed over ground for a distance from base of tree about equal to their height; distribution occasionally farther through increased wind, slope, or water.

Limber Pine.

Pinus flexilis James.

DISTINGUISHING CHARACTERISTICS.

Comparatively little known, doubtless on account of its high, inaccessible range. It is a low, thick-trunked, much-branched tree, from 25 to 30 or sometimes 50 feet in height, with short trunk from 12 to 30 inches in diameter; occasionally very old trees are $3\frac{1}{2}$ to 4 feet in diameter. Young trees are peculiar for their regular, distant whorls of short, very tough branches which stand at right angles to the trunk and extend down to the ground. Middle-aged and old trees (75 to 200 years) are characterized by extremely long and slender branches, especially near the ground and at the top; the latter are often 16 or 18 feet in length, falling gracefully at a sharp angle with the trunk. These branches appear to develop entirely at the expense of the trunk, which remains stunted. Old trunks have bark from $1\frac{1}{2}$ to nearly 2 inches thick, blackish or very dark brown, with deep furrows between wide rectangular blocks. On trunks from 8 to 12 inches thick the bark is broken into small, thin, gray-brown plates; when separated, the scales expose a dull reddish inner bark. The thin, smooth bark of young pole trees and of branches is a bright whitish gray, often silvery. The foliage, densely set at the ends of the branches, is dark yellow-green, and the needles are 5 in a cluster (fig. 5). They are from about $1\frac{3}{4}$ to nearly 3 inches long. Each year's growth of leaves persists for approximately five years. Cones (fig. 6), mature in late summer or early autumn of the second year, shed their seed in September and early in October. They are from $3\frac{1}{2}$ to 10 inches long and peculiar in having their light yellowish-brown scale tips greatly thickened; inner portions of scales, pale red.

By early winter the cones have fallen from the trees. The seeds (fig. 6, *a*) are deep reddish brown speckled with blackish brown. Seed leaves 6 to 8, sometimes 9. Wood, very dense on account of its exceedingly slow growth; light, soft; heartwood, pale lemon-yellow.

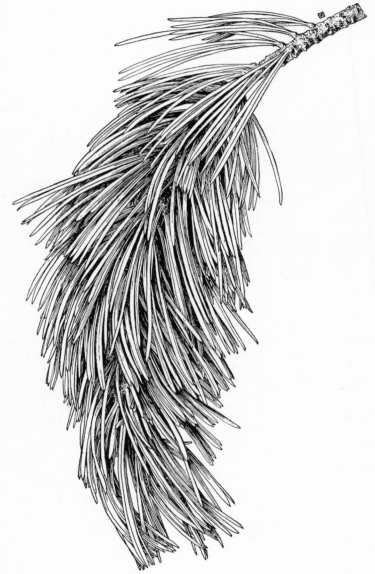

FIG. 5.—*Pinus flexilis.*

LONGEVITY.—Little is known of the longevity of this pine; trees from 200 to 300 years old and from 18 to 22 inches through are not uncommon.

On slopes of the Cordilleran Plateau from the eastern side of the Continental Divide, in Alberta and Montana, southward to New Mexico, Arizona, Nevada, and southern California.

CALIFORNIA.—Panamint Mountains, at from 7,100 to over 10,000 feet, and on summits of Inyo Mountains. On east slopes of Sierras at about 9,300 to 10,000 feet, extending in a belt from head of Tuttle Creek, southeast of Mount Whitney, to Cottonwood Creek; thence southward to slopes of Monache Peak. Occurs also at Mono Pass (east of

FIG. 6.—*Pinus flexilis: a,* cone scale and seeds.

Yosemite Valley) at 8,000 to 9,000 feet; at head of Mammoth Creek (T. 4 S., R. 27 E.), at 9,500 feet, and at Kearsarge Pass. On western slopes of Sierras along south side of South Fork of Kings River, at 10,500 to 12,000 feet. Reappears in southern cross ranges on Mount Pinos, at 8,400 to 8,826 feet; in Sierra Madre Mountains, at 8,000 to 10,000 feet; on summits of San Gorgonio and Santa Rosa mountains, in San Bernardino Mountains, and on north side of Grayback Mountain, at about 9,300 to 11,800 feet, while at Dry Lake it appears at about 9,000 feet, and in San Jacinto Mountains at 9,000 to 10,500 feet.

OCCURRENCE.

On dry, rocky, east slopes, summits, tops of ridges and foothills, and sometimes on sides of moister canyons and banks of mountain streams. Adapted to a great variety of soils and not exacting as regards depth or moisture, but grows best in moist, well-drained soils. Usually in dry, rocky, very shallow soil, appearing to prefer dry, loose, gravelly loam, with little or no humus. Reaches higher elevations on clay soils than on sandy ones.

Usually occurs singly or in small groves among other conifers, where it is of largest size ; occasionally in pure, open stands, commonly stunted, on exposed slopes and ridges. Apparently less frequent in Pacific than in Rocky Mountain range. Associated mainly with lodgepole pine and black hemlock at higher elevations, and sparingly with white fir and stunted sugar pine at lower altitudes.

CLIMATIC CONDITIONS.—Endures a variety of climatic conditions throughout range. Mean annual rainfall varies from 15 to 30 inches. Snowfall heavy, except in southern Rockies and southern California. Growing season, from 3 to 4 months in north ; somewhat longer in south. Minimum temperature from about −60° F. in north to −13° F. in south ; maximum temperature throughout range, from 90° to 97° F. Little atmospheric moisture.

TOLERANCE.—Appears to require full light. Never forms dense stands, and does not tend to crowd out other species ; only occasionally in fairly dense mixed stands. Similar in light requirement to white-bark and bristlecone pines, and less tolerant than other associated conifers.

REPRODUCTION.—Moderate seeder, varying with region and elevation. Generally bears cones abundantly in open stands at low altitudes, less abundantly in denser stands at higher elevations. Cones produced locally about every year. Seeds practically wingless and shed only near tree ; largely eaten by birds and squirrels. Mineral seed-bed most favorable for germination, which even under favorable conditions is but moderate.

White-bark Pine.

Pinus albicaulis Engelmann.

DISTINGUISHING CHARACTERISTICS.

White-bark pine has a low, long-branched, twisted or crooked trunk from 15 to 50 feet high and from 10 to 24 inches in diameter. Taller and larger trees occur in protected situations. In the high, wind-swept home of this tree it is often reduced to a sprawling shrub with enormous branches spreading over the ground. Young trees have distant, regular whorls of branches at right angles to the trunk, but in later life some of the upper whorls develop upward into long, willowy stems, giving the tree a loose, bushy crown. The branches, especially near the trunk, are exceedingly tough and flexible, so that the tree is characteristically able to withstand the fiercest storms. The bark, even that of old trees, is little broken, except near the base of the trunk, where it is rarely more than one-half inch thick. Narrow cracks divide the lower bark into very thin whitish or brownish scales, which, on falling or being torn off, reveal the characteristic red-brown inner bark. Elsewhere the bark is rarely more than one-fourth of an inch thick. Twigs of a year's and sometimes of two years' growth are slightly downy. The leaves (fig. 7), densely clustered at the ends of the branches, are dark yellow-green ; 5 in a bundle ; length, about 1⅜ to 2¾ inches. Shorter leaves occur on trees in the most exposed situations. Leaves of a season's growth remain on the tree for approximately 7 or 8 years, but some of them persist only 4 or 5 years. The cones (fig. 7) are a deep purple, with very thick scales, vary in length from about 1⅜ to nearly 3½ inches, and mature by the end of August or early in September of the second year. Usually they shed their seed during the latter month, but sometimes not until late in October. The cones dry out and open slowly in high, cold situations where this pine grows. The seeds (fig. 7, *a*), about one-half inch in length by one-third inch in diameter, are shed without their very narrow wings, which remain attached to the cone scales; the thick, hard shell is dark.chocolate brown.   Seed

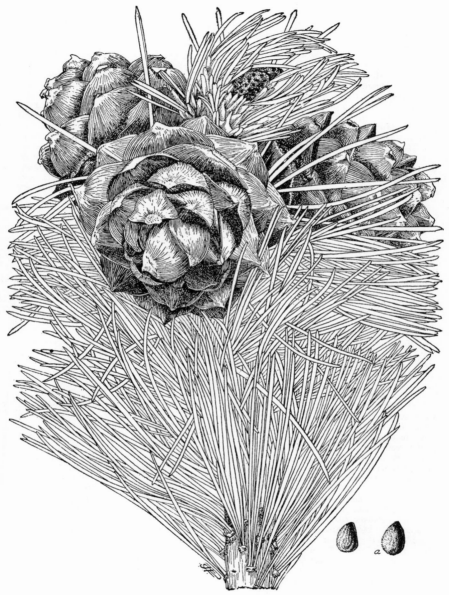

Fig. 7.—*Pinus albicaulis: a,* seed.

leaves, from 7 to 9. Wood, pale brown, light, soft, and brittle when dry; not of economic use.

LONGEVITY.—Trees attain an age of from 250 years (when they are about 19 inches in diameter) to 325 years. Very few records of longevity are available.

RANGE.

Timberline tree on the highest summits of northwestern and Pacific mountains, from British Columbia and Alberta to Montana, northwest Wyoming, Washington, Oregon, and southern California, at elevations of 6,000 to 7,000 feet toward the north, 5,500 to 9,300 feet in Oregon, 7,000 to 11,000 feet in California, and at 5,000 to 10,000 in Idaho and Montana.

CANADA.—Rocky Mountains at 6,000 to 7,000 feet, and northward to Rocky Mountains Park and Height of Land (latitude 52°). Appears as far east as Castle Mountain and the Sweet Grass Hills on the Canadian boundary. Selkirk, Gold, and southern interior ranges at 5,000 to 7,000 feet. Coast Range as far west as Silver Mountain, near Yale, at 5,000 feet; also at head of Salmon River and on Iltasyouco River (latitude 53°), but not yet found on Vancouver Island.

WASHINGTON.—Cascade Range (mainly east side), northeastern and Blue mountains, but absent from the Olympics; generally, at 4,500 to 7,500 feet. Common on eastern slopes of Cascades of Washington National Forest at 4,600 to 7,500 feet, and rare on west slopes above 6,000 feet. In Mount Rainier National Forest at 5,000 to 8,200 feet. In basins of Skykomish, Snoqualmie, Cedar, Green, White, Yakima, and Wenache rivers and of Lake Chelan; also on Mount Rainier, Mount St. Helena, Mount Adams, State and Windy passes, Early Winters Creek.

OREGON.—Frequent at timberline on both sides of Cascades and eastward to Blue and Powder River mountains, and highest ranges of Klamath River Basin; generally, at 5,500 to 9,300 feet. In northern Cascades forming timberline belt at 5,000 to 8,600 feet. Southward on both sides of main divide of Cascades, ranging from 6,000 to 9,300 feet; scarce on Umpqua-Rogue River Divide, and sparingly represented in the Siskiyous between Siskiyou and Sterling peaks. Yamsay Range only of interior Klamath River Basin and high ridges of Klamath-Deschutes Divide. On Mount Hood, Mount Pitt, Mount Scott, Mount Mazama.

CALIFORNIA.—Frequent from mountains about Shasta southward in Sierras to Kaweah peaks: generally, at 7,000 to 11,000 feet elevation. In Shasta National Forest on Mount Shasta at 7,000 to 8,000 feet, on warmest ridges up to 9,800 feet. Mount Eddy and Thompson Peak Ridge (between Canyon Creek and Salmon River, Trinity County) Mountain north of Mount Shasta and immediately east of Shasta Valley, and on Goosenest Mountain at 8,800 feet. West slope of Warner Mountains (northeastern corner of State) at 9,000 to 10,000 feet. In northern Sierras, on Lassen, Spanish, and Castle peaks, also Mount Pleasant and other high summits at head of North and Middle forks of Feather River, and elsewhere up to 7,800 feet. High peaks west of Lake Tahoe (Eldorado County). In Stanislaus National Forest, generally between 8,000 to 9,500 feet. *Tuolumne County:* Sonora Pass and above (altitude 9,600 feet) and down on west side to 8,500 feet; Mono Pass, down on east slope to 9,400 feet, and on west slope to little below 10,000 feet, thence above pass to about 11,500 feet. Trees in pass bear limbs only on east side (effect of prevailing wind). White Mountain and Mount Conness; foot of glacier at north base of Conness Peak. Tuolumne Meadows region, above 10,000 feet; upper Tuolumne River Canyon below Tuolumne Meadows; Mount Lyell, north side at 10,500 feet and thence northward on west wall of Lyell Fork Canyon; Mounts Dana and Gibbs on west slope down to Tioga and Saddleback lakes; Cathedral and Unicorn lakes and peaks (south of Tuolumne Meadows). *Mariposa County:* Sunrise Ridge, between Cathedral Lakes and Little Yosemite. *Mono County:* From summit Mono Pass eastward down Bloody Canyon to about 9,400 feet; Devil's Cauldron (east of Sierras and about 10 miles south of Farrington's Ranch). In Sierra National Forest generally between 10,000 to 12,000 feet; and southward to head of Little Kern River (latitude 36° 20'). Mount Whitney, up to 11,000 feet; Kearsarge Pass, to 12,000 feet; heads of North Fork of Kings River; rims of Granite Creek and on Middle Fork of Kings River between Dougherty and Simpson Meadows; abundant on heads of North Fork Kings and South Fork San Joaquin rivers at 11,000 to 11,500 feet; divide between Silver and Mono creeks, and from head of Silver Creek to South Fork San Joaquin, Mount Kaweah. Upper Bubbs Creek (tributary South Fork Kings River); about Bull Frog and East lakes.

Detailed range in Rockies will be given in a later bulletin.

OCCURRENCE.

Confined to narrow altitudinal limits on alpine slopes and exposed ridges to timberline throughout its range. Grows among broken, bare rocks, in disintegrated granite, and in shallow rocky soils with little superficial moisture; best in deep, well-drained, moist soil.

At north, sometimes in pure, open stands on grassy areas, but usually in open, park-like stands, preferably on north slopes with alpine fir, Englemann spruce, Lyall larch, limber pine, and lodgepole pine. On summits of Cascades, commonly pure at timberline, and often in clusters of from 3 to 7 trees, as if growing from same root. In southern Washington, with alpine fir, black hemlock, and yellow cedar; in Oregon, with black hemlock, alpine, lowland, and noble firs, lodgepole and western white pines, and Engle-mann spruce. In the Sierras, forming pure groups at timberline, on east, south, and west slopes, with patches of black hemlock and western white pine, and at lower altitudes with lodgepole pine.

CLIMATIC CONDITIONS.—Endures great seasonal and daily ranges of temperature, the former probably lying between −60° and 100° F. or more. Very heavy snowfall, exposure to fierce winds, and a short growing season are characteristic of its habitat. Its moisture requirements are moderate.

TOLERANCE.—Somewhat intolerant in youth, becoming less so with age. Rather intolerant in north, as compared with the south, where it shows a preference for north slopes. Believed to be more tolerant on good moist soils and at low altitudes, than on poor, dry ones near timberline.

REPRODUCTION.—Generally a good seeder, but varies greatly with region and locality. In north, seeds at long intervals, in south, frequently. Large quantities of seed destroyed by birds and squirrels, and reproduction therefore scanty. Seeds wingless, and reproduction confined mainly to vicinity of seed trees. Unprotected by mother trees, seedlings are often damaged by winds, which whip the stems about so that they are often worn in two by rubbing against rough granite soil.

Four-leaf Pine; Parry Pine.

Pinus quadrifolia (Parl.) Sudworth.

DISTINGUISHING CHARACTERISTICS.

This little-known nut pine is a much-branched, short-trunked, low tree, from 15 to 30 feet high and 10 to 16 inches in diameter. In old trees the trunk is often twisted and gnarled, with a wide crown of big, crooked branches; young trees are short-bodied, with dense symmetrical crowns. Bark of old trunks is reddish brown, shallowly furrowed, rough, and with wide ridges, which have close scales. The foliage is blue-green, with a whitish tinge. The leaves occur, as a rule, in bundles of 4, but clusters of 3, and sometimes of 5, are also found on the same tree; they are incurved, and from about 1⅓ to nearly 2 inches long (fig. 8). The cones (fig. 8) ripen in August of the second year and the seeds are often shed before the middle of September. Seeds fall from the cones, leaving their narrow, thin wings attached to the cone scales (fig. 8, *a*). They are chocolate brown with yellow-brown blotches. Indians gather the seeds for food. Seed-leaves, 6 to 8. Wood, light yellowish brown, moderately light, very dense, and close grained; not of commercial use.

LONGEVITY.—Trees reach an age of 200 to 280 years; those 10 to 12 inches in diameter are 130 to 150 years old. Few records of longevity are available.

RANGE.

Southern California and southward into Lower California. Arid mesas and low moun-tains southward from southeastern part of San Jacinto Mountains (30 miles north of Mexican boundary).

CALIFORNIA.—Occurs sparingly at 5,000 feet on Toro Mountain (in Santa Rosa Moun-tains, Riverside County), in Coyote Canyon, at a point a few miles to west and near Van de Venter Flat, and a single tree stands on Nigger Jim Hill between Hemet and Coahuila; 10 to 12 miles farther south it occurs on Balkan Mountains (above Julian), at head of San Diego River; also vicinity of Larkin Station (near Mexican line).

LOWER CALIFORNIA.—Near Mexican line (20 miles southeast of Campo, San Diego County, Cal.), and from point a few miles south of boundary it forms forest about 30 miles wide, extending over plateau (at middle elevations) ; on Hanson Laguna Range, and southward on San Pedro Martir Range to south end ; generally at 4,500 to 6,000 feet elevation above single-leaf piñon pine and below Jeffrey pine, completely covering

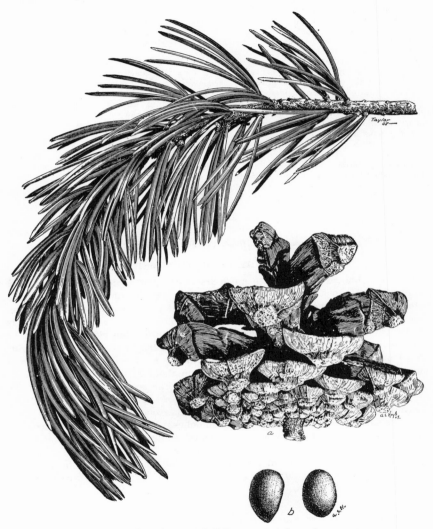

FIG. 8.—*Pinus quadrifolia: a*, cone ; *b*, seeds.

lower parts of range, but in higher parts forming belts on both ocean and desert sides. Locally noted at San Matias Spring, 4,000 feet elevation ; mesas near Mattoni ; Rosarito Divide at 5,000 feet ; El Alamo, at 3,500 feet.

OCCURRENCE.

On arid mesas, foothills, and east, west, and south slopes. Not exacting as to moisture and quality of soil. Commonly on well drained, coarse, dry, shallow soils of decomposed granite or limestone.

Never forms dense pure stands. Most abundant in chaparral on east slopes with single-leaf piñon, oaks, and juniper, and in thinner stands on west and south slopes in dense chaparral. Number of trees varies per acre from 5 to about 100. In Lower California, in open forests, often with single-leaf piñon pine. Throughout its range, heaviest growth is at higher altitudes than that of piñon.

CLIMATIC CONDITIONS.—Best growth requires moister climate, without such extremes of temperature as are endured by single-leaf piñon. Seasonal temperature of its range between 15° and 100° F. Rainfall averages between 15 and 25 inches throughout its distribution.

TOLERANCE.—Little known of light requirements, but its growth in dense chaparral indicates tolerance of shade during early youth.

REPRODUCTION.—Moderate seeder; cones often locally produced about every year. Wingless seeds, shed near tree, are largely eaten by birds and squirrels and gathered by Indians for food. Exposed soil with little humus most favorable seed-bed. Germination moderate.

Single-leaf Pine.

Pinus monophylla Torrey and Fremont.

DISTINGUISHING CHARACTERISTICS.

Unique among all American species in having single leaves, as indicated by its scientific name. Generally known as " nut " or " piñon " pine, but it is highly desirable that the distinctive mark of this tree should be fixed by adopting " single-leaf pine " as its common name. Mature trees have short trunks, rarely straight, and wide, rather flat crowns of short, heavy, twisted, and bent branches, which are given off near the ground and often hang low, giving the appearance of an old apple tree. Young trees, with their low, thick trunks, surmounted by pyramidal crowns of rather straight, rising branches, have a very different aspect. As a rule, the single-leaf pine does not exceed 25 feet in height and from 12 to 15 inches in diameter. In protected and otherwise favorable situations it may reach a height of from 35 to 50 feet, but it is characteristically a low, sprawling tree. Bark of young trunks is smooth and dull gray, while that of old trunks is roughly and irregularly furrowed, nearly an inch thick, and with thin, close, dark brown, sometimes reddish brown, scales. The general color of the foliage is pale yellow-green with a whitish tinge. The single (or very occasionally double) leaves are stiff, curved toward the branch, prickly, and from about $1\frac{1}{3}$ to $2\frac{1}{4}$ inches long—generally about $1\frac{1}{2}$ inches long (fig. 9). A season's growth of leaves remains on the tree about five years; not rarely leaves persist ten to twelve years. A striking peculiarity of seedling trees is that they continue to produce only primary leaves for six or seven years, after which they put forth normal foliage. Cones (fig. 9) are matured in August of the second season; they shed their seeds, which leave their thin, narrow wings attached to the cone scales, within about a month afterward, when the tips of the scales become shiny and a deep russet-brown. Most of the empty cones fall from the trees during the winter or spring. The seeds (fig. 9, *c*), are dark chocolate brown, with dull yellowish areas; extensively gathered by Indians for food. Seed leaves, 7 to 10. Wood, yellowish brown, very fine-grained, moderately light, and very brittle.

LONGEVITY.—An exceedingly slow-growing tree, reaching an age of from 100 to 225 years. Further records of longevity are required.

RANGE.

Desert regions of Utah, Nevada, Arizona, southeastern California, and northern Lower California.

CALIFORNIA.—In southern Sierras, on east slopes at about 6,000 to 8,000 feet from Loyalton, Sierra County (extreme northern limit probably still undetermined) and Markleeville Creek (east side of Sierras) southward to vicinity of Walker Pass, where it descends to 4,300 feet; while at Cottonwood Creek (tributary west side Owens Lake) it occurs at 7,500 to 9,500 feet. On west slopes of Sierras, limited to following places near divide: Loyalton; north slopes of Kings River, at 5,500 feet; Middle Fork of Kings River at Tehipiti Valley and above Simpsons Meadow; at head of South Fork of Kings River in main canyon, and on Bubbs and Copper creeks; Kern River from mouth of Jordan Creek (extending upstream) to Rock Creek, at about 8,400 to 9,000 feet; South

FIG. 9.—*Pinus monophylla: a,* open cone ; *b,* cone scale and seed ; *c,* seed.

Fork of Kern River, south of Monache Valley, occurs over whole basin to below Walker Pass and to mouth of Cottonwood Creek; also on Erskine Creek (branch of Kern River near junction with its South Fork); west slope of Piute Mountains; east slope of Greenhorn Mountains. *Mono County:* (East side of Sierras) most of hills in north part from Nevada boundary on both sides of Antelope Valley southward; West Walker River from

Antelope Valley southward; West Walker River region eastward to within 8 miles of Bridgeport; westward on river into mountains to Leavitt Meadow (7,150 feet); east side of Bridgeport Valley to west end of Mono Lake; Mono Basin and lower slopes west of lake up slope on entrance to Bloody Canyon, also on east and southeast sides of lake; south of Mammoth region on hills about Long Valley and between Long and Round valleys. *Inyo County:* Hills at head of Round Valley; east slopes and summit of hills north of Bishop, and opposite bottom slope of White Mountains (near Benton), here down to upper edge of valley (about 5,500 feet altitude); northeast of Benton over plateau at about 7,000 feet (between California and Nevada); south of Bishop higher on White Mountains, forming belt on middle slope, and rising until lower limit on an east slope is 6,700 feet; west side Owens Valley forms a belt between 6,000 and 8,000 feet; Panamint Range west of Death Valley, common in juniper belt on summit, and ranging (in basin above Wild Rose Spring) on northwest slope of Telescope Peak, between about 6,400 and 9,000 feet. On Providence Mountains (west Colorado River) above 5,000 feet. On southern Cross ranges at Tehachapi Pass (Tehachapi Mountains) down to 3,700 feet; on Piute Mountains; near head of Caliente Creek above 4,000 feet; north part of Tehachapi Pass (Mohave Desert side Tehachapi Basin) at 3,700 feet; lower slopes of Tehachapi Mountain, Antelope Canyon. Tejon Mountains (between Castac Lake and Cuddys Peak) in Cudahay Canyon; at Tejon Canyon and on hills near Fort Tejon, at 4,000 to 6,000 feet. Occurs also on east base of Mount Pinos, in San Emigdio and Frazier mountains at 2,600 to 7,900 feet, and on San Rafael Mountains, above 3,000 feet. Not on southern mountains of Sierra Madre, but on Mount Islip and other north slopes westward to Big Rock Creek; one tree known on Mount Lowe and another near mouth of Santa Ana Canyon. In San Bernardino Mountains, abundant on north slopes, in northeastern part, at 4,000 to 5,000—sometimes up to 7,000 feet, and extending westward to Mohave River. From San Jacinto Mountains to Santa Rosa Mountains it occurs on desert slopes above 4,200 feet, extending eastward to El Toro Mountain and Palm Springs on Colorado Desert, here growing at an elevation as low as 2,000 feet. Summits of Coast Range near Mexican boundary and Jacumba Spring (23 miles east of Campo) at 3,000 feet.

LOWER CALIFORNIA.—On east slopes (below 4,500 feet) from central table-lands to plains of Colorado Desert and several miles south of Mexican boundary.

The detailed range of this pine east of the Pacific region will be dealt with in a future publication.

OCCURRENCE.

Arid low mountain slopes, canyon sides, foothills, and mesas.

Requirements of soil moisture and quality of soil similar to those of associates, junipers and chaparral, and are less than those of other conifers in its range. Commonly in coarse, gravelly soils, shallow deposits overlying granite, limestone, or shale, often in crevices of rocks.

Usually with other species, but frequently in pure, open stands over large areas. Sparingly in chaparral; commonly with mountain mahogany, California juniper, oaks, tree yuccas, or occasionally with straggling white fir and Jeffrey pine. Largest growth and pure stands mainly at lower elevations.

CLIMATIC CONDITIONS.—Endures very great aridity, characterized by high temperature, rapid evaporation, light precipitation, and little humidity. Rainfall varies from about 16 inches in North to less than 5 inches in South. Snowfall, 4 feet in Sierras, but absent or very slight over much of tree's range. Temperature ranges from −2° F. in Sierras to 122° F. in Mohave Desert. In desert mountains of southeastern California and Nevada it endures combined moisture and heat from February to May, extreme drought from June to November, and extreme cold from December to January.

TOLERANCE.—Very intolerant throughout life; but seedlings appear to grow faster if protected for several years from hot winds.

REPRODUCTION.—Bears seed abundantly about every year. Wingless seeds fall near tree. Largely eaten by birds and squirrels and collected by Indians and whites for food. Exposed soil best seed bed. . Reproduction usually very open or scattered—never dense.

Bristle-cone Pine.

Pinus aristata Engelmann.

DISTINGUISHING CHARACTERISTICS.

Bristle-cone pine, an alpine species, and only a straggler in the Pacific country, is known in the field as " fox-tail pine " and " hickory pine," but since these names are applied also to other species it is hoped that the more appropriate name, "bristle-cone pine," may replace them. The trunk is usually short,

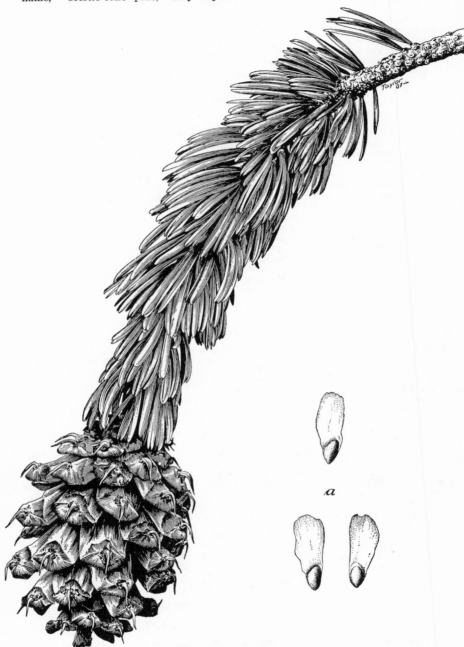

Fig. 10.—*Pinus aristata: a,* seed.

from 15 to 30 feet high and from 12 to 18 inches in diameter, with a rather wide, bushy crown of long, irregularly upright top limbs, and shorter, drooping lower ones. Somewhat larger occasionally. The bark of old trunks is a dull reddish brown and is rather shallowly furrowed, the main flat ridges irregularly connected by narrower slanting divisions, whereas the limbs, as well as the trunks of small trees, are smooth and chalky-white. The deep green foliage is densely clustered at the ends of the twigs, the needles seeming to be pressed down; in this respect closely resembling the true fox-tail pine. Five leaves, about 1¼ to 1⅜ inches long, are borne in a cluster (fig. 10). Leaves of each season's growth persist approximately twelve to fourteen years. Ripe cones, matured at the end of the second season, are from 2½ to about 3½ inches long, deep chocolate brown with a purplish tinge, the end of each cone scale tipped with a bristle-like, very fragile prickle (fig. 10) ; unexposed parts of the scales, clear reddish brown. Seeds (fig. 10, *a*), pale brown with irregular black spots, are shed from about the last of September to the middle of October. Seed leaves, 6 to 7. Wood, pale brownish red, light, usually rather coarse-grained, soft, and very brittle. On account of the poor form of the tree the wood is of no economic use ; sometimes employed for minor local purposes in the region of greatest abundance.

LONGEVITY.—Little is known of the ages attained. Trees from 16 to 20 inches in diameter are from 200 to 250 years old.

RANGE.

On high peaks from Colorado to southern Utah, central and southern Nevada, southeastern California, and northern Arizona.

CALIFORNIA.—Known only on the Panamint Range at 7,800 to 10,800 feet, and also on the adjacent White and Inyo Mountains. Reported to be on the high Sierras east of Yosemite Park and on Mount Pinos in Ventura County, but these stations require further investigation.

Range in Rocky Mountains will be described in a future bulletin.

OCCURRENCE.

Ridges, rocky ledges, and (mainly) south slopes, here often predominating. On thin, rocky soils ; often on volcanic soils of cinder cones. Usually in isolated situations where snow melts early and evaporation is rapid, so that the tree is subjected to more or less prolonged dryness of soil during summer. Rarely forms pure forest, but usually is found in scattering stand with grassy ground cover and little or no underbrush. At lower altitudes, with limber and yellow pines, white fir ; higher up, in thickest part of its belt, associated only with limber pine.

CLIMATIC CONDITIONS.—Seasonal range of temperature endured from about −50° to 95° F. Radiation rapid and daily range of temperature great. Annual precipitation from 20 to 30 inches, and very largely snow. Rainfall irregularly distributed ; dryest months, July and August. Atmosphere dry.

TOLERANCE.—Apparently intolerant of shade, never forming dense stands.

REPRODUCTION.—Trees bear cones when about 20 years old, and seed is produced practically every year thereafter. There appear to be regular seed years in which seed crop is heavier than usual. Seeding takes place to a distance of at least 600 feet from mother trees. Seeds eaten by rodents and quickly killed by fire. Best seed-bed is exposed mineral soil, but seedlings often grow in grass and litter ; they thrive best on slopes with little underbrush.

Foxtail Pine.

Pinus balfouriana Murray.

DISTINGUISHING CHARACTERISTICS.

Distinguished from its associates by a narrow, bushy crown of irregularly long upper branches, the smooth bark of which is chalky-white. The deeply fissured, bright cinnamon-brown bark of mature trunks (with squarish plates) is also very characteristic. Height, from 35 to occasionally 60 feet, and diameter, from 10 to 30 inches. Trunks are clothed with short branches, below the long upper ones, for one-half or two-thirds of their length ; fairly straight, but rough with knots and the swelled bases of branches, and usually tapering rapidly in the upper half. The foliage, which is a bright blue-green, covers the ends of the branches very densely for 10 to 20 inches; this close, tail-like arrangement of the leaves suggested the common name of the tree. The leaves, 5 in a bundle (fig. 11), are curved and closely pressed to the branch. Some of the year's growth of leaves fall during the eighth or ninth year, but most of them persist until the tenth or twelfth year. The cones (fig. 11) are matured by the middle or end of August of the second year, when they are a

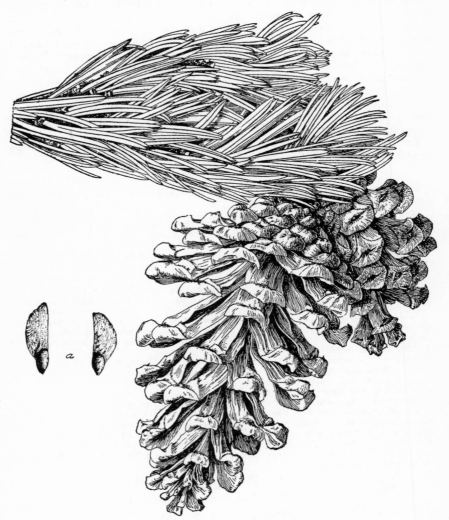

FIG. 11.—*Pinus balfouriana: a,* seeds.

deep purple. They shed their seeds (fig. 11, *a*) in September, at which time the tips of the scales are a dark red-brown or russet-brown. Cones fall from the trees during late autumn or in winter. The seeds are blotched and speckled with dull purple. Seed leaves, regularly 5. Wood, soft, light, yellow-brown, very close-grained and brittle; suitable for second-class lumber, but rarely used.

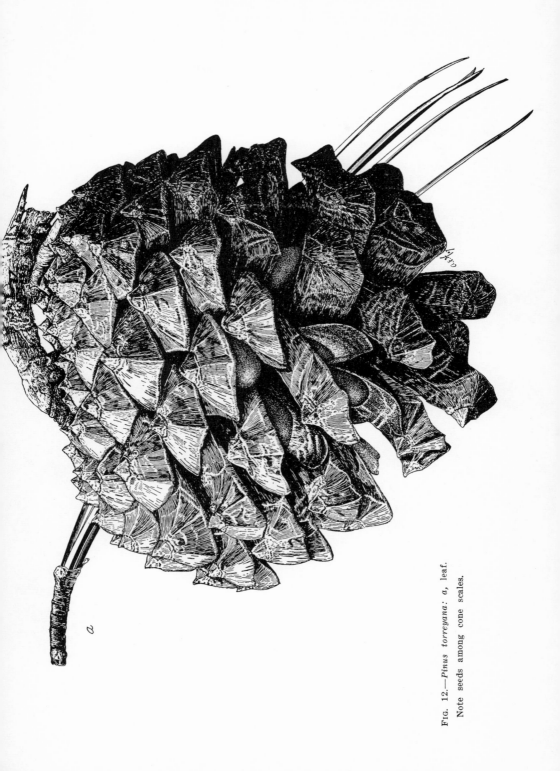

FIG. 12.—*Pinus torreyana: a,* leaf.
Note seeds among cone scales.

LONGEVITY.—Mature trees reach an age of from 175 to 310 years. Age limits imperfectly known. Trees from 18 to 21 inches in diameter are from 320 to 355 years old.

RANGE.

Confined to California at high elevations on the head of the Sacramento River, of northern Coast Range, and of the southern Sierras. On Scott Mountains, Siskiyou County, at 5,000 to 6,000 feet, Mount Eddy, and Yola Buli (Tehama County). In southern Sierras on both sides of divide between head of South Fork of San Joaquin River and that of North Fork of Kings River (in T. 8 S., R. 28 E., T. 9 S., R. 29 E). Southward it appears on west side of main divide at Kearsage Pass at the head of South Fork of Kings River, where it ascends to 12,000 feet, continuing southward to within a few miles south of Monache Peak. On Mount Silliman, ascending to 10,500 feet, on Tharpe Peak at 9,000 to 10,000 feet, at 10,000 feet on Kaweah peaks, and at 9,000 to 11,000 feet on all divides which define head basins of Middle and East forks of Kaweah, Kern, Little Kern, Middle Tule, and South Fork of Kern rivers. On upper Kern River it occurs between 10,500 and 11,500 feet, on Little Kern at elevations above 9,000 feet, on Middle Fork of Kaweah River at 10,000 to 10,500 feet. It reaches to the east slopes of the main Sierra divide only at the head of Cottonwood Creek, where it occurs at 9,000 to 11,500 feet.

OCCURRENCE.

Bare, high, rocky slopes and summits of ridges at timber line. Chiefly on broken and disintegrated granite, which is often very coarse, shallow, and quick-drying and subject to great variation in temperature. With lodgepole pine, California red fir, and black hemlock in lower part of range; at higher levels with western white pine; toward its upper limit often in open stands with white-bark pine or in pure stands which are sometimes of considerable extent; at timber line, usually the only species.

CLIMATIC CONDITIONS.—Endures great seasonal and daily ranges of temperature, short growing season, heavy snowfall, moderate spring rainfall, and extreme drought in summer. Requires but little moisture.

TOLERANCE.—Little tolerant of shade at any stage of growth; does not form dense stands; similar in this respect to limber, white-bark, and bristle-cone pines.

REPRODUCTION.—Moderate seeder. Some cones locally produced nearly every year, with especially heavy seed years. Seed widely disseminated by wind and flood waters, but eaten in large numbers by birds and rodents. Best germination in exposed mineral soil. Reproduction never dense.

Torrey Pine; Soledad Pine.

Pinus torreyana Parry.

DISTINGUISHING CHARACTERISTICS.

The Torrey pine is little known, except in its very confined seacoast range. Exposed to high winds it is a low, crooked, bent, or sprawling tree from 25 to 35 feet in height and from 8 to 14 inches in diameter. Away from sea winds it has a straight trunk and a height of 50 or 60 feet. The crown is small, rounded, and often composed of only few large, greatly developed branches. The trunk bark, about an inch thick, is roughly and deeply broken into ridges with wide, flat, pale reddish-brown scales. The bark of branches and of young trees is thick, spongy, and dull gray. The foliage is clustered in large bunches at the extremities of the stout branches, and has a dark gray-green color. The heavy leaves (fig. 12, *a*), 5 in a bundle, vary from 7½ to about 13 inches in length. Little is known of the duration of the leaves, but they are retained for at least 3 or 4 years. The cones (fig. 12) are ripe early in August of the third season. By the middle of September some of the seeds (fig. 12) are shed; a number are held in the cone for several years after the cones fall. The ends of the cone scales are a deep russet or chocolate brown. Cones are strongly attached to the branches by thick stems and usually remain on the tree for 4 or 5 years; they break away at their base, a part of which is left attached to the tree. Seeds dark brown with areas of yellow-brown. An unusually large number of seed leaves are developed by seedlings, from 12 to 14 being the usual number. Wood, pale reddish-brown, soft, very brittle, and wide-grained. This tree is of such rare and limited occurrence that the wood is of no commercial importance.

LONGEVITY.—Little is known of the longevity of this pine, which is rarely cut. Trees from 10 to 12 inches in diameter are from 75 to 80 years old. It appears to be a comparatively short-lived pine; its ordinary age is probably from 100 to 150, and not more than 200 years.

RANGE.

Confined to a limited area in San Diego County and to Santa Rosa Island, southern California. On the mainland it occurs in a strip about 1 mile wide on both sides of the mouth of Soledad River, from a point on the north 3 miles north of Del Mar, a mile and a half from the Pacific coast, to a point 5 miles south of Point Pinos.

OCCURRENCE.

Highlands adjacent to sea and on sides of deep ravines and washes leading to coast. On mainland growing in a disintegrating yellowish sand rock. On Santa Rosa Island, in a soil of mingled earth and loose rock, or sometimes in rather thick soil over unbroken rock. Largest trees on sheltered sides of hills and spurs of canyons protected from sea winds; sprawling and distorted in exposed situations. Much scattered and with little or no other growth except thin chaparral.

CLIMATIC CONDITIONS.—The temperature of its range varies annually between 25° and 95° F. About 15 inches of rain falls during the year. The air is humid and a large proportion of the days are cloudy or foggy.

TOLERANCE.—Apparently demanding full light, as shown by scanty foliage and growth in very open, scattering stands. Little is known of its silvical characteristics.

REPRODUCTION.—Prolific, annual seeder, bearing well when from 12 to 18 years old. Seeds discharged mostly during third year, the cones with remaining seeds falling about the fourth year. Germination takes place in crevices and washed mineral soil. Seedlings are rather numerous in vicinity of trees, both on mainland and on Santa Rosa Island.

YELLOW PINES.

Western Yellow Pine.

Pinus ponderosa Lawson.

DISTINGUISHING CHARACTERISTICS.

This is a massive, straight-trunked tree with a long, narrow, open crown of hugely developed bent branches. The narrow columnar crown, with scattered branches, upturned at their ends, is characteristic. Often one or two large lower branches are separated from the crown by 20 or more feet of clear trunk. Trees grown in an open stand bear branches close to the ground, retaining this long low crown throughout life. The trunk is smoothly cylindrical, with little taper until the large crown branches are reached. Height, from 125 to 140 feet, with a practically clear trunk of from 40 to 60 feet; diameter, from 3 to 4 feet. Its majestic size is surpassed among its kind only by the sugar pine. Unusually large trees are from 150 to 180 feet high, while trees are said to have been found over 200 feet high. The largest diameter recorded is about 8 feet. The bark of old trunks is marked by very broad, shield-like, russet-red plates, which may be from 3 to 4 inches thick, especially near the base of the tree. The surface of this bark is peculiar in being made up of small, concave scales. Younger trees, up to 2 feet in diameter, are quite unlike older ones in having dark red-brown or blackish, narrowly furrowed bark. Young shoots, which have a strong odor of orange when broken, are yellowish green and later brownish. The foliage, borne in heavy brush-like clusters at the ends of bare branches, is deep yellow-green. The leaves (fig. 13, *a*) occur 3 in a bundle (rarely 4 and 5, chiefly on young saplings). They vary from about 4¾

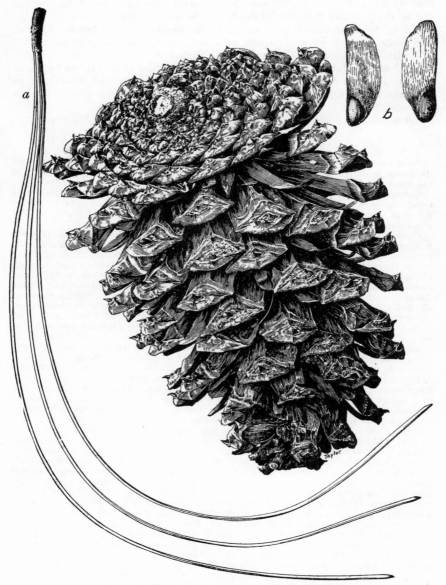

FIG. 13.—*Pinus ponderosa: a,* leaf ; *b,* seed.

to 11¼ inches. Each season's growth of leaves remains on the tree about three years. The cones (fig. 13) mature early in August of the second season and are variable also in size and color. The cones of some trees are bright grass-green when mature, while those of other trees are dark purple ; there is no other essential difference between trees bearing cones so dissimilar in color. The cones are from 2¾ to about 5¾ inches long and from 1½ to about 2 inches thick. The ends of the cone scales, after shedding their seed (mainly in September), are russet-brown and shiny. After this the cones begin falling, and by early winter they are all down. A characteristic of the cone in breaking away from the branch is that some of the basal scales are left on the tree. The seeds (fig. 13, *b*) are marked with purple spots and blotches on a dull yellowish ground; the wings are light purple-brown. Seed leaves, 5 to 9. Wood, very variable in color, from a pale lemon yellow to an orange brown or reddish yellow. Wood, usually rather light, fine-grained, and sometimes so light and so slightly resinous as to be sold as lumber for " white pine ; " of high commercial value.

LONGEVITY.—A long-lived tree, attaining an age of from 350 to 500 years.

RANGE.

From southern British Columbia to Lower California and northern Mexico, including its Rocky Mountain form (*P. ponderosa scopulorum*), occurring in every State west of the Great Plains and one hundredth meridian.

BRITISH COLUMBIA.—East of Fraser River and south of " Chasm," near Clinton and Great Shuswap Lake (latitude 51° 30′) to Gold and Selkirk ranges; in Columbia-Kootenai Valley to head of Upper Columbia Lake, to head of Lower Arrow Lake, and along Kootenai Lake to Canadian line.

WASHINGTON.—East of Cascades, between 1,800 to 3,300 feet—sometimes up to 6,000 feet, and nearly to sea level on Columbia River in Cascades. West of Cascades, limited to following localities: Dry slopes 2,000 to 5,000 feet above Lightning Creek in Upper Skagit River basin, and gravelly prairies near Roy and Hillhurst (Pierce County), south of Tacoma. East of Cascades (Washington National Forest), at 1,500 to 3,000 feet reaching 1,100 feet on Lake Chelan and 6,000 feet at head of Poison Creek and Chelan Range; southern part of Forest, watersheds of Entiat, Wenache, and Yakima rivers at 200 to 5,500 feet. Rainier National Forest, at 400 to 6,200 feet. Colville National Forest (northeastern part of State), below 4,000 feet; noted in valleys of Trout Creek, West Fork of Sans Poil River, and on Kettle River. Blue Mountains (Wenaha National Forest.), at 1,500 to 4,000 feet. Limits on west and north sides of Columbia and Snake rivers as follows: At southwest, to Bickleton and Cleveland (Klickitat County), and upper west slopes Yakima River north and northeast to Ellensburg (Kittatas County); sometimes reappearing on latter river along Northern Pacific Railroad, along both sides of Columbia River—Yakima River Divide, below 5,000 feet, sometimes down to Columbia River bottom, southward at least to Priest Rapids. Chelan, Okanogan and Ferry counties, nearly to Columbia River and often on opposite slopes. Lincoln and Spokane counties, to south slopes of Spokane River and west and south borders Spokane County. Whitman County, only near Colfax and in tongue northeastward into Idaho.

OREGON.—Cascades, Klamath River Basin, and Blue Mountains, generally at from sea level to 5,850 feet. East side of Cascades, low foothills up to 5,000 feet at north, and at 4,000 to 7,000 at south. Eastward along Columbia River from Bonneville (west limit) to The Dalles, into Deschutes River Valley west of river, to point 5 miles west of Wapinitia, down to 2,300 feet near Simnasho, 10 miles west of the river at Warm Springs Indian Agency, Metolius Canyon, west border Fly Creek Desert, upper Squaw Creek, east side Deschutes River (few miles north of Farewell Bend), Pine Mountain (half way between Pauline Lake and Bear Buttes), 3 miles below Farewell Bend (road to Prineville), Pauline Creek, East Fork Deschutes, Sinks Creek, and Klamath Marsh. West side Cascades, south only of latitude 44° 25′, extending southward into Siskiyous and on east slopes of Coast Range, at 1,300 to 6,000 feet elevation, Klamath Gap and gaps south of Lake of Woods, valley between main Cascades and mountains west of Aspen Lake, eastern base of Cascades, and eastward throughout Upper Klamath Basin to Warner and Kokeep mountains (east of Warner Lake). In Warner Mountains, east and northeast of Goose Lake to mountains east of Lakeview in gap between north and south masses of Warner Range; not on west side lower slopes of Warner Mountains, but in canyons and from Sugar Loaf Mountain southward for several miles; descends on east base of Warner Range to about 5,600 feet. Kokeep Mountains, in few canyons and elsewhere on cooler slopes; De Garmo Canyon, from 5,500 feet upward; east side of Kokeep Range, at site of old Camp Warner (Warner or Guano Creek) at 5,800 feet elevation. In Blue Mountains (low hills west of Canyon City), including Grande Ronde Basin, at from 1,500 to 4,000 feet.

CALIFORNIA.—Northern part and southward in coast ranges and Sierras to southern cross ranges. Throughout northern California from a little above sea level to 7,000 feet but not in immediate valleys of Upper Pitt, Shasta, Scott, and Hoopa rivers, southern part of Modoc lava beds, highest peaks of Salmon, Trinity, Scott, and Siskiyou mountains. Eastward to northern part of Modoc National Forest, Shafer, and Warner mountains, on latter at from 7,000 feet eastward into Surprise valley to 4,800 feet; absent from Madeline Plains and desert ranges of northern Nevada. Westward to Pacific coast fog belt, ranging over lower slopes of Scott Mountains, east and west arms of Salmon Mountains, valleys of Russian Creek and Smith River, in which it goes nearly to sea level, and southward in Modoc County to Glass Mountain (at 4,500 to 6,700 feet), Happy Valley, and 10 miles north of Lookout. Shasta and Modoc counties to ridge between Fall River and Big valleys, Hot Creek, Lassen Peak, and nearly to Haydenhill; also about Eagle Lake, Susanville, and west side of Henry Lake. North and South Forks of Salmon River, Trinity and Klamath rivers, reaching its western limits on mountains between Hoopa Valley and Redwood Creek, valley of Upper Mad River and Van Dusen Creek, and those near Sherwood (Mendocino County) ; near Cahto and Russian Valley from Willits southward. Eastward to Shasta (town) at from 1,500 to 5,000 feet, and in Mount Shasta National Forest at 2,000 to 6,000 feet. Southward in McCloud, Pitt, and Sacramento valleys to Keswick (Shasta County), south of which it descends Coast Range eastward only to 2,300 feet altitude (west of Redding) ; farther south to point 6 miles west of Beegum, and in Tehama County to 3,000 feet (west of Paskenta). Lassen Peak, Diamond Mountain, and Plumas National Forests, on ridges and flats generally at 2,000 to 6,000 feet. Northern Sierras, at 1,000 to 7,000 feet, and in Sacramento Valley above 1,500 feet. Absent from Sierra Valley. Westward on east side of Sacramento Valley (Tehama County) to point 2 miles west of Payne (1,700 feet) and 1 mile west of Lena ; Butte County to 1 mile west of Paradise (1,700 feet), ridges west of Yankee Hill, and Bidwell Bar (1,300 feet) ; Yuba County to upper Dry Creek and neighboring hills, Lafferty Peak (1,150 feet), Stanfield Hill (880 feet), Flannery Peak, and mountains east of Willow Glenn Creek, hills between Oregon House and Dobbins Creek, and Oregon Hills ; Nevada County to west of Nevada City, Grass Valley, Wolf Creek, Bear River, and Colfax ; Placer County to Weimer, Applegate, Clipper Gap, and first one above Auburn (1,500 feet) on Southern Pacific Railroad. Eastern limits : Plumas County, to Indian and Genesee valleys, Quincy, Beckwith, and mountains on east border of Sierra Valley ; Sierra County, east on west slopes Sierras to Bassett Road House (5,200 feet), on east slope from 5,800 (east of Yuba Pass) eastward into Nevada to east front of Sierras and Mount Rose above Reno, at 6,000 feet and over. *Placer County:* Eastward on west slope of Sierras to Blue Canyon and Emigrant Gap at 5,200 feet, Cisco at 5,900 feet, and beyond Forks House (5,500 feet). East side of main Sierra divide, north of Webber Peak, and south of it at Donner Pass ; also on heads of Miller and McKinney creeks, but not about Beckwith Pass. General on west slope of southern Sierras and in Stanislaus National Forest, at 2,000 to 6,000 feet, but in Lake Tahoe National Forest at 3,000 to 6,000 feet. *Eldorado County:* Westward to Coloma (1,000 feet), Shingle Springs (1,500 feet), 1 mile east of Nashville (1,500 feet) and Oleta (1,800 feet) ; eastward on west slope Sierras to Echo (5,500 feet). *Amador County:* Westward to Big Indian Creek (between Nashville and Plymouth), 4 miles east of Plymouth, Rancheria Creek at 1,200 feet (between Amador and Oleta), upper Sutter Creek, and 1½ miles east of Jackson at 1,400 feet. *Calaveras County:* Westward to 4 miles east of Mokelumne Hill at 1,500 feet, 3 miles east of San Andreas and on Mount San Joaquin and Bear Mountains ; eastward on west slope Sierras to 10 miles below Bloods at 6,600 feet. *Tuolumne County:* Westward to Robinsons Ferry (Stanislaus River), gulch between Sonora and Jamestown, Saulsbyville (or Soulsbyville?) Tuolumne, 1 mile west of Big Oak Flat, Penon Blanco Ridge (5 miles northwest of Coulterville) ; east on west slopes of Sierras to Middle Fork Stanislaus River between Cold Spring and Eureka Valley at 6,000 feet, Aspen Meadow at 6,200 feet, and Hetch Hetchy Valley. *Mariposa County:* West to Coulterville (2,000 feet), ridge west of Mariposa, Chowchilla Hill and upper Chowchilla Canyon to 2,000 feet, 18 miles northeast of Raymond at 2,000 feet ; eastward on west slope Sierras to Yosemite at 7,000 feet, Chinquapin ridge between Wawona and Yosemite at 6,200 feet, and to a few miles south of Wawona at 5,700 feet. *Madera County:* Westward to point 2 miles northeast of Wassama at 3,000 feet, Fresno Flat at 2,400 feet, ridge between Fresno Flat and Coarse Gold Gulch at 3,100, short distance west of North Fork at 2,600 feet ; eastward on west slope of Sierras to head of Fresno Creek at 5,000 feet. *Fresno County:* Westward to Tollhouse and Burr Valley, Rush Creek, mountains east of Big Creek and between Eshom Valley and Badger ; eastward on west slope Sierras to Kings River, upper Mill Creek, and Redwood Mountain. Locally noted on East Fork of Kaweah River, at 6,000 to 7,000 feet; Middle Fork of Kaweah to Buck Canyon at 7,500 feet; Sequoia National Park, at 5,000 to 6,000 feet; Middle Fork of Kings River at mouth of Crown Creek; South Fork of Kings River, from mouth of Bubbs Creek 2 miles up, and from Copper Creek 2 miles up, at 8,700 feet; Kern River canyon to point above Soda Springs; South Fork of Tule River from East Tule Indian Reservation eastward. Greenhorn Mountains; Piute Mountains and Mount Breckenridge at 6,000 to 7,000 feet. Tehachapi Mountains on most of ridges above 6,000 feet; noted in Tejon Canyon, south of which it has not been detected. Coast ranges, abundant in Stony Creek National Forest at 3,000 to 6,000 feet; scarce in Sonoma County, common in Napa County, especially on Howell Mountain plateau south of Angwins, but unknown on inner ranges bounding Solano and Yolo counties. In San Francisco Bay region, recorded only from Mount Hamilton. Santa Cruz Mountains and northward in seaward coast range to Woodside. Southern Santa Lucia Mountains, at 1,000 to 5,000 feet. Santa Barbara National Forest, only between Thorn Meadows and Pine Mountain Lodge, on San Rafael and Big Pine mountains, Mount Medulce, and in part of Alamo Mountain region, at 4,750 to 6,750 feet; near Mount Pinos (S. 12, T. 6 N., R. 22 W.), above 5,750 feet. San Gabriel National Forest, at 5,500 to 9,000 feet from head of Sheep Creek throughout Upper Swarthout Valley, as well as to some of higher parts of San Gabriel and San Antonio watersheds; also on Mount Wilson, Pine Flats, Brown Flats, and in Mount Gleason country. San Bernardino National Forest, in Little Bear Valley to Sawpit Canyon, and less abundantly nearly to Cleghorn Pass and Deep Creek; usually at 4,500 or lower, to 9,000 feet, but sometimes at 9,800 on the range fronting Mohave Desert; Santa Ana River at about 1,600 feet. San Jacinto Mountains, at 3,000 to 9,000 feet; Tahquitz Valley at 6,000 to 9,000 feet, Onstatt and Strawberry valleys; Palomar Mountain, in Doane Valley only. Farther south, noted about Julien and in San Luis Rey Canyon.

IDAHO.[a]—Northern and central parts generally at 2,000 to 7,000 feet. Priest River National Forest, at 2,000 to 4,000 feet. Coeur d'Alene Mountains, valleys, bottoms, benches, and lower slopes, up to 4,900 feet. Bitterroot National Forest, slopes and flats up to 7,500 feet; also about west and south boundaries, including a deep extension into the reserve near south and middle forks of Clearwater River. Thatuna Hills (near Pullman, Wash.). Sawtooth National Forest slopes and ridges at 2,500 to 5,000 feet.

MONTANA.—Mainly west of Continental Divide up to 3,300 feet; Flathead Valley region, up to 4,125 feet. Valley of North Fork of Flathead River, between Indian and Logging creeks, and Kootenai Valley (small areas). Bitterroot Valley up to 5,800 feet. Northern part of State, but not on east side of Continental Divide, nor on Whitefish Mountains. Farther south, east of Divide, sparingly on Little Belt Mountains between 6,000 and 6,500 feet; in Elkhorn Mountains at 4,000 to 5,500 feet, and in Absaroka Division of Yellowstone National Forest at 5,500 to 6,000 feet.

The pine occurring mainly east of the Rockies and throughout the region southward to Texas and Arizona is *Pinus ponderosa scopulorum*, the detailed range of which will be dealt with in a later bulletin.

OCCURRENCE.

On dry and moist slopes, on tops of ridges, and in canyon bottoms. Very moderate in soil requirements. Grows on all soils from glacial drift and volcanic ash to deep, loose sands and stiff clays; dry, well-drained sandy or gravelly soils most characteristic. Requires very little soil moisture; its enormously deep roots enable it to thrive in soils nearly as dry as those in which piñon pines and junipers grow.

Occurs in pure extensive stands and in mixture with other conifers and broadleaf trees. Pure large, but interrupted, forests are found on east slopes and foothills of the Cascades in Washington and Oregon; open, grassy park lands intervene; little or no underbrush or even grass occurs in these forests, on account of continued fires. Occasionally with western larch and Douglas fir. In Sierras, in scattered smaller pure stands, or, more often, variously mixed with sugar pine, incense cedar, Douglas fir, white fir, and smaller numbers of California red fir. Often associated with Kellogg oak, occasionally with bigtrees, and at lower elevations sparsely mingled with gray pine. Mixed forests usually with brushy ground cover and considerable young growth.

CLIMATIC CONDITIONS.—Great seasonal and daily variations of temperature are endured. Seasonal range between about 28° and 110° F. Mean annual rainfall in region of principal occurrence from 10 to 50 inches; an annual rainfall of less than 20 inches probably limits its occurrence in commercial quantities.

---

[a] The north Rocky Mountain range of this tree is given in order to complete the distribution of what must be regarded as the ordinary form of western yellow pine. Southward and eastward it passes imperceptibly into *P. ponderosa scopulorum*.

TOLERANCE.—Demands large amount of light throughout life, especially in older age. Stands may remain dense for from 10 to 15 years, but after that they thin out rapidly; trees above 20 feet in height require almost unbroken light. Trees in mature stands are rarely closer than 30 feet, and the crowns seldom touch. In south, seedlings do not endure intense light and heat, usually coming up in shade of old trees, in openings near logs, bowlders, and brush, which afford slight protection; in north they grow in unprotected openings.

REPRODUCTION.—Frequent and abundant seeder. Cones are locally produced every year, so that there is always some seed in a forest; good seed years occur at intervals of from 3 to 5 years. Germination of natural sowing, about 50 per cent; of artificial planting, from 60 to 80 per cent. Seed is produced by trees from 20 to 25 years old, but generally is scanty and of poor quality until trees are 50 years old. Large, thrifty trees produce over 1,000 cones; average amount of seed, from 1 to 6 pounds. Seed is not carried far in dense stands, but in open forests it is scattered from 500 to 700 feet from the tree in direction of prevailing wind. A mature tree can seed about one-fourth of an acre in an ordinary seed year. Squirrels and birds eat large numbers of seeds and disseminate considerable numbers, but can not be depended on for regular reproduction. Much seed is washed down steep slopes to stream beds and depressions, where good reproduction often occurs. Well drained, fresh soils, and a moderate daily range of temperature are necessary for germination.

Jeffrey Pine.

Pinus jeffreyi " Oreg. Com."

DISTINGUISHING CHARACTERISTICS.

Jeffrey pine is scarcely less magnificent in size than its associate the western yellow pine. Some specialists consider it a variety of *Pinus ponderosa*, which it resembles so closely in its habits and soil and climatic requirements that from the forester's point of view there appears to be no practical reason for distinguishing the two. Dendrologically, however, the typical form of Jeffrey pine (discovered in northern California in 1850 by John Jeffreys) differs in many respects from western yellow pine. It is a large-bodied, straight tree, with a long, narrow crown, the branches of which are much less stout and angled than those of its relative. Its foliage is heavier, more dense, and a distinctly dark blue-green. As a rule, the dark red-brown bark is deeply furrowed, and the ridges, often narrow, are irregularly connected with one another. On very old trees the bark is deeply broken into long, wide plates of a bright red-brown color. The leaves (fig. 14, *a*), 5 to 9½ inches long, occur in bundles of 3 and persist for from 5 to 8 and sometimes 9 years. In consequence, the foliage appears dense. The twigs of a year's growth are considerably thicker than those of the western yellow pine, and distinctly purple when young; they exhale, when cut or bruised, a fragrant, violet-like odor. The cones (fig. 14), purple at maturity, are a light russet-brown after shedding their seeds, and are from 5½ to 11¾ inches long. The seeds (fig. 14, *b*), larger than those of the western yellow pine, are similarly mottled. Seed leaves, 7 to 10—sometimes 11. Wood, light straw color and rather wide grained; similar in commercial value to the western yellow pine.

LONGEVITY.—Long-lived, reaching an age of from 300 to 410 years. Further age determinations are required.

RANGE.

Mountains of southern Oregon and southward to northern Lower California.

OREGON.—Found at only two stations—one about 30 miles south of Roseburg, in Douglas County, and the other near Waldo, in the Siskiyou Mountains.

CALIFORNIA.—Sources of Pitt River and (high levels) on Scott Mountains (near Mount Shasta), west of and on east slope Mount Eddy down to level and near Sisson; reported in Trinity Mountains at elevations above 3,500 feet, and on Snow Mountain (Lake County). East side of Sierras, in central and southern parts, between about 9,000 and

9,500 feet, and southward to head of Cottonwood Creek; also throughout western slopes, forming a similar belt, above and with *Pinus ponderosa* (usually at and near its upper limits) and extending southward through Tehachapi Mountains to southern cross ranges. On west slopes of Sierras (Stanislaus National Forest), found about Strawberry and Bear Meadow. North slope of Lassen Peak (Shasta County), eastward to 5 miles west of Quincy and Beckwith, Sierra Valley westward to Bucks Valley (5,200 feet), and 30 miles down Feather River Valley. *Lassen County:* Northwest corner between Fall River and Big Valley eastward to 6 miles west of Bieber. *Sierra County:* Eastward to ridge west of Sierra Valley (at levels between 5,700 and over 6,000 feet) to Sierraville and Truckee; westward to Bassett Road House (west of Yuba Pass) at 5,200 feet. *Nevada County:* Eastward on east slope of Sierras and into Nevada to hills west of Steamboat Valley; westward to Bowman Lake (between Middle and South forks Yuba River), and to Cisco. *Placer County:* Eastward to Lake Tahoe and into Nevada; westward to Sugar Pine sawmill (4,000 feet). *Eldorado County:* East side of Sierras; west side, westward to Echo (5,500 feet). *Alpine County:* East side Sierras from Woodfords and Markleeville to east part Mokelumne Pass; west side, from 8,400 feet westward to about 6,500 feet (Calaveras County). *Tuolumne County:* Westward to between Cold Spring and Eureka Valley (5,900 feet) and Aspen Meadows (6,300 feet); eastward on west slope of Sierras to Sonora Pass and to over 8,000 feet, and 2 miles west of White Wolf (Middle Fork Tuolumne) at 7,500 feet. *Mono County:* East side of Sonora Pass on mountains about West Walker Creek and in pass to about 8,300 feet; from little southeast of Junction House nearly to Bridgeport Valley; between latter and Antelope Valley in West Walker Canyon, disappearing several miles south of Antelope Valley; west of Mono Lake on east slopes of Sierras and on Leevining Creek nearly to lake; Walker Lake at lower end of Bloody Canyon, and sparingly to about 9,300 feet; south of Mono Lake (east side Mono Craters) on east base of Sierras to point beyond Mammoth; in valley west side of Mono Craters to a point 7,300 feet about 7 miles south of Farrington's. In belt about 15 miles wide between Mono Desert and Casa Diablo (at 7,000 to 8,000 feet) eastward from Sierras to south end of Mono Craters; south of Mammoth, on both sides of head of Long Valley, and between Long and Round valleys. *Inyo County:* Divide north of Round Valley and westward to foot of Sierras; west of Owens Lake, on east slope of Sierra between 9,000 and 9,500 feet. *Mariposa County:* Eastward to Sunset Ridge (east of Little Yosemite) at 9,000 feet, Mount Hoffman, headwaters of Snow Creek, at 8,500 feet, on Yosemite Creek (north of Yosemite Valley) to 8,500 feet, and westward to point (5,500 feet) 8 miles north of Wawona. Middle Fork of Kings River, at 9,500 feet; South Fork Kings to Bubbs Creek and Horse Corral Meadows, Cliff Creek to Deer Creek (Middle Fork Kawash River), Farewell Gap, and Kern River canyons to 9,000 feet; junction of Kern and Little Kern rivers, at 6,000 feet; Dry Creek meadow (near Kern River), at 4,800 feet. Mount Breckenridge, at 5,000 to 7,000 feet, Tehachapi Peak (Tehachapi Mountains), and Bear Mountain (west of Tehachapi Pass). Southern cross ranges (Santa Barbara National Forest), at elevation of from 4,500 to 8,800 feet, as follows: Big Pine Mountain, at 7,000 feet; Seymour Creek, at 6,700 to 7,000 feet; South Fork of Piru River, at 5,000 feet; near junction of Alamo River, at 4,500 feet; near Mount Pinos, at 5,750 to 8,800 feet. San Gabriel National Forest, on Mount Wilson and Pine Flats (Frazier Mountain). San Bernardino Mountains, at altitudes from 5,000 to 6,700 feet in Bear and Little Bear Valleys, in vicinity of Crafts Peak, and on other north slopes; also on San Jacinto Mountains; San Jacinto Peak, at 5,200 to 9,300 feet; noted in east end Round Valley, Tahquitz, Onstatt, Strawberry, and Thomas valleys: throughout Cuyamaca Mountains, being reported in Pine Valley, at 3,600 feet.

LOWER CALIFORNIA.—Mount San Pedro Martir, at 6,000 to 10,000 feet.

OCCURRENCE.

Commonly between the upper altitudes of western yellow pine and of white fir, with no sharp line of separation between its range and the ranges of these trees; usually overlapping the upper range of yellow pine and sometimes exceeding that of white fir. Best commercial growth between 5,000 and 6,500 feet elevation. Soil requirements moderate, but for best growth demands well-drained, loose, coarse, sandy or gravelly soil with abundant moisture. Occurs extensively, however, though in poor form or much stunted, on poor, shallow soils and in crevices of bare rock. Appears to require more soil moisture than white fir and sugar, yellow, and Coulter pines.

Occasionally in pure stands, and often predominating in mixture. Pure forests occur at lower altitudes where soil and moisture conditions are the best, as in bottoms and along streams, or at higher elevations, soil on rocky summits, where more exacting trees are excluded for want of sufficient moisture. At north, associates with western yellow

FIG. 14.—*Pinus jeffreyi: a,* leaf ; *b,* seed.

pine, lodgepole pines, white and red firs, sugar pine, and incense cedar; in south, associates with bigcone spruce, white fir, incense cedar, western juniper, and Coulter, sugar, limber, western white, and lodgepole pines, the last three near its upper limits.

CLIMATIC CONDITIONS.—Endures wide annual ranges of temperature, but lowest and highest in regions of best growth are about zero and 100° F. Mean annual rainfall of greater part of range varies from 20 to over 60 inches, with an average of about 35 inches where best growth occurs. Requirements of atmospheric moisture less than for white fir and sugar pine, but greater than for Coulter pine, western yellow pine, and incense cedar.

TOLERANCE.—Fairly tolerant in youth, ranking between yellow and sugar pines and permitting its seedlings and low trees to persist under shade of chaparral on east and south exposures; in later life, as tolerant of light as western yellow pine.

REPRODUCTION.—Prolific seeder. Seed years rather irregular, but seeds locally in range nearly every year. Seed of high germination (50 or 60 per cent) and persistent vitality. Produces seed only at rather advanced age, becoming less productive in old age. The heaviness of its seeds confines reproduction chiefly to neighborhood of seed trees. Range of reproduction increased as seed trees stand on slopes, down which seed is washed or blown. Birds and rodents eat large numbers of seeds and assist some in dissemination. Has vigorous reproduction at higher altitudes than has western yellow pine. Exposed mineral soil is the best seed-bed. Germination not prevented by moderate shade.

Lodgepole Pine.

Pinus contorta Loudon.

DISTINGUISHING CHARACTERISTICS.

The pine described under this name is one of the most interesting of Pacific species on account of its variable characters and on account of its enormously wide range, which extends from sea level to nearly 11,000 feet elevation. For many years a fruitless effort has been made to keep the tree which inhabits the northern Pacific coast region, extending to Alaska and eastward over the western Cascades, and known as *Pinus contorta*, distinct from the tree of the high Sierras and Rocky Mountains plateaus, known as lodgepole pine (*Pinus murrayana* and *P. contorta murrayana*). The distinctions assembled to separate these trees are one after another broken down when the trees are carefully studied throughout their great range. Differences in thickness of bark, size of cones and leaves, or size and form of the tree, are not too great to be consistently merged in one polymorphous species, as it is proposed to do here. The reproductive organs of these supposedly distinct trees are essentially the same. With no characters found in these organs to warrant a distinction of species, the other so-called distinctions depended upon are believed to be unworthy of serious consideration. Perhaps no other North American trees have given so much trouble, or left so much uncertainty in the minds of those who have attempted to hold them separate. Recent students of trees have been slow to depart from the time-honored judgment of earlier writers. It is confidently believed, however, that those writers would have taken the broader view had they been able to study the trees as they grow in all their retreats.

In its Pacific habitat this pine is a low tree with a dense rounded or pyramidal crown, the large, much-forked branches often extending down to the ground. This form is the result of an open stand, which permits other pines to produce a similar form. In very close stands it develops a tall, clean, slender shaft with a short, rounded, small-branched crown. This is its characteristic form in its more eastern range, and has there given the name of " lodgepole pine." The trunk bark of the Pacific coast form is about an inch thick over the lower half or third of the stem; it is a deep purplish red-brown and has deep, rough furrows and ridges which are sharply cross-checked; young poles and the crown branches and stems of old trees have thin, smooth, fine scaly, pale brown bark, with a grayish tinge. Bark of the latter character is borne mainly by trees growing away from the coast and by the eastern representative of this species. The thin bark results in extensive destruction of this tree by fire, which soon scorches the thickest of this bark so badly as to kill the trees. The Pacific tree is 20 to 40 feet high and from 6 to 20 inches in diameter; the trunk is short and thickly set with hugely developed branches, except in very dense stands. In its eastern range the tree attains a height of from 50 to 100 feet, and in close stands develops a smooth, clean trunk for from 30 to 60 feet; from 12 to 24 inches is the usual diameter. Taller and larger trees occur. The foliage of the coast tree is dark yellow-green, but away from the sea it becomes distinctly a bright yellow-green, which is characteristic throughout the interior Pacific and eastern range. The leaves (fig. 15), regularly 2 in a bundle, are

Fig. 15.—*Pinus contorta: a,* seed with and without wing.

from about 1 inch to nearly 3 inches long; usually about 2 inches long. A season's growth of leaves remains on the trees from six to eight years; long persistence appears to belong more to young trees, on which leaves are retained sometimes for nine years. The leaves of the Pacific form are only about one-third as thick as those of the inland and eastern representative, which are nearly an eighth of an inch wide. Cones (figs. 15, 16) ripen late in August and September. Very many trees open their cones in late fall and shed nearly all of their seeds, while the cones of other trees in the same locality may remain closed for a number of years. Open or closed they adhere to the branches for a great many years, some of the closed ones finally opening and liberating their seed. The wonderful reproductive power of this species on areas over which its stand has been killed by fire is dependent upon the ability of the closed cones to endure a fire which kills the tree without injuring its seed. After fire, the cones open and shed their seeds on the bared ground and a new growth springs up. Another remarkable adaptation insuring this tree against extinction by fire is its habit of producing fertile cones at the early age of from 7 to 10 years.

When the cones are fully ripe the scale tips are shiny and a clay-brown color, their inner portion being a bright purple-brown. The seeds (fig. 15, *a*) are deep reddish brown, with black-brown spots. Seed leaves, commonly 5, but sometimes 4. Wood varies in grain; fine in dense stands, moderately coarse in the open; commercially important. Wood of the Pacific tree is a pale reddish

Fig. 16.—*Pinus contorta.*

brown, while the eastern wood is yellow or yellowish-brown. Both are hard. The eastern wood is lighter, less resinous, and straighter-grained.

Longevity.—Attains an age of from 100 to 175 years; but doubtless it is capable of reaching from 200 to possibly 300 years, if exempt from fire, to which, throughout its range, it quickly succumbs on account of its thin bark. Many stands have in the past attained an age of only 60 years before being killed by forest fires.

RANGE.

From Alaskan coast and interior Yukon territory southward to northern Lower California and through the Rocky Mountains to the Black Hills (South Dakota) and through western Colorado. The so-called typical *Pinus contorta* (exclusive of *Pinus contorta* var.

murrayana) ranges from the coast and islands of Alaska southward mainly in the immediate vicinity of the Pacific coast of British Columbia, Washington, Oregon, and California to Point Arena, Mendocino County, and Gasquet, Del Norte County. In this range it grows commonly from near sea level to about 500 feet elevation, but forms of it are reported in Washington and Oregon up to about 3,000 feet.

ALASKA AND CANADA.—From western Coast Range in British Columbia eastward to plateau east of Rockies. At north, on Pacific slope at Chilcat Inlet, Square Island, and Skagway at sea level, and up to 1,900 feet at Glacier Station. Headwaters of Yukon River from north side of White Pass to Lake Le Barge, Lewes River, and thence down Yukon River to point a few miles below Fort Selkirk (latitude 62° 45'). East of the Yukon, northward on divide between Klondike and McQuestion rivers to latitude 64° (northern limit now known), 80 miles east of Dawson, and eastward to Mayo Lake, in same latitude; eastward on MacMillan River to a point 50 miles up the south fork, and eastward on Pelly River, to longitude 133° 30'. Plateau east of Rockies, on Dease and Liard rivers to Devils Portage, and on Peace River to hills between Athabaska River and Lesser Slave Lake and Athabaska Landing. Follows eastern foothills of Rocky Mountains southward, at about 4,000 feet elevation, on line of Canadian Pacific Railroad, occurring from Silver City to Laggan, but not reaching timberline. At south, eastward in Assiniboia to Cypress Hills, from summits of which it extends down 500 feet. Throughout interior mountain region of southern British Columbia above 3,500 feet, and below that on sandy benches and river flats.

WASHINGTON.—West of Cascades, on Pacific and Puget Sound shore and also away from coast in bogs and about gravelly prairies below 3,300 feet. Noted at Westport, McAllisters Lake. From Cascades eastward to northeastern and Blue mountains. Abundant on east side of Cascades at from 3,300 to 5,000 feet, occasionally reaching 7,100 feet and descending to 1,500 feet; occurs sparingly on west side in Washington National Forest at 3,000 to 5,000 feet near Darrington, on Suiattle River, State Creek, upper Skagit River, and northward to the Canadian boundary. On east slope of Cascades descends, on Stehekin River, to 2,100 feet; southern Washington National Forest, between 1,500 and 7,000 feet; Rainier National Forest, between 1,800 and 7,100 feet; ascends to 5,900 feet in Chelan Range; Blue Mountains, above 3,000 feet. Colville National Forest, above 4,000 feet. Noted on Mount Rainier, Mount Adams, Wenache Mountains, Falcon Valley, Pend Oreille River, divide between Columbia and Yakima rivers, near Lake Cushman, and between Union City and Shelton—south of Olympic Mountains.

OREGON.—Sea beaches, bogs, creeks, and meadows to east slopes of Cascades (below 6,000). Noted at Seaside and Clatsop Beach (near Tillamook Head). Cascades and eastward to Warner Mountains and Wallowa National Forest, generally between 4,000 to 8,000 feet; mainly on east side of Cascades, and only at high elevations on west side. In northern Cascades, at 3,500 to 5,500 feet; noted on north side at Mount Hood from 3,100 (22 miles south of Hood River Station) to 5,000 feet; also on south side of Mount Hood, above Government Camp at over 2,500 feet and down west slope to 1,700 feet (mile east of Tollgate); Camas Prairie (south of Mount Hood). In southern Cascades, on east side, at 4,200 to 8,500 feet, and at 6,200 to 8,000 feet on west side. Eastward over upper Deschutes River Valley to Lava on Paulina Creek, Paulina Lake and Pengras Ranch; farther south, to East Fork Deschutes, Walker Range, and Sinks creeks at 4,900 to 6,300 feet. Mount Mazama, at 4,800 to 6,300 feet and eastward to Fort Klamath, west shores Klamath Lake, and eastward on Klamath-Deschutes Divide and ranges of Klamath River Basin to Warner Mountains between Goose and Warner lakes. Noted in Goose Lake National Forest above 6,000 feet, east and north of Gearhart Mountain, on Swamp Creek down to 5,500 feet, Elder and Bear creeks and westward from Summer Lake to Sprague and Sycan river valleys. Reported from southern coast range in Siskiyou National Forest. Blue Mountains, at 3,000 to 6,000 feet; here on headwaters of North, Middle, and South forks of John Day River; region of Meacham; headwaters of Grande Ronde and Powder rivers; Granite Creek; vicinity of Strawberry Butte, and elsewhere. In Wallowa National Forest; noted on Big and Little Sheep creeks at 5,950 feet.

CALIFORNIA.—Klamath and Trinity mountains, Mount Shasta region and southward throughout Sierras. Immediate sea beaches southward to Point Arena (Mendocino County) and inland up Smith River (northwest Del Norte County) to Gasquet, below 500 feet. West side of Sierras to head of Little Kern River and to South Fork of Kern and main Kern River Divide; on east side, down to Cottonwood Creek. Southern cross ranges and southward to San Jacinto Mountains; westward to the coast redwood belt, and eastward to Warner Mountains. Northern California, at 5,000 to 7,000 feet; at 6,000 to 10,000 feet in central part; at 8,000 to 11,000 feet in southern part. Klamath National Forest, at 5,000 to 7,000 feet; northeast of Mount Shasta, about Black Butte and Butte Creek, at 5,000 to 5,600 feet; Goosenest Mountain and eastward to east and northeast slopes of Glass Mountain (about 14 miles south of Tule Lake on line between

Siskiyou and Modoc counties) at 6,700 to 7,500 feet, and Warner Mountains (Modoc County), here noted on South Deep Creek; west base Mount Eddy in Trinity National Forest, at 5,000 to 7,000 feet; northeast slope of Mount Shasta at 5,400 feet altitude (3 miles northeast of Ash Creek) to 5,600 feet (3 miles northwest of Inconstance Creek); between south base of Mount Shasta and Black Fox Mountain; general over Mount Shasta, Plumas, Lassen Peak, and Diamond Mountain National forests, at 6,000 to 7,500 feet, or sometimes between 4,000 and 8,000 feet. North slopes of Lassen Peak on Hat Creek, south slopes down to 5,500 feet. *Plumas County:* Eastward to Prattville and to west side of Spanish Peak range (west of Quincy), below 5,500 feet and westward to Bucks Valley at 5,100 feet. *Sierra County:* Eastward to east side Yuba Pass (above Sierra Valley); westward from 6,000 feet on west slope of main divide to 5,200 feet (Basset Road House); South Sierra Valley eastward into Nevada. *Nevada and Placer counties:* Westward from Truckee on Truckee Canyon to Donner Lake region and down west slopes of Sierras from 8,000 feet, to Cisco and Emigrant Gap below 6,000 feet. *Eldorado County:* Eastward to Tallac (south end Lake Tahoe) and southward (along Little Truckee River); westward to Grass Lake Valley at 7,800 feet; west slope Sierras from Summit (7,500 feet) westward to Echo (5,500 feet). *Alpine County:* Eastward to Silver Creek at 7,500 feet, and westward over Mokelumne Pass into Calaveras County, here extending to point 10 miles west of Bloods. Northern Sierras, at 6,000 to 9,000 feet—sometimes down to 4,500 feet on west slopes; Stanislaus National Forest, at 6,000 to 9,300 feet—rarely down to 3,500 feet or up to 10,000 feet. *Tuolumne County:* Eastward on east side Sierras over Sonora Pass (9,600 feet) to Walker Creek Valley (8,200 feet), Mono Pass (10,200 feet), and adjacent west slopes of Mount Dana, Mount Gibbs, Saddleback Lake, and Tioga Pass; westward on west side Sierras to between Cold Spring and Eureka at 6,200 feet; Aspen Meadows at 6,200 feet. *Mariposa County:* Westward to 6,400 feet (road Yosemite to Crockers), Fish Camp (3 miles south of Wawona) at 4,900 feet. *Mono County:* Eastward nearly to Mono Lake on Leevining Creek, below Mono Pass from 9,400 feet down to Walker Lake, Devil's Cauldron, and southward to Mammoth. Southern Sierra National Forest, at 6,900 to 10,500 feet—rarely down to 5,500 feet or up to 11,500 feet; generally at 9,000 to 11,500 feet on east slopes. *Fresno County:* Westward to Junction Meadow, Dinkey Creek (tributary Kings River) below 5,500 feet; eastward to Kearsarge Pass. *Tulare County:* Noted around Rowell Meadow and southward to Clover Creek divide; upper Kaweah River region; upper part of Sequoia National Park and about Alta Meadow; head basin of East Fork of Kaweah River (Mineral King to Farewell Gap); on high ridge between Cliff Creek and Deer Canyon (tributaries Kaweah River). Headwaters South Fork of Kaweah River. San Gabriel National Forest, summits of eastern part, at 8,000 to 10,000 feet—rarely down to 3,000 feet or up to 10,400 feet. San Bernardino National Forest, summits of eastern part, mainly above 8,500 feet—rarely down to 6,900; in this Forest, known on Grayback Mountain, Big Bear Valley, Bluff Lake, ridge between Santa Ana Canyon and Bear Lake, and Bear Creek Meadows. San Jacinto Mountains, above 9,500 feet on west slope, and above 7,000 feet on east slope. Only on San Jacinto and Tahquitz peaks; noted in Round Valley, between Deer Springs and San Jacinto Peak, between latter and Marion peaks at over 10,000 feet elevation.

LOWER CALIFORNIA.—Northern part of Mount San Pedro Martir at about 8,500 feet.

East of the Pacific region, this pine ranges from northern Idaho and Montana southward through Wyoming, Utah, and western Colorado, also in the Black Hills of South Dakota, and will be dealt with in a future publication.

OCCURRENCE.

On high plateaus and benches in vicinity of streams, mountain meadows, and lakes, on broad ridges, and on long, gentle slopes and bottoms of stream basins. North and east slopes are more favorable than west slopes, while south slopes, except in sheltered coves, are least favorable. Especially abundant in Sierras about mountain meadows and lakes. The typical coast form (commonly distinguished as *Pinus contorta*) occurs on sea coast in sand dunes and barrens and sometimes about tide pools and swamps. Adapted to dry, gravelly soils, but prefers sandy, moist ones of gentle slopes, depressions and plateaus, where the largest growth occurs. Stunted forms grow persistently, however, in crevices of solid rock throughout head basins of nearly all Sierra streams. It avoids limestone.

In Sierras it forms extensive pure forests, particularly about meadows, while on higher, rocky, broken ground it is associated mainly with Jeffrey pine, red fir, and western white pine, and sparingly with black hemlock and aspen. At high elevations in Oregon, with Douglas fir, alpine fir, straggling noble and amabilis firs.

CLIMATIC CONDITIONS.—Apparently intermediate in requirements between Douglas fir and Engelmann spruce. Demands more moisture in soil and air and a lower average temperature than Douglas fir or yellow pine, but probably less moisture and higher temperature than Engelmann spruce and alpine fir. Actual climatic requirements not fully determined.

TOLERANCE.—Very intolerant of shade, especially when young, but able to persist for a long time (20 or 30 years) in very dense stands or for a shorter period under specially adverse light conditions. Requires and thrives best in full light. Even aged stands with full top light, such as commonly follow complete destruction of the former forest by fire, thrive for many years (50 or 60) in dense stands with little natural thinning out, while a thinning of overtopped trees at earlier periods in uneven-aged stands is a proof of its inability to endure long-continued shade.

REPRODUCTION.—Usually a prolific annual seeder and large numbers of cones are borne. Seed of high rate of germination, and with persistent vitality. Bears fertile seed at from 6 to 10 years of age when in the open. In crowded stands cones are borne by trees from 15 to 20 years old. Small, light seed widely disseminated by wind—to about 200 yards from mother trees. Squirrels and birds destroy great numbers of seeds, but the effect on reproduction is inappreciable. Extension by natural seeding is ordinarily slow, scant, and uneven, but with aid of fire is exceedingly thick and even. Full light and exposed mineral soil are requisites of good reproduction. The latter condition is produced by fire, which, when it does not consume the cones, leaves them open or in condition to open and release their seeds. Fire is thus especially instrumental in the reproduction of this pine.

Gray Pine; Digger Pine.

Pinus sabiniana Douglas.

DISTINGUISHING CHARACTERISTICS.

Gray or Digger pine owes its common names to the pale blue-green color of its foliage and to the fact that the large seeds furnish an important food to the California Digger Indians. Its gray, thin-foliaged crown of one or two long upright forks with lower drooping small branches distinguishes it at long distances from associated trees. The meager foliage permits the big, dark cones to be seen half a mile away. Young trees form a rounded or pyramidal crown of upright branches from a short, thick stem. In middle age two or more of the upper branches grow very large and long, forming conspicuous U-shaped forks. Old trees are from 50 to 75 feet high, with a bent or rarely straight trunk from 20 to 30 feet long and from 18 to 30 inches in diameter. Larger trees are sometimes found. The bark of young trees and of branches is a dull gray; that of mature trunks is about 2 inches thick and very roughly furrowed and ridged. The ridges are scaly, wide, irregularly connected, and of a dark gray-brown, tinged with purple-red in unweathered parts. The thin, drooping clusters of leaves, a light blue or gray-green, occur two in a bundle (fig. 17, *a*), and are from 8½ to about 12 inches long. Those of a year's growth remain on the tree for three or four years. When the tree is planted for ornament in a rich, irrigated soil, within its natural range, the foliage becomes very much stouter, giving the tree an entirely different aspect from one grown in its dry native habitat; the cones of such cultivated trees are usually smaller. With the exception of the Coulter pine, the gray pine produces the largest and heaviest cones of any American pine (fig. 17). They mature by September of the second season, remaining firmly attached to the branches for a number of years. The cone scales open very slowly, so that seeds continue to be shed for several months. Indians hasten the opening of the cones by placing them in a small fire. Cones are from 6½ to 10½ inches long. The tips of the scales are a reddish or chestnut brown, later weathered and grayish brown. The seeds (fig. 17) and short wings are very dark chocolate or blackish brown. Seed leaves commonly 15, but often 16. Wood, very coarse-grained (the result of scattered or open stands), dark yellowish brown, often tinged with red; locally used for fuel.

Fig. 17.—*Pinus sabiniana*; Cone and leaf, *a*, slightly reduced; *b*, seed, natural size.

LONGEVITY.—Little is definitely known of the longevity of this pine. It appears to attain its average full growth in from 60 to 80 years; trees from 20 to 24 inches in diameter are from 40 to 50 years old. Recurring fires, to which it has been subjected, seem to prevent its longer survival. If permitted, it would probably not attain an age of over 150 years except in a broken and decrepit form.

RANGE.

CALIFORNIA.—Foothills, lower mountain slopes, and high valleys (at north) of coast ranges and Sierras.

Coast Ranges.—From upper Sacramento and Trinity rivers and Hoopa Valley (on Klamath River, Humboldt County) to southern cross ranges; generally at elevations of 500 to 4,000 feet—occasionally to 5,000 feet. *Shasta County:* North limits, delta in Sacramento River Canyon, above mouth of Pitt River, at 1,150 feet, and at point 15 miles up McCloud River; eastern limits, isolated bodies in northeastern corner of county on hills west and south of Fall River, and on Hat Creek (near Cassel), main body ending 2 miles east of Montgomery Creek (tributary Pitt River); west limit, on west side of Sacramento Valley on ridge west of French Gulch at 2,400 feet; south limit, immediately on Sacramento River at Anderson (11 miles south of Redding). *Trinity County:* North limits, Trinity River and Weaver Creek considerably above Weaverville at 2,100 feet, Canyon Creek (10 miles above Junction) at 2,400 feet; western limit, east side Mad River Valley on bottom slopes of South Fork Mountain. *Humboldt County:* Only in Trinity River bottoms, mainly in Hoopa Valley (north limit), Supply Creek Canyon and Redwood Creek (west of Hoopa Valley near Bair ranch), west limit. *Tehama County:* Eastward on west side of Sacramento Valley to point 8 miles west of Red Bluff (700 feet), and 2 miles southwest of Paskenta; on coast range (6 miles west of Beegum post-office) at 3,000 to 3,400 feet. *Mendocino County:* Westward to west slopes of Eel River, at 1,900 feet, and northward on Russian River to Hopland. *Sonoma County:* Westward to west side of Russian River; southward to Alexander Valley (Russian River, south limit in coast ranges). *Napa County:* South and southwest slopes of Mount St. Helena at 400 to 2,800 feet, southward on ridge east of Napa Valley to point several miles south of Calistoga; also on ridge west of Napa Valley nearly to Rutherford (south limits in north coast range). *Yolo County:* Eastward to east ends of ranges on both sides of Capay Valley (south limit in north coast mountains). *Colusa County:* Eastward in Sacramento Valley foothills to hills about Sites, ridge west of Antelope Valley, hills bordering Cortena Creek, to point within about 10 miles of Williams, and to one between Arbuckle and Dunnigan (Southern Pacific Railroad). *Lake County:* General between 2,500 and 3,000 feet, but on north slope of Mount St. Helena only up to 1,500 feet. South of San Francisco, on north slopes of Monte Diablo (Contra Costa County) at 800 to 3,000 feet, and on east slope near headwaters of Marsh Creek. Mount Hamilton Range (Santa Clara County), west side at 2,000 to over 4,000 feet; also farther south about Gilroy Hot Springs. Not in Santa Cruz Mountains west of Santa Clara Valley nor about Monterey Bay (Monterey County). Common in Santa Lucia Mountains, east of summit, at 400 to 2,500 feet; and also on west slopes in vicinity of Los Burros. Abundant in Reverse Canyon south of Arroyo Seco and east of Santa Lucia Peak; also on nearly all slopes on south side of divide, except on Santa Lucia Peak; south of Santa Lucia Peak about 1 mile below Milpitas schoolhouse; on San Antonio Creek to Jolon and vicinity upper San Antonio Creek slopes and tributaries to 2,000 or 2,500 feet, here meeting lower border of Coulter pine; southeast border of Monterey County on hills about Priest Valley, and eastward into west border of Fresno County. *San Benito County:* Common on Gabalan and San Benito ranges; Chelone Creek Canyon and neighboring hills; higher hills west side of Bear Valley and northward on higher parts of Gabalan Range to point opposite Tres Pinos; second ridge east of San Benito Valley (south of San Benito post-office), and farther south on hills most of the way to Hernandez and New Idria; hills about Bitter Water Valley. In San Luis Obispo National Forest, at 1,000 to 3,000 feet. Noted a few miles south of Templeton on east side San Luis Obispo Divide, but very rare on west side of San Joaquin Valley from south border of San Benito County southward to end of valley. Below 4,000 feet in San Rafael and San Emigdio mountains, and on north slopes of Mount Pinos; Santa Ynez Range, at 500 to 5,000 feet; slopes of Sierra Liebra and extending nearly down to Antelope Valley. *Sierras:* General on west side, in upper foothills, from mouth of Pitt River to Walker Basin. In northern part, chiefly at 500 to 2,500 feet—sometimes to 3,000 feet, or in canyon of South Fork of Yuba River, to 4,200 feet; in central part, range mostly 800 to 3,000 feet, but occasionally reaching 4,000 feet. *Tehama County:* West limit on Sierra foothills, 7 miles east of Red Bluff (on Sacramento River); east limit, 1 mile east of Paine post-office, at 3,000 feet, and Lyonsville. *Butte County:* Westward to point 2 miles east of Chico, 8 miles east of Nelson, and to Palermo; eastward to point 1 mile east of Magalia (2,300 feet), West Branch Feather River, Yankee Hill, Harts Mill (1,700 feet; 7 miles east of Bidwell Bar). *Yuba County:* Westward to point 12 miles east of Marysville; eastward to west base of Oregon Hills. *Nevada County:* Eastward nearly to Grass Valley and Nevada City. *Placer County:* Westward to Rocklin (22 miles northeast of Sacramento); eastward to Colfax and considerably farther in canyon of North Fork of American River. *Sacramento County:* Westward to Natoma (American River) and Michigan Bar. *Eldorado County:* Eastward 3,000 feet to point 5 miles east of Ilacerville, Pleasant Valley, canyons of North, Middle, and South Forks of Cosumnes River and Mount Orcum. *Amador County:* Westward to point 1 mile east of Carbondale; eastward to Oleta, Jackson Reservoir (1,900 feet), volcano basin (Sutter Creek), and between volcano and Oleta. *Calaveras County:* Westward to point few miles east of Wallace and some miles below Tuttletown and Angels; eastward to Rich Gold Gulch, Mountain Ranch, Mokelumne River at least to crossing between West Point and Defender, to point 5 miles east of Murpheys (3,200 feet), and farther in canyon of North Fork Stanislaus River. *Tuolumne County:* Westward to point 8 miles east of Cooperstown (1,200 feet); eastward to Cherokee Mine (east of Soulsbyville), Hetch-Hetchy Valley (on main Tuolumne River), to 3,500 feet on Middle Fork of Tuolumne River. *Mariposa County:* Westward to point 3 miles east of Merced Falls; eastward to point 5 miles east of Coulterville (3,200 feet), to point 2 miles north of Cold Springs (Mariposa road), to point on Merced River about 5 miles east of Mariposa, some distance east of Chowchilla at 3,100 feet, ridge near South Fork of North Fork San Joaquin River. *Madera County:* Westward to point 2 miles west of Raymond (900 feet) and 16 miles east of Madera (1,000 feet); eastward to point 3 miles northeast of Wassama (3,100 feet), some miles east of Fresno Flat, at 3,000 feet, ridge east of North Fork, at 2,600 feet. *Fresno County:* Westward to point 4 miles east of Pollasky, to Letcher, mouth of Mill Creek, on Kings River about 20 miles east of Sanger; eastward to Pine Ridge east of Toll House, Big Creek, and Trimmer Springs (on Kings River). Distribution interrupted in southern Sierras; occurs in valley of Kern River from point 1 mile west of Walker Pass to Kernville, at elevations of 2,500 to 5,000 feet; southward to Walker Basin at 3,100 feet, and northward on Greenhorn Mountains, continuously into Tule Indian Reservation. Abundant from Kings River northward, but absent from parts of Tule River basin, from Kaweah basin, and from region between Kaweah and Kings rivers, but reported in Eshom Valley. *Kern County:* Kernville to Havilah, Walker Basin, and nearly to Caliente; east of Caliente on north slopes about 1½ miles up Caliente Creek (1,400 feet), and to far beyond Piute post-office, going eastward to west edge of desert, here meeting upper border of tree yuccas; west of Caliente, on slopes of Bear Mountain; south of Caliente, common on slopes of Tehachapi Pass; encircles Tehachapi Basin, east of Tehachapi, on hills between Tehachapi Basin and Mohave Desert; west of Tehachapi Valley, on divides about Brite and Cummings valleys; westward from west end of Cummings Valley for about 12 miles to promontory overlooking Kern River plain.

Reported northward in Coast Mountains to south slopes of Siskiyous, eastward to Owens Valley, and southward to San Bernardino Mountains.

OCCURRENCE.

In hot, dry valleys and on dry foothills. Grows thriftily on driest, shallow, coarse, gravelly soils—often baked and cracking throughout rainless summer. Unaffected even where brush is killed by drought. Nevertheless it grows rapidly and very thriftily when planted in moist, rich soils within its range, where it becomes a much heavier foliaged tree.

Does not form forests, but occurs mainly in open groups or widely scattered at lower elevations, mostly with chaparral and foothill oaks; higher up, less abundant and mingled with scattered western yellow pine, which often extends below its main belt. Best growth between 2,000 and 3,000 feet, where it is the only pine in chaparral.

CLIMATIC CONDITIONS.—Not fully determined. Climate most suitable, apparently that only of arid regions.

TOLERANCE.—In early life endures shade, but does not require it. Seedlings come up and grow rapidly under chaparral. In late life general appearance of tree indicates need of, or adaptation to, the fullest light.

REPRODUCTION.—An annual seeder, but certain years cones are more abundant than others. Germination only moderate, and vitality of seeds (out of cones) transient. Large, heavy seeds scattered but little by wind, and falling mostly close to seed trees; hence reproduction mainly near seed trees. Seeds germinate late in winter during rainy season, usually under some shade and upon rough, bare mineral soil.

Coulter Pine; Bigcone Pine.

Pinus coulteri Lambert.

DISTINGUISHING CHARACTERISTICS.

Although a smaller tree, Coulter pine remotely resembles in general appearance young or middle-aged yellow pine, from which, however, its stiff, much heavier foliage, stouter twigs, and huge cones distinguish it at once. Ordinarily it is from 40 to 60 feet high, with an irregularly open, heavy-branched crown. The clear trunk is short (from 10 to 15 feet), and from 18 to 30 inches in diameter. Occasionally trees reach a height of nearly 75 feet and a diameter of 3½ feet. The big lower branches are long, bending downward, often to the ground, and with an upward curve at their ends; immense bunches of erect, stiff leaves conceal their extremities. The bark is early roughly broken, even on young trees. That of old trunks is roughly furrowed and ridged and of a very dark or blackish brown; the ridges are wide, roughly scaly, and irregularly connected with one another. Leaves, 3 in a bundle (fig. 18, *a*), are from 6½ to about 12 inches long; as a rule, about 9 inches. Many of the leaves begin falling during the third summer, but they persist until the fourth summer. They are a deep bluish-green. The horribly armed, extremely heavy cones (fig. 18) distinguish this pine from all of its relatives and associates. Young trees (from 20 to 30 years old) bear cones. The cones mature by August of the second summer and are from 9 to about 14 inches long. During October the cones open partly and continue to shed a few of their seed for several months afterward. Some of the cones remain attached to the branches for five to six or more years. The ends of the cone scales and their sharp, strong points are yellowish clay-brown; the inner portions of the scales are dark purple-brown. Seeds (fig. 18, *b*) and their short narrow wings are a deep chocolate brown, the latter often paler. Seed leaves, 9 to 12, sometimes 13 or 14. Wood, light, soft, coarse grained, and reddish brown; suitable for second-class lumber, but rarely cut. A comparatively short-lived tree.

LONGEVITY.—Trees from 20 to 26 inches in diameter are from 110 to 125 years old. It probably does not reach a greater age than 200 years. Further study of its longevity is required.

RANGE.

Southern California (coast and cross ranges) into northern Lower California. Only on inner coast range from Monte Diablo to Monterey Bay, south of which on western coast ranges also, south to San Diego County; generally between 3,000 and 6,000 feet elevation.

CALIFORNIA.—Monte Diablo in places to crest of main ridge. Fremont Peak at north end Gabilan Range (between Salinas and San Benito rivers) and on higher ridges of this range a few miles south of Fremont Peak; formerly over whole summit of range. Santa Lucia mountains at 550 to 4,600; Santa Lucia Peak nearly to summit and west in upper Arroyo Seco canyon, divide between head of latter and Milpitas Creek, Willow Creek (tributary Arroyo Seco) from mouth to head of Tassajara Creek, Bear Valley, Carmel River, Indian Creek, coast ridge near Sur River (above 3,600 feet), near Cone Peak (southwest Santa Lucia Peak) from 2,500 to 4,000 feet, but not in Pine valley. Summit of ridge west of Carisso Plains (San Luis Obispo County) at 1,500 to 2,750 feet. Santa Barbara National Forest on summits and north slopes from Zaca Lake to Mansana Creek (tributary Sisquoc River), on upper Sisquoc River Basin, and on Big Pine Mountain and Mount Medulce in San Rafael Mountains, at 1,500 to 2,700 feet, and on summits of Santa Ynez Mountains; noted on Rancho Nuevo Creek. San Gabriel Mountains up to 6,000 feet in vicinity of Mount Gleason, on Tujunga canyon at 3,300 to 4,000 feet, at head of Alder Creek at 5,000 feet, in vicinity of Waterman Mountain at 5,500 to 6,000 feet, and on Strawberry Peak at 5,000 to 6,000 feet. Common in San Bernardino mountains at 3,900 to 6,000 feet, sometimes down to 3,500 and up to 6,700 feet, limited to

Deep Creek and Grass valley drainages, Bear Valley (6,700 feet), south side Little Bear valley, Santa Ana and City Creek canyons, but not west of Strawberry Ridge nor east of Coxey Ranch. Common in San Jacinto Mountains at 4,500 to 6,500 feet, sometimes down to 3,500 feet and up to 7,000 feet or 7,500, as above Strawberry valley; only on south and west sides of mountains. Santa Ana Range only at head of Trabuco Canyon and southwest side Santiago Peak nearly to summit. Palomar or Smith Mountain (southwest of San Jacinto Mountains) only below Iron Spring. Common in Balkan Mountains to the south and in northern part of Cuyamaca Mountains at 4,500 to 7,000, and sometimes down to 4,000 feet; noted near Julian at 4,100 feet. Laguna Mountains (north of Mexican line), only on crest of east side.

LOWER CALIFORNIA.—Not within some miles of international boundary, but farther south in Hanson Laguna Range above 4,000 feet and south to Mount San Pedro Martir at 8,000 to highest summits (11,000 feet).

OCCURRENCE.

On dry, warm slopes and ridges, as well as sometimes on more moist, sheltered north slopes in chaparral. In dry gravelly loam soils.

Never in pure forests. At lower altitudes, singly or in groups on summits, in sheltered ravines, and hill coves; higher up (from 3,500 to 5,000 feet), with incense cedar, yellow pine, big-cone spruce, and oaks; sugar pine and white fir appear with it between 5,500 and 7,000 feet, but here Coulter pine soon thins out and disappears.

CLIMATIC CONDITIONS.—Temperature on coastal mountain slopes 25° to 35° F. and from 15° to 100° F. on inland mountains. Humidity high near coast, where cloudy, foggy days are frequent, and low toward inland, or eastern limit of range. Precipitation, from 20 to 30 inches, and chiefly rain. In southern inland mountains it sometimes endures almost arid conditions, with long drought and rapid evaporation during summer.

TOLERANCE.—Demands light except in youth, when it endures shade of chaparral.

REPRODUCTION.—Persistent, periodic seeder, bearing cones often when 10 to 15 feet high, and usually in three-year cycles. Germination of seed only moderate, and vitality (out of cones) transient. Heavy seeds; ripe in August, shed very slowly, sometimes not until or after following January; they commonly fall close to seed trees. Reproduction, never dense, is usually scattered and on exposed mineral soil and where there is little humus.

Monterey Pine.

Pinus radiata Don.

DISTINGUISHING CHARACTERISTICS.

Monterey pine is unique in its isolated sea-coast habitat, where, according to exposure and density of stand, it has a comparatively tall, clean trunk topped by a conspicuously open, irregularly long, and large branched crown. Old trees are apt to have flattish crowns, while younger trees usually have narrow, rounded crowns. The dense foliage is brilliant deep grass-green. Trees from 60 to 90 feet in height and from 16 to 24 inches in diameter are common, but a height of nearly a hundred feet and a diameter of 3½ or 4 feet, and occasionally 5 or 6 feet, is sometimes attained. Bark of adult trees is a deep reddish or blackish brown. It is broadly ridged and deeply furrowed, the flat ridges cut into close, distinct plates. Leaves of a season's growth, which are slender and about 4½ to 6 inches long, remain on the tree until the third year. They occur chiefly 3 in a bundle, with occasional clusters of two on the same branch or tree (fig. 19). A form of this tree (*P. radiata* var. (*b*) *binnata* Lemmon (1895) = *P. insignis* var. *binnata* Wats., 1876) growing on the California coast islands Santa Cruz and Santa Rosa, has most of its leaves 2 in a bundle, but not infrequently bundles of 3 on the same tree. Otherwise, the characters of this form are the same as those of the mainland tree. Other North American pines (*Pinus echinata*) exhibit similar variations, which, like those of the present tree, are deemed insufficient to establish varieties. The cones (figs.

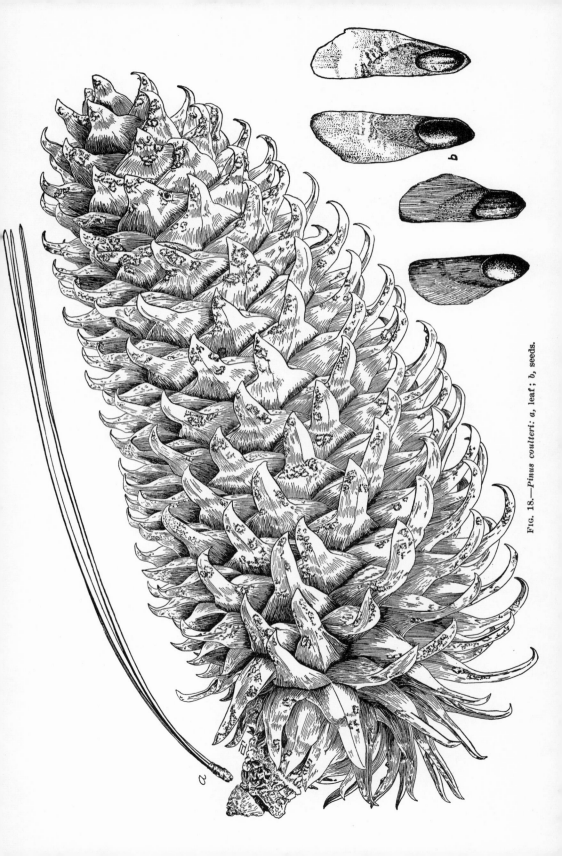

FIG. 18.—*Pinus coulteri*: *a*, leaf; *b*, seeds.

20, 21) are mature by the middle or end of August of the second season. They remain strongly attached to the branches and closed for from six to ten or more years; cut from the trees and dried in the sun, they open readily. The

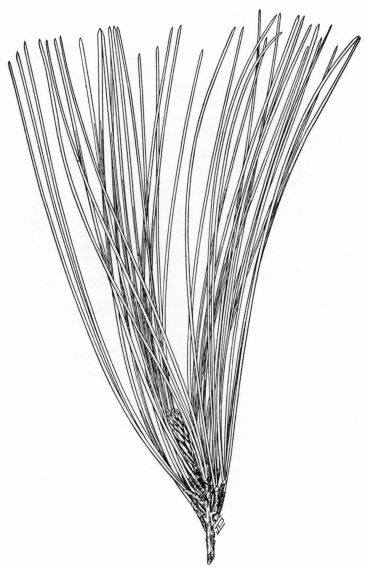

Fig. 19.—*Pinus radiata.*

tips of the cone scales are smooth, shiny, and a dark russet-brown, the inner portions being dark purple. The seeds (fig. 21, *a*), with their jet-black pimpled shells, are readily recognized. Seed leaves commonly 5 to 6; occasionally 7.

Wood, coarse-grained; annual rings often from one-half an inch to nearly an inch thick. It is soft, light, and pale yellowish brown; suitable for coarse lumber, but not used commercially.

LONGEVITY.—Short-lived. It grows very rapidly from the start, both in height and diameter, attaining its full size in from 80 to 100 years, and probably rarely passing the age of 150 years. Trees from 16 to 18 inches in diameter are from 28 to 35 years old.

FIG. 20.—*Pinus radiata,* closed cone.

RANGE.

Central California coast and islands; also Guadelupe Island off Lower California. California coast, on Point Pinos, south of Monterey Bay, from sea over Huckleberry Hill to an elevation of 800 feet, and inland also, for about 3 miles, on the summit and northeast side of the ridge (1,000 to 1,200 feet high) which connects El Toro Range with Huckleberry Hill; also on coast in Santa Cruz County; north of Monterey, from Point Ano Nuevo to Big Creek. A third tract, near coast in San Luis Obispo County, is near Cambria. Occurs also on Santa Rosa and Santa Cruz islands, off California coast, and at 2,000 to 4,000 feet elevation on Guadelupe Island, off Lower California coast.

OCCURRENCE.

Confined to slopes, bluffs, and ridges. Grows well in coast sand and also heavier inland soils. Short lived in arid situations, but does not thrive in wet soils. On coast, occasionally mixed with Monterey and Gowen cypresses; inland, forming interrupted pure forest, occasionally with groups of California swamp pine in moist places.

CLIMATIC CONDITIONS.—Seasonal temperature from 25° to 95° F. Annual average precipitation, not over 17 inches, and wholly rain. Close proximity of range to sea gives humid air, while at least one-third of days are cloudy or foggy.

FIG. 21.—*Pinus radiata, open cone: a, seed.*

TOLERANCE.—Very tolerant, growing in pure, dense stands, where trunks clean themselves well and trees maintain good crown cover, under which humus accumulates rapidly. Isolated trees usually retain low side branches, with heavy foliage until old age.

REPRODUCTION.—Prolific annual seeder. Seed with very high rate of germination and persistent vitality. Produces cones at early age. Long persistent and closed cones shed seed only after several years; often opened only by fire, which is followed by very dense reproduction, particularly in exposed mineral soil.

Knobcone Pine.

Pinus attenuata Lemmon.

DISTINGUISHING CHARACTERISTICS.

The form and size of knobcone pine varies considerably, according as it grows in exposed or in sheltered situations. It is commonly from 15 to 30 feet high and from 6 to 12 inches in diameter. Exceptionally large trees are from 60 to 80 feet high and from 18 to 20 inches in diameter. Except in very dense stands, trees of these sizes have broad, pyramidal crowns, the slender branches curving outward and upward toward the stem; the branches grow from the trunk in distant circles, giving an open aspect to the crown. Old trees are peculiar in having the trunk forked near its middle, thus forming a thin-foliaged, open, narrow crown. The bark of old trunks is thin, dull brown, and shallowly furrowed and ridged, mainly near the ground; the ridges have large, loose scales. The bark of young trunks and of branches and upper stems of old trees is smooth and light brown. The foliage is nearly always light yellow-green. The leaves (fig. 22), 3 in a bundle, are slender, often with a twist, and from 3 to sometimes 7 inches long, but mainly from 3½ to 5 inches. Leaves persist for about four or five years. The cones (figs. 22, 23) mature by September of the second season. Clusters of them, rigidly attached and bent down, encircle the main stems of even small trees (from 5 to 8 feet high) and are the most striking character of this pine. They adhere to the branches and trunk indefinitely; many trees showing that they have retained their cones for nearly fifty years (embedded in the trunk). Moreover, the cones very rarely open until the tree is killed or they are cut from it; then they open only slowly. In collecting the seed it is necessary to force the cones open by moderate artificial heat. When ripe they are a light yellow or clay brown. The seed (fig. 23, *b*) is blackish. Seed leaves, 5 to 7, sometimes 8.

Wood rather light and soft, coarse-grained, brittle, pale yellowish brown, and usually with a thick layer of sapwood.

Longevity.—But little is known of the age limits of this tree. It is commonly killed by the recurring fires which run over the dry slopes it inhabits. Considering the unfavorable conditions (barren and dry soils) under which it grows, its diameter growth, as well as its height growth, is rather rapid during early life (from 15 to 25 years old). Trees from 10 to 12 inches in diameter are from 40 to 60 years old. Probably it does not attain an age of over 100 or 150 years. Further study of its longevity is needed.

RANGE.

Throughout Coast Mountains of southern Oregon, of California, and also in southern Cascades of Oregon and northern California Sierras.

OREGON.—Southwestern part south of McKenzie River, and eastward to western slopes of Cascades, where it occurs at 1,000 to 2,000 feet elevation.

CALIFORNIA.—Klamath National Forest, at about 5,000 feet; Trinity National Forest, above 5,000 feet, extending eastward to Shasta and Whiskeytown (near Redding) and southward throughout the coast ranges. *Siskiyou County:* East slope of Scott Mountain, between Gazelle and Scott Valley, at about 4,000 feet, and thence to near summit; west slope of Marble Mountain Divide (west of Scott Valley), and thence into Russian Creek basin, scarce on North Fork of Salmon River, especially west of Sawyers Bar; extreme western Siskiyou County (between Salmon and Trinity summits, on trail from forks of Salmon River to Hoopa) up to about 5,400 feet. *Humboldt County:* West slope of Trinity Mountain (east of Hoopa Valley) between 3,700 and 4,100 feet. In Trinity County on Canyon Creek near Dedrick. *Shasta County:* Common on Sacramento River about Redding (westward also 10 or 12 miles, reaching Clear Creek), and sparingly up river to Gregory (Baird Switch); also along lower McCloud River near Baird, northward up river valley for about 15 miles. *Lake County:* East slope of Bartlett Mountain from about 3,000 feet down to Bartlett Springs, and eastward to west side of Indian

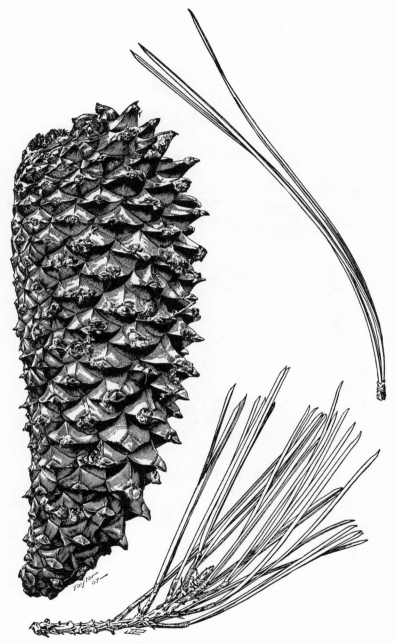

FIG. 22.—*Pinus attenuata,* closed cone.

Valley (about halfway between Bartlett Springs and Leesville) ; from Bartlett Springs southward to northern Long Valley (about 1,800 feet) ; on road between Kelseyville and Konokti Landing (west side of Clear Lake and south of Mount Konokti) ; Highland Springs, and about 5 miles west of it on road to Hopland ; saddle of Cobb Mountain (near upper Big Sulphur Creek), on road from Middletown to Geysers, and westward on Big Sulphur Canyon to Socrates Basin, Little Geysers, also between Little Geysers and Geysers (Sonoma County). *Napa County:* Top of Mount St. Helena (at junction of Napa, Lake, and Sonoma counties) ; between Toll House and south summit. Occurs

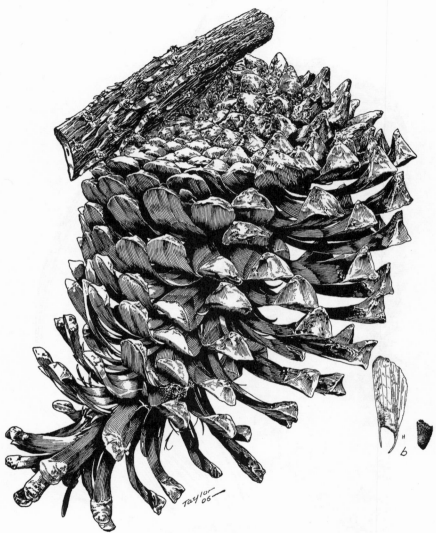

FIG. 23.—*Pinus attenuata,* open cone ; *b,* seed.

in vicinity of San Francisco Bay, in Moraga Valley, on Santa Cruz Mountains, Point Pinos (near Monterey) ; eastern slopes of Santa Lucia Mountains at head of Arroyo Seco, San Antonio and Nacimiento rivers at elevations of about 2,000 to 3,000 feet ; but in southern Santa Lucia Mountains, at Cuesta Pass, and on south side of the San Bernardino Mountains, it occurs at 2,500 to 4,000 feet, or sometimes 5,500 feet ; on East Twin Creek, at about 3,000 feet, and on City and Plunge creeks, at 2,700 to 4,600 feet.

Reported from San Jacinto Mountains. Limited area on Mount Shasta at 4,000 to 5,600 feet, between Panther and Mud creeks; eastward to Fall River. West slopes of northern Sierras, at 1,500 to 3,000 feet—occasionally to 4,000 feet, and southward to Yosemite National Park (?). Forest Hill (between forks of American River), at 2,500 feet elevation; north slope of Merced River (T. 3 S., R. 18–19 E.) in Sierra National Forest (north); Lake Tahoe National Forest, only near Lynchburg, at 4,000 feet, and on ridge above Horse Shoe Bar (T. 13 N., R. 12 E.)

OCCURRENCE.

Usually on dry, exposed, steep southeastern slopes, but often in deep gulches and protected ravines. On poor, dry, rocky, or gravelly and sandy soils. Next to digger pine it is the least fastidious of its kind regarding soil moisture. Frequently forms extensive pure forests, especially in Oregon; in foothills, it grows mainly in groups or singly, while in San Bernardino Mountains it is sparingly scattered in western yellow pine forests, with bigcone spruce, sugar pine, white fir, incense cedar, Coulter pine, and oaks.

CLIMATIC CONDITIONS.—Endures seasonal temperature of from about zero to 95° F., with occasional heavy snows and an annual rainfall up to 45 inches.

TOLERANCE.—Next to digger pine, the least tolerant of Pacific coast pines.

REPRODUCTION.—Abundant annual seeder, bearing cones at very early age. Seed with high rate of germination and with very persistent vitality in cones, no matter how old the cones are. Old trees often bear over 3.5 pounds of seed. Few cones open except by the aid of fire, which is nearly always followed by abundant reproduction. Seed germinates in the most barren soils, and seedlings are hardy from the start.

Pricklecone Pine; Bishop's Pine.

Pinus muricata Don.

DISTINGUISHING CHARACTERISTICS.

Pricklecone or bishop's pine is a little-known species which, on account of its endurance of conditions most unfavorable to the growth of other pines, deserves the forester's careful attention. Ordinarily it is from 30 to 60 feet high and from 12 to 20 inches in diameter; trees from 75 to 80 feet high and from 24 to 36 inches thick occur rarely. Young trees in an open or scattered stand have dense, pyramidal crowns and short, clear trunks. Older trees under such conditions bear a dense crown rounded at the top, with stout branches still extending low to the ground. In dense stands, in which it frequently occurs, the crown is much the same, but shorter, and the trunk is cleaner. The bark, early broken even on young trees, is deeply furrowed and rough, with dull purple-brown scales. The deep yellow-green foliage is conspicuously dense on the extremities of the numerous branches. The stiff leaves (fig. 24), 2 in a bundle, are from $3\frac{1}{2}$ to $5\frac{1}{2}$ inches long; usually $3\frac{1}{3}$ or 4 inches. Leaves of a season's growth fall from the branches during the second and third summers. The cones (fig. 25), specially characterized by their indefinite persistence, are mature in August of the second season, when their prickly scales are shiny and a rich russet-brown. Many of them open and shed their seed in September and October, while some of them remain closed for a number of years. A singular fact concerning the persistent cones is that they are rarely or never embedded in the stems of the trees, as in the case of other pines with persistent cones. The stems of the cones are broken and slowly drawn or forced from the wood by each year's growth pushing against the base of the cone, which is sometimes lightly held by the living bark. The seeds (fig. 25, *a*) are blackish or very dark brown, with a roughish surface. Seed-leaves, usually 5, but often 4. Wood, light yellowish-brown, rather heavy and hard, moderately coarse-grained; of no commercial use.

LONGEVITY.—Little is known concerning the longevity of this pine, which appears to grow rapidly in diameter for the first 40 or 50 years. Trees from

12 to 14 inches in diameter are from 75 to 80 years old. It is probably a short-lived tree, rarely exceeding 150 or 200 years. Further study of its longevity is desirable.

FIG. 24.—*Pinus muricata.*

RANGE.

California coast region from Mendocino County to San Luis Obispo County; also Lower California coast and island.

CALIFORNIA.—From Fort Bragg, Mendocino County (usually in widely separated areas), to Tomales Point—north of San Francisco Bay, ranging from near sea level to

1,000 feet and extending about 1 mile inland; south of San Francisco Bay, on summit and north side of Huckleberry Hill (near Monterey) at 500 to 800 feet elevation, and extending along coast to San Luis Obispo County.

LOWER CALIFORNIA.—Coast between Ensenada and San Quentin and on Cedros Island.

FIG. 25.—*Pinus muricata: a,* seeds.

OCCURRENCE.

In swamps, sandy plains, or steep, dry, wind-swept sandy or gravelly hills near sea; best in peat bogs (watersoaked, sandy plains with heath plants) in north part of range. Very moderate in demands on moisture and quality of soil; thrives in poor, dry, gravelly sand, in peat bogs, and grows also in cold clay soils. Occurs in pure and mixed stands. On sandy plains and gravelly slopes, in pure, crowded stands of slender trees. On cold clay soils, often with coast form of lodgepole pine and Gowen cypress; sometimes also mingled with live oaks, Douglas fir, California laurel, wax myrtle, and madroña.

CLIMATIC CONDITIONS.—Temperature of range rarely below 25° or above 95° F. Rainfall, from 20 inches in north to 11 inches in south; snow almost unknown. Atmospheric moisture, high; more than one-third of days cloudy or foggy.

TOLERANCE.—One of most tolerant pines; frequently in dense stands with fairly heavy crown cover and soil with good humus.

REPRODUCTION.—Good seeder, bearing cones when quite young and about every year. Seed of high germination and with very persistent vitality (a number of years) when held in closed cones. Seeds shed tardily; opening of cones hastened by fire, which is usually followed by dense reproduction. Aggressive, extending its range particularly over cut and burned redwood lands contiguous to it; then often replacing former forest by its dense growth.

LARIX. LARCHES.

The larches,[a] also called tamaracks, lose their leaves every fall, their branches becoming bare in winter and in the spring putting forth new foliage. Their leaves resemble somewhat those of other conifers in being needle-shaped; but they are really distinct from all the rest of our native cone-bearers in being produced in little brush-like bundles, from 12 to 40 leaves in each (figs. 26 to 28), on all but the leading shoots, on which the leaves are scattered singly. The little bud-like spurs which bear bundles of leaves are really aborted or suppressed branchlets, which, if drawn out by growth, would show their leaves disposed as in the leading shoots. Male and female flowers are borne singly on the same branches or twigs of the previous year's growth. The male, or pollen-bearing, flowers are small, rounded, or elongated yellow-green bodies about the size of a small pea, and are borne naked; the female flowers, which produce cones and seeds, are also small, but are scaly. They are usually bright purple or red, and are accompanied by a bundle of leaves.

The cones of larches mature in a single season and often remain on the trees for one or several seasons. Two winged seeds are borne under each of the thin cone scales. Larch cones open shortly after they are matured and shed their seed. Seed-leaves, 5 to 6 or 7. Succeeding these the young stem bears single scattered leaves, as do also the leading shoots of branches. This manner of leaf growth continues for several years, and then the seedling begins to produce the adult clusters of leaves.

The larches are important forest trees. They produce straight, tall stems, the wood of which is strong, moderately durable, and especially useful for round and pole timber, as well as for saw timber.

At least three species of larch inhabit the United States. One is found mainly in northeastern United States and the Canadian provinces, extending westward to southern Alaska. The two others inhabit the northwestern United States, extending northward into Canada. A fourth species is probably confined to Alaska.

Western Larch.

Larix occidentalis Nuttall.

DISTINGUISHING CHARACTERISTICS.

Western larch is the largest and most massive of North American larches. Its straight trunks grow ordinarily to a height of from 100 to 180 feet and to

---

[a] The name Larch (from *Larix*) is properly applied only to trees of the genus *Larix*. During the last twenty-five years, however, "larch" has been, and still is, applied by lumbermen and woodsmen to the noble fir, *Abies nobilis*. This tree is a true fir or "balsam" and in no way directly related to the larches. The use of "larch" as a name for this tree should be discontinued. It has led to much confusion.

a diameter of 3 or 4 feet. Not infrequently trees reach a height of over 200 feet and a diameter of from 5 to 8 feet. The tapering trunks are clear of branches for from 60 to 100 feet or more, while the crown is a narrow short

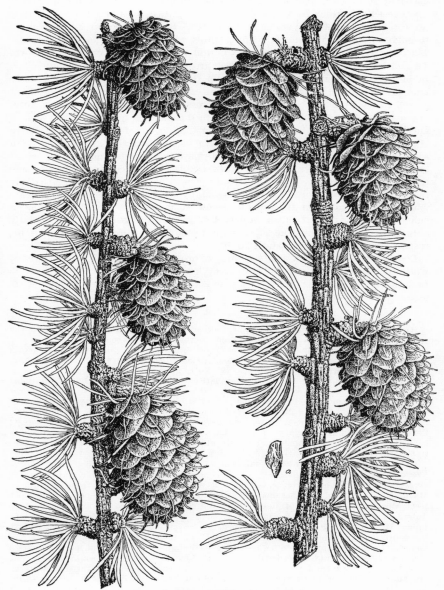

Fig. 26.—*Larix occidentalis: a,* seed.

pyramid running up to a slender point. The crown is very open and carries comparatively few small, horizontal branches, which appear thinly clad with leaves. Trees growing in specially favorable, protected situations have rather long, narrow crowns with more or less weeping branches. Middle-aged and old trunks have reddish cinnamon-brown bark, extremely thick (3 to 6 inches), deeply furrowed near the base of the tree, where the ridges are strikingly massive; 20 or more feet above, it is much thinner and less deeply furrowed. The exceedingly thick bark of old and of half-grown trees is a most important protection against fire. Very many large trees bear evidence of having passed through a number of destructive forest fires without damage to their vitality. The bark of young trees and branches is thin, scaly, and dark or grayish brown. The color of the foliage, a pale yellowish green, becoming a bright lemon-yellow in late fall, distinguishes the trees from their associates. The leaves, flatly triangular and distinctly ridged or keeled on their inner face, are from about 1 inch to nearly 2 inches in length. In cross-section they show a single fibro-vascular bundle in the center and no resin ducts. The number of leaves in a cluster, ranging from 14 to about 30, can not be depended upon as a distinctive character. The cones (fig. 26) mature in one season and are ripe early in August. They open soon afterwards and shed their seeds (fig. 26, *a*), which are light chestnut brown. By the end of October or November the cones have fallen from the trees. Cones vary from about 1 to 1½ inches in length; their foot-stalks are very short. Cone scales usually with a dense coating of delicate whitish woolly hairs on the outside, below their centers. Seed-leaves, as a rule, 6. Wood, clear reddish brown, heavy, and fine-grained; commercially valuable. It is very durable in an unprotected state, differing greatly in this respect from wood of the eastern larch.

LONGEVITY.—Long-lived, attaining an age ordinarily of from 300 to 500 years, while the largest trees are probably from 600 to 700 years old. Trees from 16 to 20 inches in diameter are from 250 to 300 years old. Further records of its age limits are required.

RANGE.

High valleys and mountain slopes of southeastern British Columbia, northwestern Montana, northern Idaho, Washington, and southward to Oregon.

WASHINGTON.—Mountains of northeastern part, Blue Mountains, and southern part on east side of Cascades. Not detected north of Omak Creek (eastern tributary Okanogan River in north central Oregon, latitude 48° 16′), nor in Cascades north of head of Peshastin Creek (tributary Wenache River, latitude 47° 30′). Mount Rainier National Forest, 2,200 to 5,600 feet on divide between Natches and American rivers; also on upper Natches, Tieton, upper Yakima, Atanum, Klickitat, and White Salmon watersheds, and on Mount Adams. Colville National Forest, northward from Columbia River to 4,000 feet in Kettle Range. General in Washington addition to Priest River National Forest; Columbia River in latitude 46° to 49°, and on Kamiak Butte, near Pullman (eastern part State). Occasional stands in Blue Mountains of Wenaha National Forest, at 2,700 to 6,000 feet.

OREGON.—Blue and Wallowa mountains, and Cascades southward to head of Squaw Creek (T. 16 S., R. 9 E., lat. 44° 8′). Cascades, mainly on east side, but extending across divide for short distance, along west side, from township 4, south (south of Mount Hood) to head of Clackamas River (T. 6 S.). On north (at 2,000 feet to 4,600 feet), east, and south sides of Mount Hood and southward, on east side of Cascades, to Tamarack Mountain (T. 6 S., R. 9 E.); here very abundant. Found next on Metolius River (T. 12 S., R. 9 E.), southeast sides of Mount Jefferson, thence extending southward to head of Squaw Creek (T. 16 S., R. 9 E.), the southmost limit now known. In Blue Mountains, on both sides of north and south ranges (included in eastern division of Blue Mountains National Forest), at 5,000 to 6,000 feet; southward to head of John Day River, and westward to township 30 east. Eastward through Wallowa Mountains to Big and Little Sheep Creeks (T. 46 and 47 E., R. 3 and 4 S.) nearly to the Idaho line.

The detailed range of western larch in Montana and Idaho will be dealt with in a later bulletin.

OCCURRENCE.

Mountain slopes, preferring north and west exposures—stream bottoms, valleys, and flats; rare in canyon bottoms and on mountain summits. Exacting in requirements of soil moisture ; best in deep, fresh, porous soils, but thrives on low, moist sites and in dry, gravelly soils.

Sometimes forms pure stands, but usually in mixed stands. Its best growth is in northeastern Washington, northern Idaho, and northwestern Montana, where it often occurs in pure open forests in valleys and slopes. In the Blue Mountains of Washington and Oregon, on typical flats. Here, also, areas of this larch and lodgepole pine are interspersed through the forest of Engelmann spruce, white and lowland firs, and Douglas fir ; the silvical characteristics of larch and lodgepole pine appear very similar in view of common association. Of largest size at lower elevations along Priest River (Idaho), in mixture with western white pine, western red cedar, Douglas fir, western hemlock, Engelmann spruce, and lowland fir. It is a more important part of Douglas fir forests somewhat higher up, where it is associated also with lodgepole and western white pines, lowland and alpine firs, Engelmann spruce, cottonwoods, and birches. In Bitterroot mountains (northern Idaho), in pure stands or with slight admixtures of Douglas fir and western yellow pine.

CLIMATIC CONDITIONS.—Seasonal precipitation, from about 20 to about 30 inches, with a moderately heavy snowfall remaining on ground until summer. Rains frequent in spring and fall, but summers hot and dry.

TOLERANCE.—Very intolerant of shade throughout life ; probably demands even more light than western yellow pine. This intolerance partly compensated for by early rapid height growth, which carries it above suppressing heavier-foliaged associates. Appears more tolerant on moist than on dry soils. In moist sites it grows in fairly dense stands, and is tall, with a clear bole, and its lower branches are early killed and dropped ; while on drier soils open stands or isolated trees occur with branches often retained to the ground.

REPRODUCTION.—A prolific seeder, but locally variable in seed production ; sterile periods of from one to several seasons are likely to intervene. Rarely bears seeds as early as the 25th year, but begins to bear prolifically at 40 or 50 years. Seed has a fairly high rate of germination and moderately persistent vitality. The thin scales of ripe cones open and close very readily with alternate dry and wet weather, so that the period and the rapidity of seed dispersion vary somewhat with local climatic conditions. Usually much seed is shed on snow. Abundant moisture required for germination and growth of seedlings. The chief competitor of larch is lodgepole pine, both finding suitable seed beds in burned-over areas with exposed mineral soil, where the kind of reproduction depends upon whether larch or pine has seeded first. If lodgepole pine has the start, it shades out the more intolerant larch. If both species start together, larch may preserve its numerical importance in the stand by more rapid growth. Its light foliage can not prevent the growth of the pines, or of spruce and firs, and the typical occurrence of larch in mixed stands is a result. Favorite areas for pure larch reproduction are those so thoroughly burned over as to preclude the immediate heavy reproduction of lodgepole pine.

Alpine Larch.

Larix lyallii Parlatore.

DISTINGUISHING CHARACTERISTICS.

The strictly alpine habitat of Alpine larch serves very largely to distinguish it from the Western larch, which it resembles in some features. It is stunted in appearance, from 30 to 40 feet high and from 10 to 24 inches in diameter, with a long, broadly pyramidal, pointed crown. Some of the branches are very long and big, forming an open unsymmetrical crown. Somewhat larger trees are sometimes found. As a rule, the ends of the branches turn upward, but frequently they droop conspicuously, while, in contrast with the brittle branches of Western larch, they are tough and withy. A notable character of the new branch shoots is their dense coating of white, fine wool, which is retained, more or less, for two seasons, and from which the tree gained the name of " woolly larch." Trunks are clear of branches for only about one-third or one-half the tree's height, and, as a result of exposure, are often crooked or bent. The bark of mature trees is rarely more than seven-eighths of an inch thick. It is indistinctly furrowed ; the irregular, flat ridges of loose scales are deep purplish or reddish brown. On young trees the bark is usually unbroken until they are 5 or 6 inches in diameter. Previously it is ashy gray, as are the crown branches of older trees. The foliage is distinctly light bluish-green, turning bright lemon-yellow late in autumn, when it is readily detected by its color on distant high, inaccessible peaks and crests. The leaves, from 30 to 40 or more in a cluster, are more or less 4-angled, and about 1 inch to 1⅝ inches in length. A cross-

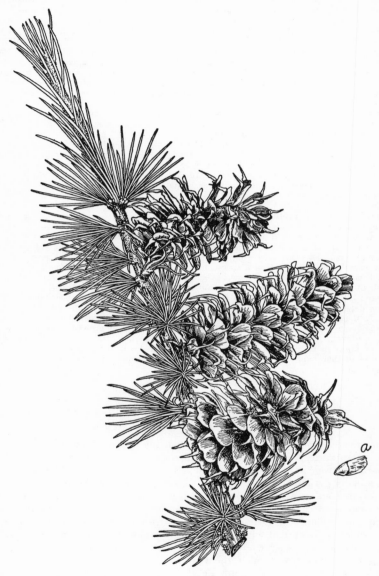

FIG. 27.—*Larix lyallii: a,* seed.

section shows one resin-duct in each of the two angles of the leaf. The cones mature in one season and are ripe early in August, opening soon afterwards and shedding their seed. By late autumn the cones have all fallen from the trees.

They are from about 1½ to 2 inches long (fig. 27). The bristly bracts that project from among the cone scales are a deep purple. The cone scales are deep purple-red, and their margins have a fringe of tangled, fine white wool, as do, more or less, the outer surfaces of the scales. The seeds (fig. 27, *a*) are pale reddish brown. Seed-leaves, usually 5. Wood, clear red-brown or deep orange-brown; fine-grained, heavy, hard, and tough; suitable for use, but not used commercially.

LONGEVITY.—Long-lived, attaining an age of from 400 to 600 years. Exceptionally large trees are doubtless 650 to 700 years old, or even older. Trees from 16 to 18 inches in diameter are from 470 to 510 years old. Age limits imperfectly known.

RANGE.

Timber line tree. Continental Divide in western Alberta and eastern British Columbia; northern Montana and southward to head of Middle Fork of Sun River and Pend Oreille Pass; northern Idaho, and southward to Nez Perces Pass and Lochsa-Selway Divide; northeastern Washington and Cascades of Washington and Oregon, southward to Mount Hood. Range still imperfectly known.

BRITISH COLUMBIA AND ALBERTA.—Eastern and western slopes of Continental Divide, at 6,500 to 7,000 feet, and northward to Mount Hector (near Laggan); eastward to Cascade in Bow River Valley, and westward to southern Selkirk Range (between Kootenai Lake and head of St. Marys River, a branch of Kootenai River) and Galton Range (near Tobacco Plains, between Continental Divide and Kootenai River), just north of Canadian boundary.

WASHINGTON.—Both sides of Cascades and high mountains of northeastern part of State. Not detected in Blue Mountains, Olympics, nor in coast ranges. In Cascades, from latitude 49° southward, probably, throughout the range, but abundant only to head of Icicle Creek (tributary Wenache River), at 6,000 to 7,400 feet; on Mount Stuart and Wenache Mountains. On east side of Cascades, in Washington National Forest, at 5,800 to 7,100 feet; abundant north of Lake Chelan at State Pass—about 6,000 feet at War Creek Pass—6,700 feet, on divides both sides of Stehekin River from Lake Chelan to head of basin; south of Lake Chelan, on Pyramid Peaks at elevations between 6,500 to 7,000 feet, and in Emerald Basin at 5,000 feet.

OREGON.—Rare in Cascades and southward to Mount Hood.

The detailed range of this tree in Idaho and Montana will be dealt with in a future publication.

OCCURRENCE.

Timber line tree, of high mountain slopes and plateaus, showing preference for north aspects and often for passes and sheltered sides of crests, and for divides. Very moderate in soil requirements, growing in rockiest soil and in crevices of rugged granite slopes, provided there is abundant soil moisture. Occurs as scattered individuals, in small, pure groves, or in open stands with white-bark pine, black hemlock, alpine fir, and Engelmann spruce.

CLIMATIC CONDITIONS.— Best climatic environment where there is heavy snowfall, beginning early and remaining well into the summer. Hardier than other alpine associates, in moist basins ascending higher and showing more vigor, while its light foliage, compact, strong trunk, and firmly anchored root system enable it to withstand, without serious damage, the rigors of high and bleak summits.

TOLERANCE.—Like western larch, very intolerant of shade.

REPRODUCTION.—Little is known definitely of the seeding habits. Sometimes produces cones abundantly, but apparently at infrequent and irregular intervals. Reproduction in the United States generally poor, and seedlings or saplings are not numerous.

Tamarack.[a]

Larix laricina (Du Roi) Koch

DISTINGUISHING CHARACTERISTICS.

In the far Northwest, where tamarack enters the Pacific region, it is a small tree often from 6 to 10 feet high and from 1 to 3 inches in diameter. East of

---

[a] Since the manuscript of this bulletin went to printer Mr. W. F. Wight has published the following new species of larch from Alaska. His illustration of the tree is repro-

the Canadian Rockies and in the Great Lakes country, trees from 60 to 80 feet high and from 20 to 24 inches in diameter were once common, but are now much rarer, the largest trees being seldom over 50 feet high and 12 or 14 inches thick. It has a single straight, slightly tapering trunk, and a narrow, sharply conical crown of slender, horizontal branches, which, during the first 25 or 30 years, and in the usual dense stands, extend down to the ground. Later the trunks are clear of branches for one-half or two-thirds of their length. The thin, scaly bark is reddish brown, but outwardly more or less weathered to an ashy brown. Twigs of a season's growth are smooth, and whitish at first, but in winter, dull yellowish brown. Mature leaves (fig. 28), scattered singly on vigorous leading shoots but elsewhere in clusters of about 12 to 20, are indistinctly triangular in cross-section—convex on the top side, with a ridge beneath—and about ⅞ inch to 1⅛ inches long. In cross-section the leaf shows 2 minute resin-ducts close to its outer edges. Cones (fig. 28) are matured in early autumn of one season, are pale russet-brown, as are the minute winged seeds (fig. 28, *f*), which escape slowly from the gradually opened cone-scales during late autumn or early winter; probably the upright position of the cone prevents the rapid escape of the seeds usual from pendent cones. Seed leaves 5, sharp-pointed, and about ½ an inch long. Wood, pale yellowish brown; in larger trees, with rather thin layer of whitish sapwood; fine-grained or moderately coarse-grained, according as the trees are grown in dense or open stands; rather hard and heavy, and elastic, used commercially chiefly for poles and ties.

LONGEVITY.—The largest trees are from 150 to 180 years old, while trunks from 10 to 12 inches through are from 60 to 75 years old. Further records of longevity are desirable.

---

duced here (fig. 28A), together with his description and notes. The writer has not been able to critically study the specimens upon which this species is based. In the absence of previous evidence to the contrary, a form of *L. laricina* has been held to be the larch commonly met with in Alaska. It is not at all unlikely, however, that the Alaskan tree is distinct, but the exceedingly close relationship of this tree with *L. laricina,* as shown by the form of the cone scales and bracts from specimens representing both species (figs. 28 and 28A) suggests that further study should be made of these trees, especially in the field.

ALASKA LARCH. *Larix alaskensis* Wight, sp. nov.

"A small tree, attaining a maximum height of about 9 m. and a diameter of 20 cm.; leaf-facicles at the ends of branches 3 to 5 mm. long; leaves pale green, 5 to 20 mm. long, about 5 mm. broad, rounded on the upper surface, slightly keeled on the lower; cones borne at the ends of lateral branchlets 3 to 5 mm. long, ovoid or short-oblong, 10 to 15 mm. long, 9 to 12 mm. broad; cone scales slightly longer than broad, the larger ones 8 to 10 mm. long, 7 to 9 mm. broad, rounded at the apex, abruptly contracted toward the base; bracts of the cone about one-third as long as the cone scales, ovate, acute; flowers not seen.

"*Distribution.*—Upper Kuskowim River to the Yukon and Tanana rivers.

"*Type-specimen:* No. 379,803, U. S. Nat. Mus.; collected August 6, 1902, at Tanana, Alaska, by A. J. Collier (No. 117).

"*Larix alaskensis* differs from *L. laricina* in its usually shorter leaves, but more particularly in its cones. The cone scales are longer in proportion to their breadth; the bracts of the cone scales are ovate and without a projecting mucronate point at the apex, while *L. laricina* has bracts short-oblong to nearly orbicular in outline, and commonly emarginate or lacerate on either side of a mucronate projection at the apex. From *L. dahurica,* the most closely related Asiatic species, it differs in its usually shorter leaves, in its smaller cones, with the cone scales less widely spreading in dried specimens, and in its narrower cone bracts.

"*Between the Yukon and Cook Inlet.*—Upper Kuskokwim, Herron, August, 1899; Tanana Valley, east of Cantwell River, Brooks & Prindle, August 27, 1902; Kaltag, on the Yukon, Collier, 1902 (No. 147); Tanana, Collier, 1902 (Nos. 117, 118); Weare, Georgeson, 1900 (No. 6)."—Reprinted from Smithsonian Miscellaneous Collections (Quarterly Issue), volume 50, 174, Pl. xvii. Published July 10, 1907.)

RANGE.

Newfoundland and Labrador to northern Pennsylvania, northern Indiana, Illinois, central Minnesota; northwestward to Hudson Bay and Alaska nearly to Bering Sea.

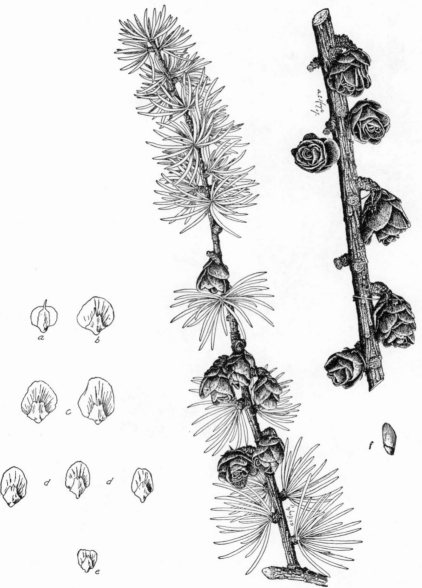

FIG. 28.—*Larix laricina:* *a,* scale at base of cone; *b,* scale near base; *c,* scales from center of cone; *d,* scales near top of cone; *e,* top scale of cone; all 1½ natural size; *f,* seed natural size.

YUKON AND ALASKA.—Pacific slope of Rocky Mountains in Yukon territory and Alaska, crossing Rockies on Liard River at about latitude 59°, and extending up Dease, upper

Liard, and Francis rivers nearly to Finlayson Lake (lat. 61° 35'). Locally noted on Francis Lake, Francis River at mouth. Reappears in central Alaska (long. 145° 45' to 158° 40') in valley of lower Yukon, upper Koyokuk, Tanana, and Upper Kuskokwim rivers, extending north to latitude 67° on Koyukuk River and south to headwaters of Kuskokwim River (lat. 63°) ; extends from river valleys to 1,650 feet. Locally noted on Yukon from

FIG. 28A.—*Larix alaskensis: a,* fruiting branch ; *b,* back of cone scale ; *c,* a cone scale with ovules ; *d,* bract of cone scale—enlarged ; *e,* bract of cone scale of *Larix americana*—enlarged.

Kaltag near Norton Bay (long. 158° 40') at least up to mouth of Tanana ; Minook Creek (southern tributary Yukon above Tanana) ; upper Koyukuk River from Bettles down at least to Bergman ; Tanana River and tributaries as follows: Main valley, one patch between Goodpastor and Salcha rivers (lat. 145° 45', east limit now known), Salcha River, two patches on small tributaries ; Cantwell River, one patch on east side near mouth; Kantishna River, one patch between head and Toklat River; Tolovana River, two patches on north tributaries; Baker Creek, one patch on head tributary; Kuskokwim River, noted on its tributary Tonzona River. Also reported from upper Copper River.

The detailed range of tamarack east of the Pacific region will be dealt with in a future bulletin.

OCCURRENCE.

Most abundant in sphagnum swamps and muskegs, but of largest size on better drained margins of swamps and lakes, moist, porous benches, and bottomlands; thrives also on well-drained hillsides. In parts of British Columbia, characteristic of damp, cool, north slopes. Grows on shallow, moist soils of nearly every consistency, from stiff clay to coarse sand. Thrives on moderately retentive loams, especially those with rich leaf mold. Occurrence in saturated soil seems to indicate not a special requirement, but ability to exist where other species more tolerant of shade can not grow. It does not do well where its roots are constantly submerged. Near confluence of Tanana and Yukon rivers in Alaska it occurs in open scattering stands, while in its eastern range it forms rather dense, pure growths. At best, the crown cover is never very dense. Commonly associated in mixed stands with black spruce, black cottonwood, alder, and willows. Other far northwestern associates have not been determined.

CLIMATIC CONDITIONS.—With the widest range of all American conifers, it experiences great diversity of climate. In the Atlantic region, it grows in a humid climate with frequent fogs and an annual precipitation of from 30 to 50 inches; and seasonal temperature is moderate—30° or over 100° F. being rare. But in north British Columbia and Alaska it is subjected to great seasonal ranges of temperature and to pronounced atmospheric dryness; temperature falls to −60° or −80° F. during winter and often goes above 100° F. in summer. The precipitation may be as low as 12 inches, and the growing season for tender vegetables may not exceed three weeks.

TOLERANCE.—Requires a great deal of light throughout life, and at no time endures heavy shade.

REPRODUCTION.—Frequent and abundant seeder. Some seed is borne annually, but especially abundant production occurs about every 2 to 4 years. Seed have only moderate rate of germination and moderately persistent vitality. Young trees often produce cones when from 10 to 20 years old. Conditions favorable to germination and growth are fresh organic or mineral soil, with a protecting cover of spare grass or herbs. Seedlings require this slight protection at first, and then grow fairly rapidly in height, so that they persist in mixture with more tolerant but slower growing species of the same age.

PICEA. SPRUCES.

The spruces are evergreen trees with sharp-pointed, pyramidal crowns and conspicuously straight, tapering trunks. The branches grow in regularly distant circles. Their stiff, often very keenly pointed, single leaves have a characteristic spiral arrangement on the branches, to which those of each season's growth adhere for from about seven to ten years. All but two of the North American species have more or less distinctly 4-angled leaves. Of the exceptions, one species has flat and only indistinctly 4-angled leaves, while the other species has flat-triangular leaves. Male and female flowers are borne on the same tree and on twigs of the previous year's growth. Male flowers, pollen-bearing only, are drooping, yellow, bright purple, or rose-red, long or short cylindrical bodies (about three-fourths inch to 1 inch by one-fourth to one-half inch), while the female flowers, which produce cones and seed, are erect, yellowish-green or bright red bodies of similar form, from three-fourths inch to about 1¼ inches in length by one-fourth to nearly three-fourths inch in diameter. The cones, which are matured in one season, are cylindrical or egg-shaped, always drooping or bent downward (figs. 29–33). Most spruces bear their cones at the extreme top of the crown, while some bear cones only on branches of the upper half of the crown. After shedding their seed, in early or late fall, the cones either drop from the trees by spring or remain on the branches for a number of years. The scales of spruce cones are thin and without prickles, in contrast to the thick, strong cone scales of pines, which often have sharp, strong prickles. The scales are firmly attached, as in the pines, to a woody central column. They never fall away until the cone is rotted to pieces. Two seeds are borne under each cone scale. The seeds are light and are provided at one end with a thin wing which enables the wind to disseminate them widely. Seed-leaves, sometimes 4, but commonly from 5 to about 15.

The spruces are exceedingly important forest trees. They yield superior saw-timber and the even-grained wood can be used for a great many purposes. For paper pulp the wood of these trees is unsurpassed by any other. Seven species are indigenous to North America, all of which are abundantly, or exclusively, represented in the United States. Four are distributed over the western half of the United States, and three range mainly through northeastern United States and Canada, while two of these extend, almost entirely in Canada from the Great Lake region, into Alaska.

Engelmann Spruce.

Picea engelmanni Engelmann.[a]

DISTINGUISHING CHARACTERISTICS.

In dense stands Engelmann spruce has a straight, clean trunk with a close, very short, narrowly pyramidal crown of small branches; the upper part of the crown has exceedingly short sprays, forming a narrow spire. Such trees are from 80 to 100 feet or more in height, and from 18 to 36 inches in diameter. Larger trees occur sometimes. Singly, or in an open stand, it forms a similar but longer crown, with drooping lower branches which may extend down to the ground. Such trees are usually from 60 to 80 feet high with very tapering trunks, and if exposed to heavy winds, the lower branches are often long and stout. From all of the main horizontal branches hang numerous tassel-like side branchlets which give the tree a very compact appearance. At high altitudes it is often not more than 2 or 4 feet high. A spike-like stem bears a few short densely-leaved branchlets while enormously long branches spread over the ground from the base of the trunk. The foliage is a deep blue-green, on some trees with a decidedly silvery or whitish tinge. This silvery tinge is very marked on young trees; occasionally, however, large and moderately old trees still retain it. The bark becomes scaly even on rather young trees. On maturer trunks it is thin, dark purplish-brown or russet-red, and outwardly composed of very loosely attached small scales. The 4-angled leaves (fig. 29) are soft to the touch, usually about an inch in length, but often longer, and are spreading on young branchlets (fig. 29) which do not bear cones, while on cone-bearing twigs they are commonly crowded and of a shorter type; they are often crowded and curved so as to appear mainly on the upper part of the branchlet. The point of the leaf is characteristically short and flat; short leaves exhibit this more strongly than do the longer ones. A cross-section of the leaf shows no resin ducts. A disagreeable odor is emitted by leaves and young shoots when crushed. Young shoots are more or less minutely hairy and may remain so for about three years. The cones, which mature in a single season, are ripe by the middle or latter part of August. Most of them are borne near the top of the crown. By October the seed is usually all shed. Cones (fig. 29) vary greatly

---

[a] Dr. George Engelmann did not name this tree in honor of himself. Parry (Trans. Acad. Sci. St. Louis, II, 122, 1863) recognizing that the tree had been referred by Engelmann to *Abies nigra* (another species), called it *Abies Engelmanni*, which proved to be a *nomen nudum*. Later Engelmann (loc. cit., 212) cited Parry's name, and in doing this formed a new name, *Picea engelmanni*, which he credited to Parry. As a matter of fact, Parry did not write *Picea engelmanni*, consequently Engelmann was the first publisher of *Picea engelmanni*, but certainly not with a knowledge that he must be cited as its author.

in length from about 1 to nearly 3 inches, the usual length being 1½ inches. The cone-scales are also very variable in form. They are commonly narrowed to squarish ends; sometimes the ends of the scales are pointed, and occasionally rounded. At maturity and shortly after shedding their seeds, the cones are somewhat shiny and from light brown to dark cinnamon-brown. They fall from the trees during autumn or early winter. The small winged seeds

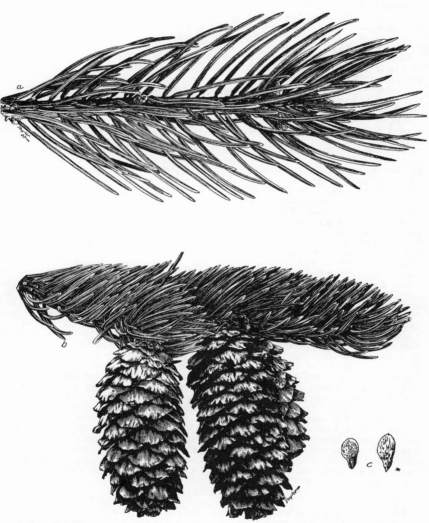

FIG. 29.—*Picea engelmanni: a,* leader; *b,* side branch and open cone; *c,* seed.

(fig. 29, *c*) are blackish brown. Seed-leaves, 6. Wood, light, soft, fine, and straight-grained, and of a very light yellowish to faintly reddish brown color; used commercially.

LONGEVITY.—Very long-lived, even in the most unfavorable situations. Trees from 16 to 22 inches in diameter are from 350 to 460 years old. Stunted trees of high wind-swept crests, from 3 to 5 inches in diameter, are from 150 to 200 years old. Extremely large trees occasionally found would doubtless prove to be from 500 to 600 years old.

RANGE.

Yukon Territory and British Columbia to southern Oregon and through the Rockies into New Mexico and Arizona. Rocky Mountains of western Canada from Peace River southward through western Montana and Idaho, western Wyoming, eastern Nevada, Utah, western Colorado, New Mexico, and Arizona; westward to east slope of Cascades in Washington and to west slope in Oregon, extending southward to California border. In Canada, at elevations from 2,500 to 6,000 feet; at 4,000 to 6,000 feet in Washington; at 8,500 to 11,000 feet in Arizona, and at 8,500 to 12,500 feet in Colorado.

WESTERN CANADA (YUKON TERRITORY, BRITISH COLUMBIA, ALBERTA).—East slopes of Rockies in Yukon Territory westward throughout British Columbia south of Peace River plateau (lat. 55° 45'); probably only to inland slope of Coast Range, and not in more arid parts of southern interior plateau nor on mountains above 6,000 feet. Northern part of British Columbia, on streams at 2,500 to 3,500 feet, reaching Babine and McLeods lakes; northern limits not yet determined. Eastern limit at south is Cascade Mountain on Bow River (along Canadian Pacific Railroad). Locally noted at Laggan, Kicking Horse Lake, Rundle Mountain (near Banff), Lake Louise, Kamloops Valley (central British Columbia).

WASHINGTON.—East slope of Cascades and northeastern mountains; generally at 4,000 to 6,000 feet elevation. Washington National Forest appears to be mainly on east side, at 4,000 to 6,000 feet; in sheltered passes occasionally up to 6,800 feet and down to 2,100 feet, as in Stehekin River valley, where it extends westward from an island about 5 miles above Lake Chelan to within 15 miles above Lake in lower edge of *Abies amabilis* growth. Other eastern limits are White River canyon (nearly to reserve line), Stamilt Creek (branch Columbia River south of Wenache River, long. 120° 20'), and divide between Yakima and Columbia rivers (Kittitas County), at 4,500 to 5,200 feet. Reported also on west side of Cascades on headwaters of Skykomish, Snoqualmie, Cedar, and White rivers. Mount Rainier National Forest, at 1,000 to 6,200 feet elevation; Mount Rainier, at about 3,500 feet. Locally noted as follows: Mount Adams; Early Winter Creek; Bridge Creek, at 4,250 feet; Stillaquamish River below Silverton; Chelan-Entiat Divide, at 6,400 feet; peak southeast of Twisp Pass; tributary Similkameen River near Windy Pass, at 6,125 feet; Rattlesnake Creek; head of North Fork of Entiat River, at 7,000 feet; Emerald Basin, south of Lake Chelan, at 5,500 feet; peaks south of Rainy Pass; Slate Creek; Falls Creek; Crater Pass, at 6,000 feet; Goat Mountain, at 4,800 feet; Upper Klickitat River, at 4,200 feet. Colville National Forest, in basins and draws, above 4,000 feet elevation.

OREGON.—Cascades southward to California line; also in Blue and Powder River mountains; in north, generally at 3,000 to 5,500 feet, but at 5,500 to 8,000 feet, in south. In northern Cascades, mainly in groups on east side of range in canyons and on high cool slopes; similarly scattered also on west side of range, on streams down to 2,500 feet. Locally noted on Mount Hood, at 3,000 to 6,000 feet, and at Badger's Lake and Brooks Meadow, Wasco County. In southern Cascades, grouped or scattered on both sides of main divide in canyons and on damp slopes, at 5,600 to 8,000 feet; limited, on east side, to few larger canyons and moister slopes, but sometimes, as in high country between Mount Pitt and Klamath Point, forming 75 per cent of stand in canyon bottoms—upper canyon of South Fork of Rogue River (T 34 S., R. 5 E). Not on Umpqua-Rogue Divide, nor in Klamath Pass, but reported on Siskiyous (Ashland National Forest) at headwaters of Ashland Creek (T. 40 N., R. 1 E); reported also from north end of Coast Range, near Astoria, at 3,000 to 6,000 feet. Blue Mountains, wide ridges and at heads of streams, above 3,000 feet; John Day River; also in Powder River Mountains (northeastern Oregon).

OCCURRENCE.

Tree essentially of high altitudes; its presence controlled to great extent by supply of soil moisture, demands for which limit its occurrence to high elevations or to land moist from springs, seepage, or overflow. Lower range limited to moist canyons or to protected north slopes, while on other exposures it finds suitable soil moisture only at higher altitudes. Owing to lower temperatures and less intense light at north, favorable moisture conditions occur there at lower elevations than in south; hence the gradual lowering of altitudinal range from 8,500 to 12,000 (south) to 6,000 feet (north), with increasing latitude. This variation is not consistent throughout the range, but is often influenced by local climatic factors. Of merchantable size at middle and lower levels; stunted or depressed at timber line. Shows little preference of soil, if sufficiently moist.

Grows fairly on dry soils, but usually gives way on porous soils to lodgepole pine, Douglas fir, and to other trees requiring better drainage. Does well on retentive, fine, loamy soils, but attains best growth on deep, rich soils of gulches and river valleys. A shallow root-system enables it to grow on thin soils of slopes and on wet margins of rivers, lakes, and swamps. Forms extensive pure forests and also occurs in mixed stands. Pure stands are somewhat more frequent in south than in north, where it chiefly meets trees of similar silvical requirements but of less extended southern range. Most generally with alpine fir and sparingly with Douglas fir near its lower limits. In Blue Mountains of Washington and Oregon, with western larch, lodgepole pine, alpine and lowland firs, and Douglas fir. In Washington, occasionally in pure stands, but usually with amabilis fir, alpine fir, Lyall larch, black hemlock, yellow cedar, and white-bark pine. In Cascades of Oregon, with alpine, noble, and amabilis firs, Douglas fir, black hemlock, and lodgepole pine.

CLIMATIC CONDITIONS.—Subject to varied climatic conditions. Annual precipitation averages over 25 inches; is largely snow. Seasonal temperature, with a minimum in north of approximately 40° F., and maximum of about 95° F. in south. Daily range of temperature great at upper levels, but less at lower altitudes and on north exposures. Near timber line the growing season is about two months, and freezing occurs almost nightly, resulting in very slow growth; while at lower elevations the growing season is about four months and frosts are less frequent, permitting a more rapid growth.

TOLERANCE.—Very tolerant of shade, surpassing most of its associates in this respect; endures years of shading and makes good growth when released from suppression. Owing to great tolerance, it forms close stands of many ages and preserves good forest conditions. Somewhat more tolerant in youth than in old age.

REPRODUCTION.—A prolific seeder over most of range. Heavy seed years occur locally at 3-year intervals. Seed with high rate of germination and persistent vitality. Produces seeds from about twenty-fifth year to an advanced age. Seeds germinate best in moist mineral soil; seedlings rarely found in humus. Notwithstanding prolific seed production, seedlings are not generally abundant. They are most numerous in small protected openings in the forest. Low branches of isolated trees also favor germination and protect seedlings, through which groups of trees are built up, and which combine with other groups to form continuous stands.

Sitka Spruce; Tideland Spruce.

Picea sitchensis (Bong.) Trautvetter and Mayer.

DISTINGUISHING CHARACTERISTICS.

Sitka spruce growing in dense stands is tall, and has short thin open conical crowns of small branches and long clean trunks of only moderate taper. In open stands, or as it occurs singly, it develops a shorter, but still tall, rapidly tapering stem with branches down to or near the ground. The crown is still open, narrow and sharp in its upper part, but very broad at the bottom, where the huge branches are often 20 or 30 feet long. The branches have many hanging slender side branchlets from 1½ to 3½ feet long. It is a very large and massive tree when fully grown, attaining a height, exceptionally, of from 160 to 180 feet, with a diameter of from 8 to 12 feet, 5 or 6 feet above ground. Still larger trees are reported. Ordinarily it is from 80 to 125 feet high and from 40 to 70 inches in diameter. Forest-grown trees are clear of branches for from 40 to 80 feet, or more. The bases of big trunks are swelled by enormous buttresses. The bark is scaly on very young trees; on large trees it is thin (one-half inch thick), is dark purple or deep reddish brown, and has big thin, easily detached scales. Twigs of the year are always smooth and dark yellow-brown. The foliage is a bright yellow-green. The bristling habit of the often keenly-pointed leaves, which stand out straight all around the branches (fig. 30), render it prickly to the touch. The leaves are flat, only very indistinctly 4-angled, stiff, and rather thick. The cones mature in one season, and hang down conspicuously from the branches. They vary in length from about 2 to 4 inches (fig. 30). Soon after maturity, during early fall, their thin papery scales open and shed their small seeds (fig. 30, *a*) in a short time. Most of the cones fall from the trees within a few months afterward, when they are light yellow-brown. The small seeds are characteristically light clay-brown, their comparatively large, thin wings adhering to them tenaciously. Seed-leaves, from 4 to

FIG. 30.—*Picea sitchensis: a,* seed.

5, slender, and about three-eighths of an inch long. Wood varies greatly in color, but it is commonly a very pale brown, with the faintest tinge of reddish. It is light, soft, from fine to rather coarse grained. It furnishes the best of saw timber, the large percentage of clear, straight-grained wood making it very useful and important commercially.

LONGEVITY.—A very long-lived tree. It grows rapidly in height in moderately dense stands, and it grows very rapidly in diameter for several centuries when alone or in an open forest. Large trees attain an age of from 400 to 750 years; such trees are from 4 to 6 feet in diameter and from 150 to 180 feet high. About 800 or 850 years is probably the age of some of the much larger trees occasionally met. Further study of its longevity is desirable.

RANGE.

Generally from sea level to 3,000 feet elevation in coast region (and inland about 50 miles) from Alaska to northern California.

ALASKA.—Islands and sea slope of Coast Range from sea level to timberline (which in the Panhandle, is 1,800 to 2,400 feet and 3,500 feet on exposed sea slopes) and westward to west shore of Cook Inlet and north end of Kodiak Island. At Lynn Canal extending up to 2,600 feet (limit of erect tree growth); west of Lynn Canal, extending from sea level to 2,200 feet. From Dry Bay to Prince William Sound at 400 to 1,600 feet, and on Prince William Sound, from about 300 feet, in gulches away from coast to over 1,450 feet on slopes facing the sound. In the interior of Kenai peninsula to an elevation of 1,500 feet. Extends around Kenai peninsula, along shores of Cook Inlet and Turnagain Arm, down west side of Cook Inlet—here scattered on lower shore and southward, in sheltered places, to Kukak Bay at bottom of Alaskan peninsula. Occurs similarly also in northern part of Kodiak Island, as far south as Ugak Bay, on east shore, and to Cape Uganuk, on west shore.

BRITISH COLUMBIA.—Islands and vicinity of coast, on western slopes of Coast Range, from about 3,000 to 4,000 or exceptionally to 5,000 feet; summit between Coldwater and Coquihalla rivers, to 3,280 feet; on Nicolume River, a few miles beyond the summit between that stream and Sumallow River; on the west side of Spioos River, near the trail crossing, and up, again, to 5,000 feet, at Taku Pass. On west coast of Vancouver Island, in Renfrew District, occurs up to 975 feet.

WASHINGTON.—Mainly at mouths of rivers and on bottomlands about Puget Sound and along the Pacific coast; also extending up valleys to the foothills of Cascades, sometimes to an elevation of 2,000 feet. In (West) Washington National Forest, scattered over river bottoms and benches below 2,000 feet; on Mount Viero (Whatcom County); in Mount Rainier National Forest, only on Nisqually River, at 1,800 feet; at Orting (near Voights Creek); in Olympic National Forest, only on Pacific coast and extending inland about 30 miles; in Soleduc Valley (at point 3 miles below Hot Springs); at a point 2½ miles south of Port Crescent, and at Elma, near Hoquiam River.

OREGON.—In northern part, along the coast and up valleys to foothills of Cascades; south of Columbia River Valley, confined to coast.

CALIFORNIA.—At mouths of streams and in low valleys facing the ocean as far south as Caspar, Mendocino County.

OCCURRENCE.

Mainly from sea level to 3,000 feet; altitudinal range determined chiefly by soil and atmospheric moisture. Contrary to habit of other trees of this region, which go to lower elevations at north, this spruce reaches higher elevations at north than at south. Generally in moist, coast alluvial and sandy bottoms, along streams, and especially on moist slopes facing sea. In north coast region it thrives on very thin, light moist soils; also follows moist soils eastward and on mountain slopes. Best growth in constantly moist, deep rich soils, and in humid atmosphere. Deficient moisture occasions stunted growth. Quantity and quality of soil more important as soil moisture and the humidity decrease, and vice versa. Endures considerable inundation in coast flood plain, but usually grows a short distance from water's edge.

Forms pure forests, especially at north, and occurs in mixed stands, most commonly with western hemlock; associated also with redwood, western red cedar, lowland fir, yellow cedar, Pacific yew, black hemlock; occasionally with Douglas fir, broadleaf and vine maples, Sitka alder, black cottonwood, willows, etc. Sitka spruce and western hemlock are the chief components of Alaskan coast forests, where one or the other becomes dominant; the spruce is usually dominant on the coast, while hemlock holds higher elevations and areas away from coast.

CLIMATIC CONDITIONS.—Climatic conditions of range very favorable to forest growth. Climate generally mild and uniform, especially through influence of sea and warm sea current from Japan. Precipitation heavy; humidity high, and dense fogs abundant;

changes of temperature, gradual; summers generally mild and winters not severe. Nevertheless, average daily, monthly, and yearly temperatures and average annual precipitation and humidity vary greatly from southern limits of range in California to northern limit in Alaska. Precipitation ranges from about 20´ inches in California to over 100 inches in Alaska. The temperature drops to −35° F. toward north limit; while over a great part of range, notably at south, and along coast, light frost occurs and temperature goes to zero.

TOLERANCE.—Tolerant, but less tolerant than western red cedar and western hemlock. Seedlings endure dense shade, competing successfully with young hemlock. Endures considerable side shade in later life, but must have overhead light for best growth after seedling stages. Grows rapidly in height after first few years, and overtakes the slower western hemlock. Alone or in mixture it maintains a dense stand. Permanently overtopped seedlings or older trees remain stunted and grow but little, but if shade be dense and persistent they die eventually.

REPRODUCTION.—Prolific seeder, especially heavy seed years occurring at intervals of two or three years, while some seed is usually borne locally nearly every year. Seed with high rate of germination and of persistent vitality. Germination and growth of seedlings best on any wet or constantly moist soil; muck, moss, duff, or decaying wood common to its habitat. Seedlings are sensitive to frost for first few years, but not in later life. Root system, shallow; in moist ground running near surface beneath moss, duff, and other débris; in drier soils, going deeper, when, for good growth, a deep, porous soil is necessary.

Weeping Spruce.

Picea breweriana Watson.

DISTINGUISHING CHARACTERISTICS.

Weeping spruce is a little-known tree, and a comparatively recent discovery. It was permanently brought to light in 1884 by Thomas Howell, but the first discovery probably dates from 1863, when Prof. William H. Brewer, in honor of whom the tree was afterward named, preserved leaves and a branchlet from a weeping spruce tree growing at the west base of Mount Shasta, California. The species has not been rediscovered in that locality. Professor Brewer's specimens can be likened only to those from weeping spruce, but the confirmatory evidence of cones, which were not collected, is required to make the identification sure.

The marked weeping habit of its lower branches distinguishes this tree from its associates. It is thickly branched to the ground, forming a long-pointed, conical crown. The trunk is greatly swelled at the base and tapers rapidly to the top. The usual height attained is from 50 to 75 feet, with a diameter of 18 to 30 inches. Trees 100 feet or more in height occur, but they are exceptional. The thin, spike-like point of the crown bears short upturned branches, while on the lower crown the branches stand out straight, becoming more and more drooping near the ground. The unique characteristic of the middle and lower crown branches is their numerous, very long, string-like branchlets, which hang down from 4 to 8 feet in length. These also have numerous pendulous side branchlets. Bark of large trunks is about three-fourths of an inch thick, dark reddish brown, and with thin, long, firmly attached scales. The dense foliage has a somewhat bright but deep yellow-green hue. The leaves (fig. 31) are flattish and obscurely triangular, the sharpest angle on the lower side. Two resin ducts are shown on cross-section of the leaf near its upper border. The cones (fig. 31) mature in one season, shedding their seed late in September or in October. When full grown, and before opening, they are dark purplish green; after shedding their seed, they are dull russet-brown. They fall from the trees slowly, many adhering until the end of the second autumn. The seeds are dark chocolate brown. Seed-leaves, as a rule, 6. Wood, little known; pale yellowish to very light brown, rather heavy, and fine-grained.

LONGEVITY.—Little is known of the longevity of this tree, concerning which further study is required. Trees from 16 to 17½ inches in diameter are from 145 to 150 years old. Probably attains much greater age.

FIG. 31.—*Picea breweriana.*

RANGE.

Southwestern Oregon and northwestern California; locally distributed in detached areas at elevations between 4,000 and 8,000 feet. Range still imperfectly known.

OREGON.—Coast Mountains, on east end of Chetco Range in Josephine County, between 4,000 and 5,000 feet; divide between Canyon Creek and Fiddler's Gulch, at head of a West Fork of Illinois River, on north slope of Siskiyous (Josephine County); Sucker Creek and high mountain tops south of Rogue River (north slope of Siskiyous).

CALIFORNIA.—Several hundred acres on north slope of Siskiyous, at about 7,000 feet, on head of small south fork of Illinois River, just south of north boundary of California and near Waldo, Oreg. South slope of Siskiyous (few miles south of last grove), on headwaters of small northern tributary of Klamath River, at 7,500 feet elevation. About 600 acres at head of Elk Creek (tributary Klamath River) on high peak 2 to 3 miles west of Marble Mountain, and 80 miles west of Mount Shasta (Siskiyou County, Cal.) ; elevation, a little below 8,000 feet ; several hundred trees on north side near summit. Summits of Klamath Mountains ; locations not determined. Trinity Mountains, crests of ridges ; noted (in T. 35 N., R. 10 W.) at head of Canyon Creek from 7 miles above Dedrick (at 4,500 ft.) to lakes at over 6,000 feet, and near divide between Stewart Fork of Trinity River and Canyon Creek, at 6,000 feet. Said to have been found in 1863 on Black Butte (north of Strawberry Valley) at base of Mount Shasta, but not seen there since. Headwaters of Parks Creek (tributary Shasta River), north slopes above 5,500 feet on north side of Shasta-Trinity Divide (T. 41 N., R. 6 W.) in Shasta National Forest. This is in neighborhood of the west Shasta station, and indicates that the early one may be found. Reported as abundant on north and east sides of Mount Shasta, but authentic records are lacking.

OCCURRENCE.

Steep north mountain slopes, ridges, and about protected heads of mountain streams. Dry, rocky soils, but best on deeper, moist, porous soils. Forms pure, rather open stands on small areas, but is commonly associated with black hemlock, straggling Douglas fir, white fir, incense cedar, western white pine, sugar pine.

CLIMATIC CONDITIONS.—Temperature moderate, rarely much below zero, or above 100° F. Precipitation, from 20 to 60 inches, snow. Snowfall often 15 or 20 feet deep and remaining on ground more than half of year. Atmosphere humid through greater part of year.

TOLERANCE.—Little is known of its silvical characteristics. Its dense foliage, and habit of retaining low side branches in rather close stand, indicates considerable tolerance of shade.

REPRODUCTION.—Information on its seeding habits and reproduction is lacking. It appears to be a fairly good periodic seeder, intervals of good production probably not less than two or three years.

Black Spruce.

Picea mariana (Mill.) B., S. & P.

DISTINGUISHING CHARACTERISTICS.

Black spruce is mainly an eastern and far northern species, included as a Pacific tree because of its occurrence in the interior of Alaska. Here it is a small or stunted tree, rarely over 12 to 15 feet high, and often only from 2 to 6 feet high ; elsewhere from 25 to 40 feet high and from 4 to 8 inches in diameter. Exceptionally it attains a height of from 50 to 80 feet and a diameter of 1 foot. The crown is characteristically open and irregular, extending to the ground except in middle-aged or old trees grown in a dense stand, in which the lower half of the crown branches are shaded out. The branches are short, slim, and often distant from each other. In forms of this tree growing in wet marshes there are tufts of short branches only, or chiefly, at the top of the stunted stem. On less wet or moist ground the crown branches are more numerous. As a rule, the branches droop at their ends, but sometimes they are peculiarly stiff and horizontal. The foliage is a deep blue-green, with a tinge of whitish, while the short leaves (fig. 32) stand out on the branches. Bark of older trees is thin and composed of small ashy-brown scales. The young twigs of a season's growth are usually a pale russet-brown, coated with small hairs of similar color. The cones (fig. 32) are ripe by the end of August, and within a few weeks afterward they shed their small winged seeds (fig. 32, *a*) ; at this time they are a pale ashy-brown. Their habit of remaining firmly attached to the branches for very many years furnishes one of the most reliable means of dis-

FIG. 32.—*Picea mariana: a,* seed.

tinguishing this tree from its somewhat similar related species. The stems of the cones are very stout, firm, and curved downward or inward toward the branch. The open cone-scales are peculiarly stiff and resistant to pressure of the hand; but are easily broken if squeezed together. The seed is a deep chocolate brown. Seed-leaves, usually 6, about one-half inch long or shorter. Wood usually a clear, very light yellow. The common color of this wood, also of that of the white spruce and to some extent of the red spruce, with which it may be mingled sometimes as lumber, is not an entirely safe character to rely upon for identification. The color of wood from different individuals of the same species often differs greatly, so that it is easy to confuse it with the pale or yellowish white wood of the two other spruces. Black spruce wood is mainly very fine-grained. Of the other eastern spruces it is the least important commercially, mainly on account of its small size.

LONGEVITY.—Doubtless a moderately long-lived tree; average observed sizes are from 125 to 200 years old. Stunted trees growing in very wet situations and scarcely 2 inches in diameter are often from 50 to nearly 80 years old, but appear to be thrifty, considering the unfavorable situation. Further records of longevity are desirable.

RANGE.

Newfoundland to Hudson Bay and northwestward to Alaksa; southward in Michigan, Wisconsin, Minnesota, and in the eastern mountains to North Carolina and Tennessee. Northwestern range very imperfectly known. It is probably much the same as that of white spruce, but further accurate field observations are required to establish the coincidence of ranges. It seems likely that black spruce will prove to be far less abundant in Alaska than the white spruce.

CANADA.—Abundant in Great Plains, especially north of Saskatchewan and on Beaver and Athabaska rivers, extending westward to eastern slopes of Rockies and southward to tributaries of Elbow River, 30 miles from Calgary. Northward, in Great Plains, through Peace and Mackenzie river valleys, to within 20 miles of Arctic Ocean and from mouth of Coppermine River (long. 116°) westward to Alaska. Crosses Continental Divide into interior plateau of Rockies farther south than white spruce, being common on high plateaus of Upper Fraser and Blackwater rivers (lat. 53°) and northward on Stikine, Dease, Liard, Frances, and Pelly rivers. Abundant from Pelly River to McQuestion River (tributary Stewart River) at about 3,500 feet elevation; at Dawson and westward on Yukon River and southward on White River to a point 212 miles from its mouth.

ALASKA.—There are no definite records for Yukon Valley, over which this tree very probably extends, northward to south slopes of Endicott Range, westward to Bering Sea, and southward to inland slopes of Pacific coast ranges. Records are available for its occurrence on Cook Inlet, an arm of the Gulf of Alaska. Here it occurs sparingly at about 2,000 feet elevation in swamps of the plateau on Kenai Peninsula, especially on Chicaloon Flats, and in peat bogs at Hope, Sunrise, and Tyonek, on Cook Inlet coast.

OCCURRENCE.

Essentially a swamp tree, characteristic of cold, wet bogs and margins of lakes; grows occasionally on high, well-drained hillsides, but is less abundant here than in wet sites, and is small or stunted. Best growth in constantly moist, alluvial, well-drained soils, but most abundant in wet soils. Depth of soil is not essential, owing to shallow root system. Grows on clay and heavy glacial drift, and sometimes even in sandy, hill soils, but of poor growth in such soils.

In east, forms pure forests over limited and extensive areas, occurring also in mixed stands. In northwest, best growth in limited or small areas of pure stand in moist, well-drained alluvial bottoms of Athabaska River, and in river valleys in Saskatchewan and north Manitoba. Valley of Yukon River, grows in wet localities, usually over buried glaciers. Not common immediately on banks of the Yukon, but abundant in Pelly River drainage on swampy parts of bottoms, on moss-covered north slopes, and at heads of streams on low, broad divides. In mixture, associated with tamarack, black cottonwood, balm-of-gilead, aspen, willows, and red alder.

CLIMATIC CONDITIONS.—At north, climate extremely severe, with low atmospheric humidity, small precipitation (sometimes not over 15 inches), great seasonal range of temperature, and occasional strong, drying winds. Annual range of temperature, rarely less than 130° F., not uncommonly falling to —60° F. in winter and sometimes above 100° F. during summer. Growing season for tender vegetation is from about four months, in western British Columbia and eastern Alaska, to three weeks on Bering Sea coast. Owing to high latitude, sunlight is less intense during growing season, but of longer daily duration than farther south. In winter, insolation is very weak.

TOLERANCE.—Very tolerant of shade, and recovers from suppression up to advanced age. In dense stands it produces heavy crown cover, and frequently shades out tamarack. Most tolerant on wet soils, which it covers with dense stands of slow-growing trees, and least tolerant in dry, well-drained situations, where it grows in more open stands. Retains side branches for a long time, producing clear trunks only in very dense stands.

REPRODUCTION.—Not a prolific seeder, although some seed is usually borne locally each year; abundant seed production only at rather long, irregular intervals. Seed of moderately high germination and with persistent vitality. Germination best on constantly moist mineral and humus soils; seed germinates well also in forest on decayed fallen trees, moss, and moist decomposed spruce leaf litter. Leaf litter in broadleaf forests not as a rule favorable to germination. Seedlings demand moderate shade for first one or two seasons.

White Spruce.

Picea canadensis (Mill.), B., S., & P.

DISTINGUISHING CHARACTERISTICS.

White spruce is considered here because of its range in the interior (at least) of Alaska. It is mainly a tree of the northeastern United States and of Canada, with a very wide distribution in the latter region. In Alaska white spruce varies, according to situation, from a stunted form from 8 to 20 feet high to a well-grown tree from 50 to 75 feet in height and from 12 to 20 inches in diameter; much larger trees occur on very favorable sites. Elsewhere it reaches from 80 to 100 feet or more in height, and from 24 to 36 inches in diameter. Trees 3 or 4 feet in diameter and over 100 feet high are rather rare. The trunk is straight, smooth, and clear of branches for one-third to two-thirds of its length, with a somewhat open, irregular, and widely pyramidal crown, the top of which, especially in old trees, may be rounded or flattened; very often, however, the crowns are sharply pointed. The branches are long and thick, and commonly curve down and then upward. A striking character of branches is their numerous small, drooping side branchlets. The dense foliage is also characteristic in its light blue-green color, which in some individuals has a distinct whitish tinge. This character has doubtless given the tree its widely recognized common name, "white spruce." Bark of trunks is thin (one-half inch thick) and is early broken into small, thin, pale, ashy-brown scales; the color varies greatly with the density of the stand. The 4-angled leaves (fig. 33) stand out all around the twigs, except at and near their ends, where they are massed on the upper side; those on the lower side are curved toward the upper ones. Twigs of a season's growth are dark yellow-brown; as a rule they are smooth, but on the far northwestern forms they are apt to be finely downy. A notable character of the young shoots and leaves is the fetid, polecat-like odor they emit when bruised; foliage a year old or older gives off a much less distinct odor. This peculiarity has given the tree its name of "cat spruce." The cones (fig. 33) ripe by the end of the summer, shed their small light clay-yellow-brown seeds (33, *a*) in September. The pendulous cones are lightly attached and usually fall during autumn or by spring. After shedding their seeds the cones are a light clay-brown, whereas just at maturity they may be light grass-green tinged with red or bright rose-red. They vary from about 1 to nearly 2½ inches in length, but they are usually about 1¾ inches long. When open and dry the cone-scales are so thin and flexible that they can be squeezed together without breaking them. Seed-leaves, about 6, very slender, and one-half to nearly three-fourths of an inch long. Wood, pale yellowish white, soft, very straight and fine-grained. One of the two most important timber spruces of northeastern North America.

LONGEVITY.—Long-lived, full-grown trees reach an age of 250 to 350 years.

RANGE.

Newfoundland to Hudson Bay and northwestward to Alaska; southward to **northern** New York, Michigan, Wisconsin, Minnesota, South Dakota, Montana, and British

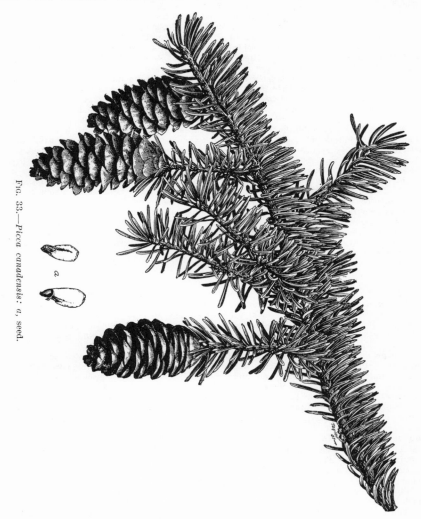

FIG. 33.—*Picea canadensis: a,* seed.

Columbia. Western range, throughout Canadian plains region from Saskatchewan River Valley northward nearly to the Arctic Ocean; extends southward, in a tongue, along east slope of Rockies, at 3,000 to 5,000 feet, through northern Montana (also in Cypress Hills, southwestern Assiniboia, and Black Hills, South Dakota); extending northwestward, at 500 to 3,000 or 4,000 feet elevation, it crosses the northern Rockies into the plateau of northern British Columbia and Yukon Territory, ranging throughout Alaska, at 2,000 to 4,000 feet, and to Bering Sea, except on the sea slope of Pacific coast ranges on the south and the Arctic watershed on the north.

WESTERN CANADA.—Crosses Continental Divide at Liard River, reaching interior plateau and extending westward to eastern slopes of Pacific coast ranges and northwestward into Alaska; southern limit now known is Stikine River, and seaward limits in Coast Ranges are Upper Stikine and Taku rivers, Shallow Lake (north of White Pass, at about 2,400 feet), point near Divide at head of Chilkat River (at about 2,600 feet), and point at timberline (about 4,500 feet) on north side of St. Elias Range. Common on rivers, islands, in sheltered valleys, hillsides, sometimes to tops of plateau (at 3,000 to 4,000 feet); in valleys of Dense Lake and River, and of Frances, Upper Liard, Yukon, Klondike, McQuestion, Pelly, and White rivers.

ALASKA.—Southward to Alaska Range, and on north slopes up to 3,500 or 4,000 feet elevation, but on south slopes, to 1,200 feet. Probably farther southward between Alaska Range and coast in valleys of Upper Sushitna and Copper rivers, reaching Pacific side of Coast Range only at Cook Inlet (long. 150°); thence extending from shores of Turnagain Arm up lower Sushitna River, on west side of Kenai Mountains, to Kenai Lake (alt. 2,000 feet); southward on west shore of Cook Inlet, about Lakes Clark and Iliamna to southern limit of timber at base of Alaskan Peninsula (possibly Kukak Bay). Abundant westward on Kokhtul and Mulchatna rivers, extending to mouths of Nushagak and Aleknagik rivers at Bristol Bay. Western limit of range is on Kuskokwim and Yukon rivers, near head of their deltas (long. 162°). Sea is reached again on northeastern shore of Norton Sound at mouth of Koyuk River, in Norton Bay, and at mouth of Niukluk River, in Golofnin Bay, but limit turns eastward in northern part of Seward Peninsula, including only head of Buckland River, and not entering Selawik River basin. Northward white spruce reappears throughout Kobuk River Basin, reaching sea on Kotzebue Sound, and reappearing still farther north on middle course of Noatuk River, here reaching its western and northern limit on west coast of Alaska (in about lat. 68°, long. 163°). Extends eastward along southern slope of Endicott Range, between Yukon River Valley and Arctic Slope, on Koyukuk River and its tributaries, to about latitude 67°, toward the international boundary, and farther northward on Porcupine River and its tributaries, to about latitude 68°; reappears in Turner River Basin, on Arctic Slope, to about latitude 69°, the northern limit in Alaska. Northward on Alatna River (tributary Koyukuk River) to point 90 miles from mouth; northward on John River (tributary Koyukuk) at about 2,500 feet elevation, to point 25 miles south of pass at head, and in valley of Chandlar River to head.

OCCURRENCE.

On river banks, terraces, dryish margins of swamps and lakes, and up adjacent sides of ridges and hills. Most frequent on sandy loam soils with moderate moisture, but grows on very shallow soils from margins of swamps to tops of mountains. Largest in moist, well-drained, finely divided porous soil; soils too dry or too wet produce dwarfed, slow growth. Forms pure, dense forests of large and limited extent and occurs in mixed stands.

The principal timber tree in Yukon drainage, occurring in dense groves and belts on alluvial flats and on islands, but in more open stands away from the river. Toward north limit in Alaska, more and more dwarfed, small clumps growing commonly in gulches. Dominant tree in Kenai Peninsula of Alaska on drier situations, but replaced by black spruce in swamps; in such localities always very scrubby. In north British Columbia generally forming extensive pure forests on rivers and lower valley slopes; it often gives way to black spruce, tamarack, or cottonwoods on flats and to lodgepole pine on dry terraces; at timberline, on inland mountains of north Canada, sometimes with alpine fir. Often in dense, pure groves and strips of forest; closely associated with birch, red alder, aspen, willows, and near streams with black cotton wood. On Kenai Peninsula, with black hemlock, balm-of-Gilead, aspen, and western birches. Toward north limit in Alaska, more and more subordinate to poplars, here single trees and small clumps being scattered among birch and poplar.

CLIMATIC CONDITIONS.—With much the same range as black spruce, white spruce endures practically the same severe features of climate.

TOLERANCE.—Tolerant of considerable shade, young trees maintaining a slow growth for many years under heavy crown cover. Marked in recovery from suppression, being surpassed in this only by black and red spruces. Retains side branches persistently; long, clear stems occur only in close stands. Thriving under light shade of poplars and birches, it often replaces these after fire or lumbering.

REPRODUCTION.—Moderately prolific seeder; considerable seed produced locally every year, while heavy seed production occurs at more or less regular, but long, intervals over parts of range. In New England, periods between seed years about eight years; seeding habits in Northwest not determined. Seed with only moderately high rate of germination, but with persistent vitality. Moist, decomposed organic, or mineral soils necessary for good germination. Natural reproduction usually abundant under mature spruce on damp moss over considerable organic soil. Reproduces poorly on thick leaf litter under broadleaf trees. Moss-covered decayed logs favor germination, as does moist mineral soil near streams. Tolerance of seedlings permits them to thrive under a crown cover which shades out most associates.

TSUGA. HEMLOCKS.

The hemlocks are evergreen trees with soft, flat or rounded triangular leaves. Their branches grow at irregular intervals from each other. The slender terminal sprays droop gracefully, and the slender leaders droop or nod conspicuously from the tops of the crowns. They are large trees with broad pyramidal crowns and long, only slightly tapering trunks, with the characteristically rough, hard bark narrowly ridged and furrowed. The bark contains tannin, which gives it an astringent taste, and when broken it displays a clear chocolate-red color. The leaves, which have small, thread-like stems, are spirally arranged around the branch, but by the twisting of their stems they appear to grow mainly from the two opposite and the upper sides of the branches; thus forming, in one western species, very flat sprays. The leaves of hemlocks are peculiar in having a single resin-duct, which is seen in a cross-section in the center near the lower surface. Leaves of a season's growth remain on the trees for about 3 to 6 years. Male and female flowers are borne separately on different parts of the same tree on sprays formed the preceding season. The female flowers grow at the ends of the sprays, while the male flowers are borne singly from buds at the bases of the leaves near the ends of the branchlets. Female flowers, producing cones and seed, are small, greenish, scaly bodies, while the male flowers, pollen-bearing only, are small yellowish bodies attached by thread-like stems. The cones of the hemlocks mature in one season, and are composed of thin overlapping scales, beneath each of which 2 winged seeds are borne; only the scales in about the central half of the cones, however, bear fertile seeds, those above and below this part being imperfect. The small seeds are easily wafted by the wind and thus may be widely disseminated. Seed-leaves of our species, 3 to 4, and very short.

Hemlocks are important forest trees both for saw timber and tanbark. As yet their wood is of comparatively lower commercial value than that of the pines, firs, and spruces, often associated with hemlock. Unquestionably, however, the commercial importance of hemlock wood will be greatly increased as the supply of other timbers, abundant now, is reduced. The true value of western hemlock timber has not been appreciated on account of its name, since it has been confused with the eastern hemlock, which produces wood of inferior quality.

Four species of hemlock are indigenous to the United States and portions of Canada. Two of these inhabit the eastern United States and the adjacent Canadian provinces, while two are found in the Pacific forests.

Western Hemlock.

Tsuga heterophylla (Raf.) Sargent.

DISTINGUISHING CHARACTERISTICS.

Western hemlock is a large forest tree. Its tall, clean, smooth-looking trunks, fine foliage, and drooping branchlets distinguish it readily from associates. The trunks taper very gradually. Forest-grown trees have small narrowly pyramidal crowns of slender branches, and are from 125 to 160 feet high and from 2 to 5 feet in diameter. Occasionally, much larger trees are found. The bark of larger branches and young trees is thin, finely scaly, and russet-brown, while that of old trunks is about 1¼ to 1½ inches thick, hard, and deeply furrowed; the ridges are wide, flat, and irregularly connected with one another by narrower cross-ridges; it is dark russet-brown, tinged with red.   The foliage is

FIG. 34.—*Tsuga heterophylla:* a, seed.

deep, glossy, and yellow-green, and clothes the branchlets thickly, but the small size of the leaves gives it a thin appearance. The leaves (fig. 34) appear to grow mainly from two opposite sides of the branchlets—a sort of comb-like arrangement. They are flat, grooved above, have a rounded end, and a distinct thread-like stem, and are about one-fourth to seven-eighths of an inch long. The leaf-bearing branchlets, especially those of the season's growth, are more or less minutely hairy. The small, few-scaled cones nod from the tips of branchlets, maturing from the middle to the end of August. They open rapidly afterwards and usually shed their small, winged seeds during September. By spring most of the cones have fallen from the trees. The cones are from about three-fourths inch to sometimes nearly 1¼ inches long, and when open are reddish clay-brown (fig. 34). Cone-scales, peculiar in being sharply narrowed from about their middle, are faintly downy on their outer surfaces. The seeds (fig. 34, *a*) are light brown. Their comparatively large wings enable the wind to carry them to a considerable distance from the parent tree. Seed-leaves 5, pointed, and about one-fourth inch long. By the third year seedlings produce foliage like that of the adult tree. In the dense, moist forests in which this tree grows best its numerous seedlings grown on moss-covered stumps and logs—often high in the air, and even in the moss on living trunks—are a familiar sight. Not infrequently seedlings extend their roots through or over their host stumps and decaying logs into the soil and become firmly rooted; many others, unable to do this, die. The ability of this tree to grow throughout its life in the densest shade explains the often almost pure stands which have followed removal of the older forest in which hemlock was widely but only sparingly represented. The hemlocks had covered the shaded ground with seedlings which later excluded other species trying to come in after the old trees were removed.

Wood, fine-grained, pale yellowish brown, with the slightest tinge of red. It is rather light, soft (works like soft pine), and very unlike the slivery wood of its eastern relative, which it otherwise resembles. The unfounded prejudice against western hemlock wood is exceedingly unfortunate, for in its best grades it is useful for many of the better commercial purposes, while its bark yields a much higher percentage of tannin than does that of the eastern hemlock (*Tsuga canadensis*), so extensively used for tanning.

LONGEVITY.—Very long-lived, growing slowly in height and diameter. Trees 16 or 17 inches in diameter are 195 or 200 years old. Large trees are from 300 to 500 years old, and it is believed that very much older trees will be noted.

RANGE.

Pacific coast region from Alaska southward to northern California; inland to southern British Columbia, northern Idaho, and Montana, and into the Cascades in Oregon and Washington.

ALASKA.—Islands and seaward slope of coast ranges westward to Cape Puget on west side of Prince William Sound; generally from sea level to timber line (3,000 feet on southeastern coast to 1,600 feet on Prince William Sound). Lynn Canal region, from elevations of 130 to 2,600 feet. South slope of St. Elias Range to 1,625 and 2,700 feet; Yakutat Bay, up to 2,200 feet on Mount Tebenkof (east end of bay), gradually dropping to sea level at Disenchantment Bay (head of Yakutat Bay). Coast from Dry Bay to Prince William Sound, up to 400 feet, and to 1,600 feet; on coastal plain, hillsides facing open water and valleys of streams, sometimes extending inland 3 to 5 miles, as at head of Cordova, Gravina, and Fidalgo bays.

BRITISH COLUMBIA.—Islands, Coast Range, and inland up river valleys to limit of abundant rainfall, from sea level to 2,000 or 3,000 feet elevation. Reappears eastward in Gold and Selkirk mountains, reaching 3,500 to 5,000 feet. Up Dean Inlet and Salmon River to point 18 miles from sea and to elevation of 600 feet; appears still farther inland, in Coast Range, sparingly on lower part of Iltasyouco River (tributary Salmon River). Inland 53 miles on Homathco River (flows into Bute Inlet) to an elevation of 2,320 feet. In lower Fraser River Valley eastern limits are Uztlihoos River (northeastern branch of Anderson River), at point 6 to 10 miles east of Fraser River, and summit between Coquihalla River (eastern tributary Fraser River) and Coldwater River. Abundant on southwest coast of Vancouver Island, reaching elevation of 975 feet about Port Renfrew. Extends into Gold Range (from eastern Washington) and into Selkirk

Mountains (from northern Idaho), stretching northward to Canadian Pacific Railway line (possibly farther), reaching 5,000 feet on west slope of Selkirk; while on east side, which it ascends to summit, its first abundant appearance is on Beaver Creek, at 3,500 feet. Eastern limit is Donald, on Columbia River, at 2,586 feet.

WASHINGTON.—Throughout western part, except on high summits, and generally extending from sea level to 4,000 or 5,000 feet elevation; westward to east slopes of Cascades; more abundant on west side middle slopes of Cascade and of coast ranges than on coast or in depression between these ranges. Mountains of northern Washington and eastward to Idaho, but not in Blue Mountains (southeastern Washington). Washington National Forest, common over west slopes of Cascades on benches and mountain sides, up to 4,000 or 5,000 feet; on east slopes only in moist valleys, at 2,100 to 4,700 feet elevation on Stehekin River, Agnes, and Early Winter creeks, on headwaters of Entiat and Wenache rivers, throughout upper Yakima and Chealum valleys and eastward to Chealum Lake. Mount Rainier National Forest, abundant on west slopes up to 5,000 feet, but scarce on east slope on Tannum Lake and on head of Klickitat River. Abundant in Olympic Mountains up to 4,500 feet elevation.

OREGON.—Throughout western part, up to about 5,500 feet, and down to sea-level on coast, but not on borders of Columbia River where it crosses Cascades nor in Willamette River Valley below 1,500 feet; extends southward in Cascades to Lake of the Woods (T. 38 S., R. 6 E.) and on Coast Range to California. Cascade National Forest (North), abundant west of range, at 1,600 to 4,800 feet, but on east side confined to headwaters of rivers and occurs only for a short distance south of Mount Hood to Beaver Creek and Warm Springs River (T. 6 S., R. 9 E.); south side of Mount Hood, up to Government Camp, at 3,600 feet, and north side from 3,500 feet northward to point 22 miles from Columbia River. Farther south in Cascades, scattered over west side only, south of Mount Thielson, occurring at elevations of 5,200 to 6,000 feet only on north and south slopes of Umpqua-Rogue River Divide, Huckleberry Mountain, headwaters of Rogue River and Big Butte Creek, Mount Pitt, about Lake of the Woods, and sparingly on mountain sides and flats eastward to east side of divide south of the lake. Not detected in the Siskiyous.

CALIFORNIA.—In fog belt on west side of Coast Range, and southward to between Elk and Alder creeks (Mendocino County), reappearing farther south sparingly in Marin County; approaches to within one-half mile of coast in Del Norte County, at Crescent City and other points; eastward in Humboldt County to ridge east of Redwood Creek, at 3,200 feet; but is farther from coast in Mendocino County, where it extends inland about 20 miles, and at Mendocino, about 10 miles inland; generally on steep slopes of canyons and tops of ridges up to about 2,000 feet.

OCCURRENCE.

A tree of the middle, moist forest zone, from sea level to 7,000 feet elevation. More abundant on west mountain slopes than on east slopes, and avoiding dry inland basins of Oregon, Washington, and British Columbia, but reappearing on west slope of Rocky Mountains. Largest growth on lower slopes, flats, stream bottoms, etc., on west slope of Cascades and coast ranges of Washington and British Columbia. At higher elevations at South in Washington, Oregon, and California than toward its north limit in Alaska; likewise, at lower elevations on coast mountains than in Cascades and on west slope of Rockies. With abundant atmospheric and soil moisture, it thrives on poor, thin soils and on any exposure, but best on deep, porous, moist soils. Soil and exposure become much more important with decrease in moisture. Lack of soil and moisture produce stunted growth, as do also high elevations, even with abundant moisture and good soils. In dryish poor soils, it seeks chiefly cooler, north situations.

Usually subordinate in association with other trees, but often dominating, especially in Alaska, where occasional pure stands also occur. Generally scattered in patches, groups, or singly through the forest. In Alaska, with Sitka spruce, western red cedar, and black hemlock, and usually dominant. In Vancouver Island, British Columbia, Washington, and Oregon, chiefly with western red cedar, yellow cedar, Sitka spruce, lowland fir, amabilis fir, yew, Douglas fir, western white pine, and lodgepole pine; while in north California it occurs with redwood. Its general and common associates are Douglas fir, western red cedar, and lowland fir, from the coast to the Rocky Mountains. Broadleaf and vine maples, black cottonwood, and red alder occur with it also at low elevations.

CLIMATIC CONDITIONS.—Climate of range, in general, favorable for tree growth, being comparatively mild and uniform, with gradual changes of temperature, which is not extreme. Precipitation generally heavy and humidity high. However, average annual precipitation, humidity, and range of temperature vary considerably from California to Alaska and from Pacific to Rocky Mountains, and from sea level to limit of elevation (7,000 feet). Average annual precipitation, from about 20 inches in California and

Oregon to over 100 inches in British Columbia and Alaska. Temperature occasionally —35° F. on west slope of Rockies in north Idaho, Montana, and British Columbia, and also in parts of Alaska, but elsewhere, especially in coast regions south of Alaska, well above zero. This hemlock generally follows humidity and precipitation of the region. Precipitation and humidity decrease from the coast to the Rockies. Precipitation is much less on east side of coast ranges and Cascades than on the sea slopes; deficient in interior basins of Oregon, Washington, and British Columbia between Rockies and Cascades; abundant on west slope of Rockies.

TOLERANCE.—Very tolerant of shade throughout life, especially in seedling stages. In later life vertical light necessary for best growth. Allowed overhead light, it recovers remarkably well from long suppression and renews rate of growth. Prolonged suppression in dense shade greatly checks growth. Thrives in cool, open, humid places with abundant soil moisture. Maintains dense stands, alone, subordinate to others, or as dominating tree with equally tolerant or slow-growing species.

REPRODUCTION.—Very prolific seeder, reproduces itself freely everywhere under favorable conditions. Produces some seed every year, but heavy seed years occur at irregular intervals. Seed with moderate rate of germination and moderately persistent vitality. Germination excellent and growth of seedlings good on wet moss, humus, litter, decaying wood, muck, and mineral soils—the latter less favorable than moist vegetable seed bed. Reproduction abundant under dense shade of mature stands and also in the open on cut-over areas with favorable moist forest floor. Restocks burned over areas at first only sparingly, where light-demanding Douglas fir, pine, larch, fir, etc., come in first.

Mountain Hemlock; Black Hemlock.

Tsuga mertensiana (Bong.) Sargent.

DISTINGUISHING CHARACTERISTICS.

Mountain or black hemlock, an alpine tree, has little general resemblance to the better-known western hemlock. Only the drooping slender branches and its bark suggest hemlock to the casual observer, by whom its foliage might be easily mistaken for that of spruce, or possibly of fir. Forest-grown trees have sharp-pointed, narrowly pyramidal crowns of slender, conspicuously drooping branches; the upper third of the crown has very short drooping branches, while the exceedingly slender whip-like leaders are gracefully pendulous. Trees grown in the open bear branches of the same habit down to the ground, rarely losing them for more than a few feet above ground, even in old age. Ordinarily, mountain hemlock is short, from 25 to 60 feet high and from 10 to 20 inches in diameter; the trunk is often rather sharply tapering; on bleak crests, it is only a few feet high or sprawling on the ground. Trees 75 or 80 feet high are not uncommon, while trees 100 or 125 feet high, with a diameter of 30 or 40 inches, are sometimes met with. On high, steep slopes the trunks are strongly bent down the slope at their bases, in the form of a sled-runner. Heavy snows annually bend or crush the slender seedlings and saplings to the ground without killing them and later growth rarely straightens the bent stems. The bark is early broken and rough on young trees. That of old trees is about 1¼ inches thick and dull purplish to dark reddish brown. It is deeply and narrowly furrowed; the rough, hard, distantly connected ridges are narrow and rounded. At some distance the trunks have a blue-gray tinge. The dense foliage varies from a dark to a pale blue-green. Foliage of a season's growth is shed about the fourth year. The blunt-pointed leaves (fig. 35) are rounded and plump looking, in this respect unlike the flat leaves of other hemlocks, but like them the leaves have small distinct stems. They clothe the branches all around, but appear thicker on their upper sides. The main branchlets are unique in having numerous short, erect side branches; both are minutely downy for several years. The cones are full grown in one season. They are usually so abundant as to almost cover the branchlets and to bend them down with their weight. Usually they are pendulous; very rarely, and chiefly on stunted trees in exposed situations, the cones, also stunted, are erect when mature. Cones (fig. 35, *a*) vary in length from about one-half inch to 3 inches; commonly they are about 2 inches long and three-fourths of an inch thick before opening. At maturity they are yellowish-green to a bluish purple. Great variation exists in the color of cones at matu-

FIG. 35.—*Tsuga mertensiana: a,* branch with closed cones; *b,* seeds.

rity. Different trees of the same forest may each have wholly different colored mature cones; but the color is a transient character and there is no other difference between such trees. When the cones open, and afterwards, they are dull to light brown, the scales spreading strongly at right angles to the cone axis (fig. 35). After the seeds are shed, usually late in September or October, the cones begin falling from the trees, and by spring most of them are down. The seeds (fig. 35, *b*) are pale brown, with large wings which enable the wind to carry them for long distances. Seed-leaves, 4, and about one-fourth inch in length. Wood, very fine-grained, soft (considerably lighter than that of western hemlock), and pale reddish brown. It is without the silvery character of eastern hemlock wood. It is practically never used for commercial purposes, and locally only occasionally on the prospector's alpine camp fire.

Longevity.—Believed to be a very long-lived tree, but much more study of its age limits is required. Trees from 18 to 20 inches in diameter are from 180 to 260 years old, while trees of high, wind-swept ridges are from 60 to 80 years old when from 5 to 7 inches in diameter.

RANGE.

Timberline tree. From the Pacific coast mountains of Alaska southward through the high Sierras of California, and to northern Idaho and Montana.

ALASKA.—Sea slope of Coast Range northward to neighborhood of Lynn Canal (in about lat. 60°), and westward to head of Yukla Creek on north of divide between Turnagain Arm and Knik Arm of Cook Inlet (lat. 61° 10′, long. 150°). Commonly at elevations of 2,000 to 4,000 feet, except when occasionally inhabiting cold sea-coast bogs from Sitka northward, and when descending to sea level at west end of its range on shores of Prince William Sound and Kenai Peninsula. Timberline in southeastern Alaska is 1,800 to 2,400 feet on exposed seaward slopes, but is considerably higher in protected inland passes. About Lynn Canal dwarf trees reach 3,250 feet, or more; westward, its upper limit ranges from elevations of 400 feet to 1,600 feet, and about Prince William Sound, at from 300 feet, in gulches away from sea, to over 1,450 feet, on warm slopes facing the Sound. On Kenai Peninsula, generally up to elevations of 1,200 or 1,600 feet, but follows Resurrection Bay across divide to Turnagain Arm, reaching 2,500 feet on inland plateau. Occurs in following localities: Hot Springs (near Sitka), Baranof Island, and Yes Bay, at sea level; Kuiu Island; White Pass, at 2,888 feet, and from inland to Shallow Lake, Long Lake, Chilkoot and valley of Chilkoot, Fort Wrangell.

BRITISH COLUMBIA.—Higher sea slopes of Pacific Coast Range and islands, generally at from 2,500 to 5,000 feet; also abundant in interior of southern British Columbia on west slopes of Selkirk Mountains. All summits of Queen Charlotte Islands above 2,000 feet, and up to 4,500 or 5,000 feet, especially those at head of Cumshewa Inlet. Fraser River Valley and inland on higher slopes above 2,700 feet to Silver Mountain (near Yale). Vancouver Island, at 3,000 to 5,500 feet elevation, especially on following summits: Mount Benson (3,000 feet); Mount Mark (3,300 feet); Mount Arrowsmith (5,500 feet); Mount Edinburgh (3,250 feet); locally noted at Vancouver, Victoria, and Port Townsend.

WASHINGTON.—Both slopes of Cascade and Olympic mountains at elevations of 5,000 to 7,000 feet, and on one peak of Blue Mountains, but not on Okanogan Highlands. Olympics, at 5,000 to 6,000 feet, and at following points: Hoh Divide; head of Bogachiel River, near pass to Jordan's Lake; near Close Call Basin; sphagnum swamp 3 miles below Hot Springs; main head of South Fork of Skokomish River. Northern part of Washington National Forest (west side of Cascades), at from 4,000 to (timberline) 6,000 feet; east side of Cascades in moist valleys and passes at 3,100 to 6,400 feet— sometimes to 7,000 feet, as on slopes above Lake Chelan, and down to 2,200 feet, as in Stehekin River Valley and on east side of Stevens Pass (mouth of Great Northern Railroad tunnel). Southern part of Washington National Forest, at 2,600 to 7,200 feet; most abundant at 4,000 to 6,000 feet in Skykomish, Tolt, Snoqualmie, Cedar, Green, White, Yakima, Wenache, Entiat river basins and of Lake Chelan. Also at following points: Cascade Pass, at 5,421 feet; headwaters of Stehekin River, at about 7,000 feet; pass between Montecristo and Index; trail to Columbia Peak; Skagit Pass; Bridge Creek. Mount Rainier National Forest, at 3,500 to 7,500 feet with best growth at 4,500 to 6,200 feet, in river basins on both sides Cascades. Locally noted as follows: Mount Rainier, at 4,000 to 6,000 feet; Mount Adams, at 6,000 feet; Cascade Divide (3 miles north of Cowlitz Pass) at 4,800 feet; at point 2 miles west of divide at Cowlitz Pass, at 4,750 feet; head of Summit Creek; Cowlitz River, at 3,650 feet; Dewey Lake (head of American River) at 5,300 feet; main divide on head of Cispus River, at 5,200 feet.

OREGON.—Both slopes of Cascades at elevations of 5,500 to 7,000 feet, and in Powder River Mountains (northeastern Oregon). Cascade National Forest (North), principal tree at 5,500 to 7,000 feet—sometimes to 7,800 feet, and straggling down to 3,000 feet. Locally noted as follows : Mount Hood (timberline) on head of East Fork of Hood River at 6,400 feet, and of Clear Fork at 5,100 feet, down on southwest side to a little below Government Camp (3,600 feet) ; on north side to about 3,000 feet ; Mount Jefferson ; headwaters of Clackamas River, at about 6,000 feet ; Salt Creek ; divide between Row River and Middle Fork of Willamette River.   Cascade National Forest (South), abundant on both sides of Cascades and on Umpqua-Rogue River Divide ; on east side, at 6,000 to 9,200 feet, and on west side, at 5,900 to 9,200 feet ; best growth at 6,200 to 7,000 feet.   High summits of Siskiyous—also on north slopes of Siskiyou Peak, but not detected east of Cascades, in Klamath ranges.   Locally noted at Crater Lake (rim of Crater), down to near Pole Bridge Creek (6,100 feet), and on Mount Scott, up to 8,000 feet.

CALIFORNIA.—Northern cross ranges and west side of Sierras southward to Bubbs Creek at head of South Fork of Kings River (lat. 36° 40'), probably also in San Jacinto Mountains,[a] generally at from 6,000 to 11,000 feet elevation.   On northern mountains from Siskiyous and Trinity Mountains eastward to ranges north of Mount Shasta and west of Butte Creek, including Goose Nest Mountain, extending northward to the Oregon line, reappearing on Glass Mountain (boundary of Siskiyou and Modoc counties) at 7,500 to 9,000 feet.   Reported in mountains east of Crescent City (Del Norte County).   Marble Mountain Divide (west of Scott Valley, Siskiyou County) on summit of pass (5,700 feet), and on higher parts of ridge.   *Trinity County:* Canyon Creek, at point about 7 miles north of Dedrick, at 4,500 feet elevation, and northward to head of creek, here mingled with Shasta fir and weeping spruce.   North part of Mount Shasta National Forest, at 7,000 to over 8,000 feet ; throughout southern part at elevations from 6,500 feet to timberline (8,000 to 9,000 feet).   Mount Shasta, at various points between 7,200 and 8,700 feet.   Abundant on west side of northern Sierras, at 6,000 to 10,000 feet ; less frequent in southern part, and at 8,000 to 11,000 feet. In Lassen Peak, Plumas, and Diamond Mountain National Forests at elevations above 6,000 feet and on such peaks as Lassen Peak, slopes near Drakes, Spanish Peak, and Mount Pleasant.   Tahoe National Forest, Mount Fillmore and southward on all summits, at elevations from 7,500 to timberline (about 10,000 feet), except on main divide between south end of Sierra Valley and north line of Sierraville Quadrangle (Sierra County) ; locally noted on Pyramid Peak (1½ miles above Fornis), near Ralston Peak, in Devils Basin (east of Pyramid Peak), and on high summits near Donner, at 7,500 to 8,500 feet.   Stanislaus National Forest, on summits at 6,900 to 9,400 feet.   Here locally noted on divide south of North Fork of Mokelumne River (9 miles north of Bloods) ; Mount Reba (north Fork of Mokelumne River) ; near Wood's place (road to Kirkwood).   Placerville Pass and adjacent peaks southwest of Lake Tahoe, at 7,500 feet to timberline.   Sierra National Forest, summits at elevations between 8,000 and 11,000 feet, and southward to Bubbs Creek (tributary, South Fork of Kings River, T. 14 S., R. 33 E.), reaching east slope of Sierras at head of Owens River ; lower part Kearsarge Pass, at north base of West Vidette Mountain and canyon between Vidette and Junction Meadows.   Locally noted as follows : Mokelumne Pass (headwaters of Silver Creek and upper Mokelumne River) ; Tuolumne Meadows, at 9,500 to little over 10,000 feet on White Mountain and Mount Conness, Lookout Knob, Lambert Dome, ridge between Dingley and Delaney creeks, old Tioga mine, upper Tuolumne Canyon, base of Unicorn Peak, Cathedral Lakes and Peak, head of Cathedral Creek, Lyell Fork of Tuolumne, at 10,500 feet ; head Snow Creek (Mount Hoffman), about May Lake, and southwest flank of mountain down to 8,500 (near Tioga road) ; near Lake Tenaya ; head of Mono Creek and Pass ; Sunrise Peak (between Tuolumne Meadows and Yosemite), at 10,000 feet ; Tuolumne Dome, at 8,000 feet ; Snow Canyon (Yosemite Park) ; Kings Creek Mountain ; head of North Fork of San Joaquin River, at 8,000 feet, and on its tributaries Silver and Fish creeks, at about 10,000 feet ; Bubbs Creek.   San Jacinto Mountains, on Wellman Flat, at 7,500 feet.

The detailed range of mountain hemlock in Idaho and Montana will be dealt with in a later bulletin.

OCCURRENCE.

Mainly at timber line, but in far north at sea level.   Southward, vertical range is determined by gradual ascent of favorable climatic and moisture conditions, until, at south, the tree is confined to high, cold, moist, mountain slopes and valleys.   Thrives in most well-drained soils, not too dry ; but best in loose, coarse, moist ones.

---

[a] This remarkable extension of range is supported by a photograph of a large tree taken in 1899 (?) by T. P. Lukens.   It is hoped that this record may be fully verified later.

Best stands on flats, gentle slopes, heads of moist valleys, or in sheltered ravines (below Crater Lake in Cascades of southern Oregon). Decidedly prefers north exposures, doubtless on account of less heat and greater soil moisture there. Exposed high slopes least favorable to best growth; although often abundant there, it is usually stunted. Commonly in limited pure stands and in mixture. At north, with Sitka spruce, western hemlock, and alpine fir. Southward, at high altitudes, with white-bark pine, alpine fir, Lyall larch, Engelmann spruce, while grand fir, lodgepole and western white pines are also occasional associates at lower elevations. Large pure stands are uncommon, but rather extensive forests with 85 per cent of hemlock are occasional. Pure patches are frequent on north slopes. In southern Alaska and British Columbia, with spruce, firs, poplars, and birches. At high altitudes in California, often in groups with patches of white-bark pine; lower, commonly with California red fir and lodgepole and western white pines.

CLIMATIC CONDITIONS.—Endures severe alpine climate. Daily and seasonal ranges of temperature great, owing to intense sunlight and rapid radiation of heat at night. Rarity of air, together with frequent high winds, cause rapid transpiration, which is modified somewhat by increased humidity due to low air temperature. Precipitation, large; chiefly snow, which often buries trees. Snow comes early and stays late; melting slowly, it supplies moisture throughout the short growing season. Rains are rather frequent in spring and fall, but summers are usually hot and dry, especially on south exposures.

TOLERANCE.—Very tolerant; excepting western hemlock, surpassing all associates in shade endurance. Its dense shade, almost excluding light from ground, usually prevents growth of seedlings, even its own, which appear to require more light than the heavy shade of mother trees affords, but which thrive under lodgepole pine, fir, etc. Seedlings and saplings bear long suppression, and rarely die under it. Trunks are not cleared readily, even in dense stands; dead branches usually persist or leave short stubs which form loose knots in timber.

REPRODUCTION.—Prolific seeder, producing cones when about 20 years old; seed is borne annually, but not every year is a good seed year. Seed has only moderate rate of germination, and its vitality is rather transient. With sufficient moisture, seed germinates on both humus and mineral soils, but apparently better on latter. Seedlings grow better in moderate shade and moist humous soil than in full light.

PSEUDOTSUGA. FALSE HEMLOCKS.

The generic name of the false hemlocks indicates a relationship to the hemlocks, which they resemble in the distinctly formed leaf stems and in the habit and character of their cones. The resin vesicles of hemlock seeds are, however, absent from the seeds of Pseudotsugas. The latter have small resinpockets, or " blisters," in the bark of young trunks and branches, in this respect being similar to the firs. Woodsmen and lumbermen know them as " varieties " of " fir " or " spruce," and even as " pines." Properly they should not be called firs, from which they differ greatly in the character of their wood, foliage, and cones. The superficial resemblance of the wood of these trees to pine is a popular reason for calling them pines, but it is a perversion of the name, for in all respects the pines are totally different trees.

False hemlocks are evergreen trees with dense, soft, flat leaves. Their branches, growing in irregular circles, form with their many side-branches wide, fan-like, densely foliaged sprays. The rough, very thick-barked trunks are tall and massive, and taper slowly. They have broadly pyramidal crowns, which in young trees extend to the ground. The flat, bluntish leaves, attached by distinct stems, are spirally and singly arranged on the branches. They appear often to grow mainly from two opposite sides and from the top of the branch; but lower leaves bend upward toward each side of the branch by a twist in their stems. Leaves of a season's growth remain on the tree about five or eight years. In cross-section the leaves of our species show two resin-ducts on the under margin near the edges of the leaves. Flowers of two sexes are borne singly on branchlets, formed the previous year, on different parts of the same tree. The female flowers are bristly, scaly bodies, developing into cones with seed; they are borne nearly or quite at the ends of twigs. The male flowers—scaly bodies bearing pollen only—grow from the bases of leaves farther back from the end of the twig. Most characteristic of the pendulous cones of these trees are their 3-pointed scale-like bracts, which protrude conspicuously from among the cone-scales (fig. 36). No other cones of native conifers, with persistent scales, have protruding bracts. The cones mature in one season, soon afterward falling from the trees. Two winged seeds are borne under each cone-scale. Their small size and large, light wings permit the wind to distribute them easily.

They are trees (mainly one species) of the greatest commercial importance, and furnish the finest and largest saw timber of any native trees, if not of any trees in the world. The slightly resinous, pine-like wood is most widely adapted for construction. Two native species of these trees are known. One is distributed more or less from the Rocky Mountain States to the Pacific coast, while the other inhabits the mountains of southern California.

Douglas Fir; Douglas Spruce.

Pseudotsuga taxifolia [a] (Poir.) Britt.

DISTINGUISHING CHARACTERISTICS.

Excepting the great sequoias of California, Douglas fir is the most gigantic tree of the Pacific forests. Under the best conditions for growth it ordinarily reaches 180 or 190 feet in height and from $3\frac{1}{2}$ to 6 feet in diameter. Trees over 200 feet high and 8 or 10 feet in diameter are to be found, but they are exceedingly rare. Under less favorable conditions, such as prevail outside of the humid Pacific coast region, it commonly attains a height of from 75 to 110 feet and a diameter of from 18 to 30 inches; while in high, exposed situations it is greatly stunted, often under 5 feet in height. The typical crown form of young trees is a broad, sharp pyramid; the lower branches are straight or drooping and the middle and higher ones trend upward, forming on the whole a rather open head. All of the branches have numerous long, hanging side branchlets, which are sometimes very long. In dense stands one-half or two-thirds of the lower branches are shaded out by the time the trees are 10 or 15 inches in diameter. Under these conditions the crowns of middle-aged and old trees lose much of their pyramidal form, and become rounded or flattened. The massive trunks, clear of branches for 80 or 100 feet (in the Pacific region), are straight, and with only a slight taper. The ashy brown bark of young trees, often chalky in patches, is thin, smooth, and but little broken, except near the ground, until the trees are 12 to 14 inches in diameter. Later, and in old trees, the bark becomes from 5 to 10 inches thick at the base of the trunk, although higher up it remains much thinner. Sometimes very old trees have bark from 18 to 24 inches thick. It is dark brown on the outside and clear red-brown within. It is often very rough, with deep, wide furrows and great ridges, which are connected at intervals by narrower cross ridges. There is great variation in the character and markings of the bark in dry and humid regions, and also in exposed and protected situations. Trees in exposed, dry

---

[a] Several authors maintain for this tree the name *Pseudotsuga mucronata* (Raf.) Sudworth, which the writer has shown to be lawfully antedated by *P. taxifolia* (Poir.) Britt. For a full discussion of the basis of this decision, see Bull. 17, Div. For. p. 23. 1898.

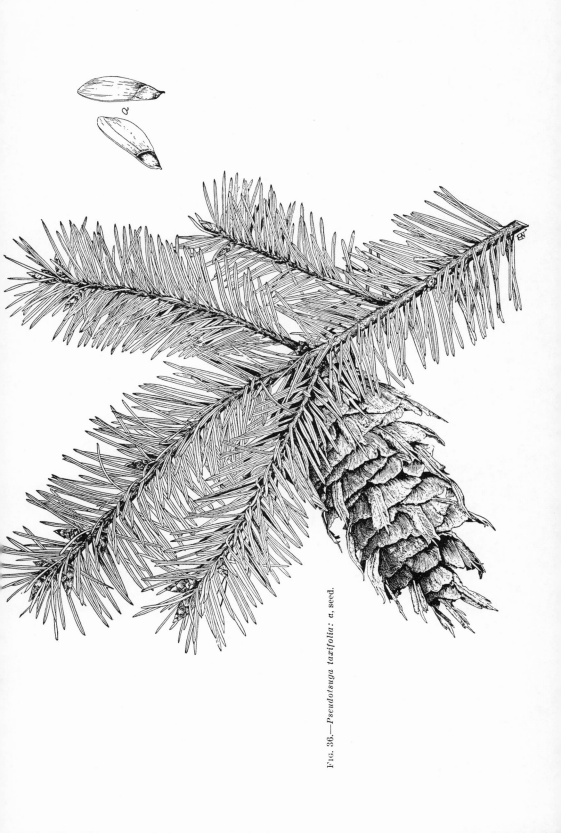

FIG. 36.—*Pseudotsuga taxifolia: a*, seed.

situations appear to have rougher and harder bark than those in the moist, deep forest. Trees of the high, very dry interior mountain slopes, particularly young trees, may have soft, cork-like, gray-brown bark. (This may well be a result of the excessively dry atmosphere, for one or two firs of that region have similar bark). Otherwise these trees are not different from those with the ordinary bark. Mature foliage is usually deep yellow-green. In the drier parts of its range Douglas fir sometimes has blue-green foliage of varying shades, especially in Rocky Mountain forms. This color is particularly pronounced during the early maturity of the leaves. Foliage of a season's growth remains on the tree about eight years, when it is shed at irregular intervals. The leaves (fig. 36) are flat, slightly grooved above and commonly blunt, or very occasionally pointed. Cones ripen early in August and by September they begin to open and shed their seed. A few weeks later the cones drop from the trees. The cones (fig. 36), which are cinnamon or reddish-brown, furnish easy and reliable means of identifying this tree. Their simplest distinction is the 3-pointed, trident-like thin bracts protruding from among the cone-scales. Cones vary from $1\frac{1}{2}$ to $4\frac{1}{2}$ inches in length, but they are commonly about $2\frac{1}{2}$ to 3 inches. The seeds (fig. 36, a) are dull russet-brown, with areas of white. Seed-leaves, about three-fourths of an inch long, are 6 to 7. Wood varies widely in character and grain, which may be very coarse, medium, or fine. Coarse-grained wood is usually distinctly reddish-brown, the "red fir" of lumbermen. Fine-grained wood is a clear yellowish brown, the "yellow fir" and "Oregon pine" of lumbermen. The botanical characters of trees furnishing these dissimilar qualities of wood are the same, and there is no foundation for the popular belief that these woods come from two different "varieties" or "species" of trees; indeed the two grades of wood may sometimes be obtained from the same tree. For the first stage of from 50 to 100 or more years diameter growth is rapid, giving coarse-grained wood, while the later stages of growth are, as a rule, slower and give fine-grained wood. The invariable difference in color between these two grades of wood is often attributed to the character of the soil, but this explanation ignores the fact that both grades may come from the same tree. The true explanation is yet to be found. Grades intermediate between these are also common, especially in trees grown outside of the humid northwestern range, from which the bulk of "red" and "yellow" timber is derived. Both grades are exceedingly important commercially, but the finer-grained, yellow wood is now being worked up for the finest grades of finishing lumber, for which it competes with high-class pine.

LONGEVITY.—Long-lived. Trees from 3 to 4 feet in diameter are from 150 to 200 years old, while those from 4 to 8 feet in diameter are from 200 to 375 years old. One tree 9 feet through showed an age of 435 years. The ages of rare trees larger than this are probably from 400 to 500 years.

RANGE.

Western North America from British Columbia southward to central California, to northwestern Texas, southern New Mexico, Arizona, and northern Mexico.

BRITISH COLUMBIA.—From east side of Rocky Mountains westward to Pacific coast and northward to Tacla Lake (lat. 55° 10′) and Skeena River (lat. 54° 20′) ; in southern part, from sea-level to 6,000 feet ; farther north, at general elevation of country, but absent from valleys of southern part of central plateau, as also from higher parts of Rocky, Gold, and Selkirk Mountains. From Rocky Mountains eastward to Calgary and Porcupine Hills ; northward to head of Athabaska and Grand Fork Fraser rivers, but absent from Cariboo Range ; northward in Fraser River Valley to McLeods, Tacla, Babine, and François lakes ; absent from headwaters of Salmon River, but on coast range northward to Skeena River. Northward on Pacific coast only as far as north end of Vancouver Island, not on coast archipelago, and rare on west coast of Vancouver Island.

WASHINGTON.—Abundant everywhere, except in Columbia River plains. West of Cascades, generally from sea level to 5,000 feet; less frequent east of Cascades. Washington National Forest (West) up to 4,000 feet, or occasionally to 6,000 feet; Washington Forest (East) at 1,100 to 6,000 feet. In Cascades, south of this reserve, up to 5,400 feet. Mount Rainier National Forest, up to 5,600 feet; on Mount Rainier and Mount Adams. Olympic Mountains, up to about 3,500 feet; Blue Mountains, at 2,500 to 4,000 feet; on Kamiak Butte, head of Grande Coulée River, and in Nisqually River Valley.

OREGON.—Throughout western part, except in a few arid valleys; from sea level to 6,000 feet. Cascade National Forest (North), sometimes up to 7,200 feet; eastward on Columbia River to Hood River; east of Mount Hood to within about 6 miles of Wapinitia (west of Deschutes River); north side of Mount Hood up to 3,800 feet and to Government Camp on south side. Occurs from Mount Hood to latitude 45°, here disappearing from east side of range. In southern Cascades, on Umpquas, Siskiyous, and west side of Cascades, up to 6,200 feet; east side of Cascades, at 4,300 to 7,000 feet from Klamath Gap northward to Klamath Marsh Terrace; Mount Mazama at 4,500 to over 6,000 feet. On north end of Upper Klamath Lake and lava flows east of this lake, at elevations above 6,000 feet, and southward to Swan Lake Point, reappearing on divide at head of Lost River. Unknown on Klamath-Deschutes Divide and elsewhere in Klamath Basin. On both slopes of coast ranges, but commoner on western.

CALIFORNIA.—In northern mountains, Sierras, and southward to San Joaquin River; also in coast ranges to Santa Lucia Mountains. Throughout northwestern California eastward to Mount Shasta, and westward to the coast; generally at 2,000 to 6,000 feet. Klamath National Forest, up to 4,000 feet. Eastward in Siskiyou County to east part of Siskiyou Mountains: Klamath River (few miles west of Hornbrook), near Klamath Hot Springs, ridge east of Shovel Creek, and eastward to near Picard (west of Klamath Lake), extreme eastern limit; farther south, eastward only to Goosenest Mountain (east of Shasta Valley and north of Mount Shasta), upper McCloud River (south of Mount Shasta) and southeastward to Fall River (Shasta County), where east limits farther south are Mount Lassen, while western limits are Sacramento River Canyon to or below Gregory, McCloud River to its junction with Pitt River, and 3 miles east of Montgomery, at 4,000 to 4,200 feet. *Lassen County:* Southern part eastward to Susanville. Mount Shasta, bottom slopes, except at north, up to 5,500 feet. In Shasta, Plumas, Lassen Peak, and Diamond Mountain National forests, at 2,000 to 6,000 feet, on west slope of range. Northern Sierras, at 2,400 to 6,000 feet on west slope, or sometimes to 7,000 feet and down to 900 feet, as in Chico quadrangle area (including Butte County); not in Sierra Valley. *Tehama County:* East of Sacramento River from point 10 miles east of Paine Creek post-office eastward. *Plumas County:* Eastward to Grizzly Mountains (west of Sierra Valley). *Butte County:* Westward to Megalia and to 4 miles north of Bidwell Bar at 1,300 feet. *Sierra County:* Eastward to mountains west of Sierra Valley, thence westward to Yuba Pass (5,800 feet); west of Yuba Pass, westward into Yuba County, where west limit is on east foothills of Sacramento Valley at Camptonville and Oregon Hills, and in Nevada County at Nevada City, Grass Valley, and Colfax on Bear River. *Placer County:* Westward to junction of Middle and North Forks of American River; eastward to beyond Blue Canyon and probably also above Emigrant Gap on main Sierra Divide, but not reported on east side of divide between Truckee and Lake Tahoe. *Eldorado County:* Westward to Placerville, Pleasant Valley, and canyon of North Fork Cosumnes River; eastward to Coloma in canyon of South Fork of American River, and to Echo (Tahoe Road), at 5,500 feet. Stanislaus National Forest, at 2,000 to 5,500 feet, and chiefly on and near Mutton Canyon, between Grizzly Flat and Indian Diggins, and on Mill Creek (tributary North Fork Mokelumne River). *Amador County:* Westward to point 3 miles east of Pine Grove and Sutter Creek Canyon (northeast of Volcano), and eastward to beyond Pioneer. *Calaveras County:* Only in central western part on branches of Mokelumne River westward nearly to Rich Gold, Esperanza Creek (near Railroad Flat); not detected between Murphys and Big Trees nor in Calaveras Big Tree groves, but it occurs on San Antonio Creek about 2 miles below Big Trees. *Tuolumne County:* Canyon of Middle Fork Stanislaus River from junction with Clark Fork at 5,500 feet eastward several miles; between Big Oak Flat and Crockers, and thence eastward to Aspen Meadows, at 6,200 feet; Hetch Hetchy Valley and Tuolumne Big Tree Grove at 5,700 feet. *Mariposa County:* Westward to near Bull Creek (10 miles east of Coulterville and a few miles east of Wassama); eastward to Yosemite Valley and Merced River (head of Nevada Fall), at 6,000 feet, Glacier Point at 7,300 feet, and nearly to Chinquapin, Bridal Veil Creek, at 7,100 feet. Southward occurs on head of Stevenson Creek (tributary San Joaquin River) at elevations of 3,000 to 5,500 feet (southern limit in Sierras) at 900 to 5,000 feet, or occasionally to 6,000 feet. In Stony Creek National Forest, at 2,000 to 5,000 feet, but mainly on west side of range. *Tehama County:* Eastward along Paskenta Road to about 3,300 feet on east side of Coast Range.

Colusa County: Northwest corner on Snow Mountain. *Lake County:* East side of Coast Range to Long Valley, Upper Cache Creek, Clear Lake, and to point near Middleton. Common in Del Norte, Humboldt, Mendocino, Marin, and Sonoma counties (coast ranges) ; abundant westward to eastern margin of redwood belt, and sparingly through it, sometimes to the sea. *Del Norte County:* Westward to Crescent City. *Humboldt County:* Sparingly among the redwoods north of Humboldt Bay ; westward south of bay to Ferndale and Bear River valleys, Petrolia, Upper Mattole River, Briceland, and south slope of King Mountain. *Mendocino County:* Westward to Kenny, Westport, Mendocino Pine Barrens, mouth of Big River, and seaward gulches from Fort Bragg to Gualala. *Sonoma County:* Westward in north part to east edge of lodgepole pine belt (on coast) to point 1 mile from beach at Fort Ross, near mouth of Russian River, nearly to Bodega Bay, Meeker, and Occidental. *Marin County:* Westward to southern part of Inverness Ridge (Point Reyes Peninsula), line of North Shore Railroad, and valleys of San Geronimo and Lagunitas. *Napa County:* Mount St. Helena, up to 4,350 feet, and southward east of Napa Valley at least to St. Helena (town), and on ridge west side of Napa Valley to point south of and to a point little beyond Oakville. Mountains about San Francisco Bay ; but not in Vaca Mountains (inner Coast Range), Oakland Hills, and Mount Hamilton, nor Monte Diablo ranges. Frequent in Santa Cruz and Santa Lucia Mountains, at 2,500 to 3,000 feet, southward to Los Burros. Throughout Santa Cruz Mountains from hills south of San Francisco and southward around north part of Monterey Bay to within a few miles of Watsonville, reappearing southward in Santa Lucia Mountains.

The detailed range of Douglas fir in Idaho, Montana, South Dakota, Colorado, Utah, Texas, New Mexico, Arizona, and Mexico will be dealt with in a later bulletin.

OCCURRENCE.

Except at high elevations and at north limit, prefers north to south exposures and sheltered slopes, canyons, benches, etc., to exposed situations. In north, and at high elevations, warmer south exposures are preferred, as. heat, not moisture, becomes the controlling factor. Lower limit in drier regions determined by lack of moisture, and upper limit chiefly by lack of heat. At higher levels on east sides of ranges than on west sides, also higher on south slopes than on north exposures ; but it is more abundant on west slopes than on east slopes, and likewise more frequent on north than on south exposures— except at north, where heat is the controlling factor. Adapted to a great variety of soils, including nearly all with sufficient moisture, from border of brackish coast water to soils where only drought-enduring western yellow pine grows. Prefers fresh, well-drained, porous, deep, loamy soils, avoiding saturated, poorly drained, heavy soils. Good soil and abundant atmospheric and soil moisture are necessary for best growth, but with abundant moisture, quantity and quality of soil are less important, and vice versa. Grows faster and larger on poor gravels and sand in the humid Puget Sound country than on best soils of Rocky Mountains with dry air and deficient precipitation ; likewise, not so large on best soils of drier California mountains, even though the climate is mild and heat and sunshine are abundant for tree growth.

Forms large pure forests and often nearly pure stands, but chiefly associated with numerous species of different habits. In California Sierras chiefly with yellow pine, sugar pine, white fir, and incense cedar, as also in Cascades of southern Oregon ; while in California coast ranges it grows with redwood and tanbark oak. In Oregon and Washington, mainly with western hemlock, western red cedar, lowland fir, western yellow pine, and on coast, with Sitka spruce, while in coast ranges and in Cascades it occurs with western white pine, western larch, and lodgepole pine.

CLIMATIC CONDITIONS.—Climate varies from moist one of Northwest to dry one in parts of interior and Southwest, and from the short growing season of high elevations to the long growing season of warm, humid coast region, and of the sunny Southwest. Winter varies from rainy season, as in parts of Pacific coast region, and an occasional snow storm and short cold snap followed by summer's heat, as in the southern Rocky Mountains, to more severe winter of the Rockies northward to interior British Columbia ; in northern Idaho and Montana winters are long and temperature drops frequently as low as −30° or −40° F. Average annual precipitation and relative humidity, extremely variable. Precipitation varies from over 100 inches (Puget Sound) to less than 15 inches (dry interior and Rockies). Amount of precipitation diminishes from coast to Rockies and from British Columbia to New Mexico ; it increases with elevation and is less on east than on west side of coast ranges, Cascades, Sierras, and Rockies. Relative humidity of air is high where precipitation is great. To sum up, this tree grows best in greatest abundance where precipitation and relative humidity of the air are greatest.

TOLERANCE.—Moderately tolerant, becoming less so with age ; endures more shade than western yellow pine, sugar pine, western white pine, and lodgepole pine, but less than western hemlock, western red cedar, white and alpine fir, incense cedar, Engelmann, blue, and Sitka spruces. Tolerance varies with locality and region, being greatest under conditions of best growth. Partial shade and shelter more necessary in early life where conditions of growth are less favorable. At moist north it thrives in the open from early youth, while in drier regions it prefers shade of weeds, brush, etc. Dense pure or mixed stands of the Northwest have clean trunks for about two-thirds of the length, while trees of open forests and in the Rocky Mountains are clean-trunked for only one-third their length, or, in scattered stands, carry branches almost to the ground. Trunks clean themselves slowly even in dense stands, which indicates tolerance of side shade ; while young trees in dense stands grow rapidly in height, showing their need of overhead light.

REPRODUCTION.—Generally a prolific seeder, producing seed every year, with specially good local seed years at intervals of three or four years. Power of reproduction and seed formation nearly as great as that of yellow pine throughout its range of distribution. Seed with moderately high rate of germination at best, but often low, and with persistent vitality. Large quantities of seed destroyed by insects and eaten by birds and squirrels. Seed matured at about same time throughout range. Warm, moist, pure mineral soil, or a mixture of the latter and humus, best for germination and development of seedlings ; reproduction rare on thick duff or vegetable matter, but abundant in humid regions after layer has been burned off or broken up by logging ; unburned, logged areas are commonly restocked by its northern associates, western hemlock and red cedar. In drier eastern range burning over ground is usually unfavorable to reproduction, lodgepole pine, aspen, and others restocking burned areas. Under most favorable conditions, reproduction is extremely dense, an acre being said to carry over 30,000 trees about 3 feet high and 11 years old, while a stand of 26-year-old trees averaged 1,068 trees per acre, 45 feet high and 3½ inches in diameter. Such reproduction is frequent in Oregon and Washington.

Bigcone Spruce.

Pseudotsuga macrocarpa (Torr.) Mayr.

DISTINGUISHING CHARACTERISTICS.

Bigcone spruce, which is a little-known tree, is distinct in appearance and conspicuous among its usually lower growing associates. It has been long considered a variety of the Douglas fir, owing mainly to the identical, but larger, form of its cones and its similar foliage. It is, however, distinct. It is generally rather stunted in appearance. The wide, pyramidal crown, extending to, or within a few feet of, the ground, is open and thin, owing to the fact that the branches grow from the trunk at very long intervals. Those of the lower part of the crown are exceedingly long, and horizontal, but somewhat drooping at their extremities, while the short top branches trend upward. Characteristic short side branchlets, sometimes erect, droop from all of the limbs. The trunk, clear of branches for only a few feet, tapers rapidly from a thick base, reaching a height of from 30 to 60 or, occasionally, 75 feet, and a diameter of from 14 to 20 inches. The bark is early roughened at the base of young trunks. It is blackish or deep red-brown, and, in old trees, from 2 to 5 or more inches thick near the bottom of the trunk. Deep, wide furrows and ridges, irregularly connected, mark the bark characteristically. The thin-looking foliage is blue-green, with an ashy tinge. The somewhat curved leaves (fig. 37) grow on all sides of the branchlets, but by a strong twisting of their stems they appear to come out mainly from two opposite sides of the twigs. They are more or less pointed, but not prickly. Leaves of a season's growth remain on the branches from 4 to 5 years—possibly longer. The cones (fig. 37), which are very distinctive, mature early in August, opening by the latter part of that month or early in September, and shedding their seeds. They vary from 3¾ to about 6 inches in length, and when open are rich dark brown. Some of the cones fall from the trees during the winter, but a good many remain for a year or longer on the branches. The

Fig. 37.—*Pseudotsuga macrocarpa: a*, seed.

large seeds (figs. 37, *a*) are dark chocolate brown and shiny on the upper side, which contrasts strongly with the dull, very slightly reddish-brown under surface. Seed-leaves, usually 6, but often 7, pointed, and about an inch long. Wood, reddish-brown, fine-grained, rather tough and hard; suitable for coarse lumber, but not used commercially. An exceedingly important tree for increasing the protective cover on dry mountain slopes of its range where few other conifers are at home.

LONGEVITY.—Little is now known of the longevity of this tree. Probably long-lived. A tree 21¾ inches in diameter showed an age of 109 years. Doubtless larger trees occasionally found would prove to be from 200 to 300 years old.

RANGE.

Southern California, from eastern Santa Barbara County and southwestern corner of Kern County to northern Lower California; range includes Santa Inez, Zaca, San Rafael, Pine, San Emigdio, Sierra, Liebre, Sierra Madre, San Bernardino, San Jacinto, Santa Ana, Palomar, Cuyamaca, and San Pedro Martir mountains. Chiefly on north and east slopes and in canyons nearly throughout these ranges, at elevations of 3,000 to 5,000 feet, but often to 6,000 or 7,000 feet, and down to 1,500 feet in canyon bottoms. Western limits are Mission Canyon (above Santa Barbara) in Santa Ynez Mountains, where one tree occurs at 1,500 feet, and Zaca Peak, in San Rafael Mountains. Northern limits are San Emigdio Mountains and south side of Tejon Canyon (west of Tehachipi Mountains). Most common in San Gabriel and San Bernardino Mountains. Not frequent in Santa Barbara National Forest, but most abundant in Matilija, Cuyama, Sespe, and Piru creek basins. Locally noted as follows: Mount Medulce, Big Pine Mountain, Pine Mountain, Piedro Blanco Peak, near Pine Mountain Lodge, south side of Sierra Liebre Range, and on mountain back of Fort Tejon. General in San Gabriel National Forest and between about 3,000 and 5,000 feet; locally noted on Mount Wilson, on Rubio Mountain, down to 2,200 feet, near Alpine Tavern, between 5,100 and 6,000 feet, and Mount Lowe, at from 2,000 feet to summits. Common in San Bernardino National Forest, on both sides of range; on north side down to 1,500 feet, and sparingly in pine belt and on plateau up to 6,000 or 7,000 feet, but up only to 3,000 feet on south side. Not detected in Santa Monica Mountains west of Los Angeles. Trabuco National Forest, at 2,000 to 3,000 feet, in bottoms at heads of canyons in Santa Ana Mountains. San Jacinto Mountains, northern and western slopes and canyon bottoms, at 3,000 to 5,500 feet; less frequent up to 6,000 or 7,000 feet. Forms 5 per cent of forest in Palomar Mountains (southwest of San Jacinto Mountains), and 10 per cent of forest in Balkan Mountains—few miles southeast, near Julian—while farther south it is very rare in Cuyumaca Mountains.

LOWER CALIFORNIA.—Sparingly represented at 5,000 to 7,000 feet on Mount San Pedro Martir.

OCCURRENCE.

Scattered in cool ravines, gulches, canyons, over north slopes; approximately intermediate in position between chaparral belt and western yellow and Jeffrey pine forest. This occurrence is often very irregular, owing to unfavorable local conditions of soil and moisture, and destructive forest fires. Generally on dry to fresh sandy or gravelly loam soils, or on rocky, shallow ones, any of which are too dry for Jeffrey pine, western yellow pine, sugar pine, white fir, and incense cedar, all common to the region. It avoids stream beds and other wet places preferred by incense cedar.

Pure small groups and patches, or single trees interspersed through pine belt, chaparral, and oak growth. Probably once occurred in much larger, pure stands, which were doubtless reduced by frequent fires. In pine belt, associated with Coulter pine, western yellow pine, Jeffrey pine, sugar pine, incense cedar, and white fir; below this, common with canyon and California live oak, and scattered through chaparral; extends into latter to limit of moisture conditions, and into pine belt as far as severe climate there permits.

CLIMATIC CONDITIONS.—Precipitation insufficient now to support good forest cover. Average annual precipitation (chiefly rain in winter at low levels, and snow at high elevations) from less than 10 inches to 30 inches; snow melts while falling, or soon after, in range of this spruce; remains only above it. Relative humidity, likewise variable and correspondingly low. Precipitation greater at high levels than at low ones, and greater on west than on east side of coast ranges facing dry interior. Snow may come at upper limit as late as May and as early as October. Fog common during rainy season (winter), depositing considerable moisture, comparatively speaking, on cool, forested slopes. Large part of precipitation and moisture from fogs never enters soil, but is quickly evaporated, only temporarily reducing general evaporation and transpiration. Summers long, hot, and dry; occasional thunderstorms, hailstorms, or cloudbursts on higher mountains. Dew generally unknown. July to October, inclusive, is dry or "danger" season, when there is great risk of forest fires, which are there very destructive and hard to control unless they burn out or meet some barrier. Once destroyed, forest cover is hard to replace.

TOLERANCE.—Intolerant of shade except in early seedling stage; throughout later life requires full overhead light for best growth; mature stands usually open, stems clear of branches for one-third or more of length, but occasionally limbed to ground in open and in chaparral. Seedlings come up and thrive in shade of live oaks and under seed trees, in open, moist, sheltered places.

REPRODUCTION.—Moderately abundant seeder, but cones are produced at rather long and infrequent intervals, though small amounts of seed are borne locally about every year. Seed of low germination, owing to large number usually imperfect; vitality persistent. Much seed eaten by rodents and birds. Reproduction generally very scanty, due probably to poor seed, loss by animals, and destruction by repeated past fires. Mature trees are protected by thick bark, but young growth is easily killed by fire. Reproduction commonly in leaf litter under shade and in vicinity of seed trees and under live oaks. Seedlings grow slowly at first, but, once well established, they increase rapidly in height, requiring more light.

ABIES. FIRS.

The firs are evergreen trees with peculiarly conical, often very spire-like, dense crowns of heavily foliaged branches, which by side branching form wide, flat sprays. The trunks are tall, very straight, evenly and gradually tapered to one or two slender, straight leaders. Whorls of comparatively small branches grow from the trunks at regular distant intervals. Their sharply defined heads of dense, often very dark foliage and arrow-like stems distinguish them among all other trees. The trunk bark, before it is broken or furrowed by age, is marked by many blister-like resin pockets, formed within and just beneath the smooth surface. These are often an inch or more long, and so numerous as to be very conspicuous. This character, which no other native trees possess so markedly, may have given them their popular name of "balsams," because of the liquid resin obtained from the pockets for medicinal purposes. The leaves, spirally arranged on the branches, persist for from five to ten years (usually nine), after which those of a season's growth gradually disappear. Leaves on the lower branches of our native firs are mostly flat (in one species triangular), rounded, or blunt, not prickly at the end (in one species needle-pointed); they appear to grow more or less distinctly from two opposite sides, or from the top, of the branch. Those of the extreme upper branches, particularly on the stout leaders, are stouter, crowded and curved toward the upper side of the horizontal twigs, and often keenly pointed or somewhat sharp-pointed. It is exceedingly important to note the very dissimilar form, habit, and character of leaves from the two parts of the crown. Leaves from the middle branches of the crown are sometimes different in form from those of either the lower or upper branches. In cross section the leaves of firs show 2 resin ducts near the lower surface of the leaves and commonly close to the edges of the leaves, but in some of our firs these ducts are in the interior of the leaf's tissue, about the same distance from the upper as from the lower surface. Flowers of two sexes, male and female, are borne on branchlets of the previous year's growth in different parts of the same tree. Female flowers, producing cones and seeds, are short, spherical, rounded or elongated scaly bodies standing erect and singly on branches of the uppermost part of the crown. Male flowers, pollen-bearing only, are elongated, cylindrical, scaly bodies hanging singly among the leaves from the lower side of branches below the female flowers. The cones, whose erect position is unique and distinctive of all firs, mature in one season. During autumn their thin, closely-packed, overlapping scales gradually become loosened from their central spike-like axis and fall away with their winged seeds, two of which are borne under each scale; no fertile or perfect seeds are borne under scales at the ends of the cones. The pointed woody axes of the cones remain attached to their branches for several years. The breaking up of mature cones on the trees is not a character of any other group of our cone-bearers, the deciduous Taxodiums of south Atlantic forests excepted. Seeds of firs are easily wafted by the wind several hundred feet from the parent trees, but they are rarely carried more than 50 or 100 feet away. The seeds have peculiar resin cells which may be seen by cutting into the seed coat. The vitality of fir seeds does not endure beyond a single season, and as a rule the percentage of germination is low (50 per cent or under). Seed-leaves, from 4 to 10, and flat.

Commercially the firs are of great importance. Some of them form protection forests on steep slopes at high elevations where few other conifers can live, while others supply excellent saw-timber of large size. They are moderately long-lived, and 350 years is probably the limit of their age, but much is yet to be learned concerning the longevity of our firs.

Seven species inhabit the Pacific forests; two of them extend far northward into Canada, while one of these and another species range through the Rocky Mountains as well.

Alpine Fir; Balsam Fir.

Abies lasiocarpa (Hook.) Nuttall.

DISTINGUISHING CHARACTERISTICS.

Alpine fir is one of the smallest of the Pacific firs and perhaps also one of the least known there, owing to the high altitude at which it grows. Among all of its associates the long, narrowly conical crown, terminating in a conspicuous spire-like point, at once distinguishes this fir from all species of its kind in the region. Its spear-like heads can be recognized at a long distance. Height, from 60 to 90 feet and diameter from 14 to 24 inches, but in exposed high situations it may be under 3 or 4 feet in height, with very long lower branches on the ground. Rare old trees attain heights of from 100 to 130 or, very occasionally, 160 feet and a diameter of 3 to 4 feet. Larger trees are reported, but they are exceedingly rare. The bark is thin, at most about 1¼ inches thick, hard, flinty, and but little broken on fairly large trees, except occasional shallow, narrow cracks near the base of the trunk. The unbroken smooth parts are ashy gray—often chalky-white. Even in old trunks, always irregularly and shallowly seamed, the flat ridges are whitish, but pale-brownish on the broken edges and red-brown on the inside. Trees on several mountain peaks in Arizona, and occasionally elsewhere in the tree's range, have peculiarly thin, soft, corky [a] bark, similar in color to the hard bark. The narrow crown usually extends to the ground, even on old trees. The dense branches, which are characteristically tough, droop at the base of the crown; when dead, often curved or bent down upon the trunk. Its low branches make it particularly susceptible to crown fires, which invariably kill it in large numbers, as do severe ground fires, which easily injure its thin bark. In very close stands old trees are occasionally free from branches for from 20 to 40 feet or more. The foilage is deep

---

[a] *Abies arizonica* Merriam is founded partly on this character and partly on a form of cone-scale which Dr. Merriam found to differ materially from that of the ordinary type of *A. lasiocarpa*. The cones and foliage of the cork-barked trees can not be distinguished by the writer from those of hard-barked trees.

blue-green, that of the season with a silvery tinge. The twigs, sometimes smooth, commonly have minute, rusty hairs for two to three years, and the buds are covered with resin. The flat leaves (fig. 38), pointless and longer on lower crown branches and keenly or somewhat pointed and shorter on uppermost branches,

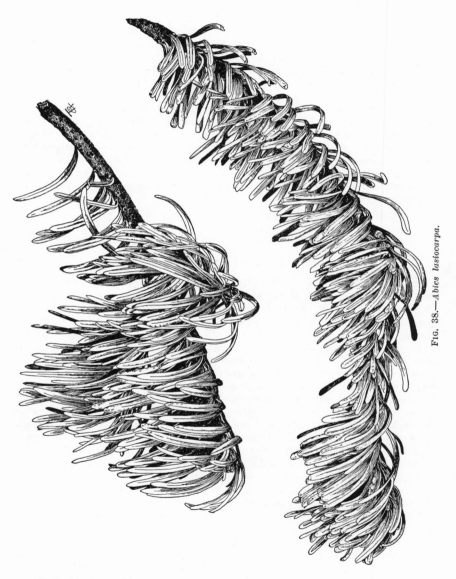

FIG. 38.—*Abies lasiocarpa.*

are distinctively massed and pointing upward on the top sides of the branches, those below and on the sides of the branches being twisted so as to join those above. The dense crowding of the leaves on the upper sides of the branches is very characteristic. Mature cones, before swelling and beginning to break up (fig. 39), are from 2¼ to about 4 inches in length by about 1¼ to 1½ inches in diameter. They are deep purple, becoming lighter by the time the scales fall. The ivory-brown seeds (fig. 39, *a*) have large, shiny, purplish or violet-tinged wings. Seed-leaves, one-third to one-half inch long, usually 4.

Wood, fine-grained, light, soft, and from pale straw color to light yellowish brown. Little clear timber is obtainable because the trunks so often retain branches down to the ground. It is fairly straight-grained and splits and works

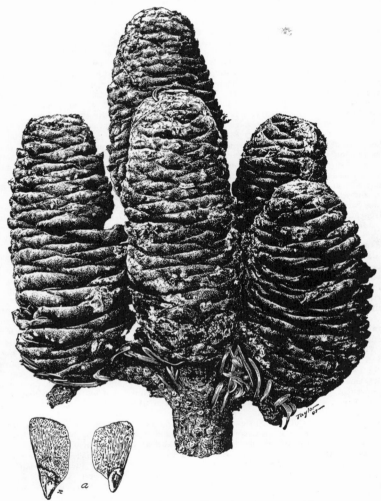

FIG. 39.—*Abies lasiocarpa:* Very ripe cones ; *a,* seed.

easily. Its dead, weathered shafts, so frequent where fires have swept, remain in sound condition for many years.

LONGEVITY.—Probably not a long-lived tree. Much more study of its age is required. Trees from 12 to 20 inches in diameter are from 140 to 210 years old. The considerably larger trees which occur are not likely to be more than 250 years old.

RANGE.

Subalpine valleys, slopes, and ridges from southeastern Alaska, British Columbia, and western Alberta southward through Washington, Oregon, Idaho, western Montana, and Wyoming to southern Arizona and New Mexico.

ALASKA.—East slopes of coast range in southeastern part; crosses divide to west slopes at Lynn Canal, where at sea-level, on west shore, it occurs in groups and extends to Chilkoot and White passes, reaching timber line at about 3,000 feet. Possibly extends farther south, at timber line, on west slope, and on sea coast, but not yet detected. Appears farther north in Copper River Valley at Mentasta Pass and Copper Center (lat. 62°, long. 145° 20′), northwestern limit.

PACIFIC CANADA.—Yukon Territory, British Columbia, and Alberta. Throughout southern British Columbia from east slopes of coast range and eastward to east side of Continental Divide in Alberta, except in southern dry parts of interior plateau. Northward in Rockies to McLeod's Lake (lat. 55°), but farther northward on interior plateau, and over eastern slopes of coast range to Lake Bennett (lat. 60°) at Lewes River (Yukon Territory) ; reappears north of Yukon River on North Fork McQuestion River (tributary Stewart River), in lat. 64° 30′, long. 136°, northern limit. Occurs in northern interior plateau and coast ranges at about 4,000 feet ; lower limits are in valleys of eastern coast ranges at Lake Bennett, descending to 2,150 feet ; occurs on Middle Lake, Lake Dease, and Lake Schütlüchroa, upper limits varying from about 3,000 feet at White Pass to 5,000 and 5,500 feet on sheltered inland passes, such as Taku Pass and mountains about Lake Dease and Telegraph Creek (upper tributary Stikine River, about lat. 58°). Not on west slopes of southern British Columbia coast range nor on Vancouver Island. On Gold and Selkirk ranges and on both sides of Continental Divide, being abundant in Bow River Pass, at 5,000 to 7,000 feet elevation, and on east slopes extending eastward on line of Canadian Pacific Railroad to Castle Mountain ; southward in Rockies, over high, cool valleys, to latitude 49° and up to timber line. Reported east of Continental Divide in Peace River region and also in that between Lesser Slave Lake and Athabaska River.

WASHINGTON.—Both sides of Cascades, Olympic, northeastern, and Blue mountains, at elevations of 5,000 to 7,500 feet. Northern part of Washington National Forest, on west side Cascades, at elevations above 4,500 feet, but on east side, at 5,000 to 6,000 feet, or sometimes up to 7,000 feet, as at Slate and Windy Passes, and down to 2,150 feet, as on Stehekin River. Locally noted as follows : Crater Pass, at 6,000 feet on west side Cascades, and at 5,700 feet on east side ; Twisp Pass Lake ; North Fork Bridge Creek ; Emerald Basin, above and south of Lake Chelan, at 5,700 feet ; North Fork of Entiat River, at 6,000 to 7,000 feet ; Entiat River, at 5,700 to 6,600 feet. Cascades in southern Washington National Forest, generally at 5,000 to 6,000 feet, but sometimes to 7,100 and down to 2,300 feet, growing on both sides of range in Skykomish, Tolt, Snoqualmie, Cedar, Green, White, Yakima, and Wenache river watersheds ; Wenache Mountains, at 4,500 to 5,200 feet. Mount Rainier National Forest, generally at from 5,500 feet to timber line, but sometimes down to 4,000 feet and up to 7,500 feet ; on both sides Cascades in White, Puyallup, Nisqually, Cowlitz, Cispus, Lewis, Wind, Little White Salmon, White Salmon, Klickitat, Atanum, Tieton, Natches, and Yakima river basins. Locally noted in this region as follows : Mount Rainier, at 4,500 to 7,900 feet ; Eagle Mountain ; Cowlitz Pass, at 4,750 feet ; head of Summit Creek (on Cowlitz River), at 3,650 feet ; Cowlitz-American River Divide (near Dewey Lake), at 5,300 to 5,500 feet ; Divide 3 miles north of Cowlitz Pass, at 4,800 feet ; Mount Adams, at 6,000 to 6,500 feet ; Upper Klickitat River, at 4,200 feet ; Little Klickitat-Tieton River divide, at 5,900 feet ; Cispus-Klickitat River divide, at 5,200 feet ; Goat and Olympic mountains, at 5,000 to 6,500 feet (timber line). Colville National Forest, along higher ridges. Washington addition to Priest River National Forest, common above 4,500 feet ; Wenaha National Forest, on broader ridges in Blue Mountains, at 7,000 feet and at heads of streams.

OREGON.—Both sides of Cascades, Siskiyous, and Blue Mountains ; generally at elevations between 5,000 and 7,800 feet ; southward to north side of Siskiyous, but absent from coast ranges. Northern part of Cascades at from 5,800 feet to timber line—sometimes to 7,300 feet, and down to 3,400. Southern Cascades, at 5,800 to 7,800 feet ; southward on east side to point 10 miles south of Crater Lake, and on west side, to Umpqua River Divide and north side of Siskiyous, where it is rare. Not on mountains east of Cascades, except those in eastern, north and south parts of Blue Mountains National Forest, and in Wallowa National Forest. Locally noted as follows : Southwest side Mount Hood from near timber line down to a few hundred feet below Government Camp ; on north side from timber line down to 3,700 feet ; Mount Mazama on Wizard Island and rim of lake down to 6,000 feet in Anna Creek Canyon ; Hidaway Creek, Granite Creek (near Alamo) ; South Fork of Rock Creek, at 6,450 feet ; head and south wall of Rock Creek ; about Greenhorn City (Greenhorn Mountains) ; at point 8 miles northwest of Alba ; head of North Fork of John Day River : Powder River Mountains ; mountains about Minam River,

The detailed range of alpine fir in the Rocky Mountain region will be dealt with in a later bulletin.

OCCURRENCE.

In cool, moist, and, in part, subalpine situations; commonly on slopes at timber line, and at its lower limits in protected valleys, at heads of streams, and about mountain lakes and meadows. Best growth on fairly deep, loose, moist soil; will grow also in wet and on poorest and driest thin soils. Main occurrence limited by requirement of soil moisture to elevations where snowfall is great. Requires less soil moisture in general than Engelmann spruce, but grows in places too wet for the spruce, as well as on Douglas fir soils, where spruce will not succeed. Does not thrive on heavy, clayey soils. Altitudinal occurrence in Alaska narrow, owing to low timber line; more abundant on east than on west slopes of Alaskan coast mountains. Throughout north coast ranges and the Rocky Mountains the vertical range is wide. Here on all slopes, but largest on high north aspects. At south, altitudinal extent is again narrow, because favorable moisture occurs only at much higher elevations.

In pure, small stands and in mixture. In Alaska, mainly with black hemlock; at higher levels in Washington, with black hemlock, occasionally yellow cedar and white-bark pine, and lower, with noble and amabilis firs; in Oregon, with black hemlock, Engelmann spruce, western white pine, lodgepole pine, and noble fir.

CLIMATIC CONDITIONS.—Endures rigorous climate, and therefore it goes farther north than any other coast fir. At far north, subject to blighting winter winds, weak insolation due to high latitude and extreme cloudiness, excessive precipitation, averaging over 60 inches of rain and from 2 to 5 feet of snow, and also to minimum temperature of about $-40°$ F. At south, sunlight is more abundant, lower humidity and smaller precipitation—averaging about 25 inches and mainly snow. Maximum temperature, about 90° F.

TOLERANCE.—Only slightly less tolerant of shade than Engelmann spruce, and more so than other associated species (except black hemlock); maintains long-suppressed reproduction under heavy shade, and with admission of light recovery and growth are rapid.

REPRODUCTION.—Moderately prolific seeder. Seed with rather high rate of germination, but of transient vitality. It begins to bear cones as early as the twentieth year. Produces some seed locally every year, with heavy production at intervals of about three years. Over large areas, however, cones often fail to mature during some seasons. Reproduction usually abundant, both in open on exposed mineral soil, and on thin and heavy moist duff under light or heavy shade. Seedlings grow most thickly on north sides of groups or forests and under branches of mother trees; small shaded openings among seed trees nearly always show reproduction. Occasionally at high elevations branches lying on ground take root (layer), from which, however, reproduction is probably rare.

Grand Fir; White Fir.

Abies grandis Lindley.

DISTINGUISHING CHARACTERISTICS.

Grand fir is commonly called "white" fir because of its conspicuously whitish, smooth bark. Other firs of the same region are known as " white " firs of a " different variety," especially *Abies concolor*, to which the name " white fir " appears to belong more fitly than to any other. It is desirable, therefore, for the sake of a distinctive common name, to coin for *Abies grandis* the name of " grand fir," which is appropriate, since it is a very stately and grand tree when fully matured. It grows to a height, in such favorable situations as bottomlands, of from 150 to 200 and, exceptionally, 250 to 275 feet, with a diameter of from 3 to 4 feet. On the less favorable hill lands its greatest height is from 80 to 125 feet, with a diameter of from 18 to 30 inches. Its trunks are remarkably straight and very gradually tapered. Standing alone or in an open forest, it carries its crown branches to within a few feet of the ground even when old, but in a close stand the crown covers only one-half or one-third of the stem. The crown is a narrow, rather open cone, pointed in young trees, but in old age is somewhat rounded at the top, and often, from the strong drooping of the lower branches, appears wider in the middle. The rounded top results from cessation of height growth in the leader and an elongation of the older, shorter top side branches. All of the branches, except the topmost, have a distinct downward and upward swing. The bark, peculiarly characteristic, is smooth and ashy brown, with chalky areas on young trunks, while on older trees it is regularly and shallowly furrowed, the long flat ridges still retaining splashes of gray-white. In old trees the bark is more deeply but narrowly furrowed, the ridges being sharper and less conspicuously flecked with white. The general

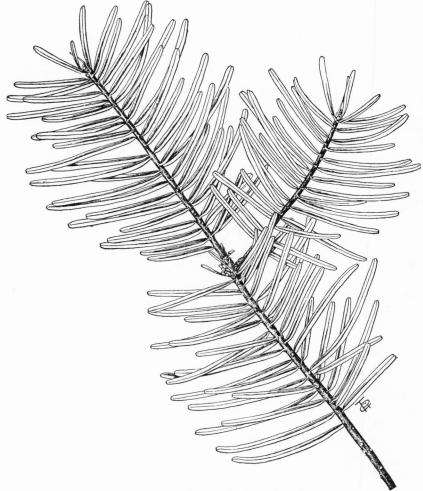

FIG. 40.—*Abies grandis,* lower branch.

tone becomes pale red-brown with an ashen tinge. The bark is very hard, close, and horny; rarely over 1¾ inches thick on old trunks, and scarcely an inch thick on trees from 18 to 20 inches in diameter.

The deep yellow-green shiny foliage is somewhat thin in appearance because of the characteristic spreading, especially of lower leaves. The leaves of the lower crown branches are flat, grooved, blunt, and distinctly notched at their ends (fig. 40) ; they appear to grow and to stand out distinctly from two opposite sides only of the branches. Many of the leaves are brought into this position by a twisting of their bases (fig. 41). Leaves of the lower crown are from 1¼ to about 2¼ inches long. Leaves of the uppermost branches are often notched, also, but are usually all more or less crowded together, pointing upward, on the top of the sprays, while the scattered leaves of the leader are sharp or keenly pointed. Leaves of the upper part of the crown are about 1

FIG. 41.—*Abies grandis,* middle crown branch.

inch or 1¼ inches long. All leaves are conspicuously white on their under surfaces. Mature buds are covered with resin, and the twigs of the season are pale russet brown and minutely hairy. The cones mature in early fall, and with their clear, light yellow-green color and slender, cylindrical form are very characteristic (fig. 42). They are about 2½ to 4¼ inches long and about 1 to 1⅓ inches in diameter. The bracts adhering to the backs of the cone-scales are squarish at their upper ends (truncated) and with a small point extending from the center. The pale yellowish brown seeds (fig. 42, *a*) have shiny, faintly yellowish wings. Seed leaves, very slender and pointed, usually 6, and about three-fourths of an inch long. Wood of this fir is little known commercially, but likely to become better known and of greater value. It is light, soft, but firm enough to be widely useful as lumber, moderately coarse-grained, and straight; varies in color from pale yellowish brown to pale brown. Its qualities deserve thorough investigation, which will probably show them to be superior to those of the softer fir woods.

Fig. 42.—*Abies grandis,* very ripe cone: *a,* seed.

LONGEVITY.—Little is known of the age limits of grand fir, concerning which further studies are urgently needed. Probably only moderately long-lived. One tree, 34⅝ inches in diameter, showed an age of 196 years.

RANGE.

Valleys and lower slopes from southern British Columbia to northern Idaho, western Montana, Oregon, and northern coast of California.

BRITISH COLUMBIA.—Mainland near coast northward to upper end of Vancouver Island; locally noted at Stanley Park near Vancouver.

WASHINGTON.—Stream bottoms and lower slopes of Cascade and coast mountains, in northeastern part and in Blue Mountains at from sea level to 5,000 feet. Both sides of Cascades (in Washington National Forest), up to 5,000 feet. Noted on Nooksak River, near Ferndale, at 30 feet elevation; East Sound at 50 feet; at Skagit and Rainey passes;

on Sauk River near Monte Cristo; head of Early Winter Creek. Both sides of Cascades in southern Washington National Forest, in valleys of Skykomish, Tolt, Snoqualmie, Green, White, Yakima, Wenache, and Entiat rivers, up to an elevation of 5,400 feet. Noted in Wenache Mountains and range between Columbia River and Yakima River, at 5,000 feet. Mount Rainier National Forest, both sides of range generally to 4,200 feet, but sometimes to 5,300 feet. Noted in Upper Nisqually Valley; Upper Klickitat River, at 4,200 feet; mouth of Hellroaring Canyon, at 3,800 feet; about Mount Adams and Eagle Mountain; on Goose Prairie along Bumping River, at 3,520 feet; on Dewey Lake (head of American River), at 5,300 feet. In Olympic Mountains from sea level to lower slopes. Locally noted at Tacoma, Port Ludlow, Lake Cushman, on shores of Puget Sound, and about Dryad, at 304 feet elevation. In Colville National Forest, Blue Mountains (Wenache National Forest), at 2,500 to 5,000 feet.

OREGON.—Stream bottoms and lower slopes of Cascade and coast ranges, Blue and Powder River mountains. In northern Cascade National Forest, on both sides of range and generally up to 4,100 feet; lower slopes of Mount Hood. Farther south (R. 5 to 17 S.) it reaches 200 to 6,000 feet. In southern Cascades National Forest, extending south-ward, on west slopes of Cascades, to headwaters of Umpqua River, and on east slopes to Mount Jefferson. Exact southern limit imperfectly known. In Coast Range south-ward into California. Locally noted in vicinity of Portland; coast of Clatsop County; from lower Clackamas River bottoms to point about 6 miles above " Hot Springs " in this canyon; Blue Mountains, at 2,500 to 6,000 feet.

CALIFORNIA.—In fog belt of northern coast, extending inland 10 to 30 miles, and southward to north of Fort Ross (Sonoma County). Locally noted in Del Norte County at Crescent City, and in bottoms of Smith River. *Humboldt County:* Inland to Hoopa Valley and ridge east of Hoopa Valley, at 3,700 to 5,500 feet; lower Mad River; Eureka; from Hydesville inland nearly to Bridgeville and Little Van Dusen River (10 miles east of Bridgeville); Ferndale to Bear Valley; between Capetown and Petrolia and thence to Upper Mattole. *Mendocino County:* Along coast from Kenny to West-port and inland along Laytonville road to point 15 miles from Westport; gulches close to coast from Fort Bragg to Gualala; Mendocino inland, on road to Ukiah, nearly to Orris Hot Springs; Navarro River up to a point 12 miles from mouth; Elk Creek, near Greenwood (12 miles south of Navarro River). *Sonoma County:* Coast north of Fort Ross with *Pinus muricata.*

The detailed range of this fir in Idaho, Montana, and Wyoming will be described in a later bulletin.

OCCURRENCE.

A tree of moist situations. On alluvial stream bottoms and their border valleys, lower gentle mountain slopes, depressions, and gulches. Best and most abundant growth in coast region on stream bottoms at low levels; small at high elevations. Its deep root system demands fairly deep, preferably moist, porous, well-drained soils. With favorable moisture and climatic conditions, it grows well on rather poor, thin soils, but better quality is necessary in soils deficient in moisture and subject to rapid evaporation.

Rarely in pure stands; usually in mixture. Most commonly with Douglas fir, and dominant over western red cedar, western hemlock, Pacific yew, and vine maple. At low levels in Oregon and Washington, with latter trees and sparingly also with amabilis and noble firs, broadleaf maple, red and Sitka alders, and black cottonwood; in low coast region with Sitka spruce, and in California with redwood.

CLIMATIC CONDITIONS.—Climate of range favorable to tree growth. Summers com-paratively cool and humid; winters ordinarily mild, and changes of temperature rather gradual; in Bitterroot Mountains (Idaho) and northward, temperature falls occasionally to −30° F. Precipitation, well distributed, except in July and August, which are usually rainless over greater part of range. Forest floor is then dry, and destructive fires often occur. Annual precipitation, from less than 20 inches to over 100 inches in different parts of range.

TOLERANCE.—For a fir only moderately tolerant of shade, being less so than amabilis fir, western red cedar, western hemlock, and California yew, but more tolerant than noble fir, Douglas fir, western white pine, western larch, and yellow pine. Seedlings endure considerable shade, but in later life full overhead light is needed for best growth. Young growth under ordinary shade remains dwarfed and dies within a few years, unless overhead light is admitted. With overhead light, but shaded from side, height growth is rapid, trunks are readily cleared of branches, and long, clean stems are formed. Shade endurance varies in general with age, moisture of soil and air, exposure, quality and quantity of soil, altitude, and latitude. With sufficient moisture, soil, and heat this fir thrives in full sunlight, and also endures considerable shade. On poor, dry soils in warm exposed places, shelter and some shade are beneficial to reduce soil evaporation and transpiration ; therefore in regions with such conditions the tree confines itself mainly to cooler, sheltered sites.

REPRODUCTION.—Moderately prolific seeder ; best in open stands. Seed of rather low rate of germination and with only transient vitality. Seeding habits not fully determined. Cones produced mainly at irregular intervals (two to three years). Occasionally few cones borne by trees about 20 years old (in open), production increasing to old age. Under favorable conditions some seed germinates soon after it is shed and seedlings may become established before cold weather. Moderately humous and shaded soils most favorable to germination, but with sufficient moisture and light, seeds sprout and seedlings thrive in humus and in mineral soils. Seedlings come up both in open and in shade.

White Fir.

Abies concolor (Gord.) Parry.

DISTINGUISHING CHARACTERISTICS.

White fir, a massive tree, is fitly and widely called by this name from the ashy hue of its bark. All of its other common names refer to its silvery or whitish appearance. It grows to its largest size in the Pacific region, where it is frequently from 140 to 180 feet and, occasionally, over 200 feet high, with a diameter of from 40 to 60 inches, rare trees being from 5 to 6 feet through. In its Rocky Mountain range it is much smaller—from 80 to 100 feet high, or rarely more, and from 20 to 30 inches in diameter. The massive trunks are conspicuously rough, with great deep, wide furrows and ridges in the ash-gray bark, which is from 4 to 6½ inches thick, and very hard and horny. The smooth, unbroken bark of the upper stem, and of young trees, is grayish, with a brownish tinge. The dense crown of heavily foliaged, short branches is an irregular, round-topped cone, extending to the ground on trees in open stands, and in dense stands covering only a third or a half of the upper stem. The trunks are straight and taper very gradually. Young trees have beautifully symmetrical, sharp crowns down to the ground, the lower limbs standing out horizontally and those above slanting upward. On old trees the lower crown branches droop conspicuously, as do also those of the middle crown ; while branches above this remain upright. In old age the more rapid growth of upper side branches than of the leader forms a rounded top. Young foliage of the year is yellow-green, with a bluish cast, but later it turns to a pale yellow green, with a whitish tinge. The leaves are flat, straight, and full and plump on the upper side, blunt or pointed—usually not prickly, but sometimes prickly on the lower crown branches of old trees. They stand out distinctly from two sides of the lower branches by a twist in their base (fig. 43) ; but very commonly the lower branches of young trees have their leaves curved and standing erect, somewhat in two lines, from the upper sides of the twigs. Leaves of the upper crown, especially on the topmost branches, are strongly curved or sickle-shaped, and appear to grow from the upper sides of the branchlets (fig. 44). These leaves and those on leaders are sharp-pointed. Lower branch leaves are usually longer (1⅓ to 3 inches long) than those of the upper branches, which are commonly about 1 to 1⅓ inches long. There is very great variation in the length form, and thickness of leaves of this fir in different parts of its wide range. The changes in form from horizontally flattened leaves to vertically flattened ones, or to those resembling a sickle-blade, are curious; they are unexplained, except perhaps by the fact that the latter form is best adapted to the dry climate in which it most often occurs. Some authors hold that Rocky Mountain trees bear longer leaves, and more commonly pointed ones, than do trees of the Pacific forests. The writer has seen trees in the latter region with quite as long leaves, while long blunt leaves are not infrequent on trees of the eastern range. The long-maintained *Abies lowiana* Murray (cultivated in England, where it was first described), the *Abies concolor lowiana* of American authors, is a form of the white fir distinguished mainly by the length of its

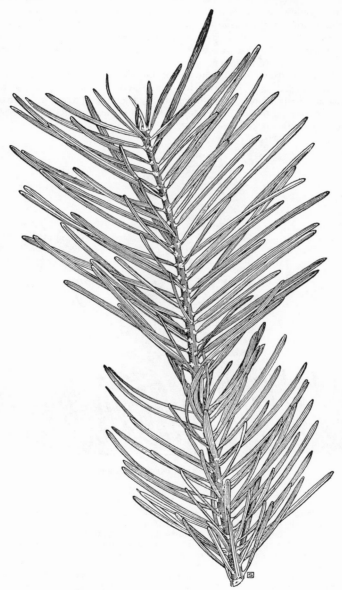

FIG. 43.—*Abies concolor,* lower branch.

leaves. It is exceedingly difficult, however, to longer maintain, even as a variety, a form based upon a character so clearly unstable. The cones (fig. 44) are mature early in September, when they are very pale olive green with an ashen tinge, or clear chrome-yellow green; sometimes purple. They vary from about 3¼ to 4¼ (sometimes nearly 5) inches in length. The bracts attached to the backs of the cone-scales are rather narrow and oblong, broad and squarish at the free end, which has a small point extending from its center. The seeds (fig. 44, *a*) are a dingy yellow-brown with shiny, clear, rose-tinged wings. Seed-leaves, 6. Wood, light, soft, rather coarse-grained, whitish to light indistinct brown; straight-grained; works easily, is strong and hard enough to be useful for saw timber, for which it is used to some extent. Many large trees are affected with "punk rot" or are wind shaken.

LONGEVITY.—It grows rapidly in height and diameter for the first 50 to 100 years, after which it grows slowly to an age of about 350 years. The limits of its age are not fully known, but very probably the largest trees are not over 350 years old. A tree 80 inches in diameter showed an age of 285 years, and one 60 inches through was 307 years old.

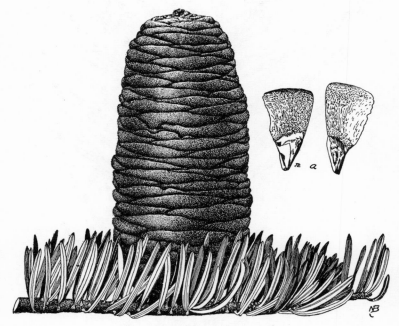

FIG. 44.—*Abies concolor: a*, seed.

RANGE.

Mountain slopes from southern Oregon through California into Lower California, and from Nevada, Utah, and southern Colorado through Arizona and New Mexico.

OREGON.—West side of Cascades southward, from about Township 22 south (headwaters of Willamette River, where it is rare at approximately 2,000 feet, but reported north of this at Fish Lake, tributary of McKenzie River), to headwaters of Umpqua and Rogue rivers; farther south, occurring at 3,000 to 6,000 feet elevation. Northern limits on east side of Cascades not known, but occurs on Matoles Creek southeast of Mount Jefferson, at 4,000 to 7,500 feet (south of T. 12 S.). Reported from southeastern slopes of Mount Hood. On Mount Mazama (Crater Lake) down Anna Creek to 5,000 feet. Extends westward in Siskiyous to coast ranges; eastward, north of Upper Klamath Lake, throughout forested upper Klamath River basin, at elevations above 5,000 feet, to mountains on east side of Warner Lake, at 7,700 feet. Noted on upper Deschutes River, on Paulina Creek, near Paulina Lake; Warner Mountains, with and above yellow pine, extending down east slopes to 6,000 feet, and to 8,100 feet or over on highest peaks; also on west side in canyons; Kokeep Mountains (east side Warner Lake) only in De Garno Canyon. Reported in Blue and Powder River mountains, northeastern part of State.

CALIFORNIA.—Northern coast ranges and southward on Sierras to southern cross ranges. Northern California eastward to Warner Mountains and westward to Siskiyous (west of railroad); westward in coast ranges to Russian Creek (west of Scott Valley), Salmon Summit southwest of forks of Salmon River, at 3,800 to 5,600 feet, Trinity Summit near meeting point of Siskiyou, Humboldt, and Trinity counties, and valley of Mad River west of South Fork Mountain. Klamath National Forest, at 5,500 to 7,000 feet; very common between Horse Creek and Klamath River (T. 47 and 48 N., R. 8 to 10 W.). Locally noted west of Scott Valley between Etna Mills and Sawyers Bar; on east slope of Marble Summit Divide, at 7,400 to 5,500 feet, and westward on Russian Creek; mountains north of Mount Shasta between Shasta Valley and Butte Creek, including Goosenest Mountain; northeast slope of Glass Mountain (12 to 15 miles south), southwest of Tule Lake, and eastward into Modoc County at Happy Camp. Warner Mountains, both sides, above 6,000 feet; head of Cedarville Canyon, from 6,000 feet up; head of South Deep Creek, Sugar Hill, and south side Fandango Valley (T. 46 N., R. 14 and 15 E.), at 6,000 feet, Big Valley on East Creek, and Blue Lake. Trinity Mountains, at 4,500 to 6,000 feet, and sometimes down to 3,000 feet, occurring throughout Trinity National Forest and nearly to Trinity River north of Yolabuli; noted on east slope of South Fork Mountain, at 3,500 feet to summit, and on west side down into Mad River Valley, which it follows to below 3,000 feet; Yola Buli Ridge; Van Dusen Canyon; Canyon Creek canyon, from near Dedrick northward 12 or 13 miles to about 6,500 feet above Twin Lakes; Bully Choop Mountain and ridge. Stony Creek National Forest, at 4,500 to 6,500 feet southward on inner coast range to Clear Lake (southern limit in these ranges), and on Sanhedrin Range to Pine Mountain; locally noted on Sheetiron Mountain, Grindstone Creek, St. Johns and Hull mountains, and Black Buttes. Shasta National Forest, at 4,000 to 7,000 feet; here noted on Mount Shasta from base of Mount Eddy (3,400 feet) to 5,700 feet (Wagon Camp), and on warm slopes to 6,700 or 7,000 feet; south of Mount Shasta, over greater part of Shasta County, and continuously from Mount Shasta to Lassens Peak; in northern Shasta County, going eastward to Soldier Mountain (near Dana), and ridge between Dana in Fall River Valley; also Big Valley in Lassen County, and from Fall River Valley westward in Pitt River region to point about 3 miles east of Montgomery. Occurs in northwestern corner of Lassen County from about 5 miles west of Bieber, and on east side of Big Valley along Willow Creek 10 miles south of Adin and a little farther south near Hayden Hill; in southern Lassen County, from Susanville westward into Shasta and Plumas counties. Tehama County, westward on Sierra foothills to about 10 miles east of Payne Creek post-office; in northern Sierras, on both slopes, and on west slope at 3,500 to 7,500 or 8,700 feet. Plumas County, in northwest corner of Sierra Valley (near Beckwith) westward on Feather River to Cromberg, and thence generally distributed; sparingly around American Valley and westward into Butte County. Here common in yellow pine belt from 3 to 4 miles north of Bidwell Bar on Feather River at about 1,300 feet elevation northwestward along North Fork of Feather River, and northeastward along Quincy Road to and beyond Quincy, in Plumas County. *Yuba County:* Oregon Hills, and eastward to Bullards Bar, Camptonville, and into Sierra County; here common in western part from Camptonville to Downieville, especially from Mount House down Woodruff Canyon to canyon of North Yuba River; also along North Yuba to Sierra City and up North Fork of Yuba. Not in Yuba Pass, but begins again on east side at 5,800 feet, continuing to west border of Sierra Valley near Sattley post-office. In southeastern Sierra County, on east slope of main Sierra Divide, and common from point several miles north of Prosser Creek into Nevada County; here abundant near Hobart Mill and Prosser Creek, and northward into Sierra County; in Truckee Canyon, southward into Placer County, and westward to Donner Lake. General in yellow pine belt of Stanislaus National Forest at 4,000 to 6,000 feet elevation, sometimes down to 3,800 feet and up to 7,500 feet. *Placer County:* About Lake Tahoe, northward into Nevada County, and southward into Eldorado County; mountains east of Glenbrook in Nevada; along railroad from near Donner (summit) westward below 6,500 feet, and on upper South Fork of Yuba River; Summit Meadows westward to Emigrant Gap; farther west in Devils Canyon between Colfax and Forest Hill, and from Iowa Hill eastward, southward, and southwestward to Forest Hill; along railroad between Dutch Flat and Towle Station. *Eldorado County:* Tallac; west and south sides of Lake Tahoe, into Glen Alpine Canyon, and southward beyond Grass Lake Valley; west slope Sierras (Placerville-Tahoe road), at 2,300 feet, to Echo, at 5,500 feet. *Alpine County:* Near Markleeville and westward to Silver Creek; west Carson River canyon. *Amador County:* North side Mokelumne River above Defender; Pioneer to 3 miles east of Pine Grove. *Calaveras County:* Bigtrees, Gardiners, and thence throughout yellow pine forest northward and northeastward on road to Blood's, up to 6,600 feet or more; west and southwest of Bigtrees to 4 or 5 miles east of Murphy's. *Tuolumne County:* On road from Sonora to Sonora Pass, and from Confidence eastward beyond Eureka Valley, reaching 8,000 feet on warm slopes (Big Oak Flat to Crockers); occurs from South Fork of Tuolumne River eastward to Crockers, Aspen Meadows, and Middle Fork of Tuolumne, at 6,800 feet; Hetch-Hetchy Valley; road from Crockers to Yosemite Valley, but not at highest elevations. *Mono County:* Sonora Pass (east side) below 8,100 feet; Mono Pass in lower Bloody Canyon, Walker Lake; 3 miles east of Mammoth, and west up slopes. *Mariposa County:* (Yosemite road from Raymond to Wawona) occurs above Wassama; from Yosemite to Crockers as far as Cascade Creek, at 6,000 feet, and also on Tuolumne side of divide; Yosemite Valley, especially west end, going eastward above Little Yosemite on warm slopes, to 8,200 feet; on west slope of Sunrise Ridge to 8,000 feet; above top of Yosemite Fall to 7,000 feet; then northward to Porcupine Flat and Tioga Road, and eastward to ridge west of Lake Tenaya, at 8,300 feet. *Fresno County:* Horse Corral Meadows; Kings River canyon eastward to Junction Meadow in Bubbs Creek canyon. *Tulare County:* North Fork of Kaweah River canyon at Bearpaw Meadow, Buck Creek canyon, head basin and canyon of East Fork Kaweah, Farewell Gap; Kern River canyon up to 7,700 feet, and Kern Lakes, 1,500 feet up canyon sides; South Fork of Tule River in eastern part of Tule Indian Reservation. *Kern County:* Throughout Greenhorn Mountains and head of Poso Creek above 5,000 feet, on Piute Mountain, between head of Caliente Creek and Kern Valley, summit of Mount Breckenridge, and possibly on other mountains south of South Fork of Kern River and Walker Pass; south slopes of Tehachapi Mountain below 7,000 feet, and down Antelope Canyon. In eastern part of Santa Barbara National Forest (southern cross ranges); noted on San Rafael Range; Mount Piños, at 4,900 to 8,000 feet; Pine and Frazier mountains. San Gabriel Mountains, on Strawberry Peak, Pine Flats, Prairie Forks, and San Antonio, at 5,000 to 10,000 feet. North slopes of San Bernardino Mountains, at 4,800 to 10,000 feet, occasionally down to 4,000 feet and up to 11,500 feet; occurs also between Skyland and Fredalba, westward to Sugar Pine Flat, and eastward to Baldwin Lake—possibly farther; Crafts Peak; Holcomb Valley, only on north slopes next desert, and down to Jeffrey Pine belt. San Jacinto Mountains, at 6,000 to 9,500 feet, or sometimes between 4,200 and 9,700 feet; noted in basin between Fullers Ridge and north spurs of Mount San Jacinto, on south walls of Round and Tahquitz valleys, in Strawberry Valley to near summit of Mount San Jacinto. Abundant on Palomar or Smith Mountain and Balkan Mountains; also on Cuyamaca Mountains above 5,500 feet.

Lower California.—Mount San Pedro Martir, at 8,000 to 11,000 feet.

The detailed range of white fir in the Rocky Mountain region will be described in a later bulletin.

OCCURRENCE.

A tree of moderate altitudes and generally on north slopes. Less particular as regards aspect in North than in South. In southern Oregon, less abundant and at higher levels on east than on west slopes. In northern California, best and in greatest density on north and east exposures, and on heads of streams; southern California, rather confined to north slopes away from stream beds. Thrives on almost all moderately moist soils, except heavy clays. Best on fairly deep, rich, moist loam; frequent on dry, nearly pure, coarse, disintegrated granite, and even among bowlders. Requires less air and soil moisture than other firs, though its best growth is in cool, moist situations.

Never in pure stands over large areas, but in Oregon and northern California often forms three-fourths of stand. In southern Cascades, scattered among yellow and sugar pines, Douglas fir, incense cedar, and sometimes with lodgepole pine; groups covering less than an acre of this and Douglas fir in nearly equal proportions are frequent throughout this forest. In California commonly with yellow, Jeffrey, and sugar pines, incense cedar, and less often with Douglas fir, in lower range; at higher levels with lodgepole pine, Jeffrey pine, and California red fir, usually forming a transition type between the former and last two types; stand toward upper limit of yellow and sugar pine, often of great density. A frequent associate also of the bigtree, together with sugar pine. At high levels in southern California, with sugar, Coulter, and lodgepole pines, and incense cedar.

Climatic Conditions.—Climate moderately humid with extreme temperatures of — 38° F. in Colorado and 98° F. in southern California, a precipitation of from 19 inches in Colorado to 40 inches in Oregon, an average precipitation throughout its range of about 25 inches, and heavy winter snows melting late in spring.

Tolerance.—Very tolerant throughout life. With favorable soil and moisture conditions, usually more shade enduring than any associated species, except Engelmann spruce and alpine fir. Owing to great tolerance, it has a close branching habit, and the trunks clean poorly. Young growth survives long suppression under heavy shade (with slow progress) and recovers readily when overhead light is admitted.

REPRODUCTION.—Fairly prolific seeder. Good seed years occur at irregular intervals (two to three years or more), but some seed is produced every year. Seed of only moderately high rate of germination, often under 40 per cent, and with only transient vitality. Seed production begins mainly at fairly advanced age; in dense stands polewood trees seed when leaders have reached full light. Seed production continues for many years, but is more abundant during rapid height growth than at maturity. Character of seed bed apparently of little importance, germination taking place on heavy litter and humus, as well as in mineral soil; but fairly abundant soil moisture is essential for establishing seedlings. Indifference to kind of seed bed renders it aggressive, for reproduction occurs over denuded lands as well as under its own shade.

Bristlecone Fir.

Abies venusta (Dougl.) Koch.

DISTINGUISHING CHARACTERISTICS.

Bristlecone fir, which is rare and little known, is unique in all of its characters, the most striking of which is, perhaps, its dense Indian-club-shaped crown, which very often extends to the ground, and ends in a long, exceedingly narrow, sharp point. The sharp spires and deep lustrous green foliage are so distinctive that the tree can be recognized among its associates several miles away. It is ordinarily from 60 to 100 feet high, or occasionally somewhat taller, and from 20 to 30 inches in diameter. The trunk, rarely clear of branches for more than a few feet, tapers rapidly to the slender, erect leader. All of the branches, which grow from the trunk in irregular circles, droop conspicuously, while their extremely long, whip-like side branchlets hang like tasseled cords among the branches. The bark of young trees is thin, smooth, and a leaden gray. On older trees it is comparatively thin, at most seven-eighths inch thick, and is irregularly broken by shallow vertical seams into flat plates, which are hard and firm. The bark of old trunks is light russet brown on the outside and clear red-brown within. The dense bright foliage is deep yellow-green. The long flat leaves (fig. 45), white-lined underneath, with their keen points are very characteristic. By a twist in their stems, leaves of lower branches (which are less densely leaved than upper ones) appear to grow from two opposite sides of the branches, while leaves from the middle and upper crown branches are rather densely arranged, mainly on the tops of the branches. The thinly scattered leaves of leaders (fig. 46) stand out straight, in strong contrast to the much less spreading habit of the other leaves. Leaves vary in length from about $1\frac{1}{4}$ to 2 inches. Lower branch leaves are usually longer than those from the upper crown branches. The large conspicuously pointed winter leaf buds are bright light chestnut-color, and without resin. The cones (fig. 47), which ripen late in August and break up in September, are one of the remarkably distinct features of this fir, particularly in the long needle-like points of their scale-bracts, which protrude from among the cone-scales. Cones are from $2\frac{3}{4}$ to $3\frac{1}{2}$ inches long, and have at maturity a faint purplish brown color. Seeds are deep chestnut-brown with shiny, light, purplish tinged, brown wings (fig. 47, *c*). Seed leaves, 7. Wood of this fir is heavier than that of any other of our firs. It is light yellowish brown, moderately soft, but very firm, and usually coarse-grained. It is least like any of the soft, light fir woods. There is nothing to commend it for commercial uses, for which at present it is barred on account of the exceedingly small number of trees in existence. The tree is, however, of the greatest importance in forming much needed protective cover for the scantily wooded slopes and dry canyons which it naturally inhabits. For this reason, and on account of its extreme rarity, as well as because it is the most curious fir tree in the world, it deserves every protection and encouragement.

LONGEVITY.—Very little is known now of its longevity; it is believed, however, to be only moderately long-lived. A tree 22¾ inches in diameter showed an age of 123 years. Further records are required.

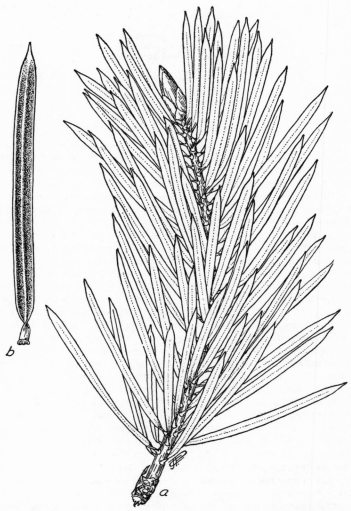

FIG. 45.—*Abies venusta: a,* lower branch; *b,* leaf twice natural size. Lower crown foliage.

RANGE.

Central California coast region; mainly in Monterey County. Scattered in patches of several or a few hundred trees in heads of canyons on both slopes of seaward part of Santa Lucia Mountains (Monterey National Forest), and at elevations of 2,200 to 5,000 feet; probably once extended higher up on slopes and possibly covered summits of range. Extends from Uncle Sam Mountain southward to Mount Mars (corresponds to Point Sur and Punta Gorda on coast) in watersheds of Sur, Carmelo, Arroyo Seco,

San Antonio, and Nacimiento rivers (T. 18 S., R. 3 E.; T. 19 S., R. 2–3 E.; southeast end of T. 21 S., R. 4 E.; north part of T. 23 S., R. 5 E.; T. 24 S., R. 5–6 E.). Locally noted in Sur Canyon above *Sequoia sempervirens;* east slope of Pine Canyon (tributary Carmelo River), and a few trees also along top of cliff on north side; upper part of Arroyo Seco Canyon above and on Willow Creek; north and east slopes near Cone Peak, at 3,500 to 4,000 feet; head of Nacimiento River, canyon north of San Miguel (tributary Nacimiento River), and in San Miguel Canyon just south of trail

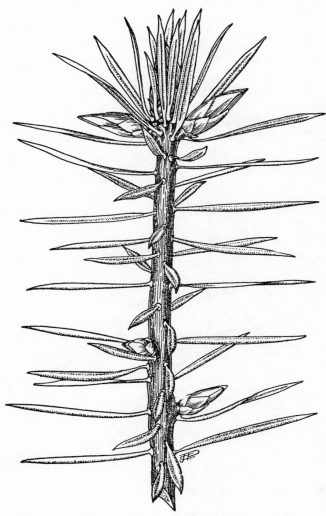

Fig. 46.—*Abies venusta,* leader.

from Kings City to Los Burros Mines; 200 trees on north slope of Bear Basin on east side of range south of Los Burros Mines and near Punta Gorda.

OCCURRENCE.

In cool, often narrow, moist canyon bottoms and their lower slopes, usually on north and west exposures; also in narrow gulches and at heads of ravines. Largest trees on west slopes, in deep ravines opening toward the sea; smaller or stunted higher up in more exposed places.   Porous, rocky, gravelly, and sandy soils; where best growth occurs, soil is moist, even in summer, from contiguous stream bed.

Probably capable of forming, under favorable conditions, pure or nearly pure stands. As now known—doubtless greatly thinned and checked by fires—only small groups and straggling lines occur, associated more or less with canyon live oak, broadleaf maple, white alder, California laurel, madroña, and somewhat less often or remotely with tanbark oak, Douglas fir, and Coulter pine.

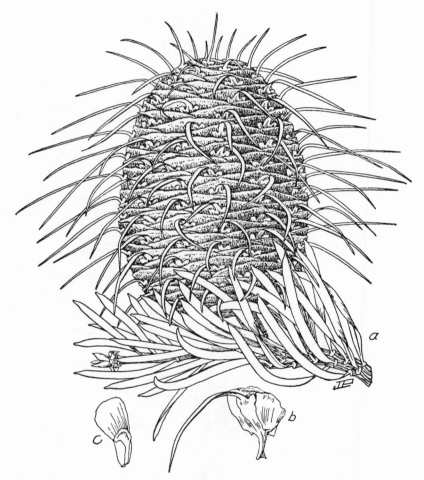

FIG. 47.—*Abies venusta:* a, cone; b, cone scale; c, seed.

CLIMATIC CONDITIONS.—Temperature in its habitat seldom goes to zero or above 100° F.   On exposed contiguous slopes, crests of ridges, where possibly this tree once grew, seasonal range of temperature is somewhat greater.   Moisture laden west winds maintain fairly high degree of atmospheric humidity during most of the year.   Annual precipitation, almost entirely rain, varies between 20 and 50 inches.   Snowfall of the region, light even at high altitudes.

TOLERANCE.—Very little is known of its shade endurance.   Appears to endure considerable shade throughout life, particularly in early growth.   Bears dense side shade, as shown by retention by old trees of vigorous lower branches in deep shade; full overhead light is doubtless required for best growth.

REPRODUCTION.—A moderately prolific seeder, but apparently cones are produced only at rather long intervals (3 to 5 or more years) ; as yet, however, little exact knowledge is available of its seeding habit and reproduction. Seed of comparatively low germination and of transient vitality. Exposed, moist, mineral soil appears to be most favorable seed bed, since most of young growth and seedlings occur on such ground. Reproduction exceedingly meager, probably, in part at least, on account of long intervals of seed production and low germination, the destruction of seed by rodents, and the falling of most of the seed in narrow canyon bottoms from which it is probably washed by flood waters.

Amabilis Fir.

Abies amabilis (Loud.) Forbes.

DISTINGUISHING CHARACTERISTICS.

Amabilis fir is known by woodsmen as " white " fir or " silver " fir, from the white, smooth bark. Woodsmen distinguished it from the grand fir (*Abies grandis*), also called white fir, as " another variety." To avoid the confusion resulting from applying the same name to two or more distinct species, it is desirable to take the name of " amabilis fir," meaning lovely or beautiful fir. The name is deserved, since the tree is one of the handsomest of its kind. A most striking characteristic is its smooth, ashy-gray, unbroken bark, conspicuously marked with large chalky-white areas. Only the old large trees (over 2 or 3 feet in diameter) are seamed at all, and then mainly at the base of the trunk. It is a straight tree, clear of branches for from 50 to 100 feet in close, dense stands. Its height in favorable situations is from 150 to 180 feet, sometimes 200 feet, and its diameter from 3 to 5 feet, or rarely 6 feet. In less favorable sites the height is from 75 to 100 feet and from 18 to 30 inches in diameter. Trees in the open, even when old, carry a wide, conical crown of dense, heavily foliaged branches down to the ground, the top of the cone being abruptly rounded. Forest-grown trees have a shorter crown of similar form. All of the branches, except the uppermost, droop strongly, those at the bottom of the crown most, and with a long curve downward and out from the trunk. The dense, deep, lustrous-green foliage is a marked feature. The leaves of lower crown branches (fig. 48) are flat and sharply grooved on the upper side, white-lined below, and usually with a notch at the end, but sometimes bluntly pointed. They are about 1¼ inches long, and, by a twist in the bases of those on the lower sides of the branches, they appear massed on the top sides. Branches of the uppermost part of the crown have shorter and stouter leaves, about three-fourths of an inch long, which are sharp-pointed and stand erect in dense masses on the tops of the sprays (fig. 49). The scattered leaves of the leader are very keenly pointed. The spherical resin-covered buds of this fir are characteristic, while twigs of the season are minutely hairy and pale yellowish brown. The dark purple cones (fig. 49), ripe in September, are about 4 to 5½ inches in length by 2¼ to 2½ inches in thickness. The bracts adhering to the backs of cone scales are rounded at their free ends, gradually narrowing into a long, thin point. The seeds (fig. 49, *a*), which fall from the trees in October, are dull yellowish brown, with shiny light brownish wings. Seed leaves bluntly pointed and three-fourths to seven-eighths of an inch long. Wood soft, light but considerably heavier than that of the white or grand firs. It is fine-grained and light yellowish brown. Rarely cut for lumber, but one of the best of the soft firs.

LONGEVITY.—Age limits undetermined. It appears to grow slowly throughout life and to be only moderately long-lived. Trees from 16 to 24 inches in diameter are from 175 to 230 years old.

Southern Alaska and coast mountains and Cascades of British Columbia, Washington, and Oregon.

FIG. 48.—*Abies amabilis*, lower branch.

ALASKA.—Extreme southeastern Alaska on sea side of Coast Range from sea level to 1,000 feet, on steep hillsides northward, on mainland, to entrance of Boca de Quadra Inlet and to Sandfly Bay, on Portland Canal.

BRITISH COLUMBIA.—Sea side of Coast Range, probably from Alaska southward, but recorded only from Queen Charlotte Islands and a point opposite north end of Vancouver Island southward, at 4,000 to 5,000 feet, on Dean or Salmon River, mountains of Fraser River Valley (below Yale) ; also in Vancouver Island, on Mount Monk, Mount Benson, and Mount Arrowsmith, and on southwest side, from sea level to about 3,000 feet.

WASHINGTON.—Both sides of Cascades, generally at 1,000 to 6,000 feet ; in Olympics, at 1,200 to 4,500 feet, and down nearly to sea level on the west side, but not in lowlands about Puget Sound. Locally noted in Olympics on headwaters of Queniult River. Washington National Forest, west section, at 500 to 6,500 feet ; east section, only along Stehekin River, Bridge, Early Winter, and Rattlesnake creeks, at 1,800 to 6,500 feet ; southern section, at 900 to 6,300 in Skykomish, Tolt, Snoqualmie, Cedar, Green, White, Yakima, and Wenache river valleys. Mount Rainier National Forest, both sides of

FIG. 49.—*Abies amabilis*, upper branch : *a*, seed.

Cascades, at 800 to 5,500 feet ; Mount Rainier, at 2,500 to 5,000 feet ; Eagle Mountain, between 5,000 and 6,000 feet ; Mount Adams.

OREGON.—Both sides of Cascades and northern coast range. In Cascades, at 2,000 to 5,400 feet and mainly on west side, but at higher elevations on east side ; southward to extreme southern headwaters of Willamette River and Old Bailey Mountain (west side of Crater Lake). North side of Mount Hood, at 3,700 feet to timber line ; southwest side, from a little below Government Camp to timber line. Coast Range southward to Saddle Mountain (25 miles south of Columbia River).

OCCURRENCE.

On well-drained, lower slopes of canyons, benches, and flats. Shows some preference generally for north exposures, but in Olympics and Cascades more abundant and at lower levels on west than on east slope. Grows in well-drained, shallow, gravelly sand to moist, sandy loam, or in porous rocky soils ; best on sandy loam ; good drainage necessary, as is also abundant, freely flowing soil moisture.

In pure, limited stands and small groups (Vancouver Island, Olympics, high levels in Cascades), but more commonly in mixture. In British Columbia, above Douglas fir with western and black hemlocks, and western white and white-bark pines ; in Washington and Oregon, at low altitudes with western hemlock, noble and lowland firs, western red cedar, and Douglas fir ; moderately high up, sparingly with lodgepole and western white pines and yellow cedar ; near upper limit, with black hemlock, alpine fir, Engelmann spruce, and white-bark pine.

CLIMATIC CONDITIONS.—Climate equable, with abundant precipitation, moderate humidity, long growing season, and small seasonal and daily variation in temperature. Annual precipitation averages about 45 inches ; 2 feet of snow, which soon disappears. Temperature rarely below zero or above 90° F.

TOLERANCE.—Moderately tolerant of shade, in this ranking close to noble and lowland firs and Engelmann spruce. Endures more shade than Douglas fir, western white pine, and western larch, but less than Pacific yew, western red cedar, yellow cedar, and western hemlock. Long suppressed young growth under dense shade eventually dies if overhead light is not admitted.

REPRODUCTION.—Prolific seeder. Some seed borne locally nearly every year, but heavy seeding occurs at rather irregular intervals of 2 to 3 years. Seed of rather low rate of germination, and vitality very transient. Considerable seed eaten by squirrels. Reproduction fairly abundant. Moist duff and moss-covered humous soil with moderate light favors best germination and growth of seedlings.

Noble Fir.

Abies nobilis Lindley.

DISTINGUISHING CHARACTERISTICS.

The woodsman's and lumberman's name for this tree is "larch," or sometimes "red fir." Why either, especially "larch," should be used it is difficult to understand. There is little, except possibly the thin foliage of this fir, to suggest likeness to any of the true larches or tamaracks, and little also about the tree to deserve the name "red fir." It is said that "larch," first applied in Oregon some twenty-five years ago, was used in order to avoid the prejudice against its admirable timber, which would have been aroused if the lumber had been offered as "fir." Perpetuation of such a misnomer is confusing, even for so good a reason. It prevents lay people from acquiring a useful and correct knowledge of the natural relationships of these important forest trees. It is hoped therefore that " larch " will be replaced by the name " noble fir," which serves to popularize the tree's technical name.

In the deep forests which this fir inhabits it is, when at its best, one of the most magnificently tall and symmetrically formed trees of its kind. The remarkably straight, evenly and only slightly tapering trunks are often clear of branches for 100 feet or more. Large trees are from 140 to 200 feet in height, or exceptionally somewhat taller, and from 30 to 60 inches in diameter ; trees 6 to 7 feet in diameter occur, but they are rare. The crown of such closely grown forest trees is an open, short, narrow, round-topped cone ; the short, stiff-looking branches stand out straight from the stem in distant whorls or groups, while the closely-leafed branchlets appear like stiff fingers against the sky. The heavy lower branches sometimes droop. Young trees 10 or 12 inches thick often bear their characteristically open, sharply conical crown down to the ground. The short branches stand out stiffly, almost straight, from the smooth grayish-brown trunks. Bark of old trees is rather thin—about 1¼ to 1¾ inches thick—and very characteristically divided by narrow seams into flat, narrow ridges. These are broken into long, irregular plates, which are soft and flake off easily, revealing a clear, dark reddish-brown beneath the ashy-brown surface. The foliage varies from a pale to a deep bluish-green, generally with a silvery tinge. The leaves, straight to curved, are plainly channeled on their upper surfaces, and arranged so that they appear to grow all in a crowded mass from the top sides of the branches (fig. 50). Those of the

FIG. 50.—*Abies nobilis*, upper cone-bearing branch.

lower branches are flat and commonly with a notch at the end, while those of the uppermost branches (fig. 50) are conspicuously 4-angled, very densely massed, and usually sharp-pointed; those of the leaders are flattish and needle pointed. Lower branch leaves are longer (about 1 inch to 1¼ inches) than the upper branch leaves, which are five-eighths to three-fourths of an inch long. The short, curved, densely massed, stiff leaves of this tree are particularly distinctive, and wholly unlike in these features those of any other Ameri-

FIG. 51.—*Abies nobilis,* slightly reduced; original 7½ inches long: *a,* seed.

can fir. Leaf buds are rounded, oblong, and resin coated. The large bract-covered cones (fig. 51) are most distinctive. None of our other firs have cones like these. They are about 4½ to 6 inches long by 2¼ to nearly 3 inches in thickness. They ripen early in September and begin to break up and fall from the trees in October. The protruding, pointed bracts, which cover the cone scales as if they were shingled, give the mature cones a light yellow-green color, which later turns to light yellow-brown. The seeds (fig. 51, *a*), dull red-brown, have shiny pale brown wings. Seed-leaves, 6 to 7, of uniform thickness through-out, with a short abrupt point.

Wood, rather heavy, being one of the three Pacific firs with the heaviest wood of any of our species. It is moderately hard, firm, of medium fine grain, very light brown, irregularly marked with reddish-brown areas, which add much to the beauty of the wood. It works easily and well, deserving much wider recognition than it now enjoys for high-grade lumber. In quality it is entirely different from and superior to any of the light, very soft fir woods. The magnificent, clean form of its trunks gives the finest of saw timber.

LONGEVITY.—Much is still to be learned concerning its longevity. From what is now known it is doubtless long-lived, probably excelling all of our other firs in this respect. Trees from 20 to 30 inches in diameter are from 290 to 365 years old. Very large trees have been observed, apparently perfectly thrifty, which would unquestionably show an age of from 600 to 700 years, if not more.

RANGE.

Coast ranges and Cascades of Washington and Oregon. Range still imperfectly known.
WASHINGTON.—Northward to Mount Baker on both sides of Cascades, Olympic, and Coast mountains. Not detected on Vancouver Island. Northern part of Washington National Forest, at about 3,000 to 5,000 feet; locally noted in Horseshoe Basin, Mount Amos, pass between Index and Montecristo. Both sides of Cascades in southern part of Washington National Forest, at 2,200 to 4,800 feet in Cedar, Green, White, Yakima, Wenache, and Entiat river watersheds. Mount Rainier National Forest, at 3,000 to 5,000 feet—sometimes down to 1,800 feet and up to 5,200 feet; abundant on Mount Rainier, at 4,000 to 5,000 feet; noted near Ashford, at 3,500 feet. Not detected on Mount Adams. North side of Olympic Mountains on Soleduc River, at about 3,000 feet, and general at higher elevations.
OREGON.—Both sides of range in Cascade National Forest (North); west side, at 1,400 to 6,000 feet; east side, southward only to latitude 45°. Locally noted on south-west side of Mount Hood at point 3 miles below Government Camp and upward, on north side at 4,500 feet; at elevations between 5,000 and 6,000 feet between North Fork of Clackamas River and Roaring Fork; this is the fir abundant on "Larch Mountain" in Clackamas watershed; Crater Lake on Wizard Island and from 4,600 feet on rim of lake to top; Browder Ridge (northernmost headwaters of McKenzie River, Lane County); north side of Siskiyous in Ashland National Forest. Reported extending southward in Coast Mountains nearly to Siskiyous.

OCCURRENCE.

Presence throughout range determined chiefly by abundant soil moisture, uniform, mild climate, and abundance of species competing with it. On gentle mountain slopes (of any aspect), depressions, benches, low ridges, and rolling plateaus. Vertical range increases from north to south and from coast eastward within a more or less fixed zone of heat and moisture. Latitude of range more restricted on east side of Cascades than on west, owing to lack of moisture and a severer climate. Thrives on moist, thin, rocky soils in cool situations, but best on deep, rich soils. Not so fastidious regarding quality of soil if abundant moisture is present.
Very rarely in pure stands of even small extent; usually with Douglas fir, western hemlock, western white pine, or less commonly with yellow cedar, amabilis and alpine firs, lodgepole pine, and black hemlock. With Douglas fir and western white pine, often growing over western hemlock, western red cedar, and other tolerant species.
CLIMATIC CONDITIONS.—Not fully determined. In general, climate of range is mild, and mainly without extreme daily or seasonal temperatures. Precipitation, heavy; considerable snow, which does not remain late.
TOLERANCE.—Rather intolerant of shade for a fir, particularly in middle and late life, when rapid height growth forces crown above slower species and maintains it in full light.
REPRODUCTION.—Moderately prolific seeder. Some seed borne locally nearly every year, but good seed years occur at rather long, infrequent intervals. Trees from 50 to 60

years old often bear cones, but seed is produced mainly by older and mature trees.   Seed production appears to increase with age and to be maintained to great age.   Seed of low germination (40 to 50 per cent), and of very transient vitality ;   much of it destroyed by an insect and eaten by squirrels.   Seed germinates freely and seedlings grow well on any moist humus or mineral soil in the open or in moderate shade ;   seedlings do not thrive in shade of mother trees.   Openings made near seed trees are readily restocked.

Red Fir.

Abies magnifica Murray.

DISTINGUISHING CHARACTERISTICS.

The common name of red fir is appropriately chosen in reference to the deep red-brown bark which it almost invariably has throughout its range.   It is a stately tree when fully grown, commonly from 125 to 175 feet high, very exceptionally 200 feet or more, and from 30 to 50 inches in diameter ; trees from 60 to 80 inches in diameter are rather rare.   Much larger trees are said to have been found, but the writer has never seen them.   At high elevations, much exposed to heavy winds, it is very often from 40 to 80 feet high and from 20 to 30 inches in diameter, or smaller.   In close stands the straight, slightly tapering trunks are clear of branches for 60 or 80 feet or more.   On high exposed slopes, smaller trees are often conspicuously bent down the slope at their base, as a result of heavy snows which yearly bend the seedlings to the ground.   Their struggle to become upright with each year's growth never wholly rids them of the mark of early vicissitudes.   The crown of old forest grown trees is a short, very narrow, round-topped cone, sometimes almost cylindrical.   The short branches droop except at the top of the crown, where they trend upward.   It has an open head, due to the distances between the regular whorls of branches.   Only in the densest stands are medium-sized trees clear of branches for half or more of their length.   In the high, fairly dense slope forests many trees bear straggling branches nearly to the ground.   Here, too, the brittle tops are often broken off by wind, when the lost member is replaced by the upward growth of one or two side branches, which soon assume the form and place of leaders.   Broken and repaired crowns of this type are familiar sights on wind-swept slopes inhabited by this fir.   Young trees (30 to 50 years old and as many feet high) have narrow, cylindrical, sharp-pointed crowns, touching the ground. All of the regular groups of branches, except the topmost, sweep down and upward at their ends in graceful curves, presenting a form which is unsurpassed in beauty and symmetry by any other of our conifers.   The bark, smooth and conspicuously chalky white on young trees and on the upper stem and branches of old trees, is from 2 to 3 inches thick on large trees ; its hard, rough, deep furrows and narrow, rounded ridges are very ·distinctive.   The latter are irregularly divided by diagonal furrows, which give a peculiar diagonal and vertical or zig-zag trend to the ridges.   No other tree in the habitat of this fir has bark in any way similar.

The dense foliage is dark blue-green, with a whitish tinge ; new leaves of the season are much lighter green and conspicuously whitened.   The leaves are 4-angled with nearly equal sides, the angle on the upper sides of the leaves being rounded.   Leaves of the lower branches (fig. 52) are flatter than those from other parts of the crown.   They are bent from the lower side of the branches so that they appear to grow from the top of the branch, mainly in two dense upright lines ; all are more or less curved.   Lower leaves, from three-fourths inch to about 1¼ inches long, are blunt and wider at their ends than at their bases.   Leaves of the upper crown branches (fig. 53), five-eighths inch to about 1⅛ inches long, are most strongly 4-sided, stouter than those below, conspicuously curved and very densely crowded toward and on the top of the branches; they are more or less distinctly pointed, those of the leader somewhat sharply so, and incurved to the stem. The leaf buds are sharp-pointed and light choco-late brown—not resinous. The cones (fig. 53) are mature by the middle or

FIG. 52.—*Abies magnifica,* lower branch.

end of August, and during September they break up and liberate the seeds. At maturity they are deep purple, often tinged with brown, varying in length usually from about 5 to 7 inches, or occasionally 8 to 9 inches long, by about $2\frac{3}{4}$ to $3\frac{1}{2}$ inches in diameter. The large-winged seeds (fig. 53, *a*) are dark brown, with shiny, purplish rose-colored wings. Seed-leaves are 9 to 13, usually 12, about five-eighths of an inch long and bluntly pointed. Wood, one of the three heavy fir woods, is about a pound heavier per cubic foot (dry) than that of

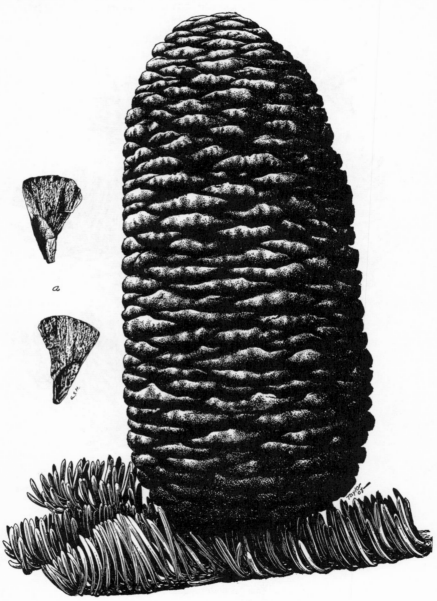

FIG. 53.—*Abies magnifica: a,* seed.

noble fir. It is soft but firm, rather brittle, straight, and usually fine-grained. Considerably more durable in an unprotected state than wood of any of the other native firs. It is yellowish brown, with a reddish tinge. The commercial value of this wood, in its better grades, is yet to be determined. Firmness and good working qualities must render it useful for a number of the purposes to which pine is put, while its clean trunks would yield saw timber of the best form.

LONGEVITY.—It appears to be rather long-lived, but much fuller investigations are required to establish age limits. Trees from 20 to 36 inches in diameter are from 225 to 370 years old. Very large trees would certainly show much greater ages. The differences to be brought out in the longevity of this fir as it grows on high exposed slopes and as it exists in heavier forests of lower and more protected locations are likely to be most interesting and profitable contributions.

The so-called Shasta red fir (*Abies magnifica shastensis* Lemmon, fig. 54) is a form of the ordinary red fir discovered and described in 1890 [a] by Prof. J. G. Lemmon. In every way, except in the form and protrusion of its cone-scale bracts, and in the usually shorter full form of the cones, this tree is identical in appearance with the type species. Moreover, the habits of the two trees are the same; in fact, may be standing side by side. The exact range and occurrence of this tree has not been fully worked out. Following its first detection on Mount Shasta, California, it was found on the coast and cross ranges of northern California, and also on the Cascade Mountains, Oregon. Later it was observed by the writer on the divides of Kaweah River watersheds and elsewhere, far south of Shasta, in the southern Sierras. The distinction of these trees, possibly so far as is now known only by the cones, is of no importance from the forester's standpoint.

RANGE.

High mountain slopes and ridges from southern Oregon and northern California southward over west side of Sierras.

OREGON.—Southern Cascades northward to mountain south of Davis Lake (lat. 43° 35′); west slope, at 5,200 to 8,800 feet; east slope (here extending 2 to 6 miles down from summit), at 6,000 to 8,800 feet. On Umpqua-Rogue River Divide and Siskiyous from Siskiyou Peak westward, but absent from coast ranges, Klamath Gap, and ridges of upper Klamath River Basin.

CALIFORNIA.—Northern part and southward in coast ranges to Lake County; also throughout Sierras, and chiefly on west side. In northern part of State eastward to mountains north of Mount Shasta between Shasta Valley and Butte Creek; here it occurs on Mount Pomeroy, at 7,000 to 7,500 feet, on summit of Goosenest Mountain, ridge east of Butte Creek, Glass Mountain, at point 14 miles south of Tule Lake at 6,700 to 7,500 feet, and probably into Modoc County. Mount Shasta National Forest, generally at 5,000 to 8,000 feet. Locally noted on Scott Mountains; Mount Eddy; Mount Shasta, at 5,500 to 7,500 feet—sometimes to 8,900 feet. Westward in Siskiyou County to Marble Mountain ridge (west of Scott Valley), where it occurs on east slope at 5,000 to 5,700 feet on Salmon Summit west of North Fork of Salmon, Trinity Summit on boundary between Siskiyou and Humboldt counties—here on west side above 4,800 feet. Klamath National Forest, above 6,000 feet. Highest summits in Trinity National Forest, between 5,000 and 8,000 feet; sometimes down to 4,000 feet, and common on Canyon Creek near lakes and on higher parts of Yola Buli Ridge. Throughout Stony Creek National Forest (Coast Range) on Sanhedrin range southward to Pine Mountain, at about 5,000 to 7,000 feet; abundant on St. Johns, Iron, and Hull mountains and headwaters of Grindstone Creek, Black Buttes, and Snow Mountain, at 7,000 feet. Lassen Peak, Plumas, and Diamond Mountain National forests have scattered bodies above 6,000 feet; south side of Lassen's Peak, above 5,500 feet. Northern Sierras, commonly on west slope at 4,800 to 7,000 feet; eastward to Grizzly Mountains and on east slope to Smithneck Creek and Sardine Valley. Locally noted in Plumas County at Bucks Valley; Grizzly Mountains and southward to Penman Peak; Spanish Creek Ridge; South side Frenchman's Hill and westward to Walker Plain. Sierra County, Yuba Pass and eastward down to 5,800 feet (west of Sierra Valley) to Sardine Valley and Smithneck Can-

---

[a] It is suspected that this tree was distinguished by Carrière as early as 1867, but it is impossible to be sure now that his description refers to this tree.

yon, and westward to Bassett Road House at 5,200 feet; Crystal Peak (east of Truckee River). *Nevada and Placer counties:* Both sides of Sierra range in Donner Lake region from Donner Lake (east slope) to Cisco (west slope); Mount Pluto, south of Truckee River; shores of Lake Tahoe down to 6,200 feet; high areas west of Summit City and westward nearly to Snow Point, and southward on divide between South and Middle forks of Yuba River to North Fork of American River, following divide between North

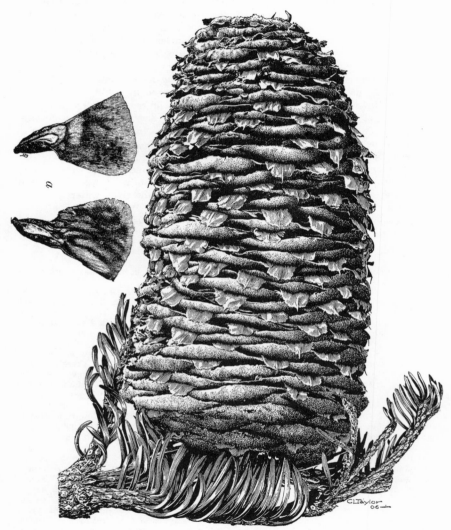

FIG. 54.—*Abies magnifica shastensis: a,* seed.

and middle forks of American River nearly to Red Point. Reported in Washoe Mountains near Reno, Nev. *Eldorado County:* From Tallac southward to Grass Lake Valley, chiefly above 7,000 feet, and from summit (7,500 feet, southwest of Tallac) down 10 miles to Echo (5,500 feet). Central Sierras (Stanislaus National Forest), at 6,000 to 8,500 feet. Calaveras County, North Fork of Stanislaus River to west of Bloods. *Tuolumne County:* From between Cold Spring and Eureka Valley, at

6,200 feet, eastward to summit; Tuolumne Meadows, up to 9,000 feet; Lambert Dome; White Mountain; Mount Conness; near Lookout Knob; ridge between Dingley and Delaney creeks; near Lake Tenaya and Cathedral Lakes; Tioga Road from 6,800 feet (in Long Gulch, 3 miles east of Aspen Meadows) to Tuolumne County. Southern Sierras southward to headwaters of Kings, Kaweah, Tule, and North Fork of Kern rivers. *Mariposa County:* North and northeast of Yosemite Valley, at 9,000 feet and up; Cathedral Lakes and southward nearly to Little Yosemite; north rim of Yosemite Valley (near top of Yosemite Falls) down to 7,000 feet, and thence northward to Tioga Road which it follows eastward from Porcupine Flat (8,100 feet) to ridges west of Lake Tenaya tributaries; Belknap Mountain (head of East and Middle Tule rivers); Freeman Creek (tributary of Kern River); head of East Fork of Middle Fork of Tule River; throughout divide between lower Kern River and Deer Creek and White River (affluents of Tulare Lake) above 6,000 feet, reaching southern limits at about Fish Creek (tributary South Fork Kern River), latitude 36° 10', and head of Poso Creek (tributary Tulare Lake and in sec. 11 to 14, T. 26 S., R. 31 E., lat. 35° 40').

The range of *Abies magnifica shastensis* is imperfectly known. At present this tree is known to inhabit the range given for the species from Mount Shasta northward, while it occurs with the species in Scott Mountains, on Mount Eddy, and in Trinity and Stony Creek National forests. South of this it is found at several points in Fresno, Tulare, and Kern counties. Locally noted in this region by the writer at Alta Meadow (near southeastern border of Sequoia National Park). Further careful observations of fruiting trees are expected to yield a wider and more connected occurrence of this form.

OCCURRENCE.[a]

Tree of high elevations, often well up to timber line. Lower, protected, gentle mountain slopes about meadows, to steep, exposed, windswept ones near high divides and crests; also in cool, sheltered ravines, gulches, and high rolling mountain plateaus. Prefers north and east exposures to drier and warmer south exposures; in such regions confined mostly to available moist, cool sites. Usually, and of largest size, on moist, porous, sandy or gravelly loam soils; but grows in very rocky, poor situations with little soil; poverty of soil and moisture produces small or stunted trees.

In large pure and nearly pure stands below timber line and above white fir belt; often in pure small stands at timber line. At upper limit, generally with black hemlock, lodgepole pine, and western white pine. In northern California and southern Oregon, with yellow pine, sugar pine, and Douglas fir at lower levels; in Sierras at lower limit, commonly with white fir, which it replaces often abruptly at white fir's upper limit. Toward upper limit, where it mingles with western white pine, lodgepole pine, and black hemlock, the latter grows mainly in gulches and ravines, lodgepole pine on borders of meadows, lakes, and moraines, and western white pine (generally scattered), while interspersed among all are frequent groups and small areas of dense pure, or nearly pure, stands of this fir.

CLIMATIC CONDITIONS.—Climate of region with comparatively short, intensive growing season, and long cold period of rest and precipitation. Average annual precipitation, about 30 to 50 inches; considerable snow, which in some parts of Sierras is over 20 feet deep and covers ground from November to June. In many parts of its range snowfall is much less, or melts before becoming very deep. Winter temperature, rarely falls to zero; summer temperature, not excessive (probably not over 80° F.) during day, with cool and generally humid nights. Frost liable to occur at any time during growing season at higher levels in range; usually, however, not until late in August.

TOLERANCE.—Only very moderately tolerant of shade at any period; much less tolerant than white fir, incense cedar, and Douglas fir; very similar to noble fir in light requirement. Rarely to any extent in intermediate or subordinate positions; nearly always in stands of equal age, which favor overhead light. Endures but little side shade, as shown by long, clean trunks universal in close stands and common in rather open stands. Tolerance appears to vary with soil, moisture, and climatic conditions; more tolerant under best conditions for growth.

REPRODUCTION.—Prolific seeder; good seed years occur about every two or three years, while some seed is borne in many localities every year. Seed production usually greatest in open stands, and by moderately old trees. Seed of fairly high germination, but of only transient vitality. Germination abundant on moist mineral soil in open or in light shade; less frequent or wanting on drier, thick duff. Seedlings grow rapidly in cool, moist, sandy soil, soon restocking high slopes and openings cleared by fire or storm.

---

[a] Includes *Abies magnifica shastensis.*

SEQUOIA. REDWOODS.

The trees composing the Sequoia group are of ancient origin. Remains of at least two sequoias, from which our species descended, have been found in the Cretaceous and Tertiary periods, during which time they lived in the Arctic Zone. Our representatives of the genus are now singularly isolated and are found almost entirely in the coast mountains and Sierras of California, far from their nearest relative on this continent—the bald cypress (*Taxodium distichum*) of the Southern States. They are the tallest and most massive of our forest trees. Indeed, one of them is easily the largest conifer in the world, widely and justly honored as the most remarkable of trees. Unlike many of our other cone-bearers, their distinguishing features remain unvarying.

On account of the restricted range of the Sierra species especially, much concern has been expressed regarding the probable extinction of these trees. Great and seemingly needless destruction has been wrought by fire and ax in these forests of incomparable grandeur. While it would be a calamity to permit the total destruction for commercial purposes of trees which number their age by thousands of years, fear need not be felt that these trees are in danger of actual extermination for want of natural reproduction. With protection against fires they perpetuate themselves indefinitely, notwithstanding the popular belief that at least the Sierra sequoia is not reproducing itself. Some of these magnificent forests should be preserved untouched as monuments of American respect and love for nature's noblest legacy. The scientific and educational value of preserving them is unquestioned. The destruction, for whatever end, of all of the great trees which it has taken thousands of years to produce could never be justified in later years.

Sequoias are evergreen trees. The leaves are narrow and lance-shaped, pointed, and arranged alternately opposite and spreading in two lines from opposite sides of the branches (fig. 57), or they are scale-like, sharp-pointed, and closely overlapping each other on the branches (fig. 56). Leaves of this type are longer, the points spreading on young shoots (fig. 55) and young trees, forming sprays somewhat similar to those of cedars. The leaves of each season's growth remain on the branches for three or four years. Flowers of two sexes, male and female, are borne each on different branches of the same tree. Both are minute or small, rather inconspicuous, scaly bodies at the ends of branchlets formed the previous year, and opening very late in winter or in early spring. The cones are egg-shaped bodies composed of closely packed, woody, persistent, thick scales, and are from about an inch to 3½ inches long (figs. 56, 57). They ripen in one and two seasons, remaining on the trees after opening (late in autumn) and shedding their seeds. Five to seven seeds, minute, brown, stiff, wing-margined flat bodies, are borne closely packed beneath each scale. The seeds can not be wafted more than a short distance by the wind. Squirrels cut down and bury thousands of the seed-laden cones, from which, under favorable conditions of light—an opening in the forest—many seedlings spring up. Seed-leaves, 4 to 6. The bark of old trees is enormously thick, red-brown, soft, and separable in very thin flakes.

The purplish, red-brown wood of the sequoias is light, very soft, straight-grained, and, except that formed during the first one or two centuries, fine-grained, often exceedingly so. It is remarkably durable under all kinds of exposure, lasting for very many years without apparent sign of decay. Its great durability and straight grain and the ease with which it can be split and otherwise worked have long made it desirable for many commercial purposes. Its huge, long, clear trunks yield saw-timber so large that it often requires to be split into quarter or half logs before it can be milled. Felling one of these monster trees requires several days' labor of two or three expert men, and when the tree goes down its weight is so enormous that not infrequently it is so completely demolished that not a foot of saw-timber is available. This is true mainly of the Sierra sequoia, the wood of which, in very old trees, is somewhat more brittle than that of the coast sequoia.

The longevity of these trees is still unsettled. Claims are made that the Sierra species attains an age of from 4,000 to 5,000 years. Many of the largest trees have been wholly or partly destroyed, making it difficult to obtain convincing records. It is safe to assert, however, that some of the largest trees are at least 4,000 years old, while most of the average large trees now standing, like many that have been cut, are about 2,000 to 2,500 years old. Their height is from 275 to 350 feet, or in very rare instances calculated to be nearly 400 feet, with diameters of from 10 to 18 feet, or unusually of from 25 to 27 feet.

Two distinct species are known. One is confined practically to the coast mountains and the other to the Sierras of California. The coast species extends a few miles into Oregon.

Bigtree.

Sequoia washingtoniana (Winsl.) Sudworth.

DISTINGUISHING CHARACTERISTICS.

What the technical name of this sequoia should be is still a matter of disagreement among authors. *Sequoia wellingtonia* Seeman (1855) was revived in 1896 by an eminent American tree botanist and again perpetuated in 1905. Ten years ago [a] the writer proposed an older name, *S. washingtoniana* (Winsl., 1854), later discussing fully the basis of his decision.[b] The argument given then has not since been overthrown, nor does it seem likely to be, if the evidence brought then is justly weighed. The unsupported assertion has, however, been made that Dr. C. F. Winslow's *Taxodium washingtonianum*, upon which *Sequoia washingtoniana* is based, was not technically published. But a careful examination of Doctor Winslow's statement (loc. cit.) should certainly be convincing, fortunately, that *Sequoia wellingtonia* is not entitled to stand for this grandest of all American forest trees.

Barring actual specific differences which abundantly distinguish the bigtree from the redwood, it seems in general appearance to be only a more massive and grander edition of the latter species. Its huge trunk, greatly buttressed at the base and very deeply and widely furrowed, bears much the same, but lighter, cinnamon-red bark. Much larger ridges and deeper furrows mark these trunks than do those of the redwood. The bark is excessively thick at the base of old trunks, often from 12 to 18 inches or more. It is soft, almost spongy, and composed of fine fibers, which are constantly breaking away through various agencies—weather, wind, and, not the least, the incessant climbing of red squirrels. Except where it has been consumed by fire, the accumulation of ages of this wearing may be seen about the trunks, where it has fallen in the form of masses of fine red-brown bark. Outer, unbroken, filmy scales of the bark are a purplish or leaden gray. Young trees from 10 to 20 inches in diameter, probably through the protection of their limbs, retain this outer film of bark and are therefore of a much grayer tone, which is the color also of the smooth, unbroken bark of still younger trees. The bark of the branches of old trees is the same color and exceedingly thin.

---

[a] See Bulletin 14, Div. For., U. S. Dept. Agr., 61, 1897.
[b] See Bulletin 17, Div. For., U. S. Dept. Agr., 28, 1898.

DIMENSIONS.—The height and diameter of these trees is popularly much over-estimated. Ordinary large trees are about 250 or 280 feet high, while exceptionally large ones are from 300 to 330 feet, with diameters of from 12 to 17 feet, or occasionally 20 to 27 feet through, measured 8 to 10 feet above the greatly swelled bases. Doubtless, exaggeration of actual dimensions is due to inaccurately measuring some of the largest trees so as to include the immense basal buttresses, which are properly no part of the trunk's thickness.

In youth the conspicuously conical trunks are densely clothed to the ground with short, slender branches which curve and point upward sharply, forming a broad, sharp-pointed pyramid. In this form it is extremely handsome and graceful. It usually retains its long crown for from 200 to 300 years, except in very crowded stands; afterwards the lower limbs gradually thin out and become drooping, with a gréater weight of dense foliage, as do also the middle crown branches; only the uppermost ones trending upward. Later, and toward maturity, the great trunks are clear of branches, except for a straggling branch here and there, for from 80 to 125 feet or more. The crown has then lost all semblance to its youthful form, and is a short, narrow, round-topped dome, irregular in outline and somewhat open. The once straight leader has died and lost its top, or the side branches have overtaken it and together round off the crown. All of the branches have become enormously large, crooked, and bent, some drooping and others horizontal, and all bearing dense masses of deep blue-green foliage. The leaves (fig. 56), sharp pointed, longer, and more spreading at their points on stouter main stems (fig. 55), overlap each other, covering the slender, drooping sprays. The smaller twigs have shorter leaves, and the larger have longer leaves. Longer, more spreading, but similarly arranged, keenly pointed leaves are borne by seedlings from one to several years old. The cones (fig. 56) are matured by the end of the second summer, when they are dark bluish to olive green. They open slowly during early autumn, the thick stiff cone scales parting only little, but sufficiently to liberate the thin, pale brown, winged seed (fig. 56, a). About 4 to 6 seeds are borne under each cone scale. Purplish grains of rosin-like substance fall from among the dried-out cone scales, and impart a deep purple to water, as do also the cones themselves. This substance contains 70 per cent of tannin, and is in this and other respects the same as that frequently found exuded in hard masses in the burned hollows of the trunks of these trees. Upon drying, after which most of the cones fall, the cones are dull yellowish-brown, the inner portions of the scales, red-brown. The minute narrowly winged seeds are not borne far from the parent tree. Thousands of ripe cones are cut down, just before they open, by indefatigable little pine squirrels. These are buried for winter food, many at the base of the parent. When fire and storm or the ax lay the parent low, some of these seeds spring up and replace it. Seed leaves, 5, five-eighths inch long, slender, and pointed; scattered, shorter but similar, leaves succeed these, topped the following year by sharp scale-like leaves one-fourth of an inch long. Succeeding growth has the longer sharp form of adult leaves.

Wood of the bigtree is brilliant rose-purple red when first cut, later becoming more and more dull purplish red-brown. It is very light (redwood is much heavier), brittle, variable in grain from coarse (the growth of the first 400 or 500 years or more) to very fine-grained (the later growth). It contains, as does the bark, a large amount of tannin, which doubtless has much to do with its remarkable durability in an unprotected state. Prostrate trunks lie for centuries on the ground with no sign of decay, except in the perishable sapwood. The wood is widely useful for commercial purposes, passing in the market as " redwood; " though lighter and more brittle than the coast redwood, it is said to be not less valuable for lumber. As already stated (p. 139), so small a percentage of saw timber is actually obtained (25 to 30 per cent) in lumbering this tree that it seems wantonly wasteful to lumber it.

FIG. 55.—*Sequoia washingtoniana.*

LONGEVITY.—Estimates and ring counts have placed the age of this tree at from 4,000 to 5,000 years. It is doubtful whether the largest of the trees now standing are over 4,000 years, while very many trees from 12 to 18 feet in diameter show ages from 1,800 to 2,500 years, or in rare cases nearly 3,000. Further studies of the longevity of this tree are required. There are abundant opportunities in the heavily lumbered southern forests.

RANGE.

CENTRAL CALIFORNIA.—Scattered areas on west side of Sierras from southern Placer

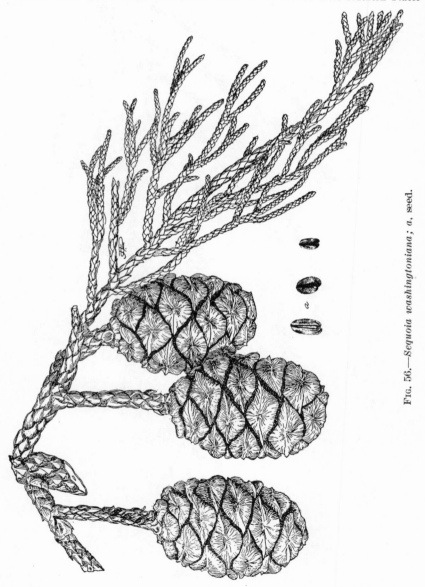

FIG. 56.—*Sequoia washingtoniana*; *a*, seed.

County to Tulare County; generally at elevations of from 5,000 to 8,500 feet; area covering, about 50 square miles. The principal groves and forests are as follows; but straggling trees often connect larger areas, especially those south of Kings River or Converse Basin forest.

(1) *North Grove:* Near southern boundary of Placer County on tributary of Middle Fork of American River and Forest Hill Divide, about 10 miles east of (town) Michigan Bluff and just inside of Tahoe National Forest; 6 trees, at 5,100 feet; private ownership (?).

(2) *Calaveras Grove:* First discovered (1854) in Calaveras County, on divide at head of Moran and San Antonio creeks, just north of North Fork of Stanislaus River and west of Stanislaus National Forest, at Big Trees post-office; elevation, about 4,600 feet; 50 acres, with about 102 trees; private ownership.

(3) *South Calaveras or Stanislaus Grove:* Tuolumne County, 6 miles southeast of last grove and southeast of North Fork of Stanislaus River on divide between Beaver Creek (north) and Griswold Creek (south—both tributaries North Fork of Stanislaus River), at about 5,000 feet; about 1,000 acres, and about 1,380 trees; private ownership.

(4) *Tuolumne or Crane Flat Grove:* Near south boundary of Tuolumne County in Yosemite National Park and 1½ miles northwest of Crane Flat Station on Yosemite trail from Coulterville, between Tuolumne and Merced rivers; about 40 trees; also single tree southwest between this grove and Merced River—exact location unknown.

(5) *Merced Grove:* Headwaters of Merced River near north line of Mariposa County and a few miles southwest of Tuolumne Grove; less than 100 trees; private ownership (?).

(6) *Mariposa Grove:* Mariposa County, between Big Creek and South Fork of Merced River (Yosemite National Park), 16 miles directly south of Lower Hotel in Yosemite Valley, and in two bodies at 5,400 to 7,000 feet; northeastern one, with 365 trees, and southwestern one, with about 180 trees, one of which is the celebrated " Grizzly Giant ;" Government ownership.

(7) *Fresno Grove:* Near north line of Madera County at head of Redwood Creek (branch Fresno River, in secs. 17 and 18, T. 6 S., R. 22 E.), about 14 miles southeast of Clarks ; 2 miles long by 1 to 2 wide, originally with about 2,000 (?) trees, many of which have been cut; private ownership.

(8) *Dinky Grove:* Fresno County, on branch of Dinky Creek (tributary North Fork Kings River, sec. 35, T. 10 S.,R. 26 E.), at 6,800 to 7,300 feet; 50 acres with about 170 trees; in Sierra National Forest.

(9) *Converse Basin Forest:* Originally one of largest south of Kings River; between latter stream and Mill Creek (T. 13 S., R. 27 and 28 E.), 6 miles north of Millwood; about 10 square miles; private ownership and almost entirely lumbered.

(10) *General Grant Grove:* In General Grant National Park; about 262 trees, and originally part of Converse Basin forest, partly Government and partly private ownership.

(11) *Redwood Mountain Forest:* A few mile south of General Grant grove on Redwood Creek (branch North Fork of Kaweah River), covering about 6 square miles, containing several thousands of trees and in parts constituting pure dense stands : considerable part lumbered; private ownership; a little-known forest.

Sequoia National Park contains following four groves, and one large forest.

(12) *Dorst Creek Groves* (northmost ones in Park), comprising two small groves on Dorst Creek (tributary North Fork Kaweah River, in northwest part of T. 15 S., R. 29 E.), with about 766 trees; Government ownership.

(13) *Swanee River Grove:* Small patch on Swanee River (branch Marble Fork Kaweah River), in southeast part of same township; contains about 191 trees; Government ownership.

(14) *Giant Forest:* On Marble Fork of Kaweah River near its mouth (T. 15 and 16 S., R. 30 E.) ; covers about 10 square miles, at 6,500 to 8,000 feet, and contains about 5,000 trees ; the largest continuous forest intact of this species; its largest tree is " General Sherman ;" Government and private ownership.

(15) *Redwood Meadow Groves:* Two separate patches about 5 miles east of Giant Forest, on Middle Fork of Kaweah River just outside of Sequoia National Park boundary and near Granite and Cliff creeks (branches of latter river) ; larger grove covers about 50 acres around and below Redwood Meadow, with about 200 trees; smaller grove, one-fourth mile below Meadow, covers a few acres with about 80 trees; a single tree also stands 1 mile north of Meadow. Private ownership.

(16) *East Fork Forests:* Two separate bodies on both sides of East Fork of Kaweah River at Redwood Creek, 3 miles west of Mineral King; northern one 3 miles long and half a mile wide, at 6,500 to 8,000 feet; large part lumbered; southern grove one-half mile wide by about one-half mile long; Government and private ownership.

(17) *A number of small groves,* a few miles west of latter forests, are on tributaries of East Fork and main Kaweah River ; they bear names of streams on which they stand and comprise groves on Squirrel Creek, Mule Creek, Squirrel and Lake creeks, Salt Creek, and in Coffee Pot Canyon (just west of Sequoia National Park) ; private ownership.

(18) *South Fork Forest:* On south Fork of Kaweah River just within west border of Sequoia National Park (in T. 18 S., R. 30 E.) and covers about one-fourth of a square mile.

(19) *North Tule River Forest:* Covers entire basin of this stream from second west-side tributary canyon to uppermost east-side one (in north part of T. 19 S., R. 30 E.), comprising about 6 square miles with north edge just within Sequoia National Park; elevation, 5,400 to 8,000 feet; large part lumbered and privately owned.

(20) *Middle Tule River Forest:* One mile south of North Tule Forest on east head basin of Bear Creek, extending over high divide, also between this basin and Middle Tule River Canyon, and over east slope of latter stream (in T. 19 and 20 S., R. 30 and 31 E.); covers an area of about 6 miles long by 5 miles wide, at 6,000 to 8,000 feet; large part lumbered; a part of this forest, but separated from it, is the Silver Creek Grove of 200 to 250 trees, on south slope of Silver Creek (tributary Middle Tule River); private ownership.

(21) *Alder Creek Forest:* One-half mile southeast of Middle Tule Forest, on Alder Creek (tributary Middle Tule River), 3 miles long by about one-half to 1 mile wide, extending from head of Ross Creek northward along summit of divide between Hassie Creek and Middle Tule Canyon to head of (south) Alder Creek, down slope to within about one half to 1 mile of Middle Tule River; elevation, 5,700 to 7,000 feet; private ownership.

(22) *East Tule Forest:* About 2 miles wide by 3 miles long, covering head basin of East Fork of Tule River (at junction between T. 20 and 21 S., R. 31 and 32 E.), at 5,550 to 7,500 feet elevation; main body begins 2 miles above Nelson's ranch, but scattered trees occur along canyon bottom to within three-fourths mile of latter ranch; also detached grove of 250 to 300 trees to southwest on divide between Bear and Marble creeks; private ownership.

(23) *Freeman Creek Forest:* On head basin of Freeman Creek (tributary East Fork of Tule River) about 3 miles long by one-half mile wide, separated by narrow divide from East Tule Forest; private ownership.

(24) *South Tule Forest:* Composed of two parts; one, in East Tule watershed, is connected with one in South Tule basin for about 1½ miles on divide and also at heads of Coy and Slate creeks; East Tule part extends from head of Coy Creek westward to Deadmans Creek; the largest area, to west of Coy and Slate creeks, is about 3½ miles long, and extends from top of divide down between East and South Tule and northward down north slope of East Tule for about 1 mile; general elevation, 6,000 to 7,600 feet; South Tule part extends from northeast corner of Tule River Indian Reservation northeastward 4 or 5 miles, with a width of 2 to 2½ miles; elevation, 5,600 to 7,500 feet; private ownership.

(25) *Dry Meadow Grove.*—Small patch east of Tule Indian Reservation, on head of Dry Meadow Creek (tributary Kern River, approximately in S. 20, T. 22 S., R. 31 E.). Government ownership.

(26) *Deer Creek Grove.*—About 30 large trees at head of South Fork of Deer Creek (tributary White River), few miles east of Deer River Hot Springs (S. 2, T. 24 S., R. 31 E.).

OCCURRENCE.

Between larger north groves there are breaks of from 40 to 60 miles. From the Kings River forest southward, groups are less widely separated; a broad belt, broken only by deep canyons, extends for 70 miles to its southern limit in the Tule River basins. Gaps between north groves correspond with glacier beds which flowed from main high crest of Sierras during the glacial epoch. Existing growth is on higher lands from which ice melted long before it did in the intervening canyons. Prefers slopes, low ridges, depressions, and draws near or on headwaters of streams, where soil moisture is present. Indifferent to exposure, growing on slopes of every aspect. Prefers conditions of dense forest, occurring only rarely and of much smaller size in exposed situations. Depth and quality of soil and abundant moisture are most favorable to best growth. Usually in deep, porous, sandy, or gravelly soils moistened by contiguous streams or slope run-off; also grows well on moist, rocky, shallow soils, but less commonly on dry gravelly or rocky soils. With moisture, the condition of soil apparently has little or no effect on growth.

Occasionally in pure stands, but usually in mixture. Mostly with sugar pine and white fir (with Douglas fir at north); western yellow pine is often mingled on drier borders of these forests and groves, as it is also at lower elevations, where also incense cedar is a very common associate. From a pure stand, big trees may form the principal part of the forest (as in larger areas), or they may (as in smaller groves) make up only a small percentage of stands. At higher levels white fir is often the only associate.

CLIMATIC CONDITIONS.—The habitat of bigtree is cooler and drier than that of red-wood. At Summit, situated some distance north of its range, at an elevation of 7,000 feet, the temperature occasionally falls to —12° F. and never exceeds 100°. Throughout its range the precipitation varies with increase in altitude and for dry and wet years from about 18 to over 60 inches. At high altitudes the snowfall is often very heavy. At Summit, an annual snowfall of nearly 700 inches, equivalent to 70 inches of rain, has been reported. The winters are long but mild, and the flowering and pollination of bigtree take place as early as February or March, although spring does not commence until considerably later. The climate varies little with latitude, because as bigtree extends southward it grows at increasingly higher elevations.

TOLERANCE.—Tolerant of but little shade at any stage; for vigorous growth, abundant overhead light required from the start. Endures more shade during early youth than in old age, when crowns are always in full light. Under dense shade young plants grow very slowly, and have sparse foilage, flat crowns, and a gnarly habit, showing need of light. Such trees, however, often survive for a number of years, recovering slowly with light. General absence of reproduction in all but openings in forest and in open ground adjacent to seed trees shows clearly that light is a most important factor in early life. Endures considerable side shade; close stands of trees, 20 to 30 years old, often retaining branches to ground, while in full light they are kept many more years.

REPRODUCTION.—An abundant seeder at short intervals, with specially heavy seed years; some seed usually borne annually in parts of range. Seed of moderately high rate germination, with persistent vitality. Open-grown trees may bear seed sparingly when 18 or 20 years old. Seed production in forest, much later; mainly when from 150 to 200 years old. Seeds are scattered in late fall and early winter. Lightness of seed permits restocking of open ground for several hundred yards from mother trees. Germination mainly and best on exposed mineral soil; seedlings rare or wanting on heavy litter, which they can not penetrate. Reproduction generally best on burned areas, where fire has cleared off litter, and exposed mineral soil, or even after light ground fire has left a layer of ashes or charcoal. Heavy stocking, which occurs only under such conditions, often amounts to 2,500 seedlings per square rod. Dense snowbrush common on burns does not prevent growth of bigtree seedlings. Usually seeded before the brush comes in, seedlings grow slowly through it. Thrifty sapling stands are frequent over this brush. Seedlings grow rapidly in clearings, under full light, sometimes reaching 6 feet in as many years, the greater part of which is attained during the third and fourth years. Such open-grown seedlings begin to branch vigorously from the first year, and assume the characteristic pointed form of rapid growth.

Redwood.

Sequoia sempervirens (Lamb.) Endlicher.

DISTINGUISHING CHARACTERISTICS.

The dark cinnamon-brown, grayish tinged trunks of redwoods are more or less buttressed at their bases and, as a result, are often marked with corresponding rounded ridges and broad hollows. The trunk is full and round higher up, and has a gradual taper throughout. Average large trees are from 190 to 280, sometimes 300, feet high, and from 8 to 12 feet or occasionally 12 or 15 feet in diameter. Exceptionally large trees are 325 or 350 feet high and 18 or 20 feet in diameter at a height of from 8 to 12 feet above the greatly swelled base. Old trunks are clear of branches for 50 or 60 feet in open stands and for 80 or 100 or more feet in dense forests. The crowns of young trees from 10 to 15 inches in diameter are narrowly conical, and extend nearly or quite to the ground. The slender, short lower crown branches droop with a downward curve, while above the middle the branches gradually trend more and more upward. On larger trees in close stands the lower limbs are shaded out, leaving a very short, round-topped or sometimes a flat-topped crown. The few branches on such trees, now long and thick, stand out rigidly from the trunk, drooping slightly—at the top not at all—forming a very open head. Bark of old trunks is from 8 to 10 or even 12 inches thick at the base of the trees, and it is very deeply and widely furrowed and ridged. The leaves (fig. 57) are flat, sharp-pointed, stiff, of unequal lengths (one-third inch to about 1 inch) on the same twig. On side twigs of lower branches and on young saplings the leaves stand out in two lines on opposite sides of the twigs, while on the main stem of these branches they vary in length down to short scale-like forms and occur in several lines, sometimes closely pressed to the branch. A conspicuous feature of these leaves is their habit of clinging to the branches for one or two years after they are dead, when they are pale dull brown. These leaves occur irregularly on branches, though they are most common on the top branches of mature trees, particularly in exposed sites. The foliage is a bright, deep yellow-green ; that of each season's growth remains on the tree about three or four years. Cones (fig. 57), which mature in one year, are ripe early in September. They open and shed their seed slowly, and remain on the trees several months afterwards. The seeds (fig. 57, *b*), about 4 or 5 of which are borne under each cone scale, are pale russet-brown. Seed leaves, usually 5 ; very slender, pointed, and about seven-eighths of an inch long. Seedlings produce similar scattered spreading leaves for several years before assuming the adult foliage. Wood (about the weight of white pine), several pounds heavier per cubic foot than that of the bigtree. It is very soft, moderately fine-grained, but variable from fine to coarse, exceedingly brittle, and a purplish, clear red-brown in color. It is of the first commercial importance on account of its great durability without protection, the ease with which it is worked, and the large sizes of clear lumber obtainable.

LONGEVITY.—Very long-lived, but greatest age undetermined. On account of the extensive lumbering in the past, followed by fire, age records of very large trees have not been obtained. Probably not as long-lived as the bigtree. A tree 20 feet in diameter and 350 feet high showed an age of 1,000 years. Another tree 21 feet in diameter was 1,373 [a] years old.

RANGE.

From southwestern corner of Oregon southward, from 10 to 30 miles inland, through California coast region to Salmon Creek Canyon (12 miles south of Punta Gorda) in Monterey County. Generally from near sea-level to about 2,500 feet elevation, and mainly on seaward side of coast mountains within the fog belt.

OREGON.—Three groves in southern Curry County ; two, aggregating 2,000 acres, on northwestern side of Chetco River, 6 and 12 miles from its mouth, a third grove, farther south, on Winchuck River only a few miles from sea and very near California line.

CALIFORNIA.—Northmost large forest is on Smith River (Del Norte County) and its tributary Rowdy Creek, from which a nearly unbroken belt extends southward. Klamath National Forest only on Goose Creek (T. 14 N., R. 2 E.). At north end of Del Norte County belt is only 5 to 6 miles wide, between which and the sea there is a belt 3 miles wide, mainly of Sitka spruce and Douglas fir. But south of Crescent City, redwood comes within a mile of coast and the belt widens to 6 or 7 miles, continuing thus to Klamath River Valley, up which it goes for 20 miles ; immediately south of this valley the belt becomes 10 to 12 miles wide and so continues until reaching Humboldt Bay, where it narrows to a width of about 7 miles, extending east to 3 miles east of Korbel, and recedes from the coast 2 or 3 miles. Southward from Humboldt Bay it continues receding from coast, until, at Eel River, the belt, here about 15 miles wide, is 15 miles or more from the sea. In southern Humboldt County (T. 3 S., R. 3 E., Humboldt meridian) the belt ends in a tapering point about 7 miles southwest of Eel River. For about 15 miles redwood is absent, but at north boundary of Mendocino County the belt begins again, close to sea, and continues about 8 miles wide to a point opposite Westport, where it extends eastward 10 miles from that town, and at a point 15 miles north of Mendocino widens to about 20 miles, reaching inland to Deep Creek (opposite Willits) on east slope of coast mountains. It continues thus, with gaps on the divide, until Sonoma County is reached, here contracting to 10 or 12 miles in width, on Russian River extending east to Forestville, and, much broken, finally ceases about opposite Santa Rosa. Through Marin County redwood appears only in groves and in ravines, but extends eastward to Napa Valley and over Howell Mountain (toward Pope Valley), here reaching its most eastern limit, more than 30 miles from the sea. In Mount Diablo range, only on

---

[a] See Forest Service Bull. 38, p. 12.

FIG. 57.—*Sequoia sempervirens: a*, branch with open cones; *b*, seed.

Redwood Peak in Oakland Hills; but south of San Francisco, on seaward coast range, covers crest and west slope, mixed with Douglas fir and other trees, extending southward through Santa Cruz Mountains. Ceases for a few miles around Monterey Bay, but in Santa Lucia Mountains (Monterey County) occurs in canyons chiefly on seaward side of range at altitudes from sea-level to 3,000 feet (the largest trees growing in Little Sur River Basin, near Pico Blanco), extending south to Salmon Creek Canyon (12 miles south of Punta Gorda, lat. 35° 50′), the southern limit.

OCCURRENCE.

Best stands and all pure stands on protected flats and benches along larger streams, sheltered, moist coastal plains, river deltas, moderate west slopes and valleys opening toward sea. At higher, more exposed levels, where it is drier, and on steeper slopes growth is smaller and gradually gives way in mixture to less exacting species. In north, often on east slopes, but in south restricted to west side of coast range. Very exacting in requirements as to soil moisture; prefers deep to shallow soils, and grows better in fresh, well-drained soils than in wet ones. Sandstone prevails in range, and soil is clayey to sandy (greasy when wet), yellowish, and capable of holding much water. Sandy to clayey loam soil, even on steep slopes, usually of fair depth and of good composition. Boggy soils near mouths of streams are not suitable, such localities being mainly given over to an irregular forest of Sitka spruce, grand fir, Port Orford cedar, and hardwoods.

Relatively small part (less than 50 square miles) of redwood forest is pure growth. This is dense, and with little undergrowth except moss and small herbaceous plants. Greater part (about 1,800 square miles) a mixture of redwood (50 to 75 per cent), Douglas fir (most abundant associate everywhere except on damp places), tanbark oak, grand fir, western red cedar, western hemlock, and madroña; Douglas fir and tanbark oak characteristic on upper slopes and hemlock on lower. Steep slope and uneven height of different species make this an open forest, and except where fires are frequent there is a dense undergrowth of huckleberry, salal, Oregon grape, thimbleberry, and ferns.[a] On rich river flats scattered Sitka spruce, Port Orford cedar, western hemlock, and grand fir are occasionally mingled. Pacific yew, California torreya, California laurel, cascara buckthorn, red alder, knobcone pine, and Gowen cypress are also more or less associated, but hold only occasional sites against the climatically more favored redwood.

CLIMATIC CONDITIONS.—Closely confined to humid region subject to frequent and heavy sea fogs; trees outside this influence are scattered and small. Fogs conserve moisture in soil and in trees by checking evaporation and transpiration from trees. In the redwood forest, therefore, soil and air are typically moist. Temperature, rarely below 15° or above 100°; annual average from 50° to 60° F. Annual precipitation, between 20 and 60 inches, mainly as winter rains. Snow lies on tops only of highest ridges.

TOLERANCE.—Moderately tolerant of shade except in early youth; even then shade is not required, most rapid growth being in full light. Has marked characteristics of intolerant trees; a thin open crown, rapid loss of side branches, and the eager bending of crowns toward openings in crown cover; seedlings not able to come up in shaded places. Yet, despite this, forms the densest of forests. Stump sprouts often exist under the densest shade for one hundred years, growing very slowly in diameter during this time, but recovering completely and growing rapidly when released from suppression. This tolerance of sprouts is, however, peculiar to trees on moist bottoms, which endure so much shade that other species are usually driven out. On drier hills, with more light, redwood generally gives way to the less tolerant Douglas fir and other drought-enduring trees.

REPRODUCTION.—Fairly prolific seeder. Very small percentage (15 to 25 per cent) of seed perfect; hence exceedingly low rate of germination; vitality moderately persistent. Sparsely reproduced by seed, but very abundantly by sprouts from old or young stumps, root collar, and (suckers) roots.[b] Sprouts grow very rapidly, are long-lived, and produce large trees of good form. Seedlings grow more slowly than sprouts and require more light.

---

[a] Redwood forests yield 10,000 to 75,000 board feet per acre, or very exceptionally 400,000 feet, while over a million feet have been cut per acre.

[b] Redwood is about the only conifer whose reproduction by sprouts is of commercial importance. The Sierra bigtree sprouts vigorously from tall broken stubs (not from stumps or roots) and thus repairs its broken crown. A number of pines produce ephemeral stump sprouts, while some of the junipers produce persistent collar sprouts after cutting and fire.

LIBOCEDRUS.

Trees of this group are characterized by their conical trunks, their thick bark, and the very strong but pleasant odor of their light, soft, straight-grained, durable wood. The small scale-like, pointed leaves (of adults) are evergreen; those of each season's growth remain on the tree four or five years. They overlap each other closely; much flattened on short side branchlets, but rounded on the larger main stems. The branchlets are arranged in one plane, forming a flat spray. Seedling leaves are scale-like, sharp-pointed, and spreading. All of the leaves are characteristically arranged in pairs, each pair placed on the branch at right angles to the preceding pair. The leaves are also distinguished by their long bases, which extend down the branch. Male and female flowers at the end of branchlets formed the preceding year are borne either on different twigs of the same branch (native *Libocedrus*) or on different trees. The small cones, which mature in one season and hang down from the branches, are composed of 3 pairs of scales (practically of only 2)—one very short pair and one, the largest pair, forming most of the cone's body and inclosing 1 or 2 winged seeds on each of its scales; the third pair is formed into a central flat, thick, woody wall, upon each face of which the seed-bearing scales clasp. The seeds are shed in early autumn, their light wings adapting them well for wide dissemination. After shedding their seeds the cones remain on the trees at least until the succeeding summer. All of the trees of this group are rather large, important forest trees, and their durable woods are commercially valuable. They are nearly all long-lived. One species only, confined to our Pacific region, inhabits the United States. Two very important species grow in western South America. The group is further interesting from the fact that in geologic times species related to those now living existed in Greenland and portions of Europe.

Incense Cedar.

Libocedrus decurrens Torrey.

DISTINGUISHING CHARACTERISTICS.

The striking characteristics of old incense cedar trees are their rapidly tapering trunks with widely buttressed bases and cinnamon-brown, deeply furrowed, and ridged bark. The bark is from 2 to 3 or more inches thick at the base of the trunks; higher up it is scarcely more than an inch thick. Young trees have thin, smooth, slightly scaly, clear, reddish cinnamon colored bark. Height, from 75 to 90 or sometimes 100 or 110 feet (very rarely more), and from 30 to 50 inches in diameter; exceptionally large trees are from 5 to 6 feet in diameter. The crowns of large trees are very open and irregular, consisting of a few scattered branches on the upper third of the stem, and several large, leader-like top branches, all with dense tufts of light yellow-green foliage. Young trees, up to about 12 inches in diameter, carry a narrow, open, columnar, pointed crown, reaching to the ground. At the bottom of the crown the branches are slender and curve down and up at their ends; higher up they gradually swing upward more and more toward the narrow pointed top. Short, flat, drooping sprays of foliage terminate the branches. A notable feature of the branches is that they shed numerous short side twigs, which die in about their second year, as the main divisions of the branch enlarge. (This is the case also with other cedars, particularly Thujas.) The scale-like leaves (fig. 58) have been sufficiently defined under the characteristics of the genus, as have also the cones (fig. 58). The flowers, male and female, are borne on the ends of separate twigs of the same branch and open in midwinter. The cones are ripe by the middle of August and usually shed their seeds (fig. 58, *c*), which are yellowish-brown, early in September. When dry and open the cones are

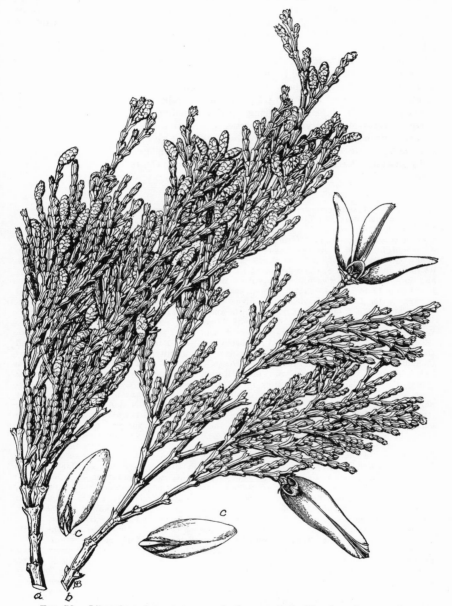

FIG. 58.—*Libocedrus decurrens: a,* male flowers; *b,* fruiting branch; *c,* seed.

reddish-brown. Most of them fall during the winter, but some always adhere to the branches until spring. The seeds, furnished with large, light wings, which adapt them admirably for wide distribution by the wind, contain glands with clear red, pungently odorous resin. Seed leaves, 2; sharp-pointed, and about 1¼ inches long and almost one-eighth of an inch wide. Wood, fine and very straight grained, pale or dull yellow brown, sometimes tinged with red. It is soft, light (about the weight of white pine), and very durable under all kinds of exposure. Its durability renders it extremely valuable for use in the water or in the ground. Large trunks, and to a much less degree small or medium sized ones also, are often riddled as if by the galleries of an insect. These injuries are supposed to result from the attacks of several little-known fungi. They do not impair the durability of the wood, however, and trunks not excessively perforated are frequently used for telephone poles, especially within the range of the tree, where it is the only lasting wood obtainable.

LONGEVITY.—Much is yet to be learned concerning the age limits of this tree. So far as is now known it is a long-lived tree, but records of very large trunks have not been made. Trees from 24 to 36 inches in diameter are from 360 to 546 years old. Larger trees would probably be from 650 to 700 years old or even older.

RANGE.

Mountains of southern Oregon, Sierras and coast ranges of California, western edge of Nevada, and northern Lower California.

OREGON.—Both sides of Cascades, Umpqua-Rogue River Divide, Siskiyous, possibly also in coast ranges, and eastward over ranges of Upper Klamath Basin to west slope of mountains east of Goose Lake; on west side of Cascades, generally at 2,500 to 5,000 feet, and on east side, at 5,000 to 6,600 feet. Northern occurrence interrupted, its limit on west side of Cascades being at head of Breitenbush River (T. 9 S., R. 7 E.), and on east side, the foothills southeast of Mount Hood near Gate Creek (T. 4 and 5 S., R. 10 and 11 E., lat. 45° 15'). Noted near Fort Klamath, sparingly thence northward toward Crater Lake, here common at about 4,600 feet; on Warm Springs Indian Reservation and about 5 miles west of Wapinitia and westward to near Camas Prairie.

CALIFORNIA.—Throughout northern part from west border of fog belt eastward to Warner Mountains and southward, nearly continuously, to Lassen Peak and Delta (Sacramento River); not present in upper Pitt River Basin, Shasta Valley, Scott and Hoopa river valleys, nor summits of Salmon and Trinity mountains. *Modoc County:* Common in Warner Mountains east of Goose Lake, and less plentiful west of Goose Lake; western Modoc County, on Turret Mountain, descending northwestward to near Happy Camp; Glass and Big Valley mountains (west of Big Valley in extreme southwest corner of county). *Siskiyou County:* Goosenest Mountain (north of Mount Shasta); north of Shasta Valley in Shovel Creek Mountains and near Beswick (or Klamath Hot Springs); also in mountains a few miles west of Hornbrook, ranging thence northward over Siskiyous, and westward and southwestward over Scott Mountains, from north part of which it descends east slope to within 5 miles of Yreka; throughout Mount Shasta up to 5,500 feet, and westward across Sisson Valley to Mount Eddy and Scott Mountains and southward into Shasta County; west of Scott Valley in Mill Creek Gulch on road from Etna Mills to Marble Mountain Divide; west side of Marble Mountain Divide in Russian Creek Basin; east slope of Salmon Summit up to about 4,000 feet, and sparingly in basin between Salmon and Trinity summits on hot slopes up to 5,500 feet. *Humboldt County:* Common on west slope of Trinity Summit ridge east of Hoopa Valley between 4,000 and 5,000 feet; west of Hoopa Valley, scattered in Supply Creek Canyon, west of which it has not been found and probably does not occur; farther south occurs along east edge of coast forest between Bridgeville and the Little Van Dusen. *Mendocino County:* Common on west slope of high ridge east of Round Valley about 20 miles east of Covelo, at 3,600 to 6,000 feet, and sparingly about Laytonville. *Trinity County:* From Weaverville southward nearly to Trinity River, and in Hayfork Mountains south of Trinity; southeast of Hayfork Post-Office on both sides of boundary between Trinity and Shasta counties; Canyon Creek from near Dedrick northward about 10 miles to near Alpine lakes; from Junction southward to Hayfork and to Post creeks and South Fork of Trinity River; South Fork Mountain and westward into Upper Mad River Valley (near and a little below Anada Post-Office); also on Upper Van Dusen River. *Glenn and Lake counties:* Throughout Stony Creek National Forest at 3,500 to 5,000 feet—sometimes down to 2,000 feet; noted on Cobb Mountain and Mount St. Helena, ranging thence to edge of Middletown Valley (alt. about 1,200 feet—southern limit in north coast ranges). *Shasta County:* Eastward to Fall River region, where it occurs near Dana and in Big Valley Mountains between Fall River Valley and Big Valley, thence southward to north slopes of Lassen Peak; south of Pitt River, westward to Montgomery; Sacramento River Canyon southward to near Gregory, and on McCloud River to near Baird. Throughout west side of Sierras, at 3,500 to 6,000 feet in northern part, but to 7,500 feet on Long Valley drainage, and at 3,500 to 7,000 feet in southern part of Sierras; reaches east side at 7,000 feet only on Washoe Mountains near Carson, Nev. Lassen Peak, Plumas, and Diamond Mountains National Forests, generally at 2,000 to 6,500 feet. *Lassen County:* Northwestern corner in Big Valley Mountains, beginning 5 or 6 miles west of Bieber; east of Big Valley on Willow Creek about 10 miles south of Adin, and thence to Hayden Hill; westward from a little west of Susanville into north Plumas County and southeastern Shasta County. *Plumas County:* Nearly throughout north part · common from Susanville westward by Mountain Meadows, Big Meadows, Drakes Hot Springs, and Morgan, and about Greenville and Indian valleys; Sierra Valley to Quincy and westward into Butte and Tehama counties. *Tehama County:* From east boundary westward down to about 3,400 feet altitude a little east of Lyonsville, and a few miles farther north stops about 10 miles east of Paine Creek Post-Office; western Tehama County, west of Paskenta at 3,700 feet, and thence westward. *Butte County:* From east boundary westward to Magalia, and farther south (Quincy-Oroville road) to within 4 or 5 miles of Bidwell Bar. *Yuba County:* Common in Oregon Hills, and down west side to ridge between Oregon Hills and Oregon House Flat, which appears to be its western limit; from Oregon Hills eastward on North Fork of Yuba River and adjacent slopes to Camptonville and on into Sierra County. *Sierra County:* Common in Woodruff Canyon north of Mountain House, and (on North Fork Yuba) to and beyond Downieville and Sierra City, thence up Yuba Pass road to about 6,000 feet; slope of Yuba Pass just east of summit, and down to near west border of Sierra Valley; south of Sierra Valley, from Sierraville southward nearly to Nevada County. *Nevada and Placer counties:* West slope of Sierras from Cisco to Emigrant Gap and Blue Canyon (in both counties), down to Colfax and to Bear River and to near Grass Valley; south of Colfax, on cold slopes of North Fork American River, and from Iowa Hill eastward to Forks House; Forest Hill and Devils Canyon (between Forest Hill and Colfax); south of Colfax a few trees as low as Weimer. Stanislaus National Forest, generally at 2,000 to 7,000 feet, but mostly at 3,500 to 5,500 feet. *Eldorado County:* Common at south end of Lake Tahoe; gulches near Placerville eastward on colder slopes; canyon of South Fork Webber Creek between Newtown and Pleasant Valley; south of Pleasant Valley, in canyon of North Fork Cosumnes River; common on road from Placerville to Lake Tahoe from about 2,300 feet up to Echo at 5,500 feet. Alpine County, noted near Hot Springs (about 4 miles west of Markleeville). *Amador County:* Noted about Oleta (about 1,800 feet) and southeastward to Deadmans Creek, Dry Creek, and Sutter Creek canyons near Volcano; common from Pine Grove eastward to and beyond Pioneer; continues southwestward from Pine Grove on ridge on south side of Middle Fork of Jackson Creek to within 4 miles of Jackson, where it stops at about 1,500 feet. *Calaveras County:* Common about West Point and northward to main canyon of Mokelumne River; southwest of West Point, on road to Mokelumne Hill, in canyon of South Fork Mokelumne River, and at point 2 miles east of Rich Gold; southeast of West Point, in canyons of Middle and South Forks of Mokelumne River and at Railroad Flat, thence to Mountain Ranch (Eldorado); west of latter, follows San Andreas road to about 1,500 feet, where it stops 6 miles east of this town; Mokelumne Pass road in extreme eastern part of county about 10 miles below Bloods at about 6,600 feet, and westward to and beyond Bigtrees, here abundant among sequoias and sugar pines. From here (on road) southwestward to within a few miles of Murphy. *Tuolumne County:* Sonora Pass road between Tuolumne and Soulsbyville, at Black Oak station west of Tuolumne, and eastward and northeastward past Cold Spring and Eureka valleys, reaching 8,000 feet on west side of Sonora Pass; north slope of ridge immediately north of Big Oak Flat, and on cool slopes in higher parts of Deer Creek canyon; on road from Big Oak Flat to Crockers from crossing of South Fork of Tuolumne River to Crockers; common from Crockers eastward and northward to Hetch Hetchy Valley, here abundant in upper part; follows Tioga road to Aspen Meadow (about 6,200 feet); common from Crockers southward for several miles on Yosemite road. *Mariposa County:* Yosemite Valley and up above Little Yosemite to about 7,000 feet; north side of valley near Yosemite Falls, about 1,500 feet above valley; on west follows road to Crockers to a little above 5,800 feet; south side of Yosemite Valley common on road to Wawona, and from Chinquapin on slope toward Glacier Point to about 7,100 feet; from Wawona on Raymond stage road down to 3,000 or 3,100 feet, to within 3 or 4 miles of Wassama (Ahwahnee); Coulterville-Yosemite road, begins on summit of plateau 4 or 5 miles east of Coulterville, at 3,000 to 3,200 feet, and goes eastward in pine forest to beyond Bower Cave and Bull Creek and into Yosemite Valley; Chowchilla Canyon and neighboring gulches down to

3,000 feet, and on cool slopes to 2,500 feet. *Madera County:* East of Fresno Flat on road to China Creek, beyond Fresno Flat, headwaters of Fresno Creek near California Sawmill at 5,500 feet. *Fresno County:* Pine Ridge and eastward into mountains; southward on Pine Ridge occurs on upper waters of Sycamore and Big creeks; eastward in bottom of Kings River Canyon into Bubbs Creek canyon; south of Kings River between Mill Creek and Eshom valleys, and east of latter on Redwood Mountain at about 7,000 feet. *Tulare County:* Sequoia National Park and east of park on warm slopes into Buck Canyon and canyon of Middle Fork Kaweah River to 7,500 feet; Kern River Canyon, in vicinity of Kern Lakes; East Fork of Kaweah River to about 7,200 feet. Southern Sierras, generally at 3,000 to 7,000 feet southward to Greenhorn and Piute mountains; not in Breckenridge nor Tehachapi ranges, except near mouth of Tejon Canyon. Not known in coast ranges of central California. *Monterey County:* Santa Lucia Mountains on north slopes; on north side of Santa Lucia Peak near summit; west of this, in Arroyo Seco Canyon about a mile above its mouth; north slopes of Cone Peak at 3,500 to 4,000 feet; also farther north on Big Pine Ridge on north slope of Bear Basin. *San Benito County:* Mount San Carlos (4,980 feet near New Idria) and neighboring peaks; Santa Barbara National Forest, San Rafael Mountains, Mount Medulce, and from near summit of Pine Mountain to Piru Creek, at 5,000 to 7,200 feet, or lower. San Gabriel National Forest, on north slopes of Mount Wilson, at 5,200 to 5,800 feet, and in Santa Anita Canyon, at 3,300 feet; Mount Islip, at 5,500 feet; Waterman Mountain, at 6,500 feet, and at point 6 miles east of Pasadena, at 4,000 feet. Highest valleys and summits of San Bernardino Mountains, as Bear Valley and Santa Ana River, at 5,000 to 7,000 feet, or sometimes to 9,500 feet. High summits of San Jacinto Mountains and at 3,000 to 8,000 feet in larger valleys and along streams. Santa Ana Mountains in Orange County. Ranges between San Jacinto Mountains and Mexican line, such as Palomar, Balkan, and Cuyamaca mountains, where noted on Cuyamaca Peak at 6,550 feet, and on Mexican boundary at Campbell's Ranch at 5,000 feet.

LOWER CALIFORNIA.—Southward on Hanson Laguna Range and Mount San Pedro Martir, at 7,500 feet and over.

OCCURRENCE.

In general, commoner on west than on east mountain slopes; but somewhat higher on east slopes, chiefly because of more moisture. Most abundant and largest on west slope of Sierras, especially where sugar pine, bigtrees, and yellow pine thrive best. As latitude increases it appears to seek lower elevations. In drier parts of range (southern California) confined chiefly to borders of streams, canyons, gulches, and cool north slopes, while at north limit it occurs mainly on warm south slopes. Adapted to a variety of soils, but usually prefers cool, moist soils (humid situations), occurring in rather dry soils (warm, open exposures) probably only because it is capable of enduring them. With deficient soil moisture, fairly deep, porous soils are essential, while with sufficient moisture the quantity and quality of soil is less important. Abundant moisture and good porous soil produce largest growth.

Seldom or never occurs pure, except in very small stands. Usually in mixture and more or less subordinate, scattered singly, in groups, or patches, and, under best conditions for growth, forming 50 per cent of stand, with yellow and sugar pine; also with white fir in lower part of latter's vertical range. In southern California, chiefly with western yellow and Jeffrey pines, and sparingly with white fir and big cone spruce, and along streams at lower elevations (at south) with red and white alder, broadleaf maple, and black cottonwood. In Oregon Cascades, with yellow pine, Douglas fir, white fir, western white pine, and sugar pine. In Sierras, with sugar pine, western yellow pine, Jeffrey pine, white fir, and bigtrees; at lower levels with Kellogg oak, red alder, broadleaf maple, and canyon live oak.

CLIMATIC CONDITIONS.—Climate variable. Insufficient precipitation and excessive heat (southern California) most unfavorable; conditions more favorable in Cascades and Sierras. Precipitation, snow in winter at high elevations, and at lower elevations rain. Average annual precipitation from less than 15 to over 50 inches. Relative humidity, variable. Fogs (chiefly from ocean) common, especially on west slope of Sierras; their influence on general climate and tree growth is considerable. Height of the dry season includes July, August, and September, with October in south, when destructive forest fires are likely to occur.

TOLERANCE.—Moderately tolerant, enduring more shade than sugar pine, yellow pine, Jeffrey pine, Douglas fir, or western white pine, and in mature stands usually intermediate or subordinate on account of slower growth and greater tolerance; often dominant in open stands and openings, or as an advance growth, at lower timber line, pushing into oak and brush. Adapted to both shade and full light. Tolerance varies with age, moisture, soil, and climate; tolerates shade well in youth, but requires more light in later life.

Endures most shade with favorable moisture, soil, and climatic conditions. Growth and size is checked ordinarily in proportion to intensity of shade endured.

REPRODUCTION.—Prolific seeder under favorable conditions, every 2 to 3 years or more; some seed borne locally every year. Bulk of seed from thrifty, mature trees in full sunlight. In exposed places, even small scrubby trees bear seed. Seed has fairly high rate of germination, and persistent vitality. Moist vegetable mold best seed-bed, but germination and growth of seedlings good on moist mineral soil. Partial shade favorable to early seedling stages. Reproduction good under old trees and in open, but especially good in openings and under thinned stands, where the dense thickets frequently exclude other more valuable trees. In cool, moist places, however, white fir often enters such thickets and predominates. Frequently the first of conifers in chaparral and oak growth at lower edge of timber belt, proving its great adaptation to different degrees of light, moisture, and soil, and its general hardihood in seedling stages.

THUJA. ARBORVITÆS.

The arborvitæs are commonly known as cedars. They are medium to very large sized evergreen trees. The foliage consists of minute, overlapping, scale-like leaves, arranged as in Libocedrus, and conspicuously flat, on short side branchlets, and the branchlets are arranged in one plane, forming a flat spray. Seedling leaves are narrowly lance-shaped and sharp-pointed, and spread widely from the stem. The very light wood has an exceedingly characteristic aromatic odor. Male and female flowers are borne on the same tree, usually on different twigs. They are minute and inconspicuous, especially the female flowers. As a rule, they open in early spring. The small solitary cones (figs. 59 and 60) mature in one season, shedding their minute, very narrowly winged seeds in early autumn. The cones, strongly bent back upon the branchlets, are light russet-brown, and composed of about 8 thin scales, arranged in pairs, each pair alternating at right angles with the preceding one, as in the arrangement of the leaves. The two or three middle pairs, which are larger than the others, bear 2 seeds under each scale. The thin, gauzy seed-wings (on two sides of the seed, and always lighter colored than the body of the seeds) are very buoyant, so that they may be carried by the wind for a considerable distance from the parent trees. Minute resin-cells in the seed-coats give the seed a strong aromatic odor.

Wood exceedingly valuable for timber. Particularly famed for its durability under all kinds of exposure, and especially useful in ground and water construction where great strength is not required.

Two species are indigenous to the United States and Canada. One, a small or medium-sized tree, inhabits the northeastern States and adjacent Canadian Provinces, while the other, a very large tree, grows in the northwestern States, where it extends far northward in the coast region.

Western Red Cedar; Red Cedar.

Thuja plicata Don.

DISTINGUISHING CHARACTERISTICS.

The lumbermen's and woodsmen's name for this tree is " red cedar," or simply " cedar." The former name, while fairly applicable to the dull, slightly reddish brown wood, is unfortunate in view of the fact that two or three widely known eastern junipers with really red wood are most persistently called " red cedar," and probably always will be, for they were known nearly a century before this western cedar was discovered.

The most prominent characteristic of western red cedar is its decidedly conical trunk form. Very old trees are enormously " swell-butted " and are conspicuously in-folded or fluted at the base and for from 10 to 20 feet above it.

Where the ridges are formed growth appears to be made at the expense of the intervening wood, and the fluted trunk is the result. This character is less pronounced on smaller trees. Height, from 150 to 175 feet, or very exceptionally 190 or 200 feet, with a diameter of from 3½ to 8 feet, or, in very old trees, rarely 10 or even 16 feet. The enormous girth of such trees is at the base; their diameter decreases rapidly, so that at 20 feet from the ground they may be no more than 9 or 10 feet in diameter. From 50 to 100 feet of clear trunk is common. Young trees are straight, with an open, narrow, conical crown reaching almost to the ground and tapering to a sharp top; the slender whip-like leader often nods in a graceful curve. Except when densely crowded, trees retain all their branches until they are 18 or 20 inches in diameter and from 50 to 80 feet high; in the open they become much older without losing their lower branches. On young trees the slender limbs all curve upward, but later they become very long, the lower ones drooping and those higher swinging down in a long, graceful curve, with an upward sweep at the ends. The flat, lace-like, yellow-green side sprays hang from the branches like lines of fringe. Old trees in dense stands have only a short, blunt, or round-topped, conical head. A notable feature in this tree is the frequent occurrence of two leaders which combine in forming a dense crown. The bark, even on old trunks, is thin, from five-eighths to seven-eighths of an inch thick, and owing to this the tree is in great danger from fire, from which it rarely escapes without fatal injury. In color the bark is a clear, reddish, cinnamon-brown, often weathered outwardly to a grayish brown. It is distinctly but shallowly seamed, with narrow ridges which in old trunks are rounded and on younger trees flat. The ridges run irregularly and continuously, with rare breaks, but are connected at short intervals by thinner diagonal ridges and fibers. The bark has a more or less stringy, fibrous appearance, and may be separated into long, thin strips on younger trees, and into shorter scales on old trunks. The inner bark is very tough and strong. Indians peel strips of it 20 or 30 feet long from young trees for basket making.

Densely crowded large trees are clear of branches for from 40 to 80 feet, but they often have scattered branches below the crown. The boles are fairly straight, but large trees are frequently bowed or slightly bent, and are rarely full and round.

The small scale-like leaves (figs. 59, 60), sufficiently characterized under the genus, remain on the tree about 3 years. As the main stems of a branch grow, its short, flat, side branchlets die and fall during their second year, in this habit resembling the similar sprays of Libocedrus. The leathery brown cones (fig. 60) mature by the end of August, and have about 6 seed-bearing scales, each of which bears from 2 to 3 seeds. After shedding their light double-winged seeds (fig. 60, b), the cones remain on the trees until the following spring or summer. Seed-leaves, 2; opposite, lance-shaped, and exceedingly small—about one-fourth of an inch long. Those which afterwards grow, 2 to 3 at short intervals, on the slender seedling are similar, but longer, widely spread, and bent downward. Short, scaly leaves similar in arrangement to those on adult stems, but longer and sharp-pointed, appear on the seedling at the end of its first or second year, and a year or two later the leaves become like those of adult trees.

Wood very light, strongly aromatic; dull, slightly reddish brown, but losing the reddish tinge with exposure. Its grain ranges from medium coarse to fine. It is very brittle and soft. Great durability under all sorts of exposure is its most important commercial quality. Large logs have lain half-buried in wet ground over fifty years with but little sign of decay in the heartwood. On account of its durability and the large clear cuts obtainable it is extensively used for shingles.

LONGEVITY.—Very little is known of the age attained by this tree. It may, however, be regarded as very long-lived. Some of the largest trees are unquestionably from 700 to 800 years old. Trees from 24 to 40 inches in diameter are from 200 to 510 years old.

FIG. 59.—*Thuja plicata.*

RANGE.

Southeastern coast of Alaska and southward to northern California; eastward, through southeastern British Columbia, through northern Washington to northern Idaho and Montana, and to Cascades of Washington and Oregon.

ALASKA.—Southeastern end, on sea side of Coast Range, from sea level to 3,000 feet, northward in small numbers, to Wrangell, on mainland, and to Sitka on Alexander Archipelago ; farther northward, sparingly represented on Douglas Island (opposite Juneau) and on Portage Bay, head of Lynn Canal (lat. 59° 20′), the northern limit. Locally noted as follows : South end of Mitkof Island (opposite Wrangell) ; entrance to

FIG. 60.—*Thuja plicata: a,* branch with open cones ; *b,* seed.

Steamer Bay (Etolin Island) ; Yes Bay (Cleveland Peninsula) ; Ketchikan Valley (Re-villagigedo Island) ; Klowak (Prince of Wales Island) ; Kaigan (Bella Bella Island).

BRITISH COLUMBIA.—Sea slopes of Coast Range and islands from sea level to about 2,400 feet ; not in interior plateau, but on slopes of southern Gold and Selkirk mountains, and on west side of Continental Divide. Coast Range region of heavy rainfall, mostly on sea slopes; Salmon River, inland 45 miles from head of Dean Inlet, at 2,400 feet, and also on east slope of Coast Range in lower Iltasyouco Valley (tributary Salmon River); on Homathco River inland 63 miles to 2,720 feet elevation; lower Fraser River Valley inland to Uztlihoos River (branch Anderson River), 6 miles east of Boston Bar; also on Coquihalla River at point south of summit between this stream and Coldwater River; farther south, sparingly on Skaist River (east branch of Skagit), and on the Similkameen at point about 13 miles below Vermilion Forks. Valleys of Gold Range westward to within 8 miles of head of Okanogan Lake, northeastern part of Shuswap Lake, down north branch of Thompson River Valley to point about 20 miles below Clearwater River; northward to Quesnelle River, Fort George (on upper Fraser), and to headwaters of Parsnip River. Not in Columbia-Kootenai Valley, but in valleys of Selkirk Mountains and on west slopes of Rockies; eastern limit, Kicking Horse Lake, at 6,000 feet.

WASHINGTON.—Throughout western part from sea level to about 4,000 feet in Olympic coast ranges, and west slope of Cascades; and more rarely, on east slope Cascades and northern ranges eastward to Idaho at elevations from about 1,500 to 4,500 feet. Abundant on Pacific coast and on east coast of Puget Sound, but rare in valley south of Sound, and on west coast of Puget Sound, except at northeastern corner of Olympic Peninsula. Washington National Forest, on west slope of Cascades sea level to 4,500 feet; east slope, at 1,000 to 4,700 feet, and only on Stehekin River, Bridge and Early Winter creeks, Twisp, Methow, Entiat, Wenache, and Yakima rivers. Locally noted as follows: Mountain View (Whatcom County) one-eighth mile from Puget Sound; Orient, at 1,188 feet (Sauk River); Skagit Pass, Big Lake (Skagit County); Cascade Creek at point 11 miles above Mount Marble; North Fork of Skagit River; Stilaguamish River, below Silverton; South Fork, below Robe; Monte Cristo, at 2,763 feet; Buck Creek, near Mineral Park; Eagle Gorge (King County); vicinity of Seattle; about Lake Chelan and Stehekin (head of Lake Chelan), at 1,108 feet; Peshastin, at 1,045 feet; Wenache River. Mount Rainier National Forest, up to 5,100 feet; on east side of range, only on two small head streams of Natches River, and on one of Klickitat River. Locally noted at Orting in Nisqually Valley, on Mount Adams, and in Falcon Valley (south of Mount Adams); Port Ludlow, at 1,800 feet; Soleduc River above Wineton, at 900 feet; Hot Springs. Both sides of Coast Range, but more abundant on west side. Locally noted in Queniult Indian Reservation, at Olympia, Black Walnut, and Elma (Chehalis County), Dryad (Lewis County). Mountains of eastern Washington southward to Kamiak Butte (9 miles north of Pullman). Locally noted in Washington addition to Priest River National Forest; Pierre division of Colville National Forest; about Colville (Stevens County), at 1,917 feet. Not in Blue Mountains.

OREGON.—Both sides of Coast Range, but mainly on west side of Cascades; not in Willamette River Valley. Coast Range, sea level to 3,500 feet, and southward into California. West side of Cascades at 1,600 to 5,000 feet, southward to head of North Fork of Umpqua River; and Crater Lake; east side, only on east and south slopes of Mount Hood and for a few miles south to latitude 45°. Locally noted on north side of Mount Hood from bridge across Hood River (1,700 feet) to Columbia River, and on south and southwest sides from Camas Prairie and Government camp west to Salmon post-office; Portland; Astoria; on North Fork of Middle Fork of Willamette River; Crater Lake to summit of rim, at 7,500 feet.

CALIFORNIA.—Sea side of coast ranges southward to Mendocino County; inland through fog belt, on south slopes of Siskiyous to northwest corner of Klamath National Forest; on Klamath River for 20 miles, and on Eel River to Dyerville. Locally noted on outer peninsula at Humboldt Bay; lower Mad River 17 miles north of Eureka; south of Ferndale on road to Bear Valley (Humboldt County), Crescent City.

The detailed range of western red cedar in Idaho and Montana will be described in a later bulletin.

OCCURRENCE.

Confined to region of abundant precipitation and humidity, chiefly to wet or constantly moist situations. Occasionally on moderately dry slopes and warm exposures, where, however, it is stunted. On moist flats, benches, gentle slopes, river bottoms, in and about swamps and wet, springy places, and in cool, moist gulches and ravines. Abundant moisture more important than quantity or quality of soil, which, however, are important for best growth. Of gigantic size on deep, rich, moist bottoms in vicinity of the coast, particularly in Washington, on Vancouver Island, and in British Columbia, while at high elevations it is shrubby.

Not in pure stands over extensive areas; usually in mixture and dominant or subordinate. Small pure patches and groups, too dense for intolerant rivals, are characteristic. Generally with redwood, Sitka spruce, western hemlock, Douglas fir, lowland fir, western white pine, western larch, lodgepole pine, Engelmann spruce, yew, vine and broadleaf maples, black cottonwood, western birch, red and Sitka alders, and occasionally with yellow cedar ; hemlock a common associate.

CLIMATIC CONDITIONS.—Climate, humid, mild, and uniform throughout commercial range and within constant influence of ocean fogs ; but at high altitudes it endures (as a shrub) a severe climate with short summers, long winters, and low temperatures (sometimes —35° F.).

TOLERANCE.—Very tolerant ; tolerance varies with age, altitude, latitude, soil, moisture, and climatic conditions.   Grows well in dense shade during earlier life, and even reaches maturity and old age in shade, but growth is retarded in proportion to density of shade, for although the shade is tolerated to high degree it is not required.   Tolerance greatest under best conditions for growth and toward south and lower limits.   Here the tree maintains a dense crown-cover throughout life and commonly forms an understory, mainly with western hemlock, alone or with redwood, Douglas fir, grand fir, western white pine, and other species.

REPRODUCTION.—Prolific seeder, with specially heavy seed years.   Seed has high rate of germination, but only transient vitality.   Seed usually germinates the autumn it is shed, and seedlings establish themselves before winter.   Germination abundant, and best on moist duff, litter, moss, decayed logs, stumps, etc., both in open and in densest shade. Under dense shade seedlings hold their ground with remarkable power.   Does not reproduce itself readily where fires have destroyed ground cover and forest cover to such an extent that soil moisture is materially reduced.

CUPRESSUS.   CYPRESSES.

The trees of the cypress group, to which belongs the cypress tree (*Cupressus sempervirens* Linn.) of the Egyptians and Romans, are closely related to the species of Chamæcyparis.   They differ from the latter group essentially, however, in having quadrangular branchlets instead of flat ones and in having them arranged not in one plane, but irregularly disposed.   The overlapping minute, scale-like leaves of both groups are arranged in alternately opposite pairs, but those of Cupressus are minutely toothed on their margins, while in Chamæcyparis the margins are entire or smooth.   Leaves of each season's growth remain on the trees from three to four years.   Flowers are similarly arranged in both groups (see Chamæcyparis).   The cones of Cupressus mature at the end of the second season, instead of in one season, as in Chamæcyparis, and bear about 15 to 20 seeds under each fertile cone scale, instead of only 4 or 5 seeds to one scale, as in Chamæcyparis.   The seeds of Cupressus (native species) have narrow, hard wings, in place of broad, gauzy wings, as in Chamæcyparis. Seed leaves in Cupressus are 3 and only 2 in Chamæcyparis.   Wood of the cypresses, which is strongly aromatic, is remarkably durable, but on account of the usually small size and poor timber form of our native species the wood is of little or no commercial value.   The cypresses are, however, of considerable importance to the forester in assisting to form protective cover on wind-swept, sandy coasts or dry, arid slopes and little-wooded canyons.

Four species inhabit the Pacific region, all confined to California.   Trees of this group are of ancient origin.   Representatives once inhabited Greenland and western Europe, where, however, they are now extinct.

Monterey Cypress.

Cupressus macrocarpa Hartweg.

DISTINGUISHING CHARACTERISTICS.

Monterey cypress owes its common name to its confined habitat near the Bay of Monterey, California.   It has a form in youth entirely different from its mature habit.   When young the trunk is sharply conical, and its crown of rigidly straight, slender branches trending upward is a wide, sharp-pointed pyramid which extends down to the ground.   Such trees are from 40 to 50 feet high and 18 or 20 inches or more in diameter. Later, the height growth, rarely more than 60 feet, ceases, and if the trees have room the branches develop into long, massive limbs, finally reaching up to the height of the leader and spreading out into a very wide, flat-topped or umbrella-shaped crown. The trunks are then short, and the large limbs often near to the ground. The crown of crowded old trees is similar, but much less broad. Exposed to the sea winds, some trunks and their enormously developed limbs sprawl on the ground, and are grotesquely bent and gnarled. The violent swaying of branches in the wind produces, in some trees, most curious enlargements at the bases of the branches (obviously serving as braces) remotely resembling the palmated divisions in the horns of a moose. Bark of mature trunks is about seven-eighths of an inch thick. Outwardly it is weathered to an ashy white, but breaking it exposes a deep red-brown beneath, the same color as that of the protected bark of limbs and young trees. Old bark is firm, and narrowly seamed, with a network of narrow, vertical ridges and smaller diagonal ones. The bark is too thin to protect the tree from severe fires. The foliage is dark yellow-green. The minute leaves (fig. 61) are closely attached to the branchlets, their sharp points sometimes standing out slightly from the twigs. Leaves of a season's growth persist about three years, usually dying the second year. They are commonly marked on the back with a minute pit and two shallow grooves. The cones (fig. 61) mature by August of the second season, when they are ashy brown. They open slowly, shedding their russet-brown seeds during autumn, after which they may remain on the trees for several or many seasons. From 18 to 20 angled seeds (fig. 61, *a*) are borne under each perfect cone-scale. They are rather heavy, and usually fall near the parent tree. Seed-leaves, 3; about three-eighths of an inch long, narrow and pointed. Similar seedling leaves, about 4 of which stand out from the slender stem at regular intervals, succeed these. During the second season the spreading leaves are followed by shorter, pointed, less spreading leaves, from one-eighth to three-sixteenths of an inch long. Later branchlets (second and third seasons) begin to have adult foliage.

Wood, very fine-grained, rather heavy (very much heavier than any of the other native cypress woods), and clear yellow-brown, with streaks of rose-red and dull yellow. It has a faint, aromatic, " cedar-like " odor. Great durability without protection is a marked feature of this wood. The poor timber form of the tree and its very limited available supply prevent the wood from becoming commercially important. It is most important, however, as one of the rare forest trees capable of forming a cover on the wind-swept coast, even down to the water's edge. In dry situations elsewhere it is most worthy of use for protective planting. Its vigorous, rather rapid height growth in early life makes it exceedingly useful for windbreaks. The full extent to which it can be used in forest planting for cover has not been determined.

LONGEVITY.—Little is known of the longevity of this tree. It is believed to be long-lived. Trees from 14 to 19 inches in diameter are from 60 to 85 years old. Some of the larger trees are doubtless over 200 years old.

RANGE.

Central California coast, for a few miles on peninsula between Monterey Bay and Carmel Bay from Point Cypress nearly to Carmel River, and on Point Lobos south of Carmel Bay; mostly in a belt a few hundred feet wide along immediate coast, but also scattered farther inland on ridge of peninsula. Extensively cultivated elsewhere in California for windbreaks.

OCCURRENCE.

Rocky sea cliffs, on clay loam soil with dry leaf litter when shaded and with grass and other herbs in openings. Soils always fresh and porous in shade, but baked, cracked, and much less moist in the open. Forms a transition zone between sea beach and Monterey pine belt.

Mainly in pure, more or less dense stand, but mingled on east with Monterey pine and occasional Gowen cypress.

FIG. 61.—*Cupressus macrocarpa: a,* seed.

CLIMATIC CONDITIONS.—Climate mild ; equable temperature, never at freezing point and rarely above 90° F. Annual rainfall about 17 inches. Strong, moist sea winds keep air humid during greater part of year, while cloudy or foggy days are frequent. Demands humid air for best growth ; grows well in fresh soils away from immediate influence of sea, but apparently much shorter lived outside its habitat. Capable of enduring wider variation in temperature than that of its natural range. If planted in dry soils, for instance, where temperature falls below freezing, it grows well and matures young wood before frost, which commonly kills back immature growth in damp, low situations.

TOLERANCE.—Decidedly tolerant of shade, but thrives in full light. Natural growth includes both widely distant, gnarled, twisted trees and extremely dense stands. In dense stands shade of crown cover is heavy, yet young growth persists under it for many years.

REPRODUCTION.—Prolific annual seeder. Seed has moderately high rate of germination and persistent vitality. Usually germinates first season, under dense stands in compact, partly decomposed leaf litter. Seedlings grow very rapidly; in cultivation, often 3 feet in as many years. Grows from cuttings made from leading twigs of year, but trees thus raised are less vigorous, branch more, and are shorter lived than those grown from seed.

Gowen Cypress.

Cupressus goveniana Gordon.

DISTINGUISHING CHARACTERISTICS.

Gowen cypress, usually a small tree, is mainly known simply as "cypress," but this name is confusing; the coined name, Gowen cypress, is preferable. Karl T. Hartweg discovered it in 1846, and later introduced it into England, where it received its technical name in honor of James R. Gowen. English writers call it "Mr. Gowen's California cypress."

It is a small, much branched, shrubby tree, about 10 to 20 feet high, and frequently much stunted and bearing cones when under 3 feet in height. Under conditions very favorable for growth, however, it is from 30 to 40 feet high, or a little more, and from 15 to 20 inches in diameter. Young trees are straight, with sharply conical stems and slender, straight branches which trend upward. When the trees are older, the lower branches stand out straight. A wide, irregular, open pyramidal crown is formed down to the ground. The crown is especially open in older trees on account of the irregular lengthening of the main branches, which become very stout. There is rarely more than a few feet of clear trunk. The bark, about one-half inch thick on old trees, is firm, and is cut by narrow seams into a network of narrow ridges connected by thinner diagonal ones. On the outside the bark is weathered to a dull reddish brown, but the interior shows a clear red-brown. The minute, closely pressed, pointed leaves (fig. 62) have a faintly marked pit (sometimes wanting) on the back, and are a dark grass-green. Those of a season's growth persist from three to four years, but die at the end of their second or third year. The cones (fig. 62), one-half to seven-eighths of an inch in diameter, mature at the close of the second season, shed their shiny, pale brown seeds (fig. 62, *a*) late in September or in October, but remain on the trees for a number of years thereafter. Mature cones are shiny and either light brown, tinged with red, or purplish brown. Nineteen or twenty angled seeds are produced under each perfect cone-scale. The seeds are not buoyant enough to be carried more than a few rods from the mother tree, even by strong winds. Seed leaves, 3, occasionally 4; about three-sixteenths of an inch long, narrow and pointed. Seedling leaves are similar, but slightly longer, and stand out from the slender stem at regular intervals in groups of 3 or 4. During the first or second season narrow scale-like leaves (about three-sixteenths of an inch long) appear on the tiny branches of seedlings. They stand slightly away from the stem, and those which succeed them, in the third and fourth years, become more and more like adult leaves in form and arrangement.

Wood, pale yellowish brown, fine grained, rather heavy, and faintly aromatic. It appears to be durable when exposed to the weather. The wood is of no commercial value, but the tree is very important in forming a cover for barren, sandy, and rocky slopes too much exposed for most other trees. Its low growth subjects it to destructive fires, but it persistently reconquers areas on which its ranks have been severely thinned.

FIG. 62.—*Cupressus goveniana: a,* seed.

LONGEVITY.—Little is known of its age, but it is believed to be fairly long-lived. Trees from 8 to 14 inches in diameter are from 55 to 97 years old. The age of larger trunks is probably 150 or 200 years, or even more.

RANGE.

California coast region in an interrupted belt from Mendocino County to San Diego County; sea-level to nearly 3,000 feet. Extends from Ukiah and plains of Mendocino County to mountains at southern boundary of the State. Ascends canyons in central California coast mountains to nearly 3,000 feet. *Sonoma County:* Noted in western part of Green Valley on road between Sebastopol and Camp Meeker (about 3 miles east of Meeker); Dutch Bill Gulch, a little below Camp Meeker, on road from Meeker to Monte Rio. *Lake County:* East side of Mount St. Helena, on road from Toll House to Middletown, extending from an altitude of about 1,500 feet down to valley level for about 5 miles south of Middletown; few miles northwest of Middletown on gulch slope north of road to Cobb Valley. *Marin County:* West end and crest of Mount Tamalpais. *Alameda County:* Cedar Mountain. *Monterey County:* Small grove on north side of Huckleberry Hill (Monterey Peninsula, near Monterey), at 300 to 350 feet (probably type locality of species). Sandy barrens and rocky slopes of Santa Lucia Mountains, at 1,000 to 3,000 feet, only near Los Burros, and extending over summit. San Luis Obispo National Forest, from Cerro Alto southeastward, as well as in main canyons trending eastward, at 1,100 to 2,500 feet elevation. *San Diego County:* In Jamul Valley between El Nido and Dulzura, near Mexican border (southern limit).

OCCURRENCE.

On sandy barrens or rocky slopes, canyons, and gulches, commonly in very dry soils of poorest kind. On summits and low mountain slopes of central California coast region, a shrub on dry, shallow soil overlying granitic or limestone rock; largest near mountain streams.

Occurs scattered, as individuals, or in groves, and often in broken forest over extensive tracts; nowhere abundant. Associates on slopes with Coulter pine, and near streams with Douglas fir and western yellow pine.

CLIMATIC CONDITIONS.--Climate mild; temperature, between 12° an 112° F., and annual rainfall from 53 inches in north to 5 inches at south. Proximity to sea insures frequent fogs and high humidity during most of year.

TOLERANCE.—Tolerates considerable shade, often growing in rather dense stands.

REPRODUCTION.—Prolific seeder, bearing cones abundantly when only 2 or 3 feet high. Seed has moderately high rate of germination and persistent vitality. Reproduction abundant near seed trees, where seedlings are often established in great numbers.

Dwarf Cypress.

Cupressus pygmaea (Lemm.) Sargent.

DISTINGUISHING CHARACTERISTICS.

Dwarf cypress, a small and unimportant species, was, until a dozen years ago, considered only a dwarfed form of Gowen cypress, which it resembles so closely, except in size and habit, that the casual or lay observer can not readily distinguish it. Stunted on extremely poor soil, it is bushy and bears cones when under 3 feet in height. In situations more favorable for growth it is from 10 to 25 feet high—very rarely 30 feet—and from 6 to 12 inches in diameter. The trunk is conical, and the crown narrowly conical, with slender branches trending upward. The shallowly seamed bark of large trunks is thin, clear red-brown, and differs from that of the Gowen cypress in having its flat ridges divided into long, shreddy scales. In general appearance the scale-like leaves (fig. 63) resemble those of the Gowen cypress, but they differ from them distinctly in being entirely without the glandular pits on the back, which are always found on some of the leaves of the other species. The cones (fig. 63) mature by autumn of the second season and remain on the branches for a long time after their seeds are shed. They vary from five-eighths to seven-eighths of an inch in the longer diameter; otherwise they are similar to the smaller cones of Gowen cypress. Cone-scales range in number from 6 to 10 (instead of 6 to 8, as in the Gowen cypress), while the smaller seeds (fig. 63, *a*) are black when mature, and only about 10 or fewer are borne under each perfect cone-scale. Wood, coarse-grained; faint reddish brown (that of Gowen cypress is pale yellowish-brown). Nothing is known now of its other characteristics; but good-sized sticks are so rare that it is not likely to be used except for local domestic purposes. The tree deserves the forester's attention, however, par-

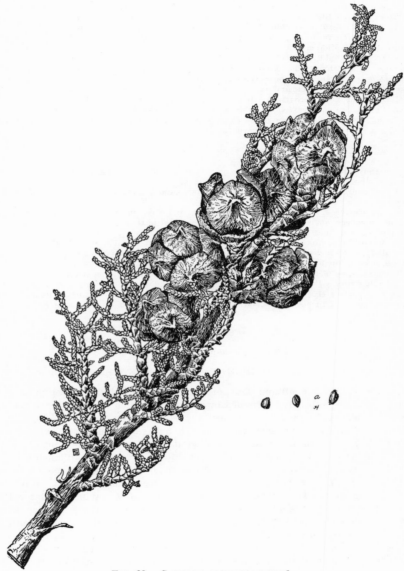

FIG. 63.—*Cupressus pygmaea: a,* seed.

ticularly on account of its remarkable ability to thrive in much-exposed coastal situations and in dry, poor soils.

LONGEVITY.—Very little is known of its age. Most of the largest trees now known in the greatly confined range are probably not over 60 years old; recurrent destructive fires have killed older trees. The early diameter growth appears to be rather rapid in protected situations, where trees from 6 to 10 inches in diameter are from 18 to about 35 years old. Probably it would be fairly long-lived, if protected from fire.

RANGE.

California coast barrens of Mendocino County from Ten-Mile Run southward to Navarro River, extending from about three-fourths of a mile of the sea inland for 3 or 4 miles.

OCCURRENCE.

In "peat swamps" in wet soil of poor, shallow sand overlying a stiff, yellow clay hardpan. The soil, wet by seepage from higher levels, supports low huckleberry and other shrubby plants, with some peat. In these situations its growth is stunted, but in better soil of borders of the barrens and of deep gullies in them, it reaches tree size.

On poor barrens, forms dense thickets, interspersed with groups of swamp pine and, occasionally, with lodgepole pine. Stunted growth of thickets is due partly to frequent fires and partly to the unfavorable soil; best growth is freer from fire.

CLIMATIC CONDITIONS.—Climate moderately equable, with temperature rarely up to 112° and never below 12° F. Annual rainfall, between 20 and 50 inches, with an average of about 35 inches. Summers are hot and dry, but the other seasons are usually humid.

TOLERANCE.—Similar to Gowen cypress; decided tolerence of shade is shown by retention of branches in the dense, over-crowded stands.

REPRODUCTION.—Prolific seeder. Seed similar in quality to Gowen cypress. Bears cones when but a foot or two high. Reproduction abundant near seed trees.

Macnab Cypress.

Cupressus macnabiana Murray.

DISTINGUISHING CHARACTERISTICS.

Macnab cypress is a very rare and little known tree, though several new stations for it have been recently discovered. It is a low, open-crowned, bushy tree, under 20 feet in height. Frequently it is only a many-stemmed, low, wide-spreading shrub. The largest trees have only a few feet of clear trunk and rarely have a diameter of more than from 6 to 12 inches. Their bark is deep chocolate-brown, tinged with red, and about one-fourth of an inch thick; firm and very distinctly cut by narrow seams into a network of rather regular, flat, connected ridges, and diamond-shaped interspaces. The thin, smooth bark of branchlets is dark-brown, or, where the scaly leaves have recently fallen and exposed it, clear purple-red. The foliage is a dark grass-green, sometimes with a whitish tinge. A minute blister-like gland distinctly marks the back of each leaf (fig. 64). Except in the case of young shoots, the leaves on all branchlets are sharply or bluntly pointed and closely pressed to the stems. On young shoots they are keenly pointed and stand slightly away from the stems. This makes the foliage prickly to the touch. Cones (fig. 64, *a*) mature at the end of the second summer, shed their light chocolate-brown, flat seeds late in autumn, and usually remain attached to the tree for several or many seasons.[a] At maturity the cones are reddish chocolate-brown, with a pale ashy coating. They vary from about three-fourths to nearly an inch in length. Sixteen to 18 seeds (fig. 64, *b*) are borne under each perfect scale. The rather heavy, very narrowly winged

---

[a] Cones recently examined were found to be full of seed after adhering to the branch for six years; moreover, the cone-scales were green and spongy, appearing to be a substantial part of the living branch.

seeds are not carried more than a few rods away from the tree.   Wood, exceedingly fine-grained, very light yellowish brown, and several pounds heavier per cubic foot than that of the Gowen cypress.   It is of no commercial use.   More-

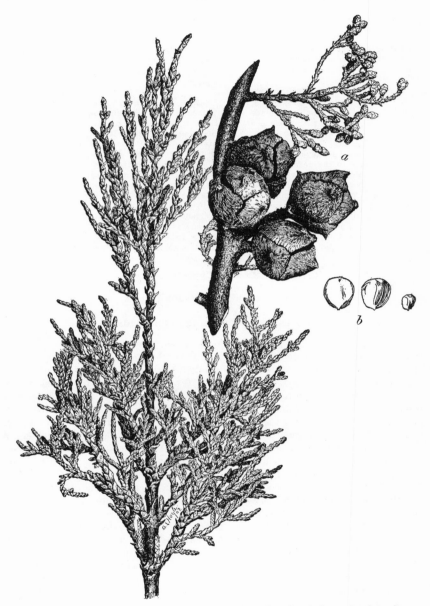

FIG. 64.—*Cupressus macnabiana;* *a,* cones; *b,* seed, natural size and enlarged.

over, the tree is too rare to have great importance in forest management, but its ability to thrive on dry, thinly covered slopes makes it worthy of investigation for planting in barren situations.

LONGEVITY.—Very little is known of its age; fuller records are required. Trees from 5 to 8 inches in diameter are from 80 to 125 years old. Probably only moderately long-lived—not exceeding 200 to 250 years.

RANGE.

In widely separated groves in coast ranges of California from Siskiyous southward to Napa County; also Sierra foothills of Shasta to Yuba counties.

Occasional groves on dry hills and low slopes of northern coast mountains, from near head of Hooker Canyon (Napa Mountains, Sonoma County) and Mount Ætna (central Napa County) northward through Lake County to Red Mountain (east side of Ukiah Valley, Mendocino County). *Lake County:* Noted in gulch on Complexion Creek, beginning on stage road about 6 miles west of Leesville, and continuing thence westward down gulch for 3 miles to Indian Valley; road from Rumsey, at head of Capay Valley to Lower Lake; exceedingly abundant along rocky gulch 2 or 3 miles beyond (north of) Manhattan Mine, whence it extends northward for about 2 miles, but not quite to south end of Morgan Valley; west slope of Bartlett Mountain, a few trees at about 1,800 feet altitude on north road from Bartlett Springs to Upper Lake; west side of Clear Lake (road Highland Springs to Hopland), in gulch about 3 miles west of Highland Springs, continuing very abundant for some distance; farther south (road Cobb Valley to Middletown), in gulch a few miles northwest of Middletown; on east base of Mount St. Helena on St. Helena Creek, from about 5 miles south of Middletown at edge of valley (altitude about 1,200 feet), southward up gulch for several miles, to about 1,500 feet; scattered on Bartlett Creek (Lake County). Common in gulch near Cook Springs (Colusa County). East Trinity Mountains, between Shasta (town) and Whiskeytown at 1,300 feet, and reported elsewhere. *Siskiyou County:* Grove near Little Shasta River about 15 miles north of Mount Shasta (Sec. 14, T. 45 N., R. 4 W.); and also one (the northmost) on west end of Siskiyous, at point about 10 miles from mouth of Seiad Creek (tributary Klamath River). Noted in Sierras as follows: *Shasta County:* Just west of Lassen Peak National Forest on plateau west of Burney Creek at 5,500 feet (southwest quarter of Sec. 24, T. 34 N., R. 2 E.); near head of North Fork of South Fork of Cow Creek at 4,000 to 5,000 feet (southeast quarter of Sec. 5, T. 32 N., R. 2 E.); Lassen Peak National Forest, small grove at base of Lassen buttes. *Tehama County:* Near Payne post-office and on Payne Creek Hill, just west of Payne Creek; 160 acres on Upper Butte Creek (near north line of Sec. 25, T. 30 N., R. 1 W.); several trees few miles southward on Inskip Butte (T. 29 N., R. 1 W.). *Butte County:* Magalia, at 2,300 feet. Three groves near Dobbin (Yuba County), on Dry and Indiana creeks.

OCCURRENCE.

On dry east and west slopes and ridges, in gravelly dry soils, which are often clayey and sometimes very shallow. In pure, dwarfed stands of limited area or in small groups.

CLIMATIC CONDITIONS.—Climate characterized by wide annual variations in precipitation, minimum being about 13 and maximum 62 inches. Temperature, rarely or never reaches zero, but often above 100° F. during the summer.

TOLERANCE.—Not determined; appears to be similar to other related species.

REPRODUCTION.—Moderately abundant seeder, usually producing cones every year. Seed similar in quality to that of Gowen cypress, but reproduction less abundant than latter.

CHAMÆCYPARIS. CEDARS.

The cedars are a little known, small group of evergreen trees, usually called " cypresses," and somewhat resembling the Thujas. They differ greatly from the Thujas, however, in having very much heavier and harder wood, without the characteristic " cedar odor," but with a peculiarly sweet or rather faintly aromatic odor. They differ from Thujas also very distinctly in their habit, and particularly in having small spherical cones instead of small, narrow, elongated cones. The seeds of Chamæcyparis, which are without aromatic resin cells, differ from the seeds of Thujas in form and character. The small, scale-like leaves, which fall from the branches in the third year, are arranged like those of Thujas. The delicate twigs or branchlets are distinctly flat, like those of Thujas, but are noticeably narrower (finer); they are arranged in one plane, forming conspicuously flat sprays (figs. 65–67). The leaves of seedlings are, like those of Thuja, long, slender, sharp-pointed, and spreading in regularly distant groups of 3 to 4; becoming shorter, more scale-like, and much less spreading on some branchlets of second and third year plants, and later assuming form of adult foliage. As a rule, the 2 seed leaves of western native Chamæcyparis are nearly one-third longer (three-eighths of an inch) than seed leaves of the western Thujas, with which the former are often associated. The flowers, which appear early in the spring, are minute and otherwise inconspicuous bodies at the ends of the twigs. The male flowers, pollen bearing only, and female flowers, which produce cones and seed, are borne on different branches of the same tree. The very small, spherical cones, which stand erect on the branchlets, are mature at the end of the first summer or in early autumn, when they open slowly to shed their seeds, after which some of them often remain on the tree for another season. From 1 to 4 or 5 minute seeds (figs. 65, 67) are borne under each cone scale. They are provided with light wings on two sides, but are less buoyant than seeds of Thuja, and usually fall near the parent trees. Seed leaves 2 and opposite.

The cedars are important forest trees. With other species, they supply much needed cover on high, exposed crests and slopes, as well as most durable and excellent commercial timber.

Two species inhabit forests of the Pacific region, one of which extends far northward on this coast.

Yellow Cypress; Alaska Cypress.

Chamæcyparis nootkatensis (Lamb.) Spach.

DISTINGUISHING CHARACTERISTICS.

Chamæcyparis nootkatensis is little known except within its range, where it is commonly called "yellow cypress" and "Alaska cypress." It is known also as "Sitka cypress" and occasionally as "Alaska cedar" and "yellow cedar." Although distinct in habit and in foliage, it may be mistaken for the western red cedar, from which, however, its clear sulphur-yellow wood plainly distinguishes it. Yellow cypress is characterized by an open, narrowly conical crown, which in the dense forest has drooping branches, few and distant from each other, and with weeping flat sprays, and by an exceedingly slender, whip-like leader, which is too weak at its tip to stand erect and which bends over gracefully. All of the branches (slender on young trees and thicker on old trees) droop more or less, and the few flat side and terminal branchlets hang down, so that the crown as a whole has a weeping habit. It is from 75 to 80 feet high (sometimes 90 or 100 feet), and from 2 to 3 feet or not uncommonly 4 or 5 feet in diameter. Forest-grown trees are clear of branches for from 30 to 50 feet, but in the open or on the border of a forest old trees may have branches nearly to the ground. On high, exposed slopes and crests it is very much smaller, often only 10 feet or even less in height, and assumes a sprawling form. The trunk is usually conical, sharply tapering from a wide base, but in very dense stands the base is little swelled. Trunks are seldom perfectly straight, and in most old trees they have one or two slight bends. They are always more or less fluted or infolded at the base, and are rarely full and round. Bark is thin on old trunks (about five-eighths of an inch thick), affording but little protection against fire, which the trees rarely survive; ashy brown on the outside, and clear, reddish cinnamon brown when broken. The surface is irregularly and rather finely broken by shallow seams; the thin, flat ridges have frequent diagonal cross connections, and flake off in long, narrow strips. The flat, blue-green sprays are noticeably harsh and prickly to the touch, in this respect unlike the smooth foliage of the associated western red cedar. The scale-like leaves (fig. 65), especially on thrifty leading branchlets, have very distinctive, sharp, spreading points. The cones (fig. 65), ripe

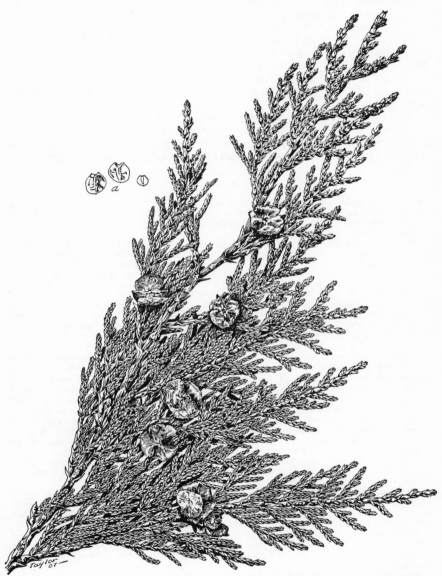

FIG. 65.—*Chamæcyparis nootkatensis; a,* seed natural size and twice natural size.

in late September or early October, are deep russet-brown, with conspicuous whitish bloom. From 2 to 4 seeds (fig. 65, *a*), of similar color, are borne under each of the perfect cone scales.

Wood, appropriately named "yellow" from its clear sulphur-yellow color, exceedingly fine-grained; though light, it is comparatively heavy for its class, being from 10 to 12 pounds heavier per cubic foot than western red cedar; elastic, but somewhat brittle, and firm, and splits and works very easily. It is remarkably durable when exposed to weather, earth, or water. Logs of yellow cypress have lain on moist ground for half a century with little decay. The firm structure of the wood, together with the ease with which it is worked and the attractive finish it takes, renders it especially useful for interior finish and cabinet work, as well as for special uses requiring soft, light, durable wood. The comparatively limited supply of this wood is likely always to confine its usefulness to a few special but, nevertheless, important purposes. Very important as an associate with other trees capable of forming protective cover on cold, high slopes.

LONGEVITY.—Little is known of the longevity of yellow cypress. It grows very slowly in height and diameter, however, and doubtless is very long-lived. Trees from 15 to 20 inches in diameter are from 200 to 275 years old. Very large trunks are probably from 500 to 600 years old. Further records are desirable.

RANGE.

Coast and islands of southeastern Alaska and British Columbia and southward on coast and in Cascades through Washington and northern Oregon. North of Vancouver Island at sea-level to 3,000 feet; in Cascades of Washington and Oregon at from 2,500 to 7,000 feet elevation.

ALASKA.—Sea slope of Coast Range and islands northward to Wrangell and to Prince of Wales Island, at from sea-level to timberline (2,000 to 3,000 feet); scattered, forming about 10 per cent of stand, and best growth between 1,000 and 2,000 feet. Farther north, only in isolated group at Sitka, at Icy Cape (just north of Cross Sound), a single tree on Khantaak Island (Yakutat Bay), a few trees on Hawkins Island at east end of Prince William Sound, and on opposite mainland, 6 or 7 miles from Orca; small area on Glacier Island (Prince William Sound, just west of Port Valdes), and on opposite mainland from Long Bay to Unganik Bay (lat. 61°, long. 147° 20'), the northern and western limits. Locally noted also on Ketchikan Creek and Shrimp Bay, at 700 feet; Revillagigedo Island; Peter's Mountain; Pearse Canal, at 725 feet; Kasan Bay; Prince of Wales Island, and at Wrangell.

BRITISH COLUMBIA.—Islands and sea side of Coast Range, at from sea-level to 2,000 and 3,000 feet elevation as far south as northern part of Queen Charlotte Sound (north end Vancouver Island), and at higher elevations farther south. Occurs sparingly on Queen Charlotte Islands, on exposed west coast near sea-level, near Massett, at head of West Arm of Cumshewa Inlet and of Rose Harbor, as well as other inlets of Moresby Island; abundant on mountains between 2,000 and 5,000 feet. Southward, leaving sea-level, it becomes general on slopes, appearing on Burrard Inlet at an altitude of several hundred feet; common in northern part of Vancouver Island, short distance inland, on plateaus and mountains, and sparingly on Lake Nimpkish; common in southern part, at from 1,000 feet up, in Renfrew district on Mount Edinburg (3,250 feet), and in Gordon River Valley; noted on Nanaimo River and Mount Benson (near Nanaimo). Inland on mainland, in Fraser Valley, to Silver Mountain (near Yale), at 4,000 to 5,000 feet.

WASHINGTON.—Frequent in Olympic Mountains and on west side of Cascades north of Mount Rainier, generally at from 2,000 to 7,500 feet; less abundant farther south in Cascades and on headwaters of rivers on east side. Ridges of Olympics below 3,500 feet, and to lowlands at mouths of rivers on Pacific coast; locally noted on upper part of South Fork of Skokomish River. Not recorded in Coast Range south of Olympics. Washington National Forest (west side of Cascades), moist slopes and benches at from 2,000 feet to 6,500 feet; locally noted in Green and White River valleys. Washington National Forest (east side of Cascades), moist valleys or slopes near main divide, at elevations of 2,100 feet to 6,000 feet; noted as follows: Skagit Pass; Methow River; Rattlesnake Creek; Stehekin River down to within about 5 miles of Stehekin; Horseshoe Basin, near Mount Amos; Stevens Pass, at head of tributary of Wenache River; Wenache River Valley; Mount Stuart; Yakima River Valley. Mount Rainier National Forest, at 2,600 to 7,400 feet, forming 1 to 2 per cent of forest in White, Puyallup, Cowlitz, and Cispus river water sheds (west side of Cascades), and extending southward to Mount Adams, but not in Columbia River basin; on east side of Cascades, only in northern part on Natches, Tieton, Atanum, and Klickitat river watersheds. Locally noted on Mount Rainier, at 3,500 to 6,000 feet—more common on north than on south side; Goat Mountains; Dewey Lake (head of American River), at 5,300 feet. Not detected on Mount St. Helens.

OREGON.—West side of Cascades southward to Deer Creek (tributary McKinzie River, T. 14 S., R. 6 E.), generally at 2,500 to 6,100 feet elevation. Locally noted on Mount Hood at Government Camp, and on north side (T. 1 N., R. 8 and R. 9 E.); valley of Santiam River, at 4,000 to 5,000 feet; between forks of Breitenbush River, at 4,150 feet. Reported extending 150 miles south of Mount Hood, but definite records of its occurrence there are lacking, as are also records of its reported existence in northern Idaho.

OCCURRENCE.

Common on bottomland, along streams, in basins, valleys, and gulches, and on mountain slopes. Where moisture is deficient, confined chiefly to north exposures and north sides of mountains, but where precipitation and humidity are great, exposure is less important, and the tree is common on south slopes. Chiefly in moist, rocky or gravelly soils of good quality; occasionally, of small size, on poor, dryish soils; very much like western red cedar in soil requirements. Quantity and quality of soil more important where moisture is deficient or where evaporation is rapid.

Mainly scattered singly or in groups; sometimes in pure stands of limited extent. Generally with Sitka spruce, western red cedar, western hemlock, grand fir, western yew, broadleaf and vine maples, and Sitka alder, in Washington, British Columbia, and south Alaskan coast region; higher up, with black hemlock, lodgepole pine, alpine, amabilis, and noble firs, Douglas fir, western larch, western white pine, and Engelmann spruce.

CLIMATIC CONDITIONS.—Climate of range generally favorable for tree growth. Summers comparatively cool and humid, and winters not severe. Average annual precipitation from 20 to 100 inches or more, from Oregon to Alaska. Changes in temperature are usually gradual, but in places mercury drops considerably below zero. In vicinity of ocean, climate is especially mild and uniform, while humidity and precipitation are particularly great.

TOLERANCE.—Not so tolerant as western red cedar and hemlock, but more tolerant than western white pine and noble fir. Under best conditions for growth it maintains fairly dense shade. Tolerance varies with soil, moisture, and climatic conditions. Less tolerant with age. Where soil and air are abundantly moist it thrives in the open; but partial shade and shelter (reducing evaporation and transpiration) are beneficial when soil moisture is deficient.

REPRODUCTION.—Seeding habits not fully known. Produces cones rather sparingly, but with occasional rather good seed years. Seed has only moderate rate of germination, with transient vitality. Reproduces itself freely under favorable conditions (moist soil and shade), but poorly in dry situations. Germination and growth of seedlings best on moist moss, muck, and mineral soils.

Lawson Cypress; Port Orford Cedar.

Chamœcyparis lawsoniana (Murr.) Parlatore.

DISTINGUISHING CHARACTERISTICS.

On account of its great beauty as an ornamental evergreen, Lawson cypress, the Port Orford Cedar of lumbermen, is widely known in this country and abroad. It is little known, however, as a forest tree. It is the largest tree of its genus and also the largest representative of its tribe (Cupressineæ) in North America. Height, from 125 to 180 feet, with a diameter of from 3½ to 6 feet. Trees 8 or more feet in diameter and nearly 200 feet high sometimes occur, but are now rare. In youth it is readily distinguished by its profusion of short, feathery, weeping branchlets of deep yellow-green, and its dense, sharply defined, pyramidal crown, which extends nearly to the ground and, in the open, is retained for many years. At first the branches all trend upward, but gradually, as the tree grows older, they become horizontal and drooping, especially at the bottom of the crown. The tips of the leading branchlets and the fringy side sprays hang down conspicuously, on old trees the leaf-covered twigs being shorter and less graceful than on young trees. Forest-grown trees carry a short but otherwise similar crown and have trunks clear of branches for 80 or 100 feet or more. Like those of the yellow cypress, trunks often have one or two slight bends and a broad, rapidly contracted base, which is somewhat flattened, hollowed or slightly fluted in places. The trunk form, however, is round and full above. The bark bears only a general resemblance to that of yellow cypress. This resemblance is due to the numerous narrow, diagonal ridges which connect the larger ridges, as in the yellow cypress. It is conspicuously thick—6 to 8 inches or more at the base of old trunks—but thinner higher up. Deep, narrow seams divide an apparently separate outer layer of bark into narrow, rather loose ridges, which separate into long strips, showing a dark red-brown underlayer of bark, which is strong and little broken. The color of the outer bark is similar, but subdued by weathering.

The minute scale-like leaves, on peculiarly flat sprays (figs. 66, 67), are soft to the touch, in strong contrast with the prickly feeling of yellow cypress leaves, and their points are shorter and blunter than those of yellow cypress. The leaves are closely pressed to the twigs, except on young trees and on main branchlets. The small berry-like cones (fig. 67) mature in one season, in the latter part of September or early in October. They are clear, dark russet-brown when they open in October. Some of them remain on the tree until the following spring. Two (occasionally 1) to 4 pale reddish brown seeds (fig. 67, *b*, *c*) are borne under each perfect cone-scale. The seeds have little buoyancy and are carried by the wind but a short distance from the mother tree. Seed-leaves are 2 and opposite, about three-eighths of an inch long, flat, one-sixteenth of an inch wide, pointed, and spreading. The succeeding leaves of the young seedling are similar, but narrower and sharper, and stand out from the slender stem at regular intervals. During the first or second season shorter, closely pressed, scale-like leaves appear on tiny branchlets, followed shortly by foliage of adult form.

Wood somewhat lighter than yellow cypress wood, very fine-grained, and faint yellowish white, with the slightest tinge of red. The wood has a most distinct, though faint, rose-aromatic odor, strong in green wood and fainter in seasoned wood and due to a resin.[a] It is rather hard and firm wood, works as easily as the choicest pine, and is very durable, without protection, under all sorts of exposure. In spite of its commercial excellence, the supply is so limited that it can hardly last long or find use outside of a restricted region. Owing to the large clear sizes obtainable, it furnishes the best of saw-timber and is a forest tree of the first importance.

LONGEVITY.—Few age determinations have been made of this tree, which is undoubtedly long-lived. Trees from 16 to 20 inches in diameter are from 186 to 225 years old. The largest trees would very probably be at least 500 or 600 years old.

RANGE.

Coast of southwestern Oregon from Coos Bay southward, within fog belt, to Mad River (near Humboldt Bay), Humboldt County, Cal., extending from within a few miles of sea to from 10 to 40 miles inland and reaching 5,000 feet elevation on seaward slopes of Coast Range. Noted at Crescent City, Cal., and in Humboldt County, on west side of Hoopa Valley, on Wilson Creek slope; on trail between Hoopa Valley and Arcata, about 4 miles west of Hoopa, at 1,800 feet; farther west, in damp gulch between Redwood Creek and Blue Lake. A few outlying stations occur farther inland, as in Siski-

---

[a] Continued inhaling of the odor from freshly cut timber produces an aggravated diuretic effect upon the system.

yous, near Waldo, Josephine County, and at a few other places in Oregon; also at western base of Mount Shasta near Sisson, Cal., on headwaters of Sacramento River, at about 3,500 feet, and in Trinity Mountains at head of Halls Gulch (tributary East Fork Trinity River, T. 37 N., R. 6 W.), around Trinity Center, at 3,300 to 4,300 feet, and probably elsewhere.

FIG. 66.—*Chamæcyparis lawsoniana.*

OCCURRENCE.

Most abundant and largest (north of Rogue River) on west slopes of Coast Range foothills from 3 to 15 miles from the ocean. Not very particular in choice of locality; on coast sand dunes, on high, dry, sandy ridges and slopes of coast hills, and on banks of streams and lakes. In mountains, best in narrow, damp, sunny ravines. Not exacting in soil requirements, yet best in moist, well-drained soils, neither dry nor swampy. In Oregon it thrives on sandy soils, growing even in dry soils of high ridges, while in north

FIG. 67.—*Chamæcyparis lawsoniana:* a, fruiting branch; b, c, seed natural size and enlarged.

west coast region of California it grows well in swampy places near the sea. In cultivation it does well in almost any porous soil, except cold peat.

In pure stands of limited extent only; commonly scattered through forest singly or in small groups. Near Port Orford (southwest Oregon) abundant in mixture with western red cedar, Sitka spruce, grand fir, western hemlock, and Douglas fir. With same species, but less abundant, in northwest California (swampy places near sea) and sometimes with redwood and California laurel. Near coast, often gives way to Sitka spruce and grand fir, growing on higher sites with Douglas fir and western hemlock. Occasionally in sugar and western yellow pine forests on rather dry, sunny slopes.

CLIMATIC CONDITIONS.—Climate characterized by moderate temperatures, heavy precipitation with slight snowfall, high humidity, and many cloudy days. Temperature on coast between 10°.and 95° F., and precipitation between 30 and 100 inches, with an average of about 56 inches ; higher altitudes have greater seasonal and daily ranges of temperature and proportionately larger snowfall. However, the generally low range keeps this tree within modifying influence of the sea. Successfully cultivated in Europe and in northeastern United States under more severe climatic conditions than those of its native range. But it is sensitive to sudden changes in temperature and humidity, and suffers from prolonged drought, especially after rapid growth. Frost hardy except in early youth, and resists late frosts better than early ones, because it starts to grow late in spring.

TOLERANCE.—Moderately tolerant of shade throughout life, but especially tolerant of heavy shade in early stages ; thrives also in open, provided the humidity of air is constant. Responds readily to side shading, so that forest-grown trees produce straight stems of considerable clear length.

REPRODUCTION.—Very prolific annual seeder, beginning when about 12 years old and continuing to an advanced age. Seed generally has a fairly high rate of germination, but often a low one ; vitality transient. Germinates abundantly in shaded moderately open places, and considerably, also, in logged and burned-over areas.

JUNIPERUS. JUNIPERS.

The junipers, some of which must, unfortunately, be called " cedars," are evergreen trees, either with branchlets closely covered by short, minute, scale-like, sharp-pointed leaves, arranged in opposite pairs, alternating around the stem (sometimes 3 in place of a pair), or with branchlets bearing much longer, needle-like leaves which bristle, or, at least, stand out loosely in groups of 3 at regular intervals.

Close, scale-like leaves are very often marked with a pit on the back (figs. 68 to 74.) When crushed the foliage emits a pungently aromatic odor. Junipers are further characterized by their fine-grained, aromatic, durable wood, which is dull yellow brown in some species and a clear rose-purple red in others. The bark is rather soft and distinctly stringy—one species only having brittle, checkered, hard bark.

The fruits of junipers, popularly called " berries," clearly distinguish them from the cypresses, which in the general appearance of their foliage they resemble. The flowers are minute and inconspicuous. Male flowers (pollen bearing only) and female (developing into fruit) are borne on different trees, sometimes, but rarely, both sexes occurring on the same tree. The " berries " are morphologically cones ; the fleshy or berry-like covering made up of fleshy flower scales (similar at first to those of conifers, which develop into woody cones) which unite in growth so as to envelop the hard seeds (1 to 12 in number ; 1 to 4 in Pacific junipers). Points of the united flower scales, or tip of the ovules, can usually be seen more or less prominently on the surface of the mature fruit (figs. 68 to 74). The berries ripen in one or in two seasons. Ripe berries are dark blue, red brown, or copper-colored, the surface covered (one Texan juniper excepted) with a whitish bloom, which may be rubbed off easily, showing the ground color. The pulpy flesh of the berries is juicy or mealy, sweetish, and strongly aromatic (due to the presence of resin cells). Birds eat the fruit of junipers, but the hard, bony seeds are entirely unaffected by digestion, which, indeed, is believed to facilitate in some degree their germination. Both birds and mammals play a most important part in the dissemination of these seeds. Without their aid dissemination would be exceedingly slow on level ground, where the heavy berries lie as they fall beneath the mother tree. On slopes, however, they may be carried far by water washing the surface soil and débris. The seed-leaves, 2 to 6, are usually needle-like, and the seedling leaves which follow these are similar in form; but as the tree grows older these are replaced by the short, close, scale-like leaves or by the lance-needle-shaped leaves of adults.

Junipers are small or, at most, only medium-sized trees. Their trunks are too short, small and poorly formed for saw-timber, though the wood possesses qualities which would otherwise adapt it for this use. They are largely used for post timber, fuel, and minor manufactures. Some of them are of the greatest value for fuel in localities where no other trees grow. Forestally junipers are highly important. Their adaptability to dry, barren slopes and exposed situations renders them exceedingly useful in maintaining and extending tree growth where few if any other trees will thrive.

Five tree junipers inhabit the Pacific region. One extends from eastern North America across the continent to the Pacific northwest. The ranges of the others lie wholly or in part within the Pacific States. Junipers are of ancient origin. Remains of them in Tertiary rocks show that they inhabited Europe ages ago.

Dwarf Juniper.

Juniperus communis Linnæus.

DISTINGUISHING CHARACTERISTICS.

Dwarf juniper is more widely distributed than any other tree inhabiting the northern half of the globe. It is one of the most singular of our trees in that throughout its world-wide range it attains tree size only in a few counties of southern Illinois, where it is from 15 to nearly 25 feet high and from 6 to 8 inches in diameter. Elsewhere on this continent it is a shrub under 5 feet in height, with numerous slender, half-prostrate stems forming continuous tangled masses from 5 to 10 yards across. It is said to sometimes become a tree from 30 to 40 feet high in north Germany, where it grows extensively also as a low shrub. As a tree it has a very unsymmetrical trunk with conspicuous rounded ridges and intervening grooves at and near the ground. It is clear of branches for only a few feet, and the crown, narrow and very open, has short, slender branches trending upward. The bark is less than one-eighth of an inch thick, deep chocolate brown, tinged with red, and composed of loosely attached, extremely thin scales.

The dark, lustrous green, keenly pointed, needle-like, or narrow, lance-shaped leaves (fig. 68), chalky white above, clearly distinguish this juniper from all of the other native species. The leaves spread widely from the triangular branchlets in groups of 3 at rather regular intervals, those of each season's growth persisting for five or six years. Sharp-pointed leaves, similarly arranged but much shorter and more slender, are found on young junipers of other species. A careful examination, however, will at once distinguish such leaves from the wider, more spreading leaves of dwarf juniper. The "berries" (fig. 68) are mature at the end of the second summer, when they are very dark blue—almost black, coated with a whitish bloom. The top of the "berry" is conspicuously marked by three blunt projections (points of the ovules). The soft flesh of the fruit is dry, resinous-aromatic, and sweet, containing from 2 to 3 (sometimes 1) hard, bony seeds. The "berries" are greedily eaten by birds and by some mammals, otherwise they may remain on the branches until the following winter or spring.

Wood, pale, yellowish brown; heavy, rather tough, very fine-grained, and exceedingly durable. The tree is too small to be of any commercial value. It has some importance for the forester, because it forms a low, matted ground cover on the highest and most exposed slopes and crests, and so retains much débris and effectively holds masses of snow.

LONGEVITY.—Very little is known of its length of life. It probably lives for several centuries. Trees from 2 to 4 inches in diameter are from 25 to 33 years old.

FIG. 68.—*Juniperus communis.*

RANGE.

From Greenland to Alaska and in the east south along the Appalachians to northern Georgia, to Ohio, Michigan, and northern Nebraska; in Rocky Mountains to Texas, New Mexico, and Arizona; in Pacific region south to northern California, in Alaska at sea level to 3,000, in California at 8,300 to 9,800 feet; also in Old World.

ALASKA.—North at least to Yukon Valley and west to Kenai Peninsula on the Pacific Coast. Noted about Arctic Circle at Walker Lake source of Kobuk River (lat.

67° 10', long. 154° 30'), Klondike River near Dawson at about 1,500 feet (Yukon), Lewes River below Lake Lebarge at base Semenow Hills (Yukon), Kenai Peninsula (west of Prince William Sound), White Pass at summit (2,880 feet), Lake Lindeman just inland from White Pass (Yukon), shores Lynn Canal, from sea level to timberline 3,330 feet, Chilkat River at Vanderbilt Point and elsewhere, Sitka.

BRITISH COLUMBIA.—Rocky Mountains of eastern British Columbia and through interior and coast ranges north to Alaska. Noted near west coast on Vancouver Island on summits of Mounts Benson (3,300 feet), Mark (3,000 feet), and Arrowsmith (5,900 feet), and at Spence's Bridge (776 feet) on Thompson River just above its junction with Fraser River.

WASHINGTON.—Mountain summits of whole State at 2,900 to 6,800 feet. Noted on northern Cascades (but not on Mount Stuart), Stevens Pass (4,050 feet at crossing of Great Northern Railroad), Olympic Mountains, Mount Rainier National Forest above 5,500 feet, Mount Rainier on Nisqually River near Longmire Springs and up to 7,500 feet, Mount Adams, Mount St. Helens, Loomis (1,200 feet, Okanogan County), but on Blue Mountains.

OREGON.—Summits of Cascades; not in Blue Mountains. Noted on Mount Hood on north side at about 6,500 feet and on Mount Mazama.

CALIFORNIA.—South in Sierra Nevadas to Tuolumne County, in coast ranges to Trinity County. Noted in Del Norte County, on Mount Shasta, encircling the peak near timberline at 8,300 to 9,800 feet, above alpine lakes at head of Canyon Creek (Trinity County), west side Mokelumne Pass (Alpine County), and Mono Pass (Tuolumne County).

OCCURRENCE.

On dry knolls, sandy flats, rocky slopes and ridges, interspersed among spruce and aspen, and enduring same climatic conditions.

TOLERANCE.—Very tolerant.

REPRODUCTION.—Fairly abundant seeder. Little known of seeding habits and reproduction in wild state.

Rocky Mountain Red Cedar.

Juniperus scopulorum Sargent.

DISTINGUISHING CHARACTERISTICS.

Rocky Mountain red cedar was long supposed to be a western form of the well-known " red cedar " (*J. virginiana*) of northeastern United States. It differs from this tree in maturing its " berries " in two seasons instead of in one season. The two trees are similar in general appearance, and the heartwood of both is of a similar dull red color; but so far as now known, the western tree has a distinctly more western range.

In open situations it is somewhat bushy, from 15 to 20 feet high, with a short trunk, from 6 to 10 inches through, and a rather narrow, rounded crown of large, long limbs, which trend upward; often there are several stems together. In sheltered canyons, on the other hand, it has a single, straight trunk from 25 to 30 or more feet high and from 12 to 18 inches through, with a slender, branched crown, and the ends of the branches and twigs are often so decidedly drooping or even pendent that in some sections the tree is known as a " weeping juniper." The somewhat stringy bark, shallowly cut into a network of narrow seams and ridges, is red brown in color or, on the outside, grayish. Much more is to be learned regarding the characteristics of this really little known tree.

The minute scale-like, pointed, often long-pointed, leaves (fig. 69) cover the slender 4-sided twigs in 4 rows of alternately opposite pairs; the back of each leaf usually has a long, indistinct pit (gland). The foliage varies from a dark green to a light green—the latter shade emphasized by a whitish bloom. Mature berries (figs. 69, 70) are smooth, are clear blue in color (from a whitish bloom which covers the thin blackish skin), and usually contain 2 seeds (sometimes 1) in a sweet, resinous pulp. Seeds (fig. 69, *a*) are pointed at the top end, conspicuously grooved, and marked at the base with a short, 2-parted scar (hilum). Number and character of seed leaves unknown.

Wood, dull red, or, more often, rather bright, rose-red; fine-grained, durable, with a thick layer of white sapwood. It is suitable for the commercial uses to which the eastern red cedar is put, but since the occurrence of the tree is somewhat rare and scattered, it is not likely to be of much economic importance. Locally prized for posts on account of its durability. The tree deserves the forester's attention for planting, since it thrives on dry soils and, especially, since

Fig. 69.—*Juniperus scopulorum: a,* seeds.

the red wood is valuable for pencils, for which the eastern supply of cedar is practically exhausted.

LONGEVITY.—Few records of its age are available. It appears to grow very slowly and to be rather long-lived. Trees from 6 to 8 inches in diameter are from 130 to 175 years old.

RANGE.

Eastern foothills of Rocky Mountains in Alberta southward to western Texas, and westward to coast of British Columbia and Washington, to eastern Oregon, Nevada, and northern Arizona; probably also in Black Hills (South Dakota) and Oklahoma; generally above 5,000 feet elevation, except near coast. Limits of range still imperfectly known.

BRITISH COLUMBIA AND ALBERTA.—Eastern foothills of Rocky Mountains westward through southern British Columbia (here in Columbia River Valley, near Donald, shores of Kamloops, François, and other lakes), to Pacific Ocean; here on heights near Vancouver (British Columbia), and at Esquinalt and Departure Bay on Vancouver Island, and on small islands in Georgia Strait. A tree juniper found as far north as Stikine River, on Telegraph Creek, just east of coast range, is probably this species.

FIG. 70.—*Juniperus scopulorum.*

WASHINGTON.—Throughout eastern part below 5,000 feet; reappears west of Cascades in arid localities, as San Juan, Orcas, Sucia, and Fidalgo islands (Puget Sound), Olympic Mountains, and Everett (Snohomish County). Locally noted, east of Cascades, at Sentinel Bluffs (on Columbia River), Peshastin and Wenache (on Wenache River), near Lake Chelan from Lake level (1,108 feet) to 1,800 feet, at Ione (Stevens County), and at Spokane.

OREGON.—Eastern part, probably including Wenaha, Blue, and Powder River and southeastern mountains. Locally noted in Wallula Gorge of Columbia River, below Juniper Canyon (Umatilla County), at 327 feet; southwestern Blue Mountains, between Ontario and Harney, above 3,600 feet; western slope of Steins Mountains, at 4,800 to 6,500 feet.

The detailed range of this tree in the Rockies and eastward will be dealt with in a later bulletin.

OCCURRENCE.

On dry exposed mesas, low, dry mountain slopes, and rather moist canyon bottoms (where best tree form occurs), in dry, rocky, sandy, or gravelly soil, but often very scanty in the latter sort.

Nothing is known now of its silvical habits in Pacific region, where it is comparatively rare; but single trees or small groups are commonly scattered among piñon pine, one-seed juniper, mountain mahogany, and narrow-leaf cottonwood, in Rocky Mountain range.

CLIMATIC CONDITIONS, TOLERANCE, AND REPRODUCTION.—Not determined. In protected canyons and other sheltered sites, it appears to endure (in most soils) considerable shade of broadleaf trees, closely resembling *Juniperus virginiana* in this respect. Usually a prolific seeder.

Western Juniper.

Juniperus occidentalis Hooker.

DISTINGUISHING CHARACTERISTICS.

Western juniper, a high mountain tree, is chiefly known simply as "juniper." Because of its uniformly higher range it is not likely to be confounded with the California juniper of a much lower zone, which it resembles in general appearance. Western juniper has a round-topped, open crown, extending to within a few feet of the ground, and a short, thick, conical trunk. Height, from 15 to 20 or, less commonly, 30 feet; only rarely 60 feet or over; taller trees occur in protected situations; diameter from 16 to 30 inches, exceptionally from 40 to 60 inches. The trunks, chunky and conical in general form, and with ridges and grooves, are usually straight, even in the most exposed sites, but are sometimes bent and twisted. With its stocky form this tree develops enormously long and large roots which enable it to withstand unharmed the fierce winds common to its habitat. There is rarely more than from 4 to 8 feet of clear trunk, while huge lower branches often rise from the base and middle of the trunk like smaller trunks. Of the other branches, some are large and stiff, standing out straight or trending upward from the trunk, while many are short ones. Sometimes the top is divided into two or three thick forks, giving the tree a broader crown than usual. In such cases, when the trees are growing in flats with deep soil, the crowns are dense, symmetrical, round-topped, and conical, and extend down to within 6 feet of the ground. Young trees have straight, sharply tapering stems and a narrow, open crown of distant, slender, but stiff-looking, long, upturned branches. Often in old age the branches are less vigorously developed and droop at the bottom and middle of the crown, but their tips continue to turn upward. The bark is a clear, light cinnamon-brown, one-half to 1¼ inches thick, distinctly cut by wide, shallow furrows, the long flat ridges being connected at long intervals by narrower diagonal ridges. It is firm and stringy. Branchlets which have recently shed their leaves are smooth, and a clear reddish brown. The bark on them is then very thin, but later on it is divided into loosely attached, thin scales of lighter red-brown.

The short, pale ashy-green, scale-like leaves (figs. 71, 72) clasp the stiff twigs closely, the longer, sharper leaves of young, thrifty shoots spreading slightly only at their points. All leaves are prominently marked on the back by a glandular pit, whitish with resin. Groups of three leaves clasp the twigs successively, forming a rounded stem with 6 longitudinal rows of leaves. The leaves produced each season die in about their second season, after which they are gradually forced off by the growth of the branchlets. The "berries" (figs. 71, 72), one-fourth to one-third of an inch long, mature about the first of September of the second year, when they are bluish black, covered with a whitish bloom;

their skin is tough, and only slighly marked at the top by the tips of
the female flower scales. The flesh is scanty, dry, and contains from 2 to 3
bony, pitted and grooved seeds, about which are large resin-cells (fig. 71, *a*).
These impart a sweetish pungent-aromatic taste to the berries. Seed-leaves 2,
needle-like, sharp-pointed, and about an inch long. Seedling leaves which follow

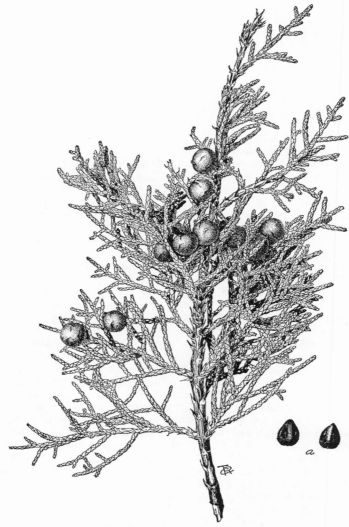

FIG. 71.—*Juniperus occidentalis: a,* seed.

these are similar in form, but much shorter, spreading in groups of three at close
intervals. These leaves grow gradually shorter and closer in their arrangement
until about the third or fourth year, when a few twigs bear short leaves of adult
form.

Wood, pale brown, tinged with red. Very fine-grained, with a slight aromatic odor, and, like all of the brown-wooded junipers, remarkably durable when exposed to weather or earth. It is soft and brittle, and splits easily. In the latter two qualities it is so similar to the wood of the eastern red-wooded

FIG. 72.—*Juniperus occidentalis.*

pencil " cedars " (*J. virginiana* and *J. barbadensis*) that it would serve excellently for lead-pencil wood; but few consumers of pencil wood are familiar with it. The short, often very knotty trunks, much used for posts and fuel, furnish poor saw timber, but would give good blocks for pencils and other minor commercial uses. As a forest tree, western juniper deserves special attention on account of its unusual ability to thrive at high elevations, on dry wind-swept situations. Few other trees can so persistently withstand such exposure.

LONGEVITY.—While the age limit of this tree has not been fully determined, it is known to be exceedingly long-lived. Its height growth is always slow, as is also its diameter growth when it is exposed, as it usually is, to fierce winds and grows rooted in crevices of rock. But even in such situations it grows persistently, producing thick trunks out of all proportion to its height. The wood of such trees is very fine-grained, indicating very great age. In protected mountain coves and on flats with deep washes of loose earth, large trunks show their more rapid diameter growth in their coarser grain. Trees of this type, from 20 to 48 inches in diameter, are from 125 to 300 years old. A study of fine-grained stems grown in exposed places would doubtless show large ones to be from 500 to 800 years or more old.

RANGE.

Idaho, southeastern Washington, and eastern Oregon southward to southern California. Arid hills and high plains of Idaho, southeastern Washington, and eastern Oregon; also high elevations in Cascades of Oregon and Sierras of California southward, in latter State, at least to San Bernardino Mountains. At north, possibly also in southern interior British Columbia, Montana, and in northern and western Nevada, but range there, as in Washington and Idaho, still imperfectly known.

WASHINGTON.—Only four localities known in arid southeastern part—at 591 feet elevation in Ryegrass Coulée (northwest of Fishhook Ferry) on Snake River, Franklin County; Yakima Canyon bottom, Kittitas County; Columbia River Canyon bottom below Sentinel Bluffs, at 1,800 feet, Douglas County; north side of Columbia River, for several miles each side of mouth of John Day River. Should be detected elsewhere in State.

OREGON.—Arid canyons, bluffs and mesas throughout eastern part and on both slopes of main divide of Cascades; generally from 500 to 6,000 feet, but sparingly on west slope of Cascades, at 1,600 to 5,200 feet, and not on Umpqua-Rogue River Divide nor on northern slopes of Siskiyous. Noted at Corvallis in Willamette Valley. East slopes of Cascades up to 6,000 feet elevation. East of Cascades, noted in Deschutes River Valley, on Columbia River and tributaries in northern Wasco County, and on Mutton Mountain plateau (between Simnasho and Warm Springs), at 2,900 feet, on Fly Creek Desert (between Matolius Creek and Squaw Creek); from a point 9 or 10 miles northwest of Farewell Bend to Prineville and eastward to Wagontire Butte, where it is especially abundant. Generally distributed over Klamath-Deschutes Divide and throughout Klamath River Basin eastward to Goose Lake National Forest, being common here on Drews, Dry, and Chewaucan creeks, and also in Warner Valley, where it grows on east and west sides of Warner Mountains. In northern part of State probably goes eastward through Blue, Wenaha, and Powder River mountains. Noted on Columbia River and branches in north Wasco, Sherman, and Morrow counties, on south side of the Columbia, near Blalocks and on John Day River (Gilliam County), in Juniper Canyon at 950 feet, and on Columbia River (Umatilla County), and in Blue Mountains, generally below pines, as in Maury Mountains and mountains south of Prineville.

CALIFORNIA.—Northeastern part and mainly on east slopes and summits of Sierras southward to the San Bernardino Mountains. At north, from ridges east of Surprise Valley (Nevada) and both sides of Warner Mountains, westward to Shasta River Valley at a point northwest of Mount Shasta; here abundant at 2,500 to 3,500 feet from point few miles east of Edgewood northward to Little Shasta Valley, lower slopes of Siskiyous, and hills east of Hornbrook. Reported in Trinity Mountains at high altitudes about alpine lakes at head of Canyon Creek. Locally noted in northern California as follows: Above Cedarville (Warner Mountains); Modoc Bluff, 6 miles west of Alturas, at 5,000 feet; west of Warner Mountains in Fandango Valley; Upper Goose Lake Valley, at 7,000 feet; Lower Goose Lake Valley; Devils Garden (west of Goose Lake), at 5,000 feet, from lake to Willow Creek—few miles southeast of Steel Swamp and southward to Warm Springs Valley, near Canby; between Tule Lake and Lost River; from point 15 miles south of Tule Lake to one 10 miles north of Lookout and eastward to Round Valley and Adin; Pitt River (Modoc County), at 4,900 feet; west of lower Klamath Lake from Brownell to Picard; Klamath Hot Springs at junction of Shovel Creek with Klamath River; ridge east of latter, at 2,700 to 4,300 feet. Southward, from northern

California, it extends east of Sierras into Nevada. In Plumas and Sierra counties, and generally in eastern Californian and trans-Sierran regions, it occurs at 5,000 and 8,800 feet throughout main and secondary ranges north of Sierra Valley; also in a narrow fringe at lowest levels east and south of this valley, as well as throughout Truckee River basin, except region around lakes Tahoe, Independence, Webber, and Donner; reaches western limits on summits of Grizzly Mountains, mountains west of Summit City, and canyon of South Fork of Yuba River. Locally noted in northeastern Shasta County, about Dana, head of Fall River, Bald Mountain (south of Fall River); northeast Lassen County western edge (5 miles west of Bieber) and eastern third of Big Valley and northward to Adin; about Susanville (southern Lassen County), at 4,500 feet, and east of Long Valley (south of Honey Lake); borders of Sierra Valley (Plumas and Sierra counties), at 3,600 feet; Feather River at Otis Ranch; from Sierraville to Loyalton; Rubicon River, 1 mile above Rubicon Springs; Canyon South Fork American River, 1 mile above Strawberry. Southward in Stanislaus National Forest, confined to summits of Sierras, at 7,000 to 8,500 feet. Here locally noted as follows: Donner Peak, at 7,000 to 8,300 feet (Placer County); Little Truckee—south of Lake Tahoe, Glen Alpine Canyon, and Loon Lake (Eldorado County); Twin Lakes (1½ miles west of Woods Ranch), at 9,000 feet; Hope Valley; Upper West Carson River Canyon; upper Silver Creek to Mokelumne Pass, and upper Mokelumne River (Alpine County); head of North Fork of Mokelumne River and Hermit Valley (on latter stream); west side of Sonora Pass, at 8,000 feet, and westward to Eureka Valley, at 6,000 feet; Tuolumne Meadows, Mount Lyell, Lyell Canyon, Unicorn Peak, Lambert Dome, Tenaya Nunitak, Tenaya Canyon, Grand Canyon of Tuolumne River, slope west of Lake Tenaya, Overhang Rock (between Tenaya and Snow Flat), and Cathedral Peak (Tuolumne County); Yosemite National Park, at head of Nevada Fall, at 6,000 feet, thence on trail from Little Yosemite to Cathedral Lakes, at 6,300 to 6,400 feet; 4 miles north of Dardanelles; Pacific Valley; Mokelumne Peak; Lily Creek (branch Middle Fork of Stanislaus River); Mount Reba, at 8,000 to 10,000 feet. On east slope of Sierras, common above Jeffrey pine at high elevations; noted in West Walker Canyon (Mono County) between Antelope Valley and Bridgeport; east side Bridgeport Meadows, and canyon southeast of Bridgeport Meadows, and thence southward to Mono Lake, hills about Long Valley, Sonora Pass, and down to 8,200 feet; Mono Pass in Bloody Canyon, Rock Creek (tributary Owens River). Abundant on ridges and summits in Sierra National Forest at 6,000 to over 10,000 feet elevation. Locally noted on headwaters of South Fork of San Joaquin River and its tributaries, Mono and Bear creeks; Kings River Basin on its North, Middle, and South forks, at 9,500 to 10,600 feet; Woodchuck Creek (tributary North Fork), Horse Corral Meadows (head of Kings River), Bubbs Creek (tributary South Fork); Kaweah River watershed, head of its East Fork, at 9,000 to 10,200 feet from Mineral King to Farewell Gap; Granite Mountain (head of East Fork), at 10,600 feet; head of Deer Creek (tributary Middle Fork); Kern River watershed, Whitney Creek at "Tunnel," headwaters of South Fork, Little Kern River (below Farewell Gap), and thence to North Fork; also near mouths of east and west forks. Abundant on Rock Creek (tributary Owens River). Reported on Panamint Mountains (east of Sierras) on north slope of Telescope Peak, at 9,300 feet, far above *J. utahensis,* upper limit of which is 8,400 feet. San Bernardino Mountains, higher parts up to 9,500 feet; locally noted on Mount San Antonio at about 10,000 feet, and in Bear Valley, at 6,700 feet; on north side of Holcomb Valley, at 6,700 feet, and near divide between Holcomb Creek and Mohave Desert, at 7,000 feet.

Extreme southern range not determined; possibly extends through San Jacinto Mountains and southward to Mount San Pedro Martir, northern Lower California, where it has been reported at 5,000 to 7,000 feet elevation.

The distribution of this tree in the northern Rocky Mountains will be given in a future publication.

OCCURRENCE.

Exposed high mountain slopes and canyon sides, in dry gravelly and rocky soils, sometimes in crevices of rock. In very open, but practically pure stands, or scattered among Jeffrey and lodgepole pines.

CLIMATIC CONDITIONS.—Similar to those of Jeffrey pine.

TOLERANCE.—Imperfectly known. Appears to be decidedly intolerant of shade in all stages of growth; always grows in full light.

REPRODUCTION.—Very abundant seeder, but seedlings are only occasional and scattered in pure mineral soil.

Utah Juniper.

Juniperus utahensis (Engelm.) Lemmon.

DISTINGUISHING CHARACTERISTICS.

Utah juniper inhabits only a small part of the Pacific region, its main range lying east of this region. Commonly a low, very short-trunked, bushy, or many-stemmed tree from 6 to 12 feet high and from 4 to 8 inches through near the ground; sometimes considerably thicker, and with a wide, rounded, rather open

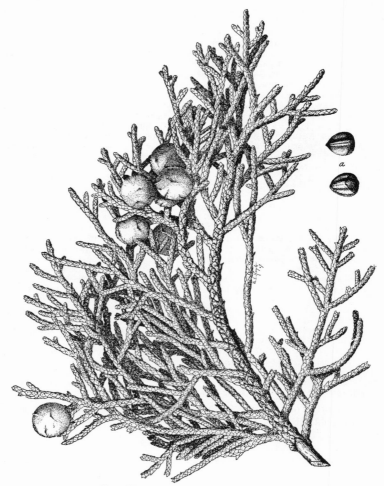

FIG. 73.—*Juniperus utahensis: a,* seed.

crown of numerous, upright, crumpled limbs. The usually short trunk is apt to be one-sided, with conspicuous hollows (or folds) and ridges. Its thin, whitish bark is cut into long, thinnish scales.

Minute, sharp, scale-like, pale yellowish-green leaves (fig. 73), generally without a pit (gland) on the back, are mostly in alternately opposite pairs, and closely overlap each other in 4 rows on the slender, stiff-looking twigs; sometimes arranged in 6 rows with three leaves at a joint. Leaves of vigorous leading shoots are much larger and keenly pointed, while those of seedlings are needle-like. The twigs appear round. Leaves of each season's growth persist ten or twelve years or more. Bark of larger twigs which have shed their leaves is pale reddish brown and scaly. Ripe berries (fig. 73), matured in the fall of the second year, are covered with a whitish bloom which, when rubbed off, exposes a smooth red-brown, tough skin. They usually contain one seed (occasionally 2), which is pointed at the top end, prominently and sharply angled (fig. 73, *a*), and marked nearly to the top by what appears to be scale-like basal covering (the seed scar), to which the thin, sweet pulp is attached. The surface of the berries shows projecting points (ends of minute flower scales). Seed-leaves, usually 5, but ranging from 4 to 6; pointed.

Wood (commonly called " cedar " or " juniper "), light yellowish brown, with a very thick, white sapwood; the durable heartwood has a less pungent " cedar " odor than that of other junipers. The tree is too small and ill-shaped for commercial use, though it finds important domestic use for fuel and posts wherever it is sufficiently abundant.

LONGEVITY.—Few records of its age are available. Probably rather long-lived. Trees from 6 to 10 inches in diameter are from 145 to 250 years old.

RANGE.

Southwestern Wyoming, Utah, Nevada, and western Colorado to southeastern California and northwestern Arizona; common throughout desert parts of this region, and generally at from 5,000 to 8,000 feet elevation.

CALIFORNIA.—Desert ranges east of Sierras. Abundant along summit of White and Inyo mountains, except highest peaks, descending on east slope of White Mountains to 6,700 feet. Common in Panamint Range on northwest slope of Telescope Peak, extending from 6,300 to 8,000 feet and sometimes higher. On Grapevine Mountains, on Providence Mountains above 5,000 feet. Less abundant in range westward, as in that part of Panamint Mountains near Jackass Spring, and on Coso and Inyo mountains; absent from Argus Mountains and not yet detected on east slope of Sierras.

The detailed range of this juniper in the Rocky Mountain region will be dealt with in a future bulletin.

OCCURRENCE.

On desert foothills and mountain slopes, in dry, rocky, gravelly, and sandy soils. In extensive, rather open and scattered pure growths, or mixed with one-leaf pine and desert shrubs.

CLIMATIC CONDITIONS.—Characterized by great aridity, high temperature, and small precipitation.

TOLERANCE AND REPRODUCTION.—Little known; probably similar to California juniper.

California Juniper.

Juniperus californica Carrière.

DISTINGUISHING CHARACTERISTICS.

California juniper is commonly known as " juniper " or " cedar." Its much lower altitudinal range serves, however, to distinguish it roughly from the western juniper. The exact lines where the two trees (similar in appearance) approach each other have not been fully determined. Casual observation might confuse one tree with the other, particularly young trees without fruit. California juniper may be distinguished by several fairly prominent characters, which should be carefully noted. Among these, and most conspicuous, is the deeply infolded or fluted trunk, which is straight and less tapering than the fuller, more rounded, and only slightly grooved trunk of the western juniper.

The crown form varies from a low, open, bushy, broad, round-topped tree under 10 feet in height to one with a conical crown 20 or 25 or, sometimes, 30 feet high. The short, clear part of the trunk is rarely more than from 10 to 20 inches in diameter. The branches often become large and greatly distorted in old trees, much as in the western juniper. The bark, outwardly weathered to a gray color and red-brown beneath, is in contrast with the clear, light

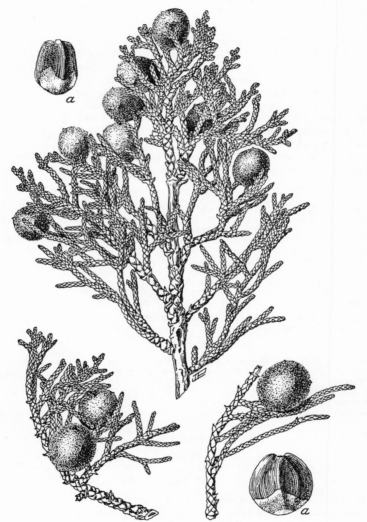

FIG. 74.—*Juniperus californica: a,* seed, twice natural size.

cinnamon-brown bark of its relative. Branchlets, after losing their leaves, have thin, scaly bark of pale ashy-brown color; those of the western juniper are reddish brown.

The pale yellowish green color of the foliage is fairly distinct from the pale ashy-green foliage of western juniper. The light, red-brown " berries " (fig. 74), one-fourth to nearly one-half inch in length, and maturing by about the first of September of the second year, are in sharp contrast with the bluish black, white-coated fruit of western juniper. The loose, exceedingly thin, papery skin of the fruit, though covered with a white bloom like that of the western juniper, is readily distinguished from the tough, thick covering of the "berries" of the latter tree. The berries are smooth except at the top end, where the tips of the female flower scales project slightly. The dry, mealy pulp, sweet and somewhat fibrous, is without resin-cells, which are a prominent feature of the other juniper's fruit. Seeds, from 1 to 2, are more or less angular and often irregularly grooved and ridged (fig. 74, *a*), but lacking the minute pits of western juniper. The minute, scale-like leaves have a glandular pit on their back and are arranged 3 in a group on the roundish stout twigs (fig. 74). The leaves of young, thrifty shoots and young seedlings, very keenly pointed and spreading, are distinctly whitened on their top side. The 4, 5, or 6 seed-leaves common to this juniper distinguish it from western juniper, which has only 2 seed-leaves. They are bristle-like, sharp-pointed, and rather rigid. The later growth of the seedling and the form and arrangement of its leaves are as described for the western juniper. Wood, hardly to be distinguished from that of western juniper. Economically, its field of usefulness is practically the same, while as a forest tree it merits special attention for its remarkable ability to thrive on low, desert slopes and plains, where, with little else but yuccas, piñon, and Sabine pines, it helps to form the only tree growth.

LONGEVITY.—No records of its age are available. It is believed, however, that it attains an age of about 200 or 250 years. A thorough study of its longevity is required.

RANGE.

Central California to northern Lower California. Inner California coast ranges southward from lower Sacramento River Valley to Tehachapi Mountains; thence up western foothills of Sierras a short distance northward to Kern River Valley, and eastward through southern coast mountains to their desert slopes; southward to Cuyamaca Mountains, and into northern Lower California; generally at 2,000 to 4,000 feet elevation.

CALIFORNIA.—North limit in Sacramento Valley unknown, but reported in Glenn County (Stony Creek National Forest) on east slope of inner Coast Range along foothills up to 4,000 feet; probably extends into Lake County. Locally noted on St. Johns and Snow mountains and Copper Buttes, at 4,000 feet; Elk Creek foothills (northwest Colusa County) from Sites to Stony Ford, and west of Fout Springs (base of Snow Mountain) northward into Glenn County. Much more abundant south of San Francisco Bay throughout coast ranges from Moraga Pass and Monte Diablo southward. Locally noted as follows: *San Benito County:* On divide between Topa Valley and San Benito, at Hernandez southward and eastward to New Idria Mine; *Fresno County:* Mountains of southwestern boundary between Coalinga and Priest Valley; hills about Priest Valley (Monterey County). *San Luis Obispo County:* On hills west of Carrizo Plain and along San Juan Creek; Santa Barbara National Forest, in Santa Maria, Santa Ynez, Santa Barbara, Matilija, Piru-Sespe, Newhall, and Elizabeth river basins; most abundant on desert (north) slopes, where, with piñon pine, it forms a belt around base and lower ridges of mountains up to 5,000 feet. Occurs similarly in canyons of Tehachapi Mountains, as in Tejon Canyon. Northward sparingly in chaparral and oak belts of Sierras to Kern River Valley, where its northern limit is the vicinity of Kernville, or possibly Trout Meadow, just south of Kern Lakes, on Kern River; southward on South Fork of Kern River from point 7 miles south of Monache Meadow down to region of Walker Pass, at elevations between 2,500 and about 5,100 feet. Reported in the Sabine pine belt of western Sierras foothills in Mariposa County, at point about 3 miles north of Coulterville at top of Merced River Canyon along road from Coulterville to Mariposa, and near mouth of Colton Creek. Locally noted on west slope of Piute Mountain just south of Kern River gap, at 3,000 to 4,000 feet; at Havilah on Clear Creek (6 miles south of Palmer Ranch); Caliente Creek to Piute post-office, at 2,000 to 5,000 feet; Walker Basin. More abundant on desert slopes of San Gabriel and San Bernardino mountains, here, with piñon pine, forming a belt around base of mountains at 3,500 to 4,000 feet elevation, extending down among tree yuccas of Mohave Desert, and southward to San Gorgonio Pass (south of San Bernardino Mountains). On north slope of Sierra Liebre

Range opposite west part of Antelope Valley, Cajon Pass up to 4,000 feet; Soledad Pass, at 2,700 feet; also occasionally in interior and on southern slopes of these ranges, as Cajon Pass, San Fernando Valley, San Gabriel Wash near Los Angeles, vicinity of Pasadena, and Mill Creek (San Bernardino Mountains). Southward, it follows coast mountains, occurring on both east and west slopes; at Mexican line from near Mountain Spring, at 2,700 feet; across Wagon Pass, at 3,117 feet, and down west side to Jacumba Hot Springs, at 2,822 feet, and possibly farther west.

LOWER CALIFORNIA.—Reported from both east and west sides of lower slopes of Mount San Pedro Martir as far south as Trinidad Valley and Las Encinas (near San Tomas).

OCCURRENCE.

On very dry mountain slopes and barrens, on canyon sides in rocky, gravelly, or sandy soils. Frequent and most typical on seaward slopes of Coast Range.

Sometimes in pure open stands, or predominating in nearly pure, very open stands of limited extent or in groups, but often mingled with one-leaf piñon pine, Sabine pine, mountain mahogany, and bigcone spruce, and occasionally with straggling western yellow pine, Douglas oak, and tree yucca; in Lower California, with piñon pine, mesquite, manzanita, and yucca.

CLIMATIC CONDITIONS.—Climate characterized by long, very dry summers, often limited or deficient precipitation, except for desert plants (mostly winter rain). Seasonal temperature, about 15° to 100° F.

TOLERANCE.—Little known of its tolerance, but apparently requires abundant light throughout life.

REPRODUCTION.—Prolific seeder. Actual seeding habits undetermined. Seed germinates on exposed mineral soil, but only when sufficiently buried by washing, or other favorable accident, to be moist. Reproduction rather scanty.

Family TAXACEÆ.

Trees (and shrubs) which belong to this family—yews or yew-like-trees—differ from the cone-bearers in producing male flowers on one tree and female flowers on another (very rarely both kinds of flowers on different parts of the same tree). Conifers have flowers of both sexes on different parts or branches of the same tree. There are fewer seed-bearing trees, therefore, since only trees bearing female flowers have seed. Moreover, in thinning a stand of Taxaceous trees care should be taken to preserve both male and female trees as near to each other as possible if reseeding is expected to take place. Pollen of the male flowers must be carried by the wind to the female flowers. If male trees are distant more than 25 or 30 yards from the female tree, only the strongest wind, blowing at the right time, will effect fertilization.

The leaves are evergreen, flat, and narrowly lance-shaped, and appear to grow (native species) in spreading lines on two opposite sides of the branches. The fruit (seed) is different from that of conifers in being almost or entirely enveloped in a pulpy covering. In the yews of this group it is a minute, berry-like cup, bright colored, juicy and sticky when broken, while in other members of the family the covering is firm, practically complete, and similar to an olive.

TUMION. STINKING CEDARS.

Stinking cedars are little-known trees which for many years were erroneously classified under the generic name *Torreya*. Only a few years ago it was found that this name had previously been applied to an entirely different plant.[a] "Torreya," "nutmeg," and "stinking cedar" are the common names for them. They are characterized by their stiff, flat, lance-shaped, needle-pointed leaves (fig. 75), which grow in two rows from opposite sides of the branches and are somewhat spirally arranged, and by the pungently aromatic or ill-smelling (fetid) odor of the leaves and of the green bark, the odor being most pro-

---

[a] Dr. Edward L. Greene, Pittonia, II, 195, 1891.

nounced when they are crushed or bruised. They form pyramidal crowns in youth, while in old age the crown becomes round-topped. The crown is somewhat open, and the branchlets droop rather conspicuously. Male and female flowers are each borne on different trees. Male flowers (pollen bearing only) are small, bud-like, and numerous on the under sides of the branches at the bases of the leaves produced the previous season. Female flowers, which develop into a greenish or purple, thin-fleshed fruit resembling an olive or a nutmeg, are also small, but much less numerous, and grow on the lower sides of the branches from the bases of new leaves of the season or of the previous season. The thin, tough skin of the fruit is resinous, and the seed has a smooth, hard shell. Seed-kernels are characteristically wrinkled, the surface appearing to be infolded, as in a nutmeg. Seed-leaves, 2. The bark is thin, and is distinctly and narrowly seamed and ridged. The trunk, rarely full and round, tapers slowly, and is usually slightly bent. A notable characteristic is the production of thrifty permanent sprouts from cut stumps. Wood, moderately light, hard, and fine-grained, clear lemon-yellow color, exceedingly durable under all kinds of exposure. Our species are so rare or are so limited in occurrence as to be of very little commercial use, for which, however, the extreme durability and good working qualities of their wood fit them. They are trees of only secondary importance to the forester, and are mainly useful for maintaining a protective cover on the borders of narrow mountain streams, in rocky coves and gulches.

Two species only are indigenous to the United States. One is confined to Florida and the other to California. Trees of this group are of ancient origin. Species of them inhabited the Arctic Zone in the Tertiary period, and later inhabited portions of Europe, where they became extinct.

California Nutmeg.

Tumion californicum (Torr.) Greene.

DISTINGUISHING CHARACTERISTICS.

California nutmeg is a rare tree of small size. It is called nutmeg from the fancied resemblance of its seed-kernel to the nutmeg of commerce, which belongs to a different and unrelated family of broadleaf plants. It is locally known as "stinking cedar" and "stinking yew," on account of the disagreeable odor emitted by its green parts and, to some extent, by its green wood when bruised.

In youth and middle age it has an open, wide, pyramidal crown which in the open extends to the ground. The slender branches stand out rather straight from the trunk in formal circles, and are somewhat drooping at their extremities. Crowded in a dense stand, it bears a short, conical crown on a clear trunk, while old trees under such conditions have rounded, dome-like tops. The trunks, which are rarely straight, are clear of branches for two-thirds of their length, and are from 35 to 50 feet high and from 8 to 20 inches in diameter. Under conditions especially favorable for growth it is 75 or 80 feet high and from 2 to 3 feet in diameter; but such dimensions are exceedingly rare. The trunk is uneven, almost never full and cylindrical. Bark, one-third to five-eighths of an inch thick, is finely checked with narrow seams and short, narrow, loosely scaly ridges, with frequent side connections; rather soft, outer layers easily scaled off; outwardly weathered to an ashy yellowish brown.

The flat, glossy, deep, yellow-green, lance-shaped, keenly pointed leaves (fig. 75), and particularly their sharp aromatic odor when bruised, distinguish the tree; green bark and branchlets also emit, when bruised, the same disagreeable odor. The fruit (fig. 75) matures by early autumn of the first season, when it is pale yellowish green with irregular dull purple areas or streaks. It is about 1 inch to 1¾ inches in length, with thin leathery covering. The seed has a thin, hard, brittle shell, while the surface of the seed kernel is deeply

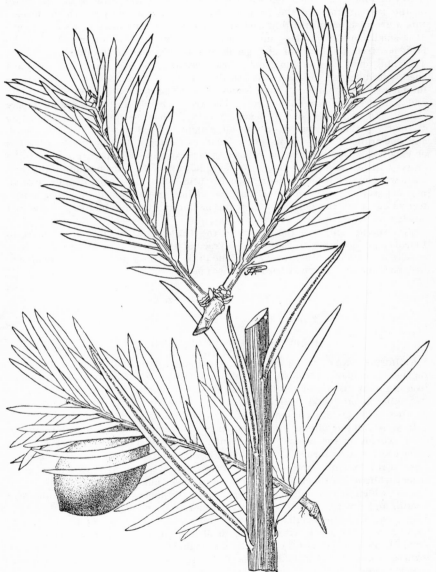

FIG. 75.—*Tumion californicum.*

wrinkled. Seed-leaves, regularly 2. Nothing can now be said of the growth and other characteristics of seedlings, which have not been studied beyond the stage of germination.   Wood, bright lemon-yellow; other characteristics of the wood and importance of the tree are given under the genus.

LONGEVITY.—Very little is known of the age, but it is believed to be a long-lived tree. It appears to grow persistently, but very slowly, in height and diameter, as shown by its small size. Trunks from 4 to 8 inches in diameter are from 60 to 110 years old, and those from 12 to 18 inches through are from 170 to 265 years old. Further study of its growth and age is required.

RANGE.

Central California, on coast ranges and west slope of Sierras.

Coast ranges, from Big River (Mendocino County) to Marin and Napa counties and south of San Francisco Bay region to Santa Cruz Mountains (Santa Clara County). Noted as follows: *Mendocino County:* West slope Coast Range north to Big River near Mendocino; on hills east of Russian River Valley bordering road from Hopland to Highland Springs, growing on both sides of Mendocino-Lake county boundary, especially on south side of gulch leading to Russian River Valley; western part Stony Creek National Forest, in lower forest belt. *Lake County:* Bartlett Springs (east Lake County); west of Clear Lake from point about 5 miles west of Highland Springs to Hopland, continuing over summit into east Mendocino County; east side of Mount St. Helena (large trees in canyon below Tollhouse); canyon of Putah Creek (road from Middletown to Cobb Valley). *Napa County:* South slope of Mount St. Helena, between 2,500 and 3,600 feet, and probably higher; Goat Rock (about a mile south of Tollhouse), on ridge forming east boundary of Napa Valley. *Sonoma County:* Big Sulphur (or Pluton) Creek Canyon (vicinity of Geysers); Dutch Bill Canyon (near Meeker). *Marin County:* Mount Tamalpais, in many gulches, canyons, basins, and chaparral main ridge; Cataract Canyon, notably near lower fall, at about 1,000 feet. *Santa Cruz County:* Near La Honda and sparingly in other localities (Santa Cruz Mountains). Sierras, west side from northeastern Tehama County, on southwest slope (Mill Creek) of Lassens Butte, at about 4,800 feet, to Tulare County (T. 21 S., R. 30 E.), occurring sparsely in gulches and canyons, at from 2,000 to 4,500 feet. Next stations southward from Lassens Butte are Deer Creek Canyon (south Tehama County) and canyons of Chico and Butte creeks (northwest Butte County); 30 miles southward, on upper Yuba and Feather rivers; noted near Dobbins (just west of Oregon Hills, Yuba County). Stanislaus National Forest, very rare in Eldorado and Calaveras counties; here noted on Empire Creek (tributary South Fork of American River), at 2,500 feet elevation; on north slopes of South Fork of Mokelumne River, at 2,000 to 2,500 feet; San Antonio Creek (tributary South Fork of Calaveras River), at 2,000 feet, and on South Fork of Webber Creek, at 3,000 feet. Southward, in Tuolumne County near mouth of South Fork at Colfax Springs; in Mariposa County, found at Mariposa and on Merced River in lower Yosemite Valley; near Dinkey Bigtree Grove (T. 10 S., R. 26 E.) and on Mill Creek (tributary of Kings River, T. 14 S., R. 27 E.) in Fresno County; in canyons along stage road to Giant Forest; in Sequoia National Park on road to Mineral King; East Fork, and other branches of Kaweah River, at 3,950 to 6,000 feet; locally noted in Coffeepot Canyon (tributary East Fork Kaweah River), on stream near Comstock Mill, and on Kaweah River between Kane Flat and Bigtree Canyon. Lower courses of Tule River branches and southward (to T. 21 S., R. 30 E.). Detailed range not fully determined.

OCCURRENCE.

In moist gravelly or sandy gulches, springy coves, and narrow watered canyons. Dependent upon soil moisture. Forms dense thickets alone or occurs in mixture with canyon live oak, white alder, western sycamore, broadleaf maple.

TOLERANCE.—Very tolerant of shade throughout life, its own dense shade often excluding other growth.

REPRODUCTION.—Seeding habits not determined. Reproduction confined to moist exposed soil or litter where seeds are fully covered by floodwaters; usually rather scanty.

TAXUS. YEWS.

The yews, very distinct as a group, are not strikingly distinct as species. There is great similarity in the appearance, structure, and qualities of the wood of different species, and also in the general appearance and form of the foliage and fruit. The shape and habit of growth, and minor differences in the form and color of the leaves, are mainly relied upon to distinguish the different species. They are world-renowned trees. The wood of one species inhabiting Europe,

Asia, and Africa was long used by ancient tribes for bows, their most important implements of war.

The leaves, which remain on the trees for many years, are flat, narrowly lance-shaped, and sharp pointed; by a twist at their bases they appear to grow in comb-like lines on two opposite sides of the branches, but as a matter of fact they are arranged somewhat spirally on the branches. Male and female flowers are each borne on different trees. (Exceptionally flowers of both sexes occur on different branches of the same tree.) Male or pollen bearing flowers are small, yellowish, bud-like, borne singly and rather abundantly on the under sides of the branches; female flowers, small and greenish, occur similarly on the branches, but are much less numerous. The latter develop into a fruit which ripens in one season and usually falls from the tree shortly after maturity. The fruit is berry-like, the single hard seed appearing to be embedded nearly to its point in sweetish, mucilaginous, bright coral-red (but not poisonous) pulp. Seed-leaves, regularly 2. The purple or brown bark is very thin. Wood, exceedingly fine-grained, and ranging in color from clear rose-red to dark reddish brown. It is extremely durable under all kinds of exposure.

Yews are small trees which live to a great age. A marked characteristic is their ability to produce permanent sprouts from cut stumps, and to grow from cuttings. Four species are indigenous to North America. Three inhabit the United States and adjacent portions of Canada, while a fourth appears to be confined to Mexico. One of our species, limited to Florida, is a small tree; another, a shrub, grows in the North Atlantic region; while one, a tree, inhabits the Pacific forests, extending northward into adjacent Canadian territory.

Western Yew.

Taxus brevifolia Nuttall.

DISTINGUISHING CHARACTERISTICS.

Western yew is little known except to woodsmen in its habitat, where it is called simply "yew." The more distinctive name suggested is desirable in view of the fact that two other yews occur in the United States.

A small tree, from 20 to 30 feet high and from 6 to 12 inches in diameter; much less commonly from 35 to 50 feet in height, and very rarely from 60 to 75 feet, with a diameter of from 18 to 30 inches. Trunks are straight and conical, but conspicuously ridged and fluted by an apparent infolding of the surface. The diameter growth is often excentric (larger on one side of the pith than on the other). Except in larger old trees, an open conical crown extends nearly or quite to the ground; the slender branches stand out straight, often somewhat drooping, while from their sides and extremities very slender branchlets hang down, so as to give a weeping appearance. This habit is strongly marked in trees growing partly or wholly in the open, where the leafy branchlets are very much more numerous and dense than in deep shade. The bark is conspicuously thin, rarely over one-fourth of an inch thick, and composed of thin, papery, purple, easily detached scales, beneath which the newer bark is a clear rose- or purple-red. The deep yellow-green leaves (fig. 76) are soft to the touch, and much paler on their under sides than above. Those produced in a season perish in about five years; occasionally a few green leaves are found on portions of 6 to 9 year old branches. The bright coral-red fruit (fig. 76), ripe in September, begins to fall during October. It is often eaten by birds for the sweetish mucilaginous covering, but the hard shell of the seed is unaffected by digestion. The attractiveness of the fruit to birds serves as an important means of disseminating the seed, which otherwise would not be carried far from the mother tree. Seed-leaves, 2; flat, short, and pointed. Nothing can now be said of the later growth and characteristics of seedlings, which have not been fully studied. Wood, fine-grained, clear rose-red, becoming gradually

Fig. 76.—*Taxus brevifolia: a,* fruit, lower side.

duller with exposure to light; dense, rather heavy, and remarkably durable in an unprotected state. Little commercial importance can be attached to the wood, on account of its scarcity. Its attractive color, durability, and elasticity render it useful mainly for such articles as canoe paddles, bows, and small cabinet work. As a forest tree, it is only of secondary importance, on account of its rarity and the fact that larger and more generally useful timber trees grow abundantly in the same range. Through its remarkable tolerance of dense shade it can assist in forming low protective cover in moist coves and canyons and at the heads of streams.

LONGEVITY.—Age limits of this yew have not been fully investigated. Growth in height and diameter are very slow, especially under deep shade, where, however, it maintains itself most persistently, indicating that it is long-lived. Few representative sizes have been studied. Trees 6 inches in diameter are from 75 to 90 years, while those from 12 to 20 inches in diameter are from 140 to 245 years old. The largest trees are believed to be about 350 or 375 years old.

RANGE.

Pacific coast region south from the southern tip of Alaska (Annette and Gravina Islands) and east to Selkirk Mountains; through western Oregon and Washington to California (coast ranges south to southern Lake County and western slopes of Sierra Nevada to Tulare County); mountains of eastern Washington and Oregon and Montana (east to western slope of Continental Divide, south at least to south end Bitterroot Mountains, Idaho, and Swan Lake, Montana).

ALASKA.—Noted only on Annette and Gravina islands at southeastern end, but probably also on neighboring islands and mainland.

BRITISH COLUMBIA.—Islands and sea side of Coast Range, extending some distance up Fraser River and reappearing farther east in Selkirk range. Queen Charlotte islands, confined to borders of inlets; noted on Cumshewa Inlet from Clew to head of West Arm, on shores of Prevost Island and south end of Moresby island, Skidegate Inlet, and near Massett. On mainland noted on lower Skeena River, on Fraser River up to Chapmans Bar near Suspension Bridge, and Coquihalla River up 20 miles above Hope. Vancouver Island common near coast, noted from sea level to 900 feet on southwest end in Renfrew district and near Victoria. Farther east on both sides of Selkirk Range north to Beaver Creek at 3,500 to 4,000 feet; noted on Kootenai Lake and west of it between Sproats Landing and Nelson.

WASHINGTON.—Douglas fir forests west of Cascades and moister parts of yellow pine forests east of Cascades, extending higher on both sides of the range into western white pine forest (at sea level to 5,000 feet). Eastward through mountains of northern and eastern parts of State. (West) Washington National Forest generally below 3,000 feet. (East) Washington National Forest only detected on Stehekin River, in Horseshoe Basin, at Nason City (Chelan County), and in some mountain passes at 3,300 to 5,000 feet. Yakima division Washington National Forest up to 6,000 feet, noted in Kittitas County. Mount Rainier National Forest generally below 4,200 feet; locally noted on upper Nisqually River, Mount Rainier between Longmire Springs and Paradise Park, and on a summit 8 miles southeast of Mount Rainier at 6,000 feet. Olympic Peninsula common; noted at Arbutus Point, in Queniult Indian Reservation and on Admiralty Inlet at Port Townsend and at Port Ludlow. Blue Mountains and infrequently along streams near Pullman (Whitman County).

OREGON.—West side of Cascades and Blue Mountains up to 6,000 feet. Not detected in Coast Range. Cascade (North) National Forest, west side below 2,100 feet in Douglas fir forest, but occasionally reaching 5,900 feet; noted locally at Portland, Clackamas River Canyon, between Portland and Mount Hood, and south of Mount Hood on Camas Prairie. Cascade (South) National Forest west side of Cascades and north side of Siskiyous; locally noted near Sawtooth Mountain (T. 25 S., R. 6 E.) above 6,000 feet, road from Rogue River to Crater Lake at 3,500 feet, headwaters of Rogue River in Cascades and of Bear Creek in Siskiyous, especially T. 38 S., R. 4 E.

CALIFORNIA.—Northern coast ranges from western Siskiyou and Humboldt counties southward to Mendocino, Mendocino County, and Mount St. Helena, Lake County. Not detected in Del Norte County and in general not extending west quite to coast; east to Marble Mountain and upper McCloud River (Siskiyou County); occurs in ravines from a little above sea level to 6,000 feet. Siskiyou County, noted in Klamath National Forest, on west slope Marble Mountain on Russian Creek, and on east slope Salmon River Mountains at 1,800 to 3,200 feet. Humboldt County, noted on west slope Trinity Mountains above Hoopa Valley as low as 4,000 feet, west of Hoopa Valley on trail to Redwood Creek, between Redwood Creek and Blue Lake, canyon South Fork Van Dusen River, Little Van Dusen, and a few miles from Briceland. Mendocino County, seaward side of Coast Range in redwood forest for 10 miles east of Westport and at a point

10 or 12 miles east of Mendocino (western limits) ; also near Cahto and Laytonville and near Willets and a few miles north of Ridgewood Summit (between Willets and Ukiah). Trinity County, noted east to canyon between Lewiston and Whiskeytown at 2,000 feet, Canyon Creek from Dedrick to Alpine lakes (5,600 feet), in gulches of Carl, Salt, and Dutch Creeks between Junction and Hay Fork and in gulches between Post Ranch and South Fork of Trinity River. *Colusa County:* On Snow Mountain and in deep canyons on Elk Mountain. *Lake County:* Noted on Sanhedrin Mountain, and east side of Mount St. Helena in canyon between Tollhouse and Middletown. Mount Shasta National Forest only detected east to headwaters of Sacramento River (Siskiyou County) and McCloud River (Shasta County) at 15 miles above Baird, at 3,000 to 6,000 feet. Not known on Mount Shasta. Lassen Peak, Plumas and Lake Tahoe National Forests infrequent in yellow pine belt of central plateau region and wet canyons of west side of main range ; noted in Placer County just south of North Fork American River east of Iowa Hill, a few miles east of Forest Hill, and in Devil's Canyon between Forest Hill and Colfax. Stanislaus National Forest, infrequent in red fir belt ; noted in vicinity of Mutton Canyon and Deep Canyon (branches of Pilot Creek, a tributary of Rubicon River) at 4,000 feet ; Big Iowa Canyon (tributary South Fork American River) at 3,000 feet, headwaters of Sly Park Creek (tributary of North Fork of Cosumnes River), and North Fork of Webber Creek at 4,000 feet, at 2,500 to 3,000 feet on the headwaters of Cedar Creek (tributary same river), at 3,500 feet on Clear Creek (tributary Webber Creek), headwaters of Mill Creek (tributary North Fork of Mokelumne River) at 3,500 to 4,000 feet. South on west side Sierras at 5,000 to 8,000 feet to Tulare County. Also reported in coast ranges south of San Francisco Bay south to Santa Cruz Mountains.

OCCURRENCE.

Near margins of low mountain streams, moist flats and benches, deep ravines and coves, in rich rocky or gravelly soils. Largest in western Oregon, Washington, and British Columbia ; much smaller in eastern range, especially in drier situations. Groves in small groups and singly, scattered sparingly with Douglas fir, grand fir, redwood, tanbark oak, vine, and broad-leafed maples.

CLIMATIC CONDITIONS.—Similar to those of Douglas fir (in Pacific range).

TOLERANCE.—Exceedingly tolerant of dense shade throughout life ; crown foliage thin and branches low to ground under deep shade ; grows well in partial or full light, but crown and foliage then much more dense.

REPRODUCTION.—Fairly prolific seeder. Vitality of seeds persistent and germination moderately high. Seedlings only occasional—often rare and mostly in deep shade on wet moss and decaying wood. Imperfectly known.

MONOCOTYLEDONES.

The trees which belong to the great class of monocotyledones differ from ordinary trees in not having their woody tissue arranged in annual concentric rings. Instead, the woody, thread-like fibers are scattered apparently irregularly throughout the trunk, on a cross-section of which the ends of these fibers appear like numerous dots. Another important characteristic is the single cotyledon or seed-leaf produced by the newly germinated seed. Other tree seedlings have 2 or more seed-leaves. The veins of monocotyledonous tree leaves are usually parallel to each other, just as in the leaves of grasses and Indian corn, also members of this class, in contrast with the feather and net like veining of ordinary tree leaves. To this group belong the palms and yuccas, which are essentially subtropical or tropical plants. The tree palms grow throughout their life with a single unbranched, column-like trunk, at the top of which the leaves are clustered. Tree yuccas are sparingly branched, much as in other trees, but their manner of producing leaves from the ends of the few branches is similar to that of the palms.

Family PALMÆ.

The trees of this family, known as palms, have single, straight, unbranched, cylindrical trunks, crowned by a cluster of spreading, fan-like leaves. The fruit, borne in branched clusters, is berry-like and usually one-seeded—seldom 2 to 3 seeded.

NEOWASHINGTONIA. PALMS.

This small group of palms, named in honor of George Washington, is composed of trees with big, column-like trunks, almost uniform in diameter

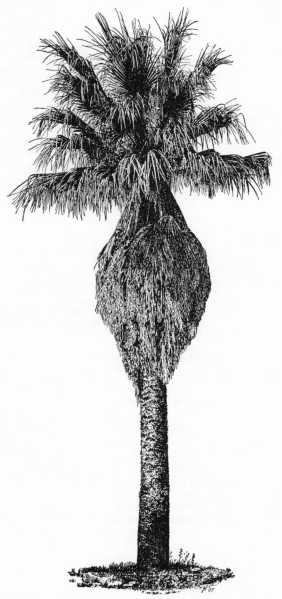

FIG. 77.—*Neowashingtonia filifera;* original 48 feet high.

throughout their length. The top of the trunk has a dense crown of very broad, fan-like, long-stemmed, circular leaves, deeply slashed into ribbon-like

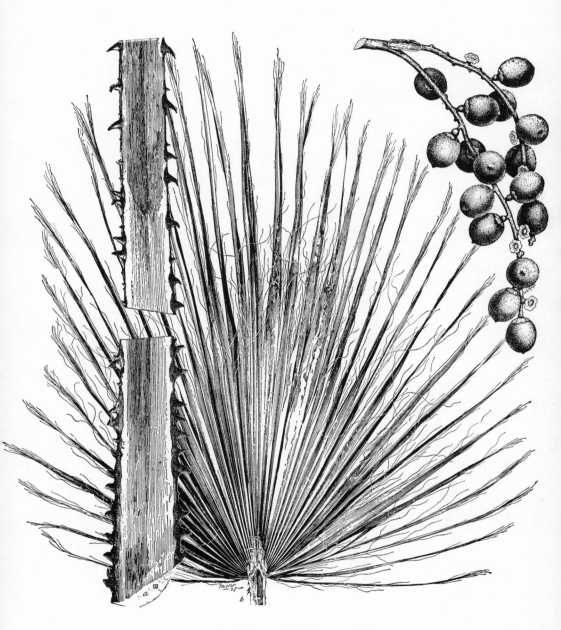

FIG. 78.—*Neowashingtonia filifera: a,* leaf stem one-half natural size;
b, leaf one-sixth natural size; *c,* fruit—part of cluster—natural size.

strips, and the tips of the strips are split in two. The stems of the leaves are armed on their two edges with irregular, straight or curved, sharp teeth. New leaves appear each year from the summit of the trunk. As those of the previous year die, they bend down, forming a dense thatch-like mass about the trunk (fig. 77). This adheres to the trunk for many years, finally falling and leaving the torn, wide overlapping bases of the leaves covering the trunk. Later diameter growth loosens these, and the trunk then becomes smooth, its rind (bark-like) being seamed and ridged somewhat as ordinary trees are.

The minute white flowers are perfect (male and female organs present in each) and borne in large branched clusters. The small, berry-like, elliptical fruit is black, with one russet-brown seed.

Only two species of these palms are known, and but one is found within the United States. This inhabits desert parts of southern California and extends into Lower California. The other species grows in Mexico and in the southern part of Lower California.

Commercially, these trees are of little importance (the trunks do not afford stable wood), except for ornamental purposes, for which they are much planted. They deserve protection and extension, however, since they are capable of forming true forest cover in desert localities where very few other trees grow naturally.

Washington Palm.

Neowashingtonia filifera [a] (Wendl.) Sudworth.

DISTINGUISHING CHARACTERISTICS.

Washington palm is known also as " desert palm " and " fan palm." It is the largest of our indigenous palms, growing to a height of from 35 to 50 or sometimes 60 to 70 feet, with a diameter of from 20 to 30 inches. The trunks taper very gradually, and sometimes appear to be of almost the same diameter throughout. As a rule they are more or less bent. The bark-like rind, marked by narrow seams, is pale cinnamon to dull reddish brown. A broad open crown of about 50 huge, fan-like, pale green leaves caps the trunk (fig. 77). If fire has not destroyed them, the drooping dead leaves of many years' growth form a dense thatch-like shroud about the trunk down to within a few feet of the ground. When the lower dead leaves have been burned off there is a mass of dead leaves just beneath the green head (fig. 77). Very many of these curious trunks are marked by fire, to which they are particularly subject until their covering of dry leaves is consumed. A remarkable resistant power apparently enables most of the trees to endure such burnings without injury, for they grow on thriftily afterwards.

The great leaves (fig. 78, *b*), about 4½ feet broad and somewhat longer, have stems 5 or 6 feet long, armed on their two edges with irregular, sharp, straight or hooked teeth (fig. 78, *a*). They are deeply slashed into stiff ribbon-like divisions (2-cleft at the ends), the edges of which are frayed into many long, thread-like fibers (fig. 78, *b*). The minute white flowers, produced every year when a tree begins to bloom, are borne in large branched clusters from 8 to 10 feet long in the crown of green leaves. At the base the flower stems and branches are noticeably flattened, forming two edges; elsewhere they are rounded.

---

[a] Since this bulletin went to press Dr. S. B. Parish has published (Bot. Gaz. 44 : 408–434, 1907) a most valuable contribution to our meager knowledge of the Washington palm. He points out that there is grave doubt as to what the plant originally described (by Wendland) as our Washington palm really is, and distinguishes the following species and varieties : *Washingtonia filifera, W. filifera robusta, W. filifera microsperma, W. gracilis, W. sonoræ.* Dr. Parish's *W. filifera robusta* corresponds with the palm described here as *N. filifera.*

Large quantities of the berry-like, spherical or elongated fruit (fig. 78, *c*), about three-eighths of an inch long, are borne every year after a tree begins to fruit. The fruit is black when ripe, in early autumn. The pale chestnut-colored seed is about one-fourth of an inch long by one-eighth of an inch thick. The single seed leaf is narrow and lance-shaped.

Wood, soft, very spongy and fibrous, and yellowish; the tough fibers dull yellow-brown. The possible commercial use of this wood is yet to be determined; if of any considerable importance it is likely to be for paper pulp.

LONGEVITY.—There is no way of determining the age of palms, since there are no annual rings to count as in other trees. The age this species attains can therefore be given only approximately. Two very large Washington palms in San Pedro street, Los Angeles, Cal., supposed to have been planted there by Jesuits, are possibly 200 years old. They are about 3 feet in diameter and said to be 90 or 100 feet high.

No arborescent plant is more popular than this for ornamental planting in the dry Southwest, and none better able to thrive and to grow rapidly where few other trees succeed without irrigation. Its many long, very strong roots descend to great depths. As a tree for clothing desert canyons and contiguous slopes, even if only an open forest can be secured, it is likely to be of no small importance.

RANGE.

Colorado Desert in southern California in central Riverside and San Diego counties and in canyons of south side of San Bernardino and east side of San Jacinto Mountains and of coast ranges farther south. South, in eastern part of Lower California, at least as far as southern end of Mount San Pedro Martir (lat. 30° 30'). In general from sea level to 2,000 feet.

CALIFORNIA.—Confined to northern and western borders of Salton Sink and its northwestern extension. At base of foothills of south side of eastern range of San Bernardino Mountains east to Indio (T. 1 to 5 S., R. 5 to 8 E). Locally noted a few miles north of Southern Pacific Railroad between Indio and Seven Palms. Northwestern limit Whitewater Canyon, in San Bernardino Mountains (lat. 34°, long. 116° 40'), which it ascends to 1,126 feet. San Jacinto Mountains locally noted Palm Canyon near Agua Caliente 10 miles south of Southern Pacific Railroad at Seven Palms at 500 feet and up, one tree in Andreas Canyon nearly at 800 feet, Dos Palmos Spring (T. 6 S., R. 5 E.), Thousand Palms Canyon (T. 9 S., R. 5 E.), Seventeen Palms (T. 10 S., R. 18 E.), and Palm Canyon north of San Ysidro Mountains (T. 10 S., R. 5 E.). Farther south, extending well up into most canyons of east side of Coast Mountains; not in canyon through which San Diego wagon road passes 5 miles north of Mexican boundary. Eastward a few trees follow line of old outlets of Salton Sea south into Lower California.

OCCURRENCE.

Margins of the inland Colorado Desert sea bed and low desert mountain canyons, in wet, sandy, alkali soil (border of sea bed), and moist, rocky, sandy ground (canyons). Forms open, extensive pure stands, with frequent rather dense groups, or is widely scattered; sometimes interspersed with occasional cottonwood, and in southern range with mesquite, yuccas, cacti, mescal, and creosote bushes.

CLIMATIC CONDITIONS.—Similar to those of Joshua tree.

TOLERANCE.—Appears capable of enduring much shade in youth, but later grows in full, strong light.

REPRODUCTION.—Very abundant seeder. Reproduction plentiful; yet less frequent in some places, probably because large quantities of seed are collected by Indians.

Family LILIACEÆ.

The trees belonging to this family differ from the palm included here in having large lily-like flowers and a capsule-like many-seeded fruit, instead of a berry-like one-seeded fruit. They differ from tree palms also in being branched to some extent when mature.

YUCCA. YUCCAS.

The tree yuccas are characterized by their bristling, stiff, upright, bayonet-like, sharp-pointed leaves, which are thickly clustered at the top of the unbranched young trunk or at the ends of the few large club-like branches of old trees. The edges of the leaves of different species are either smooth (unbroken), rough with minute teeth, or with a few thread-like fibers. Toward their ends the edges of the leaves are often conspicuously rolled or turned toward each other (on the upper side), giving the top end of the leaf a trough-like form. The leaves of each season's growth remain green for several years; later they begin slowly to bend down, close to the trunk or branch, and finally they die and within a few years fall from the tree. Bark of the tree yuccas is rather thick and cork-like, and furrowed and checked as in ordinary trees. The large wax-like showy flowers are perfect (male and female organs in same flower), and appear in big branched clusters from among the topmost leaves. With one exception (*Y. aloifolia*, which is self-fertilized), they are so constituted that they can be cross-fertilized only through the visits of insects (moths). The fruit (of Pacific species), matured in one season, resembles a small cucumber in form (about 3 to 4 inches long; fig. 81), or in some species a large butternut of the same dimensions (fig. 79). In some species it stands erect on the flowering branches; in others, it hangs down. It is indistinctly 6-sided with 6 separate cells, each containing numerous thin, flat, black seeds. The fruit may have a thin, fleshy, outer covering, which dries upon the shell when the seed chambers do not open of their own accord, or it may consist of a stiff, brittle shell, sometimes tending to split open at the top, but usually remaining closed. Such fruits fall from the tree in a dry and brittle condition and are carried some distance from the parent tree by wind or water. Finally they are broken open and the seeds scattered. Large quantities of yucca seeds are eaten by rodents. Birds, which feed on the fleshy fruit covering, also assist in distributing the seed. Many seeds are blighted by insects (moths), to the attacks of which flowers and fruits of yuccas are especially subject, but upon which the flowers depend entirely for fertilization.

The tough, fiber-like wood of yuccas is of little commercial value at present, but should be useful for paper pulp. The tree merits the forester's attention as a means of helping to maintain much-needed tree growth in arid southwestern plains and foothills.

Two tree species occur within the Pacific region, and here only in southern California; elsewhere they range eastward into the southern Rocky Mountain region and northward, one extending into Lower California. The yuccas are of ancient origin, remains of them having been found in the Tertiary period.

Joshua Tree.

Yucca arborescens (Torr.) Trelease.

DISTINGUISHING CHARACTERISTICS.

Of the two tree yuccas indigenous in the Pacific region the Joshua tree, also called "yucca cactus," is much the larger and more tree-like (fig. 79). From 18 to 25 feet, or occasionally 30 or 35 feet, is the usual height, with a diameter of from 1 to 2 feet. It is easily the most wild-looking denizen of desert hills and plains. The keenly pointed bayonet-like leaves, bristling at the ends of big clumsy branches, defy every intrusion and compel respect from many natural enemies. Young trees are unbranched (fig. 80, *a*) until they have produced flowers, which is commonly at a height of from 8 to 12 feet. Usually two branches are then formed at the top of the single stem and, in succession, each of these forms two or more, until a broad, low-branched crown results at maturity. When from 3 to 6 feet high the trunks are often set with bristling leaves down to the

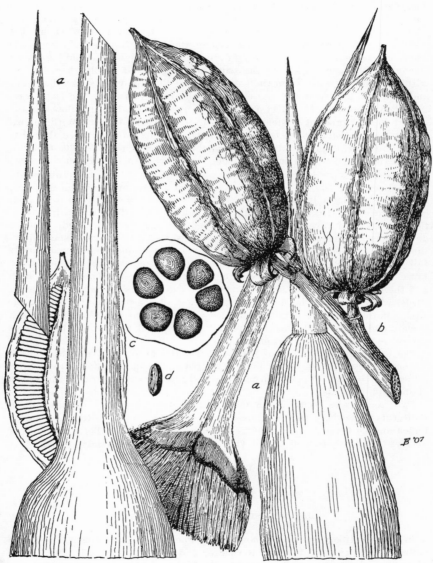

FIG. 79.—*Yucca arborescens:* *a,* leaves; *b,* fruit; *c,* sections of fruit; *d,* seed.

ground (fig. 80, *a*). No living thing intrudes upon the ground they occupy. The topmost leaves are upright in position, but as the stem increases in height the first leaves grown begin, during about their second year, to droop, finally dying and becoming closely pressed down upon the trunk in a thatch-like cover.

FIG. 80.—*Yucca arborescens:* Original 15 feet high; *a*, young tree.

Trunks 10 feet high may be entirely covered. Gradually these dead, but always stiff and prickly, leaves are forced off at the base of the trunk by the growth of the trunk and by wind, uncovering an ashy, gray, cross-checked and ridged bark. Except on old trees, the greater part of the tree is covered with dead, closely thatched leaves. This covering of formidable living and dead leaves suggests a wise protective measure through which alone the tree is able to maintain and extend itself, with little check from its enemies, in a region often lacking in other vegetation. The bluish-green leaves (fig. 80, a) are from 6 to about 10 inches long and about five-eighths of an inch wide; longer leaves occur on young trees. Leaves taper gradually from just above the base (1½ inches wide) to the point. The upper half is concave, tapering to a long, keen, reddish or blackish brown point; the lower half of the leaf is flat or only slightly concave, while the two edges have minute teeth throughout. A single stiff, branched cluster (about 15 inches long) of rather fetid flowers grows from the end of the crown branches. The fruit (fig. 79, b), usually matured early in June, is borne on short stems, at first standing more or less erect, but after maturity somewhat drooping or bent down. The fruit covering is dry and soft. It rarely opens of its own accord, but when very dry and brittle it is blown or falls from the tree, and later is blown about and broken open by the wind and its seed scattered. The six chambers of the fruit are filled with flat, jet-black seeds (fig. 79, c, d). Wood rather soft and light (when dry), but tough on account of its strong fibers; pale yellowish white. Further investigation may establish its permanent usefulness for paper pulp, for which it is suitable.[a]

LONGEVITY.—Nothing can be said definitely of the age to which this tree attains. It is very probable that an individual lives at least 100 to 200 years, and there seems little doubt that these trees may live 200 to 300 years. The growth appears to be very slow in both height and diameter, but very persistent. Its big, strong roots descend to great depths, giving the trees firm anchorage. It is frequently bent and bowed, but few trees succumb to storm, and not often to fire, which does not burn their stiff, hard leaves as readily as in the case of the thinner and more inflammable leaves or " thatch " palm trunks.

RANGE.

Southwestern Utah to the western and northern rim of the Mohave Desert in California.

OCCURRENCE.

Arid, desert plains and valleys, lower mountain slopes, benches, and plateaus, in dry, sandy and gravelly soils. Forms large pure, open or rather close stands; sometimes much scattered singly and in groups and with California juniper and single-leaf and Sabine pines. Low, scanty growths of cactus and other desert shrubs occur with the yucca.

CLIMATIC CONDITIONS.—Similar to those of California juniper (with probably higher temperature).

TOLERANCE AND REPRODUCTION.—Undetermined.

Mohave Yucca.

Yucca mohavensis Sargent.

DISTINGUISHING CHARACTERISTICS.

The Mohave yucca has been known for about fifty years, but until about eleven years ago it had been confounded with two other species, from which it is now known to be distinct. Since its most extensive and characteristic growth is found on the Mohave Desert, the common name here coined for it seems more

---

[a] Considerable local use of the wood has recently been made for physician's splints. The logs are pared into thin sheets.

appropriate and distinctive than the usual name of "Spanish dagger," which
is used for several other yuccas, some of which occur in the same range. It
is a low species, chiefly under 10 or 12 feet in height, not often branched, and
then with only a few stout limbs. The trunk is seldom over 10 inches in diameter, and where freed from dead leaves the cross-checked and furrowed bark

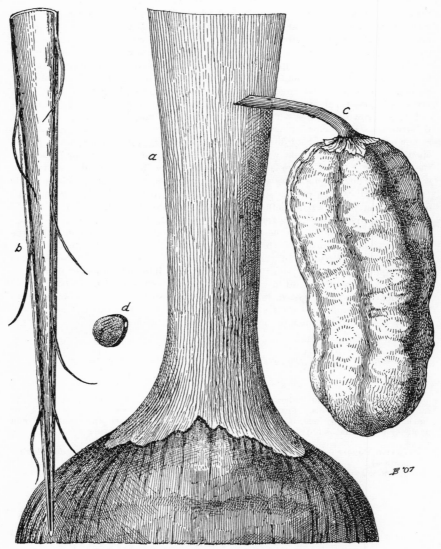

FIG. 81.—*Yucca mohavensis: a,* base of leaf ; *b,* point of leaf ; *c,* fruit ; *d,* seed.

is dark umber brown. The general aspect of the tree and the habit of its
green and dead leaves are somewhat similar to those of the Joshua tree. Distinctive characters are found in the length and form of the dagger-like leaves
and of the fruit. The yellowish green leaves, from 16 to 24 inches long, have
bases (fig. 81, *a*) about 3 inches wide, from which the blade is suddenly nar-

rowed to about three-fourths of an inch, gradually increasing in width, toward and above the middle, to about 1 or 1⅜ inches; then tapering to a stiff sharp point (fig. 81, *b*). The blade is thin and the edges are strongly curled or rolled from above the middle to the point. The edges are, moreover, conspicuously marked with thread-like fibers, which are frayed from the borders as the leaf grows older. A single branched cluster (about 14 to 16 inches long) of flowers is borne from among the uppermost green leaves. The pulpy, sweetish fruit (fig. 81, *c*), ripened late in August or early in September, is on a slender drooping stem. It is 3½ or 4 inches long, blunt at the ends, the top end having a short thick point. The flat seeds, packed in 6 chambers of the fruit, are black (fig. 81, *d*). Wood: Nothing can now be said of the wood of this yucca, except that it is lighter and somewhat softer than that of the Joshua tree.

LONGEVITY.—No definite statement can be made concerning the age limit of this yucca, which, however, can hardly be less long-lived than the Joshua tree. Messrs. C. R. Orcutt and S. B. Parish, who know the tree yuccas from long observation, both inform the writer that the Mohave yucca is an exceedingly persistent but very slow grower in its native habitat, scarcely any change having been perceived in trees under observation for the last twenty-five years.

RANGE.

From northeastern Arizona and southern Nevada across the Mohave Desert into California, and from the southern base of the San Bernardino Mountains to the coast and northward to Monterey, sometimes ascending mountain slopes to 4,000 feet.

OCCURRENCE.

Similar to Joshua tree.

DICOTYLEDONES.

The trees of the great dicotyledonous class are so called because the germinating seeds produce two seed-leaves, or cotyledons. They have broad leaves, with a central vein and a network of smaller connected veins. They are further characterized by having the non-resinous wood of their trunks in annual layers, which appear as concentric rings on a cross-section of the trunk. Each layer is formed just beneath the living bark and over the layer produced the previous year. This mode of diameter growth gave rise in earlier days to the class name "exogens," or outside growers, in contradistinction to "endogens," or inside growers, a class name then given to the trees we now more generally call "monocotyledones." The two terms, "endogens" and "exogens," originated when knowledge of how members of the two classes grow was incomplete. Later studies show that the term "exogens" is still correctly applicable to all dicotyledonous trees, but that the term "endogens" does not express the manner in which monocotyledones actually make their diameter growth. Monocotyledones were once thought to increase in diameter by the addition, each year, of scattered woody fibers at the center or pith of the tree, thus gradually crowding the woody tissue previously formed to the outside of the trunk. In other words, the outside of the trunk was believed to have once occupied the center of the stem. We now know, however, that these trees grow in diameter by laying on tissue outside of that formed the previous year, but not in a distinguishable layer as in dicotyledonous trees. Diameter growth of the gymnosperms (pines, spruces, firs, etc.) is produced in exactly the same way as in dicotyledonous trees, but the oleo-resinous woods of the former distinguish them from the latter class. It is true, indeed, that the wood of some of our broadleaf trees contains resinous matter, but it is not in any high degree oleo-resinous, as in gymnosperms. Examples of broadleaf trees with resin in their wood are the cherries, plums, acacias, mesquite, red gum (*Liquidambar*), etc., in which the character of the resin is distinctly mucilaginous.

Family JUGLANDACEÆ.

The distinctive characters of Juglandaceæ are that male and female flowers are each borne on different parts of the same tree and that the fruit is a nut (1) with a firm pulpy covering which does not break open of its own accord (walnuts), or (2) with a firm woody covering which separates at maturity into 4 nearly distinct or partly connected, rind-like divisions (hickories). The single hard-shelled nut is usually soon liberated from the latter type of covering, but the undivided pulpy covering of the former type dries and adheres to its nut until rotted away by contact with the ground. The leaves of the trees representing this family occur singly and more or less distant from each other—never growing in pairs, one leaf exactly opposite its fellow, as in trees of some other families. A very important group of timber trees.

JUGLANS. WALNUTS.

The walnuts are a small group of trees very sparingly represented in the Pacific region. They are important forest trees, some of them producing very handsome and exceedingly valuable lumber. Pungent aromatic odor is characteristic of leaves and other green parts when bruised, while the heartwood is a rich dark brown. Distinctive characters of the branches are the leaf-scars with 3 groups of minute dots, and the partition-like structure of the pith (best seen by slicing a twig longitudinally). The leaves, called compound because they differ from the ordinary simple leaf (an apple leaf) in being made up of a single central stem from which grow from 5 to 11 pairs of pointed leaflets (each appearing like an ordinary leaf). By the suppression of one leaflet of the terminal pair, the number of leaflets may be odd. The flowers appear after the leaves. Male flowers (pollen bearing) are long, flexible, cord-like, pendent bodies, borne singly or in pairs from buds of branches grown the previous season; female flowers, which develop into fruit, are bud-like bodies borne in small clusters at the ends of the new green shoots of the season, usually on the same branch as contains the male flowers. The fruit, a spherical nut (in Pacific representatives), is matured in the autumn of the first season. Its firm, pulpy husk breaks up after maturity, but with no regular divisions. The heavy nuts are dependent for their distribution upon the agency of rodents, which bury many of them for their winter food, and upon floods, which often carry them long distances.

One only of the four species indigenous to the United States occurs in the Pacific region and it is confined to western California. Other representatives of the genus are world-wide in their distribution.

The walnuts are of ancient origin. Remains of numerous ancient species, once common in Europe but now extinct, have been found in the Cretaceous and Tertiary formations, while in the northern Pacific coast region signs of ancient walnuts have been obtained from the Eocene formation, as well as from gold-bearing gravel beds of the California Sierras. No living representatives are found in these regions now.

California Walnut.

Juglans californica Watson.

DISTINGUISHING CHARACTERISTICS.

Though it ranges in size from a shrub to a tree 50 feet high and from 8 to 15 inches in diameter, California walnut is usually a low, wide-crowned tree from 12 to 20 feet high. The clear trunk is short, giving off big branches which curve upward, then down, often drooping nearly to the ground and forming a handsome dome-like crown. The bark of young trees and portions of the large branches is smooth and ashy white, while that of older trunks is blackish

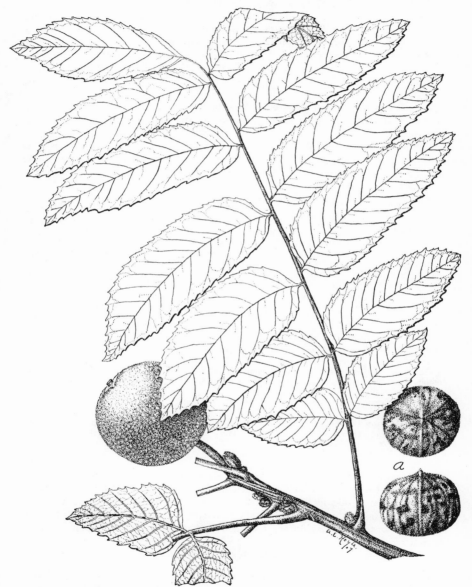

Fig. 82.—*Juglans californica: a,* nut without hull.

brown and rather deeply and sharply furrowed and ridged. The California species resembles the eastern black walnut sufficiently to suggest that tree to one familiar with it. The leaves (fig. 82), with from 9 to 17 leaflets, are light yellow-green and are smooth throughout when full grown; occasionally, however, the leaflets may have minute clusters of tawny hairs underneath in the angles formed by the veins. The spherical fruit (fig. 82) is a thinly covered nut, with a very finely but perceptibly velvety surface. Divested of its thin husk, the hard-shelled nut, its two ends appearing to be pressed together, is indistinctly and irregularly grooved (fig. 82, *a*).

Wood, rather heavy, dark brown, somewhat lighter-colored than that of the eastern tree, but similarly rich in color and grain. It is usually moderately coarse-grained, owing to the fact that it is mainly grown in the open. The tree is too poorly formed and usually too small to furnish wood of much commercial value except for local needs. When large enough for lumber it is useful as a cabinet wood on account of its handsome color and good working qualities.

As a forest tree it can be of only secondary importance, serving with a number of other riparian species in maintaining needful protective tree growth along streams.

LONGEVITY.—Few records of its age are available. It is a very rapid-growing tree in youth and gives evidence of being short-lived, probably not exceeding 150 years. Trees from 12 to 15 inches in diameter are 13 to 17 years old, while one tree 15½ inches through showed an age of 15 years.

RANGE.

CALIFORNIA.—River courses of foothills and valleys of coast region usually 20 or 30 miles from the sea, from Lower Sacramento River (noted 2 miles north of Shingle Springs, Eldorado County, at about 1,500 feet), Mount St. Helena (southern Lake County), vicinity of San Francisco and Monte Diablo (northwest base), south in coast ranges to south side of the Santa Ana (Orange County) and San Bernardino Mountains. Santa Barbara National Forest common at 800 to 4,000 feet; in watersheds of Santa Maria, Santa Ynez, Santa Barbara, Matilija, Piru-Sespe, and Newhall rivers. Santa Monica Mountains and Puente Hills, near Los Angeles; frequent in foothills below 3,000 feet; less so on south slopes of San Gabriel and Santa Ana Mountains; noted locally near Arroyo Seco west of Pasadena. San Bernardino Mountains south and west slopes up to 3,000 feet and occasionally at some distance from foot of mountains; locally noted in Waterman Canyon at 2,000 feet.

OCCURRENCE.

On margins of perpetual and intermittent streams and bottoms, usually in rather moist gravelly or sandy soil; sometimes in dry situations. Much scattered or in small, straggling groups.

CLIMATIC CONDITIONS.—Similar to those of California sycamore.

TOLERANCE.—Intolerant of shade.

REPRODUCTION.—Seeding habits undetermined. Seedlings scarce. Much of seed eaten by rodents, and carried by flood waters to places unfavorable for germination.

Family MYRICACEÆ.

The family characters of the trees of this group are thick, narrow, minutely resinous-dotted leaves, which grow from the branches in alternate positions (never in pairs, one leaf opposite the other), and the small berry-like fruit, coated with minute grains of white waxy matter. The male and female flowers are each borne either on different branches of the same tree or upon different trees.

MYRICA. WAX MYRTLES.

Wax myrtles are small trees (or shrub-like) with willow-like leathery leaves, the season's growth of which persists for about one year, when they begin to fall a few at a time. The crushed foliage and twigs exhale a resinous aromatic odor, somewhat perceptible even without bruising. The bud-like clusters of male and female flowers (of Pacific species) are each borne singly on different parts of the same tree and usually of the same branch, each at the base of a previous year's leaf, the female clusters above the larger, longer male clusters.

The small, berry-like spherical fruit is ripened in autumn; several close clusters of fruit may appear on leafless parts of the branch, the leaves of the previous year, present when the flowers open, having fallen. The surface of the berries is thickly coated with round grains of whitish waxy matter, which is an exudation.

Though of no economic value on account of their small size, these shrubby trees are of some importance in forming with other species a protective cover. The western representative is likely to be especially useful for extension on exposed coast sands and low hills, situations to which all of the species are particularly adapted.

The sole present importance of the genus is the production of the vegetable wax of commerce, which is obtained from the berries of two eastern species. Three tree species occur within the United States; two in the south Atlantic States, adjacent islands, and Gulf coast regions, and one in the Pacific coast country. A group of ancient origin, members of which once existed on this continent in the Cretaceous period.

California Myrtle.

Myrica californica Chamisso.

DISTINGUISHING CHARACTERISTICS.

California myrtle, also called "bayberry" and "wax myrtle," is mainly a bushy tree, from 8 to 20 feet high, sometimes under 5 feet, and from 3 to 6 inches in diameter; only very rarely from 25 to 30 feet high and from 8 to 12 inches in diameter. Slender upright branches form a dense, narrow crown with rounded top, exposing a short, smooth, thin-barked trunk, the bark grayish brown externally and deep reddish brown within. The very dark green glossy leaves (figs. 83, 84), light yellowish green beneath and with numerous minute black specks, are thin but tough in texture. The extreme edges of the leaves are slightly curled toward the under surface. A slight aromatic odor is perceptible from the leaves. As a rule, the female flowers appear on the upper part of a branch, below which the larger, longer clusters of male flowers are borne on a separate portion of the branch. Occasionally anomalous flower clusters, with both male and female flowers, occur between the upper and lower regular single-sex flowers, and some trees bear only, or mainly, male flowers. The clusters of berry-like nuts (fig. 84), maturing in September, are ashy white, the wax covering of the berries, however, concealing the dull purple color beneath. The shells of the nuts are very thick and hard. Commonly some of the berries remain on the branches until spring, but most of them fall during winter. Wood, pale rose-red, heavy, hard, and stiff, the whitish sapwood being comparatively thick. Of no economic value, but deserving protection and extension as a cover in the vicinity of the sea.

LONGEVITY.—Little is known concerning the longevity of this tree, which may possibly reach an age of 100 years. Trees from 6 to 10 inches in diameter are from 25 to 40 years old.

RANGE.

Pacific Coast region from Puget Sound, Washington, to near Santa Monica, Cal., never far from the sea.

Sea coast dunes and low hill slopes and on streams in moist, pure or humous sand and in dryish, poor, gravelly soil.   Occurs in clumps and dense patches of pure growth in open and in shade of swamp pine and live oak.

CLIMATIC CONDITIONS.—Similar to those of swamp pine.

TOLERANCE.—Very tolerant of shade.

REPRODUCTION.—Abundant seeder; young plants frequent both in shade and open moist ground.

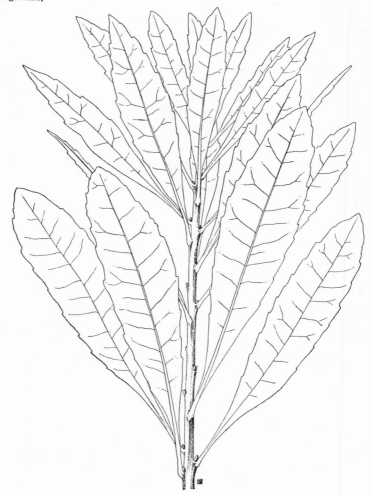

FIG. 83.—*Myrica californica,* young shoot.

Family SALICACEÆ.

A large group of trees (and shrubs) comprising the well-known willows and poplars or aspens.   The bark is characteristically bitter—especially so in the willows.   The leaves, shed in early autumn, are borne alternately on the branches (never in pairs on opposite sides of the branch).   Male and female flowers are each produced on different trees; seed is therefore borne only by female trees, the flowers of which are fertilized by insects (largely bees). The fruits, ripe in late spring as the leaves reach full size, are thin capsule-like bodies, many of which are produced in long tassel-like clusters; the capsules split open soon after maturity, liberating the minute seeds. The seeds

FIG. 84.—*Myrica californica.*

are provided with long, exceedingly fine, silky hairs, which permit the wind to carry them for very long distances.

With some exceptions, they are moisture-loving trees and shrubs, which accounts for their prevalence along streams and bottoms. A remarkable characteristic is their ability to grow readily from root or branch cuttings and to sprout vigorously and persistently from cut stumps of almost any age.

SALIX. WILLOWS.

The many trees (and shrubs) of the willow group are at once distinguished by the quinine-like bitter taste of their bark, which is harmless. Their deciduous leaves, variable in form, are most frequently long and narrowly pointed, smooth throughout, or coated with fine silky hairs on their under surfaces; their margins may be entire (uncut) or variously toothed. They grow singly on the branches at points alternating with each other on different sides of the branches (never in pairs, one opposite the other on two sides of the branch). Willow leaves are peculiar in having a pair of ear-shaped, minute or large, leaf-like growths at the base of their stems. These are larger and therefore more conspicuous on vigorous annual shoots, on which they may remain until they fall with the leaves, while on other stems they are present only during the early growth of the leaves. The leaves may fall in the autumn without much change of color, or they may first turn a lemon yellow. Leaf-scars (left by the falling leaves) are marked by three minute dots (fibro-vascular bundles severed by the parting of the leaf stem). The fruit and seed are sufficiently described under the family (Salicaceæ).

Annual sprouts of willows are exceedingly strong and withy, while older branches from the crown are often peculiarly frangible; twigs are notably frangible where they join a larger branch or fork. A frequent habit of growth among willows is to produce several trunks from a single greatly extended rootstock, while some species regularly have single, isolated trunks. Species of the latter form have been readily admitted to be trees. Those forming clusters of very large trunks have, on the other hand, been denied this rank for some time, even though the trunks were otherwise tree-like. For practical purposes, however, they certainly are trees. A striking and valuable cultural feature of the willows is their remarkable vitality, which enables them to grow persistently from cut stumps and easily from pieces of branches or roots. Through this quality some of the foreign willow trees have been pollarded for centuries, the shoots being used for coarse baskets and other economic purposes.

The willows are swamp or moist-ground species, finding their habitat from sea level to an elevation of 10,000 or more feet.

Willow wood is soft, light, usually brittle but firm, commonly pale brown, tinged with red; the heartwood of some species is very durable when exposed to water or earth. It has various minor economic uses, especially for cricket and ball bats and for gunpowder and charcoal. The greatest commercial usefulness of willows appears to have come mainly through the manufacture of baskets and furniture from shoots or rods produced in one season. Some of the tree willows produce moderately large, clear trunks, which would yield lumber, but as a rule their boles are of poor form for saw timber. Except in generally forestless regions, where willows and their allies, the cottonwoods, become useful because no other trees are available, these trees have little to commend them in comparison with many other trees of demonstrated value. They are, however, distinctly important to the forester for binding shifting sands and for holding banks of streams in soft bottoms where serious ruin of agricultural lands may result from the erosion of unprotected banks.

Tree willows attain their mature growth in comparatively few years—50 to 150 years—after which the trunks become hollow, may gradually show signs of decay, and are easily broken by storm. Their tenacious vitality, however, permits them to grow for centuries, repairing or replacing broken trunks by new stem or root sprouts.

Approximately 75 species occur on this continent, while about 20 are trees, 13 of which inhabit the Pacific region, into which one extends from the Atlantic States. The willows are of very ancient origin. Remains of them exist in the Cretaceous formations of our Middle West, while willows appear to have flourished extensively on this continent and in Europe during the Miocene period.

With few exceptions the various species of willows, which, as a class, are nearly always distinguished as willows from other trees and shrubs by laymen, are exceedingly difficult to identify, especially before they become trees. When they have attained tree size most of the important ones can be distinguished by a careful study of their mature leaves, bark, twigs, and habit of growth. But individual trees are likely to be found which will baffle attempts at identification without a close examination of the minute characters of the male and female flowers and the tiny seed capsules, all consideration of which is here omitted. Such an examination requires a strong magnifying lens and a good knowledge of plant morphology.

Black Willow.

Salix nigra Marshall.

DISTINGUISHING CHARACTERISTICS.

Black willow is the largest and most widely known of our tree willows, but much less abundantly represented in the Pacific country than in its eastern range. It is more distinctly a tree throughout its range than almost any of our other tree willows, and for this reason it is probably the most commonly recognized. Several trunks grow close together. Its usual size is from 25 to 50 feet in height and from 10 to 20 inches in diameter. Trees from 60 to 80 feet high and from 2 to 3 feet in diameter are of rather rare occurrence. The trunks (rarely straight) are usually somewhat bowed and leaning, but are clear of branches for a third or a half of their length in the open, and for two-thirds of it in close stands. The branches trend somewhat upward, forming a wide, round-topped, open crown. Rough, furrowed, blackish-brown bark, with wide, thick-scaled ridges and narrower connecting ridges, is a marked character. The slender, drooping branchlets are very easily snapped off at their bases. The leaves—very variable in size and form—from straight to scythe-like (figs. 85, 86), are from $2\frac{1}{2}$ to 5 or sometimes 6 inches long, and pale yellow-green. They may be somewhat shiny above and smooth beneath, or minutely hairy on the veins of the under surface. Wood, pale red-brown, light and soft, rather fine-grained, but firm. It has little or no actual or possible economic value, except for fuel and charcoal.

LONGEVITY.—Not much is known of its age limits, which in trees from 12 to 18 inches in diameter are from 35 to 60 years. Occasional large trees are estimated to be from 125 to 150 years old. Further study of its longevity is required.

RANGE.

New Brunswick to southern Florida and west to eastern Dakota, Nebraska, Kansas, Indian Territory, southern Arizona, southern and central California, and south into Mexico.

CALIFORNIA.—Western foothills of Sierras, San Joaquin and Sacramento valleys, north to eastern foothills of coast ranges in Colusa County, and south through southern cross ranges.

The detailed range of this species east of the Pacific region will be given in a future publication.

FIG. 85.—*Salix nigra,* seed-bearing branch.

OCCURRENCE.

On borders of streams, and on low flats, in humus-covered wet or moist gravelly and sandy soils. Forms strips and small patches of pure growth, and grows with other willows; rather uncommon in Pacific region. Climatic conditions marked by moderate temperature, which probably accounts for its rarity in this region. Decidedly intolerant

FIG. 86.—*Salix nigra: a,* male flowers.

throughout life. Abundant seeder (over greater part of range); reproduction best on wet humus or sand.

Almond Willow.

Salix amygdaloides Andersson.

DISTINGUISHING CHARACTERISTICS.

This willow, also called "peach willow" (from a resemblance of its leaves to those of the peach), produces one straight, or sometimes leaning, trunk.

Fig. 87.—*Salix amygdaloides: a,* male flowers; *b,* seed-bearing branch.

(Very rarely several clustered stems.)   Its upright branches are peculiarly straight, forming a rather compact, round head.   Ordinarily it is from 20 to 30 feet high and from 8 to 12 inches in diameter; occasionally from 40 to 50 feet high, and from 16 to 18 inches in diameter. Bark, very pale reddish brown, about half an inch thick, rather deeply furrowed, the wide ridges thick-scaled and connected by narrower ones. The straight, slender, shiny, red to orange-brown twigs are tough and can not readily be broken off where they join a branch. On their upper sides the thin leaves (fig. 87) are shiny, light yellow-green; on their under surfaces, very pale or whitish, but smooth; the minute teeth on the borders have gland-like points. The prominent mid-veins and their branches are conspicuously light to dark yellow. Wood, pale yellow-brown, light in weight, soft, brittle, and fine-grained. It has no economic value or commercial uses. Very probably this species, not yet tested under cultivation, will prove to be a good basket willow. The straight, slender annual shoots are tough and resemble in character and appearance the true almond willow (*Salix amygdalina*), which furnishes a standard basket rod.

LONGEVITY.—Little is known of the age limits. The tree grows rapidly in diameter during 25 to 30 years. Trees from 7 to 10 inches in diameter are from 20 to 35 years old. Probably attains maturity in from 40 to 50 years.

RANGE.

Quebec (near Montreal) and New York (Cayuga County) to the upper Saskatchewan; southward to Ohio and Missouri, and westward in the Plains region to the Rocky Mountains, where it ranges from southwestern Texas to Oregon, Washington, British Columbia.

OCCURRENCE.

Borders of perpetual and intermittent streams, in rocky or gravelly soil. Climatic conditions, silvical characteristics, etc., undetermined.

Smooth Willow.

Salix lœvigata Bebb.

DISTINGUISHING CHARACTERISTICS.

For want of a distinctive current common name "smooth willow" is here coined from the technical name. Smooth willow is known in its range only as "black willow," from the roughly furrowed, very dark reddish brown bark, the ridges of which are firm, narrow and connected by still narrower lateral ones; bark of the large dark brown limbs is also seamed. Commonly with one straight stem from 15 to 25 feet high (the clear portion short) and from 6 to 10 inches in diameter; sometimes 30 or 35 feet high and a foot in diameter—rarely larger. The slim branches form a somewhat irregular, broad, round-topped crown. Full grown twigs are very slender, smooth, and clear reddish yellow to reddish brown. The distinctly deep bluish green leaves (fig. 88)[a] are smooth throughout, shiny on their upper surface and whitish beneath, about $3\frac{1}{2}$ to $6\frac{1}{2}$ inches long (sometimes $1\frac{1}{4}$ inches wide) and with conspicuous yellow mid-veins, branches of which are clearly seen on the top side of the leaf—less evident beneath. Leaf stems, wide, channeled, very minutely and sparingly hairy.

Wood, pale reddish brown. Not used for commercial purposes.

---

[a] Variety *Salix lœvigata augustifolia* Bebb is a form with narrow scythe-shaped leaves with rounded bases; while the variety *S. lœvigata congesta* was distinguished by the same author by its short dense flower clusters and the spherical, cone-shaped, very short-stemmed seed capsules.

LONGEVITY.—Age limit undetermined. Grows rapidly in height and diameter during first 25 years and appears to be short-lived. Trees from 10 to 14 inches in diameter are from 28 to 40 years old.

FIG 88.—*Salix lævigata: a,* seed-bearing branch.

RANGE.

California (Siskiyou County to the southern boundary of the State). At middle elevations in coast mountains and Sierras.

Confined to wet borders of mountain and lower streams, in gravel and sand. Forms clumps and patches, often mixed with Bigelow willow and white alder. Climatic and other requirements undetermined.

Western Black Willow.

Salix lasiandra Bentham.

DISTINGUISHING CHARACTERISTICS.

Western black willow, like the preceding species, is known throughout its range simply as "black willow," on account of the color of its bark. The bark is distinctly cut by cross-seams into flat plates longer than they are wide. The form of its leaves and twigs affords the principal means of distinction. Ordinarily it is 25 or 30 feet high and from 14 to 20 inches in diameter; sometimes from 40 to 50 feet high and from 24 to 30 inches through; in some parts of its range, often a bushy tree under 10 feet high. The clear trunk, rarely straight, is short, and the long, straight limbs grow upright, producing an open, unsymmetrical crown. The mature twigs are rather large, and clear reddish yellow to brown. The leaves (fig. 89), deep yellow green at maturity and about $4\frac{1}{2}$ to 5 inches long, are shiny on their upper surface, whitish beneath, the large mid-veins reddish yellow and the leaf stems, with two or more blackish spots (glands) at their juncture with the leaf blade, smooth or slightly and minutely hairy. As a rule the largest leaves are produced at the ends of the branches, apparently on account of the more vigorous growth there.

RANGE.

California (west of the Sierra Nevada); western Oregon, Washington, and southern British Columbia (Selkirk Mountains) at middle elevations.

OCCURRENCE.

Borders of streams, water-holes, and lakes, in damp, gravelly, and sandy soil. Scattered in small groups and singly; sometimes with red and white alders, black and Fremont cottonwoods, and California sycamore. Climatic and other requirements undetermined.

A well-marked variety of this willow is the Lyall willow (*Salix lasiandra lyallii* [a] Sargent), often from 20 to 30 inches in diameter; common on streams of western Oregon and Washington. Its leaves (fig. 90) are sometimes 10 or 12 inches long, and distinctly white beneath, while the leaf stems have more glands than those of the Western black willow. Another less distinct form is *Salix lasiandra caudata* (Nutt.) Sudworth, which has smaller, more leathery leaves than the species; they are also often scythe-shaped, tapering at the base, and green throughout.

Salix lasiandra lyallii occurs in western Oregon, Washington, and southern British Columbia at middle elevations. It grows on borders and bottoms of lowland streams and of those on lower mountain slopes, in moist, loamy sand and gravel or humous, rocky, and gravelly soils of higher sites. Forms clusters in open pure stretches and patches, or is scattered singly at higher levels among other inhabitants of stream banks. Appears indifferent to altitude, but abundant soil moisture is a requisite.

CLIMATIC CONDITIONS similar to those of red alder.

TOLERANCE.—Endures considerable shade—probably one of the most tolerant of willows.

REPRODUCTION.—Abundant seeder; seedlings rather scattered, but frequent.

---

[a] Described in 1842 by Nuttall as *Salix speciosa,* from its large handsome leaves; a name which, unknown to that author, was unfortunately already assigned to another willow.

Wood of *Salix lasiandra* and its varieties is pale brown and especially brittle.

It is probable that the annual shoots of this willow, particularly of its variety *lyallii*, would, with training, prove to be good basket rods. They are worthy of trial in moist, sandy river bottoms.

FIG. 89.—*Salix lasiandra.*

LONGEVITY.—Probably reaches maturity within about 50 years. Trees from 12 to 18 inches in diameter are from 30 to 47 years old.

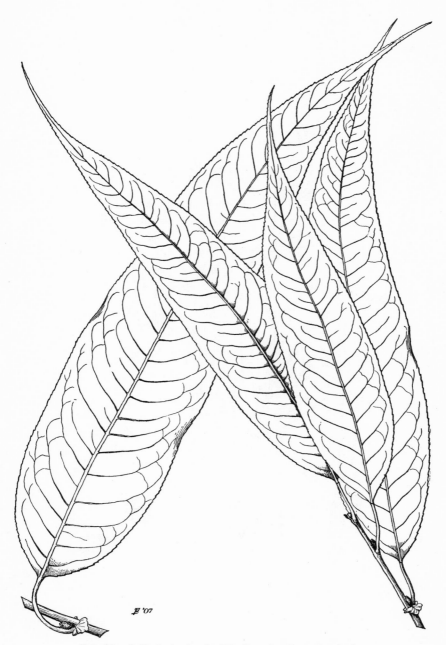

FIG. 90.—*Salix lasiandra lyallii*, three-fourths natural size.

Longleaf Willow.

Salix fluviatilis Nuttall.

DISTINGUISHING CHARACTERISTICS.

Longleaf willow is one of the most distinct of our tree willows; it can readily
be recognized by its long, very narrow leaves.   Because it forms dense thickets

FIG. 91.—*Salix fluviatilis.*

on river sand-bars, usually long before any other willow secures a footing there,
it is widely known as " sand-bar willow."   The more appropriate common name

chosen here is derived from the technical name *Salix longifolia*, which was used for it until it was found to be antedated by *S. fluviatilis*.

A slender tree under 25 feet in height, with a narrow, compact crown of short, slim, nearly upright branches; sometimes from 40 to 50 feet high and from 18 to 20 inches in diameter. A large part of the trunk is clear of branches. Over much of its range it is only a reed-like shrub growing in very dense thickets 6 or 8 feet high. The closely scaly bark is very thin (usually less than one-fourth of an inch thick), and dark grayish brown, with a faint reddish tinge; smooth on small stems. Mature leaves (fig. 91) are pale yellowish-green, the under surface lighter than the upper, smooth on both surfaces, and from about 3 to 5 inches long. A variety of this species, *Salix fluviatilis argyrophylla* (Nutt.) Sargent, is distinguished by the dense coating of silky hairs on its leaves and seed capsules; while another form, *S. fluviatilis exigua* (Nutt.) Sarg., is characterized by its very narrow leaves, $1\frac{1}{4}$ to $2\frac{1}{4}$ inches long by one-fourth to one-third of an inch broad. Both of these varieties range from northern California through the Southwest to Texas.

Wood, pale reddish brown, light, firm, and rather elastic. It is of no economic value.

The longleaf willow is one of the most useful of its kind for retaining moist sand bars and the erodable banks of streams which flow through rich bottoms. It forms the densest of pure thickets, and propagates itself largely by shoots from a mass of running roots, as well as by its seed, quickly occupying every available strip of moist sand.

LONGEVITY.—Not fully determined. Stems from 2 to 3 inches in diameter are from 9 to 14 years old.

RANGE.

Quebec (Lake St. John and Island of Orleans) and southward through western New England to the Potomac River; northwestward to the Arctic Circle (valley of Mackenzie River) and British Columbia and California; southward in the Mississippi River basin to northern Mexico and Lower California.

OCCURRENCE.

Sand bars bordering lowland streams, ponds, and lakes, in moist or wet sand and gravel, overlaid with silt, which this willow's dense reed-like stems retain. Forms extensive pure thickets and patches, in which cottonwood is sometimes mingled.

CLIMATIC CONDITIONS.—Similar to those of aspen at lower levels.

TOLERANCE.—Very intolerant of shade.

REPRODUCTION.—Exceedingly prolific seeder. Crowded masses of seedlings the first tree growth to hold wet bars and muddy shores. Strikingly even-aged stands characteristic of reproduction.

Silverleaf Willow.

Salix sessilifolia Nuttall.

DISTINGUISHING CHARACTERISTICS.

Silverleaf willow is generally known only by the name of "willow." In general appearance, and in the form of its leaves, it closely resembles longleaf willow, particularly the variety *argyrophylla*. It is sometimes 20 or 25 feet high and from 8 to 10 inches through, but usually it is a slender shrub from 6 to 10 feet high. The grayish-brown bark of larger trunks is from one-third to one-half an inch thick, with irregular shallow seams. Mature leaves (fig. 92), about 2 to $4\frac{1}{2}$ inches long by about one-fourth to one-third of an inch wide, sometimes narrower, are light pea-green, smooth or minutely hairy on the upper side, and with white, silky hairs beneath. Midveins of the leaves, lemon yellow, and the short thick stems minutely hairy.

The distinctive characters of this willow are not fully worked out. Many forms of it so closely resemble *S. fluviatilis argyrophylla*, with which it may occur, that they can be distinguished only with great difficulty. Further careful field study is required for both.

Wood, pale reddish brown.   Not used commercially.

LONGEVITY.—Not fully determined.   Stems from 6 to 9 inches in diameter are 24 to 37 years old.

FIG. 92.—*Salix sessilifolia: a,* seed-bearing branch.

RANGE.

From mouth of Columbia River, Washington, to southwestern California, ranging through western Oregon and western slopes of Sierras and coast ranges.

OCCURRENCE.

Borders of streams and moist depressions.

Mackenzie Willow.

Salix cordata mackenzieana Hooker.

DISTINGUISHING CHARACTERISTICS.

Mackenzie willow is a little-known species, probably not now distinguished by laymen. Slender, straight, from 15 to 18 feet high and from 3 to 5 inches in

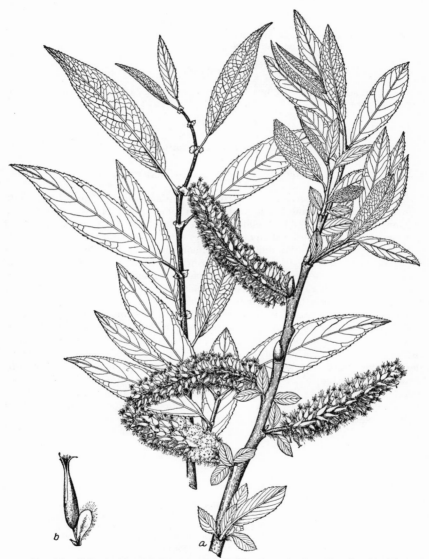

FIG. 93.—*Salix cordata mackenzieana: a,* fruiting branch ; *b,* seed pod, enlarged.

diameter, with thin, smooth, unbroken bark of an ashy gray color, and a narrow, rather compact crown of thin branches which grow upward. Mature twigs of the year are rather slender, but stiff in appearance, shiny yellow, later becoming greenish. Mature leaves (fig. 93), from 1¾ to 3¼ inches long, are deep yellow-green (paler beneath), smooth on both surfaces; the somewhat scythe-shaped form of the leaves is a notable character. Midveins and stems of the leaves are yellow. Wood, reddish brown, light, soft, and brittle.

LONGEVITY.—Not fully determined. Stems from 3 to 5 inches through are from 13 to 22 years old.

RANGE.

Great Slave Lake and southward (through region along eastern base of Rocky Mountains) to northern Idaho and California (Lake County).

OCCURRENCE.

Borders of mountain streams in rocky and gravelly soil. Climatic and other requirements undetermined.

White Willow.

Salix lasiolepis [a] Bentham.

DISTINGUISHING CHARACTERISTICS.

The white willow, so called on account of the smooth ashy gray bark (with brownish tinge) of young trunks and limbs of older trees, varies in size from a cluster of low shoots (at high elevations) to a tree from 15 to 25 feet in height (at low elevations) with a diameter of from 6 to 10 inches. Very exceptionally it is from 30 to 40 feet high and a foot or more in diameter. The slim branches trend upward strongly in a rather narrow, irregular open crown. Bark of larger trunks is less than one-half an inch thick, shallowly seamed, the wide ridges connected here and there by smaller lateral ridges; indistinctly dark brown or blackish with occasional grayish areas on the flat ridges. Mature twigs of the season, rather thick, bear numerous leaves and are deep red-brown, tinged with yellow toward their extremities, where they are very minutely downy, but smooth lower down. Mature leaves (fig. 94), from 2½ to about 5½ inches long, are somewhat thick and leathery, with yellow stems and midveins, dark yellow-green and smooth on their top sides, conspicuously silver-white beneath, where the midveins and terminal leaves are minutely hairy. Wood: Very little of the pale brown heartwood is formed, the main bulk of the trunk being sapwood. Not used commercially, but in the southern range at a low altitude, where fuel timber is scarce, it is locally used for fuel.

LONGEVITY.—Not fully determined. Stems from 5 to 9 inches in diameter are from 12 to 22 years old.

RANGE.

Northern California (Klamath River) and southward through the western part of the State to Lower California and southern Arizona (Tanners Canyon on Huachuca Mountains, and White River Canyon on Chiricahua Mountains).

---

[a] There is doubt, which can not be cleared up at present, as to whether this name is older than *Salix bigelovii* Torrey, supposed to have been published in 1856 or January, 1857, while *S. lasiolepis* Bentham appeared in February, 1857. Torrey, however, cites other species of Salix described and published by Bentham with his *S. lasiolepis*, and this seems to show conclusively that the latter's name was actually published before Torrey's *S. bigelovii,* notwithstanding the *printed* earlier date of the document containing Torrey's name of this willow.

OCCURRENCE.

Borders of lowland streams and adjacent bottoms (as a tree), and lower mountain slopes in springy places and on streams (shrubby), in moist sandy and gravelly soil. Scattered and in small groups with California sycamore and white alder.

CLIMATIC CONDITIONS.—Similar to those of white alder.

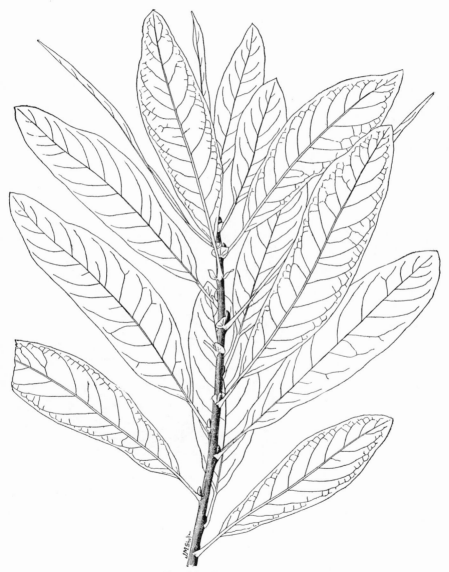

FIG. 94.—*Salix lasiolepis.*

Nuttall Willow.

Salix nuttallii Sargent.

DISTINGUISHING CHARACTERISTICS.

Nuttall willow, so called here for the sake of a distinctive common name, is mainly known as " black willow," and to some extent, because of its high moun-

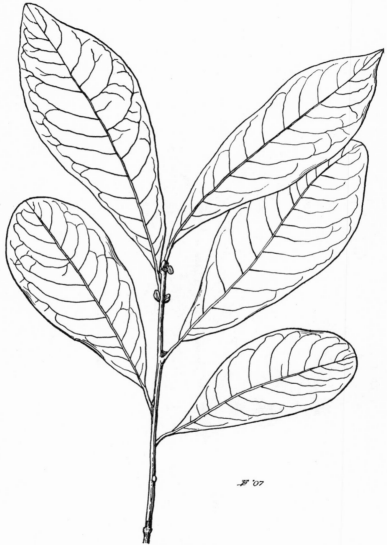

FIG. 95.—*Salix nuttallii.*

tain habitat, as " mountain willow." It has a single straight trunk, and when grown in the open its long, slim branches droop in a somewhat close, long, dome-like crown; the clear trunk is very short, even in dense stands. Its usual height is from 20 to 25 feet, and its smooth, thin-barked, dark ashy brown trunks are from 6 to 8 inches in diameter. Bark on the bases of large trunks is irregularly broken into wide ridges and is blackish brown, with a faint tinge of red. The red tinge is evident also on smoother parts of the trunk. Twigs of one or two season's growth are thick, clear reddish yellow, becoming a deep mahogany brown with age. The form and texture of the mature leaves (fig. 95) serve generally to distinguish this willow from others associated with it. They are thin, somewhat shiny, smooth, and deep yellow-green on the top sides, pale or whitish beneath (sometimes very minutely hairy), about 2 to 5 inches long, margins slightly curled toward the under surface, and the prominent yellow midveins, as well as the stems, finely hairy. The Pacific coast form of this willow distinguished as *Salix nuttallii brachystachys* (Benth.) Sargent, is generally a larger tree than that occurring farther eastward, being from 40 to 50 feet in height and from 12 to 18 inches in diameter. It has a longer clear trunk, which is more commonly ashy gray, with whitish areas, and irregularly seamed; the bark when broken shows clear red-brown. The general appearance of the trees and their foliage is, however, essentially the same; the female flower clusters only are shorter in the variety and frequently strongly curved. The coast tree is here considered only as a geographic form, inseparable, for the forester's purposes, from the type growing farther inland. Wood (of the inland tree), pale reddish brown and of somewhat lighter weight than that of the coast tree, which is of a slightly more reddish color. The wood has no commercial or domestic value, for it grows where there are many other superior woods.

LONGEVITY.—Not fully determined. Trees from 8 to 14 inches in diameter are from 25 to 48 years old.

RANGE.

From southern Assiniboia and British Columbia (Columbia River near Donald), Washington, and Oregon southward in the Rockies to northern New Mexico and Arizona (San Francisco Mountain); California (Sierras and coast ranges to the San Bernardino Mountains).

OCCURRENCE.

Headwaters and upper courses of high mountain streams; moist benches, depressions, and gentle slopes with damp, humous, rocky or gravelly soil; abundant soil moisture and well-drained situation essential. Occurs singly and in small groups, often with red alder and broadleaf maple.

CLIMATIC CONDITIONS.—Similar to those of red and mountain alders.

TOLERANCE.—Endures considerable shade.

REPRODUCTION.—Moderately abundant seeder. Seedlings frequent, but usually much scattered.

Broadleaf Willow.

Salix amplifolia Coville.

DISTINGUISHING CHARACTERISTICS.

Broadleaf willow is a new and as yet little known willow discovered in 1899. The common name is coined from the technical name, which refers to a conspicuous characteristic. Locally, the species is called "willow" only. As now known it is a shrubby tree from 20 to 25 feet high and from 8 to 12 inches in diameter. Nothing is known now of the trunk form, crown, bark, and wood, which need to be studied. Young twigs (fig. 96) are densely white-woolly, but in two or three years this covering goes off, and the dark red-purple bark is exposed. Mature leaves (fig. 97) are light yellowish-green, nearly or quite

FIG. 96.—*Salix amplifolia: a,* male flowers; *b,* female flowers; *c,* seed-bearing branch.

smooth on their top sides (sometimes slightly woolly) and whitish beneath; young and immature leaves are more or less densely white-woolly on both surfaces, the wool gradually disappearing with age later in the season.

RANGE.

ALASKA.—West shore of Yakutat Bay, near Hubbard Glacier in Disenchantment Bay and on Haenke Island and Egg Island and on the east shore at the head of Yakutat Bay.

FIG. 97.—*Salix amplifolia.*

OCCURRENCE.

Near sea beaches on sand dunes. Scattered and with Alaska willow.

CLIMATIC CONDITIONS.—Probably similar to those of black cottonwood; little known now of requirements.

Hooker Willow.

Salix hookeriana Barratt in Hooker.[a]

DISTINGUISHING CHARACTERISTICS.

The Hooker willow is not known by this name in its native habitat, but simply

Fɪɢ. 98.—*Salix hookeriana.*

as "willow."   It varies from a sprawling shrub to a cluster of trunks from 12

---

[a] This name is commonly credited to Hooker, who published it thus: "*Salix hookeriana* Barratt mst.*"*—Barratt having described and named the tree.   Hooker obviously intended

to 18 feet high and from 6 to 10 inches in diameter; rarely single trees are 25 or 30 feet high. The thin, scaly bark is pale reddish-brown, and indistinctly and irregularly seamed. Mature twigs of the season are densely coated with whitish woolly hairs, a thinner covering of which remains during another year, showing the clear red-brown bark beneath. Mature leaves (fig. 98), 3 to 6 inches long, clear, rather shiny, yellowish green and usually smooth on their top sides, except along the midveins, which are hairy; sometimes entirely covered with a hairy coat, which is always present on young leaves. The under surface of the leaves has whitish, dense wool or minute, close hairs, particularly on the large midveins and their branches.

Wood: A large proportion of the stem is heartwood, which is pale reddish-brown. Not used commercially.

LONGEVITY.—Not fully determined. Stems from 4 to 7 inches in diameter are from 18 to 35 years old.

RANGE.

Vancouver Island to southern Oregon—coast region.

OCCURRENCE.

Commonly near tide-water streams, sloughs, ponds, and salt marshes, but also about other wet places, in sandy, gravelly, or mucky soil; sometimes in dryish situations. Scattered singly and in groups.

CLIMATIC CONDITIONS.—Similar to those of Sitka spruce.

TOLERANCE.—Undetermined, but appears little tolerant of shade.

REPRODUCTION.—Abundant seeder. Young plants are frequent, especially in sand and muck.

Silky Willow.

Salix sitchensis Sanson in Bongard.

DISTINGUISHING CHARACTERISTICS.

Silky willow ordinarily has slender shrubby stems from 8 to 12 feet high. As a tree (rarely over 20 or 25 feet in height), it is greatly branched, with a crooked or variously bowed or leaning trunk from 8 to 10 inches in diameter. The thin, scaly bark is faintly reddish-brown. Mature twigs of the year are deep reddish-yellow to reddish-brown, minutely hairy; a season later they become nearly or quite smooth, but occasionally with a whitish coating. The leaves (figs. 99, 100), from 3 to 5 inches long, are clearly distinguished by their dense covering of shiny, white, silky hairs on their under surfaces, while on their top sides they are very deep grass-green, smooth, and shiny. The midveins, as well as the thick leaf-stems, are hairy.

Wood: The heartwood, pale cherry red, forms only a small proportion of the stem. Not used commercially.

LONGEVITY.—Not fully determined. Trees from 5 to 9 inches in diameter are from 16 to 30 years old.

RANGE.

Alaska (Cook Inlet and Kodiak Island) to southern California (Santa Barbara—coast region—and up to higher timber belt in mountains) and east to Blue Mountains, Oregon.

OCCURRENCE.

Borders of streams, meadows, and moist depressions; often in rich, mucky soil.

---

it to be cited as Barratt's species, since no author would deliberately name a species in honor of himself, necessitating the citation of a patronymic from his name, and his name also as its author, side by side.

FIG. 99.—*Salix sitchensis.*

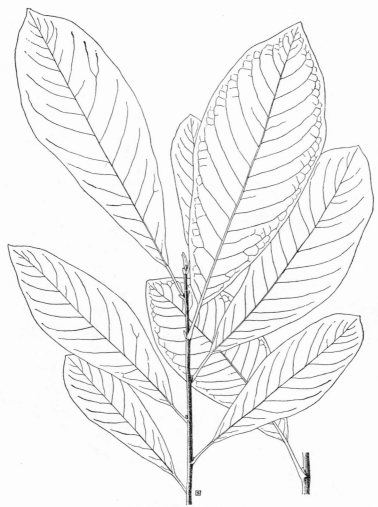

FIG. 100.—*Salix sitchensis.*

Feltleaf Willow.

Salix alaxensis (Anderss.) Coville.

DISTINGUISHING CHARACTERISTICS.

Feltleaf willow, so called on account of the felt-like, woolly covering of its leaves, was known for over thirty years as a low shrub. It was only about

FIG. 101.—*Salix alaxensis: a,* male flowers; *b,* seed-bearing branch.

eight years ago that it was found to become a tree from 20 to 25 feet high and from 4 to 5 inches in diameter in protected situations. Little is yet known of its habit when of tree size, and nothing of the character and appearance of the bark and wood, concerning which further study is required. The yearling twigs are thick and densely covered with white hairs (fig. 101) ; later the twigs

FIG. 102.—*Salix alaxensis.*

lose this covering, and the somewhat shiny, dark purple bark beneath is exposed. Mature leaves (fig. 102), yellowish-green, are rendered unique by being densely coated with pure white, shiny hairs on their under surfaces, but smooth, and slightly wrinkled by the depression of the veins on their upper sides. The wide midvein is yellow. They vary in length from about 2½ to 4 inches, and in width from 1 to 1½ inches. The hairy seed capsules are borne in a peculiarly dense, cylindrical cluster, from 4 to 5 inches long, while the top of the capsules ends in a minutely double-forked, thread-like tip (fig. 101).

RANGE.

Coast of Alaska, from Alexander Archipelago to Cape Lisbourne, and eastward to the valley of the Mackenzie River and to the shores of Coronation Gulf.

OCCURRENCE.

Little is known of its occurrence. Bay shores in newly deposited gravel (low shrub), and in gravel of older deposit (as a tree) among shrubs. Scattered, and sometimes with broadleaf willow.

CLIMATIC CONDITIONS.—Probably similar to those of black cottonwood.

POPULUS. COTTONWOODS AND POPLARS.

This large group includes the trees popularly known as aspens, poplars [a] or "popples," and cottonwoods. Several of them are very large forest trees, with rough, deeply furrowed, grayish bark ("cottonwoods"), or with smooth bark, little broken, and whitish or ashy (aspens). In their habits, their reproduction, and, to some extent, their foliage, they are closely related to the willows, with which they are most often associated. The leaves grow singly at alternate points on the branches, as in the willows. In outline, many of them are remotely triangular or egg-shaped, sometimes lance-shaped—very closely resembling the pointed-leafed willows; the borders of the leaves either have small, hooked, blunt teeth or are entire (uncut). When mature, they are most often smooth on both surfaces, but occasional species have hairy or woolly leaves. The leaf stems of many species are flattened at right angles to the leaf blade, and this causes the leaves to tremble in the slighest breeze. The leaves, after turning yellow, fall from the trees in autumn, leaving prominent leaf scars which give the twigs a knotty appearance. The scaly buds of many species are characterized by a covering of pungent, sticky resin,[b] which appears to have a protective use. Male and female flowers are each borne on separate [c] trees; only the female trees produce seed. Trees of the two sexes are unevenly distributed—frequently only one seed tree to many male or sterile trees; sometimes they are very widely separated. The flowers are fertilized by insects. With one or two exceptions (in female flowers), the flowers of each kind appear in long cylindrical clusters, which hang down conspicuously from the bases of buds on twigs of the previous year's growth. The seed-bearing flowers develop bud-like capsules (arranged on a pendent, thread-like stem) which are usually mature in early spring, before or by the time the leaves are full grown. Soon afterwards the capsules split open by from 2 to 4 divisions and liberate their minute, cottony seeds. These are provided with exceedingly fine, silky, white hairs, which render them very buoyant, so that the wind may bear them many miles from the parent trees. Of all trees, this group, together with the willows, is best

---

[a] *Liriodendron tulipifera* L., native of the East, more properly called tulip-tree, is often known as "poplar" or "yellow poplar." It is a member of the magnolia family and in no way related to the true poplars.

[b] The so-called "bee glue," with which honey bees fasten their honey combs in hives or in the hollows of trees, is gathered by bees from the buds of the cottonwoods. When hard, it is very strong.

[c] Sometimes one tree may produce clusters of male and of female flowers, or even clusters combining both male and female flowers, but this is exceptional.

equipped for effecting a wide distribution of its representatives by seeding. The lightness and abundance of poplar seed doubtless accounts for the ubiquitous presence of poplars wherever moist ground is available in all situations from sea level to nearly 10,000 feet elevation, but especially in cold, far northern regions.

The wood of the poplars is light, soft, and straight-grained. The grain is commonly fine, but is often coarse as a result of the rapid diameter growth characteristic of these trees. Its color is from whitish to a light, sometimes yellowish, brown. The wood of most species is brittle, unstable, and indurable, but that of a number of them is nevertheless of great commercial value for lumber and paper pulp. Formerly poplar wood had no economic importance, but is now rapidly coming into wider and wider use, both for pulpwood and to take the place of other woods, the supply of which is decreasing. " Yellow poplar " (tulip-tree), which some of the poplars resemble in grain and in the ease with which they can be worked, is one of the woods for which the poplars supply substitutes.

The poplars are important to the forester especially for maintaining tree growth on stream bottoms where few other trees naturally grow. They produce a forest cover and useful timber in from twenty-five to fifty years, while, like the willows, the ease and convenience with which they can be grown from root and branch cuttings and from cut stumps—even from stakes set in damp soil— renders artificial propagation particularly simple. They attain maturity in from 100 to 200 years, most of them within a century, and then begin to show signs of arrested growth, but on account of their great vitality and recuperative power some species may continue to grow for a much longer time, repairing broken trunks and other injuries to which their brittle stems are subject.

Ten poplars occur within the United States and adjacent Canadian territory, and 4 of these inhabit the Pacific region; but 3 of the latter also extend far outside the Pacific region, to the north and east.

The poplars are of very ancient origin. Remains show that they existed among the earliest tree forms of the Lower Cretaceous period in Greenland, and that many different species inhabited the central portion of this continent in the same epoch, and existed also in the Tertiary and Miocene periods in this country and in Europe.

Aspen.

Populus tremuloides Michaux.

DISTINGUISHING CHARACTERISTICS.

Aspen is the best known and most extensively distributed of our trees. Its conspicuously whitish, smooth, straight trunks and small, trembling leaves distinguish it from its associates. It is from 60 to 80 feet high and from 14 to 20 inches in diameter, more commonly from 30 to 40 feet high and from 8 to 12 inches through. In high exposed places it is small, with bent or almost prostrate stems; elsewhere the trunks are straight, unbranched, except near the summit, and of an apparently uniform diameter for one-half or two-thirds of their length. The short, slender, irregularly bent limbs stand out straight from the stem in a narrow dome-like crown, which is long in open stands and short in dense growths, in which two-thirds of the stem may be clear of branches. The hard, firm bark is little broken except near the ground. Near the ground it is broken and blackish, and, on large trunks, is nearly 2 inches thick; higher up it is thinner. Frequent black, rounded protuberances and curved, scar-like marks characterize the trunks.

The color of the bark, which is prevailingly whitish, is sometimes varied with very pale green or yellowish areas. The leaves (figs. 103 to 105) are smooth on both surfaces at maturity, somewhat shiny, and deep yellow-green above and much paler beneath. Leaf stems, yellow and flattened near the leaf blade, vary in length from about 1¼ to nearly 3 inches. In autumn the leaves become a clear lemon-yellow. Mature twigs are smooth, shiny, clear reddish brown, with similarly colored thinly resinous buds.

Wood: Silvery white sapwood forms a large proportion of the stem; the small core of heartwood is pale brown. The wood, rather fine-grained, is light, exceedingly soft, brittle, not durable in contact with the ground. Owing to its phys-

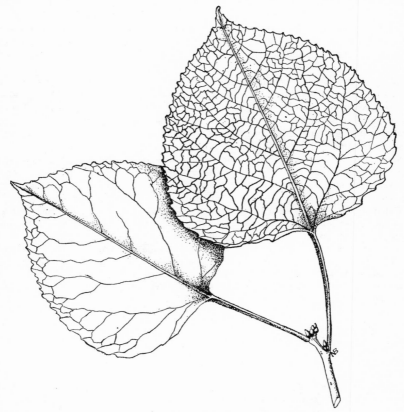

Fig. 103.—*Populus tremuloides,* eastern form.

ical fitness and the white color of its wood it is much in demand in the East for paper pulp, while its freedom from odor has made it very useful in its western range for fruit-box boards, into which large quantities of fire-killed trees are cut. Green timber is not used for the latter purpose because it warps and checks.

Longevity.—Not fully determined. Evidently a short-lived tree. Trees from 10 to 14 inches in diameter are from 21 to 36 years old.

RANGE.

Southern Labrador to Hudson Bay (southern shores) and northwest to Mackenzie River (near mouth) and Alaska (Yukon Valley); south to New Jersey, Tennessee, northeastern Missouri, northwestern Nebraska, and throughout western mountains to northern New Mexico and Arizona and central California; Lower California (Mount San Pedro Martir) and Mexico (mountains of Chihuahua).

ALASKA.—North in Yukon Valley to latitude of Arctic Circle on south slopes of Endicott Mountains, west probably nearly to Bering Sea and south to inland side Pacific Coast Range, and to its seaward side at Cook Inlet, and possibly at head of Lynn Canal. Noted near International boundary in Yukon Valley, north side Yukon basin from Fort Yukon to Deering (Bering Sea), Chandler River, Koyukuk River, Endicott Mountains up to 2,000 feet, 10 miles below Walker Lake at head of Kobuk River, Dall River to 2,500 feet, Allen, upper Kuskokwim, Matanuska, Sushitna rivers, and Copper, Tanana,

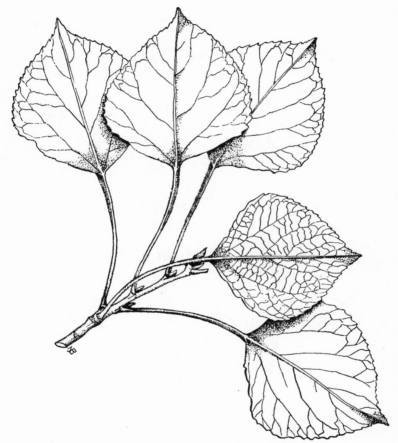

FIG. 104.—*Populus tremuloides*, Colorado form.

and White rivers up to about 3,500 feet; Lake Clark and near Nogheling River at base of Alaska peninsula, on Cook Inlet at Tyonek, and on west slope and plateau of Kenai Mountains; also reported at head Lynn Canal from Skagway to Glacier.

YUKON AND BRITISH COLUMBIA.—West to inland slopes Pacific Coast Range. Noted on Klondike, Stewart, McQuestion, and upper Pelly rivers, about Dease Lake, Liard River between Dease and Francis rivers, eastern side Cassiar Range, upper Stikine River and Skeena River above 100 miles from mouth.

WASHINGTON.—Whole State but not common; west of Cascades from sea level to 4,000 feet, and east of Cascades from 1,500 to 4,500 feet. Noted West Washington National Forest generally above 3,000 feet; locally on Slate Creek and other tributaries of Skagit River, 10 miles below Ventura, above Newby's; in East Washington National

Forest generally 1,100 to 5,000 feet; Yakima division Washington National Forest generally at 1,600 to 3,500 feet; Mount Rainier National Forest generally at 2,500 to 5,800 feet; noted locally on Natches River near mouth Nile Creek, Mount Adams, canyons Yakima River, Umptanum Creek, and Columbia River between Priest Rapids and Sen-

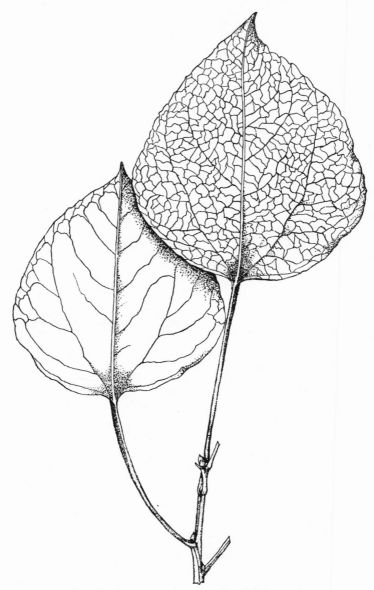

Fig. 105.—*Populus tremuloides,* California form.

tinel Bluffs in Saddle Mountains, at Wenas (Yakima County), Egbert Springs (near Trinidad on Columbia River, Douglas County), divide between Columbia and Yakima rivers (Kittitas County), Darling Mountains, Colville Indian Reservation, vicinity Pullman (Whitman County), and in Wenaha National Forest at 3,000 to 6,000 or 7,000 feet.

OREGON.—Whole State but not common. Noted on Columbia River (northeastern Wasco County), Blue Mountains, Cascade (north) National Forest, west shore upper Klamath Lake, Sprague River basin (T. 35 S., Rs. 11 and 12 E; T. 37 S., R. 11½ E.), Swan Lake Valley, Goose Lake National Forest, and Steins Mountain (southern Harney County).

CALIFORNIA.—Northern part and in Sierras south on both sides to Kern River (Kern County), at the north at 5,000 to 8,000 feet and at the south at 6,000 to 10,000 feet. Noted in Modoc and Warner Mountains National Forests, at upper end Davis Creek at 6,100 feet, Trinity Mountains at head Canyon Creek, not known on Mount Shasta; northern Sierras 7,000 to 8,800 feet, Middle Fork Feather River, about Sierra Valley above 6,500 feet, Lake Tahoe, 5,000 to 6,500 feet; Stanislaus National Forest general at 5,000 to 8,500 feet, locally noted south side of Mount Reba, Highland Creek, Rattlesnake Creek, Middle Fork Stanislaus at Mono Road crossing, head North Fork Mokelumne River, 10 miles north of Gardner 1½ miles west of Woods at 9,000 feet (timberline) (Alpine County); Yosemite National Park at Aspen Valley and elsewhere at 5,500 and 6,000 feet; Parker Creek near Yosemite Park line (Mono County) (T. 1 S., R. 26 E., sec. 18) at 7,800 feet; Sierra National Forest locally noted South Fork San Joaquin at 8,000 to 9,000 feet, Mono Creek up to head, Silver and Fish creeks (tributaries to South Fork San Joaquin), North Fork Kings River to head, Dougherty Creek (tributary Middle Fork Kings River) near Meadow, South Fork Kings River to head and its tributaries, Bubbs Creek (up to 10,500 feet) and Copper Creek (up to 9,000 feet), Crown Creek, East Fork Kaweah up to 1 mile below Farewell Gap and on its tributary Soda Canyon at Mineral King, and in Giant Forest at 6,500 feet. Kern River Canyon at 9,700 feet.

LOWER CALIFORNIA.—Plateau of Mount San Pedro Martir above 8,000 feet a few localities.

The eastern range of this species will be given in a future publication.

OCCURRENCE.

ALASKA.—On streams (drier parts), up valley slopes; protected gulches (Cook Inlet); rolling land and steep hillsides (interior); often preferring south exposures.

WEST CANADA.—Usually on streams, low-lying land; also on moderately high situations—sometimes characteristic of dry, grassy hillsides (somewhat stunted); on all slopes, but most abundant on south exposures.

WASHINGTON, OREGON, CALIFORNIA.—Prefers stream bottoms, benches, moist slopes; less abundant and smaller on dry hillsides. In Blue Mountains (Oregon), occasional groups in open spaces on high ridges. Forms part of undergrowth in yellow pine forest on east slope of Cascades—nowhere abundant. In south Oregon, as a small part of stand, and much scattered; in thickets about springs, occasionally over large areas of semiarid land. In north California (Sierras) in thickets, stunted, and at elevation of red fir, lodgepole pine, on borders of mountain meadows, moist slopes; southward in very high, rocky, moist canyons. Throughout range best growth is on moist, porous, well-drained humous soils. Grows in nearly all soils not too wet, but relatively small or stunted on poorer and drier soils.

In Pacific region generally forms pure stands only over very small or limited areas; to the east it occurs in large pure forests as well as extensively in mixture. In Alaska, commonly with balm-of-Gilead, birch, white spruce, alders, and willows (stream banks); occasionally also with lodgepole pine, Sitka spruce, black spruce, alpine fir, tamarack, birch, and black cottonwood on limited areas. On Kenai Peninsula, in forests of white spruce, with black hemlock, balm-of-Gilead, and birches; about Cook Inlet, sparingly in birch forest with small numbers of white spruce and balm-of-Gilead, mainly with latter. At Skagway, abundant with balm-of-Gilead on river bottoms over extensive areas adjacent to Sitka spruce, lodgepole pine, and alpine fir. On the lower Yukon, with birch and balm-of-Gilead on hills. South slopes of Rockies north of the Yukon carry a little aspen with white spruce and birch. In west Canada with balm-of-Gilead, black cottonwood (flats and lower slopes), birch, alders, and willows (streams), lodgepole pine (dryish terraces), and white spruce (slopes and ridges), Engelmann spruce, and black spruce. Grows with white and Engelmann spruces and with lodgepole pine singly, but mainly in groups, which fill burned or logged areas in coniferous forest. Usually subordinate in main stands of lodgepole pine. On margins of swamps, lakes, and sluggish stream banks with tamarack and with black spruce. Not abundant in Washington or Oregon, rarely occurring except singly and in small thickets, mixed especially with Douglas fir and western yellow and lodgepole pines. On Mount Rainier, near lower limit of Douglas fir; on east slope of Cascades, under Douglas fir and yellow pine from foothills nearly to summit; with lodgepole pine on west shore of upper Klamath Lake (southern Oregon). In northern and middle California, in moist places with lodgepole pine, alders, black cottonwood, and willows, and in dry places (low or bushy) with mountain mahogany and other chaparral.

CLIMATIC CONDITIONS.—The exceedingly wide range from the Atlantic to the Pacific region and from low to very high elevations shows adaptation to very varied climatic conditions, which, for the Pacific range, are essentially a combination of those already given for the many associates of aspen.

TOLERANCE.—Very intolerant of shade throughout life. Its light foliage permits growth in crowded stands, under which there is usually a more or less dense herbage. Mingled with shady conifers, intolerance of even side shade is quickly shown by long, clean stems and small narrow crowns in full light.

REPRODUCTION.—An exceedingly prolific annual seeder. Seed of high germination but of transient vitality, usually germinating shortly after being shed. Extreme buoyance results in very wide dissemination by wind. Germination best and mainly in moist, exposed mineral or slightly humous soils. The fact that its numerous seeds are quickly and widely scattered over burned and other cleared lands accounts for its being the first tree growth in many localities, where, however, it is often replaced or gradually crowded out by shade enduring associates. It is persistently present more as a result of extraordinarily prolific and constant reproduction than of power to cope with its aggressive associates.

Balm-of-Gilead.

Populus balsamifera Linnæus.

DISTINGUISHING CHARACTERISTICS.

The balm-of-Gilead, "balsam poplar," or "tacamahac," as it is also called, is distinguishable in general appearance by its lustrous, very dark green leaves, which, as they tremble and turn in the breeze, show glinting flashes of their pale green and bright rusty brown under surfaces. Height, from 75 to 80, sometimes 90, feet and diameter from 30 to 40 inches; very old trees are from 4 to 6 feet through. Stem straight and clear of branches for from 30 to 40 or more feet; the large thick limbs, trending upward strongly, form a rather long, narrow, and irregularly open crown. The bark of large trunks is slightly reddish gray and has regular deep furrows and wide ridges, while that of the limbs and young trees is brownish-gray, sometimes with a greenish shade, and is smooth. Year-old twigs are clear, shiny red-brown, with conspicuously large, sticky buds (fig. 106). End buds are about an inch long and buds from the sides of twigs are from five-eighths to three-fourths of an inch long. The bud-scales are thickly coated with a yellowish, pungently fragrant balsam, with which the young leaves are also covered. Mature leaves (fig. 106) are thin, somewhat leathery, smooth, dark shiny green on the upper surface, light green or often rust-colored, and very veiny beneath; from 3½ to about 5 inches long and 2 to 3 inches broad; leaf stems smooth, very slender, round, and from 1¾ to about 2 inches long.[a]

Wood, of light weight, soft, rather fine-grained, pale brown; not distinguishable in general appearance from that of other timber poplars. The large trunks give clear, wide lumber which is being more and more used for box and cooperage stock in place of pine and other more valuable timbers, as well as for paper pulp. Its commercial uses are likely to increase in the future.

LONGEVITY.—Not fully determined. Trees from 14 to 17 inches in diameter are from 40 to 50 years old.

RANGE.

Alaska to Hudson Bay and Newfoundland; southward to northern New England and northern New York, central Michigan and Minnesota, South Dakota, northwestern

---

[a] A well-marked variety is *Populus balsamifera candicans* (Ait.) Gray, a large tree with less upright branches, more open crown, and with wide heart-shaped leaves, which are usually silvery whitish beneath, minutely hairy on their margins, mid- and other veins, and on the leaf stems (fig. 107). It has been long cultivated for ornament in eastern United States and Canada, but nothing authentic is known of its native range.

Nebraska, northern Montana, Idaho, and Oregon. West of Hudson Bay, abundant on all Great Plains rivers of Canada, extending northward in Mackenzie River valley to (above lat. 68°) within 40 miles of Arctic Ocean, and westward in Alaska to Bering Sea. Less abundant southward in its western range.

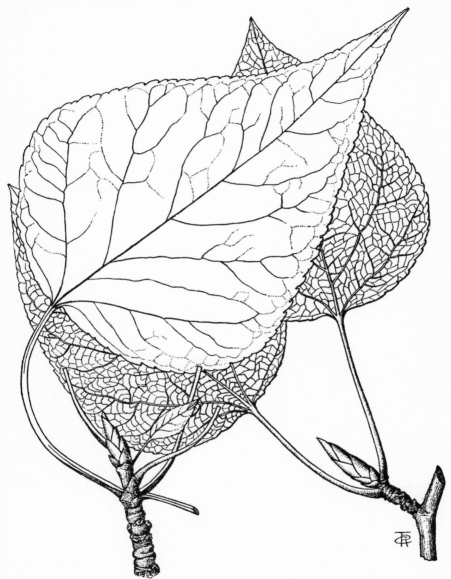

FIG. 106.—*Populus balsamifera.*

ALASKA.—Yukon River valleys and main tributaries; probably remaining north of Pacific coast ranges, except at Chilkoot Pass (head of Lynn Canal), where it may descend to south side for a short distance, and at Cook Inlet, where, from Bering Sea forest, it crosses low base of Alaska Peninsula and meets Pacific coast forest.

Abundant here about Turnagain Arm of Cook Inlet, at Hope, at mouth of Resurrection
Creek, and up west side of Kenai Peninsula to Kenai Lake, reaching nearly to timberline (1,600 to 2,000 feet), being common also at Tyonek, and probably down west

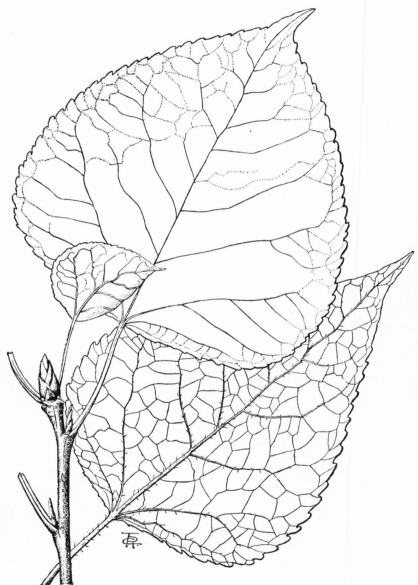

FIG. 107.—*Populus balsamifera candicans.*

coast of Cook Inlet at least as far as Iliamna Bay: reported from shores of Kodiak
Island. Western limits in Alaska are limits of tree growth (Bering Sea and Arctic
Ocean), as are also its northern limits (valley of Noatak River, lat. 68°, long. 163°),
except that *Populus balsamifera* is unknown in Turner River Valley, but occurs in

Anaktuvuk River valley (branch of Colville River), on Arctic watershed of Endicott Mountains, here reaching its northmost limit (lat. 69° 20') at 75 miles from coast. Abundant throughout Yukon River Valley bottoms and also on slopes. Extends, on south slopes of Endicott Range, to about 1,000 to 2,000 feet, on Koyukuk River to about 3,000 feet, on White and Upper Tanana rivers to about 3,500 feet, on lower Stewart River to about 2,500 feet; on south slopes of Alaska Range, near Cook Inlet, to about 1,200 feet, river bottoms on Chitina River and in Skolai Mountains, on upper Sushitna and Copper rivers to somewhat higher elevations, Skwentna River to 2,500 feet, on north and west slopes of Alaska Range to 3,500 and 4,000 feet, valley of Kobuk River (western tributary of Arctic Ocean) to 1,000 feet.

OREGON.—Reported from eastern part, but definite records are wanting.

Native range of *Populus balsamifera candicans* unknown, but the tree is cultivated and escaped from cultivation from New Brunswick to Georgia and west to Minnesota. It may possibly be met with in the Pacific region.

The detailed range of this tree east of the Pacific region will be described in later bulletins.

OCCURRENCE.

Alluvial stream bottoms, flats, borders of lakes and swamps in moist sandy and gravelly soils, which are often rich and deep. Forms pure stands and is more or less mixed with black and white spruces, birches, alders, and willows.

CLIMATIC CONDITIONS.—Characterized by humidity, heavy precipitation, very low temperature, short growing season, and long, severe winters.

TOLERANCE AND REPRODUCTION.—Not determined.

Black Cottonwood.

Populus trichocarpa Torrey and Gray.

DISTINGUISHING CHARACTERISTICS.

Black cottonwood, the largest of our poplars, under the best conditions for growth, is from 80 to 125 feet high and from 3 to 4 feet in diameter; trees somewhat taller and from 5 to 6 feet through occur much less commonly, while over much of its range it is under 50 feet and from 12 to 18 inches in diameter. The pale gray, deeply and regularly furrowed trunks are clear of branches for from 50 to 80 feet or more in the best grown trees, straight, or, often, with a long, slight bend. Smaller trees, grown under less favorable conditions, have relatively long, clean trunks, except in the open. All have rather open, short, wide crowns of thick upright branches. The furrows and ridges of the trunk bark, often nearly 2 inches thick, are distinctly and sharply defined. Young twigs are indistinctly angled, later becoming round, shiny, and reddish yellow. The similarly colored buds, from five-eighths to three-fourths of an inch long, are often curved (as if bent) and covered with a fragrant, yellowish-brown gum, from which the tree gets the name, "balsam cottonwood." Mature leaves (figs. 108, 109) are thick, leathery, and smooth; deep shiny green above, and silvery white or whitish beneath, with rusty areas and veiny. Midveins and their branches, as well as the slender, round leaf-stems, sometimes very minutely hairy. In dying, the leaves become a dull yellowish-brown. Wood, soft, straight-grained, fine-grained in dense stands; dull grayish-brown. Large logs obtainable from the best grown trees give clear, wide lumber and other materials which are extensively used in the range of the species, especially for cooperage stock. It is likely to be even a much more important soft wood in the northwest Pacific region than it is now, owing to the scarcity of other broadleaf timber trees suitable for the special purposes to which this wood can be put.

LONGEVITY.—Not fully determined. Probably attains the greatest age of any of our native species. Trunks from 2 to 3 feet in diameter are from 85 to 110 years old; one tree 43¼ inches in diameter showed an age of 112 years. The much larger trees—now very largely cut for lumber—would doubtless show ages of 150 or 175 years.

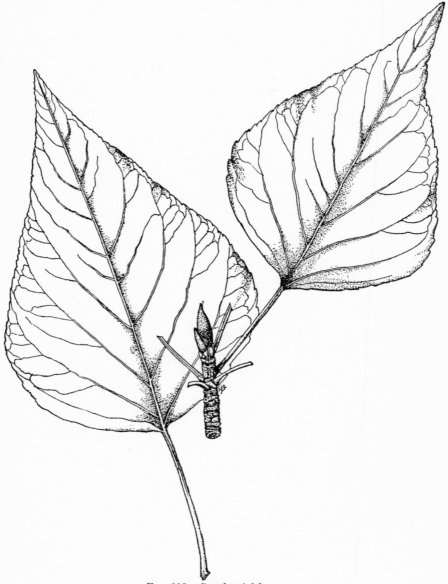

FIG. 108.—*Populus trichocarpa.*

RANGE.

Coast ranges of southern Alaska and southward through interior Yukon Territory, British Columbia, Washington, and Oregon, to southern California (San Jacinto Mountains); reported also in northern Idaho and Montana. Northern range still imperfectly known.

ALASKA.—Probably on coast from north end of Kodiak Island, Iliamna Bay, Cook Inlet, and Kenai Peninsula eastward to Lynn Canal and Stikine River, extending into the interior in British territory down Lewes, Pelly, Frances, upper Liard and probably upper Peace and Parsnip rivers, and throughout region east of coast ranges at this latitude. On

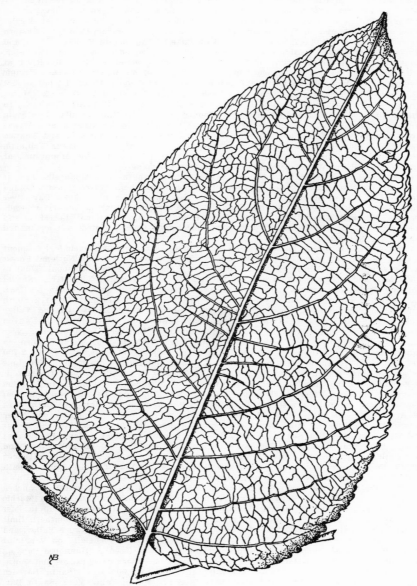

FIG. 109.—*Populus trichocarpa*, leaf of vigorous shoot.

river banks and islands of Lynn Canal, reaching 2,000 feet elevation on Kenai Peninsula. Locally noted at mouths of Lewes, Pelly, and Stikine rivers, Lake Frances, on Dease, Chichamin, Taiya, lower Chilkat, and Chilkoot rivers.

WESTERN CANADA.—Not known to, but probably does, extend southward in interior British Columbia, and possibly also on seaward side of coast mountains; unknown on Queen Charlotte Islands.

VANCOUVER ISLAND.—Noted on San Juan River (southwest coast.) In lower Fraser River Valley up to Yale, and in Columbia River Valley at Donald, and westward in low valleys of Selkirks to Kamloops Valley, here ascending to about 7,000 feet elevation.

WASHINGTON.—Washington National Forest (West) common up to 5,000 feet, locally noted at Ferndale and on Nooksak and upper Skagit rivers (Whatcom County). Eastern division at 1,100 to 4,000 feet, locally noted on Lake Chelan, mouth Stehekin River and near top Cascade Pass. Yakima division up to 3,000 feet, noted on Wenache Mountains, Mount Rainier National Forest, up to 4,200 feet, locally noted on Nisqually River at Ashford and up to a point above Longmire Springs and on Mount Adams. Olympic Peninsula, locally noted on north and south forks of Skokomish River, 12 miles west of Hoodsport and 8 miles south of Lake Cushman, and at head of South Fork (Mason County) and in Queniult Indian Reservation and at Dryad (Chehalis County). In central part of State noted in Klickitat County and in Kittitas County, locally in canyons of Yakima River and its tributaries, Umptanum Creek, Atanum and Wenas rivers (up to 4,200 feet), and on west slope of divide between Columbia and Yakima rivers; on Columbia River from Saddle Mountains to Egbert Springs (near Trinidad, Douglas County), Snake River (Columbia County) at 1,500 feet, Blue Mountains, at Almota and Colfax (Whitman County) and Spokane (Spokane County).

OREGON.—Both sides of Cascades and east, at the north to Blue Mountains and at the south to Goose Lake. Noted on Deschutes River in northern Wasco County, Columbia River in Wasco, Sherman, Gilliam, Morrow, and Umatilla counties, John Day River from Hay Creek to mouth (Gilliam County), coast region of Clatsop County, Cascade (North) National Forest up to 1,600 feet. Blue Mountains National Forest locally noted on John Day River and its tributary, Cottonwood Creek. Noted in Wenaha and Goose Lake National Forests.

CALIFORNIA.—Abundant in Sierras and southern cross ranges, but much less frequent in coast mountains; generally at 3,000 to 6,000 feet elevation. Klamath National Forest in low situations. Vicinity of Mount Shasta only on Shasta River, at about 3,000 to 4,000 feet, and near Sissons on head of Sacramento River at about 3,500 feet. Shasta National Forest on streams in yellow-pine belt. Locally noted as follows in northern coast ranges: Lewiston trail west of town of Shasta (Trinity National Forest); South Fork Eel River (Stony Creek National Forest); near Mountain House (Round Valley road from Ukiah), western limit, and occasional stations to north; Mitchell Canyon (Monte Diablo): San Leandro Creek (near Alameda). Southern coast ranges: Near Gilroy on Carnadero Creek (south end Santa Clara Valley); near Buenaventura on Santa Clara River; Monterey National Forest, on constant streams, at 500 to 2,700 feet, as on Sur, Carmelo, Arroyo Seco, San Antonio, and Nacimiento rivers. San Luis Obispo National Forest, at 500 to 2,000 feet, preferably in such perpetual stream beds as San Luis, Arroyo Grande, and Huasna rivers. Coast islands, including Santa Catalina and Santa Barbara. Sierras: Plumas, Diamond Mountain, and Lassen Peak National Forests; rare in foothills; thence throughout western slope to point on South Fork of Kern River 10 miles south of Monache Meadow (lat. 36°); abundant on larger rivers at from 3,000 to 6,000 feet elevation. Abundant in Stanislaus National Forest and on larger rivers in Sierra National Forest. Locally noted as follows in Sierras: Middle Fork Stanislaus River between Cow and Lily creeks, and on Mill Creek and in Donalds Flat; Yosemite River; Middle Fork San Joaquin River at Balloon Dome; Middle Fork Kings River near Crown and Blue creeks, and at Tehipite Dome; South Fork Kings River at Godard Creek, Converse Basin, and Simpsons Meadow; Bubbs Creek (tributary South Fork of Kings River); Big Arroyo and Soda creeks (branches Kern River); East Fork Kaweah, above Mineral King, to headwaters, and on Marble Fork Kaweah; Kern River at Funston Creek, below Little Kern Lake, and up to East and West forks; South Fork Kern 10 miles south of Monache Meadow (southern limit known in Sierras). On east slope of Sierras, only on Hockett trail to Owens Valley, and in Truckee River valley, Nevada, there ascending creeks to 7,000 feet; also on Panamint Mountains (east of Sierras in California), where trees were seen in Hannopee Canyon, at 8,500 feet. Tehachapi Mountains, in Tejon Canyon. Southern cross ranges and southward into San Jacinto Mountains; generally at 1,000 to 5,000 feet. Santa Barbara National Forest canyons of perpetual streams in Santa Maria, Santa Ynez, Santa Barbara, Matilija, Piru-Sespe, Newhall, and Elizabeth basins, at 500 to 5,250 feet, sometimes extending down into valleys. San Gabriel National Forest, not common below 4,500 feet; locally noted on foothills near Pasadena and on San Gabriel River up to 6,000 feet. San Bernardino Mountains, south slopes up to 5,300 feet; locally noted in Santa Ana Canyon from mouth to "Pines," 2,500 to 5,600 feet, and on Keller and Bear creeks. San Jacinto Mountains, noted on San Jacinto River and Tahquitz Creek at 6,000 feet.

OCCURRENCE.

At lower levels on river bottoms, sand bars, and banks, in sandy, humous, rich soils, where it is largest; at higher elevations, in canyon bottoms and gulches, in moist, sandy or gravelly soil, where it is much smaller.

Forms belts and limited forests of pure growth, or occurs in mixture. At north, with willows, red and Sitka alders, vine and broadleaf maples, lowland fir, Douglas fir; southward, at higher levels, with red and white alders, incense cedar, and occasionally Douglas fir.

CLIMATIC CONDITIONS.—Not fully determined. Climate in region of best growth is marked by great humidity and precipitation and by moderate temperatures. Beyond influence of sea and fogs, where the tree is subjected to dry atmosphere and is dependent upon soil moisture only, growth is smaller.

TOLERANCE.—Very intolerant of shade throughout life. Very rapid, persistent growth permits it to hold its own in mixture with more tolerant conifers, among which its small crown is carried high into full light.

REPRODUCTION.—Prolific annual seeder. Seed has a high rate of germination, but very transient vitality. Reproduction good on moist, bare, humous or sandy soils, but very abundant on wet bars.

Fremont Cottonwood.

Populus fremontii Watson.

DISTINGUISHING CHARACTERISTICS.

In its native range Fremont cottonwood is not known as such, but simply as " cottonwood," a name which should be replaced by the more distinctive one coined from the technical name and adopted here. This tree was long supposed to be the same as the big cottonwood (*P. deltoides*) of the Prairie and Eastern States, which it very closely resembles in general appearance. Again, until recently, there had been no stable character found by which to distinguish it from the perplexingly similar cottonwood (*P. wislizeni*) of western Texas, the Rio Grande Valley, New Mexico, and contiguous Mexican territory. Fremont cottonwood differs from the latter species in the much longer stems of its seed capsules.

Ordinarily Fremont cottonwood is from 50 to 75 feet high and from $1\frac{1}{2}$ to $2\frac{1}{2}$ feet in diameter; rarely it is from 80 to 90 feet and 4 or more feet through. The trunks, clear of branches for about half their length, are seldom straight, but are more or less bowed or leaning. Thick limbs and their drooping branchlets form a very wide, round-topped, open crown. The rough, very deeply furrowed, thick bark is externally dark grayish-brown and clear red within; the wide, distinctly cut ridges are connected irregularly by smaller lateral ridges. Bark of large limbs and young trunks is only slightly seamed and pale ashy brown. Year-old twigs are smooth, pale yellow, yellowish gray as they become older, with shiny greenish buds. Mature leaves (fig. 110) are smooth throughout, leathery, rather thick, clear yellow-green and shiny, with flat, yellow stems. In dying, the leaves become a bright lemon yellow. Wood pale, dull brown, considerably heavier than that of other cottonwoods, fine-grained, soft, brittle, not durable, and specially liable to crack badly in seasoning. Much used locally for fuel, but has no commercial use.

Fremont cottonwood is of very great service for protecting and holding the soft shifting banks of bottomland on western streams, where it is the only tree that marks their meandering courses.

LONGEVITY.—Not fully determined. Appears to grow rapidly to maturity and to be short-lived. One tree $36\frac{1}{4}$ inches (inside of bark) showed an age of only 29 years. Further investigation of this tree's age limits are desirable.

Central and southern California, through central Nevada, southern Utah, northern Arizona, and western New Mexico; in valleys and lower foothills.

CALIFORNIA.—Sacramento River Valley, foothills of Sierras and adjacent coast ranges; abundant on flats and streams up to 2,000 feet; northward to about mouth of Pitt River,

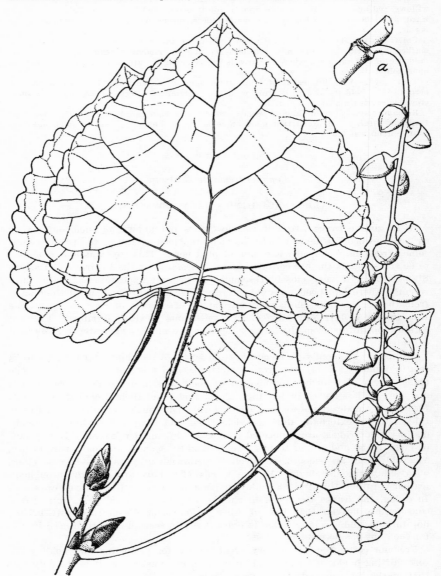

FIG. 110.—*Populus fremontii: a,* seed pods.

and westward to Whiskeytown (Shasta County). Locally noted in Tahoe and Stanislaus National forests at from 500 to 2,000 feet, near Jenny Lind (road to Salt Springs Valley, Calaveras County); Deer Creek on Lassen Peak (Tehama County). Not detected on seaward coast mountains nor in middle ranges of northern California; but abundant in

San Joaquin River Valley, on foothills of southern Sierras, and on southern coast ranges, up to 3,000 and 5,000 feet elevation.   Locally noted as common on South Fork of Kern River from below Canebrake Creek to Isabella ; on Kern River to Kernville, at a point 8 miles below Isabella and at Bakersfield.   East side of Sierras, only on Cottonwood Creek (west side of Owens Lake), and on Cottonwood Canyon in Panamint Mountains. Probably elsewhere also on southern east side slope of Sierras and on ranges east of them.   Coast ranges of southern California : Santa Lucia and San Luis Obispo mountains ; abundant generally on streams at 200 to 2,600 feet elevation, including Sur, Carmelo, Arroyo Seco, San Antonio, Nacimiento, Carriso, Salinas, and Santa Margarita rivers. Elsewhere, scattered throughout southern California on streams, on edges of deserts, and on lowlands between the mountains and sea.   Santa Barbara National Forest :   All watersheds, at 900 to 5,280 feet, including Santa Maria, Santa Ynez, Santa Barbara, Matilija, Piru-Sespe, Newhall, and Elizabeth rivers.   In all canyons of Tehachapi Moun- tains, including Cañada de las Uvas and Tejon Canyon.   Rare in vicinity of Los Angeles, occurring at Fernando.   Not detected in Santa Ana Range.   Locally noted as follows : San Gabriel National Forest, in Tujunga Canyon (2 miles from mouth), at 1,600 feet ; Mohave desert, at Victor on Mohave River ;   San Bernardino Mountains in San Ber- nardino Valley, Santa Ana Canyon and Bear, Keller, and Mill creeks.   Common in San Diego County south of San Luis Rey River, extending westward nearly to sea and eastward into desert to tree limit ; noted at Jamul Creek, 15 miles from sea, near Mexican boundary ;   Mountain Spring, east side of Coast Range and just north of Mexican boundary, at 2,500 feet ; Salton River (Colorado Desert).

The detailed range of Fremont cottonwood outside of the Pacific region will be dealt with in a future publication.

OCCURRENCE.

Confined to alluvial stream bottoms and their borders, in moist sandy and humous soils, or in moist gravelly ones.   Very dependent upon soil moisture, of which the pres- ence of this tree is always indicative.

Forms strips and small bodies of pure growth, or is scattered in mixture with willows and occasional western sycamores and white alders.

CLIMATIC CONDITIONS.—Climate marked by high temperatures and small precipitation ; air is dry in some parts of range, but humid in others, through influence and proximity of sea.

TOLERANCE.—Extremely intolerant of shade throughout life.

REPRODUCTION.—Similar to black cottonwood.

Family BETULACEÆ.

This family contains the birches and alders, well known and widely distrib- uted forest trees and shrubs.   They are characterized by their small, scaly fruit- ing cones, which somewhat resemble in form those of the true cone-bearers. The minute seeds (nuts) are produced under the scales of the cones, which in the birches fall to pieces when ripe, scattering the seed, but which in the alders remain intact, after liberating the seed by a spreading of the scales.   In this respect the cones of these trees behave almost exactly like those of some of the conifers.   Male and female flowers are each borne on different parts of the same tree, usually on different parts of the same branch.   A further striking analogy between the reproductive organs of these trees and the pines is the habit of forming either partly developed male flower clusters alone, or both male and female flower clusters, during the summer previous to their opening.   These may be seen on the leafless twigs of birches and alders in winter, during which they remain in a quiescent state until spring, when they again begin to grow and the flowers open—commonly before the appearance of the leaves, which (in our species) are shed annually in autumn.   The leaves are borne singly on the branches (never in pairs, one opposite another).

The wood of these trees is dense in structure, and its very minute, numerous pores are diffused irregularly throughout the annual rings, which are very in- distinctly defined.   All are useful forest trees, and some are especially valuable for their timber.   With few exceptions, they require moist soils.

BETULUS. BIRCHES.

Without exception, the tree and shrubs of this group are called birches. In most of the species the bark of young trees is smooth and often separable into paper-like sheets of a chalky-white, yellow, orange-brown, red-brown, or copper color; one or two species, however, have gray-brown bark, not separable into layers. Old trees have furrowed, scaly bark. The fine, dense structure of the hard wood and its comparatively indistinct annual layers are also characteristic, while most birches have beautiful, reddish-brown heartwood, which is commercially of great value. The very fine, round twigs are conspicuously marked by long-persistent, light-colored spots. Year-old twigs produce, the succeeding year, two leaves from the side buds, while from the end [a] bud a new shoot grows with only one leaf at a point. Young twigs and the inner bark of several birches have a fragrant, winter-green taste when bruised or chewed (they are not poisonous). The cylindrical male flower clusters, partly matured the previous summer and so remaining until early spring, one or several together, are long, tassel-like bodies hanging down from the ends of the twigs, back of which the very much smaller, cylindrical, quite or nearly erect female flowers proceed from the short, 2-leafed, thorn-like side twigs. Flowers appear before or with the growing leaves; female clusters develop into cylindrical or elongated cones, under the scales of which are borne very minute, brownish seeds with two gauze-like wings. The cones mature and fall to pieces in late spring or early summer, leaving on the twig a central thread-like stem, to which the scales were attached. Sown thus early, the seeds germinate at once in moist, shady places, and the seedlings mature sufficiently that season to pass the winter safely. It is best, if possible, to sow birch seed soon after it is gathered, since by storing it until the following spring much of its germinating power may be lost.

Few of the Pacific birches are of importance for their wood, because within the region most of them are too small or infrequent to form stands sufficient to supply commercial or domestic uses. When they occur with a few other small trees, they are useful as a protective cover on canyon streams, but otherwise they are unimportant for the forester. Eastern and northern representatives of the group are much more important forest and timber trees.

The birches from which our species descended existed in early geologic times. Remains of them are found in the Cretaceous rocks of the Dakota formation and in the more recent Tertiary formations. In Tertiary times they inhabited the north central and northwest coast region of this continent. Many species, now extinct, also existed in Europe during the Eocene and Miocene periods.

Nine tree birches grow in the United States and adjacent Canadian territory, of which four inhabit the Pacific region.

Western Birch.

Betula occidentalis Hooker.

DISTINGUISHING CHARACTERISTICS.

Very much confusion has existed regarding the identity of the true *Betula occidentalis*, which, so far as now known, occurs only in northwestern Washington and adjacent territory in British Columbia. To Prof. C. S. Sargent

---

[a] The last bud on a season's twig is not strictly a terminal bud, such as is produced by oaks, pines, etc., but a side or lateral bud, which appears terminal because the immature terminal part of the shoot dies and falls late in autumn or in winter. This is true of all birches.

belongs the credit of finally separating this tree from the red-brown or bronze barked tree (*B. fontinalis* Sargent) of the Sierra and Rocky Mountain regions, and also from the paper birch, *B. papyrifera*, a form of which was thought to

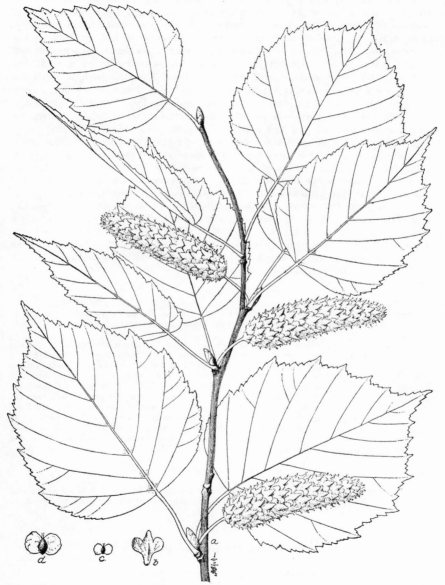

Fig. 111.—*Betula occidentalis: a,* fruiting twig ; *b,* cone scale ; *c, d,* seed, natural size and enlarged.

occur in British Columbia and Washington. The latter, a more eastern and far northern tree, is not known to reach the range of the western birch.

Not locally called "western birch," but simply "birch." It is very desirable, however, to use the more distinctive name given here, which is derived from the tree's technical name.

It is the largest of our birches and, indeed, of any known species of birch. Height, from 80 to 90 feet (not rarely 100); diameter, from 2 to 3 feet, or occasionally larger. The smooth, shiny, light orange-brown trunks are clear of branches for from 40 to 60 feet, while the branches of the spreading, open, round-topped crown droop considerably. Young trees have rather compact, conical-shaped heads. All but the lower slender branches trend upward, but with age they become more and more drooping. The thin bark is separable into thin sheets, the freshly exposed surface being a clear orange-color. Year-old twigs are clear, light yellowish-brown, more or less very minutely hairy, and with very few speck-like glands (abundant on young twigs); later, the twigs become smooth and are without hairs and very shiny. Mature leaves (fig. 111), from $2\frac{1}{2}$ to $3\frac{1}{2}$ inches long, are thin, marked with minute dots (made by resinous glands which cover the young leaves), dull deep green above (mid-veins hairy) and light yellowish green beneath, where the yellow midvein and its larger branches are minutely hairy. Leaf stems, more or less hairy and minutely glandular. Mature cones (fig. 111), somewhat erect, are about $1\frac{3}{8}$ to $1\frac{1}{2}$ inches long and one-half inch or slightly less in diameter. Cone-scales (fig. 111, b) very minutely hairy on the outside, especially on the margins. Minute seeds (nuts) with pale, very thin wings on two sides (fig. 111, c). Wood: Nothing now known of the characteristics of the wood, but since the tree occurs only occasionally, it is not likely to be commercially important.

LONGEVITY.—No records of age are available.

RANGE.

Extreme northwestern Washington and southwestern British Columbia; possibly in central British Columbia, eastern Washington, Idaho, and Montana. Range little known at present.

BRITISH COLUMBIA.—Mainly in Lower Fraser River Valley; a few trees at various points on Vancouver Island, and reported at Donald, on Columbia River (long. 118°).

WASHINGTON.—Vicinity of Puget Sound, extending inland on Skagit River (above Ruby Creek) to 4,000 feet in Cascades, and southward at least to Seattle; occurs also on islands of Puget Sound and on shores of Gulf of Georgia and Straits of Fuca. Locally noted at Sumas Prairie and Everson, in Whatcom County. Reported on Tukannon River in eastern Washington, in Blue Mountains, at a point 10 miles southwest of Pullman, and in Whitman and Stevens counties. Much more careful field study is required to define the eastern range of this tree, which appears to approach, in some individuals, occasional western forms of *Betula papyrifera*. A birch recently found in Idaho and Montana resembles the latter species, but it is suspected of being *B. occidentalis*.

OCCURRENCE.

On borders of streams, margins of meadows and lakes, in rich, moist, humous sandy and rocky soils. Nothing further known now of occurrence nor of silvical characteristics.

Kenai Birch.

Betula kenaica Evans.

DISTINGUISHING CHARACTERISTICS.

The Kenai birch is a comparatively new and little known Alaskan birch, called "red birch" and "black birch," names long used for the eastern birch (*Betula nigra*). The name "Kenai birch," coined from the technical name, is proposed to avoid confusion with names already appropriated.

From 20 to 30 feet high, with a broad crown, and a short, very deep brown to blackish brown, furrowed trunk, from 12 to 18 inches in diameter.   Season's twigs, large, clear red-brown, and dotted with minute light specks.   Mature

FIG. 112.—*Betula kenaica: a,* fruiting twig; *b,* seed, natural size and enlarged; *c,* cone scale, enlarged.

leaves (fig. 112), smooth throughout, dull deep green on their top sides and lighter beneath; both surfaces prominently marked by a net-work of veins which, with the very delicate leaf stems, are yellow.   Mature cones (fig. 112) somewhat upright, from seven-eighths inch to about 1 inch long and approximately three-eighths inch thick. Cone-scales, minutely hairy on their margins (fig. 112, *c*), and the very small seeds (nuts) with thin wings on two sides (fig. 112, *b*). Wood: Nothing is now known of the characteristics of the wood, which, however, on account of the tree's rarity, can be of little commercial use.

Longevity.—No records are available of the age of the tree or of its silvical requirements, concerning which observations are needed.

RANGE.

Only on sea side of coast mountains of Alaska from head of Lynn Canal westward to Kenai Peninsula and north end of Kodiak Island. Here, associated with *Picea sitchensis* and *Betula alaskana*, and reaching the same elevations as spruce; on Lynn Canal, growing to about 2,600 feet elevation; on Prince William Sound, to about 1,600 feet; while on Kenai Peninsula it is abundant on top of plateau, extending up slopes to about 2,000 feet. At Sunrise, on shore of Turnagain Arm, and southward on west shore of Cook Inlet to Halibut Cove, Kachemak Bay; possibly extending inland, around head of Alaskan Peninsula, into the interior and up Sushitna and Copper rivers, as well as over passes at head of Lynn Canal. Reported on Koyukuk River above the Arctic Circle. A few trees occur back of Kodiak village on Kodiak Island, while the species grows abundantly in valley at head of English or Womens Bay, 8 miles south of Kadiak village.

White Birch.

Betula alaskana Sargent.

DISTINGUISHING CHARACTERISTICS.

White birch is a little-known Alaskan species. Its possible relationship to some of the imperfectly known Asiatic white-barked birches has not been determined. The earliest record of it is from specimens collected on the Saskatchewan River in 1858, after which date its identity was in doubt until 1901. There is still much to be learned of its forest habits.

Ordinarily from 25 to 35 feet high—sometimes 50 or 60 feet, and about one-half foot to 1 foot through. The hard, firm bark of large trees is thin, occasionally almost white, but usually light reddish-brown, and is separable into thin scales. The slender twigs, reddish-brown and smooth, are conspicuously covered with minute, resinous, gland-like specks, as are also the young leaves. Mature leaves (fig. 113), thin, smooth, deep green on their top sides, lighter green beneath, and smooth or minutely hairy on the small veins, as are often the delicate, reddish leaf stems. Mature cones (fig. 113) more or less drooping, from $1\frac{1}{8}$ to about $1\frac{1}{4}$ inches long and approximately one-third inch through. Cone scales (fig. 113, *c*) minutely hairy on the margins; the very small seeds (nuts) have broad delicate wings on two sides (fig. 113, *b*). Wood: Nothing is now known of its quality and other characteristics. The fairly abundant occurrence of the tree may render the wood, which is probably similar to that of the eastern paper birch, of commercial importance for some of the same purposes (small turnery, etc.) for which that timber is extensively used.

Longevity.—No records are available of age.

RANGE.

Western British America and Alaska from Saskatchewan River and northern Rockies northward to mouth of Mackenzie River; on south side of Endicott Range, in Alaska, and westward to the Arctic Ocean and Bering Sea; and south to sea side of Alaskan Pacific coast ranges. Distribution imperfectly known.

Western Canada.—Saskatchewan River and westward from Prince Albert (about lat. 58°, long. 106°); northward (probably only near eastern base of Rockies), to

Liard River, here crossing to interior plateau west of Rockies. Throughout Mackenzie River Valley northward from Great Slave Lake, reaching its northern limit at Great

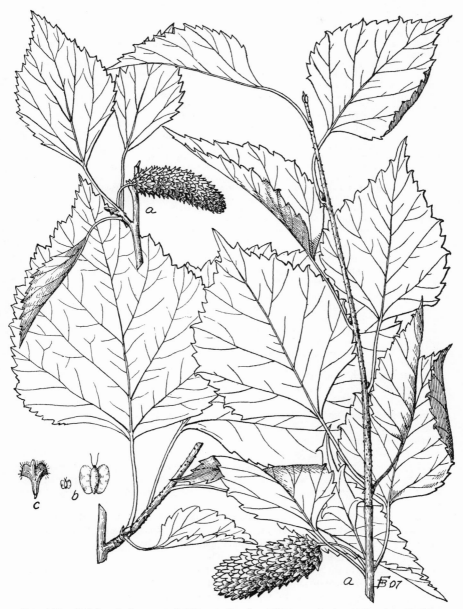

FIG. 113.—*Betula alaskana:* *a,* fruiting twig; *b,* seed, natural size and enlarged three times; *c,* cone scale, twice natural size.

Bear Lake and at the mouth of the river (about lat. 68° 30′) West of Rockies, probably extending southward in British Columbia only to Stikine River; little, however, is known now of its southern limit.   Extends down Stikine River to Kloochman Canyon (where river crosses coast range) ; occurring frequently with spruce and cottonwoods northward throughout region east of coast ranges, except on Upper Pelly River above Hoole River.   Locally noted on Dease River, headwaters of Liard River northward to Frances Lake, where timber line is about 4,000 feet ; on Stewart, Klondike, McQuestion, and Yukon rivers ; at Dawson, Fort Selkirk, on Peels River, and at Fort Simpson. Lewes River, but not above head of Fifty-mile River between Lake Marsh and Lake Lebarge.

ALASKA.—Probably not on sea side of coast mountains, except at Lynn Canal and west of it, on Kenai Peninsula and about Cook Inlet.   Common in interior valleys and throughout Yukon River Valley, in mountains, and toward west coast, northward as far as timber extends.   Noted on White and Tanana Rivers (up to 3,400 feet), Copper River (below 2,000 feet), Sushitna River to headwaters, Chicna River (tributary to Sushitna) and adjacent Skolai Mountains, Kuskokwim River from Kolmakof to headwaters, Allen, Kanuti, Dall, and Kowak rivers (up to about 2,500 feet), Koyukuk River up to Roberts Creek, and Chandler River to a few hundred feet above Chandler Lake and on head tributaries to 600 feet above main river.   Sea side of passes at head of Lynn Canal from point a short distance below summit, becoming very common at low elevations nearer sea ; locally noted at Chilkoot, Portage Bay, and on Chilkat Inlet. Abundant over Kenai Peninsula plateau, reaching timberline, with white spruce and balm-of-Gilead, at 1,600 to 2,000 feet elevation, and extending to shores of Turnagain Arm, up Sushitna River and its tributaries and also to west side of Cook Inlet ; here abundant, especially at Tyonek, reaching 2,000 to 3,000 feet elevation.   Occurs sparingly farther south on west shore of Cook Inlet at head of Iliamna Bay, and inland about lakes Iliamna and Clark (southern limit of timber at head of Alaskan Peninsula).

OCCURRENCE.

In vicinity of streams and on lower hill slopes in moist gravelly soils, mingled with spruces and other conifers of its range.   Silvical habits, etc., undetermined.

Mountain Birch.

Betula fontinalis Sargent.

DISTINGUISHING CHARACTERISTICS.

Mountain birch is a slender, graceful tree or tall shrub, long known as *Betula occidentalis* Hooker, a name which is now known to belong to an entirely different tree.   This discovery necessitated giving the mountain birch its present name, *Betula fontinalis*.   There is still some doubt, however, in regard to the true identity of at least one form of this tree.   This can be cleared up only by further field study.

This tree has several conflicting and inappropriate field names, such as " black birch," " sweet birch," " cherry birch," " water birch," and " canyon birch."   Mountain birch is proposed as more suitable, since the habitat of the tree, in contrast with that of most other birches, is distinctly a mountainous one.

Very commonly a slender-stemmed, shrub-like tree from 10 to 15 feet high (in dense thickets), but sometimes from 25 to 30 feet high and from 6 to 10 inches through.   The deep, shiny, old-copper-colored bark of the trunks distinguishes it from other asociated trees.   The thinly foliaged crown is composed of very slender branches with delicate pendent twigs.   When young the twigs are greenish and more or less thickly covered with resinous, shiny dots (glands), which disappear gradually in one or two seasons, during which the twigs become deep red-brown or copper-brown and more and more shiny.   Mature leaves (fig. 114), resinous dotted at first, are smooth, except for numerous dots on the lighter green under surfaces ; leaf stems also with glandular specks and minute hairs.   Fruiting cones (fig. 114), ripe in early summer, about seven-eighths inch to 1⅛ inches long; the minute, gauzy-winged seeds (nuts) minutely hairy at the top end (fig. 114, *b*).

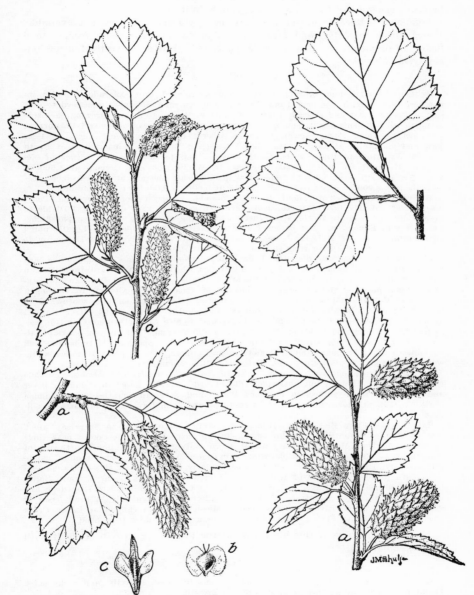

FIG. 114.—*Betula fontinalis: a,* fruiting twig; *b,* seed, twice natural size; *c,* cone scale, twice natural size.

Wood, light yellowish brown, with a very thick layer of whitish sapwood. Similar in quality to that of the eastern, brown-wooded timber birches. Owing to the small size of the trees, too little of the wood is available for commercial use.

Its dense thickets bordering rocky canyon streams and in gulches are very helpful conservers of the scanty water supply in its range.

LONGEVITY.—Records of the ages attained by large trees are not available. Young stems indicate rapid height and diameter growth; those from 3 to 6 inches in diameter are from 18 to 30 years old. Further investigation of longevity is desirable.

RANGE.

British Columbia and probably Yukon and southward into Colorado, possibly to northern New Mexico, southern Utah, Nevada, and central California; westward to east side of Pacific coast and Cascade ranges of Canada, Washington, and Oregon; east side of northern California coast mountains and east side of Sierras of central California; eastward to Upper Saskatchewan River in Alberta to such outlying ranges as Bear Paw and mountains at head of Musselshell River, in Montana, to mountains of North eastern Wyoming, to Black Hills, South Dakota, and to northwestern corner of Nebraska. Generally in valleys and canyons. In Washington and Oregon, at 1,600 to 4,500 feet elevation; at 5,000 to 10,000 feet in California Sierras; at 4,000 to 6,000 feet in Idaho; at 3,000 to 6,500 feet in Montana; at 5,000 to 9,000 feet in Colorado.

WESTERN CANADA.—Throughout British Columbia, from Upper Fraser and Peace rivers, and probably farther north, southward and eastward over Continental Divide to eastern Rocky Mountain foothills in Alberta; extending eastward, also, down Saskatchewan River to Edmonton. Not detected west of Pacific coast mountains. Locally noted on mountains east of McLeods Lake, on north Saskatchewan River from Edmonton to Victoria; on Columbia River from Golden City to Selkirk summit.

WASHINGTON.—Generally distributed, but not common on streams throughout eastern half of State, and usually at 1,600 to 4,200 feet elevation. Westward to Okanogan River, Columbia River, in its north and south course below the Great Bend and to Yakima River; possibly also to eastern foothills of Cascades; northward to Okanogan River and Colville Indian Reservation and probably into Canada, and southward to Blue Mountains. Locally noted as follows: Conconully, in Okanogan River Valley; Wenache, on Columbia River; Wenache Mountains; Coulée City (Douglas County); Columbia River Valley and divide between Columbia and Yakima River, also on banks of latter stream; Umptanum Creek (tributary the Yakima); Spokane; Hangman Creek Spokane County; Pullman, and at Almota, near Pullman, also at point 10 miles southwest of Pullman; Touchet River and Waitsburg (Blue Mountains).

OREGON.—Throughout eastern part, west to eastern foothills of Cascades. Cascade (North) National Forest, but not widely distributed. Locally noted in Columbia River and Deschutes River valleys in northern Wasco and Sherman counties, the Columbia Valley in Gilliam, Morrow, and Umatilla counties, and John Day Valley in northern Gilliam County.

CALIFORNIA.—From Siskiyou to Humboldt County and eastward to Surprise Valley, east of Warner Mountains; southward, chiefly on east slope of Sierras to near their south end. About Mount Shasta only at south end of Shasta Valley (northwest of mountain), at 3,000 to 4,000 feet elevation. On east side of Sierras, common on all mountain streams at about 4,500 to 9,000 feet, particularly those on west side of Owens Valley; south to 10 miles north of Walker Pass (northeastern Kern County), south limit; locally noted near Mono Lake, on Rock Creek (Mono County), at 4,500 to 7,100 feet, and near Lone Pine (Inyo County). West side of Sierras, detected only in head basin of South Fork of Kings River above Simpson's Meadow, and in canyon of Bubbs Creek (head tributary South Fork of Kings River) below a point 2 miles from head.

The detailed range of this birch east of the Pacific region will be dealt with in a later bulletin.

OCCURRENCE.

Borders of lower mountain streams and canyons in moist, gravelly, and rocky soils. Forms long lines and patches of pure (thicket) growth.

CLIMATIC CONDITIONS.—Similar to those of mountain mahogany.

TOLERANCE.—Requires full top light; its own moderately dense side shade produces very slender, long, clear stems.

REPRODUCTION.—Abundant seeder. Seed of medium high germination, but of transient vitality. Seedlings abundant in moist or wet washed mineral soil.

ALNUS. ALDERS.

Trees and shrubs of this group are known always as alders. The trees are of small or medium size—rarely over 75 to 90 feet in height. The bark is often smooth and gray, sometimes marked conspicuously with large, chalky-white areas; only the trunks of large trees have scaly bark—chiefly at the base. The dense, brittle wood is composed largely of sapwood, with only a small core of reddish brown heartwood.

Alders shed their leaves in autumn, but while they are still green. The leaves are conspicuously straight-veined, the veins from the midvein running to the margin of the leaf. Alder buds, formed early in summer, are peculiar in being raised on a well-defined, minute stem and in not being scaly. Male and female flower clusters, each borne on different parts of the same branch, are produced in a partly developed state the summer before they open. Both are then small, cylindrical bodies. The male clusters (the larger) become in spring from 2 to 6 inches long; they are pendent, and terminate a branchlet. Lower down on the twig are produced the very much smaller female flower clusters, which develop into small, woody, persistent cones, between the scales of which numerous very small, flat seeds (nuts) are borne. The cones are green in autumn when the seeds are mature, but later become brown, and in late fall or in early spring they gradually open their scales and liberate the seeds. The seeds of some species have very small and narrow gauze-like marginal wings, while those of others are wingless (figs. 115 to 120). Seeds of the latter type are rather heavy and are not distributed by the wind, but depend for distribution largely upon water. Winged seeds are very buoyant and easily wafted by the wind.

Commercially the alders are of scarcely more than secondary importance. Only one of the Pacific species produces useful wood; the others are too small for any purpose except fuel, for which all species are very commonly used. They grow in moist or wet situations, from sea-level to over 7,000 feet elevation. A common habitat is in river and canyon bottoms, along mountain streams, and on wet mountain slopes.

Six tree alders inhabit the United States and adjacent territory (on both the north and south), while four of these occur within the Pacific region. Many species of alders existed in the early epochs of the earth's history; remains of them are found in Eocene and Miocene rocks of the Tertiary period.

White Alder.

Alnus rhombifolia Nuttall.

DISTINGUISHING CHARACTERISTICS.

The name " white alder " is not known to be used in the range of this tree, but it is proposed for the want of a distinct common name, and refers to the tree's pale greenish foliage. So far as is now known, the tree's field name is simply " alder."

Similar in general appearance to the red alder, from which it is probably not distinguished by laymen. It differs from the latter tree in having thin, conspicuously scaly, brown bark; the scaly bark extends considerably higher up on the stem than that of red alder, which is commonly unbroken and smooth. The stems are usually straight, from 50 to 75 feet high and from 18 to 24 inches in diameter, often only 30 or 40 feet high and from 8 to 12 inches in diameter. Trunks are clear of branches for about one-half to two-thirds of their length, and the crown is rather broad, open, and dome-like, with middle

and lower branches which droop decidedly at their ends. Twigs of the year
are smooth, with distant light-colored specks, and reddish yellow; the dull
red buds are coated with light-colored, scaly down. Mature leaves are characterized by light yellow-green upper surfaces and, particularly, by their usually

FIG. 115.—*Alnus rhombifolia.*

fine-toothed, wavy borders (figs. 115, 116), which are curled a little toward the
under surface, the gland-tipped teeth, of different sizes, standing out irregularly. The toothed border, only rarely somewhat double toothed, differs greatly
from the rather regularly double-toothed borders of leaves on other Pacific

alders. Under surface of leaves, including the prominent yellow midveins, their branches, and the leaf stems, have very minute soft hairs. Mature cones (fig. 116) vary from about one-half to nearly seven-eighths of an inch in length. Most of them shed their mature seeds in midwinter, but a few shed them very

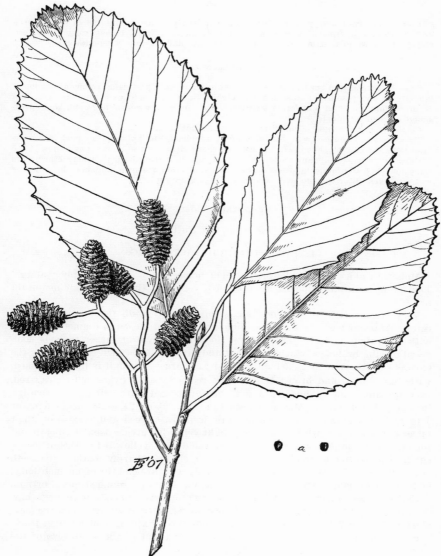

FIG. 116.—*Alnus rhombifolia: a,* seed.

late in the autumn. Ends of the cone scales, somewhat thickened, and with an intended lobe. The seeds have very thin hard borders (fig. 116, *a*). Flowers open in midwinter, when the pendent male clusters are most conspicuous, 4½ to 5½ inches long and as thick as a pipe-stem. Wood, pale yellowish-brown; of somewhat lighter weight than that of the red alder. Its principal value is for fuel, but it is suitable for cabinet work.

LONGEVITY.—Little is known of the age limits. Trees from 12 to 15 inches in diameter are from 37 to 50 years old.

RANGE.

From northern Idaho to the eastern slope of the Cascade Mountains of Washington and southeastern Oregon, and southward through California (coast ranges, western slopes Sierra Nevada, San Bernardino, San Jacinto, and Cuyamaca mountains).

OCCURRENCE.

Canyon bottoms and borders of foothill and lower mountain streams, commonly in moist gravelly or rocky soils. Forms dense stretches, lines, and patches of pure growth, and is often mingled with California sycamore, Oregon ash, western dogwood, and, occasionally broadleaf maple.

CLIMATIC CONDITIONS.—Similar to those of Oregon ash.

TOLERANCE.—Endures great deal of shade throughout life, but requires moderate overhead light for best height growth; dense side shade clears and produces long stems.

REPRODUCTION.—Abundant seeder in open stands on stream borders, where crowns are large; much less prolific in dense stands. Reproduction frequent and best in moist or wet sand, gravel, or humous soil, where seedlings grow rapidly.

Mountain Alder.

Alnus tenuifolia Nuttall.

DISTINGUISHING CHARACTERISTICS.

Mountain alder has no distinctive field name, but is called simply "alder." The name mountain alder, here proposed, refers to the tree's high mountain habitat.

Very commonly with slender, bent stems, from 6 to 15 feet high (in dense thickets), or, at best, 20 or 25 feet high, and under 6 inches in diameter (rarely with a straight trunk). The narrow, dome-like crown of larger trees is composed of slim branches which stand out and droop a little. On small trunks the bark is smooth, thin, and dark gray-brown; on larger trunks it is lightly seamed, with thin scales, and brown tinged with red. Season's twigs, with clear red, very minutely downy buds, are pale brown, tinged with purple-red, shading into gray lower down. Mature leaves (fig. 117), about $2\frac{1}{2}$ to $3\frac{1}{2}$ inches long, or 4 to $4\frac{1}{2}$ inches long on strong shoots, are deep grass-green and smooth on their upper surfaces; beneath they are very light yellowish green, usually smooth, but sometimes minutely downy; leaf stems and midveins, yellow. Borders of leaves cut into coarse teeth which are themselves finely and sharply toothed, the teeth pointing forward. Mature cones, about one-half to five-eighths of an inch long; ends of cone scales very thick and with about 4 minute rounded lobes, or subdivisions—ends sometimes without these and squarish. Seeds with very narrow, very thin borders (fig. 117, *a*). Flowers open in early spring, when the male clusters become 2 to 3 inches long and about three-sixteenths of an inch thick. Wood, light brown. Of no commercial use on account of the small size of the tree.

LONGEVITY.—Not fully determined. Stems from 2 to 5 inches in diameter are from 14 to 37 years old.

Important as a member of the forest on account of the protection it affords the headwaters and lower courses of mountain streams and springy slopes.

From Yukon Territory (Francis Lake) and British Columbia (south to lower Fraser River) through the Rocky Mountains to northern New Mexico and Lower California.

FIG. 117.—*Alnus tenuifolia: a,* seed.

West to eastern Washington and Oregon and headwaters of streams of western slope of Sierras at 6,000 to 7,000 feet.

Characteristic on heads of mountain streams, springy and boggy slopes, gulches, borders of high meadows and lakes, in wet, mucky, but usually rocky soils; abundant water (saturation) in soil essential.

Forms large, dense, pure thickets with adjacent lodgepole pine, mountain and vine maples, black cottonwood, willows, and aspen.

CLIMATIC CONDITIONS.—Similar to those of lodgepole pine (at high elevations).

TOLERANCE.—Appears to endure much shade in seedling stages, but seeks full top light later; probably less tolerant than red and Sitka alders.

REPRODUCTION.—Plentiful annual seeder. Seedlings rather abundant in wet or moist muck and litter, in shade or in open.

Red Alder.

Alnus oregona Nuttall.

DISTINGUISHING CHARACTERISTICS.

Red alder is one of the two largest Pacific alders; it reaches a height of from 60 to 90 feet, and a diameter of 18 to 30 inches—occasionally a little larger; usually 35 or 40 feet high and from 10 to 15 inches through. The trunks are straight, giving off rather slim branches which droop in a narrow, long, dome-like crown. The thin-barked, smooth-looking, light ashy gray and whitish trunks are clear of branches for one-half or two-thirds their height. Large trunks have distinctly but very shallowy seamed bark, the thin ridges being flat, narrow, and occasionally connected by smaller side ridges. Season's twigs are clear, shiny, mahogany-red, with numerous light-colored dots, and are sometimes slightly or considerably hairy, especially toward their ends; deep red buds covered with a light-colored scale-like down. Mature leaves (fig. 118) are smooth and deep yellow-green above, sometimes with minute sparse, white hairs; paler beneath and coated with very short, rust-colored hairs—often heaviest on the yellowish veins; large leaves of vigorous shoots are least hairy. Ordinarily leaves are about 3 to 5½ inches long, but are from 6 to 10 inches on strong shoots. The toothed borders of the leaves are very slightly curled toward the under surface. Tassel-like male flower clusters are from 5 to 6 inches long, and about one-fourth inch thick. Mature cones (fig. 118), which shed their seed in autumn, vary in length from about one-half inch to 1 inch; seeds (fig. 118, *a*) have very narrow, thin, wing-like margins. Ends of cone-scales, very thick and blunt—squarish. Wood, pale reddish-brown, brittle, and light when dry; newly cut the surface of the whitish sapwood soon becomes stained a red-brown. One of two Pacific alders which are large enough to furnish saw timber. The cherry-like, fine grain is attractive when finished, making the wood suitable for cabinetwork, for which it is used to some extent.

LONGEVITY.—Not fully determined. Grows rapidly during first 20 or 30 years. Trees from 10 to 18 inches in diameter are from 28 to 55 years old.

From Sitka, Alaska, through islands and coast ranges of British Columbia, western Washington, and Oregon to California (coast ranges to Santa Inez Mountains, near Santa Barbara).

Borders of streams and adjacent moist bottoms, benches, and gentle slopes; in fairly well-drained, rich, humous, rocky, or gravelly soils. Largest in Puget Sound country. Abundant soil moisture and rich soil requisite for best growth.

In extensive belts (at north), patches, and lines of pure growth, or sometimes mingled with Nuttall and other willows, black cottonwood, grand fir, broadleaf and vine maples, and western dogwood.

CLIMATIC CONDITIONS.—Similar to those of grand fir and Douglas fir.
TOLERANCE.—Appears to be the most tolerant of tree alders, especially in youth.

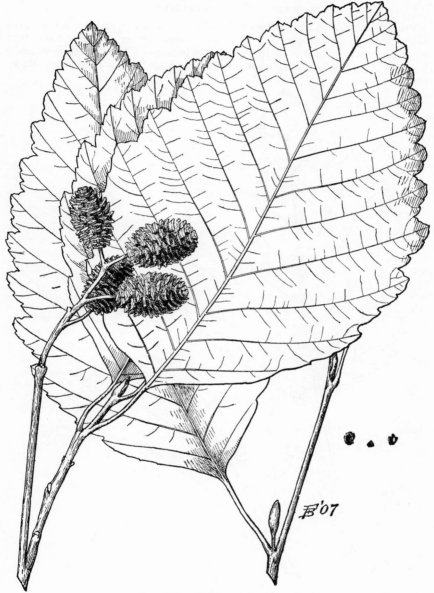

FIG. 118.—*Alnus oregona: a,* seed.

REPRODUCTION.—Moderately abundant seeder; seeding habits not fully determined. Seedlings abundant in rather dense and partial shade, in litter, and in exposed soil.

Sitka Alder.

Alnus sitchensis (Regel) Sargent.

DISTINGUISHING CHARACTERISTICS.

From lack of field knowledge, Sitka alder, a uniquely distinct species still little known to lay people, has remained in comparative obscurity from 1832 until recently. Its habitat and range are yet imperfectly known. Its field name is "alder," and it is probably not distinguished by laymen from other alders of its range.

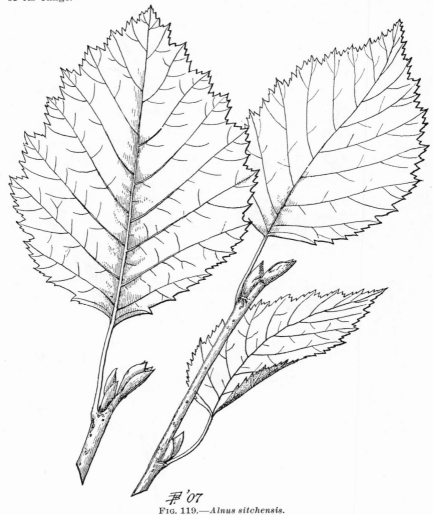

FIG. 119.—*Alnus sitchensis.*

A slender shrub from 4 to 6 feet high (in large thickets) or occasionally a tree from 20 to 30 feet high and from 4 to 8 inches through. Usually crowded in shady places, its crown of nearly straight, horizontal branches is narrow and open. The trunk bark is smooth, thin, and dull gray, with a bluish tinge.

Season's twigs, minutely hairy when young and thickly glandular-dotted, are clear, shiny, yellowish brown, and marked with rather large light-colored specks. Mature leaves (figs. 119, 120)—when young notably sticky, with numerous glandular specks—thin and papery, smooth, yellowish green on their top sides;

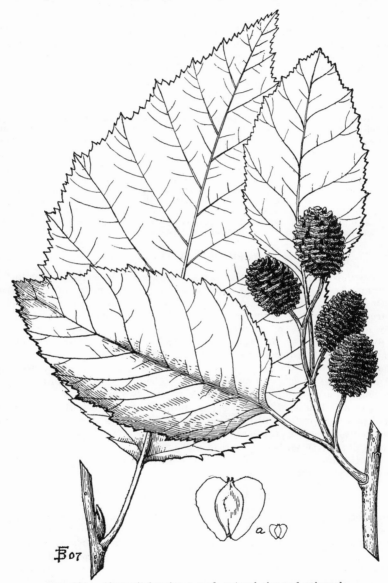

FIG. 120.—*Alnus sitchensis: a,* seed, natural size and enlarged.

much lighter yellow-green and shiny beneath, somewhat as if thinly varnished, or sometimes minutely brown-hairy on the midveins and in the corners of the side veins. Male flower clusters about 3 to 5 inches long and one-third of an inch thick. Mature cones (fig. 120), from five-eighths to three-fourths of an inch long and about three-eighths to seven-sixteenths of an inch through, have scales with blunt thick ends and minute gauze-winged seeds (fig. 120, *a*). The thin seed-wing is a very distinctive character.

Wood: Nothing is known of the characteristics of the wood, which is probably very much like that of the mountain alder (*Alnus tenuifolia*); not known to have any economic use, but, when large enough, suitable for charcoal and fuel. The tree is useful as a forest cover for its firm thickets, which protect lower mountain stream and springy slopes at lower elevations than those at which the mountain alder grows.

Longevity.—No records of age are available.

RANGE.

Northwest coast from Alaska to Oregon and to west slopes of Rockies in Alberta and Montana. From sea-level to 3,000 and 4,000 feet (timber line) in Alaska, and chiefly above 3,000 feet in British Columbia and United States. Of tree size mainly in Alaska. Range imperfectly known.

OCCURRENCE.

In moist bottoms, lower courses of mountain streams, and marshy flats, in humus-covered, rich, rocky, or gravelly soils. Forms pure stands over limited areas, or mingled with willows (at north), occasionally with western red cedar and broadleaf maple.

Climatic Conditions.—Similar in part to those of western red cedar.

Tolerance.—Endures considerable shade, especially in early life, but requires overhead light in later stages. Seeding habits and reproduction undetermined.

Family CUPULIFERÆ.

A very important family of most useful hardwood timber trees, which includes chestnuts, beeches, hornbeams, and oaks. A characteristic of their fruits, which are nuts, is that they are wholly or partly inclosed by a usually woody, separable covering, as in the prickly "burs" of chestnuts and beeches and the scaly or bristly cups of acorns. Flowers, male and female, are each borne on different parts of the same tree, often on different parts of the same branch, usually greenish or yellowish, and, with one or two exceptions, inconspicuous and unlike in appearance the showy flowers of cherries, magnolias, and many other groups of broadleaf trees. The fruits of some members ripen in a single season, while those of others require two seasons to complete their development. Fruits of all are heavy, falling only beneath the mother trees and depending for their distribution upon flood waters and streams, or upon birds and mammals which carry or store them away for food, and thus, when they do not eat them, help to spread and propagate them. The leaves, mostly shed in the autumn of each year, but evergreen in one division of the family, are produced singly, never in pairs.

CASTANOPSIS. CHINQUAPINS.

Members of the chinquapin group, as the name indicates, are chestnut-like in some of their characters, and are closely related to the chestnuts on one side and to the oaks on the other. Some of them have hard, heavy, strong wood, while others produce lighter and softer, brittle wood, unlike that of either chestnut or oak in appearance, but like that of both in containing tannin. The bark also contains tannin. Smooth twigs with scaly buds. They are characterized by their thick, evergreen leaves and (in our species) by their prickly fruit burs, which, though smaller outwardly resemble somewhat the burs of the common chestnut. The fruit (burs) require two seasons in which to mature and contain from 1 to 4 thin-shelled nuts, which (in our species) are released by the opening of the bur. Male and female flowers minute (male much more numerous than female), 3 in a minute cluster, arranged on cylindrical, long, upright stems. The male clusters grow from the bases of leaves produced that season, while the female flowers, also borne in 3-flowered minute clusters, are arranged on the base of the stems bearing male flowers (fig. 121). Flowers depend entirely upon the wind for carrying pollen from the male to the female flowers, and for this reason male flowers are much more numerous than female ones. Like the chestnuts and oaks, the trees of this group have large, long taproots. One species only, a native of the Pacific region, occurs within the United States.

Western Chinquapin.

Castanopsis chrysophylla (Hook.) A. de Candolle.

DISTINGUISHING CHARACTERISTICS.

The field name of western chinquapin is simply " chinquapin," probably from the close external resemblance of the fruit burs to those of the eastern chinquapin (*Castanea pumila*). Sometimes it is called " goldenleafed chestnut," in reference to the yellow under surface of the leaves.

Under the conditions most favorable for growth it has a straight trunk from 80 to 100 feet high and a diameter of from 3 to 4 feet, while authentic records show that it may attain a height of 150 feet and a diameter of from 5 to 10 feet. Such trees are very rare or probably not in existence now. Ordinarily it is from 30 to 50 feet high and from 8 to 15 inches through. (The high mountain form is a low shrub, with slender, half-prostrate stems, and has been distinguished as *Castanopsis chrysophylla minor*.) Large trees have fluted trunks and are clear of branches for from one-half to two-thirds of their length. The big limbs of young trees stand out in a close, pyramidal crown, while in old trees they form a dome-like crown. The bark of young trees is thin, smooth, and dark grayish, but that of large trunks is from three-fourths inch to 1½ inches thick or more, deeply seamed, and composed of very wide plates, which are reddish brown externally and brilliant red within. The evergreen leaves (figs. 121, 122), those of each season's growth persisting about three years, are thick, leathery, deep shiny yellow green on their upper sides, while beneath they are coated with minute golden yellow scales, as are the leaf stems. They are from 2½ to 3½ inches long, or on vigorous shoots from 4 to 6 inches long. Flowers open in early summer, but not uncommonly continue to open throughout this season and into midwinter. The fruit matures in the autumn of the second season, when the spiny burs (fig. 122), about 1 to 1¾ inches in diameter, split open irregularly by 4 divisions, liberating the edible nut, which is shiny, yellowish-brown, sweet, and usually single. Wood somewhat brittle, fine-grained, rather soft, pale reddish brown. Excellent saw timber is furnished by large trees, and the wood is suitable for agricultural implements. The region of large growth, though comparatively small, is one in which commercial hardwoods are scarce, so that this timber is of very considerable economic importance.

LONGEVITY.—Very little is known concerning the age, which in large trees is believed to exceed 500 years. Trees from 18 to 25 inches in diameter are from 145 to 190 years old.

RANGE.

Southwestern Washington to southern California. Cascades, from Skamania County, Wash., southward through those of Oregon (chiefly on west slope) and coast ranges and

Sierras of California to San Jacinto Mountains. Shrubby throughout its range, except in Oregon Cascades and in coast mountains of northwestern California.[a]

WASHINGTON.—At Moffat's Springs, Skamania County, the only station now known.

OREGON.—Valley of Columbia River, in vicinity of the Cascades, and southward over western slope of latter range, often crossing to east slope, as at Mount Pitt, and extending eastward to Klamath-Deschutes Divide; generally at 2,000 to 5,000 feet elevation; also in Siskiyous and westward to southern coast mountains of Siskiyou National Forest. Locally noted at Dalles of Columbia, on Mount Hood, near rim of Crater Lake and at Port Orford.

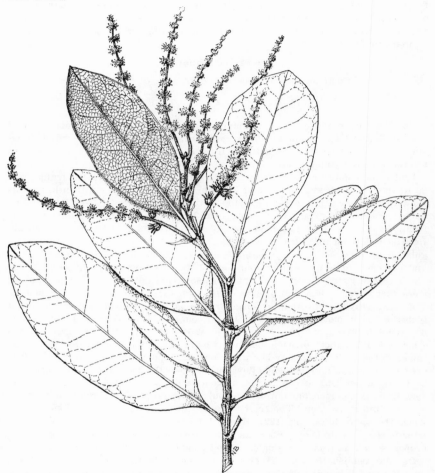

FIG. 121.—*Castanopsis chrysophylla,* flowering branch.

CALIFORNIA.—Lower mountain slopes throughout northern part, from seaward coast range, eastward to Mount Shasta, and southward on both slopes of coast ranges, and mainly on west slope of Sierras, to San Jacinto Mountains; generally at 3,000 to 6,000 feet, in north, but at 8,000 to 10,000 feet in south. High ridges of Klamath and Trinity National forests (as chaparral), but also below 3,500 feet and under Douglas fir, espe-

[a] The shrubby form of eastern California has been described as *C. sempervirens* (Kell.) Dudley, and that of the southern coast ranges has been separated as *C. chrysophylla minor* Benth.

cially on South Fork of Trinity River; locally noted on South Fork Mountain and on Canyon Creek. In yellow pine belt, at 3,000 to 6,000 feet in Mount Shasta National Forest, being locally noted west of McCloud. In Plumas, Diamond Mountain, and Lassen Peak, Yuba, Tahoe, and Stanislaus National forests, at from 2,000 tc 6,000 and 6,500 feet;

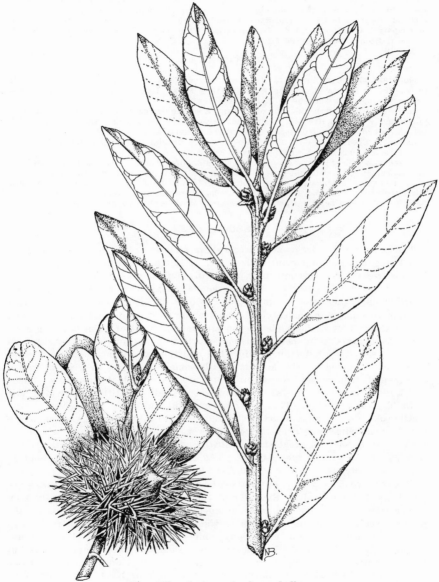

FIG. 122.—*Castanopsis chrysophylla.*

in Stanislaus Forest, at 8,000 feet. Locally noted at Glacier Point, Yosemite Valley. In Sierra National Forest, generally between 6,000 and 8,000 feet; locally noted on South Fork of Kings River from Millwood to Bubbs Creek, on Kaweah River and North Fork of Kern in Jeffrey pine belt; detected on east slope of Sierras, at point opposite Reno,

Nevada, in the yellow pine belt, at elevations of from 6,000 to 7,500 feet, and also opposite Lone Pine, at 9,000 to 9,500 feet; probably occurs at many other points on this slope. Abundant in northern coast ranges, especially near coast. Frequent about San Francisco Bay, as on Mount Tamalpais, Oakland Hills, and Mount St. Helena; as also on seaward range south of San Francisco, in Santa Cruz Mountains, and at Monterey on north side of Huckleberry Hill. Probably also in Mount Hamilton Range. Rather scarce in Santa Lucia, San Luis Obispo, Santa Barbara, and San Gabriel National forests, but frequent in San Bernardino National Forest, where it forms an important part of chaparral at 8,500 to 10,000 feet elevation, while in San Jacinto National Forest it grows at from 8,000 to 10,800 feet.

OCCURRENCE.

Mountain slopes, sheltered ravines and valleys, slopes of canyons and gulches; in rather dry or extremely dry rocky and gravelly soils. Largest in valleys of northwest California; small or shrubby at high levels elsewhere.

In dense pure-growth thickets over large areas in latter regions, interspersed with low forms of canyon live oak, western juniper, scrubby Jeffrey pine, scrub oak and chaparral; but often scattered among redwood and Douglas fir.

CLIMATIC CONDITIONS.—Combine those of white fir and Jeffrey pine (at high levels) and of Douglas fir and redwood (at lower levels).

TOLERANCE.—Very tolerant of shade; in later life endures side shade but requires overhead light for best height growth, clearing its long trunks well in close stands.

REPRODUCTION.—Abundant seeder, but less so in mixed stands, where seedlings are only fairly frequent; more plentiful at higher levels, where washing covers seed in crevices and pockets in shade of seedlings and other plants. Much seed eaten by rodents.

QUERCUS. OAKS.

The oaks form a large group, composed almost entirely of trees, some of which are the most important timber trees of North America. They are world-famous trees, which through their powerfully built trunks, branches, and roots, have earned the reputation of the greatest physical sturdiness. The great strength and other useful commercial qualities of their woods, together with the fact that many of the species occur over large areas in nearly pure forests, render these trees of the highest economic value. Most of them are long-lived and very aggressive in their persistent efforts to maintain themselves, through seed and sprout reproduction, against fire and the ax, and against other forest trees and to extend their domain. With some exceptions they grow rather slowly and require several centuries to produce the high-class saw timber which our virgin oak forests once furnished in great quantities, but which now is rapidly disappearing. They are cosmopolitan, and adapt themselves to dry, sterile soils, as well as to moist, fertile ones, and to cold as well as to temperate and tropical climates. They prefer, however, temperate regions, in which the number of species is greatest. In altitudinal range they are equally unrestricted, for they push their sturdy ranks from near the sea far up mountain slopes and canyons to nearly 10,000 feet elevation.

The two broad classes of our oaks—the white oaks and the black oaks—are popularly distinguished by the color of the wood and bark. Technically they are based upon different habits of producing fruit (acorns). The white oaks produce their acorns in one season; the black oaks produce theirs in two seasons. There are four exceptions which do not fit these classifications, namely, two Pacific oaks, which have wood resembling that of white oaks but which require two seasons to mature their acorns, and one Atlantic and one Pacific oak which have the darker wood and bark of black oaks but which mature their acorns in one season.

Many oaks have massive and straight trunks; most of them have furrowed and scaly bark and particularly large, powerful branches which often form immensely wide but storm-firm crowns.   The hard, characteristically porous wood (pores occupying mainly one portion of the annual layer) is exceedingly strong in some oaks, and, with the bark, is astringent, due to the presence of large amounts of tannin.

The leaves of oaks occur singly on the branches—never in pairs, one opposite another.   The winter buds, rounded, angled, or pointed, are formed of overlapping scales.   Some oaks shed their leaves in autumn of each year; others, have evergreen leaves, which are shed the second or third year.

Male flowers, minute, arranged singly on thread-like stems, hang down in loose, tassel-like clusters from buds on twigs of the previous year's growth.   Female flowers, minute, very inconspicuous, bud-like bodies, are produced singly or several in a stemmed cluster, from the bases of young growing leaves of the spring; they develop into a nut-like fruit (acorn) in one or two seasons. A notable exception to this arrangement of flowers is found in a section of the genus *Quercus Pasania* (treated by some authors as a distinct genus).   In these oaks, from 3 to 5 male flowers occur together, the groups are scattered along upright stems and grow singly from the bases of young leaves of the season (sometimes from the bases of the leaves of the previous year).   Single female flowers are also borne at some of these leaf-bases, usually at the uppermost ones.

Flowers of all oaks are fertilized by the wind.   The acorns which mature in a single season grow steadily to full size during that period, while those which mature in two seasons develop only very slightly the first summer (appearing as miniature acorns), and begin to increase perceptibly in size only at the opening of the second season.   Mature acorns of annual-fruiting oaks are therefore found on twigs of the year, while those of biennial-fruiting oaks are attached to 2-year-old twigs.   By inspecting the biennial oaks in autumn or winter it may always be determined whether or not they are to bear seed the following season.   Seed production is more or less periodic, at intervals ranging from one to three years: but occasional trees bear fruit for several consecutive seasons.

The fruits, called acorns, are distinctive in having a separable, scaly—sometimes bristly—cup partly or almost wholly inclosing the smooth, thin-shelled nut. Seed of the white-oak acorns is usually whitish, sweetish, and palatable, while that of black-oak acorns is yellowish and bitter with tannin.   In autumn, when the nuts are mature, either the nuts fall from the cups or, in the less easily separable fruits, both nuts and cups fall together.

Under favorable conditions acorns may germinate in autumn, but they commonly do not germinate until spring.   The seed, or firm, inner body of the acorn, consists of two seed-leaves, separated down the center, and from between these, as germination proceeds, grow both the root, or radicle, and the main stem of the little oak.   Unlike those of some other trees, the seed-leaves of the oaks do not form the first green, leaf-like organs, but remain in the split shell and furnish nutriment to the growing stem and root until their supply is exhausted, when they become black and later fall from the stem.   A characteristic of the seedling is the production of a very large, long taproot.   This grows for the first one or two years at the expense of the stem, which gains but little in height meantime.   It enables seedlings repeatedly to survive ground fires which kill the short stem.   A new shoot may be formed many times and the little tree finally establish itself.

Acorns are disseminated entirely through the agency of flood waters and animals.   Mammals and birds eat them in large numbers and so reduce the chances of reproduction, but by burying or otherwise storing them for winter use they virtually plant them.

Oaks are of ancient origin, remains of them found in the Cretaceous and Tertiary periods showing that they once occupied a much more northern habitat than their existing descendants do now.

Approximately 300 species of oaks are known in the world. About 53 species occur within the United States, and all except 3 or 4 of these are trees. Fourteen tree oaks inhabit the Pacific region. All of these enter or belong wholly to California, while one or two of them extend into the southern Rocky Mountain region. This enumeration of species does not include numerous varieties of oaks, nor hybrids, of which a good many have already been described. Others are likely to be discovered.

Valley Oak.

Quercus lobata Née.

DISTINGUISHING CHARACTERISTICS.

Valley oak, so called because it grows chiefly in open valleys, is the largest of western oaks. A striking characteristic is its scattered occurrence. Massive, short-trunked individuals, with enormously broad, often symmetrical, round-toped crowns, grow naturally far apart, forming picturesque vistas through their open ranks. The huge trunk, with grayish, deeply furrowed bark, gives off very large, rough-barked, arching limbs at from 8 to 25 feet from the ground, the drooping lower branches sometimes reaching the ground. Occasional trees have tall, undivided trunks, with small spreading or drooping short branches in a narrow, dome-like crown; generally, however, there is not more than a single length of clear saw timber in the trunks. Height, from 60 to 75 feet, sometimes 80 or 100 feet, with a diameter of from 30 to 40 inches or more. As it straggles up narrow valleys into the foothills it becomes small, often under 30 feet in height and 1 foot through. Mature leaves (fig. 123), shed in autumn, are variable in size and form on the same tree; deep green and minutely hairy (star-shaped hairs) on their top sides, lighter and minutely hairy beneath; leaf stems also hairy. Acorns (fig. 123), matured in one season and sometimes produced in very large quantities,[a] are also variable in size; bright chestnut brown when ripe. Wood, pale dull brown, very brittle, firm, often cross-grained and difficult to split or work. On account of its poor timber form the trees are rarely if ever cut for anything but fuel, for which, however, they are much used.

LONGEVITY.—Nothing is known of the extreme age attained, but it is believed to reach at least from 300 to 400 years. One tree 21¼ inches in diameter showed an age of 57 years.

RANGE.

WESTERN CALIFORNIA.—Interior plains and valleys of coast ranges and western foothills of Sierras from below mouth of Pitt River on upper Sacramento River, at the north, where it grows from sea level to 2,000 feet, southward to Tejon Pass, Tehachapi Valley, Antelope ·Valley (west end of Mojave Desert), and across southern coast mountains; here growing at elevation of 100 to 4,500 feet, and reaching its southernmost limits in Santa Monica and Lamanda Park (within the city of Los Angeles). Abundant in Sacramento Valley, extending northward to Anderson on the river and Shasta (town) in western foothills (Shasta County), reaching also valleys of lower Sierra foothills. Both sides Sacramento River and tributaries in Tehama, Glenn, and Butte counties. Northern coast ranges noted in Stony Creek National Forest northward to Gravelly Valley and other streams; in Mendocino County northward to Round Valley, Cahto, and Laytons-

---

[a] In some parts of the tree's range the sweet acorns are gathered and fed to swine in lieu of grain.

ville (headwaters of Eel River, Mendocino County) ; westward to Cahto, Russian River Valley at Willets and Ukiah (Mendocino County), and down river into Sonoma County, where west limits are Forestville (west edge of redwood belt), and farther south, Green Valley and Camp Meeker ; southward to Ignacio, San Geronimo Valley, and north base

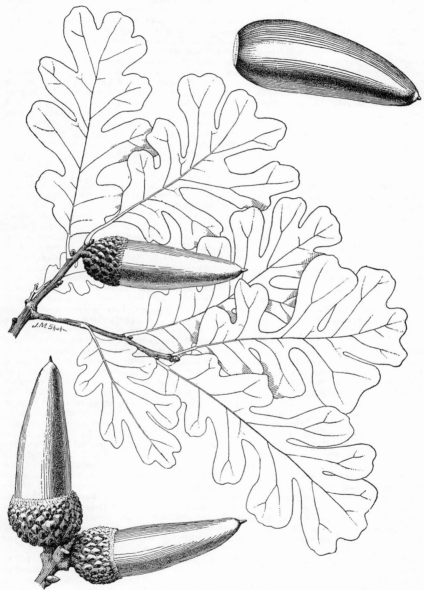

FIG. 123.—*Quercus lobata.*

Mount Tamalpais (Marin County) to Shellville (Sonoma Creek, Sonoma County). *Lake County:* In south at Middletown, Coyote, and Wennok Lake valleys and Putah Creek ; about Clear Lake, and Cache Creek from Lower Lake to Sacramento Valley ; east side of Clear Lake northward on shore to east of Lower Lake ; north side of Sulphur Bank

Arm and on Ellem Island (east end of Sulphur Bank Arm) ; west side of Clear Lake to Lakeport, Kelseyville, and Soda Bay. East of Clear Lake to North Fork of Cache Creek and to head of Long Valley. *Colusa County:* Common on Sacramento River, north and south of Colusa ; also in west Colusa County in most watered valleys ; abundant in Cortena Valley and between Cortena and Bear creeks, also throughout Bear Creek country ; westward in all valleys from Sites to Stony Ford ; west of Stony Ford, sparingly, to near foot of Snow Mountain. *Yolo County:* Knights Landing to Woodland and Davis ; throughout Capay Valley, up Cache Creek into foothills to Clear Lake ; east side of Southern Pacific Railroad between Yolo and Zamora ; from Madison westward on Cache Creek to Esparto ; between Davisville and Swingle Switch. *Sutter County:* Sacramento River and adjacent sloughs between Colusa and Marysville buttes ; north of buttes, in narrow belt (1 or 2 miles wide), but east of buttes, reaching to Marysville on Feather River. *Napa County:* Throughout Napa Valley to Calistoga and lower slopes of Mount St. Helena. *Butte County:* East to vicinity of Chico and Durham ; recedes at Durham toward the Sacramento, reappearing at Biggs, thence going southward in Sutter and Yuba counties to Marysville Buttes and to Yuba and Feather rivers ; Honcut Creek between Butte and Yuba counties ; Feather River to beyond Bidwell Bar and down river nearly to its mouth ; Yuba and other tributary rivers from Sacramento to foothills ; noted at Dry Creek crossing and 2 miles east of Oregon House (between Marysville and Camptonville). *Placer County:* Sacramento Valley to a little above Clipper Gap. *Sacramento County:* Sacramento River, American River (very abundant), Cosumnes River, Deer Creek, and about Galt. *San Joaquin County:* Sacramento River, Stockton, Lodi, and eastward to foothills ; Mokelumne River from Lockeford to Wallace. *Eldorado County:* Consumnes River between Nashville and Plymouth, and from Nashville to Eldorado ; at about 2,000 on ridge between North and Middle forks of Cosumnes ; North Fork Cosumnes River ; and Middle Fork between Pleasant Valley and Oleta ; also a little west of Mount Orcum ; near Smith Flat (east of Placerville) ; Stanislaus National Forest, at 500 to about 2,000 feet, and near Green Valley, Shingle Springs, Pleasant Valley, Calaveras River at Jenny Lind, Bear Creek Valley (west side of Bear Mountains), Garden Valley, vicinity of Coloma, Lotus, Indian Diggins, Coyoteville, West Point, Glencoe, Railroad Flat, and Sheep Ranch. *Amador County:* Jackson and Sutter creeks and between Ione and Forest Home ; Buena Vista and throughout Jackson Valley ; foothills for 3 or 4 miles east of Jackson ; and between Jackson and Plymouth and between Plymouth and Oleta ; Deadmans and Dry creeks, at point about 3 miles southeast of Oleta, and midway between Volcano and Pine Grove ; reservoir 4½ miles west of Pine Grove. *Calaveras County:* West part, particularly on Mokelumne River ; on flat 2 miles east of Valley Springs (road to San Andreas), and between latter and Mountain Ranch ; also near Wiggin's sawmill (between Mountain Ranch and Railroad Flat) ; common on Mokelumne River below Mokelumne Hill, and between latter and West Point ; lower edge of western yellow-pine belt below canyon of South Fork Mokelumne River. *Tuolumne County:* West part and on lower Stanislaus River and between Sonora and Murpheys ; east of Sonora to Soulsbyville and Carters ; Big Creek (northeast of Groveland), and eastward several miles ; also on Deer Flat (north of Big Oak Flat). *Mariposa County:* Eastward from Mariposa 3 or 4 miles in lower edge of western yellow pine (3,000 feet) ; on a branch Chowchilla Creek (below Chowchilla Hill). *Merced County:* Merced River above and below Falls and between latter and Snelling. *Madera County:* Cold Springs to Miami Sawmill and southward over Crane Valley, at Fresno Flats, about North Fork (town), between Raymond and Wawona occurring up to Wassama Valley at Ahwahnee, also in Chowchilla Canyon ; between Wassama and Fresno Flat, and from latter to Coarse Gold Gulch ; between O'Neil and North Fork. *Fresno and King counties:* San Joaquin River Canyon in most gulches and basins ; Toll House (1,900 feet) ; north of Kings River in Burrough and Watts valleys and on Sycamore Creek ; south of Kings River, in Squaw Valley and Mill Creek Valley, where it goes beyond Dunlap ; Mill Creek to Badger and Eshom Valley ; Kings River, site of old Kingston, a few miles north of Tulare Lake (Kings County) ; southward on Kings River to within about 2 miles of Hanford and to a point about 4 miles north of Lemoore ; between Armona and Hardwick belt on Kings River goes southward about 5 miles and northward about 3 miles, being 7 or 8 miles wide ; northward near Cando Switch and at Lillis. *Tulare County:* Vicinity of Visalia and to Venice Hills ; from region of Visalia toward Tulare Lake as far as Waukeena (20 miles) ; eastward to near Exeter and into foothills as on the Kaweah River and road to Aukland, going well into mountains ; about "Lemoncove" and up Kaweah River to beyond "Redstone," and to Whitney Power and Light Company's plant (East Fork Kaweah River), and probably to within 2 miles of west boundary of Sequoia National Park. Abundant in southern Coast Range valleys. *Alameda and Contra Costa counties:* Pleasanton Valley and northward to San Ramon and Walnut Creek ; eastward to Mount Diablo (in canyons, on both sides, cutting the basal slopes) ; east side of Mount Diablo, on Marsh Creek, almost to Brentwood. *Santa Clara County:* Santa Clara Valley southward to Gilroy; also on lower slopes of Mount Hamilton. *San Mateo and Santa Cruz counties:* Between south end of San Francisco Bay and base of the Santa Cruz Mountains; east base of hills west of Palo Alto and southward. *San Benito County:* San Juan Valley, particularly borders and foot of surrounding hills; common in San Benito and Bear valleys from San Benito southward; also in Dry Lake Valley. *Monterey County:* Not in Monterey region nor on coast; nor in lower part of Salinas Valley below Kings City, and probably not for some miles above Kings City, but common in hot interior valleys; Santa Lucia Mountains (Monterey National Forest), at 500 to nearly 5,000 feet elevation on watersheds of Sur, Carmelo, Arroyo Seco, San Antonio, and Nacimiento rivers; noted in upper part Arroyo Seco and Reverse Canyon; also on Milpitas Creek from foot of Santa Lucia Peak southward to old San Antonio Mission and Jolon; thence to Dani Ranch; San Luis Obispo National Forest, at 400 to 2,500 feet in Carriso, Salinas, Santa Margarita, San Luis, Arroyo Grande, and Huasna river basins; not on dry Tulare Plains to east in San Joaquin Valley, except in protected localities, where it ascends a few Sierra foothill streams to 3,250 feet; on basal slopes of Bear Mountain and eastward to Caliente; from Caliente to Tehachapi Valley; west end of Tehachapi Valley; about the borders of Cummings Valley (west of Tehachapi), and thence northwestward down mountains to plain; at Tejon Ranch and along Tejon Creek; in Cañada de las Uvas from Libre Ranch to Fort Tejon (elevation, 3,173 feet) and to Castac Lake; also in Antelope Valley (east of Tehachapi Mountains), the west end of Mohave Desert. One of the most important oaks in Santa Barbara Mountains at 100 to 4,500 feet, but only in Santa Maria, Santa Ynez, Newhall, and Elizabeth river valleys and in Ojai Valley; vicinity of Los Angeles, in Chatsworth Park, and at San Fernando; on Santa Rosa and Santa Cruz islands.

OCCURRENCE.

In low valleys (both narrow and broad) and rolling low plateaus; in fresh, rich, loamy soil, or, less commonly, in dry, gravelly soil.

In pure, very open (often distantly scattered) stands; largest in deep alluvial soils. On borders of valleys with blue oak.

CLIMATIC CONDITIONS.—Similar to those of California live oak, but under less immediate influence of sea.

TOLERANCE.—Endures considerable shade in youth, and shows tolerant qualities when old, but essentially light needing.

REPRODUCTION.—Very prolific seeder at intervals of about two years. Reproduction exceedingly scanty, due probably to the fact that trees grow on grass-covered, pastured, or wheat land, the surface of which is rarely broken where the mast falls. Seed germinates readily when well covered in fresh litter or soil, but it is seldom so covered by natural means.

Brewer Oak.

Quercus breweri Engelmann.

DISTINGUISHING CHARACTERISTICS.

Brewer oak, generally called "shin oak" because of its low, shrubby form, is rarely, if ever, a tree, but forms dense, continuous thickets, in which its slender stems are usually from 4 to 8 feet high (or, in specially favorable sites, from 12 to 18 feet high) and from 2 to 4 inches in diameter. The bark is scaly and dull gray. Season's twigs, pale reddish-brown to reddish-yellow, are minutely hairy. Mature leaves (fig. 124), shed in autumn, are deep, shiny green and roughish with very minute (star-shaped) hairs on their top sides; lighter green and minutely woolly beneath; varying in length from about 1½ to 3½ inches.

Of no commercial use, but important as an effective cover for rocky slopes, its network of creeping roots, from which its sucker-like stems originate, making irresistible barriers to run-off waters.

RANGE.

CALIFORNIA.—West slopes of Sierras, at about lower edge of yellow pine growth, from northern border of State southward to upper Kaweah River basins in Tulare County, and westward, at north, to southern Trinity Mountains, here occurring on Canyon Creek. Forms extensive thickets on upper San Joaquin River at about 6,000 feet, and to some extent also in Kaweah River valleys.

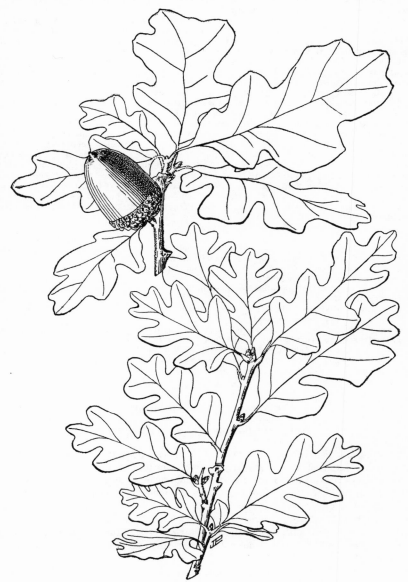

FIG. 124.—*Quercus breweri.*

OCCURRENCE.

Mountain slopes in dry gravelly and rocky soils. In extensive pure growth, or in small patches interspersed among low chaparral brush, scrubby Kellogg oak, Fremontia, etc. Peculiarly even-aged stands of great density occur at north.

CLIMATIC CONDITIONS.—Similar to those in range of western yellow pine.

TOLERANCE.—Slender, clean stems indicate decided intolerance of shade; small crowns always in full light. Seedlings endure slight shade. Seeding habits undetermined.

REPRODUCTION.—A prolific, but apparently an irregular seeder. Reproduced extensively from root sprouts.

Garry Oak.

Quercus garryana Hooker.

DISTINGUISHING CHARACTERISTICS.

Next to valley oak, Garry oak, known most commonly as "white oak," is the largest oak in the Pacific coast region. Occasionally from 75 to 90 feet high, but usually from 50 to 60 feet high and from 18 to 30 inches in diameter, with a short, clear trunk and a broad, round-topped crown; the large limbs tend upward; the lower ones, however, stand out straight and the sprays droop somewhat. On high mountain slopes it is a small, shrubby tree and on exposed situations along the seacoast a very low shrub. The light grayish-brown bark of large trunks has wide ridges and shallow, narrow furrows. Year-old twigs are conspicuously hairy—very much so when young—while the large buds, from three-eighths to one-half inch long, are thickly coated with pale rust-colored hairs. Mature leaves (fig. 125), shed in autumn, are thick and somewhat leathery, very deep, shiny green and smooth on their top sides, and pale green and usually decidedly hairy, but sometimes only very slightly so, beneath; leaf stems hairy. Leaves of some small tree or shrubby forms are thinner than those of large trees, but their twigs and buds are the same. Leaves range from 3½ to 6½ inches in length. Acorns (fig. 125), sweet; matured in one season. Wood pale yellowish brown, hard, fine-grained, strong, rather tough, and durable. Similar in quality to that of eastern white oaks. Young open-grown trees supply exceedingly tough, stiff wood, suitable for wagon tongues and other similar purposes; larger trees yield wood suitable for the same purposes as those for which standard grades of white oak are employed. Garry oak is the only timber oak of the northwest coast country, and for this reason it deserves the forester's careful attention.

LONGEVITY.—Little is known of the age limits, but it is undoubtedly a long-lived tree, probably attaining an age of from 250 to 350 years or more. Two trees, respectively 19¼ and 27 inches through (inside of bark), were 183 and 251 years old.

RANGE.

Valleys and dry, gravelly slopes and table lands from Vancouver Island southward through western Washington and Oregon into coast ranges of northern and central California; generally at elevations from near sea-level to 3,000 or 4,000 feet.

BRITISH COLUMBIA.—Only on southeastern coast of Vancouver Island, where it is large but rare and local. From Straits of Fuca, at some distance west of Victoria, northward over about one-fourth of east coast to Nanaimo, extending inward about 30 miles; on islands of Gulf of Georgia; an isolated grove on northwest end of Vancouver Island, on Quatsino Sound, and another on Fraser River (mainland) 1½ miles above Yale. Described originally from plains around Vancouver, on mainland, but not seen there since.

WASHINGTON.—Occasional slopes and prairies, in Puget Sound and Columbia River basins, also ascending west slope of Cascades to considerable elevations and extending to east slope in the Columbia and Yakima River valleys; generally below 3,800 feet. Locally noted as follows: Islands of Puget Sound; Fairhaven (Whatcom County); vicinity of Seattle; Steilacoom, and Roy (south end of Puget Sound, Pierce County), and farther south at Winlock (Lewis County); Satsop (Chehalis County); west base of Mount Rainier; near Mount Adams; Columbia River Valley eastward to The Dalles; White Salmon and Bingen (southwest Klickitat County); Tampico (central western Yakima County); Klickitat River near Hellroaring Canyon.

OREGON.—Chiefly Willamette River Valley (western Oregon), ascending west slope of Cascades sometimes to an elevation of about 3,000 feet and into lower yellow pine growth; on east slopes of Cascades at north and lower Siskiyous at the south. Not detected on sea side of coast ranges. Locally noted as follows: Beaverton, on Columbia River, and at mouth of Willamette River; Willamette bottoms near Portland; vicinity of Hood River; northeast and east slopes of Mount Hood (in T. 1 S., R. 10 E., and T. 3 S, R. 11 E.), here occurring on Tygh River Valley; head of the Willamette (T. 20 S., R. 2

FIG. 125.—*Quercus garryana.*

E., and T. 21 S., R. 3 E.); throughout Rogue River Basin, north slopes of Siskiyous, and at Waldo in western Siskiyous.

CALIFORNIA.—Northwest part, generally up to lower edge of yellow pine growth at 3,000 or 4,000 feet; westward to inland slope of seaward range, and probably not as far eastward as Mount Shasta (but reported in Lassen Peak National Forest); in Trinity National Forest, eastward to point between Lewiston and Weaverville, just west of Sacramento Valley; extends southward in coast ranges sparingly to Sonoma County—possibly to Marin County, and south of San Francisco to Santa Cruz Mountains. Locally noted on most south slopes and valleys of Trinity National Forest, such as Grouse Creek, on Humboldt Trail, near South Fork Mountain, at 2,500 feet, Rattlesnake Basin, at 3,800 feet, and creek bottom near Friends Ranch, at 3,700.

OCCURRENCE.

In alluvial high bottoms, valleys, prairies; less commonly on dry hill and (north) mountain slopes. In deep, fresh, humous soils (largest in west Washington and Oregon), and also in dry, gravelly or rocky soils (small or scrubby). Occurs only in open mixture; usually with Kellogg oak and Douglas fir, but also with madroña, western yellow pine, and Oregon ash.

CLIMATIC CONDITIONS.—Similar to those of Douglas fir.

TOLERANCE.—Endures slight shade in youth.

REPRODUCTION.—Prolific periodic seeder (about every two years). Seedlings rather scarce, most frequent on moist humous soil and litter; unbroken, grassy surfaces where seed trees often grow are unfavorable for reproduction.

Sadler Oak.

Quercus sadleriana R. Brown Campst.

DISTINGUISHING CHARACTERISTICS.

Sadler oak—named in honor of a Scottish botanist—has no common name except "scrub oak." Though it is only a shrub under 6 feet in height, it is included here because of its value as a slope cover. It produces extensive dense thickets on high, dry slopes between about 4,000 and 9,000 feet elevation. The very distinct form of its leaves (fig. 126), which are thick, deep yellow-green, smooth, and shiny on their upper surfaces, and white, smooth, or slightly hairy beneath, readily distinguish it from any other associated oaks. The leaves, though not strictly evergreen, remain on the branches until the next season's foliage is produced. Acorns are matured in one season.

RANGE.

Coast and Siskiyou mountains of southwestern Oregon and northwestern California.

OREGON.—On top of coast mountains along old Wimer road; top of Siskiyous near Happy Camp Trail.

CALIFORNIA.—Crescent City Trail, Del Norte County, near Oregon line.

OCCURRENCE.

Mountain slopes in dry, rocky and gravelly soil. In extensive thickets of pure growth.

Blue Oak.

Quercus douglasii Hooker and Arnott.

DISTINGUISHING CHARACTERISTICS.

Appropriately called blue oak on account of the blue-green color of its foliage, but known locally also as "white oak," from its light, ashy-gray bark. Trunks exposed to the sun are especially light colored, sometimes even whitish, but are considerably darker gray in sheltered situations.

Usually small or medium sized, from 30 to 40 feet high and from 10 to 15 inches in diameter; exceptionally, from 60 to 75 feet in height and 2 feet in diameter; larger trees occur, but very rarely. The rather thin, narrowly ridged bark flakes off easily. The smooth-looking trunks are short and clear of branches for about 10 to 20 feet; they are invariably leaning or bent, and give off short, thick, horizontal, contorted limbs, which form a compact, flattish, dome-like crown. Year-old twigs are exceedingly brittle, dull gray to reddish brown, and

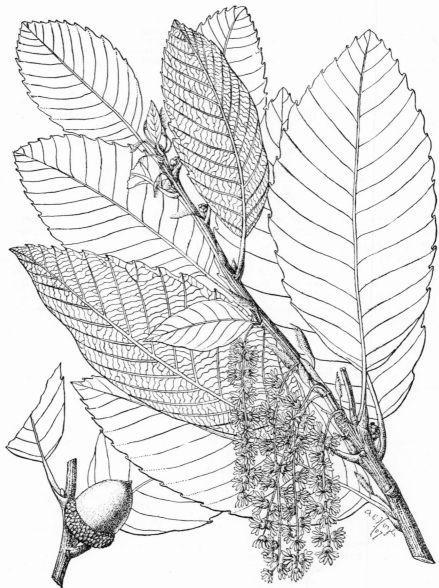

FIG. 126.—*Quercus sadleriana.*

more or less minutely hairy. Mature leaves (figs. 127, 128), extremely variable in size and form; their upper sides conspicuously tinged light blue, with minute, sparse, star-shaped hairs; beneath pale bluish or yellowish green, with very fine soft hairs; midveins and their branches also with very fine soft hairs. They are shed gradually late in autumn. Acorns (fig. 128), deep chestnut brown when ripe and exceedingly variable in form, are matured in one season.

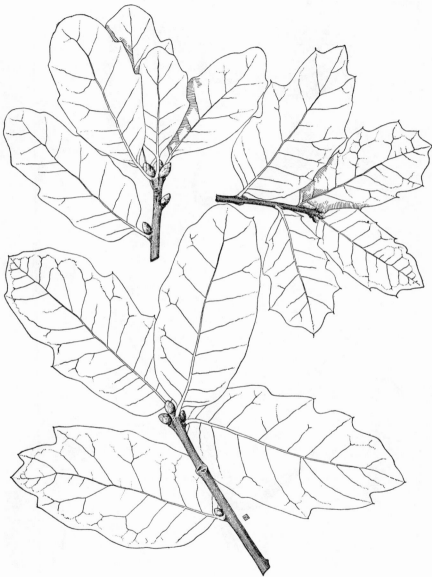

FIG. 127.—*Quercus douglasii.*

Wood, dark mottled brown, very dense, heavy, stiff, and brittle, very cross-grained and difficult to split; sapwood, uncommonly thick. Large trunks are often unsound. It is unfit for any ordinary commercial use, but is good for fuel, for which it is extensively used.

LONGEVITY.—Very little is known of the age attained. Believed to be long-lived. Trees from 14 to 20 inches in diameter are from 175 to 280 years old. Owing to the decayed heart of large trees it is exceedingly difficult to determine their age.

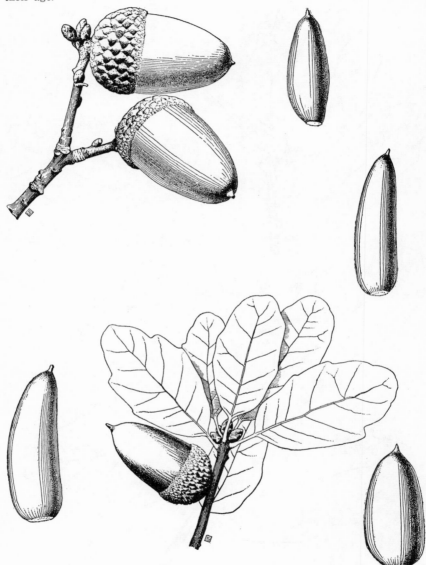

FIG. 128.—*Quercus douglasii.*

RANGE.

CALIFORNIA.—Foothills of coast ranges and west slope of Sierras from Mendocino County and mountains south of Mount Shasta southward to Santa Ynez and Tehachapi mountains and to borders of Mohave Desert. In coast ranges, common on lower foot-hills of inner mountains and rare in valleys; extends westward and northward to east slopes of seaward range at Ukiah on Russian River, becoming very abundant south of San Francisco Bay. Common in Trinity and Shasta National Forests at 500 to 2,000 feet elevation, on foothills south of Pitt River, on lower Sacramento, McCloud, and Trinity rivers, extending eastward in Trinity National Forest from beyond Shasta (town) to point just west of Redding, occurring also at point 18 miles northeast of Redding. Abundant in Stony Creek National Forest in coast ranges on lowest hills of east slope. In Santa Lucia Mountains, mainly on east slopes in Carmelo, Arroyo Seco, San Antonio, and Nacimiento river basins at 250 to 3,000 feet. San Luis Obispo National Forest, generally distributed in Carriso, Salinas, Santa Margarita, San Luis, Arroyo Grande, and Huasna river watersheds at 1,000 to 2,500 feet. Santa Barbara National Forest, only in northwestern part; in Santa Maria and Santa Ynez river basins, where it grows at elevations of 550 to 4,000 feet. Elsewhere in southern coast ranges, limited to borders of Mohave desert on north slopes of northern Sierra Liebre Mountains and in San Fernando Valley at Encino (southern part of San Gabriel National Forest), the southern limit. On west slope of Sierras it occurs very generally and abundantly in foothills at 500 to 3,000 feet, southward throughout that side into valleys of Tehachapi Mountains; common, at north, in Lassen Peak and Plumas National Forests up to 2,000 feet. Abundant in Stanislaus National Forest on lowest hills between 300 and 1,500 feet, as it is also, up to about 1,000 feet, in the Sierra National Forest.

OCCURRENCE.

On low foothills and their valleys; in dry, loamy, gravelly, and rocky soils. Forms extensive, peculiarly open, pure stands, and grows with Wislizenus oak, California white and live oaks, and Sabine pine.

CLIMATIC CONDITIONS.—Similar to those of Sabine pine.

TOLERANCE.—Very intolerant of shade.

REPRODUCTION.—Prolific periodic seeder. Seedlings scarce in ground usually grazed or cultivated, where much seed is destroyed or has little chance of germination; rather abundant elsewhere.

Alvord Oak.

Quercus alvordiana [a] Eastwood.

DISTINGUISHING CHARACTERISTICS.

So little is known now of the newly found Alvord oak that it is impossible to give an adequate account of its characters.[b]

Said to be a "small tree or shrub" with "small, brittle, and easily falling dentate [toothed] leaves," from the texture of which it is assigned to the white-oak group. The acorn is smooth, except the minutely scaly cup, which has very fine, close, whitish down. Nothing is known of the height, the form of trunk or crown, the wood, or other characters. It appears to be closely related to *Q. dumosa*, one form of which it resembles in its leaves and acorns. Careful field study of this oak is required to establish its characters.

RANGE.

Southern California. Described as occurring on "hills near the desert," and further as an "oak in the mountains connecting the Coast Range with the Sierra Nevada at the southern end of the San Joaquin Valley bordering the desert."

Engelmann Oak.

Quercus engelmanni Greene.

DISTINGUISHING CHARACTERISTICS.

Engelmann oak is a little-known tree, called "evergreen white oak" on account of its partly evergreen leaves, which remain on the trees from one spring to the

---

[a] Named in honor of William Alvord, former president of the California Academy of Sciences.

[b] Herbarium specimens, kindly sent by Miss Eastwood from a meager supply, are insufficient for an illustration.

next and begin to fall when the new leaves are being formed. It is not strictly evergreen. Its general aspect is that of a white oak with deeply furrowed, widely ridged, pale grayish-brown bark, and a big, irregular, dense, rounded

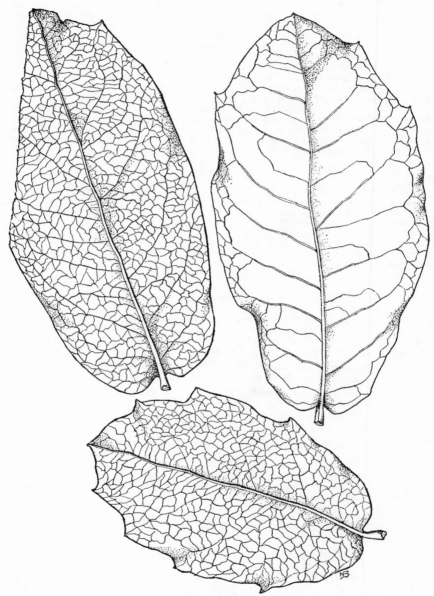

FIG. 129.—*Quercus engelmanni;* young shoot leaves.

crown. It is from 40 to 50 feet high (occasionally somewhat taller), and from 20 to 30 inches in diameter. The large limbs stand out almost horizontally above a short, clear trunk. Twigs of the first season are reddish-brown and coated with very minute, short hairs, which later disappear. Mature leaves (fig. 130), very distinctive, are thick, very deep blue-green, and either smooth or with a few star-shaped hairs on their top sides; under surfaces and leaf

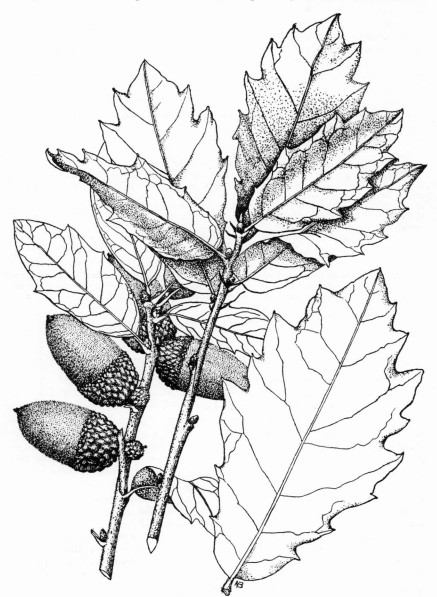

FIG. 130.—*Quercus engelmanni.*

stems light yellowish-green, and more or less coated with tawny minute hairs (which are sometimes practically absent, however); exceedingly variable in form and size, larger leaves occurring on vigorous shoots (fig. 129). Acorns are matured in one season, and when ripe are dark to light chestnut-brown; cups externally clear red-brown and minutely hairy; their scales, especially those at the bottom, having a thick, ridge-like projection on the back and sharp, hairy points.

Wood very dark brown, exceedingly heavy, dense, stiff, and brittle; green wood checks and warps badly when exposed. It has nothing to recommend it for commercial purposes, but locally it is likely to be of some importance for fuel, of which it furnishes a good quality. It is a useful desert species, and owing to the limited number of trees and their restricted range, attention should be given to its reproduction and extension.

LONGEVITY.—Not fully determined. Judged to be moderately long-lived. One tree 14½ inches (inside of bark) showed an age of only 38 years. This indicates rapid growth for a desert oak.

RANGE.

Southern California and northern Lower California.

CALIFORNIA.—Low hills in coast regions of southern part from Sierra Madre, where it extends from Altadena to Glendora, southward in a belt about 50 miles wide, beginning 15 to 20 miles from sea, to mesa east of San Diego. Forms about one-third of the stand in Palomar Mountains and is second in abundance to *Quercus californica*. Rare in Cuyamaca Mountains. At Mexican line extends from Campo to Tecate Mountain, 27 miles from coast.

LOWER CALIFORNIA.—Extends only a short distance from north boundary.

OCCURRENCE.

Low hill slopes and dry, rolling mesas, in loamy sand and gravel soils. Forms small groups and open pure patches, but usually in mixture with California live oak. Climatic conditions, silvical characteristics, and reproduction undetermined.

California Scrub Oak.

Quercus dumosa Nuttall.

DISTINGUISHING CHARACTERISTICS.

With the possible exception of the polymorphous *Quercus undulata*, of Rocky Mountain range, California scrub oak unquestionably varies more than all other oaks in the form and size of its leaves and acorns. No sort of satisfactory harmony can be established between the perplexing phases of its development, and one is likely to be hopelessly confused without a most comprehensive field study of the bushes and small trees belonging to this species. At least 3 species and as many varieties have been singled out, but the distinctions between them are hopelessly confused by the occasional occurrence of their various types of leaf and fruit on the branches of a single individual. Unless the observer has a comprehensive view of all the points that seem to compel the uniting of these diverging forms into one variable species, and one fairly constant subspecies, this reduction may seem hardly proper.

It is known as "scrub oak," for it occurs in the main, singly or massed in low thickets, with the fine, exceedingly stiff twigs and branches closely mingled. The California coast island representatives grown in sheltered places are from 20 to 25 feet high and from 8 to 12 or more inches in diameter, with scaly brown bark; while the bark of the scrub forms is scaly and light ashy-gray. The twigs, so rigid as to seem thorny to one penetrating a thicket, are branched at very abrupt angles. No adequate statement can be made of the size or form characters of the leaves and acorns, types of which are figured as fully as possible in fig. 131.

The best marked variety is *Quercus dumosa revoluta* Sargent, to be looked for especially in the northern and southern range of the species. It is distinguished by its strongly rolled or curled leaves, more or less coated with whitish hairs, and with prickly borders; the curled edges are turned toward the under surface of the leaf. Leaves of a season's growth adhere to the branches until

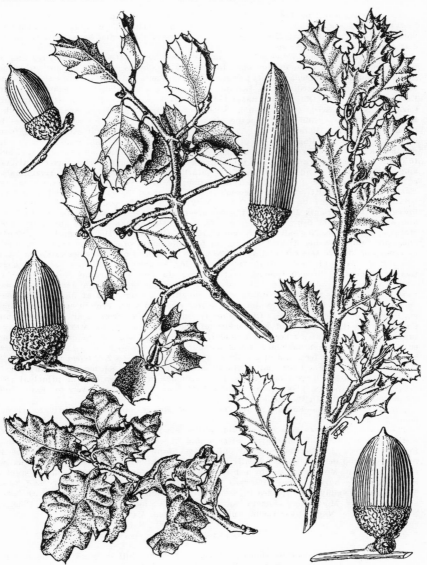

Fig. 131.—*Quercus dumosa.*

the succeeding spring, and begin to fall as the new leaves are formed. Acorns are matured in one season.

Wood light brown, hard, brittle; of no commercial use. The species useful only in assisting, with other desert hill shrubs and small trees, in forming a protective cover on the too scantily clothed dry slopes. Its strong roots go deep into rocky crevices and send up sprouts year after year, provided that the thin stems are not too severely burned.

LONGEVITY.—Not fully determined. A single stem 4½ inches through shows an age of 20 years.

Central California to Lower California. Chaparral belt of foothills from central Sierras and of coast ranges in Mendocino County and Trinity Mountains, southward to northern Lower California ; also on islands off southern California, here, only, becoming a tree of any considerable size.

CALIFORNIA.—Common scrub oak of southern coast ranges, the type definitely known northward on seaward mountains only to San Mateo County, and on Mount Hamilton range to southern Alameda County ; eastward in southern California to desert slopes of San Gabriel, San Bernardino, San Jacinto, and Cuyamaca mountains. Common in Santa Lucia and San Luis Obispo mountains between 1,000 and 4,000 feet elevation, in Sur, Carmelo, Arroyo Seco, San Antonio, Nacimiento, Carriso, Salinas, Santa Margarita, San Luis, Arroyo Grande, and Huasna river basins. In central Sierras the species is often more common than its variety *revoluta*. Locally noted in Butte County on foothills along Chico-Sterling Road ; foothills on Sweetwater Creek (Eldorado County) ; in Stanislaus National Forest, forming small thickets near bottoms of canyons at 2,500 to 3,000 feet, on headwaters of Esperanza Creek (tributary North Fork Calaveras River), and on San Antonio and Indian Creek (tributaries of South Fork of latter river) ; also at Sherlock and West Point. In Sierra National Forest, reported on canyon sides of East Fork of Tule River, below Nelson's ranch, at about 5,500 feet elevation and on Greenhorn Mountains up to 5,000 feet. Very abundant in southern mountains. Its lowest altitude in Santa Barbara National Forest is 1,400 feet, while it goes up to 5,000 and sometimes 7,000 feet ; in watersheds of Santa Maria, Santa Ynez, Santa Barbara, Matilija, Piru-Sespe, Newhall, and Elizabeth rivers. In San Gabriel Mountains, on south and north slopes facing desert, growing on foothills south of Antelope Valley (western extremity of Mojave Desert), and on Liebre ranch ; abundant on both sides of Cajon Pass, and farther west, at west end of Antelope Valley, common on hillsides facing desert ; thence southward through Cañada de las Uvas. In San Bernardino Mountains eastward to canyons facing desert. Abundant in chaparral belt of San Jacinto National Forest up to 5,000 feet on mountain sides, and often among pines at higher elevations on south side. On Santa Ana Mountains, nearer coast, in scrub growth on tops of range at 1,600 feet. Occurs in San Diego County on mountains from near sea (Temecula Canyon, near San Diego, and near mouth of Tia Juana River, on Mexican boundary) eastward to Coast Range ; here, in Palomar, Balkan, and Cuyamaca mountains, reaching east slopes ; on Mexican boundary, down to about 2,543 feet on east slope, at Wagon Pass, going to about 4,000 feet, and at Jucumba Hot Springs down to 2,822 feet elevation.

The form [a] in Santa Cruz and Santa Rosa islands, off the southern mainland coast, usually with rather large lobed leaves, is exceptional in representing the principal tree growth of this species. Its size and larger foliage are believed, however, to result from its protected habitat in these island canyons.

LOWER CALIFORNIA.—Southward on foothills of Mount San Pedro Martir to Telmo, about latitude 31°.

The range of *Quercus dumosa revoluta,* which is within that of the species, is imperfectly known. Foothills of central Sierras and of coast ranges chiefly north of San Francisco Bay. In Sierras recorded only from Stanislaus National Forest, where it forms occasional dense thickets ; locally noted near Volcanoville and Georgetown. Occurs rarely in Coast Mountains southward to Santa Lucia Mountains, but replaces species apparently only north of San Francisco Bay ; abundant to Mendocino County and Napa Valley, and probably with species in Stony Creek National Forest, north of Clear Lake, and in Trinity Mountains (Shasta National Forest) ; locally noted in Lake County, Knoxville Grade, Napa River Basin, and in Upper Conn Valley.

Low mountain and foothill slopes and sides of desert hill canyons, in the poorest and driest gravelly soils, often so sterile as to support little else.

In scattered, thick clumps and patches of pure growth, more or less interspersed with Christmas berry, mountain mahogany, ceanothus brush, manzanitas and other chaparral, of which it is essentially a part.

CLIMATIC CONDITIONS.—Similar to those of gray pine.

---

[a] *Quercus macdonaldi* Greene.

TOLERANCE.—Appears to be tolerant of but little shade.

REPRODUCTION.—Abundant seeder; apparently seeds nearly every year. Seedlings moderately abundant in exposed mineral soil of pockets where seed is well covered by washing or other accidents.

Canyon Live Oak.

Quercus chrysolepis Liebmann.

DISTINGUISHING CHARACTERISTICS.

Canyon live oak is an evergreen oak, with the soft, scaly trunk bark of a white oak. Very variable in size, from low, dense chaparral brush to a wide-spreading tree 30 or 40 feet high, with huge horizontal limbs and a short, thick, clear trunk from 30 to 60 or more inches in diameter. It develops the latter form as single individuals in open situations, but on narrow, sheltered canyon bottoms and sides it grows tall (rarely straight) and slender, with 15 or 20 feet of clear trunk and a small crown; the stems have very little taper.

Year-old twigs are dark reddish brown, more or less densely covered with fine woolly hairs, sometimes nearly or quite smooth; very woolly when young.

Mature leaves (figs. 132 to 134) of one season's growth are thick, leathery, light yellowish-green in color, and smooth on the top sides; beneath they are covered by a yellowish down. Later they lose nearly all their woolliness and become very pale bluish green beneath. Leaves of each season's growth persist from 3 to 4 years. Various forms and sizes of leaves are produced by trees of different ages. Leaves of large trees usually have very few or no marginal teeth (fig. 133), while young trees, and especially vigorous shoots, have very spiny-bordered leaves (fig. 134). Acorns are matured at the end of the second season—a notable exception to the rule among oaks which, like this species, have the sort of wood characteristic of white oak. Acorns (figs. 132, 133), without visible stems or with very short ones, vary exceedingly in the size and form of their nuts and cups, but agree more or less in having nuts of a pale chestnut color (downy at the point). The cups, rather thin (figs. 132, 133) or very thick, are densely covered with a whitish or yellowish short wool, which is so dense in some instances as to obscure the cup scales. This yellow coating has given the tree the name of "golden-cup oak" in parts of its range.

A well-marked variety is *Quercus chrysolepis palmeri* Engelmann, of the southern boundary of California. This has very thick, stiff, wide leaves, circular in outline (fig. 135, *a*), with prominent, large, spine-pointed teeth; acorns usually sharply conical, often rather long stemmed, and with very shallow, thin, sometimes thickish cups (fig. 135, *a*). Commonly it is shrub-like, from 10 to 20 feet high, and forms dense thickets. The remarkably distinct form of this variety's acorns, together with the fact that the female flowers are often borne on a long stem, indicate that this tree should be considered a distinct species.

Another distinct variety is *Quercus chrysolepis vaccinifolia* (Kellogg) Engelm., a low-massed shrub of very high altitudes, commonly called "huckleberry oak," from the resemblance of its small (three-fourths of an inch to 1 inch long), sparingly or indistinctly toothed, usually smooth leaves (fig. 135, *b*). Acorns are from five-eighths to seven-eighths of an inch long, pointed, and with very thin, shallow cups. This variety is exceedingly important for the effective low chaparral cover it produces on the highest slopes and ridges of the Sierras.

Wood of canyon live oak is of better commercial quality than that of any other species of oak in its range. It is of a light brown color, variable in grain from fine to coarse, very heavy, stiff, and exceedingly tough and strong. Its strength is well known to mountain freight teamsters, who prize wagon tongues and whiffle-trees made from it very highly. The wood is suitable for wheel stock and the woodwork of farm implements.

LONGEVITY.—Not fully determined. Undoubtedly a long-lived tree, probably reaching an age of at least 250 to 300 years. Trees from 10 to 18 inches in diameter (canyon growth) are from 98 to 156 years old.

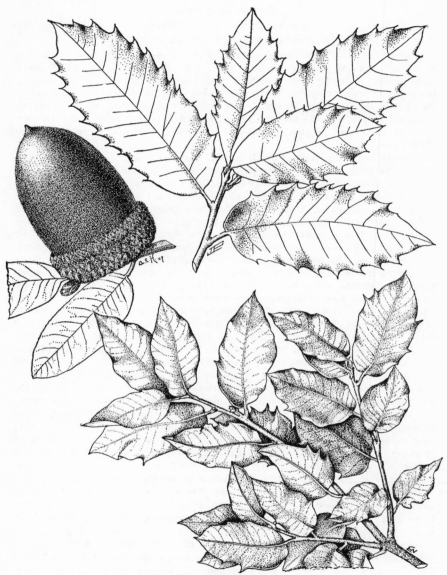

FIG. 132.—*Quercus chrysolepis.*

RANGE.

Southwest corner of Oregon and southward throughout mountains of California, except east side of Sierras and southeastern desert, to northern Lower California ; eastward through mountains of central and southern Arizona, northern Sonora, and southwestern New

Mexico; in north, at elevations of about 1,000 to 5,000 feet, and in south, at 2,500 to 9,000 feet. Reported from southern Utah and Nevada, but authentic records of its existence there are lacking.

OREGON.—Coast mountains south of Cow Creek Valley (tributary Umpqua River, lat. 42° 50′), and only as a shrub on streams and in canyons.

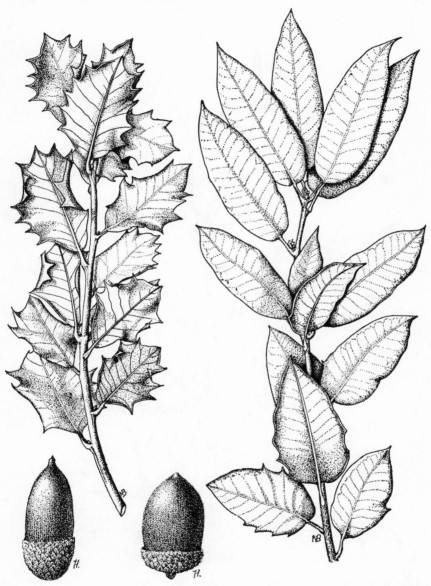

FIG. 133.—*Quercus chrysolepis.*

CALIFORNIA.—Throughout upper foothills, canyons, and summits of coast ranges and west side of Sierras, at elevations of 2,000 to 6,000 feet, altitudes at which it occurs generally throughout northern part of State, going westward probably to upper sea slope of Coast Range and eastward to about longitude of Mount Shasta, but not on that mountain.   In Klamath National Forest, reaching yellow pine belt; in Trinity Mountains, extending eastward nearly to Redding; in Shasta National Forest, chiefly on canyon slopes at 2,000 to 3,000 feet and in lower part of yellow pine belt up to about 5,000 feet; common among foothill trees in Lassen Peak and Plumas National forests.   Abundant in Sierras throughout higher foothills, generally to 6,000 feet, but very often ascending to

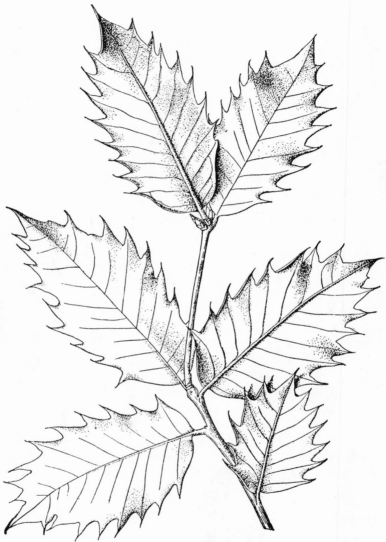

FIG. 134.—*Quercus chrysolepis.*

8,000 or 9,000 feet.   In west border canyons of Tahoe National Forest; in all principal canyons of Stanislaus National Forest, at 1,500 to 6,000 feet, occasionally spreading over high broad valleys, where large trees grow between about 3,000 to 8,000 feet elevation. Abundant in valley bottoms of Sequoia and Yosemite National parks.   In Sierra National Forest it grows in canyons and gulches far below pine belt as well as up into it. Locally noted in this region as follows: Merced River, south of Wawona; Fresno River, north of Cold Springs; Middle Fork Kings River, near Tehipiti Dome, and at mouth of Crown Creek; on the South Fork, also in head basin of this and on Bubbs Creek; Middle Tule River, at Soda Springs; East and South Forks of Kaweah River; South Fork of Kern River (opposite Weldon) in region of Cottonwood Creek, at 6,200 feet elevation,

FIG. 135.—*Quercus chrysolepis palmeri* (*a*). *Quercus chrysolepis vaccinifolia* (*b*).

Tehachapi Mountains (south end of Sierras), in such canyons as Cañada de las Uvas. Common in northern coast ranges; throughout Stony Creek National Forest, but most abundant in canyons and brushy slopes of Eel River tributaries, shrubby forms often ascending highest summits to 6,000 or 7,000 feet, as on St. Johns, Black Buttes, Sanhedrin, and Bald mountains, but a tree in west side canyons. Rare in San Francisco Bay region, and of small size on higher mountains, such as Monte Diablo, Mount Tamalpais, and in Coast Range canyons. South of Monterey, in Santa Lucia Mountains of Monterey National Forest, one of commonest trees at 1,500 to 5,000 feet elevation, in Sur, Carmelo, Arroyo Seco, San Antonio, and Nacimiento river watersheds. Farther south, in San Luis Obispo National Forest, an unimportant tree, in Arroyo Grande watershed, at 1,250 to 3,500 feet. Very common in Santa Barbara, San Gabriel, San Bernardino, and San Jacinto National forests, often associated with *Pseudotsuga macrocarpa* up to about 6,000 feet. In Santa Barbara National Forest, on watersheds of Santa Maria, Santa Ynez, Santa Barbara, Matilija, Piru-Sespe, and Newhall rivers, at elevations of 1,000 to 6,700 feet. Abundant in all canyons of San Gabriel National Forest, above 2,500 feet, as it is also in San Bernardino National Forest, occurring here on Santa Ana River (a mile below Seven Oaks) at 5,000 feet, and farther upstream, at 5,200 feet. Frequent in San Jacinto National Forest, throughout mountains, up to 6,000 feet, but as a shrub, at head of Strawberry Valley, and on Tahquitz Ridge, at 7,000 feet elevation. Abundant also in Santa Ana range (Orange County), near coast, where it grows in canyons, and as a shrub on summits; while farther south it is a frequent tree in seaward basins of San Diego County, such as of Palomar, Balkan, and Cuyamaca mountains. Reported on Providence Mountains (eastern San Bernardino County) near the Colorado River.

LOWER CALIFORNIA.—Commonest oak on Mount San Pedro Martir, above 4,000 feet elevation, and as a small tree above 6,000 feet on both sides of Hanson Laguna range (to north).

The detailed range of this oak east of the Pacific region will be described in a later publication.

Quercus chrysolepis palmeri on foothills and plateaus near southern boundary of California, forming large thickets. Noted locally in this region at point 80 miles east of San Diego, at Larkens Station, and at Las Juantas. In Lower California, from north boundary southward a short distance.

Quercus chrysolepis vaccinifolia occupies higher range of *Quercus chrysolepis,* forming extensive low thickets in Trinity Mountains and Sierras of California; probably also in other parts of the latter tree's range.

OCCURRENCE.

Commonly in narrow canyon bottoms and their steep slopes and in coves, sheltered depressions, in dry sandy and gravelly soils; or on exposed slopes, in broken rock and crevices. Largest in richer humous soils of sheltered canyon bottoms.

Sometimes in small pure clumps or patches, but usually in mixture with California black and live oaks, highland live oak, bigcone spruce; occasionally with western yellow pine and incense cedar.

CLIMATIC CONDITIONS.—Similar to those of California black oak.

TOLERANCE.—Endures considerable heavy shade, especially in youth, but later seeks top light, in dense stands producing tall, slender stems with narrow crowns, either in partial or full light. Great tolerance is shown by open-grown trees in their heavy, deep, leafy crowns.

REPRODUCTION.—Prolific seeder at irregular intervals, but reproduction scanty, apparently as frequent in open as in sheltered sites, thick leaves preventing seedlings from suffering in latter places. Silvical requirements not fully determined.

Quercus tomentella Engelmann.

DISTINGUISHING CHARACTERISTICS.

No field name appears ever to have been applied to *Quercus tomentella,* a little-known evergreen oak. It is from 30 to 40 feet high and from 12 to 18 inches in diameter. Somewhat larger trees are reported, and it is likely that still larger trees once grew in the sheltered canyons of the coast islands, to which it is confined. Nothing is known of its trunk and crown form. The trunk bark is thin, with broad, closely attached scales, which are brown, tinged with red.

Mature leaves are thick, leathery, deep green, smooth and shiny on their top sides, and beneath coated with star-shaped and jointed hairs, as are the stems;

they remain on the branches about two years before falling (figs. 136, 137). Margins of the leaves curled toward the under surface. Acorns, matured in

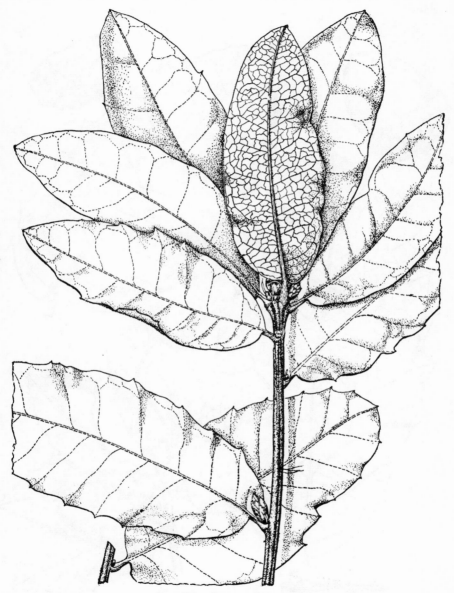

Fig. 136.—*Quercus tomentella.*

autumn of the second year, are about 1⅓ inches long and three-fourths of an inch thick, the shallow chestnut-colored cups covered with a tawny or whitish wool (fig. 137). Wood hard, fine-grained, and light yellowish brown. So little is known of this oak now that nothing can be said of its economic qualities. Probably too rare and of too limited supply to be of any importance commercially.

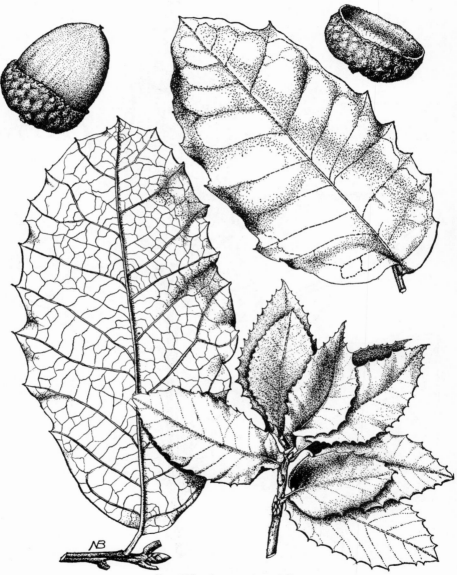

Fig. 137.—*Quercus tomentella.*

LONGEVITY.—Probably moderately long-lived. One tree 4¼ inches in diameter (inside bark) showed an age of 44 years.

RANGE.

Santa Rosa, Santa Cruz (south of Santa Barbara), Santa Catalina, and San Clemente Islands, south of Cape Vincent, off coast of California; Guadalupe Islands, off coast of Lower California.

OCCURRENCE.

In narrow canyon bottoms and on exposed slopes, in rocky or gravelly soils. Climatic, silvical, and other requirements undetermined.

California Live Oak.

Quercus agrifolia Née.

DISTINGUISHING CHARACTERISTICS.

California live oak is one of the commonest, best known of southern California oaks, as well as one of the first to attract the attention of early explorers, who called it " holly-leaved oak," from the resemblance of its leaves to the large American or European evergreen holly.

It has a short, clear trunk and a narrow or very broad, dome-shaped, dense crown, according to whether it is crowded or in the open. It usually grows in the open. Occasionally it is only a low, shrubby tree. It is ordinarily from 25 to 50 feet in height and from 1 to 2 feet in diameter. Very old trees in the open are from 60 to 75 feet high and from 3 to $3\frac{1}{2}$ feet through. Very long, thick, crooked limbs are given off from the short, clear trunk (which is often only from 4 to 8 feet long), forming with numerous fine twigs a dense, exceedingly broad crown, sometimes reaching the ground; trees in crowded stands have rather slender branches. Small trees and the large limbs of big trees have smooth, light grayish-brown bark, with frequent ashy-white areas, while large trees have very thick, hard, blackish or very dark brown, roughly furrowed bark, with wide ridges. Season's twigs, dull gray to reddish brown, with pale chestnut-colored buds, are somewhat downy, with very short, whitish hairs.

Mature leaves (figs. 138 to 140) are more or less conspicuously curled on their prickly-toothed or entire edges and are usually dark (but often light) shiny green on their convex upper sides—sometimes coated with light-colored minute, star-shaped hairs, while beneath they are paler green, smooth, somewhat shiny, and with brownish hairs in the angles of the veins, or, again, the entire under surface is downy with minute, dense hairs. The leaves are thinnish, but peculiarly stiff and brittle. The foliage appears to be evergreen, but remains on the trees only until the succeeding spring, usually beginning to fall before or a short time after the new leaves are formed. Flowers appear mainly in early spring, the acorns (fig. 140) maturing in the autumn of that season; occasional trees produce flowers in the fall and small immature acorns which drop from the trees by spring. The cups of acorns are peculiar in having their scaly edges turned in. Wood, brittle, hard, heavy, exceedingly fine-grained, reddish brown; sapwood very thick and darker than heart. It has economic value only for fuel, since the tree has a very poor timber form and the wood checks and warps badly in seasoning. Bark of this species is extensively used to adulterate the similar but much more valuable tanbark obtained from the California tanbark oak.

LONGEVITY.—Few records of the age attained are available. It is judged to be exceedingly long-lived. Trees from 12 to 25 inches through are from 26 to about 65 years old.

California and Lower California. Valleys and lower foothills of California coast ranges, inland through fog belt and southward from Mendocino, Mendocino County, to Mount San Pedro Martir, Lower California. Not in great interior valleys of California.

FIG. 138.—*Quercus agrifolia.*

CALIFORNIA.—Not common north of San Francisco Bay, but very abundant in valleys about and south of the bay. Plentiful also in southern California between mountains and sea, and also on coast islands. Going southward, it extends inland from sea to

Monte Diablo, Oakland hills, Santa Clara Valley, to valleys east of Santa Lucia and San Luis Obispo Mountains, to southern slopes of Santa Barbara, San Gabriel, eastern slopes of San Bernardino to San Gorgonio Pass, at 2,800 feet elevation, and to ranges in San Diego County.   Locally noted about Inverness and Nicasio (Marin County) and at Berkeley ; Santa Clara Valley and up western foothills ; Big Basin (Santa Cruz County), on Flea Protrero, at Monterey, Del Monte, Point Pinyos, and Carmel Bay.   In Santa Lucia Mountains of Monterey National Forest, an important tree in Sur, Carmelo, Arroyo Seco, San Antonio, and Nacimiento river watersheds, ranging throughout this Forest from sea level to 3,000 feet on hillsides and in canyons.   Locally noted in this region from

FIG. 139.—*Quercus agrifolia.*

near King City to Jolon, and at a point 5 miles north of Danis Ranch (Monterey County). Widely distributed in San Luis Obispo National Forest from sea level to 2,500 feet in watersheds of Carriso, Salinas, Santa Margarita, San Luis, Arroyo Grande, and Huasna river basins.   Common in valleys and foothills of Santa Barbara National Forest from sea level to 4,500 feet, in watersheds of Santa Maria, Santa Ynez, Santa Barbara, Matilija, Piru-Sespe, Newhall, and Elizabeth rivers.   Locally noted at Nordhoff (750 feet), Piedro Blanco Creek, Coopers Canyon at 200 feet (14 miles west of Santa Barbara). Abundant in San Gabriel National Forest from Oak Knoll into Sierra Madre Range ; here locally noted from lower hills to 1,000 and 3,200 feet at Pasadena (1,000 feet), 4

miles northwest of Pasadena, Long Canyon, and at point 1½ miles southwest of Strawberry Peak, at 3,200 feet. Frequent in Trabuco Canyon National Forest (Orange
County), in nearly all canyons, except at highest elevations. Occurs on a number of
coast islands, probably on all except San Clemente. Southward it grows in a belt about
50 miles wide, extending westward to within 15 or 20 miles of coast, and eastward to
west slope of mountains, but probably not reaching San Jacinto Mountains, though oc
curring in Palomar and Balkan mountains, and widely over Cuyamaca Mountains; here
going eastward to Jacumba Hot Springs (2,822 feet elevation.) Locally noted near
Mexican boundary in San Diego County at Alpine, 2,275 feet elevation, and Pine Valley,
at 4,200 feet.

LOWER CALIFORNIA.—More or less common in low canyons on west side of Mount San
Pedro Martir; occurs here in Encinas Canyon (near San Tomas) and at San Antonio,
at 3,000 feet, and on Santa Cruz Creek.

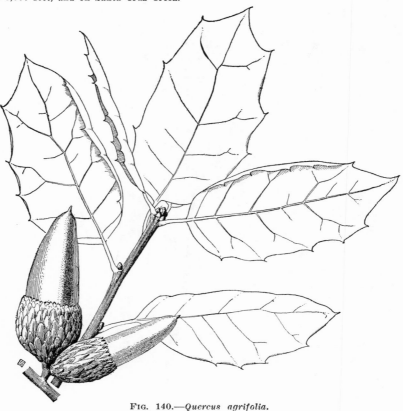

FIG. 140.—*Quercus agrifolia.*

OCCURRENCE.

Characteristic on low hills and open valleys, slopes of higher foothills, shallow canyons,
in dry loamy or gravelly soils; also (but stunted) on exposed seashore.

Forms extensive, pure, open forests, and is also mixed with valley oaks, blue oak,
Wislizenus oak, and big-cone spruce, and occasionally with canyon live oak, California
sycamore, and white alder.

CLIMATIC CONDITIONS.—Similar to those of Monterey pine.

TOLERANCE.—Very tolerant of shade throughout life.

REPRODUCTION.—Prolific periodic seeder, but reproduction generally scanty.

Wislizenus Oak.

Quercus wislizeni A. de Candolle.

DISTINGUISHING CHARACTERISTICS.

Wislizenus oak is not known by this name. It is hoped, however, that this name may be used in preference to "live oak," the present field name, which is applied to several other oaks with evergreen foliage.

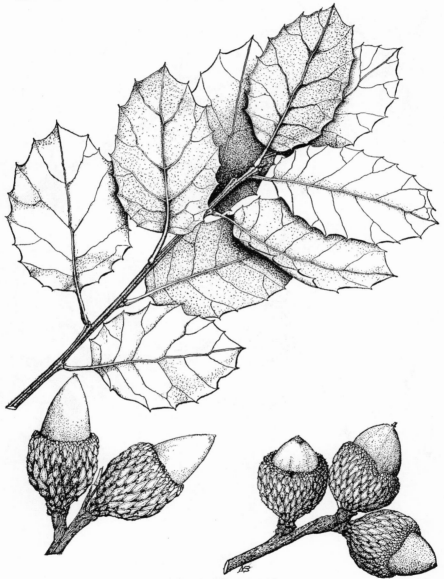

FIG. 141.—*Quercus wislizeni.*

Very similar in size, general form, and appearance of the bark to the preceding species, with which it is often associated and with which, when young, it may be easily confounded. It does not have such broad crowns nor such enormous limbs as the California live oak. Its similar, but very much thicker, leathery, shiny, perfectly smooth leaves (figs. 141, 142) are flat (never curled), deep green on their top sides and light yellow-green beneath. The leaf stems

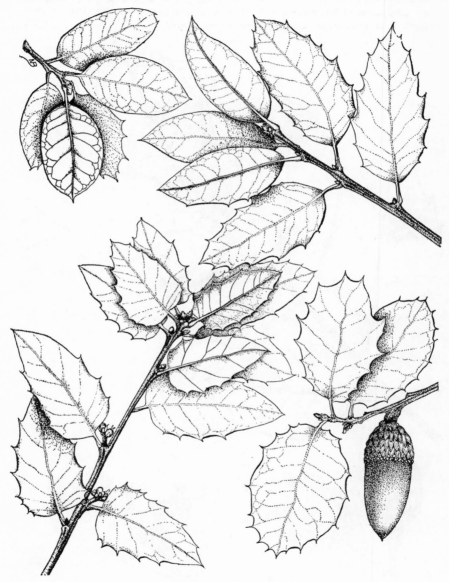

FIG. 142.—*Quercus wislizeni.*

are generally very minutely and plentifully (sometimes sparsely) hairy. Unlike those of the California live oak, the leaves of this tree remain on the branches for about two seasons and begin to fall during the second summer or autumn.

Acorns (fig. 142) mature in two seasons and are ripe in late fall. The cup scales are long and reddish brown.

Wood similar in color and character to that of the preceding, but its thick sapwood is whitish. It is of no economic use, except for local supplies of fuel, for which it is very highly esteemed and extensively used in some parts of the tree's range.

LONGEVITY.—Not fully determined. It grows slowly and persistently and is exceedingly tenacious, even where storm-beaten or pounded in the sandy and gravelly washes of streams. Trees from 8 to 15 inches in diameter are from 40 to 75 years old.

RANGE.

Northern California to northern Lower California. Foothills and valleys from near lower southern slopes of Mount Shasta (Sacramento River Valley) southward in California coast ranges and Sierras to Mount San Pedro Martir, northern Lower California. Shrubby on high summits at south.

CALIFORNIA.—Valleys and foothills in coast mountains, particularly away from coast, northward and westward to Ukiah (on Russian River), Mendocino County; northward, in great central valley of State, to foothills of southern Shasta National Forest; thence southward on lower foothills, usually at somewhat higher elevations than *Quercus douglasii*, but not in chaparral belt to any extent. In chaparral and lower canyons of Stony Creek National Forest on west side of ranges, especially on Eel River. *Sierra Nevada:* Common in foothills of Lassen Peak and Plumas National forests, at 2,000 to 2,800 feet. In Stanislaus National Forest, up to 2,000 feet elevation; confined to west border, in ravines, gulches, and canyons, and is most abundant in region of Bear Mountains, Gopher Ridge, and Bald Mountain; grows sparingly in creek canyons from Garden Valley southward to canyon of South Fork of American River, near Coloma and Lotus; also on Hangtown and Webber creeks (west of Placerville), but ceasing about 1 mile east of latter place; in Pleasant Valley southward, and in canyons from Indian Diggins westward to Coyoteville and Oleta. Common in southern Sierras on foothills and southward to Fort Tejon, in Tehachapi Mountains. In coast mountains abundant around San Francisco Bay and southward. Frequent in Santa Lucia Mountains of Monterey National Forest, in Sur, Carmelo, Arroyo Seco, San Antonio, and Nacimiento river basins, at 1,250 to 5,000 feet elevations, but shrubby above 2,700. In chaparral between 1,500 and 3,000 feet, in San Luis Obispo National Forest (T. 29 S., R. 16 E.). Generally distributed in Santa Barbara National Forest, at 1,750 to 6,200 feet, being especially common along north border on northern slopes of Cuyama River. Not in Santa Monica Mountains, but abundant on coast side of Sierra Madre Range on Mount Lowe, Mount Wilson, both slopes of Sierra Liebre Range northward to Gormans Station; in chaparral on summits of Santa Ana Range, at 1,600 feet. San Bernardino and San Jacinto mountains, here occurring in Spencer Valley at head of San Diego River, and elsewhere. Cuyamaca Mountains, near Jamacha, and at Mexican boundary, only on Hanson Laguna range. On Santa Rosa and Santa Cruz Islands.

LOWER CALIFORNIA.—North end of Mount San Pedro Martir.

OCCURRENCE.

On foothill slopes and their open valleys, in dry river bottoms and washes, and desert mountain canyons, in moderately rich, dry, loamy soils, or in poor, dry, gravelly, or rocky soils. Largest in sheltered sites, with somewhat fresh, good soil; stunted and shrubby on hot, gravelly slopes or stream bottoms.

In small, pure groups or patches, but more often mixed with scrub oak and chaparral; less frequently with blue oak and California live oak.

CLIMATIC CONDITIONS.—Similar to those of California live oak, as is also its reproduction.

TOLERANCE.—Very tolerant of shade.

Price Oak.

Quercus pricei [a] Sudworth.

DISTINGUISHING CHARACTERISTICS.

Very little is known of the Price oak, and that only from a hurried examination of a few trees found by the writer in October, 1904, on the banks of a

---

[a] Named in honor of Mr. Overton Westfeldt Price, Associate Forester, Forest Service; Forestry and Irrigation, vol. 13, p. 157.

small stream in Monterey County, Cal., on a property known as " Dani's Ranch."
The trees were closely mingled with *Quercus agrifolia*, for which they were
mistaken at a distance.   In general form they resemble that tree, especially
the small branched trees of the latter grown in close stands.   They were from
25 to 30 feet high and from 8 to 12 inches in diameter.   At the base of the trunk

FIG. 143.—*Quercus pricei.*

the bark is blackish, very hard, and roughly and irregularly broken; 3 or 4
feet higher up it is dark ashy-gray and smooth.   Mature leaves (fig. 143),
which probably remain on the trees two summers, are flat, smooth throughout,
and a deep shiny yellow-green on their upper surfaces and paler yellow-green
beneath.   The flowers are not known.   The acorns mature in the autumn of

the second year, for in addition to ripe acorns, immature ones were found on the season's smooth, reddish-brown twigs. Mature acorns (fig. 143), regarded as the most distinctive character, were invariably of the same form on all of the trees seen. The sharply pointed nut is smooth, somewhat lustrous, and a dull light brown, while the uniformly very shallow cups—on short stems—have very close, smooth, pale brown scales.

Wood, not examined, but judged to be essentially like that of *Quercus wislizeni*. Nothing is now known of the age attained.

The affinities of this oak place it between *Quercus agrifolia* and *Q. wislizeni*, and nearer to the latter. The writer has not seen the bushy trees Prof. C. S. Sargent has described and figured (Silva, VIII, Pl. CCCCVI, f. 6), occurring in Snow Creek Canyon at the base of Mount San Jacinto, which, as nearly as can be judged from the note and figure, is *Quercus pricei*. Professor Sargent considers this shallow-cupped oak (not seen elsewhere) a form of *Quercus wislizeni*. The trees found at Dani's Ranch gave every promise of later becoming very much larger.

OCCURRENCE.

Dry, gravelly banks of streams, within reach of deep soil moisture.
Forms small, pure groups.
CLIMATIC CONDITIONS.—Similar to Wislizenus oak.
TOLERANCE.—Very tolerant of shade.
REPRODUCTION.—At least an abundant periodic seeder, but fruiting habits and reproduction undetermined.

Morehus Oak.

Quercus morehus Kellogg.

DISTINGUISHING CHARACTERISTICS.

Morehus oak is a rare and little known California tree of the black oak group. It was first found about 1863, and since then many new stations for it have been and are still being discovered. It is held by some authors to be a hybrid from *Quercus wislizeni* and *Q. californica*. Its acorns bear a strong resemblance to those of the first oak, while its leaves (fig. 144) are similar in texture to those of the latter oak. The remarkably uniform shape (within reasonable limits) of the leaves borne by widely separated individuals, and the fact that the parents suggested are by no means always within the same locality—one or the other, sometimes both, often very far distant from the supposed offspring—has led the writer to treat this oak as a species. Generally from 10 to 35 feet high and 3 to 8 inches in diameter, with smooth, dark ashy-gray bark. The branches of small, shrubby trees often trend upward, while those of the larger trees stand out horizontally from the trunk, which is free of limbs for about one-third of its length. The leaves, which are shed from midwinter to spring, are dark yellow-green and smooth on the upper sides and light yellow-green and smooth or more or less covered with fine star-shaped hairs beneath. The acorns, maturing in the autumn of the second year, are usually from $1\frac{1}{4}$ to $1\frac{1}{2}$ inches long. The light reddish-brown cups inclose from about one-third to two-thirds of the nut, which is somewhat thicker than that of *Q. wislizeni*. Wood similar in general appearance to that of *Q. californica*, but the thicker, whitish sapwood is considerably tougher; not fully investigated. Of no economic importance and of slight interest to the forester, because of the tree's rare occurrence.

LONGEVITY.—Not fully determined. Believed to be rather long-lived. A single tree, $12\frac{1}{2}$ inches in diameter, showed an age of 64 years.

CALIFORNIA.—Occurs as scattered individuals and detached thickets in northern coast ranges and Sierra foothills. *Coast ranges:* A single tree at Clear Lake, and several at Sulphur Bank (Lake County) ; group at north base of Mount Tamalpais (Marin County) ; thicket on crest of Coast Range back of Berkeley, and a single tree farther north in Berkeley Hills near upper San Pablo Creek; canyon of Big Sulphur Creek between Geysers and Cloverdale (Sonoma County) at point about 3 miles below bridge ; also at point 2 miles south of Ridgewood Summit (north of Ukiah, Mendocino County). Reported in Santa Lucia Mountains in Sur, Carmelo, and Arroyo Seco river basins. *Sierra foothills:* In a belt north of Yuba River (Yuba County), running northwest from

FIG. 144.—*Quercus morehus.*

Red Bluff and lower part of Dry Creek into Butte County ; west foot of Stanfield Hill grade (about 21 miles northeast of Marysville) ; near Newcastle (Placer County) ; Eldorado County, on a head branch of Canyon Creek (tributary Middle Fork American River) 2 miles northeast of Georgetown ; North Fork of Cosumnes River (near Nashville), Middle Fork of Cosumnes (between Pleasant Valley and Oleta) ridge between North and Middle Forks Cosumnes (about 6 miles east of Nashville, elevation about 2,000 feet) ; Sacramento County ; near Folsom ; Amador County, near Plymouth, on head of Indian Creek (branch Cosumnes River), near Oleta (Sutter Creek road), and at several points on Rancheria Creek—lowest station about 3 miles from Sutter Creek, 3 miles north of Ione on low hill near Clay pit (leaves much toothed), with blue oaks, Mokelumne River west of West Point; Calaveras County, several thickets in Bear Creek Canyon (branch Calaveras River on west side of Bear Mountains), on head of Murray Creek (tributary Calaveras River) 2 miles north of Mountain Ranch, on San Domingo Creek (branch South Fork of Calaveras River) 2 to 3 miles north of Murphy, road between Mountain ranch and Railroad Flat (elevation 2,450 feet) at two points on South Fork of Mokelumne River between Railroad Flat and West Point; Tuolumne County, between Sonora and Tuolumne River, at two points (little north of Tuolumne Canyon) on road from Carters to Big Oak Flat, near head of Deer Creek—south side of Tuolumne on same road. At several places in gulch few miles north of Coulterville (Mariposa County) on road between Coulterville and Priest, with Kellogg oak and highland live oak; frequent from Cold Springs Station (Mariposa County) to Fresno Flats and North Fork (Madera County), especially in Crane Valley. Abundant also near Badger (Tulare County); very abundant on road from Raymond to Yosemite, especially within 6 or 7 miles of Raymond and eastward in edge of western yellow pine belt beyond Wassama; 2 miles west of latter is large tree at Potts's house, also one few rods north of Ahwahnee road house, and many others in vicinity among Kellogg oaks. At point 2 miles west of Eshom Valley, near east end of Burrough Valley (Fresno County). Range still imperfectly known.

OCCURRENCE.

Foothill slopes and ridges, in dry gravelly soils.

In groups and patches of pure growth interspersed with California black oak, Wislizer.us oak, Fremontia, and occasional blue and valley oaks. Nowhere abundant.

CLIMATIC CONDITIONS.—Similar to those of gray pine.

TOLERANCE.—Evidently very tolerant, its evergreen leaves being retained in dense shade.

REPRODUCTION.—Imperfectly known. Appears to seed at irregular intervals at rather early age, and but sparingly. Owing to the tree's supposed hybrid origin, the fertility of acorns requires testing.

California Black Oak.

Quercus californica (Torr.) Cooper.

DISTINGUISHING CHARACTERISTICS.

California black oak is very distinct in appearance from all other Pacific oaks. It more nearly resembles the eastern black oak (*Quercus velutina*) than it does any other species. Commonly from 50 to 75 feet high and from 15 to 30 inches in diameter, but at high elevations it is shrubby and often under 15 feet in height. Old trees are sometimes 80 or 85 feet high and from 36 to 40 inches through; such trees, as shown by their decayed, hollow trunks, often broken at the top, have long since passed maturity. The trunks are rarely straight and are often bent or leaning. They are clear of branches for from 10 to 20 feet, and then give off large limbs which form irregularly open, broad, rounded crowns. Except on young trees and large limbs (where it is smooth and dull grayish brown), the bark is blackish brown, sometimes with a reddish tint or, superficially, a weathered gray brown; it is very hard and is roughly and rather deeply furrowed on the low part of the trunk, while higher up the shallower seams fade into the smooth bark of large limbs. Year-old twigs are clear red to red-brown and usually smooth, but often minutely hairy or with a whitish tint; the prominent, scaly, light chestnut-colored buds are hairy, especially on their ends. Mature leaves (figs. 145 to 147), variable in form and size (about 4 to 6½ inches long), are thickish, a shiny deep yellow-green, and smooth on their upper sides (sometimes with star-shaped hairs); paler green beneath, smooth or minutely hairy. Small trees at high altitudes (and elsewhere also) very frequently have leaves and stems (fig. 147) conspicuously coated with minute, whitish, star-shaped hairs. Leaves are shed in autumn. Acorns (fig. 145), mature at the end of the second season, are borne on thick, short stems and are about 1¼ to 1½ inches long. The nut is pale chestnut colored, downy near and at the top end, and often indistinctly striped; the tawny brown cup has shiny scales which are thin, but often much thickened at the bases of the cup.

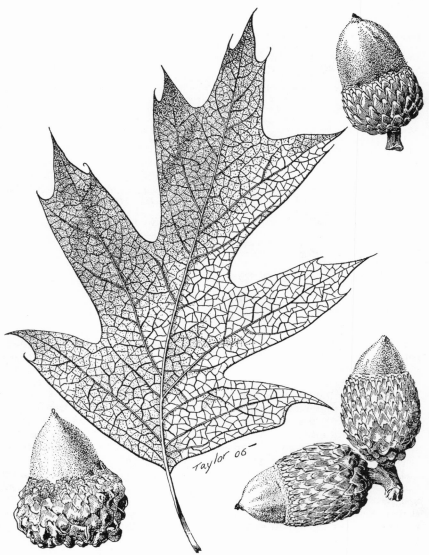

FIG. 145.—*Quercus californica.*

Wood, fine-grained, very porous, pale but distinct red, exceedingly brittle, firm, rather heavy, with large pith-rays, and having a strong odor of tannin, with which both the wood and bark are heavily charged. Large trunks are rarely sound and afford but little clear timber, and even this is inferior on account of its very porous, brittle structure. In some sections of its range the tree is important and much used for fuel. Its rather frequent occurrence in continuous patches renders it worthy of attention for this purpose.

LONGEVITY.—Age limits are not fully known. Probably moderately long-lived. Trees from 16 to 25 inches in diameter are from 176 to 275 years old. It is doubtful if this oak attains a greater age than 350 years, and it probably reaches maturity in about 175 years.

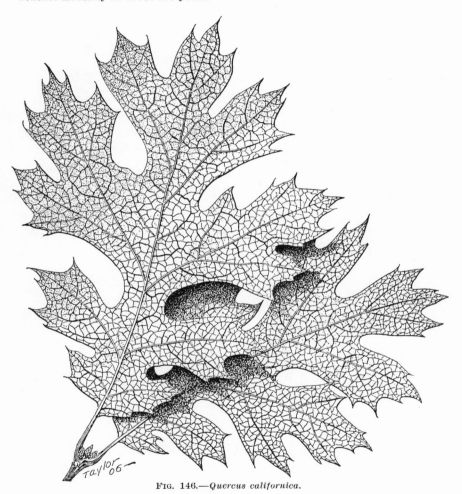

FIG. 146.—*Quercus californica.*

RANGE.

Central Oregon, in mountains, southward through California, in coast ranges and west slope of Sierras, nearly to Mexican boundary. On mountain slopes, low summits, elevated valleys and canyons, but not on plains nor near sea ; in north, usually at 1,500 to 3,000 feet elevation, and in south, at 4,000 to 7,000 feet.

OREGON.—Very abundant in valleys of central and southern part, west of Cascades, from McKenzie River (lat. 44° 15′) southward ; on mountain slopes considerably above 2,000 feet, entering lower part of yellow pine belt, and being especially frequent on streams in semiarid sections of lower Cascade and Siskiyou slopes.   Locally noted on upper Rogue River, in depressions between western spurs of southern Cascades and northern spurs of Siskiyous, and also on North Fork of Applegate Creek in Siskiyous.

CALIFORNIA.—Throughout northern part in lower part of yellow pine belt and upper range of Sabine pine; generally at 2,000 to 5,000 feet, probably going westward to inland border of coast redwood belt, and eastward at least to longitude of Mount Shasta,

FIG. 147.—*Quercus californica.*

around base of which it occurs (in Shasta National Forest) up to 4,500 feet on south and west sides; rather common in McCloud River valley, but more so about Sisson, being especially abundant northward to south end of Shasta Valley; frequent areas at elevations between 2,000 and 3,500 feet on Squaw Creek, while large pure stands occur on lower McCloud, Pitt, and Sacramento rivers.   Abundant on west slope of northern Sierras in canyons within yellow pine belt, at 3,000 to 5,000 feet elevation, but in Stanislaus National Forest ranging between 1,500 and 6,500 feet. Locally noted in Yosemite Valley, at 4,000 feet, in pure growth west of Camptonville, in Yuba County, and vicinity of Lake Tahoe. In southern Sierras, generally at 4,500 to 7,000 feet, where it occurs as follows: North Fork of Kings River; Bubbs Creek (head tributary South Fork Kings) up to Bubbs Dome; Frazier Mountain; East Fork of Kaweah River, at 4,900 to 7,200 feet, from Bigtree Canyon to point about 4 miles below Mineral King; White River (Tulare County); on crests and west slopes of Greenhorn Mountains (in T. 20 S., R. 30 and 31 E.), at 5,900 and 4,750 feet, and on Little Posey Creek, at 4,700 feet, in depression between east and west ridges of these mountains (Kern County). On east slope of Sierras, at Independence. Very abundant on southern terminal ranges of Sierras, as on Mount Breckenridge, above 4,000 feet, and probably also on Piute Mountain. Not reported from Tehachapi Mountains. In northern coast ranges, common in Trinity National Forest eastward to between Lewiston and Weaverville (west border of Sacramento Valley); locally noted on Grouse Creek Canyon near South Fork Mountain, at 2,300 and 2,500 feet. Southward in Stony Creek National Forest, very abundant in yellow pine belt at 3,000 to 6,000 feet, particularly in western part of forest on headwaters of Eel River. In vicinity of Bay, only on higher summits, such as south slope of Mount St. Helena, north base of Mount Tamalpais, upper San Pablo Creek, and east side of westmost coast range of Santa Clara Valley; not on Berkeley nor Oakland hills. Plentiful in southern coast ranges, especially in Santa Lucia Mountains of central and northern parts of Monterey National Forest, where, on both sides of range, it occurs at 2,000 to 5,000 feet elevation in Sur, Carmelo, and Arroyo Seco river basins. Not common in Santa Barbara National Forest, but widely distributed at 3,500 to 6,200 feet in watersheds of Santa Maria, Matilija, Piru-Sespe, and Elizabeth rivers, being abundant on Pine Mountain and in pure stands on summit of Liebre Mountain. Range in San Gabriel Mountains not fully recorded, but probably not there to any extent. Common in pine belt of San Bernardino Mountains; here locally noted near head of Waterman Canyon at 3,000 feet—a low altitude; on City Creek road off Plunge Creek, at 4,400 feet, and in Little Bear Valley, at 5,000 feet. Very common in pine belt of San Jacinto Mountains on west and south sides, at 5,000 to 9,000 feet; also in Strawberry Valley, at 5,200 feet; rare in Tahquitz Valley, and not detected on north side of mountains. Southward, the most prominent oak in Palomar Mountains, forming nearly half of the mixed stand on upper slopes, but in Cuyamaca Mountains less abundant than *Quercus agrifolia;* locally noted in this region on south side of Smiths Mountain at 4,100 feet, and at Campbells ranch (Laguna Mountains), at 5,496 feet. Reported from Hanson Laguna Mountains of northern Lower California at elevations above 4,000 feet.

OCCURRENCE.

On mountain slopes, benches, valleys, in canyon bottoms and lower sides, and on upper foothill slopes; in dry gravelly and sandy soils, or in very rocky places with scanty soil.

Forms pure, open groves and limited stands, or mingles (at lower levels) with gray pine, Douglas fir (Oregon), California laurel, western dogwood, canyon live oak, and straggling western yellow pine. Higher up, commonly with latter pine, incense cedar, and occasionally with bigtree. Largest in yellow-pine belt on sheltered benches, valleys, and coves, and smallest on exposed high slopes.

CLIMATIC CONDITIONS.—Not fully determined, but mainly like those of western yellow pine.

TOLERANCE.—Endures moderate shade in early life, but requires full overhead light for good growth later. In mixture with yellow pine, subordinate.

REPRODUCTION.—Abundant periodic seeder at 2 to 3 year intervals, but locally some seed is borne nearly every year. Germination scanty; best in slight shade on exposed mineral or humus.

Tanbark Oak.

Quercus [a] *densiflora* Hooker and Arnott.

DISTINGUISHING CHARACTERISTICS.

Tanbark oak is widely known in its range by this name on account of the extensive use of its bark for tanning on the Pacific Coast, where it is as important in the leather industry as chestnut oak (*Quercus prinus*) is in the East.

---

[a]Although never known to lay people as anything but an oak, for which the technical name *Quercus* stands, this tree has characters in its reproductive organs which technically permit its separation from all other oaks of the genus *Quercus* into another

A smooth-trunked tree from 50 to 75 feet high and from 1 to 2 feet in diameter; trees from 80 to 85 feet, or somewhat taller, and from 3 to 4 feet in

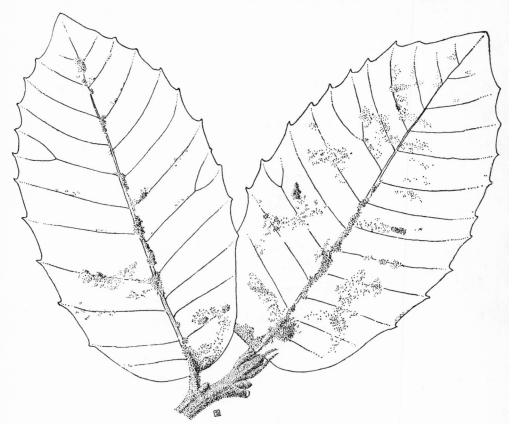

Fig. 148.—*Quercus densiflora.*

diameter sometimes occur. Though much larger trees were probably once common, they are now rare. At high elevations it is a shrub under 10 feet in

genus. It is a connecting link between the oaks and chestnuts. These minor differences are these: Its male and female flowers are borne on new shoots of the year, rarely from buds at the base of leaves of the previous year's growth; the cylindrical male clusters are thick and erect, instead of being thread-like, pendulous, and developed from buds on year-old twigs, as in other oaks; the female flowers are usually borne at the base of the uppermost male flower clusters; the male flowers are arranged 3 in a minute cluster, many of these covering the erect flowering stems, instead of being solitary as in other oaks. (The female flowers are, however, solitary, as in other oaks.) Upon these valid botanical characters Oersted proposed, in 1866, that this tree be called *Pasania densiflora.* Since then, however, it has been maintained under the name *Q. densiflora,* given to it by Hooker and Arnott in 1841. One eminent American tree botanist has recently taken up Oersted's name. But granting the technical grounds are good for such a change, it is preferable, in the writer's opinion, to still maintain this tree as a member of the genus Quercus by slightly enlarging the definition of the genus. In all other outward gross characters—foliage, fruit, wood, and habit—this tree is and always will be an oak to the lumberman and to the practical forester. Precedents for continuing to regard the tree as an oak are not wanting. Thus, box-elder (Negundo), though equally distinct from the true maples, is retained in the genus Acer.

height, with slender upright branches. The form varies greatly; in close stands, the crown is narrow, with upright branches and a long clear trunk, rarely straight; in the open, the crown is broad, with big, horizontal limbs, and the trunk is short and thick. The trunks are smooth looking, pale brown tinged with red, often with grayish areas; their thick, firm bark has deep, narrow seams cutting it into very wide, squarish plates; the bark of young trees and of large limbs is smooth and unbroken. Young twigs are densely woolly (with star-shaped hairs), but the wool disappears after the first year, when the branchlets are deep brown, tinged with red, and are often covered with a whitish

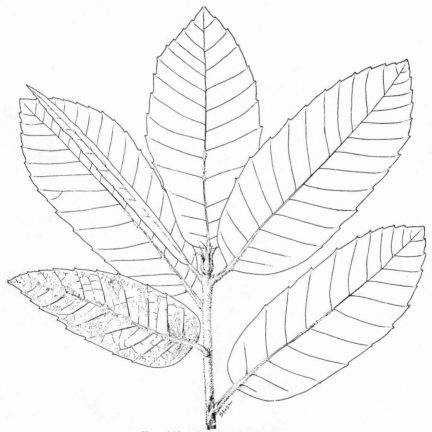

FIG. 149.—*Quercus densiflora.*

bloom. Full grown leaves (figs. 148 to 150) are light green, smooth, and shiny (occasionally with woolly areas) on their top sides, and densely woolly with reddish brown hairs beneath; in late summer the leaves become thick and leathery and the woolliness disappears except for a few hairs on the lower surface, which is then whitish with a very pale blue tint. Leaves of a season's growth persist for 3 to 4 seasons. Acorns (fig. 150) mature in the fall of the second year, when they are dull, very pale yellowish brown, usually smooth and shiny, but frequently more or less downy, while the finely hairy, bristly scales of the cup (sometimes very woolly at its base) are pale yellow brown.

The shrubby form of this oak occurring on high mountains has been described as a distinct variety, *Quercus densiflora echinoides* (R. Br. Campst.) Sargent, but it is believed not to be worthy of separation, because it is connected with the larger tree forms by numerous intermediate ones. Its leaves are from 1⅓ to 2¼ inches long, smooth on their upper surfaces and white-hairy beneath, and the margins are entire or with very indistinct teeth. Acorns are

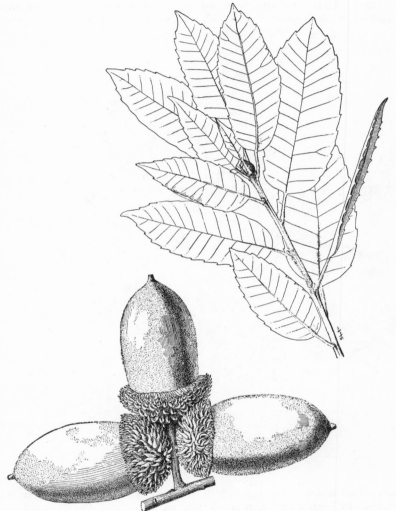

FIG. 150.—*Quercus densiflora.*

somewhat smaller than those of the tree forms and the scales of the cups are also longer. These differences seem to be due to high altitude and exposure. Wood dense and fine-grained, very hard, firm, and somewhat brittle (though brittleness varies with age), light brown, faintly tinged with red. The quality is suitable for agricultural implements and for finishing and furniture lumber. It is employed more generally for firewood.

Economically a tree of the greatest importance in Pacific forests, both for its valuable tanbark and for the promise it gives of furnishing good commercial timber in a region particularly lacking in hardwoods. The present extensive practice of destroying this oak for its bark alone, without utilizing the wood, calls for prompt conservative action.

LONGEVITY.—Full records of age limits are lacking. Forest-grown trees from 14 to 18 inches in diameter are from 80 to 128 years old; trees from 20 to 60 inches in diameter are from 150 to 250 years old. It doubtless attains a greater age.

RANGE.

Southwestern Oregon to Southern California. From coast ranges of southwestern Oregon, northern Sierras of California, and coast ranges southward to Santa Ynez Mountains (Santa Barbara County); generally at from sea level to 4,000 and 5,000 feet elevation.

OREGON.—From Umpqua River southward, probably only in coast mountains; common on streams from sea through Douglas fir forest. Locally noted at Gold Beach (mouth of Rogue River).

CALIFORNIA.—Northern coast mountains; on ridges and streams from near sea inland to Trinity Mountains, here growing under Douglas fir at elevations up to 3,000 feet or over; on South Fork Mountain, up to about 5,000 feet, and eastward to a canyon near Lewiston, where a single tree has been seen; also one in canyon (at 3,700 to 3,800 feet) between French Gulch and Deadwood. Not on Upper South Fork of Trinity River and not detected in eastern Siskiyou County nor in region between Scott Valley and Salmon River, but west of latter it occurs on east slope of "Salmon Summit" ridge at 2,000 to 3,800 feet. Locally noted near Dyerville (Humboldt County); also in a broad belt on west slope of Trinity Mountain above Hoopa Valley between 2,100 and 4,000 feet; and on lower slopes bordering Hoopa Valley and from Hoopa Valley westward to between Redwood Creek and Blue Lake; north of Humboldt Bay, in redwoods in lower Mad River valley, but not in upper part of this valley; lower Van Dusen River eastward to a point about 2 miles below Valley View Tavern, and westward, abundantly in redwoods, to Bridgeville and Hydesville; near Ferndale and in hills south of it, also about Briceland, upper Mattole, and in Mattole gulch (South of King Mountain). *Mendocino County:* Enters this county from north and is common throughout most of redwood forest; noted at Rockport and frequently between Briceland (Humboldt County) and Kenny; south of Kenny, frequent on coast in and on borders of redwoods, also among California swamp pine between Fort Bragg and Gualala; near mouth of Big River and about the Mendocino pine barrens; road between Westport and Laytonville and in canyon east of Laytonville (road to Round Valley); abundant in redwoods from pine barrens eastward cn road from Mendocino to Ukiah, also on cool north slope (south side) at head of Big River canyon; north of Ukiah, at Willits and in forest north and northwest of Willits; upper part of Redwood Canyon (northeast of Calpella). *Sonoma County:* Common throughout redwoods and considerably east of their eastern border; hill at Sea View (east of Fort Ross) and on Austin Creek, thence southward to Russian River, on which it is common from Duncan Mills to east edge of redwoods at Forestville; very abundant south of Russian River from Monte Rio to Camp Meeker and southern edge of redwoods near Freestone, thence eastward to Green Valley, where it goes to within about 3 miles of Sebastopol. Inland only to Napa Mountains, here occurring on streams, in north part of Napa County from Mount St. Helena southward; common in gulches of hills west of Calistoga, not far from which it descends to mouth of small canyon; mountains on east side of Napa Valley. Common in southwest Lake County on east side of Cobb Mountain Ridge, and also of Mount St. Helena (1,500 on St. Helena Creek to over 3,000 feet); near Adams Springs it predominates with Douglas fir. *Marin County:* Inverness Ridge (Point Reyes Peninsula) from point 5 or 6 miles south of Tomales Point southward to Olema; east of Tomales Bay, on Paper Mill and Lagunitas creeks and in San Geronimo Valley, thence southward to Mount Tamalpais—here a tree in gulches and canyons, and shrub in chaparral of upper slopes; very large near Rock Springs at west end of Tamalpais Ridge; south side of Tamalpais in Redwood Canyon and at Mill Valley. Frequent south of San Francisco Bay on seaward coast range and on Santa Cruz Mountains; west of King Pass on road from Palo Alto to sea; common from Boulder Creek to Big Basin. Northern and Central Sierras southward to Mariposa County in lower yellow pine growth and upper foothill forest; in Lassen Peak and Plumas National Forests, at 2,000 to 3,000 feet. Butte County, near Junction House (road from Bidwell Bar to Quincy), probably coming from Little North Fork of Feather River, and to point a few miles below Berry Creek (about 1,900 feet). *Yuba County:* East slopes of Oregon Hills and lower part of North Fork Yuba River Canyon from Ruths Ranch Pass to Bullards Bar, thence eastward up Willow Creek to Camptonville and beyond to at least 4,000 feet elevation (with western yellow pine). *Sierra County:* Entered from west (on road Camptonville to Mountain House), and probably also on canyons of North and Middle Forks Yuba River. *Placer County:* About 4 miles northeast of Forest Hill (road to Sugar Pine Mill), *Q. densiflora echinoides* occurs in considerable numbers. Stanislaus National Forest, locally abundant only between 3,000 and 5,000 feet, on west slope of Tunnel Hill, on headwaters of Alton Creek, Pilot Creek, near Deep and Mutton canyons, and on Big Iowa Canyon (tributary South Fork American River). Infrequent near southern limit in southern coast ranges, except in Santa Lucia Mountains of Monterey National Forest, here extending from sea level to 5,000 feet in watersheds of Sur, Carmelo, Arroyo Seco, San Antonio, and Nacimiento rivers; most important tree on streams flowing into the ocean, as it is also, but smaller in growth, of higher elevations. Not about Monterey, nor on Monterey Peninsula; few trees noted in Arroyo Seco River canyon west of Santa Lucia Peak, and in upper part of Arroyo Seco Valley above junction of Willow Creek; commoner in gulches and canyons of coast slope in Sur River region, and in isolated patches and groves of redwoods south of Carmel Bay. *San Benito County:* Canyon (few hundred feet below summit) on north side of Fremont Peak. San Luis Obispo National Forest, in basins of San Luis and Arroyo Grande rivers; locally noted near Cuesta Pass at 1,500 to 2,000 feet. Santa Barbara National Forest, on watersheds of Santa Ynez, Santa Barbara, and Matilija rivers; Mount Piños at 9,500 feet; summits of Santa Ynez Mountains, at 2,400 to 4,700 feet; in T. 5 N., R. 21 W., some distance northeast of Nordhoff; also at head of Howard Creek, and of Horn Canyon (near Nordhoff), which is probably its southern limit in the coast mountains.

The variety *Q. densiflora echinoides* ranges from Canyon Creek (Siskiyou Mountains) over northern California and southward in Sierras and coast ranges to Sonoma County; in Stanislaus National Forest, noted on north slope of Rubicon River, at 4,000 to 4,500 feet elevation.

OCCURRENCE.

Valleys and low slopes, borders of low mountain and foothill streams, coves, and ravines; in rich, moist, sandy, and gravelly soils. Sometimes in nearly pure, small stands, but chiefly in mixture with redwood and Douglas fir; occasionally with California live oak. Largest in coast region.

CLIMATIC CONDITIONS.—Similar to those of redwood.

TOLERANCE.—Imperfectly known. Endures considerable shade throughout life, but grows best with top light; dense side shade clears its tall trunks completely. Gives evidence sometimes of great tolerance.

REPRODUCTION.—Prolific seeder and seedlings often abundant in partial shade. Sprouts vigorously from cut stumps, producing permanent stems.

Family ULMACEÆ.

The elm family is composed mainly of trees, with a few shrubs. It includes the well-known elms and hackberries. Most of these have rather small leaves, borne singly—never in pairs, one opposite another—and shed them each autumn. Their flowers combine both male and female reproductive organs, though distinct male or female flowers sometimes occur with the bisexual ones, on the same tree or branch. Fruits are matured in one year, and are (1) small, flat bodies with thin, papery wings (surrounding the seed body), which render them very buoyant (elm); (2) small nut-like wingless bodies (planer-tree); (3) small, berry-like bodies with thin, sweetish flesh surrounding hard, bony seeds, which are eaten (without injuring the seed) by birds and mammals and so distributed away from the parent trees (hackberries). The berry-like fruits ripen in autumn, but the winged fruits, with few exceptions, ripen in spring or early summer. The latter usually germinate that season, while the former do not grow until the following season.

The wood of these trees is characteristically marked with wavy or zig-zag lines of minute pores, seen on cross-sections of the trunk. No other trees have this character, which is particularly marked in the wood of the elms and hackberries, the principal members of this family.

Several members of the family are large forest trees of the first economic importance, often forming the bulk of extensive forests, while others are scattered through forests of other trees or in the open. Their habitat includes wet, swampy, moist, rich soils as well as the driest and most arid ones, but all grow at low elevations.

A single group only of this family, the hackberries, is represented in the Pacific region, where its representatives are rare. Other North American trees of this family belong to eastern United States.

CELTIS. HACKBERRIES.

A small group of large or medium-sized trees and shrubs, represented in the Pacific region by two species. The rough bark is characteristically marked by projecting, knife-like ridges, and the light-colored wood is distinguished by the zig-zag lines of fine pores which mark each layer. Peculiarities of the leaves are their unequal sides, their conspicuously 3-nerved or veined bases, and their arrangement on the twigs so as to form flat sprays, which makes them appear to grow alternately from two opposite sides of the branchlets.

The minute, inconspicuous flowers (comprising those of male sex, and those which combine male and female organs—perfect flowers) are produced in spring on new twigs of the year, male flowers at the base of the twig and the perfect ones singly, usually on thread-like stems springing from the bases of the leaves at the end of the branchlet. Perfect flowers develop into single cherry-like fruits, which have a thin, dry, sweetish flesh covering a very hard-shelled, smooth or roughish seed. The seeds are rather difficult to germinate, being apt to " lie over " for a season before they grow, unless planted or falling in a soil that is constantly moist.

Wood of the hackberries is commercially of only secondary importance at present; that of the two species occurring in the Pacific region is of no value there, but one of these trees produces useful timber in eastern forests.

Hackberries are of ancient origin. Remains of those from which European species descended have been discovered in the Miocene formation of that continent.

Hackberry.

Celtis occidentalis [a] Linnæus.

DISTINGUISHING CHARACTERISTICS.

Hackberry is rare, and only a small tree or low shrub, generally under 25 feet in height and 10 inches in diameter in the Pacific region. East of the Rocky Mountains, its principal range, it is a straight, slim tree from 80 to 90 feet high and from 2 to 3 feet through when grown in the forest; in the open it has a shorter and, often, thicker trunk, and a very broad, symmetrical, rounded crown of large limbs, which are intricately branched and sometimes drooping. The trunks and limbs are grayish in open situations, and apt to be brownish gray in shaded places, and are conspicuously marked with irregularly shaped projecting ridges of bark. Young twigs are pale green, but at the end of the season they are clear reddish brown, with minute, flat, pointed buds, peculiarly dark chestnut. What appears to be a terminal winter bud is the last side, or lateral, bud, at which the immature terminal part of the twig has broken off.

---

[a] A number of varieties, and even species, have been distinguished, based mainly upon the size, texture, and teeth of the leaves, as well as upon the color and size of the " berries." These forms, the validity of which is in doubt, occur mainly, if not entirely, east of the 100th meridian. They will be considered in Parts II and III of this work, which deal with trees east of the Pacific region.

The next year the twig is lengthened by the growth of this bud.   Mature leaves
(fig. 151), shed in autumn, are somewhat thickish, stiff, veiny, and very rough
to the touch on their top sides; lighter green beneath, with or without very

FIG. 151.—*Celtis occidentalis.*

minute hairs on the veins and stems.   They vary in length from about 2 to 5
inches.   The cherry-like, slender-stemmed fruits (fig. 151) are smooth, dull
purplish brown when ripe in autumn, three-eighths to about one-half an inch

in length, with a minute point at the top. A dry, sweet, very thin, yellowish pulp covers the hard, thick-shelled seed. The fruit of this tree is extensively eaten by birds, which thus assist greatly in disseminating the seeds, which are not injured by digestive action, but on the contrary are probably better prepared for germination. Flood waters also aid in distributing the seed. Extension of the species by direct seeding from the tree is slow. Wood, rather heavy, moderately soft, brittle, and very wide-grained; the whitish sapwood is exceedingly thick and the heartwood is a bright yellowish-white.[a] Of no economic use, owing to rarity of occurrence and poor timber form 'in the far West. In the East it produces good but not extensive quantities of excellent saw timber, which is made into second-class lumber.

LONGEVITY.—The age attained by the Pacific form is unknown. It grows rapidly in the East, attaining great age, but appearing to reach maturity in about 75 or 80 years. Eastern forest-grown trees from 18 to 24 inches in diameter are from 140 to 165 years old.

RANGE.

From St. Lawrence River (St. Helens Island, near Montreal) to southern Ontario; in the United States from Massachusetts (Massachusetts Bay) to northwestern Nebraska, North Dakota, southern Idaho (Boise), eastern Washington and Oregon (Snake River), western Washington (Puget Sound), Nevada (East Humboldt Mountains), New Mexico, and south to Florida (Biscayne Bay and Cape Romano), middle Tennessee, Missouri, eastern Kansas, Indian Territory, and eastern Texas.

OCCURRENCE.

Rocky bluffs and slopes near streams; in dry broken rock, or poor gravelly soil. Lack of moisture (not a requirement) produces stunted, scraggy trees. Cultivated in moist, rich soil, it is more like the typical eastern form. Scattered singly or in small groups; not common.

CLIMATIC CONDITIONS.—Similar to those of western yellow pine.

TOLERANCE.—Endures considerable shade throughout life.

REPRODUCTION.—Fairly abundant seeder, but reproduction scanty.

Palo Blanco.

Celtis reticulata Torrey.

DISTINGUISHING CHARACTERISTICS.

The palo blanco, known almost entirely by this Spanish name, is considered by some authors to be only a variety of the eastern smooth and shiny-leafed *Celtis mississippiensis* Bosc. As palo blanco occurs in the southwest and in the Colorado Desert part of California, it is a very different tree in habit from its eastern relative, particularly in its shorter, wider, and rough leaves (fig. 152).

It ranges in size from a low, densely branched shrub to a round-crowned, short-trunked tree from 15 to 30 feet high and from 6 to 10 inches or more in diameter; the bark is bluish, ashy gray, and is rough, with prominent, thin, short, projecting ridges. Mature leaves (fig. 152), thick and leathery, are very veiny, deep green on their upper sides; very rough (like sand-paper)—sometimes only slightly rough, however, and very light yellowish green beneath, with or without minute straight hairs, and with a conspicuous network of small veins; margins of the leaves mainly without teeth. Mature fruit (fig. 152), ripe in autumn, orange red. Wood, somewhat lighter than that of *Celtis mississippiensis* and of about the same weight as that of *C. occidentalis*, is not

---

[a] See characterization of wood under genus, which holds good for this species.

distinguishable from the wood of these two species. Poor timber form of the tree renders its wood of little economic use, except as a second-class fuel wood. Of little importance as a forest tree; useful for establishing protective cover along desert streams.

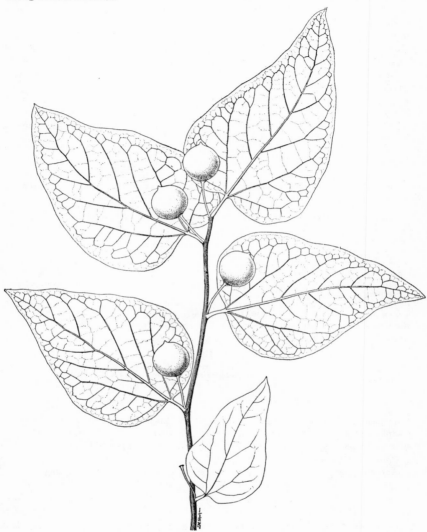

FIG. 152.—*Celtis reticulata.*

LONGEVITY.—Not fully determined. It grows very slowly, both in diameter and in height, in unsheltered, dry situations, where trees from 5 to 9 inches through are from 60 to 110 years old.

RANGE.

From eastern Texas (Dallas) to the Rio Grande and through New Mexico and Arizona to southern Utah, Nevada, California (western rim of Colorado Desert) ; Lower California (San Julio Canyon and Cerros Island).

OCCURRENCE.

Low mountain canyons, dry or intermittent water courses, desert gulches, and borders of rocky streams; in dry, gravelly soil. Scattered singly and in small groups or groves.

CLIMATIC CONDITIONS.—Similar to those of white alder.

TOLERANCE.—Undetermined, but trees show marked tolerance of shade.

REPRODUCTION.—Abundant seeder. Germination, except in constantly moist soil, tardy; seedlings rather sparse.

Family LAURACEÆ.

A small family (as represented in our forests) of trees characterized by the pungent, aromatic taste and odor of their bruised green bark and foliage. It includes the widely known camphor and bay trees of the Old World, our well-known eastern sassafras tree, and a group of "loblolly" bay trees of our southern forests, together with a single genus in the Pacific region. The foliage of some of these species is evergreen, whereas that of others is shed each autumn. The leaves of some are borne singly, those of others in pairs—one leaf opposite another. In some species the flowers combine both male and female organs, while in others male and female flowers are each borne on different trees. Fruits of our representatives are berry or plum like, with one hard-shelled seed. The wood of these trees, often hard and beautifully marked, is mainly of only minor commercial importance. Economically, the camphor trees are the most valuable of the group, all parts of the trees yielding camphor.

UMBELLULARIA. LAUREL.

Since this genus is represented by a single species only, inhabiting the Pacific forests, its characteristics are given under that species.

California Laurel; Oregon Myrtle.

Umbellularia californica (Hook. and Arn.) Nuttall.

DISTINGUISHING CHARACTERISTICS.

California laurel is an evergreen tree, distinguished at once from all others of its range by the strong camphoric-pungent odor [a] of its crushed leaves or green bark. Under the most favorable growth conditions, from 60 to 80 feet high and from $2\frac{1}{2}$ to $3\frac{1}{2}$ feet in diameter; exceptionally large trees are sometimes 4 feet through. In the dense forest it has a clean, straight trunk from 30 to 40 feet long and a narrow crown of close, small, upright branches. Elsewhere, however, and much more commonly, it has a very short, thick trunk, surmounted by large, long limbs which trend upward and form an exceedingly wide, dense, rounded crown. In moist shaded mountain canyons and gulches it appears in a many-stemmed shrubby form in clumps and thickets from 10 to 15 feet high. Bark of large trunks is thin, very dark reddish-brown, and scaly; the stems of young trees are smooth, and dull grayish-brown. New leaves are produced throughout the summer on the stems, which grow constantly in height. This results in the branches being heavily foliaged. As a rule, the leaves of

---

[a] The green bark and, particularly, the leaves possess a light volatile oil, follicles of which are given off when either is crushed, and which when inhaled through the nostrils produces severe pain over the eyes, attended often by violent sneezing. Continued inhalation of the odor of fresh leaves usually produces slight dizziness, but apparently no other alarming effects. The dried leaves produce the same effect, but less violently.

a season's growth persist on the branches for about two years, but frequently some of them are retained for five or six years.   When mature (fig. 153) they are shiny, smooth, deep yellow-green, about 3 to nearly 6 inches long and from

Fig. 153.—*Umbellularia californica: a,* fruit.

one-third inch to 1⅝ inches wide.   The yellowish-green fruit (fig. 153), re-sembling an olive, has a thin, leathery, fleshy covering which contains a large, thin-shelled seed.   The fruits mature in one season, are ripe during October, when they fall. They germinate shortly afterwards. They are frequently washed down mountain streams, and in this way a dense cover is extended along many narrow gulches, in which, in the otherwise dry foothills, grateful springs are thus maintained. Wood, very heavy when green, moderately heavy when dry, hard, very firm, fine-grained, and rich yellowish-brown, often beautifully mottled; [a] the sapwood is very thick. No other of our hardwoods excels it in beautiful grain when finished. It is a most valuable cabinet and finishing wood. Well known for this excellent quality in the rather limited region of commercial supply, where the tree deserves conservative treatment as a timber tree.

LONGEVITY.—Little is known of the age limits of this tree, which is unquestionably long-lived. Trees from 20 to 25 inches in diameter are from 160 to 210 years old; larger trees are known which should prove to be very much older.

RANGE.

Southwestern Oregon (South Fork of Umpqua River, Coos County) and southward in coast ranges and Sierras (from head of Sacramento Valley) to southern border of California. In north, at sea level to 1,500 feet; in south, 2,000 to 4,000 feet elevation.

OREGON.—Coast Range and Siskiyous.

CALIFORNIA.—Coast region. *Humboldt County:* Eastward to Redwood Creek; Redwood Creek to Blue Lake; not in lower Mad River Valley (north of Humboldt Bay); south of Humboldt Bay, from Hydesville to Bridgeville, and thence eastward to the Little Van Dusen. Nearest coast, between Ferndale and Bear Valley, and between Capetown and Petrolia; at Briceland, and in Mattole Valley. *Mendocino County:* Coast region from north part of county southward, in and about edges of redwood forest; noted near Kenny and southward to Westport, Fort Bragg, Mendocino, and Gualala; common in redwoods between Westport and Cahto; east of Laytonville and between Eel River and Round Valley, and east of this on Middle Fork Eel River; on west side of Mount Sanhedrin, between Hearst and Sawyer, and on Cave Creek and Redwood Hill; in Redwood Canyon; southward nearly to Ukiah on Russian River and northward over Ridgewood Summit to and beyond Willits; about Mendocino City, between Mendocino and Ukiah, and between head of Big River and Ukiah Valley; in valley 4 to 5 miles northeast of Ukiah, and at points on Russian River and Coal Creek. *Sonoma County:* Northeastern part on Big Sulphur or Pluton Creek Canyon slopes from Geysers to Sócrates Basin, and eastward over Cobb Mountain Divide into Lake County; also at point about 6 miles above Cloverdale in lower part of Big Sulphur Canyon; Russian River Valley north of Cloverdale; road from Hopland to Highland Springs on south side of canyon (which road follows eastward from Russian Valley); Russian River Canyon, 2 miles east of Healdsburg, and in canyon between Alexander and Knights valleys; lower Russian River from Forestville to Guerneville, Monte Rio, and Duncan Mills, and westward nearly to mouth of Russian River; southward as far as Camp Meeker and Occidental, and eastward to Green Valley (seen here nearly to Sebastopol). Southeastern part of county, on Sonoma Creek, between Sonoma and El Verano, and northward at Glen Ellen and northward to where Sonoma Valley opens on west in Santa Rosa Valley; westward into mountains separating Sonoma Valley from Petaluma Valley, and eastward in mountains between Sonoma and Napa valleys. *Napa County:* North part and southward to little below Oakville; near Calistoga on floor of valley and in gulches; at north end of Napa Valley up south slopes of Mount St. Helena. *Marin County:* Mount Tamalpais (tree in canyons and moist basins, and shrub in dense chaparral of upper slopes), especially about Rock Spring (west end of main ridge), in Cataract Canyon (north side), and in Redwood Canyon (south side); Mill Valley and Sausalito; Tomales Bay (east and west shores), and in gulch east of Marshall; on west side of Tomales Bay on east and west slopes of Inverness Ridge; in redwoods on Paper Mill Creek, at Lagunitas and San Geronimo Valley, on hills west of San Rafael, and north of San Rafael on steep canyon slopes near Corte Madera Creek. *Yolo County:* Cache Creek, Capay Valley. *Solano County:* Jameson Canyon (in hills between south end of Napa Valley and Suisun), from Green Valley westward. *Sutter County:* Gulches on north side of Marysville Buttes, and

---

[a] Green and unseasoned logs sink in water, in which lumbermen place them to produce (by soaking) the beautiful "black myrtle" lumber (Gorman).

north slope of North Butte. *Colusa County:* East slope of Snow Mountain above Fout Springs, and along Stony River to Stony Ford; Cook Springs, Bear Valley, and hills between Bear Creek and Cortena Creek. *Lake County:* Blue Lakes to Saratoga Springs and valley about Upper Lake (town) ; east shore of Clear Lake (between Upper Lake and Bartlett Landing), and up on hills into lower edge of pine forest; east side of Bartlett Mountain on spur reaching to edge Bartlett Creek Valley; about Bartlett Springs; east end of Sulphur Bank arm of Clear Lake on shore facing Ellem Island; west side of Clear Lake from old mission near Kelseyville to Soda Bay, and on base slope of Mount Konokti from Soda Bay to Horseshoe Bay ; south of Mount Konokti on west shore of Lower Lake ; west of Clear Lake, near Highland Springs and westward on road to Hopland; 5 miles south of Kelseyville, and southward to near Middletown, and at point (2,000 feet) about 8 miles northwest of latter ; near Adams Springs ; Middletown westward over Cobb Mountain Divide ; on road from Middletown to within 7 miles of Lower Lake, and along St. Helena and Putah creeks from Middletown eastward; common on St. Helena Creek from edge of Middletown Valley southward and up Mount St. Helena (3,600 feet). *Santa Clara County:* Coyote Creek near Gilroy Hot Springs; highest parts of Mount Hamilton and adjacent ridges near Lick Observatory. *Alameda County:* Canyons of Mission Peak (near Mission San Jose). *Contra Costa County:* Upper part of Marsh Creek Canyon at east base of Mount Diablo, and Mitchell Canyon ; hills near Martinez, and westward on bay shore. *Santa Cruz County:* Abundant in most parts of Santa Cruz Mountains, including Boulder Creek Valley ; on railroad from Los Gatos to Fulton Grove of redwoods ; scarce in south part of Santa Cruz hills east of north end of Monterey Bay, and for several miles northwest of Watsonville does not occur at all. *Monterey County:* Probably absent (or rare) in Monterey-Pacific Grove region ; Santa Lucia Peak to within about 600 feet of summit ; Arroyo Seco Canyon and north of peak in Arroyo Seco Valley above junction of Willow Creek. *San Benito County:* West side gulch of San Juan Valley and at north base of Fremont Peak. *Los Angeles County:* Near Alpine Tavern (Mount Lowe) and canyons lower down. *Riverside County:* Canyons on west side of San Jacinto Mountain. Noted also near Mexican line near summits of (southern limit in) Coast Range. Noted as follows on lower west slope of Sierras : *Shasta County:* Canyon of Sacramento River (few miles above Redding) ; lower McCloud River (above and below Baird). *Tehama County:* About 10 miles east of Payne post-office. *Butte County:* Westward to a little above Bidwell Bar (1,200 feet) and eastward to near Berry Creek (1,700 feet). *Yuba County:* Southwest slopes of Oregon Hills, but not west of these nor east of North Yuba Canyon (east of Oregon hills). *Placer County:* North Fork American River Canyon, near Colfax ; Devils Canyon (between Colfax and Forest Hill) ; east of latter and east of Iowa Hill ; on railroad between Dutch Flat and Blue Canyon (at about 4,000 feet). *Amador County:* Deadmans Creek to Dry Creek (road between Oleta and Volcano) ; between Oleta and Sutter Creek, and above Defender Mine in Mokelumne River Canyon. *Calaveras County:* Between Mokelumne Hill and West Point. *Tuolumne County:* Chinese to Crockers, mostly from crossing of South Fork Tuolumne River eastward ; middle fork of latter to about 3,500 elevation ; road from Crockers to Hetch-Hetchy at point between Hog Ranch and Canyon Meadow ; Hetch-Hetchy Valley and south slope (800 feet) and north side (1,500 feet). *Mariposa County:* On hill above Bull Creek Gulch, between Coulterville and Bower Cave ; near creek directly nortwest of Mariposa, and south of Mariposa in Chowchilla Canyon (at about 2,500 feet) ; abundant on north side of ridge west of Wassama, between latter and Wawona, and between Wawona and Yosemite ; Yosemite Valley and Merced River to top of Nevada Fall and into Little Yosemite Valley. *Madera County:* Fresno Flat and above latter on China Creek ; gulch (2,600 feet) on road from O'Neal to North Fork ; at latter place and on North Fork San Joaquin River Canyon near Kitanna Creek. *Fresno County:* Gulches of Pine Ridge (north of Kings River), from Sycamore Creek eastward to beyond Rush Creek ; South Fork Kings River, near Converse Basin and between Mill Creek and Badger, thence to Eshom Valley. *Tulare County:* Badger to about 6 miles of Auckland ; occasional in gulches of Kaweah River Canyon between Redstone Park and Sequoia National Park ; lower canyon of East Fork Kaweah River from Three Rivers to Mineral King ; east half of Tule Indian Reservation (South Fork Tule River Basin) (southern limit in Sierras).

OCCURRENCE.

Borders and vicinity of higher foothill streams, spring-watered gulches, lower mountain slopes and canyons ; in moist gravelly, rocky, or rich humous soil ; constant, abundant soil moisture essential. Forms dense clumps and small patches (as a shrubby tree), or is scattered singly and in groups (as a larger tree) with broadleaf maple, California sycamore, red and white alders, madroña, and tan-bark and canyon live oaks. Largest in southwest Oregon and adjacent California ; smaller elsewhere, especially in Sierras.

CLIMATIC CONDITIONS.—Similar to those of red and white alders.

TOLERANCE.—Exceedingly tolerant of shade throughout life, but partial or full overhead light necessary for best height growth.

REPRODUCTION.—Fairly abundant seeder; locally often heavily laden with fruit. Seed of moderately high rate of germination and of very transient vitality; germinates shortly after falling to ground. Clumps of seedlings frequent in dense or partial shade, where they grow rapidly.

Family SAXIFRAGACEÆ.

A very large group of mainly herbaceous plants and a few trees and shrubs of world-wide distribution. They receive their name (which means, literally, stone breaking) because they mainly inhabit dry or wet rocky situations, and are particularly prone to alpine habitats. The flowers have both male and female organs in the same bloom; the leaves occur singly or in pairs (one opposite another); and the very minute seeds are borne in small, clustered capsules. The family is represented in the United States by the following single genus, the one species of which is a tree described as recently as 1877.

LYONOTHAMNUS.

Lyonothamnus is a genus containing the only tree species of the family indigenous to the United States or North America. It is confined to the California coast islands, Santa Catalina, and Santa Cruz, in the former of which it was discovered in 1884 by William S. Lyon, forester of the first board of forestry created in California. The genus was named in his honor. The characters of this genus are given under the one species now known.

Western Ironwood.

Lyonothamnus floribundus Gray.

DISTINGUISHING CHARACTERISTICS.

Little is known of the trunk and crown form and silvical habits of western ironwood. In open, rocky sites it is only a small shrub; most commonly a tall shrub with clustered stems, occasionally a shrubby tree from 20 to 25 feet high and from 4 to 8 inches in diameter. The bark, with its deep reddish color and its thin flaky layers, is very characteristic. A number of bark layers, broken and separated, often hang in long shreds. The twigs are clear, shiny red. The fern-like evergreen leaves are opposite and vary greatly from an undivided form (fig. 155) to one split into several subdivisions (fig. 154). Individuals with only one or the other of these types occur, but trees are also found bearing both types of foliage,[a] showing that the species has remarkably variable foliage. The small flowers, produced in flat-topped, branched clusters, open in early summer, and the fruit, two very small, closely joined, bristly glandular capsules, each with four minute, long seeds, are ripe the following autumn. The capsules split open of their own accord and gradually the seeds are liberated.

Wood, very heavy, dense, fine-grained, and exceedingly hard. The name ironwood was doubtless given because of the hardness of the wood. It is distinctly red, with a slight yellowish tint. It is suitable for ornamental or fancy woodwork, but is not known to have any economic use.

The limited range and rather rare occurrence of large stems are likely to prevent the species from ever becoming important commercially. Its chief value must lie in assisting to form protective cover on steep, dry, rocky slopes, where few other trees and shrubs can maintain themselves.

---

[a] T. S. Brandegee, Zoe, I, 111.

LONGEVITY.—Imperfectly known. Stems from 2 to 5 inches through show ages from 12 to 32 years.

FIG. 154.—*Lyonothamnus floribundus.*

RANGE.

Southern California coast islands. Santa Cruz, Santa Catalina, Santa Rosa, and San Clemente. Particularly abundant on north slope of Santa Cruz. Rarely arborescent on Santa Catalina.

OCCURRENCE.

Canyon slopes; in rocky and gravelly, dry soils. Forms rather dense small, pure stands, a number of stems growing from one root.

FIG. 155.—*Lyonothamnus floribundus.*

CLIMATIC CONDITIONS.—Undetermined, but probably similar to those of Trask mahogany.

TOLERANCE AND REPRODUCTION.—Undetermined.

Family PLATANACEÆ.

A small group of trees characterized by large deciduous leaves and especially by their minute flowers, borne in closely packed, spherical or ball-like heads, attached to a thread-like; pendulous stem. From one to half a dozen of these ball-like, greenish clusters are produced on a stem. The male and female flowers (each in ball-like clusters) occur on different parts of the same tree, usually on different parts of the same branch. The male clusters are smaller (about one-third of an inch in diameter) than the female heads (about one-half inch in diameter). The female clusters develop into very characteristic, spherical, hard balls of seed, the mature balls being from three-fourths inch to $1\frac{1}{2}$ inches in diameter, one to six of which may be attached to a single pendent stem (fig. 156).

PLATANUS. SYCAMORES.

The sycamores are a small group, the members of which are strikingly alike in general appearance. Their most distinctive characteristic is the very thin, smooth, whitish or pale green bark on young trunks and on the large branches of old trees. Thin, veneer-like sheets of the bark are annually shed as a result of the diameter growth of the stems. When exposed in this way the inner bark is pale olive green at first and later a chalky white. All of the members of this genus have this characteristic, which gives them a similar appearance. Differences in the lobing of the leaves and the amount of hair on their under surfaces, the number of fruit balls, and the shape of the seed (fruit) are depended upon to distinguish the different species. The winter buds of sycamores are also very characteristic. They are inclosed by the hollow bases of leaves, which fit over them like a minute clown's cap, and when these leaves break away and fall a circle is formed around the base of the conical bud, which is enveloped by three cap-like scales. The balls of fruit are composed of long, slender, seed-like bodies, densely packed together in a spherical mass. One end of the seeds is attached to a central bullet-like body, from which they all radiate, side by side, their opposite ends forming the surface of the sphere. A circle of fine, tawny, stiff hairs is attached to the base of each seed (fruit). These heads, ripe in late autumn, usually remain attached to the branches during the winter; in the spring they break up and the hairs about each seed (fruit) spread out, after the manner of the silky hairs on a dandelion seed, adding greatly to the buoyancy of the seed. As a result the seeds are easily and widely distributed by the wind.

The pale brown, reddish-tinged wood, very similar in all of these trees, is characteristically marked by wide medullary or pith rays, most conspicuously shown in quarter-sawed or radially cut sections. The wood is, moreover, peculiarly "cross-grained," and on this account exceedingly difficult to split. Commercially it is of rather secondary importance, but is attractive and suitable for interior finish and cabinet work. The western sycamores are of little importance, except to form protective growths along streams in dry, arid regions.

Three species inhabit the United States and adjacent portions of Mexico, but only one is found within the Pacific region, extending into Lower California. Another species ranges through our Southwest into Mexico. The third is widely distributed in the eastern United States.

The sycamores are of ancient origin. Species now extinct, but very like our eastern and the present European sycamores, were once common in Greenland and in our Arctic region during the Cretaceous and Tertiary epochs; they existed also in middle Europe during the latter period, but became extinct when that period ended. During the Tertiary epoch a number of sycamores, now extinct, once existed in the central part of this continent.

Fig. 156.—*Platanus racemosa: a,* seed.

California Sycamore.

Platanus racemosa Nuttall.

DISTINGUISHING CHARACTERISTICS.

California sycamore, also called " buttonwood " and " buttonball," is small or medium sized; from 40 to 60 feet high and from 18 to 30 inches in diameter. Trunks are often very short, giving off several trunk-like branches. The branches are conspicuously irregular in the directions they take. One or more of them may reach out low to the ground, while others wind and twist in prostrate or upright positions. Thick, long, crooked, and awkwardly bent, they form an exceedingly open crown. Such trees grow mainly in the open. Crowded in the bottoms of deep canyons California sycamore occasionally reaches a height of 75 or 80 feet (rarely more) and a diameter of from 3 to 6 feet. The dull brownish bark is ridged and furrowed at the base of the trunk. At the bases of old trunks it is from 2 to 3 inches thick; a short distance above, and on all of the limbs, it is very thin, smooth, and ashy white, with greenish-gray areas. Thin layers peel off annually, broken by diameter growth, keeping the upper parts of the trees smooth and conspicuously white.

The thick leaves (fig. 156), from 5 to 11 inches long and wide, are light yellow-green, much lighter beneath; they are minutely and densely hairy, especially on the midveins and their branches, though the amount of hair is variable. From 4 to 5 male flower heads are borne on a thread-like stem which grows from a leaf cluster on branches of the previous year; and from 2 to 7 (commonly 4 to 6) female flower heads grow on a similar stem which usually terminates a new branch of the season. The latter develop into bristly fruit heads (fig. 156), three-fourths inch to nearly an inch in diameter, with a single stem 5 to about 10 inches long. The slender, bristly seeds (akenes) are from three-eighths to seven-sixteenths of an inch long (fig. 156, *a*). Wood (described under *Platanus*) is not specifically distinct from that of the other sycamores.

LONGEVITY.—Age limits not fully determined. Believed to be long-lived. A single tree 20¼ inches in diameter showed an age of 86 years. Exceedingly tenacious of life, repairing repeated damage to its crown and trunk by vigorous sprouts and growth of wood.

RANGE.

California (from the lower Sacramento River through interior valleys and coast ranges) to Lower California (San Pedro Martir Mountain). In the north up to 2,000 feet and in the south to 4,000 feet. Plumas and Lassen Peak National Forests in foothill type up to 2,500 feet. Farther south in Sierras noted at White Deer Creek (northwest tributary King's River), on King's River from Trimmer Springs up to near mouth Big Creek and thence south, in Big Creek Canyon and on Northeast Branch Mill Creek, along lower Kaweah and in Tehachapi Mountains. On Lytle Creek, Caliente Creek, lower end Cañada de las Uvas, lower part Tejon Canyon and along Poso Creek, but not down desert streams to the east. On coast ranges noted on Carmel River up from mouth and along all stream beds of Santa Lucia Mountains from sea level to 2,000 feet; San Luis Obispo National Forest up to 2,500 feet on watersheds of Carriso, Salinas, Santa Margarita, San Luis, Arroyo Grande, Huasna, and Santa Maria. Santa Barbara National Forest in watersheds of Santa Ynez, Santa Barbara, Matilija, Piru-Sespe, Elizabeth, and Newhall rivers, at 100 to 4,200 feet. San Gabriel National Forest up to above 5,000 feet; noted near Pasadena on Oak Knoll, Arroyo Seco, and canyons of San Gabriel Mountains. Santa Ana range in canyons. San Bernardino Mountains, western and southern slopes, 1,600 up to 3,000 feet. San Jacinto Mountains, western slope, below 4,800 feet. On Palomar (Smith), Balkan, and Cuyamaca Mountains, from western side nearly to summit, and west nearly to ocean.

OCCURRENCE.

Confined to or near borders of perpetual and intermittent streams and moist gulches; in poor, rocky soil. Forms sparse lines and small groups of pure growth, or is mixed with white alder, broadleaf maple, California walnut, and occasional willows.

CLIMATIC CONDITIONS.—Similar to those of Fremont cottonwood.

TOLERANCE.—Endures but little shade at any age.

REPRODUCTION.—Moderately prolific seeder. Seed of fairly high rate of germination (often tardy), and of persistent vitality. Reproduction scanty; mainly and best on moist or wet exposed sand or gravel. Dependence upon constant soil moisture (available only near stream beds) and occurrence of heavy seasonal flood waters where seed is dropped doubtless limit reproduction.

Family ROSACEÆ.

The Rosaceæ are a very large family of trees, shrubs, and herbs of world-wide distribution. Among them are some of the most important timber, fruit, and ornamental trees, including cherries, plums, apples, pears, quinces, and haw-thorns, as well as innumerable shrubs and herbs, such as roses, etc. Prac-tically only one forest tree species (black cherry), represented in eastern United States, is of commercial use. All of the other trees of the family belonging to our forests are shrubby and of little or no economic use; some of them are, however, important for the sturdy cover they form on dry, scantily clothed montain slopes.

Representatives of the family treated here have showy, perfect flowers (with male and female reproductive organs in each blosssom). The flowers open in spring or summer and the fruit is ripened the same season. A point of resemblance in the flowers is the cluster of thread-like, bead-tipped, pollen-bearing bodies (stamens) in the center of each blossom. (Compare the blooms of garden cherries, plums, peaches, etc.) Fruits of some of these trees, such as cherries and plums, are edible and well known, and are characterized by their juicy sweet or tart (in some species very bitter or astringent) pulp, which covers a hard-shelled, round or flat seed. Other groups of this family, "haws" and "crab-apples," have small, mealy, or hard-fleshed fruits resembling minia-ture apples, with very small, bony, rough, thick-shelled seeds, or smooth, thin-shelled seeds. The mountain "mahoganies," of this family, have dry fruits, which are very different in appearance from any of the others, but which are structurally related. Since the fruits of many rosaceous trees are usually lus-cious, they are extensively eaten (without injury to the vitality of the seeds) by birds and mammals, by which the seeds are principally disseminated. The dry fruits of mountain mahoganies have special hairy attachments, by the aid of which they are wafted far from the mother trees by the wind. The leaves, evergreen or shed every autumn, occur singly on the twigs—never in pairs, one opposite another.

CERCOCARPUS. MOUNTAIN MAHOGANIES.

Mountain mahoganies are a small group of shrubby trees which derive their name from their red-brown, mahogany-colored wood, which is exceedingly heavy, fine-grained, dense, and hard. They are much-branched, usually crooked, scaly-barked trees with stiff branches which have peculiar, short, spine-like twigs, and very small, thick, evergreen leaves. When bruised, the leaves give off a resinous odor. The fruit, a long-tailed, hairy, seed-like body, is inclosed in a small, striped tube (part of the flower). When ripe it escapes and is blown for consid-erable distances by the wind. Occasionally it is dislodged by grazing animals and carried away in their hairy coats.

Of little or no economic use for their wood, but of some importance for the strong, though open and scanty, cover the trees form on the driest and most exposed of high mountain slopes. Three species inhabit the arid sections of the western United States and adjacent portions of Mexico, to the dry soil and cli-matic conditions of which they seem specially adapted.

Trask Mahogany.

Cercocarpus traskiæ Eastwood.

DISTINGUISHING CHARACTERISTICS.

This rare species, only recently brought to light through the explorations of
Mrs. L. B. Trask, in honor of whom it was named by Miss Alice Eastwood, is

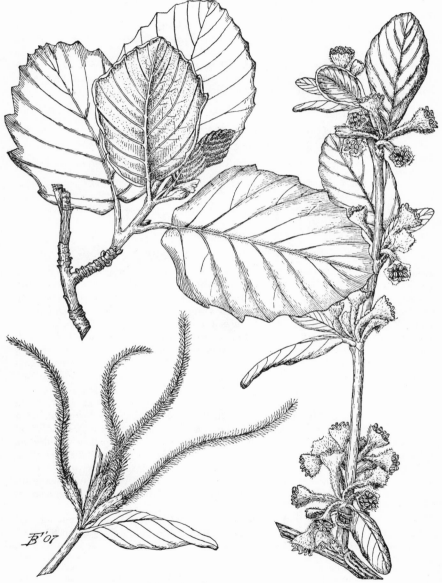

FIG. 157.—*Cercocarpus traskiæ.*

the most distinct and handsome in its foliage of our mountain mahoganies. The
short, twisted trunk, usually leaning, has hard, thin, finely seamed and ridged

bark of a grayish brown color, and is surmounted by a broad, stiff-branched crown. It only rarely reaches a height of from 20 to 25 feet and a diameter of from 8 to 10 inches, and is usually smaller, with stems from 2 to 4 inches thick. Mature leaves (fig. 157), silky white when young, are thick and shiny yellowish green; smooth and shiny on their upper sides, and densely covered with white or gray wool beneath; their margins curl under as the season advances. The hairy, long-tailed fruits (fig. 157) are inclosed at their bases with a hairy, tubular case.

Wood, pale reddish brown; otherwise very similar to that of mountain mahogany. The rarity and small size of the tree prevent the wood from becoming of economic use.

LONGEVITY.—Age limits undetermined. Two trees, respectively 3½ and 5 inches in diameter, were 17 and 35 years old. This shows an exceedingly slow growth, such as is peculiar to the other species.

RANGE.

CALIFORNIA.—Sides of a single canyon on the south coast of Santa Catalina Island.

OCCURRENCE.

Precipitous, rocky canyon sides, associated with western sumach (*Rhus ovata*) and *Adenostoma fasciculatum*.

CLIMATIC CONDITIONS (marked by high temperature) and silvical characteristics undetermined.

Curl-leaf Mahogany; [a]   Mountain Mahogany.

Cercocarpus ledifolius Nuttall.

DISTINGUISHING CHARACTERISTICS.

Ordinarily 15 to 20 feet high and 6 to 8 inches in diameter, but occasionally 25 to 30 feet high and 12 to 18 inches through—rarely much larger; very frequently only a low, broad, much-branched shrub. The trunks are generally short, more or less crooked, and large crumpled limbs stand out irregularly and with numerous stiff twigs produce a low, dense crown. The hard, firm, thin, scaly bark is reddish brown and gray tinted. Leaves (fig. 158), evergreen; those of each season's growth remain on the tree about two seasons, and are very thick, the edges curled toward the under side, which is densely covered with light brownish, minute hairs. The long-tailed hairy fruits, surrounded by a small cylindrical case, are stemless (fig. 158). Wood, very dense, fine-grained, exceedingly heavy, checking and warping badly in drying, after which it is very hard; freshly cut wood is a distinct mahogany red, browning with exposure. The poor timber form of even the largest trunks renders the wood of little commercial use, for which its rich, attractive color makes it suitable. Exceedingly important for fuel in some localities, usually where there is little or no other wood supply obtainable. It deserves the forester's attention on account of useful though open cover it forms on arid, wind-swept mountain slopes. Few other species possess its wonderful adaptability to such unfavorable conditions.

LONGEVITY.—Not fully determined. Gives evidence of being long-lived, but of very slow growth. Trees from 8 to 10 inches in diameter are from 68 to 95 years old. Further study of their age limits is required.

---

[a] Unfortunately no more distinctive common name is available for this and the succeeding species than "mountain mahogany," by which both are known in the field. They are probably not distinguished by laymen. To avoid confusion, it is desirable to call *Cercocarpus ledifolius* curl-leaf mahogany and *Cercocarpus parvifolius* birch-leaf mahogany.

The high mountain form of this species found mainly in the southern Rocky Mountains, but to be looked for elsewhere at high elevations in the range of the species, is a small, finely branched shrub with very small, exceedingly narrow, curled leaves, and smaller fruit than is produced by tree forms of lower

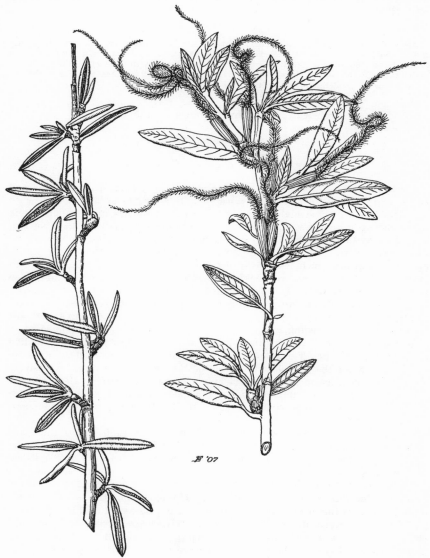

FIG. 158.—*Cercocarpus ledifolius.*

elevations. This shrub has been described as *Cercocarpus ledifolius intricatus* (Watson) Jones, on account of its densely branched habit, but it is here considered a naturally depauperate form of higher elevations, and is otherwise essentially like the larger-leafed tree.

From western Wyoming to Montana (western slopes Rocky Mountains), Idaho (Cœur d'Alene Mountains), Oregon (eastern Blue Mountains), and southward (through Wasatch Mountains and ranges of the Great Basin) to California (eastern slopes Sierra Nevada and northern slopes of San Bernardino Mountains), and to northern New Mexico and Arizona.

Arid mountain slopes; in poor, dry, gravelly and rocky soils, or less often in moist, richer soils, where it is of largest size (hills of central Nevada). In pure open, or rather dense stands, or mingled with chaparral; commonly with one-leaf piñon.

CLIMATIC CONDITIONS.—Undetermined, as are also its silvical characteristics. Appears to be decidedly intolerant of shade throughout life.

Birch-leaf Mahogany; Mountain Mahogany.[a]

Cercocarpus parvifolius Nuttall.

DISTINGUISHING CHARACTERISTICS.

Birch-leaf mahogany is usually shrubby, with several long, sparingly branched stems, and under 10 feet in height; occasionally a tree 15 to 25 feet high, with a rounded crown of straight, upright, stiff, slim branches and a short trunk 4 to 8 inches in diameter. The bark of large limbs and small trunks is smooth and dull gray to brownish; that of large trunks is thin, flaky, and reddish-brown. The more eastern form appears to have much firmer bark with shallow seams, and its scales are much less easily detached. Mature leaves (fig. 159), with prominent straight veins, are thickish, smooth, sometimes minutely hairy, deep yellowish-green on their top sides and whitish, occasionally brownish, beneath. Leaves of a season's growth persist as a rule for about two seasons; very commonly, however, they persist only for one summer and winter, falling as the new ones appear the succeeding spring. The long-tailed, hairy fruits are inclosed in a tubular case which has a distinct slender stem, instead of being stemless like the preceding species. The silky young twigs have a pleasant slightly aromatic flavor. Twigs of the low shrubby forms of this species are often extensively eaten by cattle, in some sections furnishing a considerable part of the mountain browse on which range animals depend for food. Wood, of somewhat lighter weight, is otherwise very similar to that of the preceding tree; rarely used except locally for firewood.

LONGEVITY.—Very slow-growing tree. Stems from 5 to 6 inches thick are from 50 to 60 years old. Further study of its growth and age limits is desirable.

Three varieties of this species have been described. These are distinguished on the basis of characters which the writer believes to be only such natural modifications in leaves and fruit as are to be expected in individuals growing under varying soil and climatic conditions. Through all of the forms it seems possible to trace the marks of one variable species; no essential differences can be found in the wood of the different trees. *Cercocarpus parvifolius betuloides* (Nuttall) Sargent, the California coast and Sierra foothill form, has wider leaves, smooth above, and larger fruit than are produced elsewhere. *Cercocarpus parvifolius breviflorus* [b] (Gray) Jones is distinguished by very small flowers and small, narrow leaves with entire slightly curved or very finely toothed

---

[a] See footnote under preceding species.
[b] This is Dr. Gray's *Cercocarpus breviflorus*, which, by inadvertence or otherwise, is frequently written *C. brevifolius*.

borders. This form occurs in the Southwest. *Cercocarpus parvifolius pauci-dentatus*, a form of the same region, is characterized by leaves with few or no marginal teeth.

FIG. 159.—*Cercocarpus parvifolius.*

RANGE.

From western Nebraska to Oregon (Siskiyou Mountains), south to western Texas and northern Mexico ; California (west of Sierra Nevada and south to San Jacinto Mountains ; Santa Cruz Islands) ; Lower California (mountains).

OCCURRENCE.

Habitat and silvical characteristics similar to those of mountain mahogany.

MALUS. APPLES.

The apples form a group of small trees. They are of little forest importance, but are of very great economic value on account of their edible fruits, which include the many varieties and races of cultivated apples. They are hard, dense-wooded trees, with small leaves arranged singly on the twigs (never in pairs, one opposite another), and shed every autumn. Their principal distinctive characteristic is the more or less globe-like form of the fruits, which are sunken at the stem end, as in the common crab or other cultivated apple, and which have a homogeneous flesh. The chestnut-colored, smooth, shiny seeds of apples are inclosed (1 to 2) in each of the 3 to 5 cells. Their near relatives, the true pears (*Pyrus*), have fruits which taper at the stem end (pyriform), and have flesh with minute or large stony grains, though these are less pronounced in highly cultivated pear fruits than in those of wild trees.

Three tree species occur in the United States and adjacent Canadian provinces, one of which inhabits the Pacific region, to which it is confined.

Oregon Crab Apple.

Malus rivularis (Dougl. in Hook) Roemer.

DISTINGUISHING CHARACTERISTICS.

The Oregon crab apple is a small tree, with thin, scaly, reddish—often grayish brown—bark and slender, spreading branches. At best it is rarely more than 25 or 30 feet high and from 8 to 12 inches in diameter; very frequently a slender-stemmed shrub from 6 to 10 feet high, forming dense thickets. Year-old twigs are clear shiny red. Mature leaves (figs. 160, 161) are veiny, thickish, smooth, and deep green on their top sides, and very light green and minutely hairy—sometimes whitish—beneath; leaf stems hairy. Fruit (figs. 160, 161), maturing late in autumn and having a slightly acid, palatable taste, is variable in color from greenish to clear lemon yellow splashed with bright red on one side or red all over; edible. Wood exceedingly fine-grained, dull, light reddish brown; sapwood very thick. Suitable for tool stock and small turnery, but unimportant.

LONGEVITY.—Appears to grow very slowly in diameter and height. Age limits not fully determined. One tree 11 inches in diameter showed an age of 102 years; while one 6 inches through was 57 years old.

RANGE.

From the Aleutian Islands south along the coast and islands of Alaska and British Columbia through western Washington and Oregon to California (Sonoma and Plumas counties).

OCCURRENCE.

Low river bottoms and adjacent low slopes, on borders and in vicinity of smaller lowland streams, in moist or rather wet sandy or mucky soil. Grows in large, dense, pure thickets and also scattered among red alder, willows, cascara sagrada, occasionally broadleaf maple and western dogwood, and lowland shrubs.

CLIMATIC CONDITIONS.—Similar to those of Sitka spruce and red alder.

TOLERANCE.—Not fully determined. Endures moderate shade throughout life, and rather dense shade in youth.

REPRODUCTION.—Fairly abundant seeder in central and southern range and in less exposed situations; appears less prolific northward. Seed germinates tardily. Seedlings frequent in moist mucky soil.

Fig. 160.—*Malus rivularis*.

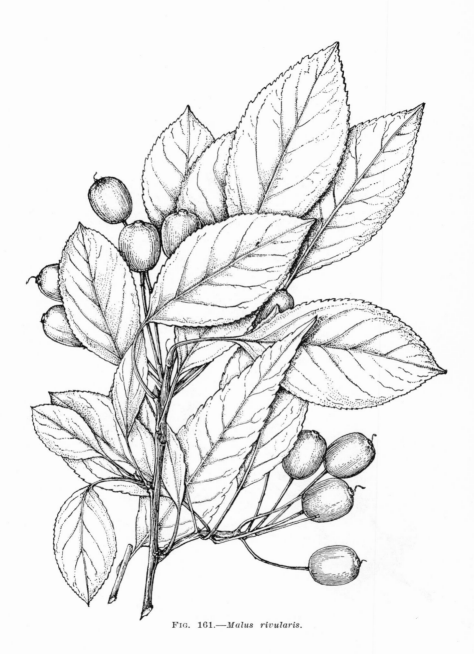

FIG. 161.—*Malus rivularis.*

AMELANCHIER.　SERVICEBERRIES.

The serviceberries are small, slender, scaly-barked trees and shrubs of world-wide range, but nowhere of forest or economic importance. The heartwood is brown or reddish brown, very fine-grained, hard, firm, and heavy; there is a large proportion of whitish sapwood. Twigs are very small. The showy, nodding, or erect clusters of white flowers, which usually appear in early spring before the leaves, make the trees conspicuous in the leafless forest. Flowers (male and female reproductive organs in each), with five white divisions, are visited by insects, which aid in their cross-fertilization. The small, symmetrically formed leaves, shed in autumn, are arranged singly on the twigs (never in pairs, one opposite another). Fruit, deep red or dull purple, and borne in small branched clusters, ripens early or late in summer and resembles a huckleberry; it has a somewhat juicy, sweetish, edible pulp, with from 5 to 10 very minute, dark brown seeds. For their distribution the seeds depend almost entirely upon birds and mammals, which eat the berries, but with little injury to the seeds. Trees of the group are confined to North America, where 3 or 4 species occur, one of which ranges from the Rocky Mountains into the Pacific region.

Western Serviceberry.

Amelanchier alnifolia Nuttall.

DISTINGUISHING CHARACTERISTICS.

Western serviceberry is a tall, slender-stemmed shrub from 8 to 10 feet high and about an inch thick; very commonly under 3 feet in height, forming vast thickets; it seldom becomes a tree as much as 25 or 30 feet high and from 4 to 8 inches through, and then has a slender, straight, clean trunk and a narrow, open crown. The bark is dull grayish or slightly reddish brown and indistinctly seamed near the ground—usually quite smooth. Season's twigs are clear red, smooth (though with white hairs when young), with sharp-pointed, russet-brown buds. Mature leaves (fig. 162), thin in shady places but thickish in the open, are deep or pale green and smooth on their upper surface, and smooth and grayish, sometimes minutely and sparsely hairy, beneath. The blue-black, sweetish fruit, with a whitish bloom, matures (according to the locality) from about July to August, and is about one-half to five-eighths of an inch through (fig. 162). When not overripe the edible fruit is agreeable to the taste, and where abundant is often gathered by settlers (who call the tree "sarvice"), as well as by Indians, for food. Birds and mammals, especially bears, consume large quantities of the fruit. Wood, pale yellowish brown; of no economic use. The only value of the tree to the forester lies in the fact that it forms dense thickets, with other brush, at high elevations, where its rigid, often closely browsed stems, help to prevent run-off. Its tree forms, which are rare, are of no commercial value. Shrubby forms, quickly killed by ground fires, sprout from the roots, and otherwise endure with persistent growth the constant browsing of range cattle, its stems only becoming more and more intricately and densely branched.

LONGEVITY.—Not fully determined. Stems from 2 to 4 inches in diameter are from 9 to 20 years old.

RANGE.

From Alaska (Yukon River, latitude 62° 45') to California (southern boundary); eastward through British Columbia, Saskatchewan, and Manitoba to Lake Superior (western shores), northern Michigan, Nebraska, Colorado, and New Mexico (Rocky Mountains).

OCCURRENCE.

Alluvial bottoms and prairies, moist valleys, dry mountain slopes, benches, borders of streams, water holes, and mountain meadows in variety of soils from rich to poor; largest in fresh rich soil (lower Columbia River region) and shrubby in dry, gravelly, poor ones (mountain slopes). Forms small groups and extensive pure thickets, interspersed with aspen, western choke-cherry, bitter cherry, Oregon crab, and ceanothus, manzanita, and other chaparral brush.

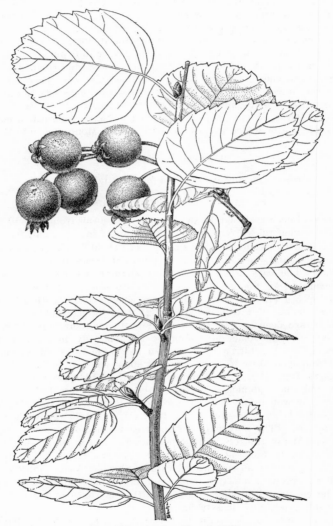

FIG. 162.—*Amelanchier alnifolia.*

CLIMATIC CONDITIONS.—Similar to those of western chinquapin; mild, long, warm growing season appears to determine range of largest growth.

TOLERANCE.—Endures considerable dense shade when young, but needs abundant overhead light for best growth.

REPRODUCTION.—Abundant seeder nearly every year. Seedlings often numerous in moist, humous soil in partial shade; much scattered and infrequent on dry slopes.

CRATÆGUS. HAWS.

The haws are a very large group of small, thorny trees and shrubs, widely distributed in this and the Old World. From the abundance of their keen, often very long, woody thorns, they are everywhere known, and generally distinguished from other woody plants, as " hawthorns," " haws," or " thorns." Excepting the few western species, which form useful chaparral cover, the other representatives are of little forest value and of no commercial importance. They produce dense, heavy, sappy, exceedingly tough wood, which warps and checks badly in drying. Excepting occasional use for small tool-handles and other turned articles, the wood is of no economic value.

In eastern North America, where a vast number of species are known, they are aggressive in taking possession of abandoned farm or cleared lands. Their sharp thorns protect them from grazing animals. Later these impenetrable thickets are gradually invaded by commercial species through the agency of wind and animals, and finally, under denser shade, the thorns succumb.

Their usually small leaves, shed every autumn, are arranged like those of the apples, while the small apple-like fruits, bright red, yellow, or black, in branched clusters, have dryish, unpalatable—but occasionally tart and palatable—flesh with from 1 to 5 joined (but separable), very hard, bony seeds, which, on account of their thick shells, germinate tardily, often " lying over " for a season. The white to rosy flowers (similar in appearance and structure to pear and apple blossoms) are produced in flattish, branched, erect clusters at the ends of new shoots, after the leaves are grown. Myriads of insects visit the flowers and assist in their cross-fertilization ; birds and mammals, which devour the fruits, assist in disseminating the seeds of many species.

Exclusive of shrubby thorns, there are about 100 species now known to occur in the United States and adjacent territory. These include a number of little-known forms which may be separated as distinct species upon later study. Only one species is known to inhabit the Pacific region.

No other group of North American trees presents such almost insurmountable difficulties in point of distinctive characters. It is impossible, and, fortunately, unnecessary for the practical forester to know them all, and exceedingly difficult even for the specialist. The points relied upon to distinguish the species are, unfortunately, too often found mainly in the organs of the flowers and in the ripening and falling of the fruit—characters which are observable only at special times. A number of thorns can be distinguished by their mature leaves, but a very large number of them can not. Students of western forests have a comparable problem in the polymorphous oaks, but nature has luckily spared them such perplexities as those offered by the haws.

Black Haw.

Cratægus douglasii Lindley.

DISTINGUISHING CHARACTERISTICS.

Black haw is mainly a low, much-branched shrub, or else a shrub with taller, slender stems, forming dense thickets. In rich, moist soil it becomes a tree from 20 to 30 feet high and from 10 to 20 inches in diameter, and then has a straight, slightly seamed, reddish brown trunk and a densely branched, dome-like crown. Mature twigs of the season are a clear, shiny red. Mature leaves (fig. 163) are thick, somewhat leathery, smooth (sometimes shiny) ; deep green on their upper sides and paler green beneath. The very characteristically black or black-purple, shiny fruit (fig. 163), sweet and edible, matures in early autumn, when it is rapidly shed.   Wood, fine-grained, brownish rose-red, with a large proportion of sapwood.   No commercial use is made of it.

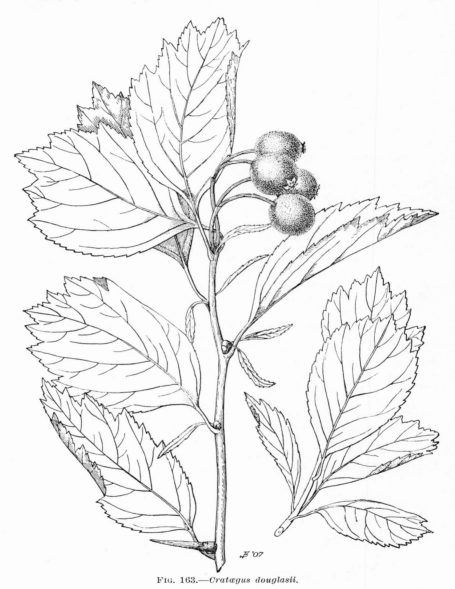

FIG. 163.—*Cratægus douglasii.*

As a chaparral cover along washable banks of streams the brushy form of this haw is of considerable use.   The firm, spreading roots of closely grown stools hold fast and resist tendencies to erosion.   Its tree form is unimportant in a region where other useful trees abound.

Longevity.—Not fully determined. Like many other large tree thorns it appears to be long-lived, as shown by its exceedingly fine-grained wood and persistent growth. A tree 13⅜ inches in diameter showed an age of 83 years.

A well-marked variety of this thorn, *Cratægus douglasii rivularis* (Nutt.) Sargent, is commonly a low shrub, sometimes nearly without thorns; it is frequent in western Washington and Oregon and southward to Sierra and Plumas counties, Cal., where it is less common. It is distinguished from the species mainly by its narrow leaves, which are finely toothed, not deeply lobed and slashed as in the species. It was described long ago as a species (*C. rivularis* Nuttall) and is by some authors still maintained as such; but since intermediate leaf forms are not hard to find, connecting the species over its entire range, the writer believes that this form should be treated as a variety only.

RANGE.

From British Columbia (Parsnip River) through Washington and Oregon to California (Pitt River), and through Idaho and Montana (Flathead River at western base of Rocky Mountains).

OCCURRENCE.

Borders and bottoms in vicinity of lower mountain streams; in moist, gravelly and sandy soils, or in deep, rich soils (where, in Oregon, it is large). Grows in very dense, large, pure thickets, patches, and small clumps, mingled with choke cherry, black cottonwood, longleaf willow, red alder, etc.

Climatic Conditions.—Similar to those of choke cherry; adapted to very wide range of conditions.

Tolerance.—Shows signs of great tolerance; not fully determined.

Reproduction.—Very abundant seeder, and young plants numerous in shade and open on borders of thickets.

HETEROMELES.

A genus containing but a single evergreen species which is confined to California and adjacent islands. In general appearance it is very unlike any of the other related generic groups of the family (Rosaceæ), as indicated by its name (Heteromeles). The characters of this genus are given under the species, which follows.

Christmas Berry.

Heteromeles arbutifolia Roemer.

DISTINGUISHING CHARACTERISTICS.

Christmas berry, also called " California holly," " tollen," and " toyon," is best known as a low shrub throughout most of its range on the mainland. In the coast islands, however, especially on Santa Catalina Island, it becomes a small tree from 15 to 25 feet high, but with a very short trunk from 10 to 15 inches thick at the ground. The crown form of the shrub is peculiarly similar to that of the tree, in which many upright branches are given off at the end of the short, thick trunk. The smooth-looking, pale, ashy gray bark is indistinctly seamed, and the ridges are connected. Mature leaves (fig. 164) thick, leathery, smooth throughout, deep shiny green on their upper surfaces, lighter beneath, and usually with two minute glandular teeth on the stem at the base of the blade. Leaves of a season's growth remain on the twigs until the end of the second winter. The smooth, bright red berries (fig. 164), which have a dry, tart flesh, ripen from October to February; they are borne in large clusters which are very attractive among the glossy green leaves. One or two ridged, brown, dotted seeds occur in each of the two cells of the berries. Wood, deep reddish brown, with thin sapwood ; exceedingly heavy, dense, and fine-grained. Very suitable for small ornamental turnery and other woodwork, but not used for any purpose.

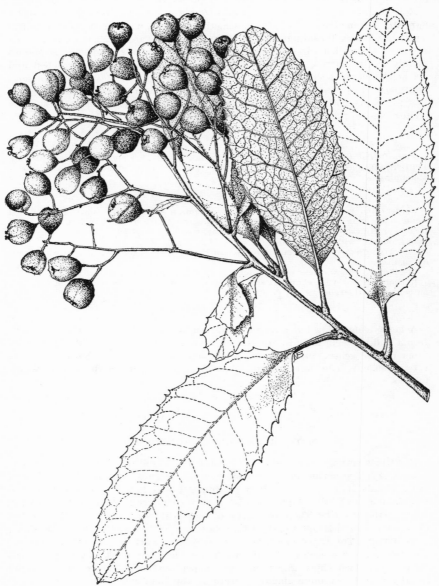

FIG. 164.—*Heteromeles arbutifolia.*

As a part of the chaparral cover of low, dry slopes and rocky gulches, or in the groves formed by its larger growth, this species is of considerable service in a region too scantily protected against erosion.

LONGEVITY.—Not fully determined. It grows very persistently and appears to be long-lived. A single stem 5½ inches in diameter was 48 years old.

RANGE.

California coast ranges and Sierras (chaparral belt) southward from Mendocino and Shasta counties to northern Lower California ; also on southern California coast islands.

CALIFORNIA.—Coast ranges northward on coast to Mendocino County, and to Trinity Mountains on inland ranges, where it has been noted as far north as between Redding and Whiskeytown (Shasta County). In Sierras, on foothills in Lassen Peak, Diamond Mountain, Plumas, Tahoe, and Stanislaus National forests. Southward in coast ranges to San Francisco Bay, and in southern coast ranges eastward to San Bernardino ; also in islands off southern coast. South of Monterey Bay, noted on Point Piños, in Pescadero and a few other canyons, and in Santa Lucia Mountains in chaparral of Sur, Carmelo, Arroyo Seco, San Antonio, and Nacimiento river basins from sea-level to 4,250 feet. San Luis Obispo National Forest (to southeast), from 250 to 2,250 feet elevation in watersheds of Carriso, Salinas, Santa Margarita, San Luis, Arroyo Grande, and Huasna rivers. Santa Barbara National Forest, below 3,000 feet in watersheds of Santa Maria, Santa Ynez, Santa Barbara, Matilija, Piru-Sespe, Newhall, and Elizabeth rivers. Santa Ana range. All coast islands except San Clemente. General in San Gabriel National Forest ; noted on south slope Sierra Liebre Range, near Pasadena, Arroyo Seco. San Bernardino Mountains. San Jacinto Mountains and Palomar, Balkan, and Cuyamaca Mountains (San Diego County). Mexican boundary, noted on west slope of coast range up to 4,500 feet.

LOWER CALIFORNIA.—Northern part, in Hanson, Laguna, and San Pedro Martir ranges.

OCCURRENCE.

Frequent on north slopes of low mountains and foothills in vicinity of watercourses, in gulches, or on exposed sea cliffs ; in dry, rocky, and gravelly soils. Grows in scattered, pure clumps and patches on mainland slopes (shrubby), and in small pure stands, as a tree, in its island range.

CLIMATIC CONDITIONS.—Similar to holly-leaf cherry. Tolerance and other silvical characteristics undetermined.

REPRODUCTION.—Very prolific seeder. Young plants abundant in soil-filled crevices, pockets, and in other places of lodgment.

PRUNUS. CHERRIES AND PLUMS.

As here constituted, a large group containing such well-known and widely distributed trees and shrubs as the plums, peaches, almonds, apricots, and cherries, most of which do not produce useful timber, but are among the most valuable fruit trees. The plums and cherries are the only native trees of the group to be considered here.

For the sake of reducing the number of generic names, the latter-day practice of subdividing this long-maintained composite group into *Prunus* (including the plums only) and *Cerasus* (including only the cherries) will not be followed. It is thought best to treat these trees under *Prunus*, as has been done for a long time. The cherries differ from plums principally in having a rounded fruit seed or " stone " in place of more or less flat seeds ; plum fruits are, moreover, usually covered with an easily removed, whitish bloom, which is absent from cherry fruits.

Prunus contains but one tree species (black cherry) of commercial importance ; the remaining representatives are small trees or shrubs of little economic use. Some of the western plums and cherries, however, are useful in helping to form protective covers on otherwise thinly clad mountain slopes.

Wood of the plums and cherries is fine-grained, dense, evenly and finely porous, rather heavy, and rich light or dark brown. Green twigs and bark are characteristically bitter, and have, when crushed, a more or less strong peach-pit odor possessed by no other group of plants.

Flowers of Prunus, appearing from buds on twigs of the previous year, either with the leaves, or before or after them, are similar in general appearance to those of the hawthorns, apples, and pears, but different in structural details. They depend for cross-fertilization entirely upon insects. The fruits, more or less juicy and sweet, acid, or very bitter, are matured in one season, either in early or late summer. Luscious in flavor or attractive in appearance, plum and cherry fruits are eaten extensively by birds and mammals (without injury to the seeds) and thus widely disseminated; otherwise these trees depend for distribution of their seeds upon flood waters. The leaves are arranged on the twigs as in the apples and haws, and are either shed every autumn or, in some species, are evergreen.

Sixteen species of Prunus occur in the United States and adjacent territory, 4 of which inhabit the Pacific region.

Western Plum.

Prunus subcordata Bentham.

DISTINGUISHING CHARACTERISTICS.

The name " western plum," suggested here, is not the field name of this tree, which is " plum " or " wild plum," indefinite names which are applied also to several eastern wild plum-trees. To avoid confusion, it is hoped " western plum " will be used.

Generally a stocky, crooked-stemmed shrub from 2 to 10 feet high in dry situations, but in moist, rich soils a tree from 15 to 20 feet high and from 4 to 6 inches (sometimes more) in diameter. The short, clear trunk, ashy brown, seamed, and scaly, gives off thick limbs, which stand out nearly at right angles to the stem, and have many short, stubby twigs, some of which are spine-like. Season's twigs are clear red to deep purple-red, usually smooth (sometimes minutely hairy), with sharp-pointed red buds. Mature leaves (fig. 165), shed in autumn, are commonly smooth on their top sides but very often minutely hairy, as they always are beneath; about $1\frac{1}{4}$ to nearly 3 inches in length; in dying they become bright red and yellow. The white flowers appear before the leaves in early spring. Mature fruit (fig. 165), ripe in early autumn, is deep purple-red, three-fourths inch to about 1 inch long, with a pointed flat stone, which has a conspicuous, thin, keel-like edge on one side only, the opposite side being grooved. The flesh of the fruit is edible and much used locally, is juicy and somewhat tart; variable in quality.

Wood, fine-grained, very dull light brown, with thin sapwood; of no economic use.

With other chaparral the tree sometimes forms good protective slope cover on dry slopes.

LONGEVITY.—Not fully determined. A tree $6\frac{1}{4}$ inches in diameter showed an age of 48 years. Probably short-lived.

A variety of this plum, *Prunus subcordata kelloggii* Lemmon, is distinguished by its yellow sweet fruit and in its nearly smooth foliage; especially abundant in Shasta and Sierra counties. Yellow fruited forms of other wild plums and of cherries are known.

RANGE.

Southern Oregon to central California (west of the Cascades and Sierra Madre Mountains).

OCCURRENCE.

Borders and vicinity of low mountain and higher foothill streams and valleys; in sandy, fertile, fresh soils (here largest), or in dry, gravelly ones (shrubby). Grows in extensive pure thickets and clumps, interspersed with black haw, Oregon crab, Garry oak, western choke cherry, and occasional gray pine.

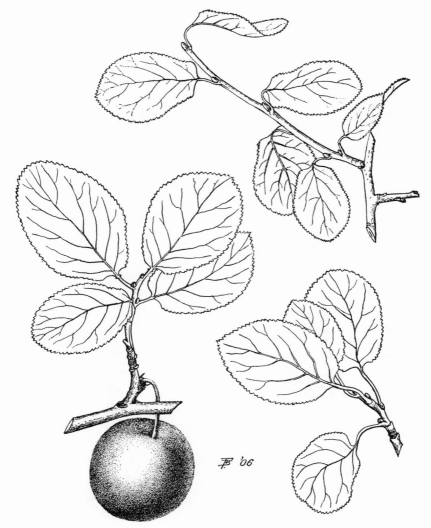

FIG. 165.—*Prunus subcordata.*

CLIMATIC CONDITIONS.—Similar to those of choke cherry.

TOLERANCE.—Endures light shade, which is helpful in seedling stage.

REPRODUCTION.—Prolific periodic seeder in better soils, but fruits sparingly and irregularly in poor, dry soils. Seedlings fairly abundant in fresher soils; very scarce in dry places.

Bitter Cherry.

Prunus emarginata (Dougl.) Walpers.

DISTINGUISHING CHARACTERISTICS.

Bitter cherry varies greatly in size; from a slender-stemmed, much-branched, tall or low shrub, much bent in high rocky, exposed sites, to a straight clean-stemmed tree from 35 to 40 feet high and from 6 to 12 inches, or more, through.

Fig. 166.—*Prunus emarginata.*

The thin bark is smooth, very dark brown on large trunks, but grayish brown on small stems. Season's twigs are deep red, which fades into reddish brown lower down. Mature leaves (fig. 166) very variable in size and texture, are smooth throughout and smaller in most of the shrubby high mountain forms with gray-brown stems, larger and finely hairy beneath on the larger darker-barked trees which are usually grown in moist, rich places; 2 glandular, minute projections mark the leaf-stem where it joins the blade. The leaves of both forms agree in their distinctly minute, rounded, marginal teeth.[a]

Mature fruit (fig. 166), one-fourth to three-eighths of an inch in diameter, clear coral red; ripe from about July to September, according to the locality and elevation; extremely bitter, as are the green twigs, leaves and inner bark; with a pointed stone, sharp-ridged on one side only and round or minutely grooved on the opposite side. Wood, dull brown, with very thick sapwood, of very light weight, and exceedingly brittle; it rots quickly in contact with the earth. Large trees, which often occur abundantly, useful chiefly for firewood.

The greatest value of this species is probably the dense chaparral cover which it forms on dry, rocky and springy slopes at high elevations, where its persistent stems, often bent low by heavy snows, form effective barriers to rapid run-off.

LONGEVITY.—Not fully determined. Apparently short-lived. A tree $9\frac{3}{8}$ inches in diameter showed an age of 42 years.

RANGE.

From Montana (upper Jocko River), through mountains of Idaho and Washington and southern British Columbia (Vancouver Island) ; south through western Washington and Oregon to southern California, western Nevada (vicinity of Carson City and Washoe Mountains), and northern Arizona (San Francisco Mountains). In north at sea level to 3,000 feet and in south at 5,000 to 9,000 feet.

BRITISH COLUMBIA.—South coast Vancouver Island, and Rocky Mountains at source of Columbia. Noted at Victoria (Vancouver Island), at Yale on Fraser River, and at Nelson on Columbia River between Kootenai and Lower Arrow lakes.

WASHINGTON.—Whole wooded portion of State east of Cascades, in yellow pine and bunch grass regions, at 1,600 to 4,200 feet and west of Cascades in Douglas fir region up to 3,800 feet. Noted in Washington National Forest at 49° latitude and farther south on west side of Cascades on lower slopes and on east side at 1,100 to 3,500 feet, in Clallam County on north side of Olympic Peninsula, at Montesano (Chehalis County, south of Olympic Peninsula), on west side of Puget Sound at Port Ludlow (Jefferson County), Tacoma, and Admiralty Head (east of entrance to Admiralty Inlet), at Lilliwaup on Hood Canal of Puget Sound, in Mount Rainier National Forest on Upper Nisqually River, and elsewhere; on Mount Adams, Klickitat River (Klickitat County), canyons of Yakima River, and Umptanum Creek, and at Ellensburg (altitude 1,550 feet) (Kittitas County) ; on Snake River east of Pasco (500 feet) (Franklin County), Wenache Mountains, Peshastin (Chelan County), White Bluff (on Columbia River, below Lake Chelan), Lake Chelan (1,100 feet), Stehekin River, 3 miles above Lake Chelan ; Kettle Falls of Columbia (Stevens County), Mount Carlton (Spokane County), and Blue Mountains on streams.

OREGON.—Whole wooded portion of State at lower elevations. Noted at Astoria, in Cascade (North) National Forest, on Columbia River in northeast Wasco, and Northern Sherman, Gilliam, and Morrow counties, and in Wallula Gorge below mouth of Walla Walla River at 327 feet ; John Day River (Gilliam County), Blue Mountains at Union and elsewhere, Silvies and Steins mountains (Harney County), and Goose Lake National Forest.

---

[a] It is believed that the true status of this cherry has not yet been satisfactorily determined. Further field study is necessary to determine the exact relationship between the gray-barked, smooth, and smaller tree or shrub common on the western high slopes of the Sierras and in Oregon and Washington, and the larger, dark-barked tree of lower, moist situations. The two forms are strikingly unlike in habit and general appearance, and the large downy leaves of the bigger tree are difficult to reconcile with the smooth, brighter green leaves of the smaller one.. I have not seen specimens from the type locality (Columbia River Valley, where Douglas discovered this tree in 1825), but most probably they are of the downy-leafed, larger tree form, so that the name *Prunus emarginata* should include this common form. On the other hand, it is probable that *Prunus emarginata californica* (Greene) (=*Cerasus californica* Greene) should be taken up for the smaller smooth form now included in the species.

CALIFORNIA.—Water courses and chaparral of middle elevations, south on Sierra Nevada to head of Kern River, on north coast ranges to San Francisco Bay, and on south coast ranges from Santa Cruz Mountains to San Jacinto Mountains, at the north at 3,500 to 5,500 feet and at the south at 5,000 to 9,000 feet. Noted in Mount Shasta National Forest, base of Mount Shasta at 3,500 to 5,500 feet and south to the "Loop" on Sacramento River; Wagon Camp (5,750 feet on Mount Shasta), Sissons (3,500 feet), and Upper Soda Springs (Siskiyou County); coast ranges, rare in Humboldt County and southward, Trinity and Stony Creek National Forests' highest ridges such as Canyon Creek lakes, and Black Buttes, Mount Tamalpais, and Oakland Hills around San Francisco Bay; Sierra Nevadas frequent, Plumas, Diamond Mountain and Lassen Peak National Forests; near Quincy (Plumas County), mountains east of Chico and Oroville (Butte County), Yuba River at 4,500 to 5,500 feet, Donner Lake, Lake Tahoe National Forest. Emigrant Gap (Placer County), Lake Tahoe, Placerville (Eldorado County), Stanislaus National Forest, frequent at 6,500 to 8,500 feet; Mud Springs (Amador County), Yosemite Valley, mountains of Fresno County at 8,000 feet, South Fork King's River, Middle Fork Kaweah River at 8,000 feet, Kaweah River road below Mineral King and between Kern River lakes and Trout Meadows; southern California coast ranges, hills of Santa Clara County up to 1,000 feet, ridges west of Los Gatos, Santa Lucia Mountains at 3,000 to 4,000 feet, San Rafael Mountains, San Bernardino Mountains at Bear Valley and elsewhere, San Jacinto Mountains, abundant at 5,000 to 9,000 feet in Tahquitz Valley and elsewhere. The variety *villosa* Sudworth occurs with the type, especially on the headwaters of the Columbia in British Columbia, Montana, and Idaho; in Washington and Oregon chiefly west of the Cascades and in the southern California coast ranges.

The distribution in Montana and Idaho will be described in a later publication.

OCCURRENCE.

Near streams on low and high mountain slopes and on moist benches; in dryish to moist gravelly soils at high levels, and in rich, sandy, or gravelly soils at lower elevations, where it is largest. Forms large, dense, pure shrubby thicket in higher range within upper white fir and red fir belt, and nearly pure stands on limited areas lower down, where it often occurs with scattered Douglas fir and western dogwood; sometimes especially abundant on cutover and burned Douglas fir lands.

CLIMATIC CONDITIONS.—In lower range, similar to those of Douglas fir, but in higher range it endures a climate like that of California red fir.

TOLERANCE.—Intolerant of shade.

REPRODUCTION.—Abundant seeder and scattered seedlings frequent in moist mineral soil and humus.

Western Choke Cherry.

Prunus demissa (Nutt.) Walpers.

DISTINGUISHING CHARACTERISTICS.

It is desirable to establish for *Prunus demissa* the more distinctive name of "western choke cherry," in place of "choke cherry," its ordinary field name, since the latter is also applied to the closely related eastern *Prunus virginiana* Linnæus, of which it is held by some to be a geographical form or a variety.

Very commonly a short or tall tree-like shrub (in dense thickets), from 4 to 10 feet high, or, in rich, moist situations, a slender, crooked-stemmed tree from 20 to 25 feet high and from 6 to 8 inches through.

Bruised twigs, leaves, and green bark have a strong scent, similar to that of peach-pits. Season's twigs (greenish, smooth or minutely hairy at first) are smooth and light reddish brown, with pointed, light brown buds. Bark, smooth and gray on old trunks and brown on young ones, is irregularly seamed and rough, with hard, deep reddish-brown scales. Mature leaves (fig. 167) are thick, somewhat leathery, deep, dull green; smooth and shiny on their upper sides; usually more or less minutely hairy and pale beneath (occasionally smooth); the borders have straight, sharp teeth. The white flowers are borne in dense cylindrical clusters, as are also the shiny blackish cherries, which are one-third to one-half an inch in diameter (fig. 167) ; the fruit [a] ripens in late summer or early autumn, when it is sweet, with an astringent after-taste, from which comes the name " choke cherry." The fruit is greedily eaten by birds, to which, it is believed, the wide general distribution of the species

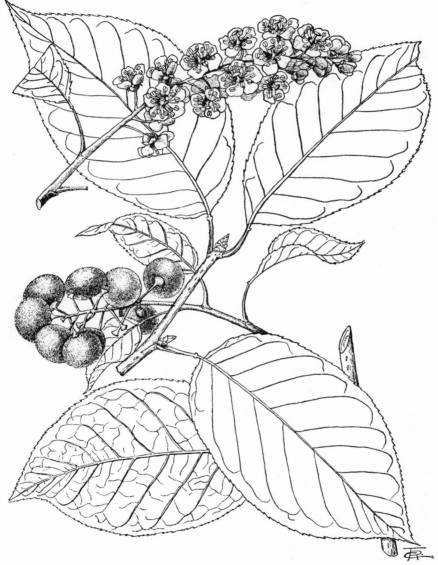

FIG. 167.—*Prunus demissa.*

is due. Wood, pale yellowish brown, fine-grained, firm, but brittle, with a thick layer of whitish sapwood. Not used for any economic purpose.

---

[a] Settlers in many parts of the West gather and preserve the fruit, which is excellent when cooked, but with slight astringent taste.

Useful with other shrubby trees in forming thick, retentive cover on the sides of mountain streams and on moist slopes otherwise devoid of woody growth.

LONGEVITY.—Not fully determined. Probably short-lived. Two trees, respectively 3 and 6 inches in diameter, were 10 to 22 years old.

RANGE.

Rocky Mountains to Pacific States and British Columbia, at the north from sea level to 4,000 feet, at the south from 5,000 to 7,000 feet.

BRITISH COLUMBIA.—To northern part on coast and in interior as far as Cache Creek. On Vancouver Island in isolated patches.

WASHINGTON.—Common east of Cascades below 4,000 feet, and west of Cascades only occasional on arid prairies, such as Whidby Island and Yelm Prairie. Noted in Washington National Forest at 1,100 to 3,500 feet, east of Cascades locally at Wenache (Chelan County), on west bank of Columbia from Priest Rapids to Sentinel Bluffs in Saddle Mountains, in gorge of Umptanum Creek (Kittitas County), on west slope of Divide between Columbia and Yakima rivers, in Yakima Canyon, at North Yakima, and Sunnyside, on Upper Columbia, in Spokane Valley, at Rock Lake (head of Palouse River), Pullman and Wawawai (Whitman County), along Snake River east of Pasco (Franklin County), and in Blue Mountains.

OREGON.—Chiefly to the east of Cascades, but also in arid parts west of Cascades. Noted on Columbia River from northeastern Wasco to Umatilla County, on John Day River in Gilliam County, in Cascade (North) National Forest, in Goose Lake National Forest, and in Blue Mountains.

CALIFORNIA.—Whole State, except on seaboard, chiefly in foothills, at the north up to about 3,500 feet, and at the south at 5,000 to 7,000 feet. Noted in chaparral of Klamath, Modoc, and Warner mountains National Forests; at Yreka (2,635 feet) (Siskiyou County), Mount Shasta on its south slope above McCloud Mill, near Sisson (3,500 feet) and at south end of Shasta Valley (3,500 feet) (Siskiyou County), Sacramento Canyon at Shasta Springs (2,538 feet) (Siskiyou County), southern Trinity Mountains east as far as hill between Whiskeytown and town of Shasta (Shasta County), and also locally noted near Lewiston and on Canyon Creek (Trinity County); in Sierras in Plumas, Diamond Mountain, Lassen Peak, Yuba, Tahoe National Forests, in Stanislaus National Forest in general at 2,500 to 4,000 feet, locally noted in canyon of South Fork of American River at 4,000 feet and on north slope of Mokelumne River at 2,500 feet, Lake Tahoe National Forest in T. 17 N., R. 13 E., and in Yosemite Valley; west border of Sierra National Forest on dry pine hills, locally noted near Hávilah (Kern County) at 3,150 feet. In coast ranges noted in Napa Mountains, in San Francisco County, on Oakland Hills, Mount Hamilton, in chaparral of Monterey National Forest in watershed of Nacimiento River, in Santa Barbara National Forest in watersheds of Santa Maria, Santa Ynez, and Piru-Sespe rivers, and in San Rafael Mountains, also in San Antonio and San Bernardino mountains in upper portion of chaparral belt and in pine belt, in San Jacinto Mountains, at 5,000 to 7,000 feet on Fuller's Ridge and in Onstatt Valley, and in Laguna Mountains at Campbell's ranch (5,500 feet), about 15 miles north of Mexican boundary.

The distribution in the Rocky Mountain region will be described in a future publication.

OCCURRENCE.

Lowest mountain slopes, ridges, benches, and borders of streams (most common), canyon bottoms; less frequent on dry hill slopes. Usually in fresh or moist, rich gravelly or rocky soils where it is largest; shrubby in dry, poor soils. Forms dense thickets of pure growth; often more or less scattered, singly or in clumps, with Douglas fir, red and mountain alders, aspen, black cottonwood, mountain maple, western serviceberry, bitter cherry, chinquapin brush, and occasionally yellow pine.

CLIMATIC CONDITIONS.—Similar to those of red alder and aspen.

TOLERANCE.—Undetermined, but apparently intolerant of shade at any time, as shown by its slender stems and small crown in dense stands, where it struggles for top light.

REPRODUCTION.—Very abundant seeder nearly every year. Seedlings plentiful in moist litter, and advancing rapidly in old burns among willow-weed and low herbage.

Hollyleaf Cherry.

Prunus ilicifolia (Nutt.) Walpers.

DISTINGUISHING CHARACTERISTICS.

Hollyleaf cherry is the most distinct of Pacific cherries on account of its evergreen holly-like foliage (fig. 168). Locally known as "islay," "Spanish wild cherry," and "Mountain evergreen cherry."

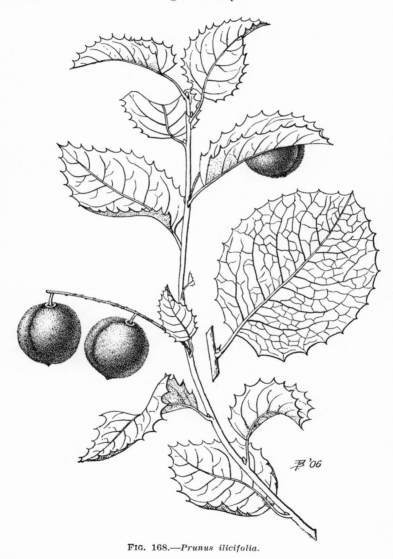

FIG. 168.—*Prunus ilicifolia.*

Most often a dense, prickly shrub from 2 to 4 feet high on dry, rocky slopes, but in sheltered canyons sometimes from 20 to 25 feet high and from 10 to 12 inches through; as a tree, more often about 10 feet high, with a very thickly branched crown and only a short trunk. The deep reddish-brown bark of large trunks is deeply furrowed and cut into little squarish divisions. The small twigs are smooth, reddish yellow to red brown. Mature leaves (fig. 168), thick, leathery, glossy deep green on their top sides, and much lighter green beneath; marginal teeth prickly. Leaves of a season's growth remain on the

FIG. 169.—*Prunus ilicifolia integrifolia.*

trees about two summers. The fruit (fig. 168), ripe from October to November, is a clear deep red, becoming red-purple and very dark with age; pulp exceedingly thin, tart, and palatable. The large, thin-shelled, pale yellowish stone prominently veiny. Ripe fruit is carried away by birds, which thus assist in disseminating the seed, and extensively eaten by mountain rodents, which cut the cherries from the branches and store them, thus also effecting considerable distribution and unintentional planting. Wood, exceedingly heavy, dense, fine-grained, tough, pale brown tinged with red, has only a very thin layer of sapwood. The heartwood is handsome and suitable for small ornamental woodwork, but not known to be used. A useful chaparral on steep, dry slopes.

LONGEVITY.—Not fully determined. From records, however, of trees planted in southern California nearly a century ago, and now 10 to 12 inches in diameter, it is estimated that this cherry may attain at least 100 years and still be growing. Its early growth in height in moist, rich soils is surprisingly rapid. A forest-grown tree 6⅝ inches in diameter showed an age of 56 years.

A very distinct variety of this species, *Prunus ilicifolia integrifolia* [a] Sudworth, inhabits California mainland and coast islands (off Santa Barbara), especially Santa Catalina, and also San Julio Canyon, Lower California. It differs from the species in having entire or, rarely, spiny margined leaves (fig. 169), longer flower clusters, and larger, more fleshy fruit. It becomes a small tree also, but its wood appears to be of considerably lighter weight than that of the species. It may possibly prove to be a distinct species.

RANGE.

California (from San Francisco Bay through the coast ranges, also on western slopes of San Bernardino Mountains and on Santa Cruz and Santa Rosa islands) to Lower California (San Julio Canyon).

OCCURRENCE.

Low mountain and high foothill slopes and plains, canyon sides and bottoms; in dry, rocky or gravelly soils (shrubby), but preferring moist sandy soil (largest). Forms clumps and small patches mingled with chaparral brush (species of *Ceanothus, Rhus laurina, R. ovata, Quercus dumosa, Arctostaphylos, Adenostoma, Yucca*).

CLIMATIC CONDITIONS.—Similar to those of big-cone spruce.

TOLERANCE.—Very tolerant of shade.

REPRODUCTION.—Abundant periodic seeder. Seedlings most frequent in moist bottoms of gulches and canyons where seed is covered by litter and washed soil. Less abundant and scattered on dry slopes, where seed lodged in pockets or buried by rodents affords reproduction.

OCCURRENCE.

Prunus ilicifolia integrifolia.—Similar to hollyleaf cherry. Silvical and climatic requirements undetermined; probably very like those of latter tree, but notably less aggressive. Requires further study.

Family LEGUMINOSÆ.

A very large family, containing such well-known trees and shrubs as locusts, acacias or "mimosa-trees," as well as a vast number of herbaceous plants, such as beans, peas, and clovers, which comprise some of the most important food and forage plants in the world. The trees supply heavy, strong, durable woods of excellent commercial qualities, while a number of them are notable because they produce mature timber in a remarkably few years. They are, therefore, important forest trees, particularly for artificial planting.

According to the structure of their flowers and fruits they are technically divided into several subfamilies. As popularly characterized here, however, they can usually be recognized by the compound form of their leaves (simple

---

[a] Miss Alice Eastwood has proposed for this variety, which she holds to be a species, the name "*Prunus Lyoni* n. nom" (Handbook of the Trees of California, 54 1905), citing as a synonym "*Prunus integrifolia* Sargent," a name which, by the common law of priority, must stand in place of Miss Eastwood's *Prunus lyoni*, should this variety be raised to the rank of a species. Lyon originally referred specimens of this tree to *P. occidentalis* Swartz, which was later shown to be a different species, leaving the California tree without a name. The writer regrets exceedingly now that in naming this cherry (Gard & For., IV, 51, 1891) he did not dedicate it to Mr. Lyon, who first brought the tree to light.

in only one genus of our trees). These consist of a prominent central stem which either directly gives off a number of pairs of rounded or pointed leaves (leaflets) along its two opposite sides or gives off branches and subbranches which in turn bear their leaves in this way. The central stem corresponds morphologically with the midveins of simple leaves, such as those of maples and oaks, and when shed in autumn parts from the twigs just as in these latter trees. Leguminous trees are further and most distinctly characterized by their beans, or bean-like fruit pods, all matured in one season, some of which resemble ordinary garden peas and beans and some of which have jointed or twisted pods in which each seed is separated from its fellows by intervening constrictions; while in some members the fruit is structurally a bean-pod, but unlike ordinary ones in containing but a single seed, this, however, bean-like in shape. Flowers of many members of this family are pea-like or bean-like and combine male (pollen bearing) and female (seed bearing) organs, or the organs of one sex are suppressed and the flowers are male or female only. They are borne on different parts of the same tree or branch or on different trees. In one section of Leguminosæ the flowers (bisexual in each blossom) bear no resemblance to pea or bean flowers, but appear like bristling, stiff, yellow, white, red, or pink threads, arranged in ball-like or cylindrical bodies.

PROSOPIS. MESQUITES.

The mesquites form a group of small or medium-sized trees and shrubs, all of which inhabit subtropical or tropical countries, with few representatives in the United States. Their wood is heavy, very hard, strong, durable, and of considerable local economic use; but on account of the small size and poor timber form of the trees it is of only secondary and limited commercial importance.

They are characterized usually by their 2-forked, sometimes 4-forked leaf stems, with from 5 to 20 or more pairs of small leaflets and often a pair of slender keen spines at the base of the bud from which the leaf stems grow. At the base of the main leaf stem and of its forks minute glands (dots) are usually found. The leaves are shed every autumn. Flowers (bisexual), minute and densely arranged in long cylindrical clusters (in our species), with slender stems from buds on twigs of the previous year's growth. Fruit, a long slender, and flat bean-like pod (fig. 171), or a cylindrical, spirally marked pod (fig. 170), neither of which opens of its own accord to liberate its smooth, small hard beans, each of which lies in a separate cell of the pod. The seeds depend for their distribution upon flood-waters and upon cattle and other animals which feed upon them and thus assist in disseminating and sometimes in planting them. Seeds do not, however, germinate except when covered by or placed in contact with continuously moist soil. The ripe, dried pods, made into coarse flour, have long been used for food by southwestern Indians and Mexicans. Two species and two well-marked varieties occur in southwestern United States and adjacent territory on the south.

Screwpod Mesquite.

Prosopis odorata [a] Torrey and Fremont.

DISTINGUISHING CHARACTERISTICS.

Sometimes a short-trunked tree from 15 to 20 feet high, and from 3 to 8 (rarely 10 to 12) inches in diameter, but usually shrubby, with numerous stems; bark of large trunks pale reddish brown, shaggy with loose strips. Year-old twigs

---

[a] The technical name maintained by other writers is *Prosopis pubescens* Bentham (1846); *Prosopis odorata* T. and F. was published in 1845 and is clearly entitled to recognition on the ground of being the first name applied to this tree, except for the

are hoary with more or less dense, minute hairs. A pair of sharp spines marks the point from which one or two 2-forked leaf stems issue; each spine bears from 5 to 8 pairs of small, whitish-hairy leaflets (fig. 170). The greenish,

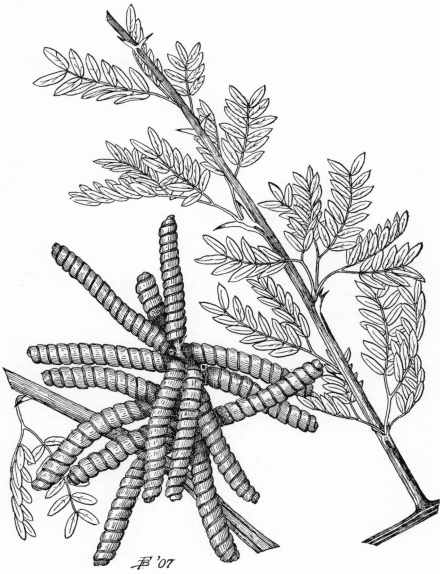

FIG. 170.—*Prosopis odorata.*

inodorous flowers bloom from spring to late summer, producing successive crops of pods. Mature pods, pale yellow, cylindrical, spirally twisted (fig.

---

unfortunate fact that the authors of it give in their description and plate characters of both *Prosopis juliflora* DC. and of the screwpod mesquite. It is probable that a foliage and flowering branch of the former was used, with fruit of the latter species. There is

170)—a most distinctive character—and containing from about 10 to 20 small, smooth, hard seeds (fig. 170). Wood, pale yellowish brown and otherwise similar in its qualities, including weight, to that of the succeeding species.

LONGEVITY.—Age limits not determined. Trees from 6 to 8 inches in diameter are approximately from 50 to 75 years old, while the larger trees found occasionally are estimated to be from 100 to 150 years old.

RANGE.

Western Texas (valley of Rio Grande, from Devils River to El Paso) ; west through New Mexico, Arizona, southern borders of Utah and Nevada to California (arid region of Colorado basin to San Diego County) ; northern Mexico.

OCCURRENCE.

Desert river bottoms, waterholes, and canyons ; in dry sandy, loamy, or gravelly soils. Forms close and open, often nearly pure stands, but frequently with mesquite.

CLIMATIC CONDITIONS.—Similar to those of hackberry (*Celtis reticulata*).

TOLERANCE.—Endures very little shade at any stage.

REPRODUCTION.—Very abundant seeder. Large quantities of pods infested by grubs. Seedlings sparse in exposed places, but frequent in sheltered canyon bottoms and valleys where seeds have been well covered by washed soil.

Mesquite.

Prosopis juliflora glandulosa [a] (Torr.) Sargent.

DISTINGUISHING CHARACTERISTICS.

The shrub and tree commonly called "mesquite," which ranges from eastern Texas to Utah and Colorado and southwestward into southern California, Lower

---

enough in the description to unmistakably point to the screwpod mesquite as the plant for which the name *Prosopis odorata* was intended, and there is absolutely no doubt that the fruit figured is of this tree. By all past and present usages among just authors there is every reason for and great justice to Torrey and Fremont in taking up their name and only the most trivial pretext for preceding it by a later name. *Prosopis juliflora* DC., with which it was confounded, in part, by these authors, had long previously (1825) been published, so that whatever of Torrey and Fremont's description applies to that tree is synonymous. There still remains the incontrovertible fact that these authors' plate, at least, contains separate and distinct figures belonging unmistakably, the fruit to the screwpod mesquite, and the flowers and foliage to the common mesquite. The very common and unassailable practice of all taxonomists, in dealing with composite species of this type, is to maintain the name given for the plant which was new when the author dealt with the plants ; while in a case where one name has been applied to two plants new at the time, the usage is to apply the name given to one of these plants and to rename the other. One recent case of this kind is of interest here. *Betula occidentalis* Hooker includes, in part, a birch native of northwestern Washington and southwestern British Columbia, and the red barked birch of a more eastern range. Only lately it was discovered that these two species were really included. *Betula occidentalis* Hooker was, therefore, at once taken for the northwestern tree, because the first part of Hooker's description applied to that tree, the latter part to the red barked birch, to which a new name, *Betula fontinalis* Sargent, was very properly given. The fact that the description was divided gives no more support for this procedure than is afforded in the case of the plate of *Prosopis odorata* T. and F., the figures of which are distinctly separated, and in reality present a simpler case, because the plant of one figure has already been named *Prosopis juliflora* DC. The possible argument against maintaining *P. odorata* T. and F. because it must be cited as a synonym, in part, of *P. juliflora* DC., applies equally well, if need be, against maintaining *Betula occidentalis* Hooker, which must also be cited as a synonym, in part, of *B. fontinalis* Sargent.

The writer's act in thus disposing of composite species is believed to rest firmly upon the universal law of priority which does full justice to every discoverer.

[a] This variety is Torrey's *Prosopis glandulosa* (1828) supposed by him to be a distinct species, one of the characters of which given being the minute glands (dots) at the base of the main leaf stem and its forks : characters now known to be present on the leaves of all species of Prosopis. In relating this tree as a variety to *Prosopis juliflora* DC., Torrey's specific name must of course be retained, although it refers to an indistinctive character.

California, and Mexico, is most perplexing in its characters. What may be called *Prosopis juliflora* (Sw.) DC., inhabiting western and eastern Texas and commonly a shrub with many stocky stems from a very large rootstock, or sometimes a short-trunked low tree, may be distinguished fairly well by its 15 or 20 pairs of much-crowded, very narrow, smooth leaflets, one-third to about one-half inch long, and by the smooth outer parts (calyx) of its flowers. Diverging from this plant are two varieties which appear distinct in their extreme forms, but which are more or less directly connected with the species through intervening transitional forms. While taxonomically it is important, for the sake of exactness, to trace and define these varieties, the main excuse for doing so here is in the possible forest value one or both of these varieties may possess.

One variety, *Prosopis juliflora velutina* (Woot.) Sargent, is a tree from 30 to 40 feet high and from 12 to 20 inches through, inhabiting dry valleys of southern Arizona and the State of Sonora, Mexico. It is the largest of our species. The leaf stems, their branches, and the 12 to 24 pairs of small, narrow, crowded leaflets are gray-hairy; outer parts (calyx) of the flowers minutely hairy.

The other variety, *Prosopis juliflora glandulosa* (Torr.) Sargent, the mesquite with which this manual is directly concerned, inhabits southern California, extending into Lower California and Mexico, thence eastward to eastern Texas and northward into southern Kansas. This is a shrub or small short-trunked tree from 15 to 20 feet high, and from 6 to 10 inches or more through, with a rounded crown of arched or drooping branches. The leaf stems, their branches, and the 6 to 60 pairs of narrow leaflets are generally smooth, the leaflets usually being distant from each other (but not infrequently crowded) and one-fourth inch to nearly 2 inches long (fig. 171). Outer parts (calyx) of the flowers smooth. This is the most reliable distinctive character, but it is not invariable, since these parts are sometimes minutely hairy. The fragrant yellow-green flowers are produced from about May to July. Mature pods (fig. 171) yellowish, 3 to 9 inches long (usually 4 to 6 inches) by one-fourth to about one-half an inch wide, somewhat flat but plump; very flat and thin at first, narrowed between the 6 to 20 seeds; pulp about seeds, which are pale brown, shiny and hard, is sweet and edible. Woods of the two varieties and species are indis-tinguishable; usually a deep red-brown, dense, close-grained, very hard and heavy, but somewhat brittle; exceedingly durable under all sorts of exposure; sapwood very thin and lemon yellow. It has many important local economic uses for building, cabinet work, and fuel in regions where it is practically the only available hardwood, while the wood of the enormously developed roots also supplies fuel. Only its small size and poor timber form prevent the wood from being of wider commercial importance.

For the forester mesquite is the most interesting and important tree of the arid Southwest, where through the phenomenal growth of its huge deep roots it defies drought conditions which kill other trees. Development of its enormous roots appears to be out of all proportion to the often insignificant stems above ground, and is a subject for most profitable and interesting investigation. As a rule, however, the larger the stem above ground, the smaller the root develop-ment; low, shrubby stems commonly have huge taproots descending to water at a depth of 50 or 60 feet or more.

A remarkable fact concerning the root wood is that it is heavier than wood from the trunk. The wood of both roots and trunk contains nearly as much tannin as ordinary tanbarks. A clear, yellowish gum exudes from the trunks when they are wounded. This hardens with exposure, and has the mucilaginous qualities of gum arabic, as a substitute for which it is sometimes used.

Longevity.—The life limits of mesquite, below and above ground, have not been worked out fully, but the tree is unquestionably long-lived, though of

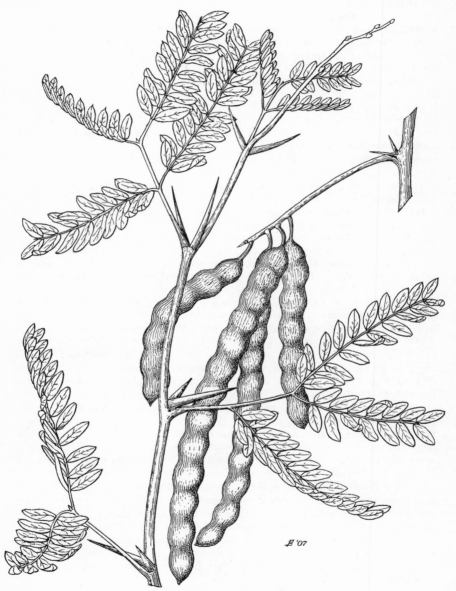

Fig. 171.—*Prosopis juliflora glandulosa.*

exceedingly slow growth. Trunks from 10 to 12 inches in diameter are from 100 to 125 years old, while the larger trunks occasionally found are likely to be very much older.

Eastern Texas to southern Kansas and southward into northern Mexico. Reappearing in Arizona, southern California, and Lower California.

OCCURRENCE.

Desert plains, valleys, mesas, and canyons, under soil and climatic conditions like those of screwpod, to which it is also similar in silvical characteristics.

CERCIS. JUDAS TREES.

Cercis forms a group of small trees and shrubs popularly known as red-buds or Judas trees. It contains about 7 species, which occur in parts of Asia, Europe, and North America. All of the 3 species of this continent are trees, one inhabiting eastern United States, one Texas and Mexico, and one California. The eastern and southwestern species are the largest of our representatives. They have dense, hard, brown, heavy woods, but are commercially unimportant trees, chiefly because of their small size and rather rare occurrence. Several are highly prized, and are much planted as ornamental trees on account of their bright rose-colored, pea-like flowers, which cover the branches with a brilliant flame of color in early spring, before the leaves appear. The eastern species grows in moist, rich forests, while the western ones often inhabit dry, poor, rocky, and exposed situations. The thickish, single-bladed, heart-shaped leaves have from 3 to 5 prominent veins, and are shed in autumn. The fruit, ripe in autumn, is a very thin and flat bean-like pod with small, brown, hard, bean-like seeds.

California Red-bud.

Cercis occidentalis Torrey.

DISTINGUISHING CHARACTERISTICS.

California red-bud is not generally regarded as a tree, but it occasionally grows to tree size in sheltered places, and then has a single, smooth, grayish trunk from 10 to 12 feet high and from 2 to 3 inches through. Much more frequently, however, it grows in dense clumps with slender stems from 2 to 4 feet high. The small, pea-shaped flowers (fig. 172) are a clear magenta color. Mature leaves (fig. 172), smooth throughout (as are the twigs and branches). In autumn the twigs and branches often bear many clusters of pointed, flat, very thin, russet-brown pods (fig. 172) ; in ripening, the pods are first purple. Wood, fine-grained, dark yellowish brown, with a rather thin layer of whitish sapwood. Of no economic or domestic use.

It is worthy of the forester's notice only for its aid, with other foothill brush, in forming a scanty cover along dry, rocky borders of streams.

LONGEVITY.—Undetermined.

RANGE.

CALIFORNIA.—Along streams from Mendocino County and the region about Mount Shasta southward to San Diego County.

OCCURRENCE.

Borders of foothill streams, low mountain slopes and canyons, in dry, or rather dry, gravelly and rocky soils. Grows singly and in shrubby clumps interspersed with California buckeye, ceanothus, manzanita, and other chaparral brush in gray pine belt ; tree forms occur in sheltered situations.

CLIMATIC CONDITIONS.—Similar to those of gray pine.

TOLERANCE.—Endures a good deal of shade in early life and light shade when older; tolerance appears greater with increased soil moisture.

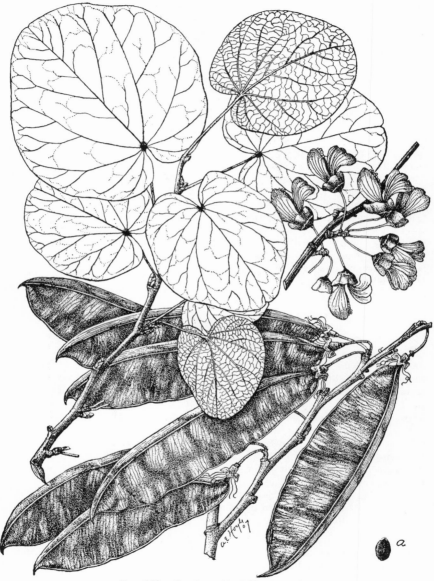

FIG. 172.—*Cercis occidentalis: a,* seed.

REPRODUCTION.—Plentiful seeder. Seed of high rate of germination (60 to 70 per cent), but tardy; vitality persistent. Young plants frequent in crevices, pockets, and little benches where seed has been well covered with mineral soil.

ACACIA.

Acacia is a very large group of widely distributed, world-famous trees, shrubs, and herbaceous plants. Over 400 species are known in different parts of the Old and New World, three-fourths of them in Australia. About a dozen trees and shrubs occur in the southwestern United States and adjacent territory. The group now contains fewer representatives than formerly, a number of acacia-like members having been classed under related genera. Several leguminous trees, such as the locusts (*Gleditsia*) and others, are popularly called acacias, but technically they are not true acacias. It is exceedingly difficult to find characters by which acacias may be popularly distinguished from other closely related groups, which are technically separated mainly by such inconspicuous characters as the structure of their flowers.

True acacias have astringent bark, which in some cases is very valuable for tanning. When punctured, the trunk exudes a mucilaginous gum. The gum of some foreign species is known in commerce as gum arabic. The true leaf is compound, comprising one main stem with 2 to 3 pairs of small side branches which bear several or many pairs of opposite tiny leaflets.[a] Leaves of our acacias are shed every year. Their twigs have one or two keen spines (sometimes long and straight, and sometimes short and curved), commonly at points where leaves or flower stems grow (fig. 173). When there are two spines they form a pair. Flowers minute, often arranged in bright colored, slender, single-stemmed balls, or in long, single-stemmed cylindrical clusters. An important technical distinction is that the flowers, each of which usually combines both male (pollen bearing) and female (fruit bearing) organs, have more than 50 of the bristly, usually bright yellow, thread-like organs (stamens) protruding from the flower body; each stamen is entirely or practically separate from its fellows. Divisions of the inner flower cup (petals) are united into a cup or divided above and united at their bases (rarely, entirely separated). The fruit pods, bean-like, are flat or full and rounded when mature, straight, but in our species commonly twisted or crumpled, and their hard, smooth seeds usually bear an oval or circular depression on each of their broad surfaces, an important distinctive mark. They are all peculiarly adapted to growth, usually very rapid, in poor dry soils and in hot or warm climates. As a rule, our native acacias are little more than chaparral brush; they are too rarely trees to be of economic importance.

Acacias are of ancient origin, many species having existed in an early geologic period.

Only two of the dozen species indigenous in our Southwest, together with one naturalized species, are trees, and only one of these occurs within the Pacific region.

Cats Claw.

Acacia greggii Gray.

DISTINGUISHING CHARACTERISTICS.

Cats claw receives its name from the keen hooked spines on its twigs (fig. 173). Very often it is only a low shrub, but usually it is a short-trunked, much-branched tree from 10 to 20 feet high and from 6 to 8 inches through; occasionally it is somewhat taller and thicker. The angled twigs are minutely hairy and

---

[a] Some exotic acacias produce simple, leaf-like organs (phyllodia) which are morphologically only leaf stems dilated into the form of a simple leaf blade.

light reddish brown.   Mature leaves (fig. 173) grow singly and alternately from
the young twigs, but one or two issue at a point on older twigs; the 3-nerved
leaflets (fig. 173) are more or less hoary with minute hairs.   The pods (fig. 173)
ripen in August, when they are pale brown, containing flat, shiny, deep brown,
almost circular seeds—a most important character.   The pods usually remain

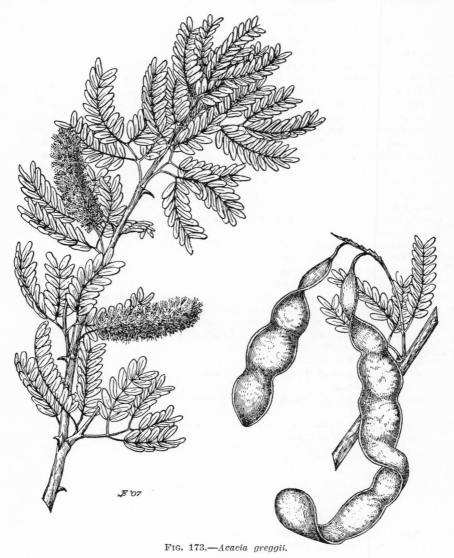

FIG. 173.—*Acacia greggii.*

on the branches for from six to eight months.   Wood, dull red-brown, dense,
heavy, hard, and with a thin layer of lemon-yellow sapwood.   Not known to be
used for any economic purpose, probably because of the scarcity of sizable trees,
but it has economic value on account of its good quality and its durability.

Ability to thrive in the driest and poorest soils renders it worthy of the forester's attention, though the cover it affords is open and scanty.

LONGEVITY.—Not fully determined. A tree 8½ inches in diameter showed an age of 49 years.

RANGE.

From Western Texas (Rio Grande) through southern New Mexico and Arizona to southern California.

OCCURRENCE.

Borders of low desert mountain streams, in low canyons, on benches, and mesas; in dry, gravelly soils. Similar otherwise in occurrence, climatic, and silvical requirements to mesquite. Seeding habits and reproduction undetermined.

PARKINSONIA.

The Parkinsonias form a small group of shrubby or low trees of little forest or economic importance. They are characterized by smooth, thin bark; the twigs have one or three pronged sharp spines, or are themselves spine-like and sharp; and the very thin foliage is composed of clusters of long or very short two-forked leaf-stems (forking close to the twig), each of which bears from five to thirty pairs of very small leaflets (fig. 174). The small, showy, yellow flowers (each with male or female organs) are borne in long or short, exceedingly slender branched clusters (the bottom flowers opening first), and bloom from spring to late summer. The fruit matured during one season is a pointed cylindrical pod (fig. 175), jointed by constrictions between the seeds and conspicuously striped longitudinally; 1 to 8 hard, smooth, brownish seeds in each pod.

Wood, dense, fine-grained, brown or yellowish brown, hard, and moderately heavy. Small size of the trees renders the wood of little economic use.

They are little known, but should prove worthy of attention on account of their ability to thrive in hot situations, one species particularly in dry, arid places. Grazing animals browse extensively upon the twigs.

The group comprises but three species, two of which occur in southwestern United States and within the Pacific region; a third species is African.

Horse-bean; Ratama.

Parkinsonia aculeata Linnæus.

DISTINGUISHING CHARACTERISTICS.

The horse-bean is a short-trunked, smooth-barked tree from 15 to 25 feet high and from 4 to 8 inches through, with thin, willowy, drooping or arched branches. The thin bark is reddish brown. Year-old twigs are greenish and very minutely hairy, later becoming smooth and grayish or reddish yellow; older parts of the branches bear from 1 to 3 pronged, long, keen spines at the joints, from which issue 1 or 2 pairs of very long (6 to 18 inches), flat leaf-stems (each pair attached to the branch by a very short, spine-pointed stem). Each stem bears from 20 to 30 pairs of extremely small, scale-like leaflets (fig. 174). A most interesting morphological feature in the development of the spines is that when they first appear on young twigs they are the short basal parts (spine-tipped) of the leaf stems, from which are given off 1 or 2 pairs of flat leaflet-bearing branches. These branches are later shed, as the spine grows, leaving on its sides conspicuous scars. The fragrant yellow flowers, three-fourths inch to 1 inch broad, and on very slender branched stems, bloom from spring throughout the summer; upper central division of each blossom red-dotted inside (fig. 174). Mature pods (fig. 174), yellowish brown, from 2 to 6 inches long, longitudinally veined, and with 1 to 8 seeds. Wood

FIG. 174.—*Parkinsonia aculeata: a,* seed.

of the horse-bean is pale brown; yellowish sapwood thick; not used for any commercial purpose.

Longevity.—Not fully determined. A tree 7 inches in diameter was 24 years old.

Texas (lower Rio Grande) ; Arizona and California (in valley of Colorado River) ; northern Mexico and Lower California.

About lagoons (Colorado River Valley) ; in rich, wet silt or mud. Scattered singly or in groups.

Climatic Conditions.—Similar to those of mesquites. Nothing is known of its tolerance and reproduction.

Little-leaf Horse-bean.

Parkinsonia microphylla Torrey.

DISTINGUISHING CHARACTERISTICS.

So far as can be discovered, this tree, which is generally shrubby, has no field name, probably because it is not recognized by laymen as a relative of the preceding species. For want of a better one, "little-leaf horse-bean," coined from the technical name, is proposed.

At best 15 or 20 feet high, with a short trunk from 6 to 10 inches through ; very often only a shrub from 3 to 6 feet high, with numerous stems. The crown is always intricately branched, and the limbs are armed with many short, stiff, spine-pointed twigs. Bark of branches and trunk smooth and pale reddish yellow ; the greenish twigs are densely covered at first with minute woolly hairs, most of which disappear by autumn. The pale yellow flowers, borne in short, delicate, branched clusters, appear before the leaves in late spring from minute buds on thorny twigs formed the previous year (fig. 175) ; upper central division of the flower, white. The minutely hairy leaves (fig. 175) appear in early summer, but fall shortly after reaching maturity, so that the twigs, as ordinarily seen in middle or late summer, are bare, save for clusters of striped pods (fig. 175), which commonly remain on the branches until the following spring. The pods contain from 1 to 3 (as a rule, 2) seeds. Wood, very dense, fine-grained, hard, deep yellowish brown, often mottled and streaked with dull red ; a large part of the stem is yellowish sapwood. Sizable trees are so rare as to render the wood of no commercial or domestic use.

Owing to its shrubby, leafless form and generally rare occurrence, it can hardly prove of any importance to the forester, even though it thrives in the hottest and most arid situations.

Longevity.—Not fully determined. One tree $9\frac{5}{8}$ inches in diameter showed an age of 50 years.

Southern Arizona (desert region) ; southern California (desert region adjoining Arizona ; Lower California (adjoining California) ; Mexico (Sonora).

Desert hill slopes; in gravelly and rocky dry soils.   Scattered singly and in small groups.

CLIMATIC CONDITIONS.—Similar to those of leather-leaf ash (*Fraxinus coriacea*).

FIG. 175.—*Parkinsonia microphylla: a,* seed.

TOLERANCE.—Decidedly intolerant of shade.

REPRODUCTION and other silvical characteristics undetermined; fairly abundant seeder.

CERCIDIUM.

Cercidium forms a small group of low, shrubby, thorny, green-barked trees, somewhat similar in habits and form to the Parkinsonias, with which our

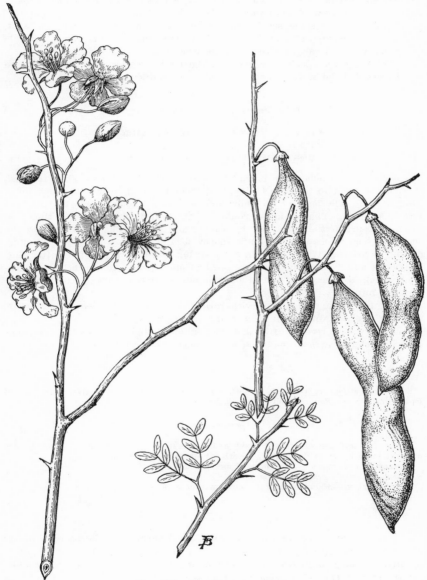

FIG. 176.—*Cercidium torreyanum.*

three southwestern species were once, and by some authorities still are, combined. The 2-forked leaf-stems with few pairs of very small leaflets, and the yellow, similarly clustered flowers are closely similar to those of *Parkinsonia microphylla*. Cercidium is best distinguished by the flat, unconstricted pods, which are more like bean fruits than the round, jointed pods of *Parkinsonia*. This, together with some minor structural differences in the flowers, make it desirable to maintain *Cercidium* as distinct from *Parkinsonia*. Like the latter, trees of this group are desert-loving shrubs and trees. For this reason they are of some service to the forester, since they form persistent, though thin, chaparral in arid places. The moderately heavy, hard wood is occasionally used locally for fuel, but not otherwise.

One of the three species occurring in the United States (two of which are small trees and the other a shrub) inhabits the southern Pacific region.

Palo Verde; Green-bark Acacia.

Cercidium torreyanum (Wats.) Sargent.

DISTINGUISHING CHARACTERISTICS.

Green-barked acacia is a much-branched, generally leafless, short-trunked, thorny tree from 15 to 25 feet high, and from 10 to 15 inches through; sometimes larger. The bark of all limbs and of young trunks is smooth and light yellowish green. That of large trunks is light brown with a reddish tinge; on the lower part of the trunk lightly seamed and scaly. The somewhat zig-zag, smooth, green twigs (fig. 176) are thorny at the angles. The pale, minutely downy leaves (fig. 176) appear in early spring, but fall very shortly after they reach full size. Since the pods are shed in midsummer, the branches, as generally seen, are therefore bare, though a few scattered leaves occasionally remain in autumn.

Wood, pale yellowish brown with rather thick sapwood; heavy, but brittle and cuts easily. Not known to have any economic use.

LONGEVITY.—No records of its age are available. Judging from the persistent slow diameter growth of small stems, it appears to be long-lived.

RANGE.

Southern California (Colorado Desert) and Arizona (lower Gila River Valley) and south into Mexico (Sonora) and Lower California.

OCCURRENCE.

Sides of desert canyons, about sinks and depressions in arid sandhills, and on dry washes; in rocky or sandy ground. Scattered singly and in small groups.

CLIMATIC CONDITIONS.—Like those of mesquites.

TOLERANCE.—Intolerant of shade.

REPRODUCTION.—Abundant seeder; reproduction undetermined.

DALEA.

The genus *Dalea* contains a large number of shrubs and herbaceous plants and but one tree species. The tree occurs in our southwest. Most of the representatives belong to Mexico and South America. Foliage marked with minute glandular dots (fig. 177). The small blossoms, which resemble pea flowers in general appearance, combine male (pollen bearing) and female (fruit bearing) organs. Fruit, a small one-seeded pod, which adheres unopened to the kidney-shaped seed. Of no economic or forest importance.

Indigo Bush.

Dalea spinosa Gray.

DISTINGUISHING CHARACTERISTICS.

Mostly a spiny-twigged, small, much-branched shrub; sometimes a very short and thick trunked, bushy tree from 12 to 18 feet high and from 8 to 12 inches

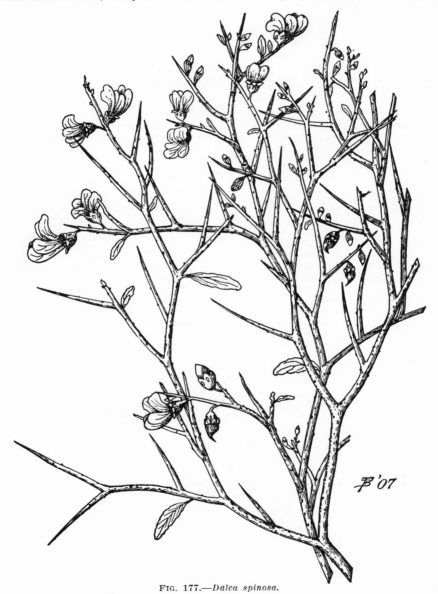

Fig. 177.—*Dalea spinosa.*

in diameter—occasionally thicker. The trunk is usually twisted or gnarled, and the rather large limbs, as well as numerous slender, needle-like twigs, trend upward strongly. Gray or whitish throughout, especially the limbs and twigs, which are more or less coated with very minute white down. The trunk bark of large trees is deeply and narrowly seamed, hard and rough, with small scales. Very few leaves (fig. 177) are produced, and these, white-downy and gland-dotted, are shed soon after reaching mature size, so that the tree or shrub commonly appears leafless. Flowers deep indigo blue (hence the name " indigo bush "), the outer basal covering of the blossoms (calyx) 10-ribbed, with a glandular spot between each of the six upper ribs. The calyx adheres to the small beaked, one-seeded pod (fig. 177), which is also gland-dotted. The shiny, light brown, kidney-shaped seeds are mottled with dark brown.

Wood, rich chocolate brown, with a thin layer of sapwood; moderately wide-grained, soft, and rather light. Not used for any purpose.

LONGEVITY.—Not fully determined. A tree 11¾ inches in diameter showed an age of 40 years.

RANGE.

Southern California (Colorado Desert—at Agua Caliente and Toras) and eastward into Arizona (to lower Gila River) ; south into adjacent Mexico (Sonora) and Lower California (to Calamujuet).

OCCURRENCE.

Desert plains in dry rocky or gravelly soil. Scattered and in small groups.
CLIMATIC CONDITIONS.—Similar to those of mesquite.
TOLERANCE.—Requires full light.
REPRODUCTION.—Seed production rather small. Seedlings sparse and in washed mineral soil.

OLNEYA.

Olneya is a genus confined to arid parts of our southwest and containing but one species which enters the Pacific region. Characters of the genus are given under the following species.

Mexican Ironwood.[a]

Olnea tesota Gray.

DISTINGUISHING CHARACTERISTICS.

Olnea tesota is commonly called " ironwood " in the United States on account of its cross-grained, exceedingly heavy, hard wood. To avoid confusion, the name " western ironwood " is proposed. " Ironwood " was applied to several eastern hard-wooded trees long before this species was discovered.

A short, thick-trunked, bushy tree from 15 to 20 feet high and from 8 to 12 inches in diameter; sometimes of larger diameter. Green-gray throughout its crown of thick, upright limbs and spiny twigs, and with thin, deep red-brown flaky bark. Thorny twigs (fig. 178), at first densely covered with minute, close hairs, which gradually disappear with age. One or a pair of thorns, which fall off in about their second year, grow from just below the leaf-stems; the latter bear from 7 to 15 white-hairy leaflets (fig. 178), in pairs, except the terminal one. The leaves, partly evergreen, remain on the twigs from one spring to another, falling as the succeeding foliage appears. The purplish, small flowers, appearing with the new leaves, resemble pea-blossoms, and grow in short, small, hairy clusters. Mature pods (fig. 178), ripe in late summer, are light russet brown and densely covered with close gland-tipped hairs; the thick, leathery

---

[a] Often called *arbol de hierro,* especially in Sonora, Mexico, where the tree was discovered in 1852.

halves of the pod, slow in splitting, open and liberate flattish, oval, shiny, russet brown, hard seeds. Unlike many other leguminous seeds, these grow rather quickly after they are planted.

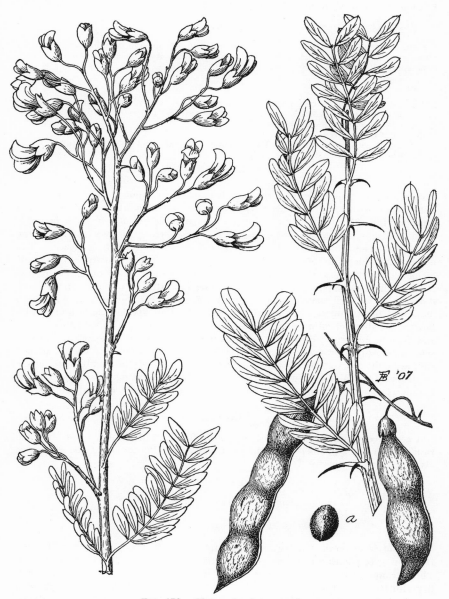

FIG. 178.—*Olneya tesota: a,* seed.

Wood, deep chocolate brown, mottled with red; sapwood, very narrow, lemon-yellow; exceedingly hard to split or to work. The short trunks yield but little clear wood, which serves only locally for fuel and for some minor purposes,

The ability of this tree to thrive in hot desert regions makes it worthy of attention for planting in arid, treeless localities within its climatic range.

LONGEVITY.—Not fully determined. Believed to be long-lived. A tree 8 inches in diameter showed an age of 77 years.

RANGE.

Southern California (from Colorado River south of Mohave Mountains) to southwestern Arizona and through adjacent Mexico (Sonora) and Lower California (between Comundee and Calamujuet).

OCCURRENCE.

Along desert water courses (especially intermittent streams), depressions, and washes in dry gravelly soil. Grows singly and in open patches, mingled sometimes with mesquite, palo verde, and desert shrubs.

CLIMATIC CONDITIONS.—Like those of mesquites.

TOLERANCE AND REPRODUCTION.—Undetermined ; appears decidedly intolerant.

Family CELASTRACEÆ.

Celastraceæ comprises a large number of trees and shrubs widely distributed over the world. The North American representatives are small and unimportant. The popularly best-known groups of this family include the ornamental shrubs and bushy trees known as spindle-trees (*Evonymus*), and the woody climber "bittersweet" (*Celastrus*) of eastern North America. The characters which relate members of this family are drawn entirely from their inconspicuous flowers, the distinctions in which are not easily observed by laymen. Simple distinctive characteristics are wanting. In some species the flowers—which are usually small and inconspicuous—are perfect, with both male and female organs in the same flower ; in other species, male and female flowers are distinct on different parts of the same tree ; and in yet others, male and female flowers are each on separate trees. The fruit, ripened in one season, is berry-like or a dry capsule ; the evergreen or deciduous leaves, of one simple blade, may grow in pairs (one opposite another) or singly, alternately on different sides of the twigs. The one genus representing this family in the Pacific region is so unique in its characters as to be easily recognized.

CANOTIA.

A genus containing but one species of a limited and little-known southwestern range, including a small part of the Pacific region. Characters of the genus are given under this species.

Canotia.

Canotia holacantha Torrey.

DISTINGUISHING CHARACTERISTICS.

Canotia holacantha is a tree or shrub anomalous in its entire lack of leaves ; the thin green bark of its twigs seemingly performs the functions of leaves. This strange modification appears greatly to help the plant to endure the hot, dry climate of its range. At best, a shrubby tree from 15 to 20 feet high with a very short, stocky trunk from 4 to 6 inches through ; very occasionally, almost a foot in diameter. Greenish bark of the branches somewhat streaked, that of large trunks pale brown and seamed. Twigs very slender, round, tipped with a sharp point, growing singly from the branches, never in pairs (one opposite

another). Small short clusters of white (bisexual) flowers appear near the
ends of the spiny twigs (fig. 179), producing a dry woody capsule (fig. 179),
which splits open at the top, liberating the small winged seeds. Wood, heavy,

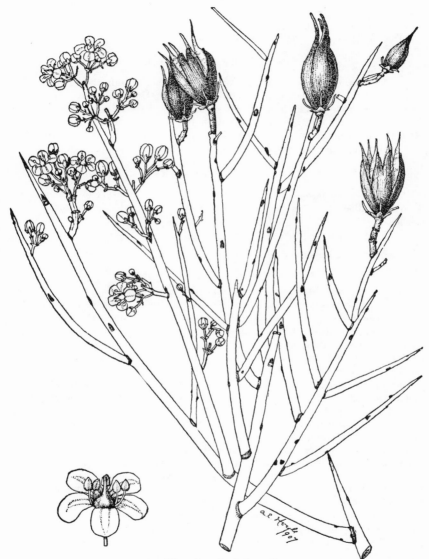

FIG. 179.—*Canotia holacantha.*

fine-grained, light rich brown, very hard. Not used for any purpose, chiefly
because of its rarity.

LONGEVITY.—Not fully determined. An exceptionally large tree 10 inches in
diameter showed an age of over 72 years.

RANGE.

Arizona (from White Mountain region to the Bill Williams (River) Fork) ; southern California (Providence Mountains).

OCCURRENCE.

Low mountain slopes, foothills, and mesas in dry gravelly soils. In groups and scattered among chaparral and occasional small desert trees.

CLIMATIC CONDITIONS (marked by high temperature) and silvical habits, etc., undetermined.

Family STERCULIACEÆ.

Sterculiaceæ contains a large number of genera, but these are mainly represented in tropical regions outside of the United States. The West Indian tree, from which chocolate of commerce is derived, is a member of this family, as is also the sycamore-leafed Sterculia, indigenous to China and so often planted for ornament in the frostless, warmer parts of the United States. One genus only, the following, belongs to this country.

FREMONTODENDRON.[a]

The genus *Fremontodendron* is represented by only one species, which is confined to California. The generic characters are included with those of its species.

Fremontia.

Fremontodendron californicum (Torr.) Coville.

DISTINGUISHING CHARACTERISTICS.

The commonest field name of *Fremontodendron californicum* is " slippery elm," which refers to the mucilaginous tough bark and twigs. These taste like those of the true slippery elm (*Ulmus pubescens*) of the East. It is also called " silver oak," because of the white undersurface of its leaves, and " leatherwood," because of its tough twigs and bark. All of these names, however, were used for eastern trees and shrubs long before they were applied to this California tree. Fremontia is desirable to avoid confusion.

Usually a small tree from 10 to 20 feet high, with a short trunk from 3 to 6 inches through and an open crown of wide-spreading limbs ; occasionally somewhat taller and with a thicker trunk. Very often, however, it is a much branched shrub, from 4 to 6 feet high, forming dense thickets with other foothill brush. The trunk bark is rough, deeply seamed, and blackish brown, sometimes reddish ; year-old twigs are smooth and pale reddish brown, and when young are densely covered with rust-colored down. Mature leaves (fig. 180), borne singly at a point on the twigs, are thick, veiny, rusty-downy beneath and more or less hairy above. The leaves of each season's growth remain on the twigs about two winters. Mature fruit (fig. 180), preceded by a bright yellow, rose-like flower, is a densely woolly 4 or 5 celled capsule, splitting open at its point when ripe in midsummer. The deep reddish brown small seeds are slowly shaken from the open pods by the wind or browsing animals. Wood, deep, often clear, reddish brown, fine-grained, dense, rather soft, cutting easily, and with a very thick layer of whitish sapwood. Not used for any economic or domestic purpose. Both tree and shrubby forms are of considerable service for the tenacious protective cover they form on dry rocky foothill slopes. Range cattle browse upon the twigs, which are very nutritious.

---

[a] Formerly written *Fremontia,* a generic name recently found to have been preoccupied for another group of plants, but which fortunately could be modified so as to retain its dedicatory reference to General J. C. Fremont, through whose early western explorations the one species representing this genus was discovered.

LONGEVITY.—Not fully determined. Two trees, respectively 5¼ and 3½ inches in diameter, were 43 and 39 years old.

RANGE.

California (from Mariposa) to Lower California.

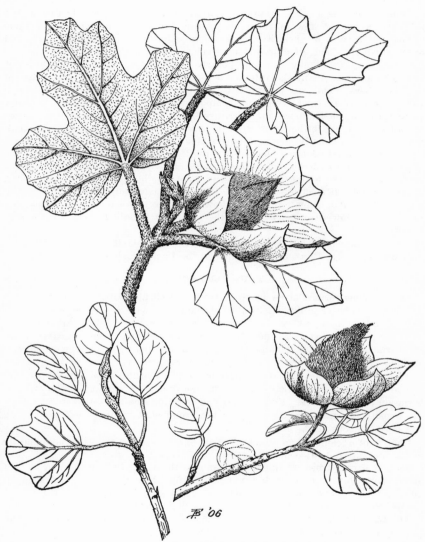

FIG. 180.—*Fremontodendron californicum.*

OCCURRENCE.

Lower mountain and higher foothill slopes and ridges; in dry, gravelly, and rocky soils. Forms extensive pure shrubby thickets, or groups (small trees) mingled with scrub oak, mountain mahogany, hollyleaf cherry, manzanita, ceanothus, and other chaparral brush. Largest on Sierra foothills.

CLIMATIC CONDITIONS.—Similar to those of gray pine.

TOLERANCE.—Appears capable of enduring considerable shade, but rarely subjected to it.

REPRODUCTION and silvical requirements undetermined; usually an abundant seeder. Seedlings grow in exposed mineral soil where seed has been covered by wash.

Family ANACARDIACEÆ.

Anacardiaceæ is a large group of small trees and shrubs, widely distributed over the world. A few of them are of some economic importance for their woods, but several of them are more valuable for their commercial gums and other products. The gum-producing species are, however, not indigenous to this country. Chief among our popularly known members are the sumachs. The juice of these plants is resinous, becoming sticky as it dries, while that of some members is violently poisonous to the human skin.[a] The leaves are simple (as in the garden "smoke-tree") or compound (subdivided into pairs of leaflets, as in the common staghorn sumach), are borne singly on the branches (never in pairs) and are either evergreen or are shed every autumn. The small flowers occur in usually large, dense, terminal clusters, and usually form large, dense, often bright-colored, masses of fruit. In some species, however, the clusters are thin and the fruits like berries. In some species male flowers are borne on one tree and the female flowers on another tree; in other species, some trees bear perfect flowers (each containing male and female organs), and some trees bear only male or female flowers, while in some cases one tree may bear perfect flowers mingled with either male or female flowers on separate twigs.

Four genera comprising the trees of this family are found in the United States, only one of which, *Rhus*, is represented in the Pacific region.

RHUS. SUMACHS.

The sumachs form a large group of trees and shrubs with a resinous—sometimes poisonous—or milky, sticky juice, large pithy twigs, and often large leaves (compound) with many pairs of pointed leaflets and an odd terminal leaflet; only one of our species with mainly simple, single-bladed leaves. Leaves of all are borne singly, never in pairs (one opposite another); those of most species are shed in autumn, but in one they are evergreen. The clusters of greenish flowers (in some cases large) are practically of separate sexes (by suppression or abortion of the male organs in one and the female organs in the other), each borne on different trees. Fruit, massed in large or small close clusters, spherical, smooth or hairy; coating thin; dry or somewhat resinous, and containing one hard, smooth seed.

Rhus is of ancient origin; remains of its extinct species are found abundantly in the Eocene and Miocene formations of Europe.

Several exotic trees of this group, among them the famous lacquer-tree of Japan and China, are exceedingly valuable for their commercial products of gum, wax, etc., and for their wood. Of the nearly 20 species native to the United States, none is of commercial importance, chiefly on account of their small size. The wood of most of our sumachs is, however, very rich and handsome in color and grain, and except for lack of size is very suitable for cabinet work. Five or six of these become small trees, and one of these inhabits the Pacific region.

---

[a]A saturated alcoholic solution of acetate of lead removes all trace of the poison if the inoculated skin is thoroughly washed with it immediately or within an hour after the contact. This solution is less effective a few hours after the poisoning takes place. Thorough washing of the poisoned skin with pure alcohol is also a preventive if applied within an hour after contact with the plant. Following either treatment the skin should be thoroughly washed with soap and water.

Mahogany Sumach.

Rhus integrifolia (Nutt.) Bentham and Hooker.

DISTINGUISHING CHARACTERISTICS.

The field name of mahogany sumach is simply "mahogany," and refers to the brilliant red color of its wood. To avoid confusion with the true mahogany

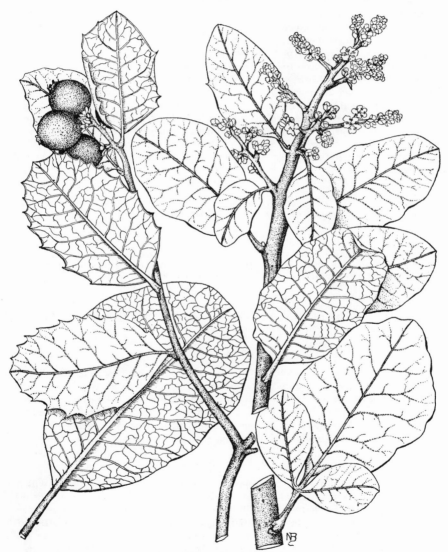

Fig. 181.—*Rhus integrifolia.*

(an unrelated tree, a native of Florida and adjacent islands), the name "mahogany sumach" is suggested.

A popularly little known evergreen species, occurring mainly as a very low bush producing dense thickets, and only occasionally and in protected places becoming a tree from 10 to 20 feet high, with a very short, stocky trunk from 8 to 15 inches through; sometimes taller and thicker. The crown, open and irregular, is composed of many wide-spreading limbs and stiff twigs. Year-old twigs are clear red-brown and more or less downy—densely so at first. Mature leaves (evergreen) are thick, leathery, usually of one simple blade (fig. 181); sometimes (compound) consisting of three leaflets (fig. 181); borders of leaves slightly curled toward the under side; smooth on their top sides, paler yellowish green beneath and somewhat downy on the veins and leaf stems. Leaves of one season's growth persist about two years. Mature fruit (fig. 181), ripe in late summer and few in number, is circular or oval in outline, flattish, and densely covered with deep red, fine down, the thin, sticky, resinous pulp covering a smooth, hard, pale brown stone (fig. 181). Wood red, heavy, hard; with very thin, light colored layer of sapwood. It is sometimes used locally for firewood, for which it is said to be very excellent. The beautiful, rich, red color and good working quality of the heartwood renders it suitable for small ornamental work.

The shrubby form is useful as an enduring chaparral cover on exposed seacoast sands, where few other shrubs are able to exist.

LONGEVITY.—Not fully determined. One tree 21½ inches in diameter showed an age of 62 years.

RANGE.

Coast of southern California (from Santa Barbara) to southern Lower California (Magdalena Bay); Santa Barbara and Cedros Islands.

OCCURRENCE.

Low mountain and foothill slopes, and on exposed seacoast bluffs; in dry sandy and gravelly soil; also in sheltered coves and gulches. Forms extensive dense thickets of pure growth (low shrub) in very exposed places; in groups or small patches as tree in protected sites; sometimes with *Rhus laurina*.

CLIMATIC CONDITIONS.—Similar to those of Torrey pine.

TOLERANCE.—Undetermined; probably very tolerant.

REPRODUCTION.—Abundant seeder. Seedlings frequent, sparsely distributed, or often very numerous where washing has covered seed.

Family ACERACEÆ.

This family consists mainly of trees, comprising such widely distributed and well-known economic and ornamental representatives as the maples, and also one Asiatic genus. Some of them are large, commercial forest trees, producing very useful timber, and the sap of several yields hard sugar, the making of which is an important North American industry. Further characters of the family are included under the following, its principal genus.

ACER. MAPLES.

The maples embrace all of our representatives of the family Aceraceæ, which, with the exception of box-elders or ash-leafed maples, are universally called maples. Maples are characterized by usually simple, single-bladed leaves (figs. 182 to 187) or by compound leaves with from 3 to 5 leaflets (fig. 188). Leaves of both types always occur in pairs on the twigs. The leaves of all maples are shed in autumn. The flowers, which appear before, with, or after the leaves, are, in some representatives, male (by abortion of female organs) or are female (by abortion of male organs), each kind being borne on separate trees; in other cases, blossoms of these types occur on different parts of the same tree

FIG. 182.—*Acer macrophyllum.*

or branch. They are not often perfectly bisexual, or strictly of one sex and borne on separate trees. It happens, therefore, that not all trees are seed bearing. Flowers are small or minute. Those of some maples are borne in long, conspicuous, many-flowered clusters, while those of others appear in small few-flowered bunches. All maples are dependent for the fertilization of their flowers upon insects, which throng about their nectar and pollen-bearing blooms.

The fruit (of our representatives) is readily recognized. It is composed of a pair of one-winged seeds, joined together but more or less easily separable when mature. The fruit is ripened in spring or late summer, and is disseminated mainly by wind and flood waters, and to some extent by animals. Seed matured in spring falls shortly after ripening and germinates, while that ripened in late summer remains on the branches through winter, or falls late in autumn and germinates in the spring. The vitality of the seeds is generally transient, the more precocious seeds depending for their life upon reaching a suitable place to sprout shortly after maturity; but the autumn-ripened seed retains its vitality until spring on the cool ground or hanging from twigs in the cold winter air.

Nearly all maples have fine-grained, dense, evenly and finely porous woods, some of which are hard, often beautifully curled and mottled, and highly prized for finishing and cabinet work.

Of approximately 70 maples known in the world, 13 occur in the United States, and 4 of these inhabit the Pacific region.

Broadleaf Maple.

Acer macrophyllum Pursh.

DISTINGUISHING CHARACTERISTICS.

Broadleaf maple is the only large maple tree of the Pacific region, where it is called "Oregon maple" and "bigleaf maple." The name "broadleaf maple," derived from the technical name, seems preferable. It varies greatly in form and height in different soils and situations, from a short-stemmed crooked tree from 25 to 30 feet high and under 1 foot in diameter to one from 60 to 80 feet high with a straight, long, clear trunk from 14 to 30 inches through; occasionally of larger diameter. Open-grown trees have short trunks and broad, dense, round-topped crowns, while those in dense stands produce trunks clear of branches one-half or two-thirds of their height, and a short, narrow crown. Old trunks have rough bark with hard, scaly ridges of a pale grayish to reddish-brown color. Mature leaves (fig. 182), unmistakable in their large size, are thickish, smooth, and somewhat shiny on their top sides, paler green beneath, and 7 inches to occasionally 14 inches wide, with stems 6 to 12 inches long. Before falling they become clear reddish yellow. The large, drooping clusters of fragrant yellow flowers appear after the leaves are grown. Mature fruit or "seeds" (fig. 182), produced in large quantities by trees in the open and at a comparatively early age, is tawny or yellowish brown when ripe in late autumn, often remaining on the branches until winter or later; body of the seeds covered with sharp bristle-like hairs. Wood, fine-grained, rather hard, firm, light brown with pale tint of red; of an excellent commercial quality and suitable and used for the same purposes as eastern hard maple. A timber tree of the first importance in the Pacific region, where commercial hard wood is scarce.

LONGEVITY.—Long-lived, the largest trees attaining an age of from 150 to 200 or more years. Forest-grown trees, from 12 to 20 inches in diameter, are from 50 to 85 years old.

RANGE.

Coast of Alaska (south of latitude 55°), British Columbia, Western Washington and Oregon, and California (south to San Bernardino Mountains).

ALASKA.—Northern limits not definitely known.

BRITISH COLUMBIA.—Islands and seaward side of coast range, rare northward. Noted Queen Charlotte Islands, Fraser River Valley at Mission Junction and Yale (inland limit), islands of Gulf of Georgia, Vancouver Island (locally noted on San Juan and Gordon rivers).

WASHINGTON.—Mainly west of Cascades below 3,500 feet. Eastern limits Peshastin (Chelan County) and Bingen (Klickitat County) on Columbia River. Noted on Puget Sound at Seattle, Tacoma, Lilliwaup, and Union (Mason County), Mason and North Fork Skokomish River up to mouth of South Fork (Mason County), Clallam County, Olympic Mountains below 1,500 feet, Queniult Indian Reservation, Norton (Lewis County); (West) Washington National Forest up to 2,000 feet, locally noted Silverton (Snohomish County), and Skagit Valley 10 miles below Marblemount (Skagit County); (East) Washington National Forest at 1,100 to 3,500 feet, locally noted Stehekin River, Lake Chelan, Stehekin, Peshastin, and Peshastin Canyon (Chelan County); Mount Rainier National Forest below 3,300 feet, locally noted Cowlitz bottom, Ashford (Pierce County).

OREGON.—Wholly on west side Cascades, though extending east on Columbia River to Sherman County between mouth Deschutes River and Grants. Noted Cascade (north) National Forest whole west slope up to 1,600 feet, Cascade (south) National Forest below 2,250 feet, Grant's Pass (950 feet, on Rogue River, Josephine County), Siskiyou National Forest. General in Coast Range.

CALIFORNIA.—Throughout coast ranges from north to south border of State, Sierra Nevada only west side south to Sequoia National Park, and southern cross ranges only south and west sides, at the north up to 4,000 feet, and at the south at 3,000 to 6,000 feet. East limits in northern part of State, Siskiyou Mountains near Southern Pacific Railroad, Scott Valley between Yreka and Fort Jones (Siskiyou County) below 3,500 feet, Mill Creek gulch west of Etna, upper canyon Sacramento River from Sissons (3,500 feet) (Siskiyou County), to Kennett (Shasta County) and McCloud River for 15 miles above Baird. Also noted in Siskiyou County on Salmon Summit from below 1,800 to 5,100 feet and in Del Norte County on Smith River and at Crescent City. Eastern limits in north coast ranges, mainly eastern slopes of inner range, on hill between town of Shasta and Whiskeytown (Shasta County), probably eastern boundaries southern Trinity and northern Mendocino counties, Stony Ford, Fout Spring at base of Snow Mountain and Cook Springs (northwest Colusa County), Cache Creek above Rumsey (Yolo County), Napa Valley north of Calistoga, hills west of Calistoga, and southwest slopes Mount St. Helena, below Toll House (Napa County), and Sonoma Creek between Glen Allen and Sonoma (Sonoma County). Humboldt County, noted Hoopa Valley and up west slopes Trinity Mountains to 3,700 feet. Redwood Creek, Carson's lumber camp 17 miles north of Eureka, and south in redwood forest to southern border of county, also east up Van Dusen and Mad rivers beyond east line of county. Trinity County, noted from east side Trinity Mountains to Lewiston, at Canyon Creek, Junction City, Dutch and Carl creeks south of Junction City, Post and Second creeks south and southwest of Hayfork, and thence to South Fork Trinity, Mad, and Van Dusen rivers. *Mendocino County:* Noted in coast redwood belt mainly in gulches, Laytonville to Covelo, borders Round Valley, Middle Fork Eel River, Cave Creek to Redwood Hill, Redwood Canyon, Russian River from Ridgewood Summit to south border of county, near boundary Lake County on road from Hopland to Highland Springs. Lake County, noted on northeast slopes Mount St. Helena on St. Helena Creek from Toll House to south end Middletown Valley (1,500 feet or lower), mountains north Mount St. Helena to beyond Cobb Mountain at 1,700 to 2,200 feet, canyons upper Putah and Big Sulphur creeks and divide between them, near Adams Springs, road from Middletown to Lower Lake, west of Highland Springs, northeast of Upper Lake on Bartlett Mountain down to Bartlett Springs, east and southeast of Lower Lake on road to Reiff and Rumsey. *Sonoma County:* Noted on lower Russian River from eastern edge of redwood belt at Forestville, west to Gurneyville and Duncan Mills, and more sparingly west of Duncan Mills, Austin Creek from Duncan Mills to and above Cazedero, Gurneyville to Occidental, Camp Meeker, Green Valley, between Sebastopol and Camp Meeker, upper Russian River northward from Cloverdale, canyon between Knight's and Alexander valleys, canyon Big Sulphur Creek for 6 miles above Geysers. *Marin County:* Throughout, noted between Sausalito and San Geronimo, Lagunitas and Paper Mill Creek, Mount Tamalpais north and south sides. *Contra Costa County:* Noted in canyons of Mount Diablo, Mitchell Canyon and upper Marsh Creek. *Alameda County:* Noted in Niles canyon and canyon on Mission Peak. Coast ranges south of San Francisco Bay; noted on Mount Hamilton (Santa Clara County) at 3,000 feet, and on road from Gilroy Valley to Gilroy Hot Springs; seaward coast range (mainly east side), in San Mateo, Santa Clara and Santa Cruz counties, noted west of Palo Alto, Boulder Creek, Big Basin; San Benito County, on north side Fremont Peak, south of San Juan; Monterey County, not on Monterey Peninsula, but in Santa Lucia Mountains, at 800 to 4,200 feet, noted on coast slope in watershed of Sur River; at head of Arroyo Seco west of Santa Lucia Peak and above junction of Willow Creek, and in watersheds of Carmelo, San Antonio and Nacimiento Rivers; San Luis Obispo National Forest at 250 to 2,000 feet, in watersheds of Santa Margarita, San Luis, Arroyo Grande, and Huasna rivers. Northern Sierras not reported in Lassen Peak National Forest. *Butte County:* Noted Chico Creek eastward from Chico. *Plumas County:* East to American Valley near Quincy, Spanish Peak ridge (up to 5,400 feet on west and southwest slopes), and Mohawk on Upper Feather River. *Sierra County:* East in north Yuba canyon to Sierra City and some distance up North Fork of North Yuba, and to a canyon between Goodyear and Mountain House. Yuba County common throughout yellow pine belt west to Oregon Hills and Bobbins. *Placer County:* Noted in canyon North Fork American River, near Cape Horn at Blue Canyon, Colfax, Forest Hill, between Iowa and Forks House, Devils Canyon, between Forest Hill and Colfax. *Eldorado County:* Noted near Placerville. *Amador County:* Noted at Pine Grove, from Oleta southeast to Deadmans Creek, on road to Volcano and south to Dry Creek Canyon and ridge north of Volcano. Stanislaus National Forest in general at 2,000 to 4,500 feet. *Calaveras County:* East to West Point, Railroad Flat, Mountain Ranch, between Bigtrees and Murphy, at 2,100 to 3,800 feet, and Murphy, west to 5 miles south of San Andreas on Calaveras River, also noted Mokelumne Canyon, between West Point and Defender, and on North Fork Calaveras, between Mountain Ranch and Mokelumne Hill. *Tuolumne County:* Noted between Big Oak Flat and Crockers and between Big Creek and South Fork Tuolumne. *Mariposa County:* Noted near Bower Cave and on Bull Creek between Bower Cave and Coulterville, Yosemite Valley up to Nevada and Yosemite Falls (5,600 feet), and from Yosemite to Wassama. *Fresno County:* Noted in canyons of Kings and Middle Fork Kings River, Dinky Creek, and at mouth of Bubbs Creek. *Tulare County:* Noted in lower part Sequoia National Park and in upper Kaweah canyon (southern limit in Sierras). *Southern cross ranges:* Noted in Tejon Mountains; Santa Barbara National Forest, in watersheds of Santa Maria, Santa Ynez, Santa Barbara and Matilija rivers at 200 to 4,280 feet, noted in Cooper Canyon 12 miles west of Santa Barbara, upper Cherry Creek, Upper North Fork Matilija and main Matilija, and Zaca Lake and vicinity; San Gabriel National Forest canyons of south side between 3,000 and 6,000 feet, noted near Los Angeles and Pasadena, Mount Lowe at 5,100 feet, Santa Anita Canyon at 3,200 feet, canyon West Fork San Gabriel River at 2,500 to 3,000 feet (Santa Ana County), upper parts of canyons; San Bernardino Mountains, canyons of south and west sides; noted in canyon Santa Ana River and on Hemlock, Bear, and Keller creeks.

OCCURRENCE.

Borders of foothill and low mountain streams and in alluvial river bottoms (here largest); in moist, gravelly, and rich humous soils. Best growth in Oregon and Washington coast region. Forms practically pure dense stands over large areas, but often with California laurel and lowland fir.

CLIMATIC CONDITIONS.—Similar to those of Douglas fir (in Pacific range).

TOLERANCE.—Endures a good deal of shade during early life. Requires top light for best growth; dense side shade produces long, clear trunks.

REPRODUCTION.—Seeds very abundantly in the open; much less in close stands. Seedlings fairly frequent on rocky streams, but plentiful on rich bottoms.

Vine Maple.

Acer circinatum Pursh.

DISTINGUISHING CHARACTERISTICS.

Vine maple is so called because of the often sprawling, crooked vine-like appearance and habit of its slender, weak stems. The branches occasionally root where they touch the ground, and are covered with moss or leaf mold. It rarely stands erect with a straight trunk. Trunks usually from 15 to 20 feet high and from 3 to 6 inches thick. Often shrub-like. At best, in moist, rich bottoms and mountain flats, from 25 to 30 feet high and from 8 to 10 inches through. The largest trunks are slightly seamed near the base, but elsewhere the bark is smooth, thin, and dull grayish brown, tinged with red. The crowns are irregular, open, with slender, crooked or crumpled limbs and twigs. The shapeless form of this tree is probably due to its growth mainly under dense shade, of which it is extremely tolerant, where it can produce only long, weak stems, which, annually

bent to the ground by the heavy snows prevalent in its range, struggle each year
to grow erect, giving the stems many curious crooks. In the open and on borders
of forests it is apt to be shorter and more erect. Mature leaves (figs. 183, 184),

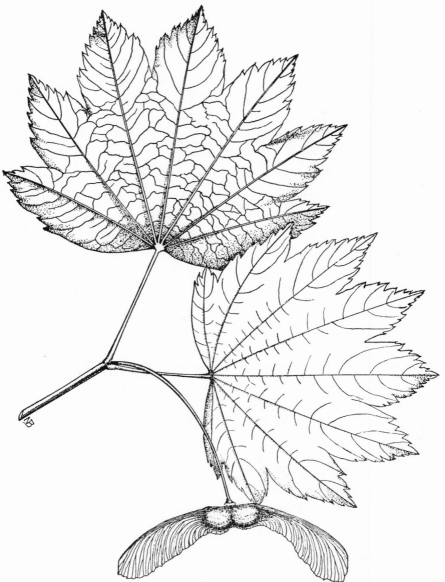

FIG. 183.—*Acer circinatum.*

rose red when young, are smooth above; minute tufts of hairs only in the angles
of the veins on the paler, lower surfaces; in the fall beautifully colored reddish
yellow or bright scarlet. The ripe " seeds " (fruit) (figs. 183, 184) are light yel-

low-brown in early autumn; earlier the wings are bright rose-red, a short time before falling. Wood very pale brown to almost white, with thick sapwood; very fine-grained, dense, and hard, checking badly in drying. Locally used for fuel, for which it is excellent, and for some minor domestic purposes; of no commercial use.

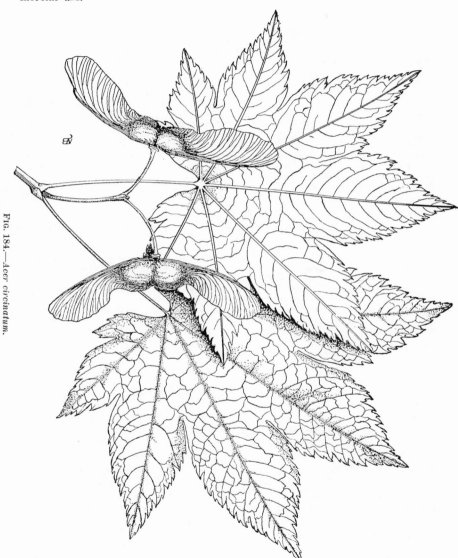

FIG. 184.—*Acer circinatum.*

LONGEVITY.—Not fully determined. A very persistent but slow grower; large trees reach 80 or 90 years of age. Trees from 4 to 5 inches in diameter are from 60 to 70 years old.

From the coast region of British Columbia south through Washington, Oregon, and California (to Mendocino County).

BRITISH COLUMBIA.—Coast west of Coast Range, not far north, and on Vancouver Island. Noted in lower Fraser River Valley and on Chilliwak Lake.

WASHINGTON.—Mostly west of Cascades, below 2,000 or 3,000 feet. Noted east of Cascades in Stehekin Valley at 1,150 to 4,000 feet, and on Nason Creek in Chelan County, and near Martin, Kittitas County (alt. 2,775 feet). Noted west of Cascades in Washington National Forest below 2,000 feet, Silverton (Snohomish County), Seattle, at Tacoma, Lilliwaup on Hood Canal, Olympia (Thurston County), Montesano and Grays Harbor (Chehalis County), in Clallam County, Olympic National Forest below 2,000 feet, Mount Rainier National Forest lower red fir type, Upper Nisqually River, Yakima Pass (east boundary King County), Mount Adams, White Salmon (on Columbia River at west boundary Klickitat County).

OREGON.—Confined to part west of Cascades, which it ascends along streams in Douglas fir forests to 5,000 feet. Noted along Columbia River on flats above dunes between McClures and The Dalles, Wasco County, on Mount Hood, in Cascade (north) National Forest, all over west slope, and in Siskiyou National Forest.

CALIFORNIA.—South at least to Mendocino County on the Coast and Lewiston on Upper Trinity River (alt. 1,750 feet) (Trinity County), and east to McCloud River, Upper Sacramento River just above Dunsmuir (Siskiyou County), altitude 2,280 feet, and near Sissons (Siskiyou County), altitude 3,500 feet, and in Modoc County to Warm Springs. Noted also in northwestern part of Klamath National Forest.

Alluvial bottoms (mainly above inundation), flats, benches, depressions, borders of mountain streams, and lower meadows; in moist, rich (often heavily humous), rocky soils.

Always subordinate, undergrowth in pure clumps and patches, or mingled with broad-leaf maple, western dogwood, grand and amabilis firs, Douglas fir, western hemlock, western white pine, yew, and western serviceberry.

CLIMATIC CONDITIONS.—Similar to those of Douglas fir (in Pacific region).

TOLERANCE.—Exceedingly tolerant of shade—often very dense.

REPRODUCTION.—Only moderate periodic seeder, but some seed borne locally about every year. Seedlings occur generally, but scattered sparingly in dense and partial shade where they persist.

Dwarf Maple.

Acer glabrum Torrey.

DISTINGUISHING CHARACTERISTICS.

Dwarf maple is only rarely a tree from 20 to 30 feet high and from 6 to 12 inches through, its narrow crown of straight, slender limbs trending upward sharply. Very generally it is a small-stemmed shrub from 4 to 6 feet high or a slender tree from 10 to 12 feet high. The trunks are smooth, red brown, with a grayish tint. Mature twigs of the season are smooth, rich reddish brown, as are the buds. Mature leaves[a] (figs. 185 to 187) are smooth and shiny on their top sides; very pale green beneath; smooth, the yellowish veins appearing prominent; leaf stems frequently clear red. Mature "seeds" or fruit (fig. 187), ripe in early autumn and soon shed, are light russet brown—bright rose-red before ripening. Wood, almost white, with very thick sapwood,

---

[a] By some authors the deeply 3 to 5, mostly 3, lobed leaves are held to belong to a distinct species, *Acer douglasii* Hooker. The fact, however, that throughout the range of this maple deeply cut leaves are frequent with the ordinary form—often on the same tree—would seem to show that the character is unreliable.

fine-grained, dense, hard, and rather heavy. Of no commercial use on account of
the mostly small size of its stems. Of little importance to the forester except
for the thin, scattered brush cover its shrubby stools form.

FIG. 185.—*Acer glabrum*.

LONGEVITY.—Not fully determined. One tree $3\frac{1}{8}$ inches in diameter showed
an age of 15 years.

RANGE.

From southeast Alaska on the coast south to British Columbia (Vancouver Island
east to Kananaskis), and eastward and southward over the mountains of the west to

California (southward on Sierra Nevada to east fork of Kaweah River), Idaho, Montana, and Colorado (eastern slopes of Rocky Mountains), western Nebraska (Sioux and Scotts Bluff counties), eastern New Mexico, and Arizona. A tree on coast of Vancouver Island, Blue Mountains of Oregon, and in canyons of Idaho, New Mexico, and Arizona ; elsewhere shrubby. In general, at 5,000 to 6,000 feet, but at north down to sea-level.

ALASKA.—North along coast to head of Lynn Canal (lat. 60°), along rivers, probably only extending inland to altitude of few hundred feet, though also noted on east side of Coast Range on Stikine River above its canyon. Noted on Prince of Wales Island and

FIG. 186.—*Acer glabrum.*

at Lynn Canal at Chilkoot at outlet of Chilkoot Lake, at mouth of Chilkat River, and at Pyramid Harbor.

CANADA.—Usually below 6,000 feet. East to east side of Continental Divide at Kananaskis (altitude 4,200 feet) in Bow River Valley and to South Kootenai Pass. North about to latitude 51°. Noted above Morley (altitude 4,067 feet) and at Banff (altitude 4,521 feet) in Bow River Pass, mountains near Waterton Lake, at Spence's Bridge (just above mouth of Thompson River), and on Vancouver Island at Victoria, Esquimo, Gordon River Valley, and Renfrew region.

WASHINGTON.—Whole wooded portion of State. To sea-level on Puget Sound (noted at Hoodsport), at 1,100 to 4,500 feet on east slopes Cascades in Washington National Forest. Noted Skagit Pass at head of Skagit River, Mount Rainier, Nisqually Valley, Mount Adams, and on east side of Cascades in Yakima County, on west slope of divide between Columbia and Yakima rivers, in Yakima Canyon, at Tampico, Wenas, Cleman Mountain, and Saddle Mountains, on west bank of Columbia River between Priest Rapids and Sen-

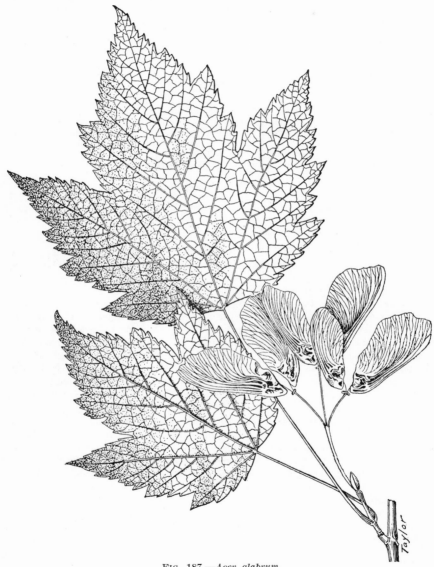

FIG. 187.—*Acer glabrum.*

tinel Bluffs, in Kittitas County on divide above Ellensburg, and in Wenache Mountains, and in Chelan County in valley of Stehekin River, 5 miles above Lake Chelan. Also noted in eastern Washington in Colville Indian Reservation at Fort Colville (Stevens County), altitude 1,917 feet, Davis Ranch at foot of Mount Carlton (Spokane County), Sprague (Lincoln County), altitude 1,899 feet, and in Blue Mountains at 4,000 feet.

OREGON.—Whole wooded portion of State except Goose Lake region. Noted along Columbia River in Sherman County, Blue Mountains, Mount Hood, Crater Lake on inner slope of crater.

CALIFORNIA.—Northern part of State, Sierra Nevada, probably only on west slopes, and ranges east of southern Sierra Nevada at high elevations. Noted at 3,000 feet at south end Shasta Valley, on Mount Shasta up to 5,600 or 6,000 feet, especially in Mud Creek Canyon and Squaw Creek, near Sissons and in McCloud Valley; in Trinity County, on lakes at head of Canyon Creek; Lassen Peak, Plumas, and Tahoe National Forests; Stanislaus National Forest at 5,000 to 7,500 feet, Yosemite Valley, Bubbs Creek (tributary South Fork Kings River), East Fork Kaweah River at 8,000 to 9,000 feet, east of southern Sierras in Grapevine Mountains in Wood Canyon, in Panamint Mountains, in Death Valley Canyon at 6,000 to 7,000 feet, or higher. Also reported in San Jacinto Mountains, in canyon on east side below Round Valley at 7,500 to 8,000 feet.

OCCURRENCE.

Rocky cliffs and canyon sides, gulches, borders of high mountain streams, and meadows, usually where soil is thin, gravelly, and often poor. Scattered singly and in small clumps with broadleaf maple, mountain alder, birch (Alaska), aspen, and western serviceberry. Occasional large trees in southeastern Alaska, Vancouver Island, and Blue Mountains of Washington.

CLIMATIC CONDITIONS.—Similar to those of aspen.

TOLERANCE AND REPRODUCTION.—Undetermined. Appears little tolerant of shade; seeds rather sparingly.

California Boxelder.

Acer negundo californicum (Torr. and Gr.) Sargent.

DISTINGUISHING CHARACTERISTICS.

California boxelder is usually called simply "boxelder," but it should be distinguished from the eastern boxelder (*Acer negundo* L.), of which the Pacific tree is a variety.

A short and stocky tree from 20 to 50 feet high and from 10 to 30 inches in diameter; sometimes taller and thicker. The clear trunk is short, the crown broad, dense, and round-topped, and the bark of the trunk pale grayish brown, with regularly deep furrows and narrow ridges. Mature twigs of the season thickly coated with down, as are the mature 3-parted leaves (fig. 188) on their under sides and sometimes on both surfaces. (Foliage and twigs of the eastern tree are smooth or only slightly hairy.) Mature "seeds" or fruit (fig. 188) are also downy. The greenish flowers of boxelder differ from those of simple-leafed maples in being strictly male and female, and those of each sex are borne on separate trees; therefore only the female trees produce seed. Male flowers occur in clusters of drooping, unbranched thread-like stems, while the female flowers are on a drooping branched stem, both from buds on twigs formed the previous year. The seeds, ripe in autumn, usually remain on the twigs until or during the winter, their dead stems adhering to the branchlets in spring. Wood, very pale lemon yellow or creamy white, the sap and heartwood scarcely distinct from each other. Variable from fine-grained to moderately coarse-grained, light, soft, firm, but brittle. Suitable for second-rate finishing, box-boards, and paper pulp, but the poor timber from and scattered supply of the trees render the wood of little commercial importance.

LONGEVITY.—Not fully determined. One tree 12 inches in diameter showed an age of 36 years. Gives evidence of being short-lived.

RANGE.

Southern California (valley lower Sacramento River; valleys and coast ranges from Sonoma County to Santa Barbara County, and western slopes San Bernardino Mountains).

Noted in Sonoma County, Contra Costa County. Rare in coast ranges south of San Francisco Bay; noted near Soledad in Santa Lucia Mountains, Goleto and Gaviota Passes in Santa Ynez Mountains (Santa Barbara County), and below Fort Tejon, Cañada de las Uvas, in Tehachapi Mountains.

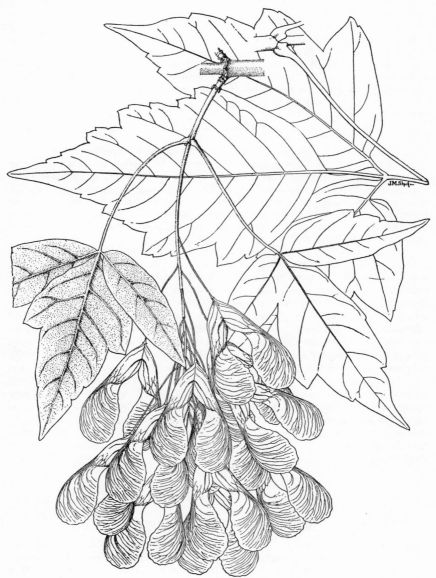

FIG. 188.—*Acer negundo californicum.*

OCCURRENCE.

Borders of streams, bottoms of moist canyons and gulches, in sandy or gravelly soils—best in humous sandy soil. Often in strips and patches of pure growth, but commonly with white alder, western sycamore, and willows.

CLIMATIC CONDITIONS.—Similar to those of Fremont cottonwood.

TOLERANCE.—Moderately tolerant of shade, especially in early life.

REPRODUCTION.—Prolific seeder, bearing good crop nearly every year. Seed has fairly high rate of germination (but often tardy) and persistent vitality. Germinates well only when covered by moist litter or soil. Reproduction rather scanty.

Family HIPPOCASTANACEÆ.

Hippocastanaceæ is known as the horse-chestnut family, which is popular through the wide cultivation for ornament of its best-known representative, the common Grecian horse-chestnut. They are nearly all small or medium-sized trees, which belong chiefly to the genus Æsculus, and, with the similar Mexican and Central American genus Billia, make up the entire family. Characteristics of the family are given under Æsculus, which is well represented in the United States.

ÆSCULUS. BUCKEYES.

The buckeyes comprise trees, and a few shrubs, which are called " horse-chest-nuts " and " buckeyes ;" the latter name, however, is applied to all of our native species. The trees are principally unimportant forest trees, their wood being soft, light, not durable, cross-grained, and hard to work ; a number of them are, however, very highly esteemed and much planted for ornament, on account of their showy flowers and handsome foliage. They are all strikingly similar in the form of their opposite leaves, which are composed of one long stem with from 5 to 9 separate, leaf-like leaflets radiating from its end. The foliage is shed in early autumn every year. The usually large fruits of buckeyes are also similar to each other and easily recognized by their thick, leathery, smooth, warty, or prickly covering (a capsule), which, when mature (in late summer), splits open by regular seams and liberates one or two (often large) thin-shelled, shiny, rich brown, chestnut-like seeds. The fancied resemblance of the big, glossy brown seeds to the eye of a buck is the probable origin of the popular common name " buckeye." The heavy, fleshy, bitterish seeds, rarely eaten by any animals, are distributed almost entirely by flood waters, whenever carried away from the mother tree. Buried in earth or débris they retain their vitality only until spring, when they germinate, if at all. Winter buds are brown and scaly, those on the ends of the twigs often large and conspicuous. The showy red, yellow, or white (usually erect) clusters of flowers are produced as a new shoot from the ends of last year's twigs. Some of the flowers (on upper part of the cluster) are male or pollen bearing, while others (at the base of the cluster) are bisexual and the only ones producing fruit. Four species occur in the United States ; 3 are in the East, and one in the Pacific region, confined to California.

California Buckeye.

Æsculus californica Nuttall.

DISTINGUISHING CHARACTERISTICS.

California buckeye is shrub-like ; it has several stems from 10 to 20 feet high and from 3 to 6 inches through, growing together from a common root. Some-times it is from 25 to 30 feet high and from 8 to 20 inches in diameter, with a short, smooth, gray—often whitish—trunk and a flat-topped, open crown of wide spreading limbs. Leaf-stems from 4 to 5 inches long and commonly with 5 (sometimes 4 to 7) leaflets (fig. 189), which are from 3 to 7 inches long, smooth throughout when mature, except for minute hairs in the angles of the veins on the paler green lower sides. They fall in early autumn, leaving the large pear-shaped fruits (fig. 189), 2½ to 3 inches long, hanging down conspicuously from the tips of the branches. The fruit capsule usually contains one seed, about 2 inches thick. Wood, fine-grained, white to very pale yellow, the heart and sapwood scarcely distinct from each other; of no commercial use.

FIG. 189.—*Æsculus californica.*

The chief usefulness is in forming considerable open but helpful cover on exposed dry, rocky foothill slopes, in gulches, and along hill streams where few other trees grow.

LONGEVITY.—Not fully determined, but undoubtedly short-lived. One tree $7\frac{1}{2}$ inches in diameter showed an age of 43 years. Maturity is doubtless reached in about 100 years.

RANGE.

California (from Sacramento River in Mendocino County along coast ranges to San Luis Obispo County; western foothills of Sierras to northern slopes of Tejon Pass in Kern County; Antelope Valley north of San Gabriel Mountains in Los Angeles County).

North Coast Ranges: Lower foothills (500 to 2,000 feet) northward into Mendocino County, Shasta County, at least to Redding in Sacramento River Valley. Locally noted on Russian River (Mendocino County); in canyons and on hills near Ukiah; at Lewiston and on Canyon Creek (Trinity County); hill between Shasta (town) and Whiskeytown (Shasta County); lower hills of Stony Creek National Forest; valleys south of Clear Lake (Lake County); Mount Tamalpais (Marin County). *South Coast Ranges:* Probably throughout lower foothills to San Luis Obispo Mountains, but noted only on seaward range west of Santa Clara Valley (500 to 1,500 feet), where it is common; near Santa Cruz; foothills of Santa Cruz Mountains; near Monterey on foothills just above Carmel Mission; Monterey National Forest (Santa Lucia Mountains), at 600 to 4,000 feet, but not common, in basins of Sur, Carmelo, and Arroyo Seco rivers; San Luis Obispo National Forest, only in basin of Salinas River. *Sierra Foothills:* Common from Shasta County to Tehachapi Mountains; in the north, at 500 to 2,000 feet, and in the south, at 1,000 to 3,000 feet. Locally noted in Shasta County; near Chico (Butte County); near Ione (Amador County) at 200 to 5,000 feet; Stanislaus National Forest, throughout lower belt; Northfork and vicinity (Madera County); South Fork of King's River, below Millwood; Kaweah River, foothills; Kern River basin, below oaks; at Havilah; Kernville to Walker Basin. *Southern Cross Ranges:* Abundant in Tehachapi Mountains in canyons and nearly up to summits; extends eastward and southward to the north slopes of Santa Barbara Mountains above Antelope Valley, where it occurs in basin of Elizabeth Lake at 2,400 to 4,500 feet, reaching the foot of Sawmill Mountain. Locally noted from Havilah to Fort Tejon and in Cañada de las Uvas, and reported on south slope of Santa Barbara Mountains in Matilija Creek basin.

OCCURRENCE.

Foothill and lower mountain slopes; frequent on borders of streams and canyon sides, in dry gravelly soils. Forms spreading clumps interspersed with scrub oak, redbud, occasional live oak, blue oak, and gray pine, manzanita, and other chaparral brush; largest in sheltered coves and gulches.

CLIMATIC CONDITIONS.—Similar to those of blue oak and gray pine.

TOLERANCE.—Seedlings endure slight shade for several years, but later growth demands full light.

REPRODUCTION.—Fairly abundant seeder. Young plants moderately frequent. Seed germinates only when it is well covered in soil.

Family RHAMNACEÆ.

Rhamnaceæ is popularly known as the buckthorn family, which is widely known chiefly from its representative genus Rhamnus, an exotic species which is particularly famous as a medicinal plant. They are all small trees or shrubs, some of them generally distributed throughout the world. They are characterized by their bitter bark, their often scaleless (naked) buds, their single-bladed leaves, evergreen or shed every autumn, and their small, greenish, usually bisexual flowers and berry-like fruits. Six genera, containing trees, occur in the United States, and two of them, *Ceanothus* and *Rhamnus*, are represented by eastern and Pacific species.

RHAMNUS.   BUCKTHORNS.

The buckthorns form a large group containing trees and shrubs characterized by their intensely bitter, pungent bark and twigs. The twigs do not have strictly terminal or end buds, the last bud being a side one at the base of the last leaf-stem. The leaves, evergreen or shed each autumn, occur singly on the twigs or seemingly in pairs, the two leaves nearly but rarely exactly opposite each other.   Minute flowers, bisexual, or some of them male and others female, and each kind borne on different trees, occur in small branched or unbranched clusters at the bases of leaf-stems, coming after the latter are grown.   Fruits matured in one season (usually in late summer) resemble berries and have a thick, juicy pulp covering from 2 to 4 very hard seeds, somewhat like a coffee grain.   The succulent, often attractive fruits are greedily eaten by birds and mammals (without injury to the seeds).   They are widely disseminated, chiefly in this way.   Wood of the buckthorns is fine to coarse grained, moderately heavy and firm, of ordinary quality, and of no economic value, principally because the trees are small.   The best known species of the group is the European Buckthorn (*Rhamnus cathartica* L.), popular for hedges and as a small ornamental tree.   Several of our native species are planted for ornament, but one only, a tree of the Pacific region, is of commercial importance on account of its medicinal bark.   Three tree species and one variety occur in the United States, and two of these inhabit the Pacific region.

Evergreen Buckthorn.

Rhamnus crocea Nuttall.

DISTINGUISHING CHARACTERISTICS.

Evergreen buckthorn has glossy, prickly, evergreen leaves, and is very commonly only a straggling or massed shrub from 2 to 4 feet high, but in protected situations it is sometimes a slim tree from 12 to 15 feet high, with a smoothish, dull ashy gray trunk from 3 to 6 inches through; crown branches few and distant.   The smooth, red-brown twigs are straight, stiff, some of them spine-like.   Mature leaves smooth throughout (fig. 190), thinnish but leathery, shiny yellowish green on their top sides, and much lighter, sometimes reddish green beneath; occasionally very minutely hairy on the veins and leaf stems.   Fruit (fig. 190), ripe in late summer, dull red, and smooth; the very thin pulp covers from 1 to 3 little nuts, which split open and liberate a hard, grooved seed pointed at one end (fig. 191, *a*).   Wood, light yellowish-brown, fine-grained, and brittle. Of no economic use.

LONGEVITY.—Not fully determined.   One tree $3\frac{5}{8}$ inches in diameter showed an age of 29 years.

A distinct variety of this species which possibly deserves to rank as a species is *Rhamnus crocea insularis* (Greene) Sargent, which occurs on Cedros and Santa Barbara islands and the adjacent mainland of California.   It differs from the species in its longer and less distinctly toothed leaves (fig. 191), sometimes with entire borders; in its somewhat larger flowers and bright red fruit; and particularly in the uniformly grooved, rounded, and abruptly short-pointed top end of the seed.   Said to be 25 or 30 feet high and to flower six weeks later than *Rhamnus crocea*.   Specimens of this variety have not been compared with those upon which *Rhamnus pirifolia* Greene, found on Santa Cruz Island, is based.   The latter appears to be a form of this variety.

What is probably another, but less well known, variety is *Rhamnus crocea pilosa* Curran, found in Santa Maria Valley near San Diego, Cal.   It has narrower leaves with curled borders, and the twigs and leaves are covered with dense, minute, soft hairs.   Nothing is known of its size.

RANGE.

California; upper Sacramento River, west of Sierra Nevada Mountains (to latitude 29°) to Lower California (Guadalupe Islands).

Prefers north mountain slopes, in shelter of forest borders, gulches, ravines, but occurs elsewhere on warm exposures; in dry, or moderately moist, gravelly soils. In groups or scattered among chaparral and shrubby trees.

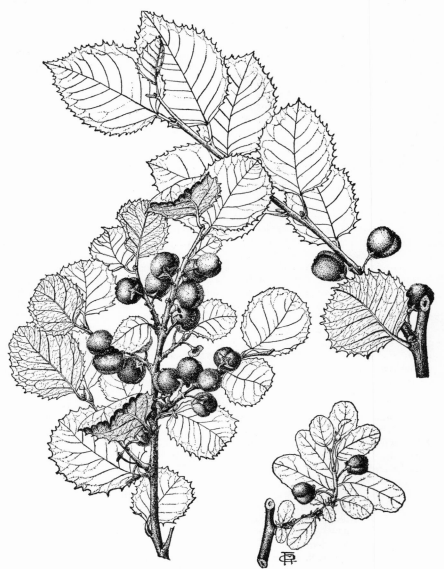

FIG. 190.—*Rhamnus crocea.*

CLIMATIC CONDITIONS.—Climate hot and dry in part, but in part influenced by proximity of sea.

TOLERANCE.—Very tolerant of shade, as shown by its growth for years under dense shade of tolerant trees.

REPRODUCTION.—Usually a prolific seeder, beginning at young age. Seed of high possible germination (under favorable conditions) and of very persistent vitality. Germina-

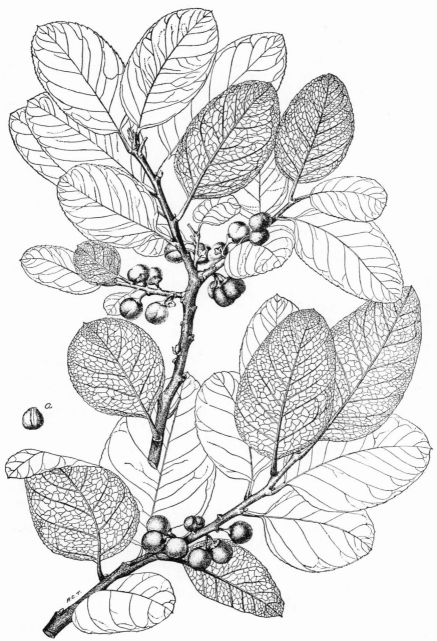

FIG. 191.—*Rhamnus crocea insularis: a,* seed.

tion rather scanty, owing probably to rare accident of seed being sufficiently buried to permit sprouting. Best conditions for reproduction imperfectly determined.

Cascara Sagrada.[a]

Rhamnus purshiana De Candolle.

DISTINGUISHING CHARACTERISTICS.

Cascara sagrada varies in size and form in different parts of its wide range, where it occurs in dry or moist soils, in the open or crowded in a shady forest of other large trees. In moist rich soils of the north coast region, forest-grown trees are from 20 to 30 feet high, with a straight, smoothish, ashy gray, or sometimes brownish, trunk from 6 to 15 inches through, and a narrow open crown which has only a few branches standing out straight from the undivided bole ; occasionally somewhat taller ; in open places, with a very short trunk from 20 to 30 inches in diameter, giving off very large, upright limbs. Farther south, in poor, dry soils of open situations, usually a slender-stemmed [b] shrub in dense clumps from 3 to 6 feet high ; sometimes bent to the ground. Mature twigs of the season are smooth or slightly and minutely downy, and usually dull reddish brown.

Mature leaves (fig. 192) in its northern and moister range are commonly thin, large, prominently veiny, with sparse, very minute hairs above and beneath on the larger veins and on the leaf stems ; they are shed regularly in autumn. In its drier, southern distribution to and through central California, mature leaves (fig. 193) are smaller, thicker, and somewhat leathery ; the hairiness is decidedly more pronounced, and the veins are smaller but conspicuously connected in a network ; foliage of this type often persists more or less during late autumn or winter. Seen separately, the two extreme forms almost appear to be distinct species, but shade, soil, and atmospheric moisture seem to account for distinctive characters of the northern form, while exposure, dry soils, and dryness of atmosphere seem to account for the smaller, hairier, thicker-leafed southern form, which, moreover, is connected with the northern one by intermediate forms. Flowers, fruits, and seeds of both forms are essentially alike.

There is good reason, however, for separating from the thicker-leafed form one which inhabits southern California (sometimes the central part) and extends into Arizona and New Mexico. It is *Rhamnus purshiana tomentella* (Gray) Brandegee, distinguished by the dense coating of whitish down on the twigs and lower sides of the usually narrow leaves ; a wide-leafed form of this variety has been found,[c] however, in Lake and Colusa counties, Cal.

Mature fruit (figs. 192, 193) smooth and black (previously red) with juicy, rather thin, sweetish pulp, which contains 2 or 3 hard, smooth, olive-green seeds. When there are two seeds they are flat on one side like a coffee grain, and when three they are triangular ; bottom end of seeds notched and top end rounded.[d] Wood, pale yellowish brown, with faint tinge of red ; moderately heavy and soft ; firm but brittle, rather coarse-grained ; layer of whitish sapwood thin in forest-grown trees, but thick in those grown in the open. Of no economic use.

---

[a] Also called bearberry, bearwood, coffeeberry, coffee-tree, bitter-bark, wahoo, and shittimwood.

[b] In the northern part, especially of the lower west slope of the Sierras, occurs what is here considered a form of this species, with very slender, wand-like stems, clear red twigs, and thinnish, narrow, sharply pointed leaves. It has been described as a distinct species (*Rhamnus rubra* Greene, Pittonia, I, 68, 160) and deserves further careful study in the field.

[c] Discovered first by Prof. T. S. Brandegee.

[d] See dissemination of seeds under *Rhamnus,* p. 401.

On account of its medicinal (tonic and laxative) properties the bark is collected extensively from trees in its northern range, to the amount, annually, of at least half a million pounds. In Oregon and Washington especially, collecting the bark has become an important local industry, to meet the increasing

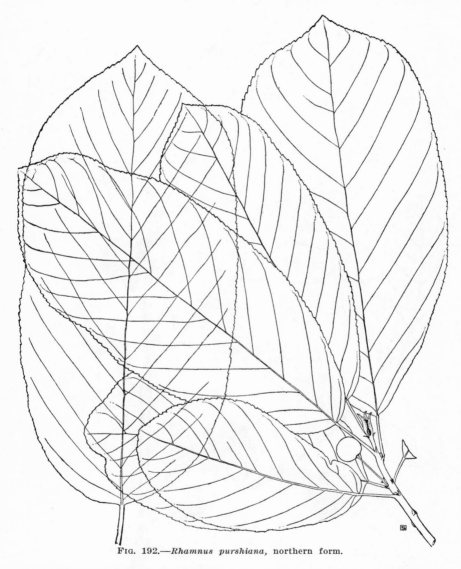

Fig. 192.—*Rhamnus purshiana,* northern form.

demand for bark both in this country and in Europe. Large numbers of trees are destroyed annually by peeling. The cut stumps sprout vigorously, so that, with conservative management the supply can be maintained.[a]

---

[a]An investigation looking to such management is now under way.

LONGEVITY.—Not fully determined for large trees. Those from 6 to 12 inches in diameter are from 18 to 40 years old, when grown in dense stands, but not overtopped.

FIG. 193.—*Rhamnus purshiana,* southern form.

RANGE.

From Puget Sound southward into Lower California; eastward through northern Washington to Idaho (Bitter Root Mountains), Montana (Flathead Lake); eastern slopes Sierra Nevada Mountains; mountains of Colorado, Arizona, New Mexico, and western Texas.

OCCURRENCE.

Low river bottoms, flats, valleys, borders of slow streams (at north), and high foothill slopes (southward) ; in former habitat in rich, rocky, or humous soils (best growth) and in dry gravelly or sandy soils throughout southern range (here shrubby) ; abundant moisture and rich soil required for largest growth. Mixed (usually as an undergrowth) with Douglas fir, red alder, western red cedar, hemlock, broadleaf and vine maples, Oregon crab, in alluvial bottoms, but often with manzanitas, live oaks, chaparral brush elsewhere on open hill slopes.

CLIMATIC CONDITIONS.—Similar to those of red alder and Douglas fir.

TOLERANCE.—Exceedingly tolerant of dense shade in humid air and moist soil ; apparently much less so in drier and exposed situations ; the two habitats, different in climatic and soil conditions, producing two very unlike forms.

REPRODUCTION.—Prolific seeder. Seed of medium high germination (often tardy) and of very persistent vitality. Scattered seedlings fairly abundant in moist forest litter and mucky soils ; scanty in drier habitat except in depressions where seed has been deeply covered by accident. Growth slender in dense shade ; branched and bushy in open ; shrubby in dry places.

CEANOTHUS. MYRTLES.

The myrtles are a small group of low, slender trees and shrubs confined to North America. One eastern shrubby species is called "New Jersey tea," while most of the western species are known as "lilacs" and "myrtles." As trees they are unimportant, but as shrubs they often form a large and conspicuous part of the useful chaparral cover on dry mountain slopes throughout the western United States, where, in addition to assisting much in preventing rapid run-off, a number of them furnish the principal browse in summer for range cattle and sheep. The greater number of them grow in the open, but some mingle with forest trees. They grow near sea level or ascend high mountain slopes, frequently becoming conspicuous features in burned areas among mountain pines, spruces, and firs.

The twigs are smooth and unarmed (sometimes with spines or spine-pointed) and frequently angled. The leaves are simple (with one blade) and borne singly. Prominently characteristic of the leaves, annually deciduous or evergreen, are their 3 veins, consisting of the main central vein, on both sides of which a vein extends from near the base of the leaf nearly or quite to its top end (figs. 194 to 196). The minute, blue or white, perfectly bisexual flowers, often fragrant, occur in small, dense, branched clusters. The colored divisions (petals) of the flowers resemble minute tobacco pipes. The fruits are small, dry, berry-like bodies, with three rounded, bulging lobes, which are three little nuts. These are joined together, but are separable when ripe ; the thin, dry, brittle covering of each splits open and liberates a thin, hard-shelled seed. A curious fact concerning the dissemination of the seeds is that, in a number of species, the seeds are quite forcefully thrown [a] from their outer shells. This provision insures their being cast upon the ground, often a little way from the parent tree. Flood waters and browsing animals further assist in distributing the seeds.

Six or seven species, all found in the Pacific region, have been classed as trees, but so far as can be satisfactorily determined only three of these are true trees. This number is likely, however, to be increased by careful field studies of some of the large, shrub-like species.

Species of this genus are often difficult to identify in all of their variably shrubby or tree forms, particularly such closely related species as *C. arboreus* and the shrubby *C. velutinus.* Moreover, it is now known that several species hybridize and so produce very perplexing forms.

---

[a] Parry, Proc. Davenport (Iowa) Acad., v. 164.

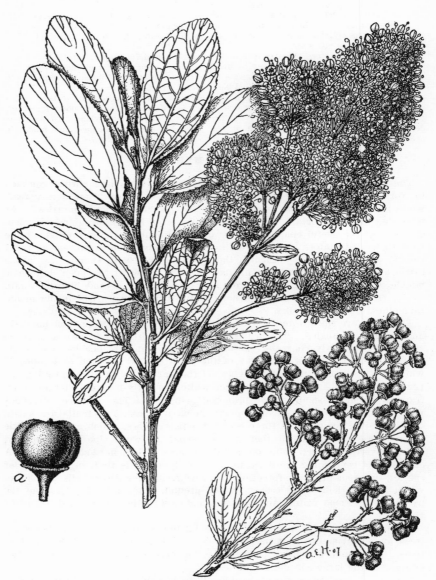

FIG. 194.—*Ceanothus thyrsiflorus: a,* fruit enlarged.

Blue Myrtle.[a]

Ceanothus thyrsiflorus Eschscholtz.

DISTINGUISHING CHARACTERISTICS.

Variable in size, from a fruiting shrub from 2 to 4 feet high to a very short, thick-trunked, bushy tree from 12 to 25 feet high and from 4 to 12 inches in diameter; occasionally somewhat taller. Thin trunk bark, clear reddish brown, with thin scales. The branches, and especially the twigs, are prominently angled. Mature leaves (fig. 194) are evergreen, smooth and shiny on their top sides, lighter green beneath, and minutely hairy, particularly on the midveins. Fragrant flowers, usually light blue, sometimes white. Mature fruit (fig. 194), ripening from mid-summer to early autumn, is dead black and smooth.

Wood pale yellowish brown and usually with a very thin layer of sapwood; moderately heavy, fine-grained. Of no economic use.

LONGEVITY.—Not fully determined. One tree 5 inches in diameter showed an age of 12 years.

RANGE.

Western California (from Mendocino County to San Luis Rey River).

OCCURRENCE.

On protected slopes, edges of forests, and near streams; at south, on exposed border of sea, here only a shrub. Largest on hills above Noyo River swamps (Mendocino County), and in redwoods on Santa Cruz Mountains. In moist or dryish gravelly and sandy soils, scattered with Douglas fir, redwood, oaks, western dogwood, vine maple, and willows.

CLIMATIC CONDITIONS.—Not determined.

TOLERANCE.—Fairly tolerant of shade, which it prefers especially in youth, but with greater soil moisture exists in open. Seeding habits and reproduction not fully known. Appears to seed plentifully about every year.

Tree Myrtle.

Ceanothus arboreus Greene.

DISTINGUISHING CHARACTERISTICS.

Tree myrtle, an island species, has no common field name. The one here given, for want of a better one, is derived from the technical name.

As a rule, a low, short-trunked, bushy tree from 10 to 20 feet high, with a deep brownish, scaly trunk from 3 to 8 inches thick; the small bark scales are rather thick, and squarish. Young twigs, faintly angled, grayish with minute down, and later becoming reddish. Mature leaves (fig. 195) thickish, deep green, with exceedingly fine, soft hairs on the top sides, and thickly woolly beneath; leaf stems also more or less hairy; margins of leaves with blackish, gland-tipped teeth. Pale blue flowers in rather large, dense clusters from early to late summer. Mature fruit (fig. 195) is wrinkled and black. Wood, pale brown, tinged with red; very thin, whitish sapwood; fine-grained, dense, hard and heavy. Of no economic use.

LONGEVITY.—Not fully determined. Very persistent slow grower, giving evidence of being rather long-lived. One tree 2⅝ inches in diameter showed an age of twenty-seven years.

---

[a]Also called " blue blossoms," " California lilac," and " tick-tree."

Off coast of southern California (Santa Catalina, Santa Cruz, Santa Rosa Islands).

FIG. 195.—*Ceanothus arboreus.*

OCCURRENCE.

High north slopes (Santa Cruz Island) in dry, gravelly or rocky soil, where it is largest and most frequent as a tree; smaller on other islands. Silvical habits undetermined, as are its requirements of climate, light, its seeding habits, and reproduction.

Lilac.

Ceanothus spinosus Nuttall.

DISTINGUISHING CHARACTERISTICS.

Lilac has long been known as a shrub only, but recently it has been found to reach a tree size of from 12 to 15 feet in height and from 3 to 5 inches in

FIG. 196.—*Ceanothus spinosus.*

diameter. It has a short, clear trunk with deep reddish-brown, scaly bark, and a narrow scanty-leafed, open crown of upright limbs. Mature twigs of the season, somewhat angled, reddish brown, usually spine-tipped; often growing horizontally from the branches. Mature leaves (fig. 196) usually without marginal teeth, thickish, somewhat leathery, smooth, and partly evergreen; leafstems either slightly and minutely hairy or quite smooth. Leaves on young, vigorous twigs are often toothed, with the 3-veined character at the base more prominent than in the other entire-margined leaves. Fragrant, pale to deep blue flowers are borne in long (5 to 6 inches), wide bunches, the small clusters of blossoms densely crowded. Mature fruit (fig. 196) smooth and black. Wood of the arborescent form has not been examined. Not likely to be of any economic use on account of the rarely large size of trees.

LONGEVITY.—Not fully determined. Record of one stem 3½ inches in diameter showed it to be 20 years old.

RANGE.

California. Canyons near the coast of Santa Barbara, Ventura, and Los Angeles counties.

OCCURRENCE.

Low mountain canyons; in gravelly and rocky soils. Forms patches and groups mainly under and interspersed with California live oak and walnut, white alder, pale elder, California sycamore, and laurel.

CLIMATIC CONDITIONS.—Similar to those of California sycamore.

TOLERANCE.—Not fully determined, but species endures a good deal of shade.

REPRODUCTION.—Abundant seeder and young plants frequent.

Family CORNACEÆ.

Cornaceæ is commonly known as the cornel family, members of which are widely distributed throughout the world, but most abundantly in temperate regions. It contains shrubs and trees, some of the latter large and valuable for their timber. The family is represented in the United States by two groups, *Cornus*, the cornels and so-called dogwoods, and by *Nyssa*, the pepperidge or tupelo gum trees. Only *Cornus* is represented in the Pacific region, while members of *Nyssa* belong wholly to the Atlantic region. They have simple single-bladed leaves which are borne in pairs (one opposite another), or singly, and are shed every autumn. Their small, inconspicuous flowers are either perfectly bisexual or of separate sexes, each kind borne on different trees (only the female trees producing seed). Some of the fruits resemble small berries, others cherries, and contain a one or two seeded stone.

CORNUS. DOGWOODS AND CORNELS.

The dogwoods and cornels are a group of shrubs and small, rather unimportant hardwooded trees, with more representatives in North America than in any other country. The most popular and widely known members of the group are the English cornel tree (*Cornus mas* L.) so much cultivated for its acid, cherry-like fruit, and the so-called flowering dogwood of our eastern woodlands, prized and planted for its showy, white-scaled flowers.

The bark of cornels is bitter and tonic. Cornel wood is very suitable and useful for small turnery requiring hardness, strength, and wearing qualities; special care in seasoning (slow drying) is needed to prevent checking. The pointed leaves occur mostly in pairs, rarely one at a point, while twigs and branches are given off in pairs at every joint (except in one eastern species). The leaves have prominent, deeply impressed, straight veins, and characteristic wavy margins, and are always clustered at or near the ends of the twigs. Flowers, perfectly bisexual, very small, greenish, closely crowded, and stemless, in small flat bunches at the ends of twigs, each cluster appearing to be the center of a large white flower, the showy 4 to 6 divisions of which are not parts of a true flower, but large petal-like [a] scales (fig. 197). In other members (native trees) the small, white flowers appear loosely and without showy scales, in broad, minutely branched (2-forked), flattish-topped clusters. Fruits produced by the first type of flowers appear in crowded clusters at the ends of the twigs (fig. 198), while the larger, broad, flat clusters of flowers produce similarly arranged clusters of berry-like fruit. Cornel fruits, often bright colored, are eaten by birds and mammals (with little or no injury to the seed), and thus the seeds are widely distributed; otherwise, they are distributed only by flood waters.

They are chiefly moisture-loving plants, growing either in naturally wet or moist soils, or in forests where shade and ground cover conserve soil water. Species of *Cornus* existed in early geologic periods. Of the three tree cornels native to the United States, only one inhabits the Pacific region.

Western Dogwood.

Cornus nuttallii Audubon.

DISTINGUISHING CHARACTERISTICS.

Western dogwood, the only tree of its genus in the Pacific forests, is easily recognized in spring when in flower by the large, conspicuous, petal-like [a] scales, or in late summer and early autumn by its clusters of bright red fruit and brilliant red and orange foliage. From its general appearance it might easily be mistaken for its eastern relative, *Cornus florida* L., from which, however, it differs widely in details. The western dogwood is a smooth-looking tree ordinarily from 20 to 30 feet high, and from 6 to 8 inches through, but not uncommonly from 30 to 50 feet high, with a fairly straight trunk from 10 to 20 inches in diameter. Much of the thin, dull, ashy brown or reddish bark is smooth; only the bark of large old trunks is broken into very small, thin scales. Crown branches are short. Young trees in the open have rather short trunks and long, narrow crowns, which in older trees become rounded, while in close stands the crowns are short and narrow, and the trunks long and clean. Twigs of a season's growth, minutely hairy when young, are mostly smooth and dull red-purple, often with greenish areas; the small, pointed, leaf-buds are clasped by two opposite, long-pointed, narrow scales (fig. 198). Mature leaves (fig. 198) are thin, with minute, very close hairs on their top sides, and beneath lighter with fine, soft hairs, as also have the leaf stems. Leaves are from $3\frac{1}{2}$ to 5 inches long; midveins and their side branches conspicuously impressed on the upper sides of the leaves. The button-like clusters of very small, greenish-yellow flowers, which bloom in early spring, are surrounded by from 4 to 6 showy white or, sometimes, faintly pinkish scales (fig. 197), which are popularly taken to be parts of a real flower. They are, however, flower-bud scales which, with the flower cluster, are partly formed during the previous summer, and are situated just beneath [b] the immature flower cluster; they remain in this undeveloped state until the following spring, when they grow with the

---

[a] Showy like one of the inner parts of a flower which, in ordinary blossoms, are colored as in the rose.

[b] In the eastern "flowering dogwood" (*C. florida* L.) these scales completely cover the cluster of immature flowers. When full grown, scales of this species differ greatly from those of western dogwood in being deeply indented at their ends (somewhat heart-shaped).

flowers, becoming large and showy when the latter open. Autumnal flowers
are not uncommon. From 25 to 40 shiny red berries are matured in a dense
cluster (fig. 198) at the ends of the twigs; the thin, dryish pulp of the berry
contains one hard-shelled, 1 or 2 seeded stone. Wood, very pale reddish-brown,
with thick sapwood; moderately heavy, dense, and very hard, fine-grained,

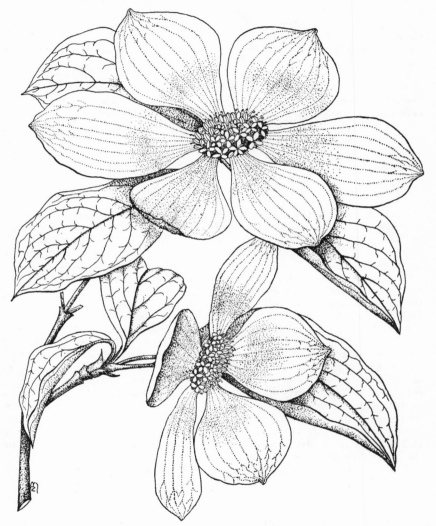

Fig. 197.—*Cornus nutallii.*

checking badly (if seasoned rapidly in the open air). Considerably lighter and
less dense than wood of the eastern dogwood; suitable for turnery and small
cabinet work, but little used at present, and not likely to be of much economic
importance.

LONGEVITY.—Records of the age attained by the largest trees are not available. Trees from 6 to 12 inches through are from 45 to 90 years old. The largest trunks are probably from 125 to 150 years old.

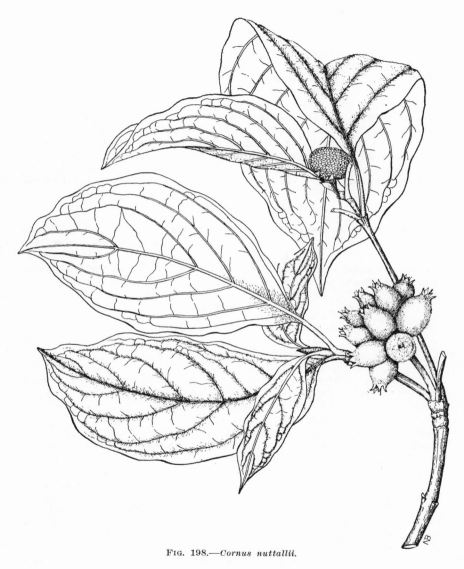

FIG. 198.—*Cornus nuttallii.*

RANGE.

From southern coast of British Columbia (Lower Fraser River and Vancouver Island) through Washington, Oregon, and California (coast ranges to San Jacinto Mountains and western slopes of Sierra Nevada Mountains).

OCCURRENCE.

Low bottoms, lower gentle mountain slopes, valleys, coves, ravines, borders, and well-drained bottoms of mountain streams, in rich, fresh, loamy, gravelly, or rocky soils;

largest in fresh, porous soils.   Mixed, singly or in small groups, under Douglas fir, red-wood, and western hemlock, with broadleaf and vine maple, Nuttall willow, red and white alders; sometimes under western yellow pine and sugar pine.   Largest in heavy Douglas fir forests of Puget Sound country.

CLIMATIC CONDITIONS.—Similar to those of Douglas fir.

TOLERANCE.—Very tolerant of dense shade.

REPRODUCTION.—Abundant annual seeder.   Seed of medium high rate of germination (but tardy) and of persistent vitality; requires constantly moist seed bed for good germination.   Seedlings scattered; most abundant in deep shade or on moist stream borders.

Family GARRYACEÆ.

A small and little-known group of trees and shrubs represented in our Pacific country, adjacent southern territory, and in the West Indies, by one genus, *Garrya*, which commemorates the name of Garry, who facilitated the early northwestern explorations of David Douglas, discoverer of the type species. The general aspect of these plants suggests close relationship to the cornels (Cornaceæ), in which *Garrya* is usually placed; but the very different character of the flowers and fruit is good reason for separating *Garrya* from that family.

GARRYA.

About a dozen species (chiefly shrubs) comprise this group.   Two of them occur in the Pacific region, and one of them sometimes becomes a tree.   Important characters of the group are opposite leaves and flowers (of two sexes) borne on separate individuals (only the female individuals producing seed). Other characters of the genus are given under the following tree species.

Quinine Bush.

Garrya elliptica Douglas.

DISTINGUISHING CHARACTERISTICS.

Quinine bush gets its name from its bitter bark, leaves, and, especially, fruit. It is known also as " silk-tassel bush," and as " fringe-tree," in reference to the tassel-like clusters of flowers and fruit.

Ordinarily a low, evergreen chaparral shrub,. but in parts of its northern coastal range, sometimes a short-trunked tree from 20 to 30 feet high and from 6 to 20 inches through.   Little is now known of its trunk and crown form, for it is only rather recently that tree forms were first found.[a]   Mature leaves (fig. 199) are thick, leathery, smooth above and white-woolly beneath, the margins particularly wavy.   Mature fruit (fig. 199), ripe in late summer or early autumn, is berry-like, with a thin brittle case covering an acid, slightly bitter, purplish pulp, in which there are 1 or 2 seeds.   Male clusters of flowers (fig. 199) are from 3 to 5 inches long and fringe-like.   Wood, not used commercially because of its rarity.   It has not been studied fully, but is known to be heavy, dense, and hard.

As a shrub quinine bush assists, with manzanita and ceanothus brush, in maintaining a scanty but tenacious cover on dry, gravelly, and rocky mountain slopes. Nothing is known of its silvical characteristics as a tree in moist, rich soils.

LONGEVITY.—Age limits undetermined.

---

[a] The late A. J. Johnson, a tireless explorer of Oregon forests, first brought this fact to the writer's notice, and upon his statement the sizes here given are based.   He reported finding especially large trees in Coos County, Oreg., in 1889.

RANGE.

RANGE.—Oregon through California south to the Santa Lucia Mountains in Monterey County. Range imperfectly. known.

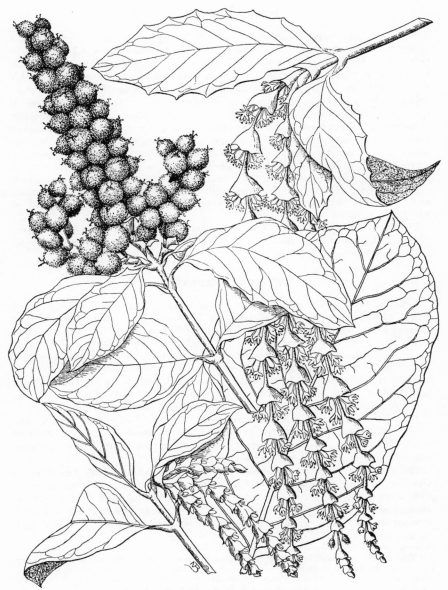

FIG. 199.—*Garrya elliptica.*

OCCURRENCE.

Mountain slopes of medium elevation and on foothills ; in dry, gravelly soils (shrubby), or occasionally in sandy loam soils (largest). Grows singly and in clumps. At higher levels, sometimes under western yellow pine with manzanita, ceanothus, and other brush; silvical habits elsewhere imperfectly known now.

CLIMATIC CONDITIONS.—Similar to those of redwood and yellow pine. Tolerance (evidently endures a good deal of shade) and reproduction undetermined.

Family ERICACEÆ.

Ericaceæ, popularly called the "heath" family, contains a large number of shrubs and a few small or medium-sized, hard-wooded trees, all widely distributed in the warm and temperate regions of the world. Among its well-known members are the huckleberries, blueberries, and cranberries; the popular trailing arbutus, wintergreen, and manzanitas; and the azaleas and rhododendrons, which are among the most beautiful flowering shrubs and small trees in the world. While many of the shrubs, wild and cultivated, are commercially important for their fruit or for ornamental planting, but few of the trees supply wood of value, except for minor purposes. They vary greatly in their requirements of soil, moisture, and light, some of them inhabiting cool, shady forests, or cold, wet bogs from sea level to high mountains, while others thrive in arid soils of hot mountain slopes. They have simple, single-bladed leaves, which are evergreen or shed annually in autumn. The flowers are perfectly bisexual, and the fruits vary from juicy berries to dry, small-seeded capsules, all of which are matured in one season.

The family contains nearly 70 genera, about 20 of which inhabit the United States. Eight or ten of these are trees, represented in the Pacific region by *Arctostaphylos* [a] and *Arbutus*.

ARBUTUS. MADROÑAS.

Arbutus is a small group of evergreen-leafed shrubs and chiefly small trees, with peculiarly thin, red bark on branches, large limbs, and smaller trunks; bark of large tree trunks thicker, brown, and scaly. The leaves, borne singly, are thick and leathery, while the small, urn-shaped flowers (5-lobed at top) are in rather large, open, branched clusters, the main stem thick and stiff. The fruit, berry-like in appearance, dry and mealy, is spherical, one-third to one-half inch in diameter, bright red or orange-red, with a finely warty surface, and 5-celled, with several or numerous small seeds. The attractive looking "berries" are eaten by birds, which assist in disseminating the seeds.

Members of this group have dense, rather heavy, close-grained, often very strong, stiff wood, which is apt to check badly if dried rapidly and without special treatment. That of our representatives is not especially valuable, except for charcoal and minor domestic uses.

Three of the dozen known species occur in the United States and Mexico, and one of these inhabits only the Pacific region. Some of them grow in rich, dry or moist soils from sea-level to several thousand feet elevation, sometimes forming a considerable part of the shady cover along mountain streams and in coves, while others grow on poor slopes of low hills and high mountains.

---

[a] This group contains the chiefly shrubby, well-known manzanitas so frequent on dry slopes in the Pacific region. At least 3 or 4 (particularly *A. manzanita* Parry, *A. glauca* Lindley, and *A. viscida* Parry) of the known species occasionally become veritable trees or tree-like, and eventually should be included among the Pacific trees. In the writer's opinion, however, the whole group requires much more careful study than has yet been given to it in the field before this can be done properly. For the present, therefore, consideration of *Arctostaphylos* is omitted from this work.

Madroña.

Arbutus menziesii Pursh.

DISTINGUISHING CHARACTERISTICS.

Madroña is often a stately tree from 60 to 80 feet high, with a straight, clean trunk from 2 to 3 feet in diameter; sometimes, but rather rarely, considerably taller and thicker. Very frequently low and shrubby, or from 25 to 40 feet high, with a crooked or leaning trunk from 8 to 15 inches through. Its red-brown trunks, red branches, and shiny, evergreen foliage distinguish it at once from all other trees or shrubs in its range. The crown form varies from a narrow, dense, columnar one in younger trees to a broad rounded one in old trees. The thin, reddish-brown bark of old trunks is loosely scaly, mainly only on the lower trunk; that of the upper stem, limbs, and twigs, and of young trunks, very thin, smooth and red, peeling off in thin, irregular, flakes, much as in the sycamores. The showy, large clusters of flowers resemble lilies of the valley. Mature leaves (fig. 200) are thick, leathery, smooth throughout, shiny on their upper sides, whitish beneath, and 2½ to 5 inches long. The brilliant orange-red, berry-like fruit (fig. 200), ripe late in fall, and often borne in great abundance, makes the trees most beautiful in autumn. Wood, pale reddish brown, with a thin whitish sapwood; rather heavy, dense, fine-grained, hard (when dry), but cuts like soft wood when green, and is usually quite brittle. Suitable for cabinet work and an excellent charcoal wood. At present not important for commercial purposes, but, with a better knowledge of how to season it, the wood should be of more economic value in a region so lacking in hard woods.

LONGEVITY.—The age attained by very large trees is unknown. Gives evidence of being long-lived. Grows very slowly, especially in diameter, but with little loss of vigor. Trees 12 to 16 inches through are 60 to 85 years old. Further study of age limits is desirable.

RANGE.

Coast region of southern British Columbia and Washington to southern California; reported also in northern Lower California. Range still imperfectly known.

BRITISH COLUMBIA.—East coast of Vancouver Island, and sparsely northward to Seymour Narrows, and around south end nearly to Port San Juan. Adjacent islands and immediate mainland coast. Noted on Vancouver Island at Victoria, near Nanoose Bay and at Departure Bay; not in Port Renfrew region.

WASHINGTON.—Frequent in coast region, especially on Puget Sound. Noted in valley of Elwha River; shores of Hood Canal in vicinity of Union City; Mat Mats Bay; vicinity of Seattle.

OREGON.—Common along coast, up rivers, and inland on southern coast ranges and slopes of Siskiyous eastward to head of Bear River (T. 40 S., R. 2 E.); also northward on west slopes of Cascades to Umpqua-Rogue River Divide (T. 33 S., R. 1 W. and 1 to 3 E.), and reported farther north on Lost Creek (T. 22 S., R. 1 E.). Locally noted at Astoria and Gold Beach.

CALIFORNIA.—Northern cross ranges and coast ranges southward to San Gabriel Mountains; also southward in Sierras to head of Tuolumne River (lat. 37° 45′); generally from sea level to about 3,000 feet elevation. Northern cross ranges eastward to yellow pine belt in Shasta National Forest; southern slope of Siskiyous eastward at least to railroad crossing. Klamath National Forest, in Siskiyou County; noted on west slope only of Marble Mountain up to 4,000 feet and westward into basin of Russian Creek, valley of North Fork Salmon River, to Sawyers Bar, Forks of Salmon River, and up east slope of Salmon Summit to 4,700 feet. Noted in Humboldt County on west slope of Trinity Summit above Hoopa Valley at elevations below 4,000 feet, and westward into Hoopa Valley, Supply Creek Canyon, Miners Creek Canyon, Redwood Creek, Korbel, and Blue Lake; farther south in Little Van Dusen Canyon and westward to Bridgeville and Hydesville; also in McNutts Gulch (south of Domingo Hill) on road from Capetown to Petrolia, and south of Petrolia on Upper Mattole to Briceland; lower slopes King

Mountain and southward into Mendocino County. Trinity National Forest, generally distributed from valley bottoms, at 1,500 to over 3,000 feet, eastward to a canyon near Lewiston, and extending up Canyon Creek to first falls; locally noted in vicinity of Wildwood, Hayfork Mountains, Post Creeks, South Fork of Trinity River, Mad River, Hayfork (Post-Office), on Post creeks to South Fork. *Mendocino County:* Coast from

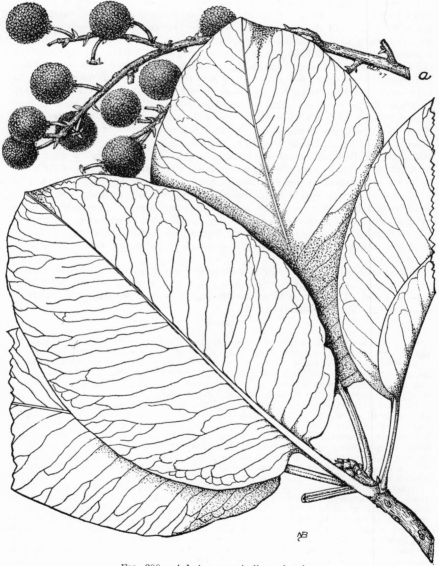

FIG. 200.—*Arbutus menziesii: a,* berries.

Kenny southward to Westport, eastward to Cahto and Laytonville; road from latter to Round Valley; between Eel River and Poonkinny, divide between Eel River and Round Valley, Round Valley hills north of Indian Agency and gulches; canyon on west slope Mount Sanhedrin, Tomki gulch, Upper Redwood Canyon; hills east of Redwood Valley, and on Russian River at north end of Ukiah Valley to and beyond Willets; rare near sea, growing 5 or 6 miles back; noted between Gualala and Fort Bragg, Upper Big River, and divide between Ukiah and head of Big River. *Sonoma County:* Near coast on road to Plantation House; Austin Creek Canyon (south of Cazadero); Lower Russian River from Duncan Mills nearly to mouth, and eastward to Guerneville and Forestville; Dutch Bill gulch, Camp Meeker, Occidentalis to south edge of redwood forest, near Freestone; east of Occidentalis to Green Valley; between Meeker and Sebastopol; Middle Russian River (southward from Mendocino County). *Southeastern Sonoma County:* Sonoma Creek northward in Sonoma Valley; Glen Ellen, Beltane, Sonoma Mountains and those between Sonoma and Napa Valley; canyon between Knights and Alexander valleys; extreme northeastern Sonoma County; Big Sulphur Creek at Geysers, and up canyon to Socrates Basin and over divide into Lake County. Here about Russian River, east of Healdsburg, and north of Cloverdale. *Marin County:* Mount Tamalpais, common; Kentfield and westward; San Geronimo and Lagunitas valleys, Paper Mill Creek; hills west of San Rafael; Mill valley to Sausalito; south end of Tomales Bay, and on Inverness Ridge on west side of bay. Stony Creek National Forest, only on Eel River drainage of western border. *Lake County:* From Mount St. Helena eastward to within 2 miles of Middletown, and from west of Middletown westward up Cobb Mountain and into Sonoma County. *Napa County:* Southward in Napa Valley, on west side, to and beyond Oakville; upper Napa Valley to and beyond Calistoga; east of St. Helena, and on south side of Mount St. Helena up to Toll House; on west side of ridge south from Mount St. Helena on east side of Napa Valley. *Solano County:* Few isolated trees in Jameson Canyon from Green Valley westward, and perhaps elsewhere. *Alameda County:* Canyon about Mission Peak southeast of old San Jose Mission. *Santa Clara County:* Hills bordering Coyote Creek near Gilroy Hot Springs; Mount Hamilton range. *San Mateo and Santa Cruz counties:* Common on both sides of Santa Cruz range; noted from Boulder County to Big Basin and on road from Los Gatos westward, west of Stanford descending to east base of range and common about Portola; following Santa Cruz Mountains southward from sea level to summits occurs in hills east of Monterey Bay nearly to Watsonville. *Monterey County:* Not detected about Monterey nor on Monterey Peninsula, except a few trees in canyons on Point Piños at 400 to 500 feet. Common on coastal summits of Santa Lucia Mountains, at 800 to 4,250 feet, in watersheds of Sur, Carmelo, Arroyo Seco, San Antonio, and Nacimiento rivers; noted at north base of Santa Lucia Peak in gulch leading to head of Milpitas Valley, and west of Santa Lucia Peak in canyon of Arroyo Seco. *San Benito County:* Locally noted on north side of Fremont Peak only a few hundred feet below summit; also lower down on east slopes of San Juan Canyon and in other gulches about north base of mountain; in a gulch on west side of San Juan Valley 2 miles north of San Juan. San Luis Obispo Mountains, in Salinas, Santa Margarita, and San Luis river basins; noted at San Luis Obispo at 2,000 feet. Southern cross ranges eastward to San Gabriel Mountains; north slope of Santa Ynez Range, at 1,000 to 3,500 feet, with best growth at Refugio Pass, and at head of Rattlesnake Creek (Cold Spring trail), at 2,500 feet; in San Rafael Range, only on west slopes of Big Pine Mountains and on Mount Medulce, in cool canyons at 3,000 to 4,000 feet; Santa Monica Mountains, a few shrubby plants in Los Tuñas Canyon; San Gabriel Range, small group on Mount Wilson and in narrow belt on the Sturtevant Trails, at about 3,000 feet. Reported also from San Bernardino Mountains. Sierra foothills, abundant but usually distributed in patches and small areas. Rare in Shasta County; occurs sparingly along McCloud River for about 15 miles north of fish hatchery at Baird, and near Winthrop on Squaw Creek. General in foothills of Lassen Peak and Plumas National forests up to about 2,500 feet. *Butte County:* On the road from Oroville to Quincy from a gulch about 4 miles north of Bidwell Bar, at an altitude of about 1,200 feet, northeastward to "Junction House" (deserted station—altitude, 3,500 feet) about 3 miles south of Merrimac Stage station, thence into Little North Fork Canyon. *Yuba County:* Yuba Pass road, abundant in canyon of North Fork Yuba River on east side of Oregon Hills, thence to and beyond Camptonville, above which it enters west end of Sierra County. *Nevada County:* Common near Grass Valley, particularly on north slope of ridge about 1½ miles east of Grass Valley. Tahoe National Forest, in lateral canyons of North Fork of Feather River and between Camptonville and Middle Fork of Yuba River, at 2,300 to 3,200 feet. *Placer County:* Common on road from Colfax south to Forest Hill; also on south side of North Fork American River Canyon between Colfax and Iowa Hill, and for several miles east of Iowa Hill. Stanislaus National Forest, rather abundant at a few points in middle timber belt at about 2,500 to 4,000 feet, but especially so and of large size on headwaters of Sutter, Pioneer, Mill, and Jesus Maria creeks; smaller and less frequent on Empire Creek, between Garden Valley and Georgetown, and on Otter Creek (tributary Middle Fork American River); **extensive area in southern part of Amador County beginning about 3 miles east of Pine**

Grove, and extending eastward to Pioneer, and for about 3 miles along summit of ridge on north side of Mokelumne River Canyon (above Defender) at 2,700 to 3,000 feet. Sierra National Forest, one grove of large trees on north slope of Pilot Ridge on Packards Camp Stream (tributary South Fork Tuolumne River, lat. 37° 45'), southern limit now known in Sierras.

OCCURRENCE.

Foothill and low mountain slopes of every aspect, borders of streams, cool canyons and valleys; in well-drained, moist, rich, rocky, or loamy soils (here largest) to dry, loamy, or poor gravelly soils (here small or shrubby). Best growth near sea under influence of fogs. Forms small pure stands, but more commonly an undergrowth with redwood, tanbark oak, Douglas fir, California laurel, goldenleaf chinquapin, broadleaf and vine maples, California live oak; frequent in open stands of western yellow pine and Kellogg oak, and less often with gray pine.

CLIMATIC CONDITIONS.—Similar to those of yellow pine and Douglas fir.

TOLERANCE.—Appears very tolerant of shade throughout life. Endures dense shade, but requires at least partial top light for best growth; dense side shade cleans long, slender trunks.

REPRODUCTION.—Abundant seeder. Exact seeding habits undetermined, especially in the open. Seed has moderately high rate of germination, and persistent vitality. Germination best and most abundant in moist soil when seed is well covered; otherwise (as in drier places) tardy and seedlings scarce.

Family OLEACEÆ.

Popularly known as the olive family, an important group of forest trees and shrubs, widely represented in warm and temperate countries, particularly those of the northern half of the world. It includes the world-famous olive-tree, cultivated centuries ago in Syria and Palestine, later in the Mediterranean country, and now, in addition, in our southwest and in California; it includes also the ashes—very valuable timber and ornamental trees—and such popular shrubs as the lilacs, the gorgeous yellow-flowered Forsythias, sweet jessamines, and the privets, the latter much planted for hedges. All are similar in having their leaves arranged in pairs (one opposite another). Flowers of some are all perfectly bisexual, those of others are either male or female, each kind borne on different trees; those of yet others are both bisexual and unisexual on the same tree.

Some 20 different genera are known in the world, 5 of which are represented in the United States. Three groups of these contain tree species. One genus, *Fraxinus*, has species distributed from the Atlantic to the Pacific region, whereas the other groups belong entirely to our eastern forests.

FRAXINUS. ASHES.

All the ashes except one are trees, and without exception all are known as ashes. Some are very large trees, commercially valuable for their timber, which is straight-grained, hard, and elastic. They grow naturally in a variety of soils, from wet, boggy swamps to the driest and poorest uplands, but most of them thrive best in moist, rich soils. A few form a large part of the forest in which they grow, while others constitute considerable, but only scattered, elements in it. Still others are unimportant stragglers, often confined to narrow rocky banks of stream courses.

With few exceptions, they have straight, evenly tapered trunks, and grayish, regularly and rather finely ridged bark. Their leaves, arranged in pairs, are all of one type, a principal leaf stem with few or many pairs of (leaf-like) leaflets arranged on two opposite sides and a single leaflet at the end, so that the total number is always odd. The twigs and branches, also, have a characteristic arrangement in opposite pairs at every joint. Flowers appear in early spring, usually before the leaves. They are usually small or minute and inconspicuous, though densely clustered and are either perfectly bisexual or of separate sexes. When of separate sexes the sexes are borne on separate trees. Occasionally some bisexual flowers and some of one sex only are borne on the same tree.

Fruits or "seeds," borne in branched clusters, have a general similarity in form in all the ashes and are always produced in one season, ripening in early autumn, but often remaining on the trees for several weeks afterward. The "seed" has a thin wing at one end which adds greatly to its buoyancy and enables the wind to waft it to considerable distances from the mother tree. Seeds are also disseminated to some extent by streams and flood waters. At least a small proportion of the crop is eaten by mice and other small rodents. Falling to the ground in autumn or winter they germinate, if at all, the following spring, very rarely retaining their vitality for a longer time.

Nearly 40 species are known, 16 of which occur in the United States, and all are trees except one, a shrub. Three arborescent and one shrubby species inhabit the Pacific region. One tree is confined to that region, while the other two barely extend into it from their principal, more eastern range. The largest and best timber ashes belong to the eastern United States.

Leatherleaf Ash.

Fraxinus coriacea Watson.

DISTINGUISHING CHARACTERISTICS.

Leatherleaf ash has no field name. The one suggested here is derived from the character of its leaves, to which the technical name refers.

It was distinguished about thirty years ago under its present name, but until recently it has been confused with *F. velutina*, the range and habits of which are much the same. Still imperfectly known, especially as regards range and silvical characteristics. Similar in size and general appearance to *F. velutina* (but occasionally of large diameter). It differs in having thicker, leathery, longer-stemmed, broader leaflets, 5 in number, which are $2\frac{1}{2}$ to 3 inches long and $1\frac{1}{4}$ to 2 inches broad (fig. 201), deep green and smooth above, lighter beneath, with minute soft hairs (sometimes smooth). Occasional leaves have 3 leaflets, or are simple and single bladed. Margins of the leaflets rather coarsely toothed, the teeth far apart. Twigs of a season's growth are covered with fine, soft down. The flowers are as in *F. velutina*, but they appear a few weeks earlier, and usually before the leaves come out, but sometimes with them. Clusters of mature fruit (fig. 201) are narrow, $2\frac{1}{2}$ to 3 inches long, and the seeds few. Wood, not yet studied. The tree is of too rare occurrence in the Pacific region to be of economic importance there.

LONGEVITY.—Not fully determined. Record of one tree $11\frac{1}{4}$ inches in diameter shows an age of 48 years.

RANGE.

Desert regions of southern Utah, northern Arizona, southern Nevada, and southeastern California.

OCCURRENCE.

On borders of desert streams and sinks; in gravelly or loamy soils. Forms open groups and patches of pure growth, or occasionally interspersed with desert willow and cotton-wood.

FIG. 201.—*Fraxinus coriacea.*

CLIMATIC CONDITIONS.—Endures climatic conditions marked by high summer temperature, rapid evaporation, small rainfall, dry atmosphere, and mild winters. Nothing is known now of silvical characteristics and reproduction.

Oregon Ash.

Fraxinus oregona Nuttall.

DISTINGUISHING CHARACTERISTICS.

Oregon ash, the only timber ash of the Pacific region; is recognized everywhere in its commercial range as one of the most useful hardwoods. Lumbermen call it " Oregon ash," but it is often known simply as " ash."

Forest-grown trees have long, clean trunks and narrow, short crowns of small branches, and are from 60 to 75 feet high and from 16 to 30 inches in diameter; sometimes larger. Trees on the open borders of streams have short trunks and very wide, round-topped crowns with large limbs. In drier parts of its range it is often a crooked tree under 25 feet in height and only from 6 to 8 inches through. The trunk bark, rather thick and soft on the surface, is deeply and regularly furrowed, the wide ridges connected by thinner side ones, and dull gray to grayish brown. Twigs of a season's growth are usually covered with whitish—sometimes brownish—dense, soft, fine woolly hairs, but occasionally are only very minutely hairy or even smooth, with a whitish bloom. Mature leaves (fig. 202), about 6 to 12 inches long, with from 5 to 7 thick, yellow-green leaflets, which are about 3 to 6 inches long by about seven-eighths inch to $1\frac{1}{2}$ inches wide and more or less woolly or downy beneath, as are the grooved leaf stems (fig. 202). Male and female flowers, each borne on separate trees, appear as the leaves begin to come out; only the female trees bear " seed " (fig. 202), which matures in early autumn in large, full clusters. Seeds vary from about $1\frac{1}{4}$ to occasionally 2 inches in length, and the wings from one-fourth to one-third inch wide. Wood, dull yellowish brown with whitish sapwood. The wood of forest-grown trees is moderately fine-grained and rather brittle, but that of open-grown trees is coarse-grained and elastic—particularly the sapwood of young trees. Of slightly lighter weight than the eastern timber ashes, but in general appearance and quality it compares favorably with them, and is suitable for the same commercial uses for which those timbers are employed.

LONGEVITY.—Age limits of very large trees have not been determined. Trees from 16 to 25 inches in diameter (grown in the forest) are from 95 to 155 years old. The largest trees appear to grow much more slowly after the first century and probably attain 180 to 250 years before becoming decrepit.

RANGE.

From Puget Sound (shores) southward through Washington, Oregon, and California (coast region to San Francisco Bay; on foothills of Sierra Nevada Mountains to mountains of San Bernardino and San Diego counties). Also reported from the southern part of British Columbian coast.

WASHINGTON.—Western part west of Cascades, but not on Olympic Mountains, from sea level to 2,000 or 3,000 feet. Columbia River, not above The Dalles. Noted at White Salmon on Columbia River in Klickitat County, Seattle, Satsop, Mount Rainer National Forest up to 2,500 feet, especially in the " Big Bottom " of Cowlitz Valley.

OREGON.—Western part west of Cascades, in valleys. Noted on Willamette River bottoms near Portland, on Columbia River flats above dunes between McClures and The Dalles (Wasco County), in Cascade (North) National Forest, in Bear Creek, and other valleys of Siskiyou National Forest at about 2,000 feet.

CALIFORNIA.—Noted in Klamath, Mount Shasta, Lassen Peak, Plumas, and Stanislaus National Forests up to about 2,000 feet; in Sacramento River canyon just west of Mount Shasta and at Middle Creek just north of Redding, in Shasta County; in northern coast ranges west of Sacramento River, near Lewiston, Trinity County, and elsewhere; in Stony Creek National Forest on all tributaries of Eel River; at Cazadero, in Sonoma County, and at Ross Valley, in Marin County, near coast; in Napa Valley, Napa County, and at Stockton in San Joaquin County. Also reported south of San Francisco in coast ranges in San Mateo County and elsewhere ; in Sierras also noted in Kaweah River Valley, and in southern California coast ranges near Los Angeles, in San Gabriel and Lytle Creek Canyons.

OCCURRENCE.

In vicinity of streams, on alluvial bottoms and flats ; in rich, deep, humous, sandy soils or in moist, rocky, gravelly ones ; largest in richer sites (southwestern Oregon) and correspondingly small or stunted in poorer situations. At north, occasionally in very small pure patches, but usually in rather close stands with red alder, broadleaf maple, California laurel, occasional grand fir, and Pacific post oak ; at south, with white alder and California sycamore.

CLIMATIC CONDITIONS.—In north, similar to those of grand fir, and in south, to those of Fremont cottonwood.

TOLERANCE.—Decidedly intolerant of shade throughout life, except in very early seedling stages, which endure only slight shade. Side shade quickly cleans its stems of limbs and in close stands produces long trunks with small crowns in full light.

REPRODUCTION.—Abundant annual seeder in open stands or when isolated. Seed has medium high rate of germination and persistent vitality. Germination best and usually abundant on moist or rather wet humous soils ; scanty in sandy and gravelly stream bottoms, owing to fact that much of seed is carried to unfavorable places by seasonal flood waters. In richer soils early height growth is very rapid.

Fraxinus velutina Torrey.

DISTINGUISHING CHARACTERISTICS.

Fraxinus velutina has no field name, except " ash," and has no prominent characters upon which to base a good common name. Probably not distinguished by laymen from other southwestern ashes. Ordinarily a rather slender, short-trunked tree from 20 to 30 feet high, with a grayish, sometimes faintly reddish, regularly seamed and broadly ridged trunk from 5 to 8 inches through ; surface of the bark is rather soft and scaly. The dense crowns of large trees are broad, rounded, and symmetrical. Twigs of a season's growth are usually reddish brown—sometimes dull grayish and covered with matted, fine woolly hairs, but often smooth and with a whitish tint, which can be rubbed off. Mature leaves (fig. 203), about 4 to 6 inches long, have from 3 to 9 thickish, somewhat leathery leaflets, which are smooth, deep yellowish-green on their top sides, lighter and more or less softly downy beneath. Angles of veins also hairy. Leaflets are from 3 to 4, sometimes 5, inches long, and one-third to seven-eighths inch wide ; partly entire ; indistinctly and distantly toothed, mainly above the middle, the points of the teeth turned in. Flowers appear with the growing leaves and are of two sexes, male and female, each kind borne on different trees, only the female trees bearing seed. Mature fruit (fig. 203) is in thick clusters $3\frac{1}{2}$ to 5 inches long, the wings about one-fourth inch wide and as long as the body of the seed. Wood, pale brown and with a very thick layer of sapwood ; moderately heavy, firm, fine-grained ; cuts and works easily, but is rather brittle. Although usually finer-grained, it resembles the white ash timber of eastern markets. Except for the small size of available sticks, the quality is suitable for many of the same uses. The occurrence of the tree in the Pacific region is too rare to give the wood economic importance there. In the writer's opinion this is one of the best southwestern ashes for experimental planting in arid regions.

LONGEVITY.—Not fully determined. One tree $15\frac{1}{8}$ inches in diameter showed an age of 114 years.

RANGE.

From western Texas (mountains) through southern New Mexico and Arizona to southern Nevada and southeastern California (Panamint Mountains and Owens Lake).

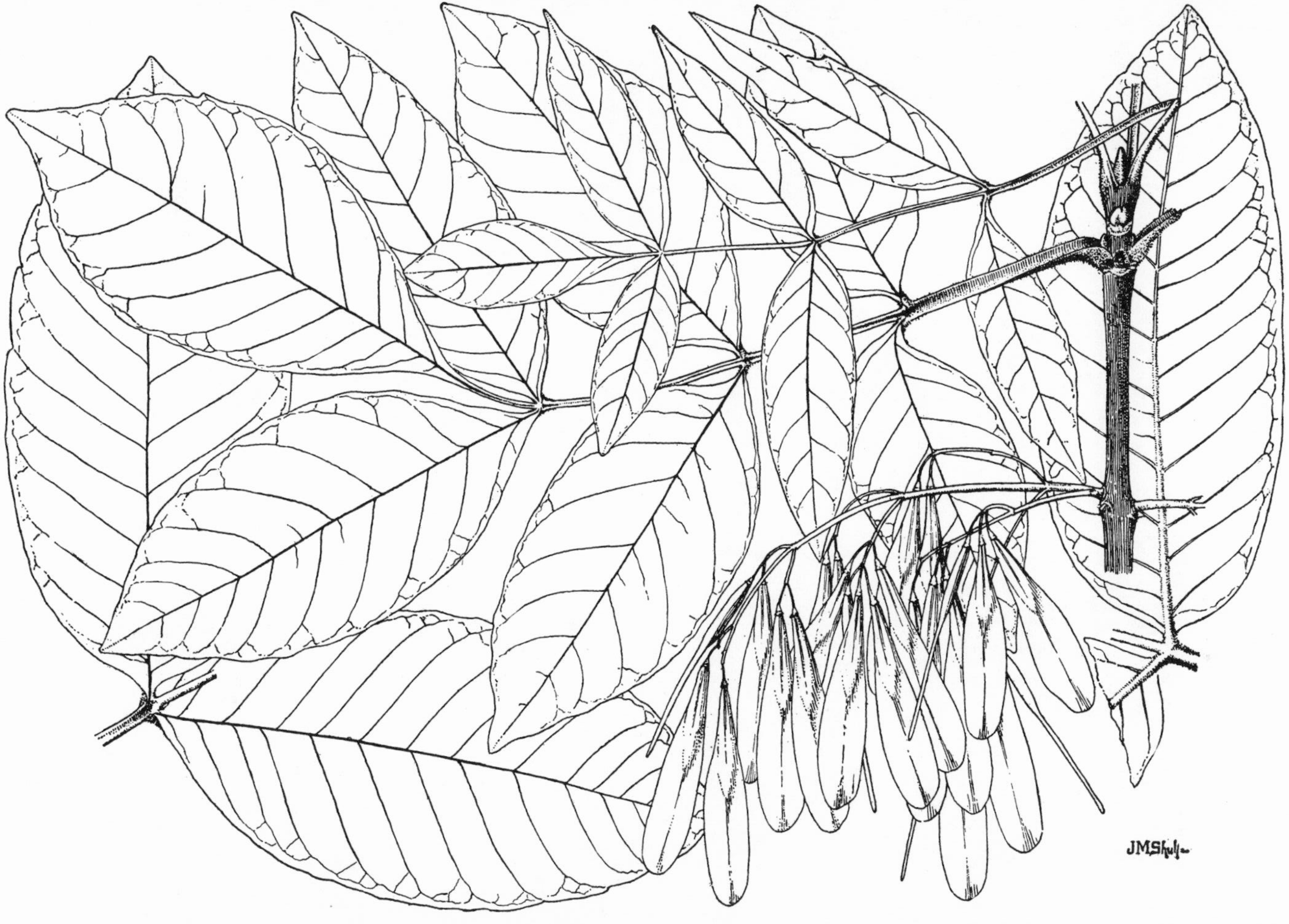

FIG. 202.—*Fraxinus oregona.*

OCCURRENCE.

In vicinity of streams, on lower sides and in canyon bottoms and gulches, desert water-holes and lakes, and sometimes on dry benches; in gravelly, sandy, and loamy soils. Grows with cottonwood and in small, pure groups.

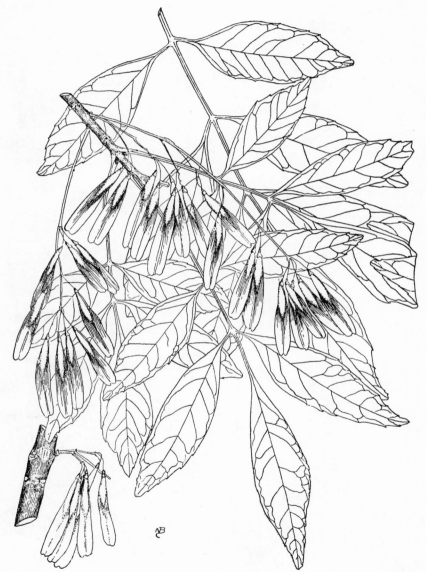

FIG. 203.—*Fraxinus velutina.*

CLIMATIC CONDITIONS (characterized by high summer temperature) and silvical characteristics undetermined. Prolific seeder.

Flowering Ash.

Fraxinus dipetala Hooker and Arnott.

DISTINGUISHING CHARACTERISTICS.

Flowering ash is not known to reach tree size. It flowers and fruits as a shrub, with numerous, slender stems from 6 to 10 feet high; occasionally single

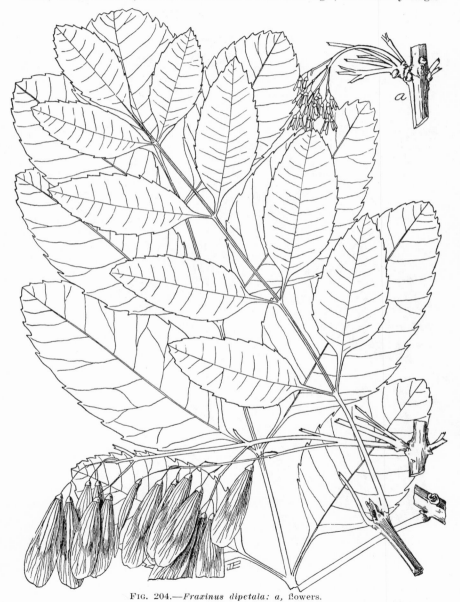

FIG. 204.—*Fraxinus dipetala: a,* flowers.

stems are tree-like in form. It is included here in order to give a full account of the ashes in this region.

The flowers (usually bisexual), appearing in spring with the leaves, differ from those of other Pacific ashes in having their parts white and showy, as in ordinary plant blossoms (fig. 204, *a*). The conspicuous part of the flowers is, as the technical name indicates, of two white divisions (petals). Twigs of a season's growth are more or less distinctly 4-angled and smooth. Mature leaves are smooth throughout, with from 5 to 9 (sometimes 3) thick leaflets (fig. 204). Mature fruit (fig. 204), variable in the length of its wings, is ripened in late summer.

Upon the occasional occurrence of individuals with leaves of 3 leaflets is based the variety *Fraxinus dipetala trifoliolata* Torrey, while *F. dipetala brachyptera* Gray is based on exceptionally short fruit (one-half to three-fourths inch long), the wing being about one-half as long as the body of the seed.

RANGE.

CALIFORNIA.—Along streams of the inner coast ranges and foothills of the Sierra Nevada.

OCCURRENCE.

On borders and in vicinity of foothill streams and in gulches; in dryish or slightly moist rocky and gravelly soils. In clumps and mingled with chaparral.

Family BIGNONIACEÆ.

Bignoniaceæ is a large group popularly known as the bignonia or trumpet-vine family. It contains such popular climbing shrubs as the trumpet-vine and the well-known catalpas—so valuable for their quickly grown, durable wood. Representatives of the family are particularly numerous in the tropical regions of the western hemisphere. The family comprises nearly 100 genera, 5 of which occur in the United States, while 3 of these, *Crescentia*, *Catalpa*, and *Chilopsis*, are groups of trees; the latter genus only is represented in the Pacific region. The flowers are large and showy, trumpet-like, or funnel-shaped, and the leaves of all (except *Crescentia*) are alike in being arranged on the twigs in pairs. The fruits (except in *Crescentia*) are long pods which split in half and have very light, flat, often fringed seeds, with two delicate wings.

CHILOPSIS.

This genus contains but one species, and its characters are included in the following description of its representative.

Desert Willow.

Chilopsis linearis (Cav.) Sweet.

DISTINGUISHING CHARACTERISTICS.

Desert willow is little known except to those who travel in its arid range, where it is called " desert willow " because of its narrow, willow-like leaves.

Ordinarily from 10 to 20 feet high, with a narrow crown of slim, upright branches, and a short, often crooked or leaning trunk from 2 to 6 inches through; sometimes larger; very often shrubby, with several or many slender stems from 5 to 6 feet high. Bark of even the smaller stems is regularly cut by seams into a network of deep yellowish-brown, shallow, connected ridges. Twigs of a season's growth are smooth (sticky or densely woolly at first), and pale yellowish to reddish brown. Mature leaves (fig. 205), which persist from spring until about midwinter, are smooth (often sticky when young), usually about 5 to 6 inches long, though sometimes nearly a foot long; mainly opposite on the lower parts of the twigs, but more or less alternate or diagonally opposite toward

FIG. 205.—*Chilopsis linearis: a,* seed pod; *b,* seed.

the ends of the slender, willowy stems. The large, funnel-shaped, violet-odored flowers (fig. 205) are white, faintly tinged with purple, and with bright yellow patches in the throat. Mature fruit pods (fig. 205, *a*), ripe in early autumn, about

5 to 10 inches long. They remain on the twigs more or less during the winter, gradually splitting open and liberating their small, flat, fringe-winged seeds (fig. 205, *b*), which are light and easily wafted by the wind, the principal agent of dissemination. The pods, which contain a very large number of seeds closely resembling catalpa seeds, have a flat central partition running their entire length, and upon two sides of which, as in catalpa pods, the seeds are borne. Wood, very much like that of catalpa in color and structure, is light and soft, yellowish brown, frequently with yellow areas, and durable in contact with the ground.   Not used for commercial purposes, but sometimes locally used for fence posts, for which it is highly prized on account of its durability in the ground.

LONGEVITY.—Not fully determined. Record of one tree 8⅝ inches in diameter shows an age of 43 years. Maturity is probably reached in less than 50 years. Old trees grow persistently for a long time, but show they have passed maturity by their hollow old trunks.

RANGE.

Through southwestern (from near Laredo) and western Texas, southern New Mexico, Arizona, southern Utah and Nevada, and southern California (San Diego County) ; northern Mexico.

OCCURRENCE.

Borders of desert and low mountain water courses, moist sinks, and water holes, in rather dry, well-drained, sandy and gravelly soils. Scattered and in groups.

CLIMATIC CONDITIONS.—Similar to those of mesquites.

TOLERANCE.—Intolerant of shade.

REPRODUCTION and seeding habits undetermined.

Family RUBIACEÆ.

Rubiaceæ is popularly known as the madder family, to which belong the world-famous madder plants of India and of the Mediterranean country, whose roots yield the most permanent red dyes known. Other important representatives are the coffee and cinchona trees of South America, the latter yielding the alkaloid tonic drugs cinchonidia and quinine, so much used in medicine. The family comprises shrubs, trees, and herbs of some 350 genera, natives mainly of tropical countries. Four genera, containing trees and shrubs, are represented in the United States by arborescent species. One of these, *Cephalanthus*, occurs from the Atlantic to the Pacific.

CEPHALANTHUS.

Cephalanthus forms a small group of unimportant species, one of which inhabits the Pacific region, extending also throughout the eastern United States. Characters of the genus are given under its one widely distributed species.

Button Bush.

Cephalanthus occidentalis Linnæus.

DISTINGUISHING CHARACTERISTICS.

Perhaps no woody plant is more widely known as a common shrub forming thickets on the borders of swamps, ponds, and streams than button bush. It has been known since the seventeenth century, but not until comparatively recent years has it been found to attain tree size, as in parts of southern Arkansas, eastern Texas, and at a few stations in California.   Tree forms may be discovered at other points. In this form it is from 20 to 30 feet high, with a clear, straight trunk of 10 or 15 feet in length, and from 6 to 8 inches in diameter ; taller and thicker trees sometimes occur. Elsewhere, so far as now known, it is only a shrub from 3 to 8 feet high. Bark of the trees is blackish brown, with a grayish overcast, and rough with deep furrows and wide broken ridges.

FIG. 206.—*Cephalanthus occidentalis: a,* flower ; *b,* fruit.

Twigs and leaves have a characteristic arrangement, 3 (or sometimes 2) growing from each joint of a main stem. Mature leaves (fig. 206, *b*) are smooth on their upper sides, lighter green and smooth or very minutely hairy beneath,

3 to 6 inches long and three-fourths inch to 3 inches wide. The perfectly bisexual, minute, cream-colored, fragrant flowers are densely packed in spherical, long-stemmed heads (fig. 206, *a*), which grow chiefly in threes from the ends of the branchlets. Likewise, the minute, long (inversely conical), grooved fruits are densely packed in spherical, dark brown heads (fig. 206, *b*) ; as the fruiting heads fall to pieces late in autumn or winter each little dry, pod-like fruit splits upward from its base into from 2 to 4 one-seeded parts. Wood of tree forms has not been studied; that of shrubby stems is light brown, with reddish tinge, hard, moderately heavy, and fine-grained. Rare occurrence of tree forms prevents the wood from being of more than incidental use.

LONGEVITY.—No records of the age attained by tree forms are available.

RANGE.

Lowlands in the water from southeastern Canada, Florida, westward to eastern Nebraska and Kansas, Texas, New Mexico, Arizona, and California, extending south to Cuba and Mexico.

OCCURRENCE.

Borders of lowland streams, marshes, and ponds ; in moist and wet sandy, gravelly, and mucky soils ; sometimes in dry streambeds within gray pine belt. Forms extensive pure thickets, interspersed with willows and other moisture-loving plants. Occasionally a small tree in river bottoms (Sacramento and San Joaquin).

CLIMATIC CONDITIONS.—Similar to those of sandbar willow.

TOLERANCE.—Endures considerable shade in wet soil, but requires top light for best growth.

REPRODUCTION.—Prolific seeder ; young plants abundant in shade and open.

Family CAPRIFOLIACEÆ.

Caprifoliaceæ is popularly called the honeysuckle family. Representatives are especially abundant in the temperate parts of the northern half of the world ; there are a few in the warmer regions. Small trees and shrubs, those occurring in the United States being unimportant. Well known and principal members of the family are the bush and climbing honeysuckles, snowberries, elderberries, and the familiar snowball. Of the 10 known genera, 2, *Sambucus* and *Viburnum*, contain tree species. *Sambucus* alone is represented in the Pacific region. Common characters of the family are their opposite leaves and small, often juicy, berry-like fruits.

SAMBUCUS. ELDERBERRIES.

The elderberries are small unimportant trees and shrubs represented by about 13 species, 5 of which occur in the United States. Two of the latter are arborescent and inhabit the Pacific region. They are commonly known as elderberries, and are distinguished by the large, soft pith of their twigs and branches, their large opposite (compound) leaves consisting of one main stem and several pairs of (leaf-like) leaflets, with an odd one at the end, and by their large, flat-topped, dense, branched clusters of small flowers, which produce similar conspicuous clusters of small, juicy, berry-like fruits with from 3 to 5 seed-like, stony nutlets, each 1-seeded. Most of them grow best in moist, rich soils with plenty of light, but one or two grow in dry soils. Our tree species occur too rarely and are of too small size to be of economic use, save for local domestic purposes.

Blue Elderberry.

Sambucus glauca [a] Nuttall.

DISTINGUISHING CHARACTERISTICS.

Blue elderberry is known in the field simply as " elder." The name here suggested for the sake of distinctness has reference to the pale, bluish berries, which differ in color from the fruit of any other Pacific elder.

FIG. 207.—*Sambucus glauca,* one-half natural size.

In favorable locations it is commonly from 15 to 20 feet high, often with a slender, straight trunk from 4 to 8 inches through, and a rather dense, round

---

[a] It is most probable that Rafinesque's *Sambucus cerulea,* two years older than Nuttall's *S. glauca,* and based upon the Lewis and Clark reference to an " alder," with " pale sky blue " berries, is the rightful name for this species. These explorers were in the region now known to contain the common glaucous-berried elder, to which alone their short but unmistakable description could have been applied. For the present, however, it seems advisable to retain Nuttall's name.

crown; less frequently, from 30 to 40 feet high, and from 10 to 15 inches in diameter; exceptionally large individuals are sometimes 2 feet through. At higher altitudes chiefly a tall, many-stemmed shrub. Lower branches are often arched and drooping, while large limbs are frequently sharply crooked ("elbows"), owing to upright shoots growing out from points where the limbs are broken off. Bark of tree forms thin, dark yellowish-brown—sometimes faintly reddish—rather regularly and deeply cut into a network of connected, narrow ridges. Twigs of a season's growth are smooth, sparsely white-hairy at first, shiny reddish brown, somewhat angled—strongly so when young—and marked with large, horseshoe-like leaf-scars, which have 5 minute pits (ends of woody fibers of the parted leaf-stem). Mature leaves (fig. 207), shed in autumn, are smooth throughout, composed of 3 to 9 leaflets which are lighter green beneath. Mature "berries" (fig. 207), whitish with a chalky bloom which, when rubbed off, reveals a smooth, blue-black skin; the berries are 1 to 3 seeded, sweetish and edible.[a] The seeds are disseminated very largely by birds and a few mammals which eat the berries for the juicy pulp. Wood, pale brownish yellow, with thin, whitish sapwood; usually wide-grained, rather light and soft, and very brittle. Not used for economic purposes.

LONGEVITY.—The age limits of the largest trees are not fully known, but it is undoubtedly a short-lived tree. Smaller trunks studied indicate very rapid height and diameter growth, while a record of one planted tree shows it to have attained about 40 feet in height and 28 inches in diameter in approximately fifty years. Record of a forest-grown tree 12 inches in diameter shows an age of thirty-five years.

RANGE.

From southern British Columbia (Fraser River) and Vancouver Island to the southern borders of California and eastward to the Blue Mountains in Oregon and the Wasatch Mountains in Utah.

OCCURRENCE.

Bottoms of mountain canyons, valleys, and adjacent slopes, on mountain streams, in ravines, and moist hillsides; in rich, porous, gravelly soils. Largest in northern low valleys; shrubby at high levels. Scattered among Douglas fir, western yellow pine, grand fir, madroña, red alder, broadleaf maple (at north), and sometimes with live oak, California sycamore, and white alder (at south).

CLIMATIC CONDITIONS.—Similar to those of Douglas fir (in northern range) and California sycamore (in southern range).

TOLERANCE.—Endures very little shade at any period.

REPRODUCTION.—Abundant seeder; reproduction frequent, but scattered.

Mexican Elder.

Sambucus mexicana Presl.

DISTINGUISHING CHARACTERISTICS.

Mexican elder is known in the field simply as "elder," but it should have a more distinctive common name, and Mexican elder is proposed.

Nearly always of tree form, from 15 to 25 feet high and from 6 to 10 inches through above the swelled base; the clear trunk, with yellowish brown (sometimes faintly reddish), finely ridged bark, is short; the crown is broad and rounded. Lower branches arched, drooping, and angled, as in the blue elderberry. Twigs of a season's growth nearly always with dense, whitish, fine hairs when young, pale reddish brown and usually smooth. Mature leaves, very similar in general appearance to those of the preceding elder, containing

---

[a] Settlers use the berries as a fruit, which is excellent when cooked.

usually 5 thickish leaflets which are smooth above and lighter green and hairy, or at least somewhat hairy on the veins, beneath (sometimes almost or quite smooth). Mature " berries," of similar form and size to those of the blue elder, are smooth and almost black [a] never with pale bloom of the latter species. The edible fruit is highly prized locally. Wood, pale yellowish brown, and otherwise similar to that of blue elder. Not used commercially.

LONGEVITY.—Not fully determined. Appears to grow much more slowly than the preceding tree. Record of one tree $7\frac{1}{2}$ inches in diameter shows an age of 32 years. Record of a planted tree in Sonora, Mexico,[b] 20 inches in diameter (26 feet high) shows an age of 34 years. This indicates, as for the blue elder, that Mexican elder grows rapidly under cultivation.

RANGE.

From western Texas (Nueces River) through southern New Mexico and Arizona to southern California ; also in northern California (Plumas County) ; southward through Mexico to Central America.

OCCURRENCE.

Borders and bottoms of mountain streams and springs, in wet or moist gravelly soil.

CLIMATIC CONDITIONS.—Similar to those of yellow pine and tolerance and reproduction as in blue elder.

Red-berried Elder.

Sambucus callicarpa Greene.

DISTINGUISHING CHARACTERISTICS.

Red-berried elder is said to attain tree size occasionally, but in the main it is a shrub, bordering streams and ravines in the coast mountain region of California. Distinguished by its bright red (sometimes yellow) berries. The leaflets are smooth above and hairy beneath. Excepting the occasional tree form of this plant, its characters, as found in California, are perplexingly close to those of the northern red-berried elder, *Sambucus pubens* Mchx., which is probably best considered the same as *S. racemosa* L., a tree form of which (var. *arborescens*) was described by Torrey and Gray (Fl. N. A. II, 13, 1840). Much further ʌtudy of this California elder is required before its true status can be determined. Nothing can now be said of its tree size, the character of its wood, or its growth and silvical requirements.

---

[a] Berries of the common and mainly eastern bush elder, *Sambucus canadensis* L., are black-purple and in this respect are closely similar to those of this southwestern species, the range of which it enters in the southern Rocky Mountain region. The shrubby form is distinguished, however, by its smooth twigs and leaves, and particularly in its non-arborescent habits.

[b] E. A. Mearns.

TABLE OF CHANGES IN NOMENCLATURE

The text of this Dover edition is that of the 1908 edition of Sudworth's work. During the 57 years since its initial publication, taxonomists, guided by established rules of botanical nomenclature, have made numerous changes in both the common and technical names of trees. Others, in careful study of certain generic groups, have developed new concepts of the validity and limitations of many species which are described in Sudworth's work. In some instances this has led to combining closely related forms into one large polymorphic species.

Thus, in the interests of technical accuracy, and with a view toward making this work of even greater utility to the serious student of American arborescent vegetation, the publisher is happy to provide a supplementary listing of all genera, species and/or varieties in which there have been significant changes in nomenclature.

This Table of Changes in Nomenclature has been prepared especially for this Dover edition by E. S. Harrar, Dean of the School of Forestry, Duke University.

1965   *Dover Publications, Inc.*

Page	Line	For	Read
3	13	Coniferae	Pinaceae
3	20	White-bark pine (*Pinus albicaulis* Engelmann)	Whitebark pine (*Pinus albicaulis* Engelm.)
3	21	Four-leaf pine; Parry pine (*Pinus quadrifolia* Parl. Sudworth)	Parry pinyon (*Pinus quadrifolia* Parl.)
3	23	Single-leaf pine (*Pinus monophylla* Torrey and Fremont)	Singleleaf pinyon (*Pinus monophylla* Torr. & Frem.)
3	24	Bristle-cone pine (*Pinus aristata* Engelmann)	Bristlecone pine (*Pinus aristata* Engelm.)
3	25	(*Pinus balfouriana* Murray)	(*Pinus balfouriana* Grev. & Balf.)
3	28	Western yellow pine (*Pinus ponderosa* Lawson)	Ponderosa pine (*Pinus ponderosa* Laws.)
3	29	*Pinus jeffreyi* "Oreg. Com."	*Pinus jeffreyi* Grev. & Balf.
3	30	(*Pinus contorta* Loudon)	(*Pinus contorta* Dougl.)
3	31	Gray pine; Digger pine (*Pinus sabiniana* Douglas)	Digger pine (*Pinus sabiniana* Dougl.)
3	32	(*Pinus coulteri*) Lambert	(*Pinus coulteri* D. Don)
3	33	(*Pinus radiata* Don.)	(*Pinus radiata* D. Don)
3	34	(*Pinus attenuata* Lemmon)	(*Pinus attenuata* Lemm.)
3	35	Pricklecone pine; Bishop's pine (*Pinus muricata* Don.)	Bishop pine (*Pinus muricata* D. Don)
3	37	(*Larix occidentalis* Nuttall)	(*Larix occidentalis* Nutt.)
3	38	Alpine larch (*Larix lyallii* Paralatore)	Subalpine larch (*Larix lyallii* Parl.)
3	39	(*Larix laricina* (Du Roi) Koch)	[*Larix laricina* (Du Roi) K. Koch]
3	41	(*Picea engelmanni* Engelmann)	(*Picea engelmannii* Parry)
3	42	(*Picea sitchensis* (Bong.) Trautvetter and Mayer)	[*Picea sitchensis* (Bong.) Carr.]
3	44	Weeping spruce (*Picea breweriana* Watson)	Brewer spruce (*Picea breweriana* S. Wats.)
4	2	Coniferae	Pinaceae
4	4	(*Picea mariana* (Mill.) B., S. & P.)	[*Picea mariana* (Mill.) B.S.P.]
4	5	(*Picea canadensis* (Mill.) B., S. & P.)	[*Picea glauca* (Moench.) Voss]
4	7	(*Tsuga heterophylla* (Raf.) Sargent)	[*Tsuga heterophylla* (Raf.) Sarg.]
4	8	(*Tsuga mertensiana* (Bong.) Sargent)	[*Tsuga mertensiana* (Bong.) Carr.]
4	10	Pseudotsuga — False hemlock	Pseudotsuga — Douglas-fir
4	11	Douglas fir; Douglas spruce (*Pseudotsuga taxifolia* (Poir.) Britton)	Douglas-fir [*Pseudotsuga menziesii* (Mirob.) Franco]
4	13	Bigcone spruce (*Pseudotsuga macrocarpa* (Torr.) Mayr)	Bigcone Douglas-fir [*Pseudotsuga macrocarpa* (Vasey) Mayr]
4	15	Alpine fir; Balsam fir (*Abies lasiocarpa* (Hook.) Nuttall)	Subalpine fir [*Abies lasiocarpa* (Hook.) Nutt.]
4	16	Grand fir; White fir (*Abies grandis* Lindley)	Grand fir [*Abies grandis* (Dougl.) Lindl.]
4	17	(*Abies concolor* (Gord.) Parry)	[*Abies concolor* (Gord. & Glend.) Lindl.]
4	18	(*Abies venusta* (Doug.) Koch)	(*Abies bracteata* D. Don)
4	19	Amabilis fir (*Abies amabilis* (Loud.) Forbes)	Pacific silver fir *Abies amabilis* (Dougl.) Forbes]
4	20	(*Abies nobilis* Lindley)	(*Abies procera* Rehd.)
4	21	Red fir (*Abies magnifica* Murray)	California red fir (*Abies magnifica* A. Murr.)
4	23	Bigtree (*Sequoia washingtoniana* (Winls.) Sudworth)	Giant sequoia [*Sequoia gigantea* (Lindl.) Decne.]
4	24	(*Sequoia sempervirens* (Lamb.) Endlicher)	[*Sequoia sempervirens* (D. Don) Endl.]
4	26	Incense cedar (*Libocedrus decurrens* Torrey)	Incense-cedar (*Libocedrus decurrens* Torr.)

Page	Line	For	Read
4	28	Western red cedar; Red cedar (*Thuja plicata* Don.)	Western redcedar; Red cedar (*Thuja plicata* Donn)
4	30	(*Cupressus macrocarpa* Hartweg)	(*Cupressus macrocarpa* Hartw.)
4	31	(*Cupressus goveniana* Gordon)	(*Cupressus goveniana* Gord.)
4	32	*Note;* Dwarf cypress [*Cypressus pygmaea* (Lemm.) Sarg.] is now included as a part of Gowen cypress (*Cupressus goveniana* Gord.) without benefit of variety ranking.	
4	33	Macnab cypress (*Cupressus macnabiana* (Murray)	MacNab cypress (*Cupressus macnabiana* A. Murr.)
4	35	Yellow cypress; Alaska cypress (*Chamaecyparis nootkatensis* (Lamb.) Spach)	Alaska-cedar [*Chamaecyparis nootkatensis* (D. Don). Spach]
4	37	Lawson cypress; Port Orford cedar (*Chamaecyparis lawsoniana* (Murr.) Parlatore)	Port-Orford-cedar [*Chamaecyparis lawsoniana* (A. Murr.) Parl.]
4	40	Dwarf juniper (*Juniperus communis* Linnaeus)	Common juniper (*Juniperus communis* L.)
4	41	Rocky Mountain red cedar (*Juniperus scopulorum* Sargent)	Rocky Mountain juniper (*Juniperus scopulorum* Sarg.)
4	42	(*Juniperus occidentalis* Hooker)	(*Juniperus occidentalis* Hook.)
4	43	(*Juniperus utahensis* (Engelm.) Lemmon)	[*Juniperus osteosperma* (Torr.) Little]
4	44	(*Juniperus californica* Carrière)	(*Juniperus californica* Carr.)
4	46	Tumion — Stinking cedars	Torreya — Torreyas
4	47	California nutmeg (*Tumion californicum* (Torr.) Greene)	California torreya (*Torreya californica* Torr.)
4	49	Western yew *Taxus brevifolia* Nuttall)	Pacific yew (*Taxus brevifolia* Nutt.)
4	52	Neowashingtonia	Washingtonia
4	53	Washington palm (*Neo-washingtonia filifera* (Wendl.) Sudworth)	California washingtonia [*Washingtonia filifera* (Linden) H. Wendl.]
5	4	Joshua tree (*Yucca arborescens* (Torr.) Trelease)	Joshua-tree (*Yucca brevifolia* Engelm.)
5	5	(*Yucca mohavensis* Sargent)	(*Yucca mohavensis* Sarg.)
5	9	(*Juglans californica* Watson)	(*Juglans california* Carr.)
5	11	Myrica — Wax myrtles	Myrica — Bayberries
5	12	California myrtle (*Myrica californica* Chamisso)	Pacific bayberry (*Myrica californica* Cham.)
5	15	Black willow (*Salix nigra* Marshall)	Goodding willow (*Salix gooddingii* Ball)
5	16	Almond willow (*Salix amygdaloides* Andersson)	Peachleaf willow (*Salix amygdaloides* Anderss.)
5	17	Smooth willow	Red willow
5	18	Western black willow (*Salix lasiandra* Bentham)	Pacific willow (*Salix lasiandra* Benth.)
5	19	Longleaf willow (*Salix fluviatilis* Nuttall)	River willow (*Salix fluviatilis* Nutt.)
5	20	Silverleaf willow (*Salix sessilifolia* Nuttall)	Northwest willow (*Salix sessilifolia* Nutt.)
5	21	(*Salix cordata mackenzieana* Hooker)	[*Salix mackenzieana* (Hook.) Barratt]
5	22	White willow (*Salix lasiolepis* Bentham)	Arroyo willow (*Salix lasiolepis* Benth.)
5	23	Nuttall willow (*Salix nuttallii* Sargent)	Scouler willow (*Salix scouleriana* Barratt)
5	24	Broadleaf willow (*Salix amplifolia* Coville)	Yakutat willow (*Salix amplifolia* Cov.)
5	26	Silky willow (*Salix sitchensis* Sanson in Bongard)	Sitka willow (*Salix sitchensis* Sanson)

Page	Line	For	Read
5	27	*(Salix alaxensis* (Anderss.) Coville)	[*Salix alaxensis* (Anderss.) Cov.]
5	29	Aspen *(Populus tremuloides* Michaux)	Quaking aspen *(Populus tremuloides* Michx.)
5	30	Balm-of-Gilead *(Populus balsamifera* Linnaeus)	Balsam poplar *(Populus balsamifera* L.)
5	31	*(Populus trichocarpa* Torrey and Gray)	*(Populus trichocarpa* Torr. & Gray)
5	32	*(Populus fremontii* Watson)	*(Populus fremontii* S. Wats.)
5	35	Western birch *(Betula occidentalis* Hooker)	Water birch *(Betula occidentalis* Hook.)
5	36	*(Betula kenaica* Evans)	[*Betula papyrifera* var. *kenaica* (W. H. Evans) Henry]
5	37	White birch *(Betula alaskana* Sargent)	Alaska paper birch [*Betula papyrifera* var. *humilis* (Reg.) Fern. & Raup]
5	40	*(Alnus rhombifolia* Nuttall)	*(Alnus rhombifolia* Nutt.)
5	41	Mountain alder *(Alnus tenuifolia* Nuttall)	Thinleaf alder *(Alnus tenuifolia* Nutt.)
5	42	*(Alnus oregona* Nuttall)	*(Alnus rubra* Bong.)
5	43	*(Alnus sitchensis* (Regel) Sargent)	*(Alnus sinuata* (Reg.) Rydb.)
5	44	Cupuliferae	Fagaceae
5	45	Castanopis – Chinquapins	Castanopis – Chinkapins
5	46	Western chinquapin *(Castanopsis chrysophylla* (Hook.) A. de Candolle)	Golden chinkapin [*Castanopsis chrysophylla* (Dougl.) A.DC.]
5	49	Valley oak	California white oak
5	50	*(Quercus breweri* Engelmann)	*(Quercus breweri* Engelm.)
5	51	Garry oak *(Quercus garryanna* Douglas)	Oregon white oak *(Quercus garryana* Dougl.)
5	53	*(Quercus douglasii* Hooker and Arnott)	*(Quercus douglasii* Hook. & Arn.)
5	54	*(Quercus alvordiana* Eastwood)	[*Quercus dumosa* var. *alvordiana* (Eastw.) Jeps.]
6	4	*(Quercus engelmanni* Greene)	*(Quercus engelmannii* Greene)
6	5	*(Quercus dumosa* Nuttall)	*(Quercus dumosa* Nutt.)
6	6	*(Quercus chrysolepis* Liebmann)	*(Quercus chrysolepis* Leibm.)
6	7	*(Quercus tomentella* Engelmann)	*add:* Island live oak *(Quercus tomentella* Engelm.)
6	9	Wislizenus oak *(Quercus wislizeni* A. de Candolle)	Interior live oak *(Quercus wislizenii* A.DC.)
6	10	*Note:* Price oak *(Quercus pricei* Sudworth) is now included as a part of California live oak *(Quercus agrifolia* Née) without benefit of variety ranking.	
6	11	Morehus oak *(Quercus morehus* Kellogg)	Oracle oak *(Quercus X moreha* Kellogg)
6	12	*(Quercus californica* (Torr.) Cooper)	*(Quercus kelloggii* Newb.)
6	13	Tanbark oak *(Quercus densiflora* Hooker and Arnott)	Tanoak [*Lithocarpus densiflora* (Hook. & Arn.) Redh.]
6	16	*Note:* Hackberry *(Celtis occidentalis* Linnaeus) is now included as a part of netleaf hackberry *(Celtis reticulata* Torr.) without benefit of variety ranking.	
6	17	Palo blanco *(Celtis reticulata* Torrey)	Netleaf hackberry *(Celtis reticulata* Torr.)
6	19	Umbellularia – Laurel	Umbellularia – California-laurel

Page	Line	For	Read
6	20	California laurel (*Umbellularia californica* (Hook. and Arn.) Nuttall)	California-laurel [*Umbellularia californica* (Hook. & Arn.) Nutt.]
6	23	Lyonothamnus	Lyonothamnus – Lyontree
6	24	Western ironwood (*Lyonothamnus floribundus* Gray)	Lyontree (*Lyonothamnus floribundus* A. Gray)
6	27	(*Platanus racemosa* Nuttall)	(*Platanus racemosa* Nutt.)
6	29	Cercocarpus – Mountain mahoganies	Cercocarpus – Cercocarpuses
6	30	Trask mahogany (*Cercocarpus traskiae* Eastwood)	Catalina cercocarpus [*Cercocarpus betuloides* var. *traskiae* (Eastw.) Dunkle]
6	31	Curl-leaf mahogany (*Cercocarpus ledifolius* Nuttall)	Curlleaf cercocarpus (*Cercocarpus ledifolius* Nutt.)
6	32	Birch-leaf mahogany *Cercocarpus parvifolius* Nuttall)	Birchleaf cercocarpus (*Cercocarpus betuloides* Nutt.)
6	34	(*Malus rivularis* (Doug. in Hook.) Roemer)	[*Malus diversifolia* (Bong.) Roem.]
6	37	Western serviceberry (*Amelanchier alnifolia* Nuttall)	Saskatoon serviceberry [*Amelanchier alnifolia* (Nutt.) Nutt.]
6	38	Crataegus – Haws	Crataegus – Hawthorns
6	39	Black haw (*Crataegus douglasii* Lindley)	Black hawthorn (*Crataegus douglasii* Lindl.)
6	40	Heteromeles	Photinia – Christmasberries
6	41	Christmas berry (*Heteromeles arbutifolia* Roemer)	Christmasberry (*Photinia arbutifolia* Lindl.)
6	43	Western plum (*Prunus subcordata* Bentham)	Klamath plum (*Prunus subcordata* Benth.)
6	44	(*Prunus emarginata* (Dougl.) Walpers)	(*Prunus emarginata* Dougl.)
6	45	Western choke cherry (*Prunus demissa* (Nutt.) Walpers)	Common chokecherry (*Prunus virginiana* L.)
6	46	(*Prunus ilicifolia* (Nutt.) Walpers)	[*Prunus ilicifolia* (Nutt.) D. Dietr.]
6	49	Screwpod mesquite (*Prosopis odorata* Torrey and Fremont)	Screwbean mesquite (*Prosopis pubescens* Benth.)
6	50	Mesquite (*Prosopis juliflora glandulosa* (Torr.) Sargent)	Honey Mesquite [*Prosopis juliflora* var. *glandulosa* (Torr.) Cockerell]
6	51	Cercis – Judas trees	Cercis – Redbuds
6	52	(*Cercis occidentalis* Torrey)	(*Cercis occidentalis* Torr.)
6	53	Acacia	Acacia – Acacias
6	54	Cat's claw (*Acacia greggii* Gray)	Catclaw acacia (*Acacia greggii* A. Gray)
7	3	Parkinsonia	Parkinsonia – Parkinsonias
7	4	Horse-bean; Ratama (*Parkinsonia aculeata* Linnaeus)	Jerusalem-thorn (*Parkinsonia aculeata* L.)
7	5	Little-leaf horse-bean (*Parkinsonia microphylla* Torrey)	Yellow paloverde [*Cercidium microphyllum* (Torr.) Rose & Johnst.]
7	6	Cercidium	Cercidium – Paloverde
7	7	Palo verde; green-bark acacia (*Cercidium torreyanum* (Watson) Sargent)	Blue paloverde (*Cercidium floridum* Benth.)

Page	Line	For	Read
7	9	Dalea	Dalea — Daleas
7	10	Indigo bush (*Dalea spinosa* Gray)	Smokethorn (*Dalea spinosa* A. Gray)
7	11	Olneya	Olneya — Tesota
7	12	Mexican ironwood (*Olneya tesota* Gray)	Tesota (*Olneya tesota* A. Gray)
7	14	Canotia	Canotia — Canotias
7	15	(*Canotia holocantha* Torrey)	(*Canotia holocantha* Torr.)
7	20	Rhus — Sumachs	Rhus — Sumacs
7	21	Mahogany sumach (*Rhus integrifolia* (Nutt.) Bentham and Hooker)	Lemonade sumac [*Rhus integrifolia* (Nutt.) Benth. & Hook. f.]
7	25	Broadleaf maple	Bigleaf maple
7	27	Dwarf maple (*Acer glabrum* Torrey)	Rocky Mountain maple (*Acer glabrum* Torr.)
7	28	California boxelder (*Acer negundo californicum* (Torr. and Gr.) Sargent)	Boxelder (*Acer negundo* L.)
7	32	(*Aesculus californica* Nuttall)	[*Aesculus californica* (Spach) Nutt.]
7	35	Evergreen buckthorn (*Rhamnus crocea* Nuttall)	Hollyleaf buckthorn [*Rhamnus crocea* var. *ilicifolia* (Kellogg) Greene]
7	36	Cascara sagrada (*Rhamnus purshiana* De Candolle)	Cascara buckthorn (*Rhamnus purshiana* DC.)
7	37	Ceanothus — Myrtles	Ceanothus — Ceanothuses
7	38	Blue myrtle (*Ceanothus thyrsiflorus* Eschscholtz)	Blueblossom (*Ceanothus thyrsiflorus* Eschsch.)
7	39	Tree myrtle	Feltleaf ceanothus
7	40	Lilac (*Ceanothus spinosa* Nuttall)	Spiny ceanothus (*Ceanothus spinosa* Nutt.)
7	43	Western dogwood	Pacific dogwood
7	45	Garrya	Garrya — Silktassels
7	46	Quinine bush (*Garrya elliptica* Douglas)	Wavyleaf silktassel (*Garrya elliptica* Dougl.)
7	48	Arbutus — Madroñas	Arbutus — Madrones
7	49	Madroña	Pacific madrone
7	52	*Note:* Leatherleaf ash (*Fraxinus coriacea* Watson) is now included as a part of velvet ash (*Fraxinus velutina* Torr.) without benefit of variety ranking.	
7	53	(*Fraxinus oregona* Nuttall)	(*Fraxinus latifolia* Benth.)
8	4	*Fraxinus velutina* Torrey	Velvet ash (*Fraxinus velutina* Torr.)
8	5	Flowering ash (*Fraxinus dipetala* Hooker and Arnott)	Two-petal ash (*Fraxinus dipetala* Hook. & Arn.)
8	7	Chilopsis	Chilopsis — Desertwillows
8	8	Desert willow	Desertwillow
8	10	Cephalanthus	Cephalanthus — Buttonbushes
8	11	Button bush (*Cephalanthus occidentalis* Linnaeus)	Common buttonbush (*Cephalanthus occidentalis* L.)
8	13	Sambucus — Elderberries	Sambucus — Elders
8	14	Blue elderberry (*Sambucus glauca* Nuttall)	Blueberry elder (*Sambucus glauca* Nutt.)
8	16	Red-berried elder	Pacific red elder
13	15	*Picea engelmanni*	*Picea engelmannii*
13	34	*Sequoia washingtoniana*	*Sequoia gigantea*
19	17	Family CONIFERAE	Family PINACEAE
19	19	False or bastard hemlocks	Douglas-firs
30	28	White-bark Pine	Whitebark Pine
30	29	*Pinus albicaulis* Engelmann	*Pinus albicaulis* Engelm.
33	26	Four-leaf Pine; Parry Pine	Parry Pinyon

Page	Line	For	Read
33	27	*Pinus quadrifolia* (Parl.) Sudworth	*Pinus quadrifolia* Parl.
35	16	Single-leaf Pine	Singleleaf Pinyon
35	17	*Pinus monophylla* Torrey and Fremont	*Pinus monophylla* Torr. & Frem.
37	56	Bristle-cone Pine	Bristlecone Pine
37	57	*Pinus aristata* Engelmann	*Pinus aristata* Engelm.
39	48	*Pinus balfouriana* Murray	*Pinus balfouriana* Grev. & Balf.
42	32	Western Yellow Pine	Ponderosa Pine
42	33	*Pinus ponderosa* Lawson	*Pinus ponderosa* Laws.
47	22	*Pinus jeffreyi* "Oreg. Com."	*Pinus jeffreyi* Grev. & Balf.
49	21	*Pinus contorta* Loudon	*Pinus contorta* Dougl.
54	22	Gray Pine; Digger Pine	Digger Pine
54	23	*Pinus sabiniana* Douglas	*Pinus sabiniana* Dougl.
57	2	*Pinus coulteri* Lambert	*Pinus coulteri* D. Don
58	35	*Pinus radiata* Don.	*Pinus radiata* D. Don
62	2	*Pinus attenuata* Lemmon	*Pinus attenuata* Lemm.
65	24	Pricklecone Pine; Bishop's Pine	Bishop Pine
65	25	*Pinus muricata* Don	*Pinus muricata* D. Don
68	47	*Larix occidentalis* Nuttall	*Larix occidentalis* Nutt.
71	42	Alpine Larch	Subalpine Larch
71	43	*Larix lyallii* Parlatore	*Larix lyallii* Parl.
73	53	*Larix laricina* (Du Roi) Koch	*Larix laricina* (Du Roi) K. Koch
78	14	*Picea engelmanni* Engelmann	*Picea engelmannii* Parry
79	Fig. 29	*Picea engelmanni*	*Picea engelmannii*
81	34	*Picea sitchensis* (Bong.) Trautvetter and Mayer	*Picea sitchensis* (Bong.) Carr.
84	23	Weeping Spruce	Brewer Spruce
84	24	*Picea breweriana* Watson	*Picea breweriana* S. Wats.
86	34	*Picea mariana* (Mill.) B., S. & P.	*Picea mariana* (Mill) B.S.P.
88	19	*Picea canadensis* (Mill.), B., S., & P.	*Picea glauca* (Moench.) Voss
89	Fig. 33	*Picea canadensis*	*Picea glauca*
91	43	*Tsuga heterophylla* (Raf.) Sargent	*Tsuga heterophylla* (Raf.) Sarg.
95	24	*Tsuga mertensiana* (Bong.) Sargent	*Tsuga mertensiana* (Bong.) Carr.
99	34	FALSE HEMLOCKS	DOUGLAS-FIRS
100	16	Douglas Fir	Douglas-Fir
100	17	*Pseudotsuga taxifolia* [a] (Poir.) Britt.	*Pseudotsuga menziesii* [a] (Mirb.) Franco
100	Fig. 36	*Pseudotsuga taxifolia*	*Pseudotsuga menziesii*
104	29	Bigcone Spruce	Bigcone Douglas-Fir
104	30	*Pseudotsuga macrocarpa* (Torr.) Mayr	*Pseudotsuga macrocarpa* (Vasey) Mayr
107	22	Alpine Fir	Subalpine Fir
107	23	*Abies lasiocarpa* (Hook.) Nuttall	*Abies lasiocarpa* (Hook.) Nutt.
111	42	*Abies grandis* Lindley	*Abies grandis* (Dougl.) Lindl.
116	12	*Abies concolor* (Gord.) Parry	*Abies concolor* (Gord. & Glend.) Lindl.
121	15	*Abies venusta* (Dougl.) Koch	*Abies bracteata* D. Don
122	Fig. 45	*Abies venusta*	*Abies bracteata*
123	Fig. 46	*Abies venusta*	*Abies bracteata*
124	Fig. 47	*Abies venusta*	*Abies bracteata*
125	10	Amabilis Fir	Pacific Silver Fir
125	11	*Abies amabilis* (Loud.) Forbes	*Abies amabilis* (Dougl.) Forbes
128	26	*Abies nobilis* Lindley	*Abies procera* Rehd.
129	Fig. 50	*Abies nobilis*	*Abies procera*
130	Fig. 51	*Abies nobilis*	*Abies procera*
132	7	Red Fir	California Red Fir
132	8	*Abies magnifica* Murray	*Abies magnifica* A. Murr.
135	12	*Abies magnifica shastensis* Lemmon	*Abies magnifica* var. shastensis Lemm.

Page	Line	For	Read
136	Fig. 54	*Abies magnifica shastensis*	*Abies magnifica* var. *shastensis*
137	16	*Abies magnifica shastensis*	*Abies magnifica* var. *shastensis*
139	18	Bigtree	Giant Sequoia
139	19	*Sequoia washingtoniana* (Winsl.) Sudworth	*Sequoia gigantea* (Lindl.) Decne.
141	Fig. 55	*Sequoia washingtoniana*	*Sequoia gigantea*
142	Fig. 56	*Sequoia washingtoniana*	*Sequoia gigantea*
145	35	*Sequoia sempervirens* (Lamb.) Endlicher	*Sequoia sempervirens* (D. Don) Endl.
148	27	Incense Cedar	Incense-Cedar
148	28	*Libocedrus decurrens* Torrey	*Libocedrus decurrens* Torr.
153	41	Western Red Cedar	Western Redcedar
153	42	*Thuja plicata* Don.	*Thuja plicata* Donn
158	47	*Cupressus macrocarpa* Hartweg.	*Cupressus macrocarpa* Hartw.
161	15	*Cupressus goveniana* Gordon	*Cupressus goveniana* Gord.
163	33	*Note:* Dwarf cypress [*Cupressus pygmaea* (Lemm.) Sarg.] is now included as a part of Gowen cypress *(Cupressus goveniana* Gord.) without benefit of variety ranking.	
165	25	Macnab Cypress	MacNab Cypress
165	26	*Cupressus macnabiana* Murray	*Cupressus macnabiana* A. Murr.
168	23	Yellow Cypress; Alaska Cypress	Alaska-Cedar
168	24	*Chamaecyparis nootkatensis* (Lamb.) Spach.	*Chamaecyparis nootkatensis* (D. Don) Spach.
171	44	Lawson Cypress; Port Orford Cedar	Port-Orford-Cedar
171	45	*Chamaecyparis lawsoniana* (Murr.) Parlatore	*Chamaecyparis lawsoniana* (A. Murr.) Parl.
176	19	Dwarf Juniper	Common Juniper
176	20	*Juniperus communis* Linnaeus	*Juniperus communis* L.
178	29	Rocky Mountain Red Cedar	Rocky Mountain Juniper
178	30	*Juniperus scopulorum* Sargent	*Juniperus scopulorum* Sarg.
181	13	*Juniperus occidentalis* Hooker	*Juniperus occidentalis* Hook.
186	2	*Juniperus utahensis* (Engelm.) Lemmon	*Juniperus osteosperma* (Torr.) Little
186	Fig. 73	*Juniperus utahensis*	*Juniperus osteosperma*
187	42	*Juniperus californica* Carrière	*Juniperus californica* Carr.
190	44	TUMION. STINKING CEDARS	TORREYA. TORREYAS
191	27	California Nutmeg	California Torreya
191	28	*Tumion californicum* (Torr.) Greene	*Torreya californica* Torr.
192	Fig. 75	*Tumion californicum*	*Torreya californica*
194	25	Western Yew	Pacific Yew
194	26	*Taxus brevifolia* Nuttall	*Taxus brevifolia* Nutt.
198	1	NEOWASHINGTONIA	WASHINGTONIA
198	Figs. 77, 78	*Neowashingtonia filifera*	*Washingtonia filifera*
199	21	Washington Palm	California Washingtonia
199	22	*Neowashingtonia filifera* [a] (Wendl.) Sudworth	*Washingtonia filifera* (Linden) H. Wendl.
201	40	Joshua Tree	Joshua-Tree
201	41	*Yucca arborescens* (Torr.) Trelease	*Yucca brevifolia* Engelm.
202	Figs. 79, 80	*Yucca arborescens*	*Yucca brevifolia*
203	45	*Yucca mohavensis* Sargent	*Yucca mohavensis* Sarg.
206	48	*Juglans californica* Watson	*Juglans californica* S. Wats.
208	48	WAX MYRTLES	BAYBERRIES
209	19	California Myrtle	Pacific Bayberry
209	20	*Myrica californica* Chamisso	*Myrica californica* Cham.
213	17	Black Willow	Goodding Willow
213	18	*Salix nigra* Marshall	*Salix gooddingii* Ball
214	Fig. 85	*Salix nigra*	*Salix gooddingii*
215	Fig. 86	*Salix nigra*	*Salix gooddingii*
216	1	Almond Willow	Peachleaf Willow

Page	Line	For	Read
216	2	*Salix amygdaloides* Andersson	*Salix amygdaloides* Anderss.
217	25	Smooth Willow	Red Willow
219	4	Western Black Willow	Pacific Willow
219	5	*Salix lasiandra* Bentham	*Salix lasiandra* Benth.
222	1	Longleaf Willow	River Willow
222	2	*Salix fluviatilis* Nuttall	*Salix fluviatilis* Nutt.
223	40	Silverleaf Willow	Northwest Willow
223	41	*Salix sessilifolia* Nuttall	*Salix sessilifolia* Nutt.
225	2	*Salix cordata mackenzieana* Hooker	*Salix mackenzieana* (Hook.) Barratt
225	Fig. 93	*Salix cordata mackenzieana*	*Salix mackenzieana*
226	14	White Willow	Arroyo Willow
226	15	*Salix lasiolepis* [a] Bentham	*Salix lasiolepis* [a] Benth.
228	1	Nuttall Willow	Scouler Willow
228	2	*Salix nuttallii* Sargent	*Salix scouleriana* Barratt
228	Fig. 95	*Salix nuttallii*	*Salix scouleriana*
229	42	Broadleaf Willow	Yakutat Willow
229	43	*Salix amplifolia* Coville	*Salix amplifolia* Cov.
232	2	*Salix hookeriana* Barratt in Hooker [a]	*Salix hookeriana* Barratt [a]
233	25	Silky Willow	Sitka Willow
233	26	*Salix sitchensis* Sanson in Bongard	*Salix sitchensis* Sanson
236	2	*Salix alaxensis* (Anderss.) Coville	*Salix alaxensis* (Anderss.) Cov.
239	35	Aspen	Quaking Aspen
239	36	*Populus tremuloides* Michaux	*Populus tremuloides* Michx.
244	18	Balm-of-Gilead	Balsam Poplar
244	19	*Populus balsamifera* Linnaeus	*Populus balsamifera* L.
247	25	*Populus trichocarpa* Torrey and Gray	*Populus trichocarpa* Torr. & Gray
251	20	*Populus fremontii* Watson	*Populus fremontii* S. Wats.
254	1	BETULUS	BETULA
254	41	Western Birch	Western Paper Birch
254	42	*Betula occidentalis* Hooker	*Betula papyrifera* var. *commutata* (Reg.) Fern.
256	45	*Betula kenaica* Evans	*Betula papyrifera* var. *kenaica* (W. H. Evans) Henry
257	Fig. 112	*Betula kenaica*	*Betula papyrifera* var. *kenaica*
258	21	White Birch	Alaska Paper Birch
258	22	*Betula alaskana* Sargent	*Betula papyrifera* var. *humilis* (Reg.) Fern. & Raup
259	Fig. 113	*Betula alaskana*	*Betula papyrifera* var. *humilis*
263	37	*Alnus rhombifolia* Nuttall	*Alnus rhombifolia* Nutt.
266	20	Mountain Alder	Thinleaf Alder
266	21	*Alnus tenuifolia* Nuttall	*Alnus tenuifolia* Nutt.
268	13	*Alnus oregona* Nuttall	*Alnus rubra* Bong.
269	Fig. 118	*Alnus oregona*	*Alnus rubra*
270	2	*Alnus sitchensis* (Regel) Sargent	*Alnus sinuata* (Reg.) Rydb.
270	Fig. 119	*Alnus sitchensis*	*Alnus sinuata*
271	Fig. 120	*Alnus sitchensis*	*Alnus sinuata*
272	23	CUPULIFERAE	FAGACEAE
272	40	CHINQUAPINS	CHINKAPINS
273	12	Western Chinquapin	Golden Chinkapin
273	13	*Castanopsis chrysophylla* (Hook.) A. de Candolle	*Castanopsis chrysophylla* (Dougl.) A. DC.
278	11	Valley Oak	California White Oak
281	41	*Quercus breweri* Engelmann	*Quercus breweri* Engelm.
283	6	Garry Oak	Oregon White Oak
283	7	*Quercus garryana* Hooker	*Quercus garryana* Dougl.
285	36	*Quercus douglasii* Hooker and Arnott	*Quercus douglasii* Hook. & Arn.

Page	Line	For	Read
289	30	*Quercus alvordiana* [a] Eastwood	*Quercus dumosa* var. *alvordiana* [a] (Eastw.) Jeps.
289	46	*Quercus engelmanni* Greene	*Quercus engelmannii* Greene
290	Fig. 129	*Quercus engelmanni*	*Quercus engelmannii*
291	Fig. 130	*Quercus engelmanni*	*Quercus engelmannii*
292	28	*Quercus dumosa* Nuttall	*Quercus dumosa* Nutt.
295	6	*Quercus chrysolepis* Liebmann	*Quercus chrysolepis* Liebm.
295	34	*Quercus chrysolepis palmeri* Engelmann	*Quercus chrysolepis* var. *palmeri* (Engelm.) Sarg.
295	42	*Quercus chrysolepis vaccinifolia* (Kellogg) Engelm.	*Quercus chrysolepis* var. *vaccinifolia* (Kellogg) Engelm.
299	Fig. 135 (a)	*Quercus chrysolepis palmeri*	*Quercus chrysolepis* var. *palmeri*
299	Fig. 135 (b)	*Quercus chrysolepis vaccinifolia*	*Quercus chrysolepis* var. *vaccinifolia*
300	48		*Insert above:* Island Live Oak
300	48	*Quercus tomentella* Engelmann	*Quercus tomentella* Engelm.
307	1	Wislizenus Oak	Interior Live Oak
307	2	*Quercus wislizeni* A. de Candolle	*Quercus wislizenii* A.DC.
307	Fig. 141	*Quercus wislizeni*	*Quercus wislizenii*
308	Fig. 142	*Quercus wislizeni*	*Quercus wislizenii*
309	54	*Note: Price oak (Quercus pricei* Sudworth) is now included as a part of California live oak *(Quercus agrifolia* Née) without benefit of variety ranking.	
311	24	Morehus Oak	Oracle Oak
311	25	*Quercus morehus* Kellogg	*Quercus* X *moreha* Kellogg
312	Fig. 144	*Quercus morehus*	*Quercus* X *moreha*
313	31	*Quercus californica* (Torr.) Cooper	*Quercus kelloggii* Newb.
314	Fig. 145	*Quercus californica*	*Quercus kelloggii*
315	Fig. 146	*Quercus californica*	*Quercus kelloggii*
316	Fig. 147	*Quercus californica*	*Quercus kelloggii*
317	54	Tanbark Oak	Tanoak
317	55	*Quercus* [a] *densiflora* Hooker and Arnott	*Lithocarpus densiflora* (Hook. & Arn.) Rehd.
318	Fig. 148	*Quercus densiflora*	*Lithocarpus densiflora*
319	Fig. 149	*Quercus densiflora*	*Lithocarpus densiflora*
320	Fig. 150	*Quercus densiflora*	*Lithocarpus densiflora*
323	30	*Note:* Trees of the Pacific region formerly identified as Hackberry *(Celtis occidentalis* Linnaeus), an eastern species, are now included in Netleaf Hackberry *(Celtis reticulata* Torr.).	
323	31	*Celtis occidentalis* [a] Linnaeus	*Celtis reticulata* Torr.
324	Fig. 151	*Celtis occidentalis*	*Celtis reticulata*
325	31	Palo Blanco	Netleaf Hackberry
325	32	*Celtis recticulata* Torrey	*Celtis reticulata* Torr.
327	23	LAUREL	CALIFORNIA-LAUREL
327	26	California Laurel	California-Laurel
327	27	*Umbellularia californica* (Hook. and Arn.) Nuttall	*Umbellularia californica* (Hook. & Arn.) Nutt.
331	16	LYONOTHAMNUS	LYONOTHAMNUS. LYON-TREES
331	23	Western Ironwood	Lyontree
331	24	*Lyonothamnus floribundus* Gray	*Lyonothamnus floribundus* A. Gray
335	2	*Platanus racemosa* Nuttall	*Platanus racemosa* Nutt.
336	38	MOUNTAIN MAHOGANIES	CERCOCARPUSES
337	1	Trask Mahogany	Catalina Cercocarpus
337	2	*Cercocarpus traskiae* Eastwood	*Cercocarpus betuloides* var. *traskiae* (Eastw.) Dunkle
337	Fig. 157	*Cercocarpus traskiae*	*Cercocarpus betuloides* var. *traskiae*
338	20	Curl-leaf Mahogany; [a] Mountain Mahogany	Curlleaf Cercocarpus
338	21	*Cercocarpus ledifolius* Nuttall	*Cercocarpus ledifolius* Nutt.

Page	Line	For	Read
340	13	Birch-leaf Mahogany; Mountain Mahogany[a]	Birchleaf Cercocarpus
340	14	*Cercocarpus parvifolius* Nuttall	*Cercocarpus betuloides* Nutt.
340	41	*Cercocarpus parvifolius betuloides* (Nuttall) Sargent	*Cercocarpus betuloides* Nutt.
340	43	*Cercocarpus parvifolius breviflorus*[b] (Gray) Jones	*Cercocarpus breviflorus*[b] A. Gray
341	Fig. 159	*Cercocarpus parvifolius*	*Cercocarpus betuloides*
342	17	*Malus rivularis* (Dougl. in Hook.) Roemer	*Malus diversifolia* (Bong.) Roem.
343	Fig. 160	*Malus rivularis*	*Malus diversifolia*
344	Fig. 161	*Malus rivularis*	*Malus diversifolia*
345	19	Western Serviceberry	Saskatoon Serviceberry
345	20	*Amelanchier alnifolia* Nuttall	*Amelanchier alnifolia* (Nutt.) Nutt.
347	1	HAWS	HAWTHORNS
347	40	Black Haw	Black Hawthorn
347	41	*Crataegus douglasii* Lindley	*Crataegus douglasii* Lindl.
349	4	*Crataegus douglasii rivularis* (Nutt.) Sargent	*Crataegus douglasii* var. *rivularis* (Nutt.) Sarg.
349	27	HETEROMELES	PHOTINIA. CHRISTMAS-BERRIES
349	32	Christmas Berry	Christmasberry
349	33	*Heteromeles arbutifolia* Roemer	*Photinia arbutifolia* Lindl.
350	Fig. 164	*Heteromeles arbutifolia*	*Photinia arbutifolia*
352	14	Western Plum	Klamath Plum
352	15	*Prunus subcordata* Bentham	*Prunus subcordata* Benth.
352	42	*Prunus subcordata kelloggii* Lemmon	*Prunus subcordata* var. *kelloggii* Lemm.
354	2	*Prunus emarginata* (Dougl.) Walpers	*Prunus emarginata* Dougl.
356	38	Western Choke Cherry	Common Chokecherry
356	39	*Prunus demissa* (Nutt.) Walpers	*Prunus virginiana* L.
357	Fig. 167	*Prunus demissa*	*Prunus virginiana*
359	2	*Prunus ilicifolia* (Nutt.) Walpers	*Prunus ilicifolia* (Nutt.) D. Dietr.
360	Fig. 169	*Prunus ilicifolia integrifolia*	*Prunus ilicifolia* var. *integrifolia*
362	43	Screwpod Mesquite	Screwbean Mesquite
362	44	*Prosopis odorata*[a] Torrey and Fremont	*Prosopis pubescens* Benth.
363	Fig. 170	*Prosopis odorata*	*Prosopis pubescens*
364	19	Mesquite	Honey Mesquite
364	20	*Prosopis juliflora glandulosa*[a] (Torr.) Sargent	*Prosopis juliflora* var. *glandulosa*[a] (Torr.) Cockerell[*]
366	Fig. 171	*Prosopis juliflora glandulosa*	*Prosopis juliflora* var. *glandulosa*
367	7	JUDAS TREES	REDBUDS
367	23	California Red-bud	California Redbud
367	24	*Cercis occidentalis* Torrey	*Cercis occidentalis* Torr.
369	1	ACACIA	ACACIA. ACACIAS
369	41	Cats Claw	Catclaw Acacia
369	42	*Acacia greggii* Gray	*Acacia greggii* A. Gray
371	12	PARKINSONIA	PARKINSONIA. PARKINSONIAS
371	31	Horse-bean; Ratama	Jerusalem-thorn
371	32	*Parkinsonia aculeata* Linnaeus	*Parkinsonia aculeata* L.
373	11	Little-leaf Horse-bean	Yellow Paloverde
373	12	*Parkinsonia microphylla* Torrey	*Cercidum microphyllum* (Torr.) Rose & Johnst.
375	1	CERCIDIUM	CERCIDIUM. PALOVERDES

[*] Far western trees formerly included in this variety are now separated as Western Honey Mesquite (*Prosopis juliflora* var. *torreyana* L. Benson).

Page	Line	For	Read
375	Fig. 176	*Cercidium torreyanum*	*Cercidium floridum*
376	12	Palo Verde; Green-bark Acacia	Blue Paloverde
376	13	*Cercidium torreyanum* (Wats.) Sargent	*Cercidium floridum* Benth.
376	38	DALEA	DALEA. DALEAS
377	1	Indigo Bush	Smokethorn
377	2	*Dalea spinosa* Gray	*Dalea spinosa* A. Gray
378	25	OLNEYA	OLNEYA. TESOTAS
378	29	Mexican Ironwood	Tesota
378	30	*Olneya tesota* Gray	*Olneya tesota* A. Gray
380	32	CANOTIA	CANOTIA. CANOTIAS
380	37	*Canotia holocantha* Torrey	*Canotia holocantha* Torr.
382	20	Fremontia	California Fremontia
384	26	SUMACHS	SUMACS
385	1	Mahogany Sumach	Lemonade Sumac
385	2	*Rhus integrifolia* (Nutt.) Bentham and Hooker	*Rhus integrifolia* (Nutt.) Benth. & Hook.
387	23	Broadleaf Maple	Bigleaf Maple
392	36	Dwarf Maple	Rocky Mountain Maple
392	37	*Acer glabrum* Torrey	*Acer glabrum* Torr.
396	23	California Boxelder	Boxelder
396	24	*Acer negundo californicum* (Torr. and Gr.) Sargent	*Acer negundo* L.
397	Fig. 188	*Acer negundo californicum*	*Acer negundo*
398	41	*Aesculus californica* Nuttall	*Aesculus californica* (Spach) Nutt.
401	17	Evergreen Buckthorn	Hollyleaf Buckthorn
401	18	*Rhamnus crocea* Nuttall	*Rhamnus crocea* var. *ilicifolia* (Kellogg) Greene
401	35	*Rhamnus corcea insularis* (Greene) Sargent	*Rhamnus crocea* var. *pirifolia* (Greene) Little
402	Fig. 190	*Rhamnus crocea*	*Rhamnus crocea* var. *ilicifolia*
403	Fig. 191	*Rhamnus crocea insularis*	*Rhamnus crocea* var. *pirifolia*
404	1	Cascara Sagrada [a]	Cascara Buckthorn
404	2	*Rhamnus purshiana* De Candolle	*Rhamnus purshiana* DC.
407	17	CEANOTHUS. MYRTLES	CEANOTHUS. CEANOTHUSES
409	1	Blue Myrtle [a]	Blueblossom
409	2	*Ceanothus thyrsiflorus* Eschscholtz	*Ceanothus thyrsiflorus* Eschsch.
409	28	Tree Myrtle	Feltleaf Ceanothus
411	1	Lilac	Spiny Ceanothus
411	2	*Ceanothus spinosus* Nuttall	*Ceanothus spinosus* Nutt.
413	16	Western Dogwood	Pacific Dogwood
416	19	GARRYA	GARRYA. SILKTASSELS
416	25	Quinine Bush	Wavyleaf Silktassel
416	26	*Garrya elliptica* Douglas	*Garrya elliptica* Dougl.
418	24	MADROÑAS	MADRONES
419	1	Madroña	Pacific Madrone
423	23	*Note:* Leatherleaf ash (*Fraxinus coriacea* Watson) is now included as a part of Velvet ash (*Fraxinus velutina* Torr.) without benefit of variety ranking.	
423	24	*Fraxinus coriacea* Watson	*Fraxinus velutina* Torr.
424	Fig. 201	*Fraxinus coriacea*	*Fraxinus velutina*
425	2	*Fraxinus oregona* Nuttall	*Fraxinus latifolia* Benth.
426	21		*Insert below:* Velvet Ash
426	22	*Fraxinus velutina* Torrey	*Fraxinus velutina* Torr.
428	1	Flowering Ash	Two-Petal Ash
428	2	*Fraxinus dipetala* Hooker and Arnott	*Fraxinus dipetala* Hook. & Arn.
429	10	*Fraxinus dipetala trifoliolata* Torrey	*Fraxinus dipetala* var. *trifoliolata* Torr.

Page	Line	For	Read
429	10	*F. dipetala brachyptera* Gray	*Fraxinus dipetala* var *brachyptera* A. Gray
429	31	CHILOPSIS	CHILOPSIS. DESERT-WILLOWS
429	34	Desert Willow	Desertwillow
431	36	CEPHALANTHUS	CEPHALANTHUS. BUTTONBUSHES
431	40	Button Bush	Common Buttonbush
431	41	*Cephalanthus occidentalis* Linnaeus	*Cephalanthus occidentalis* L.
433	35	ELDERBERRIES	ELDERS
434	1	Blue Elderberry	Blueberry Elder
434	2	*Sambucus glauca* [a] Nuttall	*Sambucus glauca* [a] Nutt.
436	20	Red-berried Elder	Pacific Red Elder

INDEX OF COMMON AND SCIENTIFIC NAMES.

A CATALOGUE OF SELECTED DOVER BOOKS
IN ALL FIELDS OF INTEREST

AMERICA'S OLD MASTERS, James T. Flexner. Four men emerged unexpectedly from provincial 18th century America to leadership in European art: Benjamin West, J. S. Copley, C. R. Peale, Gilbert Stuart. Brilliant coverage of lives and contributions. Revised, 1967 edition. 69 plates. 365pp. of text.
21806-6 Paperbound $2.75

FIRST FLOWERS OF OUR WILDERNESS: AMERICAN PAINTING, THE COLONIAL PERIOD, James T. Flexner. Painters, and regional painting traditions from earliest Colonial times up to the emergence of Copley, West and Peale Sr., Foster, Gustavus Hesselius, Feke, John Smibert and many anonymous painters in the primitive manner. Engaging presentation, with 162 illustrations. xxii + 368pp.
22180-6 Paperbound $3.50

THE LIGHT OF DISTANT SKIES: AMERICAN PAINTING, 1760-1835, James T. Flexner. The great generation of early American painters goes to Europe to learn and to teach: West, Copley, Gilbert Stuart and others. Allston, Trumbull, Morse; also contemporary American painters—primitives, derivatives, academics—who remained in America. 102 illustrations. xiii + 306pp.
22179-2 Paperbound $3.00

A HISTORY OF THE RISE AND PROGRESS OF THE ARTS OF DESIGN IN THE UNITED STATES, William Dunlap. Much the richest mine of information on early American painters, sculptors, architects, engravers, miniaturists, etc. The only source of information for scores of artists, the major primary source for many others. Unabridged reprint of rare original 1834 edition, with new introduction by James T. Flexner, and 394 new illustrations. Edited by Rita Weiss. 6⅝ x 9⅝.
21695-0, 21696-9, 21697-7 Three volumes, Paperbound $13.50

EPOCHS OF CHINESE AND JAPANESE ART, Ernest F. Fenollosa. From primitive Chinese art to the 20th century, thorough history, explanation of every important art period and form, including Japanese woodcuts; main stress on China and Japan, but Tibet, Korea also included. Still unexcelled for its detailed, rich coverage of cultural background, aesthetic elements, diffusion studies, particularly of the historical period. 2nd, 1913 edition. 242 illustrations. lii + 439pp. of text.
20364-6, 20365-4 Two volumes, Paperbound $5.00

THE GENTLE ART OF MAKING ENEMIES, James A. M. Whistler. Greatest wit of his day deflates Oscar Wilde, Ruskin, Swinburne; strikes back at inane critics, exhibitions, art journalism; aesthetics of impressionist revolution in most striking form. Highly readable classic by great painter. Reproduction of edition designed by Whistler. Introduction by Alfred Werner. xxxvi + 334pp.
21875-9 Paperbound $2.25

THE ARCHITECTURE OF COUNTRY HOUSES, Andrew J. Downing. Together with Vaux's *Villas and Cottages* this is the basic book for Hudson River Gothic architecture of the middle Victorian period. Full, sound discussions of general aspects of housing, architecture, style, decoration, furnishing, together with scores of detailed house plans, illustrations of specific buildings, accompanied by full text. Perhaps the most influential single American architectural book. 1850 edition. Introduction by J. Stewart Johnson. 321 figures, 34 architectural designs. xvi + 560pp.
22003-6 Paperbound $3.50

LOST EXAMPLES OF COLONIAL ARCHITECTURE, John Mead Howells. Full-page photographs of buildings that have disappeared or been so altered as to be denatured, including many designed by major early American architects. 245 plates. xvii + 248pp. 7⅞ x 10¾.
21143-6 Paperbound $3.00

DOMESTIC ARCHITECTURE OF THE AMERICAN COLONIES AND OF THE EARLY REPUBLIC, Fiske Kimball. Foremost architect and restorer of Williamsburg and Monticello covers nearly 200 homes between 1620-1825. Architectural details, construction, style features, special fixtures, floor plans, etc. Generally considered finest work in its area. 219 illustrations of houses, doorways, windows, capital mantels. xx + 314pp. 7⅞ x 10¾.
21743-4 Paperbound $3.50

EARLY AMERICAN ROOMS: 1650-1858, edited by Russell Hawes Kettell. Tour of 12 rooms, each representative of a different era in American history and each furnished, decorated, designed and occupied in the style of the era. 72 plans and elevations, 8-page color section, etc., show fabrics, wall papers, arrangements, etc. Full descriptive text. xvii + 200pp. of text. 8⅜ x 11¼.
21633-0 Paperbound $4.00

THE FITZWILLIAM VIRGINAL BOOK, edited by J. Fuller Maitland and W. B. Squire. Full modern printing of famous early 17th-century ms. volume of 300 works by Morley, Byrd, Bull, Gibbons, etc. For piano or other modern keyboard instrument; easy to read format. xxxvi + 938pp. 8⅜ x 11.
21068-5, 21069-3 Two volumes, Paperbound $8.00

HARPSICHORD MUSIC, Johann Sebastian Bach. Bach Gesellschaft edition. A rich selection of Bach's masterpieces for the harpsichord: the six English Suites, six French Suites, the six Partitas (Clavierübung part I), the Goldberg Variations (Clavierübung part IV), the fifteen Two-Part Inventions and the fifteen Three-Part Sinfonias. Clearly reproduced on large sheets with ample margins; eminently playable. vi + 312pp. 8⅛ x 11.
22360-4 Paperbound $5.00

THE MUSIC OF BACH: AN INTRODUCTION, Charles Sanford Terry. A fine, nontechnical introduction to Bach's music, both instrumental and vocal. Covers organ music, chamber music, passion music, other types. Analyzes themes, developments, innovations. x + 114pp.
21075-8 Paperbound $1.25

BEETHOVEN AND HIS NINE SYMPHONIES, Sir George Grove. Noted British musicologist provides best history, analysis, commentary on symphonies. Very thorough, rigorously accurate; necessary to both advanced student and amateur music lover. 436 musical passages. vii + 407 pp.
20334-4 Paperbound $2.25

DESIGN BY ACCIDENT; A BOOK OF "ACCIDENTAL EFFECTS" FOR ARTISTS AND DESIGNERS, James F. O'Brien. Create your own unique, striking, imaginative effects by "controlled accident" interaction of materials: paints and lacquers, oil and water based paints, splatter, crackling materials, shatter, similar items. Everything you do will be different; first book on this limitless art, so useful to both fine artist and commercial artist. Full instructions. 192 plates showing "accidents," 8 in color. viii + 215pp. 8⅜ x 11¼. 21942-9 Paperbound $3.50

THE BOOK OF SIGNS, Rudolf Koch. Famed German type designer draws 493 beautiful symbols: religious, mystical, alchemical, imperial, property marks, . ι nes, etc. Remarkable fusion of traditional and modern. Good for suggestions of timelessness, smartness, modernity. Text. vi + 104pp. 6⅛ x 9¼.

20162-7 Paperbound $1.25

HISTORY OF INDIAN AND INDONESIAN ART, Ananda K. Coomaraswamy. An unabridged republication of one of the finest books by a great scholar in Eastern art. Rich in descriptive material, history, social backgrounds; Sunga reliefs, Rajput paintings, Gupta temples, Burmese frescoes, textiles, jewelry, sculpture, etc. 400 photos. viii + 423pp. 6⅜ x 9¾. 21436-2 Paperbound $3.50

PRIMITIVE ART, Franz Boas. America's foremost anthropologist surveys textiles, ceramics, woodcarving, basketry, metalwork, etc.; patterns, technology, creation of symbols, style origins. All areas of world, but very full on Northwest Coast Indians. More than 350 illustrations of baskets, boxes, totem poles, weapons, etc. 378 pp.

20025-6 Paperbound $2.50

THE GENTLEMAN AND CABINET MAKER'S DIRECTOR, Thomas Chippendale. Full reprint (third edition, 1762) of most influential furniture book of ·all time, by master cabinetmaker. 200 plates, illustrating chairs, sofas, mirrors, tables, cabinets, plus 24 photographs of surviving pieces. Biographical introduction by N. Bienenstock. vi + 249pp. 9⅞ x 12¾. 21601-2 Paperbound $3.50

AMERICAN ANTIQUE FURNITURE, Edgar G. Miller, Jr. The basic coverage of all American furniture before 1840. Individual chapters cover type of furniture— clocks, tables, sideboards, etc.—chronologically, with inexhaustible wealth of data. More than 2100 photographs, all identified, commented on. Essential to all early American collectors. Introduction by H. E. Keyes. vi + 1106pp. 7⅞ x 10¾.

21599-7, 21600-4 Two volumes, Paperbound $7.50

PENNSYLVANIA DUTCH AMERICAN FOLK ART, Henry J. Kauffman. 279 photos, 28 drawings of tulipware, Fraktur script, painted tinware, toys, flowered furniture, quilts, samplers, hex signs, house interiors, etc. Full descriptive text. Excellent for tourist, rewarding for designer, collector. Map. 146pp. 7⅞ x 10¾.

21205-X Paperbound $2.00

EARLY NEW ENGLAND GRAVESTONE RUBBINGS, Edmund V. Gillon, Jr. 43 photographs, 226 carefully reproduced rubbings show heavily symbolic, sometimes macabre early gravestones, up to early 19th century. Remarkable early American primitive art, occasionally strikingly beautiful; always powerful. Text. xxvi + 207pp. 8⅜ x 11¼. 21380-3 Paperbound $3.00

ALPHABETS AND ORNAMENTS, Ernst Lehner. Well-known pictorial source for decorative alphabets, script examples, cartouches, frames, decorative title pages, calligraphic initials, borders, similar material. 14th to 19th century, mostly European. Useful in almost any graphic arts designing, varied styles. 750 illustrations. 256pp. 7 x 10. 21905-4 Paperbound $3.50

PAINTING: A CREATIVE APPROACH, Norman Colquhoun. For the beginner simple guide provides an instructive approach to painting: major stumbling blocks for beginner; overcoming them, technical points; paints and pigments; oil painting; watercolor and other media and color. New section on "plastic" paints. Glossary. Formerly *Paint Your Own Pictures*. 221pp. 22000-1 Paperbound $1.75

THE ENJOYMENT AND USE OF COLOR, Walter Sargent. Explanation of the relations between colors themselves and between colors in nature and art, including hundreds of little-known facts about color values, intensities, effects of high and low illumination, complementary colors. Many practical hints for painters, references to great masters. 7 color plates, 29 illustrations. x + 274pp.
20944-X Paperbound $2.50

THE NOTEBOOKS OF LEONARDO DA VINCI, compiled and edited by Jean Paul Richter. 1566 extracts from original manuscripts reveal the full range of Leonardo's versatile genius: all his writings on painting, sculpture, architecture, anatomy, astronomy, geography, topography, physiology, mining, music, etc., in both Italian and English, with 186 plates of manuscript pages and more than 500 additional drawings. Includes studies for the Last Supper, the lost Sforza monument, and other works. Total of xlvii + 866pp. 7⅞ x 10¾.
22572-0, 22573-9 Two volumes, Paperbound $10.00

MONTGOMERY WARD CATALOGUE OF 1895. Tea gowns, yards of flannel and pillow-case lace, stereoscopes, books of gospel hymns, the New Improved Singer Sewing Machine, side saddles, milk skimmers, straight-edged razors, high-button shoes, spittoons, and on and on . . . listing some 25,000 items, practically all illustrated. Essential to the shoppers of the 1890's, it is our truest record of the spirit of the period. Unaltered reprint of Issue No. 57, Spring and Summer 1895. Introduction by Boris Emmet. Innumerable illustrations. xiii + 624pp. 8½ x 11⅝.
22377-9 Paperbound $6.95

THE CRYSTAL PALACE EXHIBITION ILLUSTRATED CATALOGUE (LONDON, 1851). One of the wonders of the modern world—the Crystal Palace Exhibition in which all the nations of the civilized world exhibited their achievements in the arts and sciences—presented in an equally important illustrated catalogue. More than 1700 items pictured with accompanying text—ceramics, textiles, cast-iron work, carpets, pianos, sleds, razors, wall-papers, billiard tables, beehives, silverware and hundreds of other artifacts—represent the focal point of Victorian culture in the Western World. Probably the largest collection of Victorian decorative art ever assembled—indispensable for antiquarians and designers. Unabridged republication of the Art-Journal Catalogue of the Great Exhibition of 1851, with all terminal essays. New introduction by John Gloag, F.S.A. xxxiv + 426pp. 9 x 12.
22503-8 Paperbound $4.50

How to Know the Wild Flowers, Mrs. William Starr Dana. This is the classical book of American wildflowers (of the Eastern and Central United States), used by hundreds of thousands. Covers over 500 species, arranged in extremely easy to use color and season groups. Full descriptions, much plant lore. This Dover edition is the fullest ever compiled, with tables of nomenclature changes. 174 full-page plates by M. Satterlee. xii + 418pp. 20332-8 Paperbound $2.50

Our Plant Friends and Foes, William Atherton DuPuy. History, economic importance, essential botanical information and peculiarities of 25 common forms of plant life are provided in this book in an entertaining and charming style. Covers food plants (potatoes, apples, beans, wheat, almonds, bananas, etc.), flowers (lily, tulip, etc.), trees (pine, oak, elm, etc.), weeds, poisonous mushrooms and vines, gourds, citrus fruits, cotton, the cactus family, and much more. 108 illustrations. xiv + 290pp. 22272-1 Paperbound $2.00

How to Know the Ferns, Frances T. Parsons. Classic survey of Eastern and Central ferns, arranged according to clear, simple identification key. Excellent introduction to greatly neglected nature area. 57 illustrations and 42 plates. xvi + 215pp. 20740-4 Paperbound $1.75

Manual of the Trees of North America, Charles S. Sargent. America's foremost dendrologist provides the definitive coverage of North American trees and tree-like shrubs. 717 species fully described and illustrated: exact distribution, down to township; full botanical description; economic importance; description of subspecies and races; habitat, growth data; similar material. Necessary to every serious student of tree-life. Nomenclature revised to present. Over 100 locating keys. 783 illustrations. lii + 934pp. 20277-1, 20278-X Two volumes, Paperbound $6.00

Our Northern Shrubs, Harriet L. Keeler. Fine non-technical reference work identifying more than 225 important shrubs of Eastern and Central United States and Canada. Full text covering botanical description, habitat, plant lore, is paralleled with 205 full-page photographs of flowering or fruiting plants. Nomenclature revised by Edward G. Voss. One of few works concerned with shrubs. 205 plates, 35 drawings. xxviii + 521pp. 21989-5 Paperbound $3.75

The Mushroom Handbook, Louis C. C. Krieger. Still the best popular handbook: full descriptions of 259 species, cross references to another 200. Extremely thorough text enables you to identify, know all about any mushroom you are likely to meet in eastern and central U. S. A.: habitat, luminescence, poisonous qualities, use, folklore, etc. 32 color plates show over 50 mushrooms, also 126 other illustrations. Finding keys. vii + 560pp. 21861-9 Paperbound $3.95

Handbook of Birds of Eastern North America, Frank M. Chapman. Still much the best single-volume guide to the birds of Eastern and Central United States. Very full coverage of 675 species, with descriptions, life habits, distribution, similar data. All descriptions keyed to two-page color chart. With this single volume the average birdwatcher needs no other books. 1931 revised edition. 195 illustrations. xxxvi + 581pp. 21489-3 Paperbound $3.25

AMERICAN FOOD AND GAME FISHES, David S. Jordan and Barton W. Evermann. Definitive source of information, detailed and accurate enough to enable the sportsman and nature lover to identify conclusively some 1,000 species and sub-species of North American fish, sought for food or sport. Coverage of range, physiology, habits, life history, food value. Best methods of capture, interest to the angler, advice on bait, fly-fishing, etc. 338 drawings and photographs. 1 + 574pp. 6⅝ x 9⅜.

22383-1 Paperbound $4.50

THE FROG BOOK, Mary C. Dickerson. Complete with extensive finding keys, over 300 photographs, and an introduction to the general biology of frogs and toads, this is the classic non-technical study of Northeastern and Central species. 58 species; 290 photographs and 16 color plates. xvii + 253pp.

21973-9 Paperbound $4.00

THE MOTH BOOK: A GUIDE TO THE MOTHS OF NORTH AMERICA, William J. Holland. Classical study, eagerly sought after and used for the past 60 years. Clear identification manual to more than 2,000 different moths, largest manual in existence. General information about moths, capturing, mounting, classifying, etc., followed by species by species descriptions. 263 illustrations plus 48 color plates show almost every species, full size. 1968 edition, preface, nomenclature changes by A. E. Brower. xxiv + 479pp. of text. 6½ x 9¼.

21948-8 Paperbound $5.00

THE SEA-BEACH AT EBB-TIDE, Augusta Foote Arnold. Interested amateur can identify hundreds of marine plants and animals on coasts of North America; marine algae; seaweeds; squids; hermit crabs; horse shoe crabs; shrimps; corals; sea anemones; etc. Species descriptions cover: structure; food; reproductive cycle; size; shape; color; habitat; etc. Over 600 drawings. 85 plates. xii + 490pp.

21949-6 Paperbound $3.50

COMMON BIRD SONGS, Donald J. Borror. 33⅓ 12-inch record presents songs of 60 important birds of the eastern United States. A thorough, serious record which provides several examples for each bird, showing different types of song, individual variations, etc. Inestimable identification aid for birdwatcher. 32-page booklet gives text about birds and songs, with illustration for each bird.

21829-5 Record, book, album. Monaural. $2.75

FADS AND FALLACIES IN THE NAME OF SCIENCE, Martin Gardner. Fair, witty appraisal of cranks and quacks of science: Atlantis, Lemuria, hollow earth, flat earth, Velikovsky, orgone energy, Dianetics, flying saucers, Bridey Murphy, food fads, medical fads, perpetual motion, etc. Formerly "In the Name of Science." x + 363pp.

20394-8 Paperbound $2.00

HOAXES, Curtis D. MacDougall. Exhaustive, unbelievably rich account of great hoaxes: Locke's moon hoax, Shakespearean forgeries, sea serpents, Loch Ness monster, Cardiff giant, John Wilkes Booth's mummy, Disumbrationist school of art, dozens more; also journalism, psychology of hoaxing. 54 illustrations. xi + 338pp.

20465-0 Paperbound $2.75

INCIDENTS OF TRAVEL IN YUCATAN, John L. Stephens. Classic (1843) exploration of jungles of Yucatan, looking for evidences of Maya civilization. Stephens found many ruins; comments on travel adventures, Mexican and Indian culture. 127 striking illustrations by F. Catherwood. Total of 669 pp.
20926-1, 20927-X Two volumes, Paperbound $5.00

INCIDENTS OF TRAVEL IN CENTRAL AMERICA, CHIAPAS, AND YUCATAN, John L. Stephens. An exciting travel journal and an important classic of archeology. Narrative relates his almost single-handed discovery of the Mayan culture, and exploration of the ruined cities of Copan, Palenque, Utatlan and others; the monuments they dug from the earth, the temples buried in the jungle, the customs of poverty-stricken Indians living a stone's throw from the ruined palaces. 115 drawings by F. Catherwood. Portrait of Stephens. xii + 812pp.
22404-X, 22405-8 Two volumes, Paperbound $6.00

A NEW VOYAGE ROUND THE WORLD, William Dampier. Late 17-century naturalist joined the pirates of the Spanish Main to gather information; remarkably vivid account of buccaneers, pirates; detailed, accurate account of botany, zoology, ethnography of lands visited. Probably the most important early English voyage, enormous implications for British exploration, trade, colonial policy. Also most interesting reading. Argonaut edition, introduction by Sir Albert Gray. New introduction by Percy Adams. 6 plates, 7 illustrations. xlvii + 376pp. 6½ x 9¼.
21900-3 Paperbound $3.00

INTERNATIONAL AIRLINE PHRASE BOOK IN SIX LANGUAGES, Joseph W. Bátor. Important phrases and sentences in English paralleled with French, German, Portuguese, Italian, Spanish equivalents, covering all possible airport-travel situations; created for airline personnel as well as tourist by Language Chief, Pan American Airlines. xiv + 204pp.
22017-6 Paperbound $2.00

STAGE COACH AND TAVERN DAYS, Alice Morse Earle. Detailed, lively account of the early days of taverns; their uses and importance in the social, political and military life; furnishings and decorations; locations; food and drink; tavern signs, etc. Second half covers every aspect of early travel; the roads, coaches, drivers, etc. Nostalgic, charming, packed with fascinating material. 157 illustrations, mostly photographs. xiv + 449pp.
22518-6 Paperbound $4.00

NORSE DISCOVERIES AND EXPLORATIONS IN NORTH AMERICA, Hjalmar R. Holand. The perplexing Kensington Stone, found in Minnesota at the end of the 19th century. Is it a record of a Scandinavian expedition to North America in the 14th century? Or is it one of the most successful hoaxes in history. A scientific detective investigation. Formerly *Westward from Vinland*. 31 photographs, 17 figures. x + 354pp.
22014-1 Paperbound $2.75

A BOOK OF OLD MAPS, compiled and edited by Emerson D. Fite and Archibald Freeman. 74 old maps offer an unusual survey of the discovery, settlement and growth of America down to the close of the Revolutionary war: maps showing Norse settlements in Greenland, the explorations of Columbus, Verrazano, Cabot, Champlain, Joliet, Drake, Hudson, etc., campaigns of Revolutionary war battles, and much more. Each map is accompanied by a brief historical essay. xvi + 299pp. 11 x 13¾.
22084-2 Paperbound $6.00

MATHEMATICAL PUZZLES FOR BEGINNERS AND ENTHUSIASTS, Geoffrey Mott-Smith. 189 puzzles from easy to difficult—involving arithmetic, logic, algebra, properties of digits, probability, etc.—for enjoyment and mental stimulus. Explanation of mathematical principles behind the puzzles. 135 illustrations. viii + 248pp.

20198-8 Paperbound $1.25

PAPER FOLDING FOR BEGINNERS, William D. Murray and Francis J. Rigney. Easiest book on the market, clearest instructions on making interesting, beautiful origami. Sail boats, cups, roosters, frogs that move legs, bonbon boxes, standing birds, etc. 40 projects; more than 275 diagrams and photographs. 94pp.

20713-7 Paperbound $1.00

TRICKS AND GAMES ON THE POOL TABLE, Fred Herrmann. 79 tricks and games— some solitaires, some for two or more players, some competitive games—to entertain you between formal games. Mystifying shots and throws, unusual caroms, tricks involving such props as cork, coins, a hat, etc. Formerly *Fun on the Pool Table*. 77 figures. 95pp.

21814-7 Paperbound $1.00

HAND SHADOWS TO BE THROWN UPON THE WALL: A SERIES OF NOVEL AND AMUSING FIGURES FORMED BY THE HAND, Henry Bursill. Delightful picturebook from great-grandfather's day shows how to make 18 different hand shadows: a bird that flies, duck that quacks, dog that wags his tail, camel, goose, deer, boy, turtle, etc. Only book of its sort. vi + 33pp. 6½ x 9¼.

21779-5 Paperbound $1.00

WHITTLING AND WOODCARVING, E. J. Tangerman. 18th printing of best book on market. "If you can cut a potato you can carve" toys and puzzles, chains, chessmen, caricatures, masks, frames, woodcut blocks, surface patterns, much more. Information on tools, woods, techniques. Also goes into serious wood sculpture from Middle Ages to present, East and West. 464 photos, figures. x + 293pp.

20965-2 Paperbound $2.00

HISTORY OF PHILOSOPHY, Julián Marias. Possibly the clearest, most easily followed, best planned, most useful one-volume history of philosophy on the market; neither skimpy nor overfull. Full details on system of every major philosopher and dozens of less important thinkers from pre-Socratics up to Existentialism and later. Strong on many European figures usually omitted. Has gone through dozens of editions in Europe. 1966 edition, translated by Stanley Appelbaum and Clarence Strowbridge. xviii + 505pp.

21739-6 Paperbound $2.75

YOGA: A SCIENTIFIC EVALUATION, Kovoor T. Behanan. Scientific but non-technical study of physiological results of yoga exercises; done under auspices of Yale U. Relations to Indian thought, to psychoanalysis, etc. 16 photos. xxiii + 270pp.

20505-3 Paperbound $2.50

Prices subject to change without notice.
Available at your book dealer or write for free catalogue to Dept. GI, Dover Publications, Inc., 180 Varick St., N. Y., N. Y. 10014. Dover publishes more than 150 books each year on science, elementary and advanced mathematics, biology, music, art, literary history, social sciences and other areas.